The Mental Health of the Child

The Mental Health of the Child

Program Reports of the National Institute of Mental Health

ARNO PRESS

A New York Times Company

New York / 1973

Reprint Edition 1973 by Arno Press Inc.

Manufactured in the United States of America

———◆———

Library of Congress Cataloging in Publication Data

United States. National Institute of Mental Health.
   Program Analysis and Evaluation Branch.
   The mental health of the child.

   Reprint of the 1971 ed., which was issued as Public
Health Service publication no. 2168.
   1. Child psychiatry--United States. I. Segal,
Julius, 1924-   ed. II. Title. III. Series:
United States. Public Health Service. Publication
no. 2168.
[RJ501.A2A55 1972]   614'.08s   [618.9'28'900973]
ISBN 0-405-03149-1   72-1302

The Mental Health of the Child

Program Reports of the National Institute of Mental Health

Julius Segal, Ph.D., Editor

Authors:

Antoinette Gattozzi
Gay Luce
Maya Pines
Clarissa Wittenberg
Herbert Yahraes

Program Analysis and Evaluation Branch
Office of Program Planning and Evaluation
National Institute of Mental Health
5600 Fishers Lane
Rockville, Md. 20852

June 1971

Public Health Service Publication No. 2168
Printed 1971

Contents

Foreword

In every age, men have recognized the special importance of the child's role in society. Whether through ancient tribal initiation rituals or the pronouncements of contemporary psychoanalytic theorists, each succeeding civilization has acknowledged that the child will carry after us the imprint of the world we create around him. Paradoxically, however, the child has also been a traditional victim of our neglect and abuse. An inability and unwillingness to respond to the special needs of the child haunt us in the ghettos and suburbs of twentieth-century America as they did in the factory towns of the industrial revolution. Tonight, thousands of American children will fall into a troubled sleep, bearing the scars of emotional trauma and physical pain inflicted by adults no less misguided and ill than those who nurtured the cruel children's prisons of eighteenth-century England. We have not yet matched our best instincts and insights with comparable action—and nowhere is this more apparent than in the field of mental health.

Over one half of the U.S. population is now under 25 years of age, and it is estimated that over 10 percent of this precious resource—about ten million of our youth—require mental health services. Their needs range from hospitalization to treat and reverse serious psychopathology, to the early interventions of doctors, teachers, counselors, and parents able to handle mild, transient problems and thus prevent later developmental crises.

The child's mental health needs have challenged our best efforts to date. In the State mental hospitals of our Nation where, for the past fifteen years, the number of adult patients has been declining steadily, both the first admission and the resident population rates for children have increased at an accelerated pace. While many children are receiving the mental health care they require—some 52,000 in community mental health centers, 33,000 in public and private mental hospitals, 26,000 in residential treatment centers, and 526,000 in psychiatric outpatient clinics—millions more are going without help. Of the Nation's approximately 2,300 mental health clinics in 1968, somewhat less than one tenth were child guidance clinics; moreover, only 40 percent of the 268,000 patients under 18 years seen at such clinics were actually treated, the remaining 60 percent receiving no more than a diagnosis. A large proportion of all counties in the United States are without mental health clinics altogether, and most of these also lack agencies that substitute in some measure for such services. The cost to society—in wasted resources and human suffering—can only be guessed. But in 1969 nearly one million children aged 10 to 17 were brought before juvenile courts, and during the past two decades the suicide rate among adolescents and young adults has increased by 60 percent.

These data do not minimize the success of efforts to date conducted or supported by the National Institute of Mental Health. From its very inception, NIMH has devoted a large part of its program to activities relating to the mental health of children, many of them reflected in this report. Contributing to the overall effort today is the entire range of the Institute's resources.

• Community mental health center programs now not only provide mental health services directly to troubled children and their families, but also serve as a rich vehicle for acquainting a variety of community agencies with mental health principles and practices, thereby enabling them better to foster the well-being of our young. In nearly two thirds of the community mental health centers funded to date, specialized services to children are highlighted.

• Projects designed to improve the Nation's mental hospitals have focused heavily on upgrading the quality of institutional care provided to seriously disturbed children.

• Interdisciplinary training programs directed at developing skilled child therapists have been expanded, many of them emphasizing the prevention of child behavior disorders. Such programs have led to a significant increase in the number of professionals and paraprofessionals qualified to work with children and their families in both preventive and remedial activities.

• New light on the dynamics of child development—and on our ability to influence its course—has been shed by scientists devoted to child research. Our understanding of the complex biological, psychological and social factors involved in mental illness has considerably increased; we are better able to detect incipient emotional trouble and therefore to take preventive and curative measures early, when they are most likely to be effective. A number of promising approaches have been tested and demonstrated for building in the very young a strong foundation for both emotional health and intellectual competence.

• And, finally, we now have more hopeful treatments for the whole range of childhood disorders—from problem behavior to childhood schizophrenia.

Despite such advances, much more must be done. Activities directed at improving the mental health of children now carry the highest priority for NIMH. Our intent is to provide a base of knowledge, techniques, manpower, and services that will not only reduce significantly the number of our mentally and emotionally ill children, but also enhance the well-being and productivity of all our youth.

This volume, issued as the Institute marks the 25th anniversary of the National Mental Health Act, is intended to display the range of the Institute's current and past efforts in the child mental health field. Rather than an exercise in self-celebration, the report serves as a reminder of the beginnings that have been made—and of what more we can do. It is intended to stimulate further the creative approaches of research personnel, and to provide information of value to clinicians and all those others who deal directly with the child. A number of studies and demonstrations reported here may well serve as models for future efforts elsewhere.

Highlighting its importance, the area of prevention is the focus of the first section of this volume. Emphasis here is on the child in his normal environment—the family, the school, the community—where the task is to so enhance the child's environment that mental health is maintained and pathology is aborted at the primary source, before the child must be separated from the general population. A number of NIMH efforts in this direction are reported here—including attempts to demonstrate methods for enriching the intellectual and emotional world of deprived and minority children and to show how the corrosive effects of prejudice can be prevented early in the life of the child. Another goal is to help the older disadvantaged youth, often troubled and embittered, to work for his dreams and realize his capabilities. One team of investigators has provided dramatic evidence that worldly wise, angry young people in the ghetto need not live without hope; properly motivated and placed in a college setting, they demonstrate untapped depths of wisdom and ability.

The second section of this volume is concerned with a variety of circumstances that can affect a child's mental health—and thus relates not only to the etiology of behavior problems, but to their prevention as well. Reported here are a number of the Institute's efforts to learn precisely which factors in early life either enhance or reduce the potential for intellectual growth and emotional well-being. These projects include, for example, detailed observations of the effects of various relationships existing between infants and mothers, as well as long-range studies of the connection between certain characteristics of parents and the psychological development of their children. One study is concerned with the influence of visual media—in particular, of television—on childhood behavior, while another deals with child-rearing practices and outcomes in societies other than our own. The section ends with three studies of factors contributing to schizophrenia—the most serious and devastating form of mental illness, which so often and so cruelly afflicts young people.

The third section presents an array of projects concerned both with improving the diagnosis and treatment of disturbed children and adolescents, and with increasing our understanding of some of the conditions leading to disturbed behavior. The studies reported here deal with a broad range of problem children—including those diagnosed as schizophrenic, neurotic, and hyperkinetic, as well as seriously disturbed boys, members of delinquent gangs, narcotic addicts, young criminals, and suicidal adolescents. The range of efforts in their behalf is also very broad, embracing, for example, behavior therapy, brief psychotherapy, psychiatric drugs, a foster home program, hospitalization and counseling for potential suicides. The children of poor, unmarried, teenage girls, one recent study shows, need not be victimized by the nature of their beginnings—nor are the mothers themselves without the capacity for psychological growth and maturation. Another report describes attempts to understand and deal with the problem of child abuse, and still another provides a demonstration of how young criminals might be reeducated in a prison setting.

The foundation of all our efforts in child mental health must be basic research—an effort to understand both normal and abnormal development and behavior—and the final section of this volume includes reports of some of the Institute's endeavors in this area. The studies described here explore such fundamental variables as the biology of learning and memory, the effects of hormones on behavior, normal and abnormal patterns of sleep at various age-levels, the influence of heredity on behavior under stress and on intelligence and personality, and the growth of intelligence in babies. Findings from such studies considerably strengthen our ability to prevent and treat mental disorders in children.

The NIMH efforts in the child mental health field clearly cannot be encompassed in a single report, for they involve the varied activities of research scientists, clinicians, community agencies, and training institutions. The program includes work in the most basic sciences—for example, in biochemistry, genetics, and experimental psychology—along with clinical and community studies. The examples reported here, however, will help provide the reader with an appreciation not alone of the scope and complexity of the NIMH program in behalf of children, but also of its guiding purpose. Underlying all of the Institute's varied efforts—from basic research to community consultations—is the endeavor to meet our children's mental health needs.

In pursuing its child mental health program, the Institute seeks every opportunity to collaborate with programs and agencies whose efforts complement our own. The factors affecting the mental health of children are too vast and complex to be dealt with by any one organization alone. Mental health problems make themselves felt in virtually every aspect of a child's life—at home, at school, in the world of work—and their solution, therefore, requires the contributions of agencies with varied missions and programs, each emphasizing different dimensions of the child's world.

The mental health of our children rests, ultimately, on the health of our total society—from the smallest unit to the largest. The stability of the home and the well-being of the family, the compassion of the surrounding community, the social conscience and social action of our Government and its citizens—all of these are crucial. The twenty-five years past are viewed with satisfaction, but also with an awareness of the formidable tasks not yet completed. Our pledge is to continue and expand these efforts, now well begun, to improve the mental health of children, and thus to enhance the quality of their lives—and our own.

Bertram S. Brown

Bertram S. Brown, M.D.
Director
National Institute of Mental Health

Prefatory Note

This volume, intended to provide examples of past and current efforts by NIMH in the child mental health field, includes primarily reports published earlier in the Institute's *Research Project Summaries* and *Program Reports* series. Seven reports, describing more recent advances, appear here for the first time. They begin on pages 3, 44, 113, 310, 343, 463, and 479. The earlier reports are presented as originally published, though in many cases the investigators have done further work on their projects, and in some instances the locations of the investigators, their titles, or the official designation of their institutions have changed.

The 42 reports included here are grouped into four major areas, covering prevention, etiology, diagnosis and treatment, and basic research. To a considerable extent, however, the groups overlap; work reported in one group, in a number of cases, could have been included with equal justification in another. It should be emphasized also that the projects described here were chosen simply as representative of NIMH activities in the field of child mental health. They do not deal with more important subjects and they do not present more useful findings than do scores of other Institute-supported projects in the area.

Studies and Demonstrations in Prevention

Bitter are the tears of a child:
  Sweeten them.
Deep are the thoughts of a child:
  Quiet them.
Sharp is the grief of a child:
  Take it from him.
Soft is the heart of a child:
  Do not harden it.

Lady Pamela Wyndham Glenconner

Nursery Schools in the Service of Mental Health

Investigator:
Mary B. Lane, Ed.D.
San Francisco State College
San Francisco, California

Prepared by:
Herbert Yahraes

Introduction and Summary

An Institute-supported program in San Francisco has been quietly fighting racial prejudice—regarded as a major mental health problem—through the medium of little children. In an area of the city known as the Western Addition, where slum neighborhoods are being replaced by urban renewal projects, to the resentment of the predominantly poor and predominantly black population, this program has demonstrated that a special kind of nursery school can bring together all kinds of people.

Mary B. Lane, professor of education at San Francisco State College, who conceived the program, calls this kind of nursery school *cross-cultural* or multi-cultural. By this she means a school that enrolls children of different races and socioeconomic levels and uses special curricular and organizational devices to promote interfamily, interrace relations.

In 1966, Dr. Lane and her associates opened three nursery schools for 60 children, selected in door-to-door canvassing, who had recently passed or soon would pass their second birthday. The racial and socioeconomic background of the children reflected those of the community. About 60 percent of the youngsters were black, 30 percent white, and 10 percent Oriental, meaning Chinese, Japanese, or mixed. About one-third of them came from families living in low-cost public housing; one-third of the children came from new, cooperatively owned, apartment development for people of middle income; and the rest from families in individual dwellings. This last group—designated for research purposes as the "random housing" group—ranged from families of unskilled workers to those of professional men. In each racial group, the families represented several socioeconomic levels.

The schools were known as Nurseries in Cross-Cultural Education, or NICE. They were in rooms lent by the Buchanan Y.M.C.A., the Christ United Presbyterian Church, and—in a public housing unit named the Westside Courts—by the San Francisco Housing Authority.

Each school was staffed by a professionally trained nursery school leader, an assistant who had had experience with children, though not as a teacher, and a part-time aide who was from the community. The staffs

3

were racially mixed—white and black. An effort to recruit Oriental teachers failed. One teacher or aide at each school was a man because Dr. Lane thought that the many children, about a fourth of the total, without a male figure in the home should have one at school.

The general aim was to assess the schools as instruments for promoting mental health in a community subjected to the stresses of redevelopment. Results were to be appraised in terms of factors related to mental health such as basic trust, autonomy, initiative, cognitive development, and social competence, in the case of the children, and, in the case of the families, social competence, intergroup acceptance, and utilization of community resources.

The program stressed parent involvement. Mothers gradually took on the role of aides during the sessions—three hours every morning—and participated in a number of after-school activities, sometimes with fathers. During the second year, responding to mothers' requests for more information about techniques of teaching, Dr. Lane gave a 30-hour training, course, modelling it on one of her courses at San Francisco State for prospective nursery school teachers. To meet the demand the following year, two such courses had to be given.

During the second year also, both to promote closer ties between school and home and to help mothers become better teachers of their children, the program developed a series of "home tasks"—things to be made, experiments to be tried, stories to be read, games to be played. One of these was taken to each home each week by a member of the staff, or by students from San Francisco State, and explained to the mother. The following week it was picked up and the experiences of mother and child recorded.

Before the start of the third year, the parents formed the Parent Advisory Council to help guide NICE activities during the final year and to decide the program's future when Institute support ended.

A PARENT SPEAKS

Following is a slightly abridged version of an interview with a mother who had two daughters in one of the cross-cultural nursery schools. One girl attended the full three years of this NIMH-supported project. The other was enrolled during the final two years and now attends the project's independently-financed successor, in which the mother is a teacher's aide.

Mother: Everytime I talk about it, I get sort of shook up inside because they learned so much, and I have learned so much. I don't mean only about toys and things like that but the most important—that I have learned how to raise children. Because I sort of talk and raise my girls differently from what I did my older boys. And because I didn't know −.

Here is an instance. I was a very over-protective mother and I'm a very firm mother. Well, in the NICE project I was taught how to help the situation. I used to spank a lot, you know. But I learned you can talk to children—sit down and talk to them just like you and I talk.

Like when we first went to the nursery school. When the children was all 2 and 2 and 1/2, they would hit each other a lot-and the teacher would

4

The NICE schools closed in 1969, after three years, and the children went off to kindergarten in public schools. Thanks to decisions by the Parent Advisory Council and the commitment of Mary Lane and her associates, however, the end of NICE was the beginning of CCFC, which stands for Cross-Cultural Family Center. This is an organization with the same goal as the original program—the promotion of interfamily, inter-race relations—and a membership comprising 33 of the families who were in NICE and a number of new ones. It operates a nursery school taught largely by mothers who were trained on the job in the original cross-cultural schools, and a kindergarten-supplement program for the original NICE children. It also offers afternoon and evening programs for other children and for parents. The Center depends on fund-raising activities by its members and on tuition fees from the children of nonmembers. It is pleasantly housed in the new church school building of the Unitarian Church, in the area served by the original project.

The accomplishments of NICE may be summarized as follows:

1. The children at 5 seemed to be without racial or class prejudice. As a matter of fact, on the basis of observations by project and teaching staffs, the children got along throughout the project at least as well as any homogenous group of children. Friendships across group lines were common. During the second year, teachers reported 31 "best friend" pairs. In more than half the cases, these were inter-racial. Since the children were 2 years old when the project began, they have little or no conscious memory of associations in groups of children before that time. They will remember only playing with children of cross-cultural backgrounds.

2. The children made gains in intellectual development, as shown in Table 1. On the Stanford-Binet intelligence scale the average I.Q. gain over three years was nine points—from 102 to 111. On the Peabody Picture Vocabulary Test, which tests a child's understanding of words, it was 24 points—from 90 to 114. The gains in all cases were significant at the .01 level, and there were no significant differences between housing groups.

---

walk up and say: "She doesn't want you to hit her. It hurts when you hit." And I'm just looking and observing. And then when the child would hit again, the teacher would say: "No, that hurts, and she doesn't want you to hit and we're not going to let you hit." It was so fascinating to me, I really wanted to stay every day just to watch how they handled the children.

You would have acted differently?

Right, I would have wanted to say: "Now listen, you know better than to hit," and I would have said, "Now you hit her back!" But that's not the way, I've learned. There was my little girl and another little girl, which is a little Japanese, Neisha. Every day this little girl, sometime during the day she would walk over and just hit my little girl. And my little girl would start crying. You know me—I'd say, "This is just killing my child!" So one day I got so mad about it I went to the teacher and I told her, "Now listen, I'm just sick and tired of my child getting beat up every day," and I said, "Something should be done about it." And the teacher, very calmly: "Well, have you any idea why Neisha hits her all the time?" And I said I'd

White children as a group went from 108 on the Binet test to 121; black children, from 97 to 103. On the Peabody, white children went from 93 to 117; black, from 83 to 110. These differences between racial groups were significant at the .01 level, with the white children scoring higher than the black children at all time-points. The staff points out, however, that it is impossible to group the children on the basis of a single factor, either race or type of residence, without the other factor entering in. Oriental children were omitted from analyses involving racial groups because there were too few for proper statistical treatment.

TABLE 1

Average IQ Scores by Type of Residence, First and Last Tests

	Public Housing[1]		Random Housing[2]		St. Francis Square[3]	
	First	Last	First	Last	First	Last
Stanford-Binet	98	103	100	113	108	117
Peabody	83	115	92	108	94	117

1. Low income; black.
2. All income levels; about half black, half white and mixed.
3. Middle income; about 2/3 white, 1/3 black.

3. The children made significant gains in social competence as measured on the California Preschool Social Competency Scale. This scale covers a wide range of behaviors such as response to routine, response to the unfamiliar, following instructions, making explanations, helping others, initiating activities, reacting to frustration, and accepting limits.

not even thought about why she was hitting her. And the teacher said, "She wants to be loved." The teacher went on to tell me: "When they are that little, they don't know how to talk; this is their way of communicating with one another. That's it. And the only thing she is trying to tell Mary is: 'I want to play with you. I want to be your friend.'" And within a month and a half those two were playing together every day. But you know, my concept of it was a completely different thing, but the wrong thing.

I wish the project had come around sooner, that my older children wouldn't have had to suffer so much because I din't know. And I think that the parents in this project got out of it just as much as these children or even more.

My oldest girl was in the nursery school for three years. Well, I'm just so proud of her in the kindergarten. She's marvelous in her class, and they are getting her ready to read. Because all the stuff that the older children have done, she's had it. You know, too, at times she helps the teacher a lot—to help the other children. And so I'm very proud of my children, those who were in the project. Because they have learned education-wise and they have learned one of the things —.

The national norms for this scale are based on teacher ratings of children in preschool programs. On the first test, the average score placed the NICE children at the 38th percentile; on the last test, at the 78th. The gains were significant for each housing group, and the differences among groups were also significant. Over the three-year period, there was no significant difference between white children, who went from the 41st percentile to the 77th, and black children, who went from the 35th percentile to the 76th.

TABLE 2

California Preschool Social Competency Scale (Percentiles)

	First Test	*Last Test*
Public Housing[1]	31	72
Random Housing[2]	43	82
St. Francis Square[3]	42	78

1. Low income; black.
2. All income levels; about half black, half white and mixed.
3. Middle income; about 2/3 white, 1/3 black.

4. The children made significant gains, too, on three scales developed by the project in an effort to guage three qualities it was trying to instill—basic trust, initiative, and autonomy. Among the housing groups no significant difference appeared except in autonomy, where the St. Francis Square children rated higher than the other groups at all times. When first tested, white children scored significantly higher than black in trust and initiative but not on autonomy; on the last test, the scores for whites and

Just like my older daughter, she can tell the difference between a Japanese and a Chinese. And I can't. Because she has been with these little Japanese and Chinese children. I'll say: "Oh, that's a Japanese," and she'd say, "Oh, Mamma, that's not a Japanese—that's a Chinese!" And this really shocked me because I couldn't tell the difference. But through us having all the different races of the children, and them playing with them —. Sometime you'll kind of look at a child and they'll be looking at a child and looking at the child—they're really looking at the child, different from the way we look at it. They look at how the eyes are made, and how the nose, and how everything, you know.

Anybody tell you that?

No—but I sort of learned from my children. Children look at each other in a different way than we look at each other. And then, you know, they'll go up and touch, you know, to make sure that the hair—they want to know why is her hair different from mine. And they have to touch it to really feel and see that that is different and everything. So kids is just amazing. And when I started in the nursery I would go almost just for black on each of the characteristics were virtually identical. The three scales are experimental and their validity untested.

5. In their attitudes toward members of other racial and socioeconomic groups, the parents have become considerably more open-minded and accepting. This is the impression of the staff and of persons who talk to representative parents. It is substantiated by an analysis of ratings for each mother on several experimental scales measuring "intergroup acceptance." The ratings were made at the start of the project and again at the end. Over the three years, both the average score of all the mothers and the average score of the mothers in each housing group increased significantly. The groups had the same relative positions at the end as at the beginning: first, St. Francis Square; second, Random Housing; third, Public Housing.

6. The mothers have become more skilled as parents and more competent as members of society. Ratings on experimental scales to measure child-rearing practices and general social competence showed significant increases over the three years. The St. Francis Square group again rated first and the public housing group third. Four of the mothers have become assistant teachers in the CCFC nursery; another is in charge of the Center's kindergarten-supplement program; another supervises the after-school activities for older children at the Center. One mother has been employed by the San Francisco Unified School District as a school aide. A mother who was on welfare when the project started has become a secretary to a Y.W.C.A.

7. Through open meetings, social affairs, membership of parents in community organizations, and other ways, the project's influence has extended beyond the families immediately involved. Staff and parents have been called on to consult Head Start staff, participate in panels, appear on TV, and help the State prepare for the 1970 White House Conference on Children and Youth. The NICE schools were used in the training of psychiatric social workers, teachers, home economics students,

observation and then the more I went, then the more I wanted to go. I wanted to learn. Then I started working in the school with some of the children, which was very rewarding, because you teach them a lot, and you learn a lot from them.

Has it been easier in kindergarten for your girl than for your boys?

It's a lot easier. It's so much different in boys and girls anyway: girls seem to be a little bit more advanced than boys when it comes to learning. But my daughter, she is as much different in her going to the kindergarten than when my sons went as day and night. Because when she went in there she didn't have this fear of being away from me, for a time, because she had learned that, and then she had learned how to play with other children and she had learned all these different kind of peoples. Just like a teacher in kindergarten is a Japanese and they have an aide in there that's a Negro. Well, she goes in and she doesn't even think about race or why is a person different.

She notices that —?

In the Nice project, even when they was two and a half and three they noticed. And they wondered and they questioned the teachers to some health personnel, and members of the Teachers Corps and the Neighborhood Youth Corps.

8. Materials useful to other projects concerned with preschool children have been developed. These include descriptions of the home task program, which has been widely followed by Head Start and other projects for disadvantaged children, and of suggested processes and materials for a "multicultural curriculum," and a film, "Swimming in the Nursery School." Two films are being developed from NICE video tapes—on the introduction of a child into an ongoing program and on the use of cognitive materials to stimulate thinking. A series of pamphlets on various aspects of the program is planned.

If money becomes available, the team that directed NICE—Mary Lane and two research associates, Mary S. Lewis and Freeman F. Elzey—expect to follow the NICE children through the fifth grade of public school.

Birth of NICE

One day eight years ago, Mary Lane received a telephone call from an acquaintance of hers, a young mother who had recently moved into St. Francis Square. This is the cooperative apartment development, for families of middle income, that in 1962 replaced several blocks of old, three-story houses occupied mainly by low-income black families. Other blocks of similar houses had been torn down earlier to make room for luxurious high-rise apartments. The San Francisco State professor, an authority on the education of young children, was asked to talk with a group of "the Square" parents about the troubling experiences they were having.

Dr. Lane knew that the development had been planned as an integrated community for people committed to inter-racial living and that, while the majority of the residents were white, a number of middle-income black

---

length about why, you know. You know, just like the cartoon—they would rub the black children's skin; they would just rub it to see would it come off. And then they ask a lot of questions. Just like in my daughter, she wanted her hair to be long like Enrica's hair, and so I had to press hers out so hers would be long like 'Rica's hair.

Do they ask questions of you?

Yes. Because they are interested in things. And there she was, sort of questionning. She'd say: "Am I really a black person or am I a blue person?" The way I feel about it she is a Negro, but sometimes other people call the Negro a black. And then she said: "Well, I think I want to be a Negro." I felt kind of fine. You know. And after the questions, it wasn't no problem at all. They played with each other. They'd even come and they'd say: I'm a Negro, or black," and "You're a Caucasian," and "You're a Japanese," and "You're so and so."

How did the teachers explain?

Well, they'd say at times: "Some of us are one way and some of us the other, you know, but we're all human beings because we are all boys and girls."

families lived there, too. She now learned that many, probably most, of the parents in the Square felt frustrated and rebuffed. They had moved in considering themselves liberals in racial matters and eager to get along with the black people in the surrounding neighborhood, mainly in public housing. But facilities in the development such as laundry rooms and playgrounds were being vandalized, and children from the Square were being attacked and chased home from school by public housing children. Further, a group of parents had started a cooperative nursery school in a nearby Y.W.C.A. and had hoped that some of the black public housing residents would participate, thus giving children from the Square an opportunity to associate with other children who would be entering kindergarten or first grade with them. The public housing people had not responded. Residents of the Square were beginning to feel themselves on an island surrounded by hostility.

The Square children, Dr. Lane was told, were doing very well in elementary school, where almost all of the pupils were black. The teachers liked the newcomers and were pushing them ahead. "And," one mother reported, "27 of us have been appointed room mothers!" Apparently it had not occurred to her to wonder about the women who had been the room mothers before. And apparently it had not occurred to most of the parents to wonder how public housing people might feel when they looked out of their stark concrete dwelling place and saw the Square—with its attractive buildings and the neighborhood's only grass and shrubbery—occupying the site where they or relatives or friends once had lived.

Says Dr. Lane, "I thought to myself: *Here are all these middle-income children—200 preschoolers alone—in the Square. And here are all these children in public housing. How wonderful if we could get a cross-cultural thing going, and see if we could break down some of the barriers.*"

A family-centered nursery school for 2-year-olds would be an ideal "cross-cultural thing," she felt, because even people of the most diverse

---

I was prejudiced before I went to the nursery school. Because when my older sons would come home and would talk about their friends, I would say: "Is he a Negro or white?" And one day my oldest asked me: "Well, Mamma, what difference does it make?" And that gave me something to think about. And then I said: "Well, really what difference does it really make?" And then I stopped asking him that.

This NICE project has helped me to overcome my prejudice, because we often have discussions and one discussion was on prejudice, and I think three or four sessions were on it. And at the first meeting, everybody was sort of, you know, not really saying what they really feel. So, Mrs. Lane, she was there. "Now," she says, "You should be fair—you really feel one way or the other about it." And by the time we got to the second meeting, it really came out, what you really feel. And then we learned about each other. I'm prejudiced to a certain extent. Here's you; you are prejudiced to a certain extent. Because it brings you back to how we was raised. You know, and do we want our children to be raised this way? Well, we don't want our children to be raised this way.

10

interests, if properly approached, would surely work together more or less harmoniously for the welfare of their children. And working together, they would learn to understand and appreciate one another. Their children would accept inter-racial activities as a matter of course. Additionally, the children from disadvantaged families probably would enter the public school system, after three years in the nursery school, much better prepared intellectually and emotionally than could be expected otherwise.

With the moral support of a number of community organizations and financial backing from NIMH, through a grant to the College, Dr. Lane spent a year developing her ideas, finding sites for the schools, talking to families with children of the right age (only two such families declined to enter their children), and selecting and training the teaching staff. Assisting her through the life of the project were the research associates mentioned earlier, Freeman Elzey and Mary Lewis. The three worked together as a team, Elzey designing the research projects and analyzing results, Mrs. Lewis conducting the interviews and creating the home tasks program, and all three sharing administrative duties. A psychiatric social worker, Stanley Seiderman, joined the staff some months after the schools opened and became a part of the team in a counselor role.

Key Philosophy: Complete Acceptance

Members of the teaching staff faced more problems than usual because, in addition to being teachers, they were expected to act as counselors to parents and researchers, a function that obliged them to make daily notes and write a weekly record of both child and parental behavior. During much of the first year, too, they sometimes found themselves acting as social workers, guiding low-income families to medical, housing, and other community services. Even after a social worker was added to the project

---

Are you from San Francisco?

No, I'm from the South. Houston. And I remember one of the things that used to hurt me—when my mother would say Yes, ma'm and No'm to a 12-year-old Caucasian. That used to break my heart, because that isn't right, you know. *How're you . . . How're you . . . .* And as a child coming up, it would break my heart, because we were taught at home that you respect age. And you know, I could understand that. But a person younger than me! And I would ask my mother, but she never could really explain to me, to my satisfaction. Or she'd say: "Well, you have to," or "That's the rules." And I have always questioned things like that.

There were things that came out during the group discussions here, that one race don't really know what the other one really thinks until you really get down and start talking about things. Because just like some of the white persons would say they were taught you shouldn't marry out of your race and everything, and a whole lot of this *your parents don't want you to.* And they were shocked to know that these Negro parents didn't want their children to marry out of their race. You know, and different things like this.

3087

11

staff, some of the families preferred to take their troubles to the teachers. A summer of intensive training preceded the opening of the schools but could not altogether prepare the teaching staff for what lay ahead.

Probably the most important feature differentiating these cross-cultural schools from other nursery schools was unconditional acceptance of the parents as well as the children. It was also the teachers' heaviest burden. Unconditional acceptance meant, for one thing, putting up cheerfully with lackadaisical observance of schedule. Children and their mothers were welcomed any time they arrived. Mothers who wanted to take children home before the session was over were permitted to do so. Mothers who failed to pick up their children on time found them being cared for.

More disturbing practices also were accepted. One mother spanked her 2-year-old daughter for wetting her pants. One father, finding his boy reluctant to leave at the end of a session, took off his belt and threatened him. A woman, watching her son, not yet 3, color a picture, insisted that he stay within the lines. In each case the teachers felt shivers running up and down their spines but said nothing.

In staff meetings, where problems associated with unconditional accept-ance were often raised, Mary Lane and her team took the position that if parents were ever to be open to change, in either child-rearing practices or racial attitudes, they first had to be accepted as they were. Some staff members found it harder than others to go along. One head teacher left after a few months.

Before the end of the first year, the staff had evidence that the concept of complete acceptance was paying off. Families were changing their time habits to conform with the schedule of the schools. Parents were asking teachers why they didn't punish the children for wetting themselves, threaten them for not doing immediately what the teacher wanted, insist on neat performances. And the parents were beginning to listen to the answers.

Making the Parents Welcome and Useful

When the three schools opened, parents were invited to stay with their children as long as they wished or felt it necessary. Each school had a parents' corner, fitted out with comfortable chairs, coffee-making

---

I owe a lot to this project. I had a distrust for professional people, you know—that they were one way, and you were another way. But then in this project I learned that although they are professional people they are just human beings, like I am. You know, we call the staff by their first names, and everybody always looks at me when I say Mrs. Lane. Most of us call her "Mary," but I don't know—I have so much respect for her. I just come from old-fashioned teaching that when you really respect a person, and admire a person—. When I say, "Mrs. Lane," well, this is my way of saying I respect her as a person for what she stands for and the things that she has done. It's not because there is a difference in race or anything like that; it just comes out of respect. I suppose there is something in me that I just can't come to call her "Mary." I just can't.

materials, and magazines. Some of the mothers, delighted at the opportunity to watch their children and to talk with other adults, lingered half the morning. After a while the "bag lunch" became an institution. On a certain day each week, mothers would drop in with a lunch bag during the morning and stay to observe the rest of the session and to eat with the staff. These informal get-togethers gradually moved from general talk about children to guided discussions of such subjects as sibling rivalry, art activities in the home, discipline, and toy selection.

Mothers became more and more deeply involved in school operations. After a few months, some of them were asked to volunteer as additional aides because, even with one or two student teachers in each school, the ratio of adults to 2-year-olds was not high enough to give the children as much individual attention as they needed. Later, with the approach of summer and the departure of the student teachers, all mothers were asked to serve one day a week during the summer session. Most of those whose time was not otherwise committed agreed. They were invited to bring along their children, so the workday became also a family outing day. The following fall, Dr. Lane explained at a parents' meeting that writing research reports and attending teachers' meetings required a sizeable amount of the teaching staffs' time. So one day a week the schools would close unless the parents could take over. Teams of mothers signed up to do this, each team obligating itself for one day a week for six weeks.

Home Tasks

At the end of the first year, project staff members and teachers wondered what else could be done to bring home and school together. In about half the families, parents rarely visited the schools except to drop off or pick up the child. And some of the parents who did stay longer were either uninterested in or puzzled by what was going on, in spite of staff efforts to communicate. These were parents who in the main thought of learning only in terms of reading and writing. Some way of getting into the homes and talking to the mothers individually seemed necessary if NICE was to be sure it was reaching at least most of the families. The staff decided on an educational intervention scheme it called the Home Task Project.

Home Tasks would help parents see and make use of the learning potential in the play activities of their young children. Parents then would

---

I would just like to see that this family center could be continued, because I think it has helped my children and so many of the children that need help. And not only the children, but the parents. There was one mother in particular. Her children were enrolled in the nursery school, and the first two years she wasn't really concerned about taking care of them. You know—their eating right and things like that. And since working with the NICE project and the teachers in it, I have seen a big change in her. She's a completely different person. And then you ponder. You see a parent that don't care, and after three years, this parent has just turned about. It's the sort of thing that makes you stop and think.

have greater understanding of the school's task and of the way the school uses materials to help the child learn. Also, by working with the child a few minutes each day, the mother would begin to view herself as the child's teacher as well as his mother.

Mary Lewis spent the summer developing the home tasks and the explanatory materials to accompany them. The tasks were designed to extend knowledge, sharpen perception, develop motor skills, or expand concepts. They included seeds to be planted, a scrapbook to be filled, a plank to be balanced on, picture books to be looked at, puzzles to be worked, pieces of wood to be joined, drawings to be colored, games to be played, and a turtle to be cared for. At Halloween every family would get a pumpkin, along with a recipe for pumpkin cookies, a candle, and a list of suggestions on how a pumpkin could be used to help the child grasp such concepts as round, orange, hard, and hollow. Altogether, 60 such tasks were developed.

Every week, at a regular, mutually satisfactory time, each home was visited by a member of the staff or a student teacher bringing the week's task and typewritten instructions for its use. The visitor demonstrated the task, explained the instructions, and discussed the educational value. A bean bag game, for example, was intended to develop not only eye-hand coordination but also such space-relation concepts as inside, outside, to the right, to the left, over, and in front of. A "feel kit" included the book, "What Is Your Favorite Thing to Touch?", a bag for holding small objects to be identified by touch, and instructions for playing the "comparison game," in which the child is encouraged to name things that are "as smooth as ——," "as sticky as ——," "as soft as ——," and so on. One task called for mother and child to take a short walk, talk about what they saw, and draw a rough map locating some of the things seen. Mothers were encouraged to use the tasks with their children at least once a day. The following week the visitor returned with the next task and asked about the child's experiences with the last one and the mother's ideas for expanding its usefulness as an educational item. Expensive items such as books or puzzles were picked up for delivery to other families.

The staff reports that the home task project, which continued through the second year and 18 weeks of the third, was not without headaches. Items were lost, broken, or kept for longer periods than scheduled, and visits were missed because of forgetfulness either by the visitor or the family. From the comments of the mothers, however, the staff believes that the project succeeded both in drawing parents closer to the schools and in demonstrating the potential of the parents as teachers. Visitors reported increasing interest on the part of most families. Many mothers reported that home task day had become a special occasion for the whole family. Even middle-class mothers were surprised at the variety of ways open to them to develop their children's abilities. After each visit certain information was recorded on IBM cards. It is now possible to determine, among other things, which tasks were most used and how a given task was regarded by mothers and children.

14

A Training Course for Parents

At the request of mothers who said they would like more information on how to work with young children, the project staff decided midway through the second year to offer a course in preschool learning and education. It reasoned that such a course would make the women both better mothers and more competent aides at the schools. Mothers were told the course would run two hours a week for 15 weeks and that they would be expected to work one day a week in the nursery. Out of 32 mothers who were not working, 15 signed up—8 of them black, 4 white, and 3 Oriental.

Asked by Dr. Lane, the instructor, why they wanted training, those who signed up said they would like to learn, among other things:

To talk to my children so they will want to mind.
To get rid of the feeling that I can't handle my child.
To read books with more feeling.
To stay calm.
Educational spots in the city for children.
What to expect of children.
To understand myself better.

The mothers were asked to take notes; readings were assigned and reported on; small groups were formed to make a special study of one area of interest chosen by the members (such as books, trips, toys); and each mother had a semester project—to study and report upon one child, not her own.

To set the tone for the course, Dr. Lane wrote each mother a letter in which she said, in part:

You are your child's most important teacher. Did you ever stop to think what life-long learnings come from you? First of all, he learns the *feel* of mother as you feed him, change him, bathe him. He remembers this always. From you he learns how much he can trust the world.

Then he learns his language from you. His voice tone and the way he pronounces words will be much like yours. What he first talks about will be what he has heard and seen at your knee.

Very important is what he learns from you about how you feel about people. If you are friendly and helpful and think people are pretty fine, he is likely to feel this way, too.

He learns very early from you how you feel about *him*. If you feel your child is just great for a two- or three-year-old, he'll feel great about himself. These attitudes that he "catches" from you when a child, he is likely to keep for all his life. . . .

The course included sessions on child study, art activities, music and fantasy, books and story-telling, educational trips and toys, and science. Dr. Lane or another San Francisco State faculty member would discuss the topic and answer questions. Then a few of the weekly reports written by the mothers as part of their semester project—to observe a child—would be read and discussed. During the following week the mothers were expected to try out in the schools something they had learned during the session. If the topic had been music, for example, they were asked to lead a small group in a song or a dance.

"I thought we were just going to learn from Mary Lane," says one mother, whose views of her experiences during the course were typical. "And that would have been fine. But we learned also from each other. One of us would have a problem with children, and we'd lay it in front of everyone, and people would come up with some very good ideas. You learn ten times more with people sitting around a table with you. You let all your feelings out, and everybody gains."

The course was so popular that next year Dr. Lane offered it again. And, to meet the demand from working mothers, Mrs. Lewis offered a similar course in the evening, which was attended by a few fathers as well as by mothers. All in all, about 35 parents took one of the courses and earned credits from the extension division of San Francisco State for doing so. The credits were appreciated particularly by half a dozen of the mothers who wanted to work in day-care centers and had to meet the requirements for a license.

Developing Self-Esteem

In the beginning, NICE made no effort to develop a cross-cultural curriculum for its children. Since the project was serving a cross-cultural population and had a cross-cultural staff, it assumed that the curriculum was bound to be cross-cultural. The staff put its conscious emphasis on developing skills—perceptual, motor, cognitive—and trust, autonomy, initiative, and social competence.

Because many of the children had culturally poor backgrounds, the project did place more than the usual emphasis on building self-esteem—on helping each child see himself as someone special and as a member of a special family. The staff followed a number of fairly common procedures, such as hanging a full-length mirror low enough for children to see themselves, using the children's names in talking and singing, and identifying and exhibiting work produced by the children. Going farther, the teachers also gave special attention to children with markedly low self-esteem, sometimes even assigning one staff member to care exclusively for one child. For example, a student teacher was assigned to Buddy, who was too fearful to talk or even, at snack time, to reach out for a glass of fruit juice. The teacher took him on walks, read to him, played with him. Half a year later, Buddy was talking a blue streak but articulating poorly, so the staff guided him and his mother to the college's Communication Disorders Clinic. By the end of the year, Buddy's self-concept had improved dramatically.

16

For deepening and expanding a child's good feelings about himself and his family, NICE regards photography as its most important activity. Each school had a simple camera, which the teaching staff was encouraged to use for portraits, candid shots, and group activity pictures. Since the project had access to a dark room at the College, processing was inexpensive. The schools usually had many pictures on display. In one school, children's photographs were used to identify lockers; in another, each child had his own bulletin board, on which were displayed his photograph, samples of his work, and group photographs of classmates. All the schools displayed family pictures. The photographs were often the subject of discussion among children, teachers, and parents.

Special events such as birthdays, picnics, and trips were photographed and the prints put on display for use as learning materials. And occasionally pictures taken a year or two earlier would be brought out for comment. "When a child has a opportunity to see himself in this way through time and space," Dr. Lane comments, "He views himself as a changing person. We feel he gains a sense of openness about himself and his potential. These are important factors in the self-concept."

During the second year, families, teaching staff, and children cooperated to produce a "Self Book" for each child. This was a collection of photographs that the child wanted to have in his own book, together with his own comments about them. Each book began with a photograph of the child and a typed transcript of the story he dictated about himself. Then came other photographs—usually of members of the child's family, his teachers, and his favorite toys. The photographs at home had been taken by someone from the school in accordance with the child's wishes. With each picture was a story the child had dictated. The Self Books were kept in school. Often a child would ask a teacher or a parent to read to him from his book; he would listen delightedly. From this project, Dr. Lane is sure, the child learned not only that his family was something special but also that someone cared enough about him to record what he said.

Later, staff members and parents under the guidance of Mary Lane produced for each child "My NICE A B C Book," which opened with his photograph and included, under F, a photograph of his family. Each of the other pages had a verse about one of the letters of the alphabet, together with photographs of the children or teachers whose first name began with that letter. Thus a child could learn the ABC's and at the same time the names of all those who shared with him three years in the nursery school.

A Cross-Cultural Program

It was apparent from the start that some of the children noticed differences in one another, for they would feel another child's hair as through to verify its differentness, and touch and comment on each other's skin. Late during the second year, when the children were approaching their fourth birthdays, the teachers noticed that they were becoming more consciously aware of differences, or at least talking more often about them. One noon as one of the black mothers was leaving school with her daughter—after a session in which the music hour had included a song about black being beautiful—the little girl said: "Mommy, you and I are white, aren't we?" She was one of several black children who identified rather strongly with one or another of the white teachers. On the other hand, one of the white boys kept telling his mother he wished he were "dark, like Michael," because he liked Michael very much.

So the staff began thinking perhaps it should be paying more conscious attention to the cross-cultural elements of the curriculum. The feeling was that children should not only become aware of differences between one ethnic or cultural group and another but also come to accept and appreciate these differences. In addition, a child's image of himself and his family should be tied to that of his group. As Dr. Lane puts it: "We hoped each child would come to feel that 'I am Bobby Lewis. My folks are the Lewis family. And the Lewises are — black, white, Oriental, mixed, or whatever.' "

Parents were urged to attend staff meetings to talk about these goals and what more might be done to attain them. The parents were to constitute the Parent Advisory Council. Only nine accepted, but these were outspoken in their comments. For example:

> "There are people I don't want him to identify with, no matter what color they are—people, you know, of lower character."

> "How can you explain to your child that you get angry with people in high office and that you don't like a certain person even if he is President?"

> "Yeah, it's hard to build respect, especially in a black home. They're always talking about bad white people—they do this to us, and they did that, and we're going to get 'em. Like she knows somebody white killed Martin Luther King, but she's kept her white friends."

> "You know, it's a funny thing, I never even thought of it that way myself—a white man killed Dr. King, but I guess it's a way of thinking about it. I think I would say it was an individual not a white or black man, and it's wrong no matter who did it."

> "I think the children need to know blacks do bad things and they do good things, just like white people and pink people. But I think when my little girl sees a black do bad things she thinks it too bad."

> "Well, I want my kid to feel good about herself and if she does that, maybe she won't have to hate other people."

All of the parents were kept informed of the Council's discussions. The attending parents, as well as some of the others, contributed ideas for the third year's program. In the end, the staff had many suggestions for ways of teaching differences, particularly in matters of food, dress, games, customs, and holidays. Through its own research it also had a list of books and another of recorded music and songs, from many cultures, considered appropriate for prekindergartners.

As the result, the third-year program included:

• Development of a multicultural calendar that marked such dates as Martin Luther King's birthday, Chinese New Year, Japanese Children's Day, and Jewish and Christian holy days. The calendar was intended primarily for home use, but some of the special days were observed in the schools.

• Visits to the library during Negro History Week to see an exhibit of photographs of people around the world.

• Showing of a moving picture about a black boy and a white boy attempting to span an ocean inlet by building a bridge together. ("Bridge Tomorrow," written, filmed, and produced by Oscar Williams, San Francisco State College.)

• Displays of photographs of prominent people—white, black, Oriental.

• Games and songs from different cultures.

• Exchange of recipes among the mothers and the sharing of characteristic dishes—such as chittlings, teriyaki, sweet and sour pork—at the weekly school lunches.

Services for the Family

The teachers frequently encountered problems that could not be handled with simply a few minutes of advice. For instance, a mother was sick, and her family needed homemaker assistance; a marriage was on the rocks; a family had to move but could find no place to move to; a credit agency was threatening suit; an older child was in trouble with the police. Particularly during the first half year teachers often spent part of their afternoons, which had been set aside for planning and report-writing, and even some of their free time, consulting with such families and bringing them together with the appropriate community services.

The addition to the staff of a psychiatric social worker eased the situation. He acted as a consultant to the teachers and a counselor and advocate of the families requiring help. With the aid of two graduate students in social work, he studied the public resources of the area—health, employment, legal aid, and the like—and told people about them in a meeting to which the parents in particular were invited but which was open to all. A number of the poorer families hadn't known what was available to them almost next door, free.

During the three years of the NICE schools, the project helped 35 families to deal with specific mental health problems through counseling by the social work staff or action by other community agencies, or both. About two-thirds of the cases were child behavior problems, half of them involving nursery school children and the other half, older brothers and sisters.

In other ways, too, the project became involved with a family's older children. For boys whose parents said they needed something to do, it organized a club led by students in educational sociology at San Francisco State. One activity was going to baseball games with their fathers. If a boy's father couldn't attend, the boy went with another father in the project. A black boy might be picked up by a white father, a white boy by a black one. Other activities included trips on foot or by bus to interesting places in the city. For older girls, the project formed the Girls' Friendship Group, which met weekly with a student leader. For a dozen older children who were having trouble in school, it procured tutoring by student teachers. During the project's last summer, the social work staff arranged for 19 youngsters to attend good, small camps.

In addition, the schools provided intervention almost continuously and as a matter of course as the teachers identified special needs. If a child always hung back from group activities, he was encouraged in a number of ways to join in. If a child lacked a male model at home, he was chosen more often than others to go with the man teacher to buy fish for the acquarium or food for the guinea pigs. If a child just sat and looked blank, though his hearing was normal, teachers made sure that some smiling, interested person was near him, often talking to him. Because staff members knew children and families so well, the project estimates that all but half a dozen families received special help directly related to mental health.

The project was concerned with physical health as well, the purpose being to see that each family knew how to get the medical services it needed. To this end, the project required annual physical examinations for both children and mothers, and when necessary it guided the families to facilities where the examinations—and any treatment required—could be obtained at little cost. It won the cooperation of the Health Department in providing vision, hearing, and dental screening services. It arranged for a comprehensive serology test of all the children, primarily to screen for sickle cell anemia, which has a relatively high incidence among black people. Several children were found to have the condition and their families were helped to get the necessary medical care. The project arranged also for parents to participate in several discussions of cancer.

Other activities included:

Swimming classes for nursery school children and their older brothers and sisters.

A dancing class for mothers.

Swimming parties for mothers.

A sewing class for mothers, with aid and instruction from home economic majors at San Francisco State.

An art class for mothers and fathers.

Moving pictures on family life and education.

A monthly meeting for mothers, where the topics discussed included "Prejudices and How to Discourage Them" and "What Advice Would You Give to an 18-Year-Old Mother-To-Be?"

School and tri-school suppers and picnics.

Involvement in the Community

The project was alert for ways to facilitate the involvement of families in community affairs. One opportunity occurred early when the play yard of the West Side Courts Nursery School was subjected to vandalism, including the partial burning of a playhouse. At a meeting of the residents of this public housing unit, quickly arranged by the staff, people who were not members of the project had an opportunity to voice hostility toward the school for serving "white kids" as well as black. And parents with children in the school had an opportunity to explain the goals of the project and thus win for it greater acceptance by their neighbors.

Beyond that, the discussion brought out a legitimate grievance: the lack of recreational facilities, particularly for children from 9 through 13, who seemed to have done most of the damage. Through the efforts of the head teacher, a second meeting was attended by the staff of a nearby neighborhood center, and arrangements were made to bring Westside Courts youngsters into that center's recreational program. As an outgrowth of this experience, staff and parents worked with community leaders to obtain better planning for the use of a small park for the Westside Courts area and became more involved in the Police Community Relations Program. Also, one of the teachers at the nursery school started a woodworking class for older boys and this developed into a club for young teenagers, girls as well as boys. The burned play house, incidentally, was rebuilt and the other damage repaired by a group of the fathers—black, white, and yellow—in the course of a "work Saturday."

During interviews with staff members before the nursery schools opened, many of the parents—of all the ethnic and socioeconomic groups represented—expressed concern about the area's public school facilities and programs. So a Public Education Committee of parents and staff members was set up. It arranged for meetings at which school issues were explained and discussed; organized a program of parent-school visits, under which parents visited the kindergartens their children would attend; and sent representatives to meetings of the city's School Board. The Committee became an area-wide group.

One mother—black, six children, on welfare—represented NICE as a board member of the Mental Health Consortium, formed to work for better use of the area's mental health facilities. Another participated in a charrette, a community-based meeting open to the expression of the residents' wishes and complaints, organized by the Far West Educational Laboratory. The social worker represented NICE on a community planning group, where he helped develop a program for the sick children of working parents.

Several months after the schools opened, a white couple invited all the other parents from one of the schools to a party in their home in St. Francis Square. It was the first parents' party. One black couple from public housing decided not to go because they could not believe they would be welcome. Another got as far as the host's door. "If anybody looks funny at me when they open the door and see who's here," said the man to his wife, "I'm turning around." Today, according to staff members, the idea of rejection would never occur to any of the parents, because they have come to trust one another.

The development of trust was a rather slow process. Until the schools had been in operation a year, there was little mingling by the parents across either racial or income lines. The mixing process speeded up during the first summer, when more of the mothers were helping at the schools and getting to know one another better, and whole families were being thrown together at school picnics. During the final two years, middle-income parents, who were predominantly white, habitually picked up low-income parents, who were predominately black, and took them to parents' meetings and other activities. And some of the women with a car in the family organized car pools so that working mothers, generally from low-income families, would be saved the trouble of getting their children to and from school.

Comments from parents tell this part of the story best.

One mother who had never associated with white people ("oh, we had little friendships in school but it was always kept in school, you know—they didn't come to visit me at home and I didn't go to visit them at home") found herself liking almost everybody she met in the project. "And, someway, it's not a forced like: I've gotten to know them and it's a real friendship—not just having something to talk about, mostly school. They like me, and I like them." She and her children go to dinner at white families' homes and the white families and their children go to dinner at her home.

"We are meeting people on a social level that we wouldn't have met before, except possibly on a business level," said a professional man of chinese ancestry. "This is the most magnificent part of it." He recalled the first time he and his wife had been invited to a social occasion—an anniversary—at the home of one of the black families. The father managed a clothing store. "The thing that struck us very profoundly," said the professional man, "was that these people have as much capability as I have, yet they are not able to live nearly so well for their efforts as I am. And there are many black families who live even less well—in one of those very inhuman monoliths that architects have created to house those families. When you get them that kind of housing, how can you expect high-class citizenship performance?"

Said the wife of a lawyer: "We didn't go out of our way to solicit friends among the parents, just as we don't go out of our way to solicit friends among our neighbors. It was just a natural happening, and it took time. It's genuine." Her husband noticed a couple of plainclothesmen looking on at a fund-raising dance given by the new Cross-Cultural Family Center. "It must seem odd to them," he remarked, "this peculiar mix of people, having a good time, drinking and dancing and talking and laughing." His wife reported: "It was really beautiful."

Another mother, asked what she thought of cross-cultural education, said: "I think it's wonderful, because I think that's the answer to every-thing—all the problems that we're having now. The more you are together the more you really know it's no mystery.... You find out that people are actually doing the same things and having the same type problems, regardless. You really find that out."

One woman said that even before NICE she had been acquainted with a number of people different from her. "But I just didn't have—I'd say 'Yeah, it's a nice day,' and I'd be finished." She mentioned a nursery school mother who had been born in Japan. "One day I met her in the wash house, and we started talking. She was the sort of person I could say, 'It's a nice day,' and we were finished—after that—I don't know what it was. I think it was a change in both of us. The races don't make too much difference—it depends on how they act. That should be a thing we should remember. She talks about the classes where people were talking about how they grew up and what happened to them—their way. And I sort of look at a lot of people and say, 'Yes, that's how you become you are what you are.' And that helps. It just helps in knowing a lot of people in general." This mother said she was joining the Family Center because "I might learn to know somebody else that I didn't know this year at all."

The New Family Center

The nursery schools closed in the summer of 1969, as scheduled, and that fall the Cross-Cultural Family Center opened as the successor to NICE. The Parent Advisory Council and the project staff had spent half a year planning for it.

The two biggest problems had been where to locate the Center, since none of the school sites was adequate, and how to finance it, since NIMH was unable to continue support. The site problem was solved providentially. Some of the nursery school parents appeared on a television program, dealing with battered children, and told what they had learned from NICE about child-rearing and children's education. Impressed, members of the Unitarian Church, which had recently finished building a new education center, asked what the project was going to do next, and offered the use of classrooms, play space, and an auditorium. The church representatives explained that NICE, more than some other worthy organizations which had been considered, seemed particularly able to carry out the church's commitment — to use its new plant for the good of the community.

Some members of the project staff were not eager to accept. Dr. Lane, notably, felt that being in a church might put a damper on activities. She also felt that the superior, almost luxurious, facilities being offered might intimidate some of the persons who would be using them. She expressed herself at a meeting of the Parent Advisory Council and suggested that the search for a location be continued. The Council voted her down. One member remarked: "It won't take me long to get used to a little luxury." Dr. Lane soon felt altogether happy with the decision.

The financial problem was tougher. For the first year it was met largely through contributions of time and talent by parents and by members of the original project staff from San Francisco State, and through money raised by cake and rummage sales and by benefits — a dance, a concert, a fashion show. The fund-raising efforts were so extensive and exhausting that for 1970-71 the Center decided to operate the school in two sessions, morning and afternoon, and to admit children of non-members and charge tuition for them. Fund-raising efforts are still necessary but should be less arduous. Some members of the Center are opposed to this direction but have been unable to suggest a viable alternative.

The head teacher of the Center's nursery school was an assistant teacher in the original project, and her assistants are mothers who were trained as part of that project. The Center's activities include a kindergarten-supplement program for the original NICE children three times a week; individual tutoring in the afternoon for elementary school children who need help in order to keep up with their classmates; afternoon classes in sculpting, dancing, and science for children of 6 and older; and evening classes in cooking and sewing for children of 10 and older. For boys and girls from 7 to 10, there are clubs that meet weekly. For adults, there are discussion groups, pot-luck suppers, occasional socials.

The Parent Advisory Council for the NICE schools became the Board of Trustees of the Family Center, which is a non-profit corporation. The chairman of the board, a man of Chinese ancestry, says: "The three years of the nursery schools simply started something that we expect to grow — to become increasingly more beautiful." Another member, a black woman, adds: "The Family Center speaks stronger and louder about the value of NICE than anything we can say."

Research Grant: MH 14782
Dates of Interviews: November 1969 and September 1970

Reducing the Effects of Cultural Deprivation

Investigators:[1]
Msgr. Paul H. Furfey, Ph.D.
Thomas J. Harte, Ph.D.
The Bureau of Social Research
Catholic University of America
Washington, D.C.

Prepared by:
Herbert Yahraes

Introduction and Summary

During the first 15 or 18 months of life, a number of investigators have reported, children from one racial or socioeconomic group score about the same in tests of intellectual functioning as those from another. By school time, though, different groups have reached different levels; in particular, children from families of low socioeconomic status have a lower average IQ than children from families of higher status. The schools do not change this difference.

Other studies have shown that intellectual level, as measured by mental tests, is closely related to verbal ability, as measured by tests of vocabulary and information, and that disadvantaged groups score lower on these verbal tests than on others. It has also been shown that the children in these groups receive less verbal stimulation from parents—through being talked to, read to, taken on trips, etc.—than children in middle-class groups, and that the parents are usually not very good examples for children to follow in learning language.

These findings suggest that:

• Children from low socioeconomic groups develop deficits in intellectual functioning because they lack adequate intellectual, particularly verbal, stimulation.

• One reason many disadvantaged families remain disadvantaged, generation after generation, is the lower ability of their children to profit from our educational system and, therefore, a lower ability as adults to compete in our economic system.

• If adequate stimulation can be provided early enough, it should prevent deficits in intellectual functioning and thereby help break the cycle of poverty and cultural deprivation.

---

[1] This research was planned by Earl S. Schaefer, Ph. D. of NIMH and carried out in consultation with him. Doctor Furfey served as project director as well as Co-Principal Investigator.

To test one means of providing such stimulation, Earl Schaefer, Ph.D. of NIMH's Center for Studies of Children and Family Mental Health, initiated the Infant Education Research project in 1965. This is a project guided and financed by the Institute but carried out by a staff directed by Msgr. Paul H. Furfey, Ph.D. research associate, Bureau of Social Research, Catholic University. Under it individual tutoring—an hour a day, 5 days a week—was provided to a group of 28 Negro boys from slum areas of Washington, D.C.

The tutoring began when the youngsters were 15 months old and continued for 21 months—the period in which differences between groups in their average level of intellectual functioning first appear, and also the period of early verbal development. The tutors were young women, who talked to the children, read to them, played with them, brought them toys and puzzles and picture books, took them on walks and trips—in short, tried to provide the kinds of mental stimulation necessary to a child's development but not commonly found among the most disadvantaged families. The tutors dealt with emotional and behavioral problems as well. When the children were 3, most of them were enrolled in nursery schools, and monthly discussion groups were set up for the mothers. Serving as controls were 30 Negro boys from similar neighborhoods, who received the same tests as the others but were not tutored.

The investigators hoped to learn whether or not this kind of experience between the ages of 15 months and 3 years makes a difference in intellectual functioning and, if so, whether or not the difference persists.

The results to date show that the project has indeed favorably affected the mental development of the tutored youngsters for at least a time. When the infants were tested at the age of 14 months, a month before tutoring began, both groups scored above normal on the Bayley Infant Scales, which are concerned mainly with sensory and motor development and with alertness and interest. The children in the experimental group were found to have an average IQ of 105; those in the control group, of 108.

At 21 months, after half a year of tutoring, the average IQ of the experimental group was 97; of the control group, 90, a difference significant at the .05 level (it would occur by chance only 5 times in 100). The test this time had a number of verbal and cognitive items, which are included in the Bayley scales for this age level. Scores on such items, which are closely linked to success in school, are strongly affected by environment. Presumably the environment had affected both groups adversely, but 6 months of tutoring had brought the experimental group close to normal.

At 27 months, the average IQ of the experimental group, as measured by the Stanford-Binet test, had advanced to 101, and at 36 months, to 106. For the control group, the scores were 90 and 89. The difference between the groups was significant each time at the .01 level. At 4 years, on the same test, the children who had been tutored rated exactly normal, 100, as a group; the other group rated 90.

In addition to the IQ test at 36 months, the investigators used:

The *Johns Hopkins Perceptual Test,* in which the child is given a form—a triangle, say—and asked to match it with one of several other forms.

The *Peabody Picture Vocabulary Test,* in which the child is shown several pictures at a time and asked to point to the one illustrating a given activity or object ("show me running" * * * "show me horse" * * * "show me vegetable").

A *preposition test,* developed by Schaefer, which asks the child to place something *over* something else, *behind* it, *by* it, and so on.

The tutored children scored significantly higher on the perceptual and vocabulary tests than the other children, but not on the preposition test.

After each test, the children were rated for *task orientedness,* meaning their attention to the job at hand and their cooperation with the tester. At three, this factor was found to correlate with the test results, as expected. More important, both this factor and the test results were found to correlate highly with the mothers' interest in the children, as rated by the tutors. Where maternal interest was rated high—as judged, for example, by the mother's efforts to adequately feed and clothe the child and to express herself verbally with him—the child's test scores were also likely to be high. Mothers rated low in this respect were likely to rate high on a child neglect factor, whose elements included inadequate care, irregular meals, inadequate clothing, sickness, accidents, and beatings. The children of such mothers tended not only to do poorly on mental tests but also to display behavior marked by belligerence, irritability, and negativism.

Nothing in the family—income, parents' education, presence or absence of the father—correlated with the intellectual functioning of the child except the mother's interest. At four, maternal interest no longer correlated with task orientedness, but it did still correlate with the children's IQ.

Just why the experimental group dropped from above normal in intellectual functioning at the age of 3 to normal (although still 10 points above the control group) at age 4 is a matter of conjecture. Doctor Schaefer thinks it is because the tutoring stopped, except for sessions twice a month. "It is quite clear," he observes, "that if we tutor a culturally deprived child for 21 months we increase the rate of his intellectual growth during that period. But it is not clear that he will stay at the level he reaches then unless the extra stimulation is continued; the evidence at this point is that he will not.

"The question is not how to offset a poor genetic potential. The project demonstrated that these lower-class black children had the genetic potential for an adequate level of intellectual functioning: with only 5 hours a week of stimulation, they scored above the norms during the period of stimulation. The question is, how can we foster that genetic potential over the long run?" Schaefer's answer, set forth more fully in a later section, is: by early and continued stimulation—to be achieved by educating future parents to be good parents.

The Infant Education Research Project is continuing. When the children are in kindergarten, between the ages of 5 and 6, tutors will visit the homes of those in the experimental group twice a week, primarily to work with the mothers in the use of educational materials. The mothers will also be taken on visits to the school, in the hope of developing better relations between home and school, and they will continue to meet monthly. Both the experimentals and the controls will be tested during the first year of elementary school to learn if the benefits of the intervention program continue. Also, younger children in the families are being tested to learn if there has been a carryover from the tutoring. (At present there is only anecdotal material. For example, one mother spoke of the child being tutored as "your" child and of her new baby as "my" child. When the tutor came to teach the older baby, the mother would sit in the next room and play with and talk to the new baby. This one became quite precocious in language, speaking in sentences at the age of 13 months.)

Staff members believe that a program based on the one reported here but not intended as a research project could be mounted in any community at no great cost. The tutors could be either mature women or high school girls, chosen for their ability to relate to children and properly trained and supervised. Most of the recordkeeping and psychological testing could be eliminated.

However, staff members also believe, on the basis of the work so far, that ways should be found of working with everybody in the family—not just with the youngest child and to some extent his mother. If the whole family were brought into an educational project, they think, the older children and the parents would become more interested in and capable of carrying on measures that stimulate intellectual growth. So the project should have a broader and longer lasting effect.

Two subsidiary studies likely to be of help in future work with disadvantaged groups are under way. One, by Doctor Furfey and Doctor Mary Elizabeth Walsh, of the Bureau of Social Research, is an analysis of the children's cultural background, based on the tutors' observations of daily life in the homes of their charges. The other, by Doctor Edna O'Hern, of the Department of Sociology, St. Francis College, New York, is an analysis of the children's language, based on their taped responses to pictures.

Findings of Earlier Studies

When Schaefer, working with Catholic University's Bureau of Social Research, proposed the Infant Education Research Project in 1965, considerable evidence had accumulated that the intelligence level of children in poor environments could be raised. The most dramatic example had been reported by Harold M. Skeels and Harold B. Dye in 1939.

Skeels and Dye studied 25 children who as babies had been committed to an orphanage which had few attendants and provided little stimulation. At ages running from 7 months to 3 years, 13 of the children—all of them showing evidence of marked retardation—were transferred to an institution for the mentally handicapped and placed in wards of the older and brighter women, one or two babies to a ward. These women, with mental ages of 9 to 12, gave the babies adoring attention. Over the next year or two, the children made extraordinary IQ gains, ranging from 7 to 58 points. Most of the children were later placed in adoptive homes. Of the 12 children in a contrast group, left in the orphanage, only one showed an IQ gain, of 2 points; the others had losses ranging from 8 to 45 points.

In 1966 Skeels published the results of a followup study made while he was at NIMH. As adults all 13 persons in the experimental group showed average or better than average achievement "as indicated by education, occupation, income, family adjustment, intelligence of the children, and contribution to the community." Of the 12 persons in the contrast group, one had died in a home for the mentally retarded, four were in institutions, one was self-sufficient at a middle-class level, and the other six had such jobs as dishwasher, part-time cafeteria worker, and assistant to the gardener in an institution. Most or all of the 12, Skeels believed, would have achieved within the normal range had they been placed early in infancy in suitable adoptive homes provided with equivalent stimulation.

Other investigators, among the many who influenced the planning of the Infant Education Research project, had reported:

• No differences between Negroes and whites in mental tests given during the first 15 months.—Nancy Bayley.

• Negro elementary children in five southeastern states have a stable average IQ of 81 for the years 8 through 11.—W. A. Kennedy, V. Van de Riet, J. C. White, Jr.

• Infants whose mothers had been instructed to read and talk to them began at 17 months to produce more speech sounds than babies in a control group.—Orvis C. Irwin.

• The intelligence of children reared by foster parents was more like that of the foster parents than of the less educated, lower socioeconomic true parents.—Marie Skodak.

• At 18 months, the IQs of 170 London children were virtually identical, regardless of social class. At 3 years, children in the upper class showed a gain of about 22 points; those in the middle class, of about 9 points. Lower-class children dropped about four points.—C. B. Hindley.

• Groups of Negro children of different socioeconomic classes showed consistent class differences in language skills.—Vera P. John. Later came the finding that the teaching skills of 160 Negro mothers and the performance of their 4-year-old children differed greatly according to the families' socioeconomic level.—Robert D. Hess and Virginia Shipman.

• Among 292 children, both lower class and minority-group status were associated with poorer language functioning.—Martin Deutsch.

• Fifteen children committed to a State institution as feebleminded and given a special 2-year training program showed an average gain 2 years later of 10.2 points on the Stanford-Binet IQ test and 10.5 points on the Vineland Social Maturity Scale. Children in a control group dropped 6.5

points on the IQ test and 12 points on the social maturity scale; in other words they were more retarded at eight than they had been at four. Follow-ups showed that six of the first group but none of the second had been permanently paroled from the institution.—S. A. Kirk.

• All gifted children apparently have received intensive early stimulation. This special stimulation may be indispensable to the development of high abilities. There is no evidence the children suffered ill effects of any kind.—William Fowler.

• "* * * it appears that the counsel from experts on child-rearing during the third and much of the fourth decades of the twentieth century to let children be while they grow and to avoid excessive stimulation was highly unfortunate. * * * It is no longer unreasonable to consider that it might be feasible to discover ways to govern the encounters that children have with their environments, especially during the early years of their development, to achieve a substantially faster rate of intellectual development and a substantially higher adult level of intellectual achievement. * * * The fact that it is reasonable to hope to find ways of raising the level of intellectual capacity in a majority of the population makes it a challenge to do the necessary research."—J. McV. Hunt.

Training the Tutors

The tutors were chosen because they were intelligent, outgoing women interested in working with children. All had had experience in jobs— teaching, social work, nursing—that brought them in touch with children. A few were mothers. With the exception of a woman who was still in college, all were college graduates. Five were black and four white. They worked together beautifully, a project official reports, and those of one color seemed to get along with the children as well as those of the other. (Each child had two tutors—generally one of them black, the other white—who alternated weekly in working with him. This arrangement was intended to lessen disruptive effects in case a tutor left or was changed, to reduce any feeling on the part of the mother that the tutor was competing for the child's affection, and to provide two different observers of the child and his family.)

During the initial training period, which ran for about 2 months, half-time, the tutors heard and discussed lectures by Schaefer, Furfey, and others on child development, the special problems of the disadvantaged child, and means of overcoming those problems . The need to develop and maintain a relationship that would foster the child's interest, happiness, and success in his new experience was emphasized. If this need were to be met, the tutors were told they would have to accept the child's interests, praise his achievements, and enthusiastically explore new learning opportunities with him. The interaction between tutor and child was to be playful, spontaneous, and pleasant; formal instruction would be avoided. A tutor must be aware that a child's early learning involves a great deal of looking, listening, tasting, smelling, and feeling. She must also be aware

30

that she is a model for the child—and the mother—to imitate. She will name things casually but often—toys, household objects, pictures in books, events, clothes, the child's body.

"We are all investigators, researchers, experimenters together," Schaefer told the tutors. "We are searching for a method of early education which will raise the intellectual functioning of children and increase their ability to do well in our American school system. We think we know some of the characteristics which help children to succeed in school. We think it helps a child to be cooperative, outgoing, verbal, friendly, helpful to others, resourceful, curious, attentive, to have a goal-directed behavior and be able to concentrate and persevere. It helps if he has developed a feeling of competence and of human worth, if he is able to assert himself in a positive way and make a worthwhile contribution to a group. It is of great value that he have good comprehension and a good vocabulary. We hope to find ways of developing at least some of those characteristics."

Examples of a number of specific activities that might be used during the tutoring sessions were discussed—among them, blowing bubbles, playing with beads, making things with pipe cleaners, playing a guessing game, making a pull toy, having fun with paper plates, and playing a sorting game. The tutors were asked to encourage the child to participate in any activity as much as possible and to talk to him about what was going on. If tutor and child were making a bean bag, for example, the talk might go something like this:

> We will make a bean bag.
> Please hold the cloth for me.
> I will cut it.
> Be careful. The scissors are sharp.
> Move your hands.
> That's it.
> Now we can sew it.
> Look at this needle.
> See the tiny hole.
> We have to get the thread in this tiny hole—the eye of the needle.
> Look at my thimble.
> Try it on your finger.
> See how it fits on mine.
> Please hold the cloth while I thread the needle.
> Watch me thread it.
> You can string beads. Some day you will be able to thread a needle.
> Now, I will hold the bag open while you put the pebbles in.
> Put in one; now one more.
> Put a whole bunch in at once if you can.
> Now we will sew up the last side.
> We must sew it so no pebbles will fall out.
> See, it's all done.
> Thanks for helping, Johnny. Johnny helped to make a bean bag.
> See, isn't it pretty. We're all finished.

Now move back, so I can throw it to you, etc.
Now let's try throwing it into that pail. Let's take turns, etc.

Making a bean bag would be fun. It would also help the child build his vocabulary. And it would help him in learning to count, learning goal-directed activity, learning that a combination of materials can make something different from the original materials, and learning that a person can create something and then have fun with it.

Emphasis throughout was placed on language stimulation. Schaefer urged the tutors to get the children "hooked on books."

The technique of *transfer,* too, was emphasized. "Children are happier and more comfortable with the familiar," Schaefer pointed out. "They can even become frightened by something entirely novel. Begin work with something familiar to the child. If it is something he likes and enjoys you will soon be able to transfer to a slightly different use or activity and thus capitalize on the child's initial interest and pleasure.

"For example, if he finds it fun to shake jingle bells because he enjoys the sound, you may later be able to transfer to sorting jingle bells according to size or color, counting them, making things with them, etc., and still maintain his interest and joy, while at the same time stimulating new learning."

As part of their training, the tutors observed the activities of children in day centers, an orphanage, an institution for delinquent children, and the homes of middle-class families having children of roughly the same age as those in the project. The tutors also recruited the families for the research program, by knocking on almost 200 doors in several of Washington's worst slum areas, and thus became acquainted with the types of homes they would be going into. And each worked for two weeks with a pilot case, a child who was a little too old to be chosen for the project.

There was in-service training, too. Each tutor discussed cases frequently with the leader of the tutoring team (in the beginning a speech therapist who had been a teacher of preschool deaf children, and since mid-1967 Mrs. Lillie Davidson, formerly a nursery school teacher, a supervisor of teachers, and a supervisor of children's counselors in a center for homeless children). Case conferences involving Schaefer, Furfey, the head of the tutoring group, the tutors, and sometimes a mother and her child were held frequently. All the tutors met weekly with other staff members to discuss problems and to give and receive suggestions about educational materials and techniques.

The Children and Their Families

The effect of certain environmental factors upon intellectual functioning has been found to differ according to sex.[2] Since the project could not

---

[2] The Effect of Childhood Influences Upon Intelligence, Personality and Mental Health in *Mental Health Program Reports—3.*

afford a large enough sample to study both sexes, it limited itself to boys because lower-class black boys and men seem to have a more difficult time in school and society than girls and women.

The subjects were chosen from census tracts selected because they had high rates of crime, delinquency, infant mortality, joblessness, dilapidated housing, and families on welfare. The neighborhood environment as well as the typical home environment was deprived. Though the experimentals lived in a slightly worse neighborhood than the controls, the children from one area had been scoring much the same as those from the other on the Metropolitan Readiness Test, given to children on entering school. The median scores were approximately at the 20th percentile on national norms, meaning that they fell in the lowest fifth.

Families having a boy of the right age were invited to participate if the home situation was relatively stable—that is, if it did not look too chaotic for daily tutoring session—and if the family met two of three other qualifications: its yearly income was less than $5,000, the mother had not finished high school, the mother had never been employed as a skilled worker.

Among the 98 homes the tutors visited to select the experimental group, 12 were rejected by the staff as unsuitable (because they were considered unsafe for the tutors or too crowded to work in, or because the family's attitude was judged likely to present unduly severe problems). Five other homes were ruled out because either the income or the mother's education was too high. Most of the other rejections were made because the children were not of the right age. Four families refused to participate.

The control group was selected from 89 homes in a slightly better area. Ten were rejected by the staff as unsuitable, and 12 were ruled out because the economic or educational level was too high.

Stipends—$10 for each testing session and $1 for each tutoring session—were offered primarily in the hope of reducing losses from the sample, particularly losses of children with poorly motivated mothers. Since losses were expected to be high in any case, and the project wanted to retain at least 20 in each group, 31 children were chosen to be tutored and 33 to serve as controls. A number of the families have broken up and some have moved, as many as five times. But only three in each group have been lost. (Among the experimental families, one moved out of town; one placed the baby in a day center so the mother could take a job, and the center refused to admit the tutors; and one notified the project that the tutors would no longer be safe: the wife's mother had moved in and she liked to throw things.) This unusual record is attributed both to the interest of most of the mothers in having something done for their children and to the tutors' persistence in following families and staying on the job in spite of any unpleasant circumstances. The staff now thinks that without the financial inducement, no more than three or four of the families in each group would have been lost.

The homes as a rule had neither toys nor books, and the mothers at first seemed to think it a joke to suppose that anything could be taught to a child as young as 15 months. Some of the parents, even some of those on welfare and with half a dozen children, were well organized. The families always had food; the children were sent to school daily; the mother knew how to go to second-hand stores and buy clothes. Other parents seemed overwhelmed by their problems.

The following quick sketches of representative cases are drawn from tutor's reports:

W. lived with his parents, a brother, a sister, an uncle, and an aunt—7 persons in all—in a three-room apartment on the third floor of a rapidly deteriorating house. The rats were so bad, his mother said, that she had to beat on a pan to frighten them away before she entered the kitchen. They had chewed the nose off a doll. The father had a steady job as a truck driver, and the mother worked part-time as a counter girl in a nearby drugstore. She kept the apartment tidy, showed her love for her children, and participated in the tutoring sessions.

At 15 months, J. was a shy, neglected, poorly dressed child who lived with his baby sister and his 17-year-old mother in a dingy six-room apartment, part of an old house. It was occupied by his grandmother, who worked as a domestic, an unemployed uncle, and the uncle's 4-year-old daughter. J.'s father was in jail. The apartment was uncrowded but unpleasant. Fumes from an oil stove, which supplied inadequate heat, made the eyes smart. Chunks of plaster had fallen from the walls. The bedroom floors were littered with soiled clothing. Cockroaches crawled all around. There were no toys or books, but there were newspapers, a television, a radio, and three telephones which had been disconnected. The mother, a high school dropout, was quiet and timid, knew little about raising her children, and was apparently unable to show affection for them. She was interested mainly in going to school and getting a job. J. was cared for by the grandmother, a warm and friendly person and apparently the only member of the household bringing in money, and a babysitter.

When the tutoring began, V. lived with his parents in a spacious one-bedroom apartment and slept with them in a double bed. His father had a steady job, and his mother worked in the afternoon until her husband asked her to quit so she could spend more time with the boy. This was one of the few homes with books and toys. V. was as spoiled as any middle class only child could be. When the tutor and he went for a walk and passed a store without going in and buying something, he had a temper tantrum. One night some men came to the apartment, threatened V.'s father with a gun, and chased him out. The next day the family moved to another section of the city. This was near the end of the tutoring program. The mother seemed despondent over the course of events, and the boy showed hostility toward the tutors.

A. and his mother, brother, and sister lived in a two-bedroom basement apartment that reeked with the odor of urine because the mother washed clothes and diapers together and did not properly rinse them. Sometimes the odor was so bad that the tutor had to take the boy outside. Cockroaches added to the discomfort. The mother, strict and brutal, would punish the children either by striking them or locking them up in a room.

34

E. was a happy, sociable child who readily sought and gave affection. He lived with his five brothers and sisters and his parents in a two-room apartment, which needed repairs but was kept in reasonable order. His mother worked nights in a carry-out restaurant. She loved him and did a good job of caring for him. E.'s parents separated during first year of tutoring, and the mother moved with all the children to another two-room apartment. When E. entered nursery school, she began going to night high school so she could get a better job.

R.'s mother showed the tutor a scar on the boy's upper thigh that had come from a rat bite. She had four other children but managed to sit in on many of the tutoring sessions, often went along on trips, and was proud of R.'s accomplishments. There were books in the house. The family seemed to pay little attention to R.'s father, who did not work regularly. When the mother got a job as a teacher's aide in a Head Start center, the children were sent to a baby-sitter's home and the tutoring continued there.

T.'s mother separated from her husband during the course of the project and moved with her six children into a one-bedroom apartment. Three boys and their 8-year-old sister slept in a double bed, another boy in a crib, the newest baby in a bassinet, and the mother in a single bed in the same room. A bed in the living room was often used by overnight guests. The mother, who seemed disturbed as a result of problems first with her husband and then with a new man, constantly screamed at the children and threatened them with belts but got no response. The toilet was usually broken. Some of the children had ringworm. T. kept complaining of being hungry. The tutors found it difficult to get him to concentrate.

Working With the Children

The tutors set out to build friendly, easy relationships with the children by playing with them and talking to them—activities in which some of the mothers had engaged only rarely. Some children made friends almost immediately. Others hung back. With one boy, shy almost to the point of being withdrawn, the tutors had to work almost a year to establish rapport. In other cases, productive relationships developed only after the tutors had worked to change maternal attitudes and behavior.

At the start, the children were given manipulative toys—blocks, pop beads, nesting sets—which they learned to put together and to separate. One toy would lead to a number of activities. Given pop beads, for example, a child would feel them, swing them in the air, and chew or suck on them. Perhaps he would learn by accident that they could be pulled apart. This delighted him. Putting them together was too difficult for most of the children at 15 months, so the tutor would show how to do it and then guide the child's hands till he could do it himself. Other activities with beads included hiding some of them around the room for the child to find and add to the string, using a long string of them as a pull toy, counting, naming colors, and matching according to color or shape. Along

35

with the simple manipulative toys, the child was given opportunities to play with balls of various sizes, a kiddie-car, a pounding bench, and other toys that helped develop the larger muscles.

Always the tutor talked to him about what was going on. When a new toy—for instance a ball—was presented, she would name it. The games that could be played with the toy gave the child opportunities to hear, imitate, and learn other new words—for instance, *roll, throw, catch,* and *kick.* As the child matured, the tutor would talk about the different sizes, kinds, colors, and number of balls.

If a boy liked a toy car, the tutor would talk about that car and other cars. Then she would get a book containing pictures of cars and talk with the child about what he saw on each page. When tutor and child went for a walk, they would talk about the cars seen. Looking at picutres of cars in a book helped develop an interest in books, too. One tutor was surprised and pleased to find the children associating one make of automobile with her. When they saw this auto in a book or on the street, the response would be, "Tha' teacher's car!"

Toys were used not only to aid physical development and to teach language but also to develop two of the characteristics essential to the mastery of schoolwork—attentiveness and perception. Here puzzles were considered especially valuable. First came simple, isolated-object puzzles—for example, a board containing pictures of three kinds of fruit, to be taken out and put back in—which were introduced between the ages of 15 months and 2 years. More difficult puzzles followed. One tutor, Betty Pair, describing her experiences for the benefit of other persons working with children, wrote:

"We talk about the puzzle while it is still intact; then dump out the pieces (this act I leave to the child, because he seems to derive great pleasure from the dumping); then talk about the side with colors on it and the dark, rough side; then trace with our fingers around the inside of the puzzle; then attempt to fit the pieces in the puzzle.

"It is important that the child complete the task, but it is imperative that he not become so frustrated in his attempt to do so that he sets up a negative block against the activity. For this reason, I initially put the pieces back slowly in the puzzle so that the child can observe me. This is the 'I Can Do It' part. We then see if he can do it, with the assistance he may require to prevent overt frustration. When there are signals that assistance is required, I put my hand over the child's hand on the puzzle piece, and I explain, 'Turn it around,' or 'Turn it over,' or 'try another space,' as we do what each command directs."

Another tutor, Lucile Banks, offered these suggestions:

1. Present puzzles as enjoyable games.
2. Demonstrate how pieces are placed.
3. Give each piece a name.
4. Begin by taking only one piece out of the board at a time.
5. Finish one puzzle before starting another.

6. If frustration persists, direct the child to a more relaxing activity—such as painting or a favorite toy.
7. Praise the child.
8. Present puzzles already mastered for relaxation and reinforcement.

Through playtime activities, the tutors also worked to modify undesirable behavior. If a child were hyperactive, the tutor would try to get him interested in one activity—like putting rings on a stick, arranging animals, building a wagon—and would work with him to see it completed. "Well, Bobby," she'd say, "let's finish this. I will help you. * * * No, we aren't going to play with that until we've finished this" or "until we've picked this up and put it away."

Toys are credited with having aided social development, because they usually had to be shared with other children in the house, either during the tutoring sessions or between them. Generally a toy was left in the home for several weeks. If it became a favorite it might be left longer, or one like it bought as a birthday or Christmas present.

Tutors and mothers worked together to make toys. Milk cartons—cut into squares and the squares covered with paper—became blocks; oatmeal boxes, drums; pierced bottle caps on a string, a tambourine. Bleaching compound bottles were shaped for use as dolls' cribs. A roll of shelf paper filled with sketches ("This is Jim * * * he lives in a house * * * he has 3 brothers * * *") became, as it was slowly unwound, a movie. Two cans and string made a walkie-talkie. Tutors and mothers also spray-painted cartons for use in storing toys, and they cut down large soap-powder boxes to make cases for children's books.

Books were introduced early in the project, though the attention span of these 15-month-olds was very short. To win the children's interest, the tutors tried to relate things seen in books to things known in daily life. Sometimes they would carry books with them on walks and point to a picture of a dog or a tree, bird, truck, and then to the real thing. Adults and children in illustrations showing family groups would be named after the persons in the child's family. Books that a child found especially appealing would be presented again and again, unless he showed boredom; books that had no attraction for him would be taken away but might be introduced again later.

One boy clearly preferred books about horses. So his tutors dug up as many horse books as they could find and they took him on trips to see horses and to ride ponies. Whenever a tutor showed him a picture of a horse, he would tell her about these trips. Sometimes he would sit for an hour looking at a book with pictures of horses in it. A boy who preferred books about animals in general was taken not only to the zoo several times, but also to the Rock Creek Park Nature Center, the natural history exhibits at the Smithsonian, and the circus. And his mother took him to the country.

With the child, and sometimes his mother, watching and helping, the tutors made books by cutting pictures from magazines and pasting them in scrapbooks. Some of the books were concerned with a single subject —babies, for example, or automobiles. Others had pictures chosen because they would remind the child of things he and the tutor had seen at the zoo, or in a store, or during a walk around the block. Scrapbooks were also made to illustrate such concepts as big and little (an elephant and a mouse), one and many (automobile tires), old and new (shoes), and circle and square. Other scrapbooks were used to teach numbers. A picture of one sheep would be headed, "This is 1"; of two donkeys, "This is 2," and so on. The numerals were cut out of sandpaper so the child could feel as well as see them. The homemade books were left in the home for use whenever the child liked. So were some of the others, particularly the cloth ones.

The tutors also told stories, read stories, and used the combination of story book and record player.

During their third year, most of the children went to the library a number of times and checked out, carried home, and kept for a few days a book of their own choosing. The children by this time had come to expect the presentation of at least one book, old or new, during each session, and books often took up more of the session than toys. "Hey, Teach," some of the children would say as the tutor entered, "I wanna book."

Music, too, was part of the curriculum. The tutors would sing to the children, play songs and other music on a record player, and use home-made or inexpensive children's instruments—drum, tambourine, bells, xylophone—to help the youngsters express rhythm and time.

"When the babies were young (15-18 months)," reports one of the tutors, Patricia Chernoff, "I held them in my lap or arms, facing me, and moved my body or knees to the rhythm of the song, at the same time articulating the words carefully and drawing the child's attention to my singing by holding him close and using exaggerated facial expression. I repeated the same songs until eventually the child attempted to sing. At this point, I simplified the words, concentrating on those which were repeated most often in the song and therefore easiest to perceive and repeat. For example, in presenting "Shoo, Fly, Don't Bother Me," I sang *Shoo Fly* with greater emphasis and volume than the rest of the words, expecting the child to repeat only those two words. Gradually, when he was able to sing *Shoo Fly* in the correct places throughout the song. I encouraged him to add the remainder of the phrase, *don't bother me.* The phrase, *for I belong to somebody,* because of its length and the rhythm with which it is sung, comes much later. When the child is unable to perceive the words from the recorded presentation, I have repeated them more slowly, later without the recording.

"Once the child has become interested in the actual singing of the songs, I have lessened body contact and emphasized the rhythm, con-centrating only on the words. When the child becomes tired of singing, I terminate the music session rather than changing the emphasis to clapping, etc.

"I have found that the length of time required to learn a song has lessened considerably (in some cases, the child enters in during the first presentation) as the children become able to focus their attention on the

38

words and as I continually reinforce with praise and enthusiasm their attempts to sing the words."

A child's birthday was always recognized, usually by a party and a book or a toy from the tutor. If a party could not be arranged, tutor and child would walk to a store to pick out a present.

Influence on the Mothers

The tutors believe that they have reached each family to some degree. One mother related with pride that whenever she took her boy to the store, he dragged her over to the display of books, and she sometimes bought him one. Another would sit in on the tutoring sessions and often ask questions about aims and techniques. Though she herself could not read, she took out a library card at the tutors' suggestion, and began borrowing books for her three youngest.

At the start, one mother kept screaming at her 15-month-old, who liked to get into things: "You are bad—I'm going to beat you." Her attitude was hostile, almost rejecting. As she watched the boy's progress under the tutors, though, she came to recognize his inquisitiveness as a mark of intelligence, and her attitude turned to one of acceptance and even pride. Another woman frequently made out-of-town visits, leaving her boy with a relative. During these absences he was obviously upset; even when the mother was at home he seemed to feel insecure. He became a happy interested youngster only after the tutors persuaded the mother that he loved and needed her, and she began staying home. Under the influence of the tutors, A.'s mother, mentioned earlier, eased her harsh discipline and became so interested in learning how to help children that she took a volunteer job in a nursery school. A.'s IQ, which had dropped from 116 at 21 months to 89 at 36 months, rose to 102 at 4 years.

Some of the women would buy a toy or a book like one brought in by the tutor, or they would ask what they ought to buy. One displayed a 28-piece puzzle she had bought as a Christmas present. Since the boy in the program was only two and a half, the tutor supposed it was for the older children. "No, it's for *him,*" said the mother. She dumped the pieces on the floor, and the youngster put them together in a few minutes. The boy's older sister found it difficult at times to keep up with him. The mother called her silly or dumb, till the tutor explained that the girl was smart enough—she just had not had her brother's training.

A number of the families began taking more trips with their children. Some mothers had not known that such resources as libraries, museums, and a zoo existed; others had not known how to get to them. A few mothers hadn't even known what bus to take to go downtown, and one never left the house to go anywhere unless one of the children went along: she didn't think she could find her way back.

The tutors often encountered problems that were outside their province as tutors but not as human beings. For instance, they would find a family sitting around in winter coats because the heat had been turned off. Or the mother would be distraught because the family faced eviction. Or the mother and father had quarrelled, and the mother had gone off to visit relatives. The children in such cases would be upset—fearful, or apathetic, or quarrelsome; one child kept asking his tutor to take him with her.

One woman with half a dozen children had an especially difficult time with her money. (Says a tutor: "To budget welfare money—which is too low anyway—for a month is really a challenge even to someone who has taken a home economics course in college. When the welfare checks come out, food stores raise their prices, and people go around in cars trying to get you to buy nice looking but flimsy clothes that won't last over a month.") After the first two or three weeks of the month, this woman would run out of both food and money. Several times a tutor found the children picking crumbs from the floor and eating them. The project had no funds to feed the family, but the tutors sent the mother to agencies that could give her emergency help. They also went shopping with her and showed her how to choose economical foods, and they brought in snacks for the children.

When the children were three, the tutoring ended, except for twice a month visits, and the project tried to place them in nursery schools. It succeeded in all but two cases, where the family situation was particularly unstable. (An effort to place children from the control group succeeded in only half a dozen cases, partly because the effort was less intensive and partly because the families were little motivated to send their children to nursery school.)

At the same time the mothers were invited to meet once a month, in groups of four or five, for a planned program of discussions of subjects in which they were interested as well as subjects about which the project thought they needed to be informed. Most were pleased to accept and one was delighted: she had always wanted, she said, to belong to something.

All kinds of problems have been discussed—for example, how to tell older children about sex (some of the women said that their own mothers had been too shy to talk to them, so they hadn't known about having a baby until they'd had it); what to do about a child who is having trouble in school or refuses to go to school; how to cope with poor health, bad housing, marital problems. The tutors conducting the meetings have felt equipped to answer some of the questions themselves. They have handled the others by giving out pamphlets on the subject or suggesting that the mother talk with her child's counselor at the school. Movies have been shown—about differences between children at different ages, about sibling rivalry, and about how parents are teachers, too. Mothers with jobs have told how they went about getting them, what training they took, and how they met the transportation problem. Only two mothers have failed to attend any of the meetings.

As one result of the project, at least in part, a number of the mothers are trying to better themselves economically and socially. Using skills learned largely from the tutors, one is working in a parent and child center setup under an Office of Economic Opportunity program, and several as aides in nursery schools. With advice and encouragement from the tutors, others have gone back to school or have entered training programs, in order to get better jobs. Some have sent their children off to school or a day care center, traveled an hour or an hour and a half to attend a training program across town, and hurried home late in the afternoon. After the children entered nursery school, several of the mothers coupled an all-day job with a training program at night. They would leave their children at a sitter's home five days a week, picking them up on Friday night and returning them on Sunday.

During the kindergarten year, the homes of working mothers will be visited on Saturdays, and the children of these mothers will be seen at the babysitter's during the week.

Implications for Educational Policies

To summarize, the Infant Education Research Project found that:

1. A tutoring program beginning at the age of 15 months for Negro boys from disadvantaged families and continuing, 1 hour a day, for 21 months significantly raised their level of intelligence until they were 4 years old, at least.

2. The average reached at the end of the third year, 106, dropped six points during the next year but was still significantly higher than the control group's average.

3. When maternal interest was high, a child's IQ was likely also to be high.

How long the benefits from the additional stimulation will continue remains to be seen. But the drop in the peak IQ level after the tutoring stopped, at 3, suggests to Schaefer that short-term programs of early education are not sufficient to develop and sustain the child's potential over the long run. Other studies using different programs of stimulation point to the same conclusion.

The investigator thinks the answer lies in both early and continued education. "Genetics may determine the potential range of a child's intellectual level," he points out, "but the quality of the environment determines the actual level. Evidence is accumulating rapidly that because of physical, social and emotional, and cultural deprivations, many children are not developing their genetic potential, and therefore do not function effectively in school and in society."

Physical deprivations include inadequate medical care, insufficient and low-quality food, poor housing, and inadequate clothing. Social and emotional deprivations stem from the lack of stable and supporting relationships with the mother and father or their substitutes. Cultural deprivation occurs when parents fail to provide a stimulating environment. Children who lack pencils, paper, crayons, books, games, and other educational materials do not receive enough training in certain qualities and abilities—such as attention, concentration, perseverence, and perceptual-motor skills—that make for success in school. Children who are not encouraged to talk about their experiences, who do not have models of good language use to follow in their early years, and who have little or no opportunity to make visits beyond their immediate neighborhood are likely to reach school age lacking the language skills, the interest, and the knowledge of more fortunate children.

As Schaefer sees it, the intellectual development of the typical child can be viewed as having four basic stages. In the first, the parent develops a loving acceptance of the child and a positive involvement with him. In the second, this involvement elicits from the child the development of a positive relationship with the parent. In the third, the parent and the child engage together in activities, such as piling up blocks, rolling a ball, looking at a picture book, and the parent by word and by example teaches the child language, skills, and task-oriented behavior. From this early experience with the parent, the child reaches the fourth basic stage—he has acquired the interests and the skills that enable him to learn on his own. "Successful achievement of these early developmental stages in the home," says Schaefer, "may be a necessary basis for a successful education in the school. But deprivation during their own childhood may leave parents without the personal resources to support the optimal development of their children."

Do we then need more nursery school? More child-care centers that will take children at 15 months and even younger? A spread of tutoring programs, like the one in Washington but lasting longer and made part of the public education system so that every child will be reached?

"We do need to recognize that education goes on from birth," Schaefer answers, "but I think it would be more fruitful in most instances to support parents in their educational role than to set up educational institutions to supplant them. Parents, or at least the mother, are there early and continue to be there. This study found that both tutoring and the quality of maternal care were related to the children's intellectual development at three and four. Tutoring can be thought of as supplementary maternal, or parental, care because in the middle class a good mother, and a good father, does what the tutors have done."

As one hopeful development, Schaefer points to a new Institute-supported project in Prince Georges County, Maryland, that seeks to integrate the educational efforts of home and school. When children are infants, teachers will go into the home to work with the parents; later on the parents will go into the school. But he thinks we ought to look even farther ahead. "If you assume that almost everyone becomes a parent and that one of the most important jobs for each generation is to rear the next generation," he says, "it follows that we should be giving children, beginning in kindergarten and running through the twelfth grade, some of the skills needed if they are to be competent as parents. We should have programs for future parents."

The Washington project has demonstrated that lower-class black infants can benefit from additional stimulation. Could other infants also benefit? Schaefer answers that we cannot be sure until programs of stimulation are tested with other ethnic and socioeconomic groups. "Some people say that middle-class parents are doing as well as they can with their children

—that nothing else they could do would lead to higher levels of intelligence and achievement. I don't believe that, but it needs to be tested."

"Many parents—and I think they can be found in all social classes—don't have the skills to be effective in their roles as teachers. We need to develop methods of improving the education of young children, and we also need to develop better ways of communicating what we learn—and what we already know, for that matter—to all parents and future parents. If the whole culture became aware of the importance of parents as teachers, I believe it would lead to an educational revolution, and to a better adjusted, more competent, and more intelligent population."

Research Grant: MH 9224
Dates of Interviews: August and September 1969

References:

Bayley, N., and Schaefer, E. S. Correlations of maternal and child behaviors with the development of mental abilities: data from the Berkeley Growth Study. *Monographs of the Society for Research in Child Development,* 29:6, 1964.

Schaefer, E. S. Home tutoring program. *Children,* 16:2, 1969.

Skeels, H. M. Adult status of children with contrasting early life experiences. *Monographs of the Society for Research in Child Development,* 31:3, 1966.

U.S. Office of Education, Department of Health, Education, and Welfare. Infant Education Research Project. Washington, D.C.,: Superintendent of Documents, U.S. Government Printing Office.

U.S. Department of Health, Education, and Welfare. PHS Health Services and Mental Health Administration. The edge of education. *HSMHA World,* 4(1): 18-23, Jan-Feb 1969.

A Pre-School Program for Disadvantaged Children

Director:
Constance N. Swander
Co-Director:
Gladys R. Blankenship
The Good Samaritan Center
San Antonio, Texas

Prepared by:
Herbert Yahraes

Introduction and Background

Carmen, David, Pablo, Maria, and the dozen other 3-year-olds playing in the courtyard of the Good Samaritan Center in San Antonio strike an observer as happy, energetic, and bright. And they are. However, were it not for a special educational program developed and tested by the Center, with financial support from NIMH, many of them would be destined at 6 to enter the public school system so poorly prepared as to be considered and treated as slow—a few of them, possibly, as retarded. Typically, their course through the school system would grow increasingly difficult, and a number would drop out early, prepared only for living at the low socioeconomic and cultural level into which they were born.

The Good Samaritan Center is a neighborhood center serving about 20,000 people on San Antonio's west side. This is a low-income area, more than 90 percent of whose residents are of Mexican descent. Though the neighborhood is clearly poor, it is not a slum. About 650 families live in two public housing projects; the others in small, one-story houses— some of them little better than shacks—covering block after block. Most of the houses, which would sell for perhaps $6,000, are owned by the families living in them or by a relative. They are usually neat, but crowded; living rooms must often double as bedrooms.

In the four census tracts surrounding the Center, the median annual family income in 1960 ranged from $2,830 to $4,190. More than 60 percent of the families being served in the Good Samaritan's health and guidance clinics had monthly incomes of less than $200 to support from 5 to 15 persons. Among the families of children now being served by the pre-school project, about a third are on relief. Fathers are absent in about a fifth of the homes. The men typically are unskilled or semi-skilled workers; the women typically do not work outside the home.

Good Samaritan, located in the midst of the area it serves, is housed in half a dozen simply designed, one-story structures built around a court- yard. It is sponsored by the West Texas Diocese of the Episcopal Church and is supported by the church and by the United Fund of San Antonio and Bexar County.

Studying the problems common to the people of its neighborhood, the Center found them to be rooted in lack of education, which in turn was rooted in lack of preparation for school. Sixty percent of the children in first grade were considered problem children; 15 percent of all the children had been held back at least one year. Many of the teen-age dropouts could read and write English only haltingly; they could not express themselves adequately even in their first language, Spanish. Half of the adults in the neighborhood had not completed fifth grade.

Constance N. Swander, executive director of the Center, decided in 1964 that the long-run solution to the area's poverty and associated problems lay in preparing the children for success in school. She planned to do this through a pre-school program that would teach English while preserving and reinforcing the children's use of Spanish, and at the same time would develop the children's ability to learn by guiding them through planned learning experiences.

The program, which won NIMH support and opened in 1965, had those two principal objectives because Mrs. Swander recognized that the children had two principal handicaps—lack of an opportunity to learn English and also lack of the verbal stimulation necessary for a child to develop whatever intellectual capacity he was born with. In the typical disadvantaged home of San Antonio's west side, as in many disadvantaged homes elsewhere, children are likely to be ignored unless they misbehave, and language is used more for controlling their behavior than for telling them about objects in their environment or for otherwise instructing them. So they grow up lacking real facility even in their native language. And without language facility, points out Shari Nedler, until recently the project's psychologist, "the child cannot organize his concepts, he cannot reason at abstract levels, he cannot describe, analyze or synthesize; he cannot solve any but the simplest problems."

The 16 children who enter the program each year are chosen at random from the neighborhood's eligible 3-year-olds, who are found by a house-to-house canvass. To be eligible, a child must come from a low-income,* Spanish-speaking family that has lived at least five years in the city and two years in the neighborhood. This residential requirement makes for a stable sample; in four years the project has lost only two children. Until the 1969-70 class of 3-year-olds was chosen, there was also a requirement that the child be able to speak only in Spanish. This requirement has been dropped, partly because most of the neighborhood's children do know a little English, picked up from television and from brothers and sisters who go to school, and partly because the Center wishes to emphasize that the program is potentially valuable for any

---

*The Orshansky poverty index is used. A family is considered in the low-income group if, for example, it numbers seven persons and has an annual income of $4,700 or less.

culturally disadvantaged child, whatever the language he hears at home. When the eligible children—there were 54 of them out of the 130-3-year-olds found in the most recent canvass—have been identified, a table of random numbers is used to choose the 16 whom the program can accept.

During the first two years, the staff had some difficulty persuading families to let their children participate. Several families, indeed, flatly refused. Others had to be visited as many as half a dozen times by the Center's principal emissary, Gladys R. Blankenship, who is of Spanish descent herself and thoroughly bilingual. Mrs. Blankenship is superintendent of the school and co-director of the project with Mrs. Swander. The families knew and trusted the Good Samaritan Center; many of them just did not think a child of 3 was old enough to be parted from his mother, even if she did have—as she generally did—too many other children to pay him much attention. Today, mothers throughout the neighborhood are eager to have their children accepted in the program. And "Los Ninos," a weekly television show starring Mrs. Blankenship and several children from the Center, undertaken in 1969 at the request of Station KENS, is popular in San Antonio and neighboring communities.

In 1968, with the grant from NIMH due to expire in two years, the Office of Education made the project an arm of the Southwest Educational Development Laboratory, in Austin, Texas, one of the Office's 16 regional laboratories, and the laboratory named the project's psychologist, Mrs. Nedler, as its program director for early childhood education. Known now as the San Antonio Urban Educational Development Center, the project is serving as a model for other efforts with pre-school children from disadvantaged groups. As of early 1970, programs to further test the methods and curricula developed under the NIMH grant were going forward:

—in San Antonio with 400 Mexican-American children, a program conducted with Model City funding in the public schools;

—in McAllen, Texas, with 150 children of migrant Mexican-American farm workers;

—in Dallas, Texas, with 3-year-old Negro children in a recently established school for disadvantaged children;

—in Bossier City, Louisiana, with 50 Negro children.

Children from disadvantaged Negro families, Mrs. Nedler points out, have basically the same problems as those from disadvantaged Mexican-American families: they are not learning good English at home, and they are not getting the intellectual stimulation necessary for the development of language skills and cognitive abilities.

School sessions at the San Antonio center run for three hours each morning, five days a week. Each class of 16 has one young woman as teacher and another as assistant teacher. The teachers are college women who have majored in education or in child development and who speak Spanish fluently. The assistants are high school graduates from the same neighborhood as the children. Trained on the job, they serve not so much as aides—if this term connotes someone who helps with coats, serves snacks, carries messages—but as second teachers.

Building Confidence

Children in the Good Samaritan area, like children in other disadvantaged neighborhoods (and some children in more favored neighborhoods), typically receive little encouragement to begin a task and can have small hope of a reward for completing it. As long as a child is doing what he's supposed to do, his parents say little or nothing to him; they wouldn't think of praising him. But let him do what he is not supposed to do, and he is reprimanded. Such conditions stifle initiative and promote passivity. They may promote misbehavior as well, because misbehavior becomes one way of getting attention.

Through all its many activities, the school tries to develop a child's confidence and wholesome self-regard. At the very start, for example, each child is introduced to the class and given a name tag, which he wears proudly. Also, he is taken on a tour of the classroom and shown where things are kept, how to put them away, how to care for books, and how to carry a chair. Putting this information to use not only promotes good classroom discipline but also gives the child a feeling of accomplishment.

Classroom performance checklists, along with other observations, are used to assign the children to three smaller groups based on ability levels. Such grouping gives each child opportunities to experience success in work geared to his ability or readiness. The groupings vary for different activities and are adjusted throughout the year. The teacher leads one group and the assistant another; members of the third group engage in individual projects—painting, building, cutting out designs, and so on.

Another aid to building self-confidence and a feeling of identity is "tell time," a period right after roll-call during which a child may come before the class and say anything he wants to say. The children don't have to participate, but most of them usually do. They talk about their mother or father, or something that happened at home, or a cut finger—anything. Even the 3-year-olds are eager to express themselves.

Children are praised when they answer correctly. They are also praised for working hard and behaving appropriately. A child who is unusually shy or passive is given special attention.

Teaching English

In the beginning, the Center thought that the children would learn English much as they had learned Spanish, by being exposed to it. As they took part in nursery school activities, the teacher would talk to them in English, using Spanish to explain. They would repeat her English words and gradually begin to use them: they would "pick up" the new language. Tests at the end of the year, however, showed that while the children had made progress on other fronts, they had advanced hardly at all in their knowledge of English.

The school then began developing a program for teaching English systematically. Based on its first-year experience and on word lists used in

47

the public schools, it drew up a 2,800-word vocabulary and organized it by topical units—words dealing with the body, with food, with clothing, with transportation, and so on. Vocabulary building, however, is not an end in itself. The school's aim is to develop a child's competence in his first language by expanding his basic fund of information through new labels, or words, and new concepts, or ideas, and then to introduce him to English by using the same labels and concepts.

During the first 15 weeks of school the 3-year olds hear nothing but Spanish, for these children typically have a poor vocabulary even in their own language. As their teacher expresses it, they lack labels. Their mothers, unlike most middle-class mothers, have not been inclined to name things—and thus to teach the names—when talking to their children. They have been saying, "Get me that," instead of "Get me the apple," and "Put it here," instead of "Put the apple on the table."

Lessons on body awareness, which is the first topical unit, begin with the use of a mirror to aid in self-identification, a pre-requisite of self-esteem. Many of the children have not used a mirror to any extent—some, not at all—and are not fully aware of their own features. The teacher asks, in Spanish, "Whom do you see?" Generally the child responds, "Me." So the teacher asks, "Well, what is your name?" Then she asks everyone to say, "Good morning, Juan."

After other members of the group have been similarly introduced, labeling begins. The teacher points to her nose, eyes, mouth and names them; then she has the children, one by one, say *nose, eyes, mouth*—in Spanish— and point to these parts on their own faces. Next the teacher touches a child's arm. "Este es el brazo," she says. "Este es el brazo, verdad?" Touching his ears, she says, "Y, estas son sus orejos—orejos, si." When she asks a child where his ears are, he may hesitate. At home, undoubtedly he has heard the word *orejos,* but he has not quite connected it with his own orejos. The teacher comes back to him every once in a while until it is clear that the connection has been made.

As part of the body awareness unit, the class makes a life-size puzzle. The teacher traces around a child; then asks, "What is missing—what does he need to be able to see? To be able to hear?" and so on. Once the missing features are put in, the teacher cuts the figure into parts, and each child gets the opportunity to put it together. He is encouraged to talk about what he is doing.

Games such as Simon Says are also part of the curriculum. As with every new activity, the teacher and the assistant teacher first demonstrate how the game is played. Then they lead groups in playing it. Eventually, as a means of building self-esteem, each child takes his turn at being the leader.

At the conclusion of a unit, a performance checklist is administered. In the case of body awareness, the teachers ask, "Can this child identify himself by name? Label parts of the body? Locate them on a doll and on himself? Describe simple functions?" Lagging children receive special attention.

From body awareness, the curriculum proceeds to clothing. The teacher introduces the unit by giving the rule for this class of objects: "If you can wear it, it's clothing." She then labels articles of clothing. "Who has a dress on?" she asks. "I have," several girls respond. Says the teacher: "How do we know the dress is clothing? Because we can wear it." After she has labeled several pieces of clothing, she points to a chair and asks, "Is this clothing?" "Why not?" "Can we wear it?"

The clothing lessons introduce the children to the concept of fasteners. "Can you find buttons on your dress?" asks the teacher. "What do you suppose would happen if you didn't have buttons on your dress?" "What other ways can you fasten clothing?"

Sometimes a child will point to a zipper and name it in English. "Yes," the teacher will say, "that's very good. That's the way it is in English— *zipper*. Now, do you know how we say it in Spanish?" They want to know, so she teaches them: *segadura*.

The children are also taught the labels of such things in the house as stove, sink, chair, and table. The 3-year-olds have a model kitchen where they look at and touch the objects they are labeling.

In many learning situations, action is required because it strengthens the learning process. Half a dozen 4-year-olds, for example, gather with their teacher in a screened-off corner of the classroom for an English lesson. "We are standing," the teacher says, and places each child on his feet. "We are standing," the teacher repeats. "We are standing," say the children. The teacher begins jumping up and down, and the group follows. "We are jumping," the teacher says. "We are jumping," say the children. "That's right," says the teacher. "We are jumping. Now say it again: 'We are jumping.' " "We are jumping," say the children. The teacher sits down, and the group follows. "We are sitting," she says. "We are sitting," the class repeats. "Good," says the teacher, "very good."

All age groups study the same topical units—food, clothing, house, and so on—but the older the children, the more deeply each subject is explored. In the case of fasteners, for instance, the 3-year-olds learn the labels for some types of them, and the 4-year olds expand this vocabulary. The 5-year-olds are led to consider the purpose of fasteners. The teacher holds up a child's shirt and asks first David and then Maria to try it on. They can't get into it, though, because the front has been sewn up. "What can we do about this?" the teacher asks. "How can we make this shirt easier to put on?"

"Cut it," one child suggests.

"Tear it open," says another.

"Fine," the teacher says, and proceeds to rip the shirt down the front.

But now when the children try it on, it doesn't function as a shirt. Again the teacher asks for suggestions. "What can we do now? How can we make this shirt stay together?"

"A button," somebody ventures.

Somebody else says: "A zipper."

"Good," says the teacher. "Let's see what a button will do." She sews one on. The group talks about what a button does and then generalizes to other kinds of fasteners.

Lessons are based on what the child already knows. When English lessons begin for the 3-year-olds in January, the introduction of words and concepts in English is preceded by a short review of the same words and concepts in his first language. For instance, starting a unit dealing with vehicles, teacher and children talk about *un carro, un aeroplano,* and *un bus.* Then the teacher announces that everyone will speak in English.

Teacher, holding up a picture of an automobile: "This is a car."

Children: car.

T: All right. Say it, "This is a car."

C: This is a car.

T: All right. This is a car. Good.

T: holding up a picture of an airplane: This is an airplane.

C: Airplane.

T: Good. Again—

C: This is an airplane.

T: All right, Martin, say "airplane."

Boy: Airplane.

At each age level the teacher listens to each child in the group as he tries to reproduce a new word.

Children, as teacher displays a picture of a bus: "This is a bus."

Teacher: A bus. Again—

C: This is a bus.

T: All right. Let's have Martin say it.

Boy: Bus.

T: Bus. Good. Now let's say the whole thing.

C: This is a bus.

T: Very good.

Then the teacher asks questions requiring a "yes" or "no" answer ("Is this a car?") and other questions testing whether or not the child has related the word to the picture ("All right, Martin, show me the airplane").

The next year, when the children are 4, the language lesson is entirely in English.

Teacher (displaying pictures of an airplane, a truck, and a ship): "These are vehicles."

Children: Vehicles. These are vehicles.

T: Good. Why are these vehicles?

Several children: Because they have motors.

T: Because they have motors and because we can ride in them.

T: (showing airplane): Do you ride in this?

C: Yes.

T: Then it is a vehicle. Say it.

C: Then it is a vehicle.

T: (showing ship): Can you ride in this?

C: Yes.

T: Say it. Then it is a vehicle.

C: Then it is a vehicle.

T: Listen, if you can ride in it, it's a vehicle.

T: (with picture of a shirt): Can you ride in this?

C: No.

T: So?

C: Not a vehicle.

T: It's not a vehicle. That's very good.

T: This vehicle is a truck.

C: This vehicle is a truck.

T: Good for you. This vehicle is a truck. Cynthia?

Girl: This vehicle is a truck.

T: Good.

The teacher varies the pace of presentation in order to keep the children involved. They must listen carefully if they are to answer correctly:

T: Is this a vehicle: Is this a ship?

C: Yes.

T: Okay. I want Martin to show me a vehicle that is an airplaine . . . . Very good. I want Cynthia to show me a vehicle that is a truck . . . . Good. I Want Juanita to show me a vehicle that is a banana.

Girl: It's not a vehicle.

T: No, you're right and I couldn't fool you. That's very good . . . . I want Olga to show me the *vehicles* . . . . Very good. She pointed to all of them because they are all vehicles. But are they all ships?

C: No.

T: Are they all airplanes?

C: No.

T: Are they all trucks?

C: No.

T: What are they all? What can you call all these things?

C: Vehicles.

T: Vehicles. That's very good.

A year later, when the children are 5, they learn that *vehicles* includes still other types and even sub-types. After the group has discussed the function of a passenger train—it carries people places—the teacher shows them a freight train.

Teacher: What kind of train do we call this one?

Child: Where are the people?

T: There are no people on this train. What does this train take?

Children: Food, Gasoline . . . .

T: Food, gasoline. What else could this train take?

Child: A refrigerator.

T: A refrigerator. You're right. This is a freight train. Say it . . . . Say it, Gonzalo, what kind of train is this?

Boy: Freight train.

T: Say the whole sentence.

Boy: This is a freight train.

T: Very good.

The lessons on vehicles—and on the other units—provide opportunities for taking up language differences that present special problems. One of these problems has to do with differences in length; *largo* and *mas largo* in Spanish become, when translated literally, *long* and *more long* in English.

Teacher: This train is short. Say it.

Children: This train is short.

T: (pointing to picture of a long train): Is *this* train short?

C: No.

T: This is not short. So what could we say about this train?

C: It is long.

T: It is long. Say it.

C: It is long.

T: (pointing to picture of a longer train): *This* train is . . . .

C: More long. Longer.

T: Longer. Say it, This train is longer.

C: This train is longer.

T: (pointing to longest train): What can we say about *this* train?

C: *More* longer.

T: No, we're going to say this train is . . . .

Child: Longest.

T: Good. Longest. This train is longest. Say it.

Language lessons for the 5-year-olds also include a review of prepositions (the children learn, for example, that in English an airplane is *on* the ground but *in* the sky) and a sequence of questions enabling the child to relate present, past, and future tenses (the airplane is in the sky; before that it was on the ground; when the airplane on the ground takes off, it will be in the sky).

Expanded Language Program

Complementing the language lessons in all three years is what the Center and the Southwest Educational Development Laboratory call "the expanded language program." This is so planned as to arouse the children's interest in talking about the topics they have encountered in the language lesson, and about related topics. It gives them practice in the new words—and concepts and structures—and at the same time requires them to use their memories, reasoning powers, and imaginations. An English lesson dealing with fruits, for example, is followed by a discussion of these and other foods. The teacher gets the talk started by asking questions: What fruits do you peel before eating? Does an orange have more juice than a banana? What would happen if you squeezed a banana? Another expanded language activity involves the cooking of rice and corn, in order to find out—and talk about—how cooking affects their volume. Food also is used to help teach the concepts—and the labels—of hot and cold (oatmeal and cornflakes) and big and little (apples).

As part of this program, books pertaining to the unit being studied are placed in the classroom for the children's use, and at story time each day the teacher reads from one of them. If the lesson unit deals with houses, for example, the teacher reads a story about houses. Then the children are encouraged to talk about their own home, or a friend's home, or anything that the story has brought to mind. Five-year-olds may spend three or four periods on the same story. The first day they may just look at the pictures and talk about what may be happening. The second day, the teacher reads the story and asks the children to compare their predictions with what actually happened. The third day the children draw a picture—the scene or event they liked best—and the next day they talk about it to the group.

For the 3-year-olds, the expanded language program is in Spanish throughout the year; for the 4-year-olds, much of it is in English, but the story period remains in Spanish. For the 5-year-olds, practically everything is in English. Daily music and art periods also serve the language program.

Developing Perceptual Motor Abilities

Many disadvantaged children reach first grade deficient not only in language skills but also in perceptual skills, which are even more basic to intellectual growth. The Good Samaritan school seeks to develop these abilities through planned daily exercises.

Training in attentiveness and auditory skills begins during the first week of school, when the 3-year-olds learn a rule about listening—that when they hear the bell, which is used to signal a change in activities, they will stop what they are doing and listen. Each child rings the bell and repeats the rule. Another time the teacher demonstrates two bells having different tonal qualities; then the children close their eyes, the teacher rings one of the bells, and the children tell her which one it is. In another exercise the teacher plays one of four instruments—bell, drum, triangle, or cymbals—and a child who has been blindfolded is asked to walk to it. Other lessons deal with sounds in the home—a door closing, dishes rattling, a window being opened, water running. Such exercises get the children accustomed to paying attention to the differences between sounds and to locating the source of a sound. Many of the children, from crowded, noisy homes, may have learned to tune out; now they are learning to tune in. Later on, more advanced auditory discrimination lessons will sharpen their ability to detect and recognize differences in the sounds of words.

The visual training program includes practice in discriminating among objects on the basis of size, color, shape, or function; paying attention to the boundaries of objects, as in cutting out or coloring a picture; and noticing and reproducing patterns, as with blocks, pegs, and beads. Thus, the program strengthens visual skills and reasoning ability and at the same time helps prepare the child for an important task that he will face when learning to read—distinguishing one letter from another. Under visual training, too, come many exercises to strengthen attentiveness and memory. In one, for example, the teacher displays three pictures, then asks the children to close their eyes as she turns one over. Can they remember which one is missing? When there are four pictures, can they remember? Five? Seven? Another exercise uses letters instead of pictures. Another calls on the children to reproduce from memory patterns they have been shown—simple ones, like circles and triangles, at first; later on, numbers and letters.

While the typical disadvantaged child is proficient in such gross motor activities as running, jumping, and climbing, he lags in the development of the fine motor skills needed for classroom success, particularly in writing. The Center's daily schedule, therefore, includes such activities as lacing shoes, tieing ribbons, manipulating small building blocks, dropping buttons through a narrow opening, using a pair of scissors, tracing, coloring, and pasting.

Evaluating the Project

By the time the children have completed two years at the Center, most of them—whether at play in the courtyard or at work with another child on some project in the classroom—are using both Spanish and English. There is no conscious choice, the teachers think; the children use the words that come to mind first.

Will these children, after the third pre-school year, be able to compete in first grade with children who have learned English at home? The staff feels that they will. In substantiation, the teacher of the 5-year-olds points out that in first grade, where she taught for four years, teachers are supposed to begin the reading readiness program immediately, a very difficult matter with children who know little English. The 5-year-olds at the Center, she thinks, are ready for such a program even before they have finished half of their last year. They have been trained to listen, which is one of the goals of the public schools' reading readiness program. They have learned enough English to be able to follow instructions; for example, they know when the teacher is talking about the top of the page and when she is talking about the bottom. They have learned other concepts and the English words for them. Give some first-graders from disadvantaged homes two or three objects and ask whether they are the same or different, and the children will just look at the teacher or say "Maybe." But the children at the Center, she says, "can tell you right off." The Center's children have also had experience in a common reading-readiness exercise: "Let's look at this picture and you tell me what you see." The Center's children have done this many times; they know the labels in English— "boy," "girl," "father," "mother," "house," "car"—for what the pictures show, and they have had practice in expressing themselves.

Approximately 30 of the Center's graduates are now in first or second grade, in half a dozen different schools. Two teachers have spoken highly of the few they have encountered, and at least a dozen mothers have dropped by the Center to report that the Good Samaritan graduates are doing considerably better in school than their older brothers and sisters.

54

For lack of funds, the Center notes, a systematic follow-up of these children has not yet been undertaken. However, under a program financed by the Southwest Educational Development Laboratory, an effort has been made to evaluate the San Antonio project on the basis of (a) changes in the children attending its classes during the 1968-69 school year, and (b) a comparison of these changes with those experienced by children in two other groups. One of these groups came from three day-care centers in San Antonio funded as Head Start programs under the Office of Economic Opportunity and concerned with children from Mexican-American families of low-economic status. These centers offered some of the elements of the Good Samaritan program but were concerned in the main with providing all-day care and supervised play. The second comparison group comprised 16 3-year-olds who were eligible for the Good Samaritan's regular program but could not be admitted. The parents of these children were encouraged to participate in a parent-involvement program; through it, the Center hoped to learn whether or not the children could be affected indirectly by increasing the parents' interest in child development. As it turned out, the fathers and mothers involved in this program attended the scheduled semi-monthly meetings quite irregularly, and the discussions—though they included such topics as hygiene, mental health, and story-telling techniques—were not so specifically concerned with child development as had been planned. Essentially, the children in this group may be considered controls—that is, as having experienced no significant intervention.

To try to determine the intellectual development of the children in the three groups during the nine months between September 1968 and May 1969, the staff used:

1. The Leiter International Performance Scale, a non-language test relying heavily on visual discrimination. Some items call for matching one object with another; others, for grouping objects that belong together. The examiner demonstrates what is to be done—for example, he takes a red block and puts it with a red square. Then he gives the child other items in the same category to do by himself.

2. The Peabody Picture Vocabulary Test, which provides an estimate of the child's verbal intelligence although the child himself is not required to talk. The examiner names an object (such as "dog") and then asks the child to point to it in one of several pictures presented to him. In addition to the standard English version of this test, the Center developed and used a Spanish version.

The results are shown in Table 1.

In the first examination, as expected, since all the children came from educationally deprived, non-English-speaking homes, all three groups scored well below the national average in a test—the Peabody—requiring the use of English in its administration. Each group fell below the average by at least 40 points. Even in the Spanish version of this test, the groups scored from 12 to 25 points below standard. On the instrument not requiring language in its administration—the Leiter—all three groups fell within the normal range. This result, too, had been expected.

55

Table I

AVERAGE SCORES BEFORE AND AFTER NINE MONTH TRIAL PERIOD

Test	Good Samaritan		Day Care		"Controls"*	
	Sept.	May	Sept.	May	Sept.	May
Leiter	107	121**	99	101	97	96
Peabody— English	59	68	60	63	58	58
Peabody— Spanish	88	102**	76	77	75	80

*Children in Parent-Involvement program. See text.

**Significant at less than the .01 level, meaning that the results would have occurred by chance less than 1 time in 100.

Nine months later, only the children who had attended the Good Samaritan Program showed marked gains. On the English version of the Peabody Test, this gain was not—by a slight margin—statistically significant; on the Spanish version and on the non-verbal test, it was. The scores on these tests were also significantly greater than those made by the other groups.

In sum, the Center's program for 3-year-olds significantly increased their intellectual performance as compared with what it had been and as compared with the performance of children in a traditional nursery school program and with that of children not involved in a program.

The staff emphasizes that these findings are for a single year only and for small samples. It points out, too, that the evaluation tests used so far are not ideal by any means. Though the Leiter eludes the language barrier, the test is time-consuming and those who administer it may unwittingly provide clues to answers unless specially trained. The experience at San Antonio suggests that the vocabulary of the Peabody Picture Vocabulary Test is too advanced for disadvantaged pre-school children and contains too few items at each age level for accurate measurement of differences between groups.

Improved evaluation measures. In conjunction with child development authorities in Texas universities and the public school system, the Southwest Educational Development Laboratory is developing and standardizing several tests intended to measure a pre-school child's proficiency in language more adequately than tests now available. One such effort is modeled on the Peabody but has a vocabulary drawn from the same list of words used in building the school's language lessons. The new tests, which have both English and Spanish versions, are to be made available nationally after they have been standardized. Tests to indicate a youngster's achievement after a given lesson or lesson unit are also being developed. As another means of evaluating the program, children in the San Antonio project will be followed for several years after they have entered the city's schools.

Working with Parents

The Center keeps in touch with parents through monthly meetings to which all fathers and mothers are invited and through conferences with individuals when desirable. The meetings are quite informal, almost like family gatherings; mothers even bring their new babies to be admired. At one recent session, the talk got around to how children ought to behave when they got to public school. One mother expressed the opinion that the teacher was always right. "Keep quiet," she said she told her first-grader; "then the teacher is going to like you, and you'll pass into second grade." The other parents seemed to agree. Mrs. Blankenship suggested, though, that it was healthy for a child to ask questions, that he had a right to ask them, and that, in fact, a teacher would like him to ask them.

When a problem arises that the Center alone cannot meet, the people who know the child and his family—generally at least one teacher, her assistant, and Mrs. Blankenship—talk it over and decide how to advise the parents. Usually the mother will be asked to drop in; sometimes a staff member will visit the home. The mother of an extremely timid girl was advised to scold her less, praise her more, and give her some opportunity to talk. The parents of a boy who had no motivation because at home his older brothers and sisters did everything for him, were advised to let him have more responsibility and to praise him whenever he undertook a new task.

Parent Education Program. This program, a revision of the parental involvement project noted earlier, is for 16 mothers of 3-year-olds who are not included in the regular pre-school course. At the start, each mother was video-taped as she taught her child simple tasks, such as sorting blocks, and as she read to him. The staff wanted to learn how well the mothers explained a task to their children, how they organized information, to what extent they used praise, and how much affection there was between mother and child. Now the Center is trying to train the mothers to work with their children more effectively. This involves showing them how they can present educational activities, such as comparing fruits of different color and size and labeling and counting common household objects. In many cases it also involves changing certain behavior patterns, the most common of which is to ignore good behavior and punish bad behavior, so that the only way a child gets attention from his mother is to misbehave.

Mrs. Blankenship, working with mothers at the Center, demonstrates a different activity each week. Once a week another staff member visits the homes and observes how the mother works with her child and whether or not the child has learned the activity for the week. The Center plans to continue this program for three years so that it can compare the effects of working directly with children in the classroom and working indirectly with them through their mothers. Evidence that the children of the mothers in the Parent Education Program are substantially benefitted would be welcome, would point toward a way of reaching educationally

57

disadvantaged children at a cost considerably below that of establishing classroom programs.

Materials for National Use

Instruction manuals presenting the curriculum day by day for each of the three years have been prepared so that the San Antonio program can be readily adopted elsewhere, the Spanish-language sections being omitted where English is the children's native language.[1]

A training program for teachers includes film strips on the Center's program and philosophy and a manual.

Research Grant: MH 14988
Date of Interviews: November 1969

References:

A rationale for the bilingual early childhood program. Southwest Educational Development Corporation, Austin, Texas, 1969.

"The Crucial Years" and "Bridging the Gap," filmstrips developed by Good Samaritan Center, San Antonio, and Southwest Educational Development Laboratory, Austin, Texas, 1969.

---

[1] Requests for curriculum and training materials should go to Mrs. Shari Nedler, Program Director, Early Childhood Education, Southwest Educational Development Laboratory, Austin, Texas.

Baker's Dozen: A Program of Training Young People as Mental Health Aides

Project Director:
Jacob Fishman, M.D.
Institute for Youth Studies
Howard University
Washington, D.C.

Co-investigator:
Lonnie E. Mitchell, Ph.D.
Baker's Dozen

Prepared by:
Clarissa Wittenberg

The broad avenues which lead to Baker's Dozen are as handsome as any L'Enfant designed for the city of Washington, but the area around them is far from grand. It is marked by decrepit rowhouses hung with "condemned—no trespassing" signs. Store-front churches and a Black Muslim mosque characterize the neighborhood. One small store nearby has a sign "Buy Black." In this area of 104,000 people, 95 percent are Negro. Most of them have very low incomes, but there is a small group of professional people and businessmen there as well. This area had the highest incidence of poverty, unemployment, substandard housing, delinquency, and school dropouts in Washington. In short, it is a ghetto. It is a place where groups of idle men stand around on street corners, even in the snow. For people in Washington, it is the "Cardozo" area, the "Shaw" area. These are the names of schools infamous for their disrepair and troubles. This is the Watts of Washington. Baker's Dozen[1] is a youth center, a new type of child-guidance clinic. It is located in this area in two joined Victorian rowhouses similar to others in the block. It is here that an unusual experiment in improving mental health is being carried out.

Nine young men and women, all of whom have grown up in this area and whose families still live there, have been working for a year and a half in a rigorous training program. They each have one or more groups of about eight to ten disturbed, needy adolescents with whom they work.

[1] Baker's Dozen is connected with the Institute for Youth Studies at Howard University. The institute is an interdisciplinary center for research, training, graduate work, and professional studies. It was begun as a settlement house and now is deeded to Howard for the purposes of this study. The name Baker's Dozen derives from the group of 13 women, all Howard graduates, who began it during World War II to give "an extra measure of service" to this area.

The program is double-barreled in that it helps a group of deprived, socially disadvantaged, poverty-inhibited adolescents who then, each in turn, provide a significant mental health service to the community. Help is given at less cost and more effectively than it could be given by a program limited to traditional use of professionals.

The area has an acute lack of clinical facilities for children and adolescents. However, it is obvious that the resources of such facilities, primarily oriented as they are to the middle class, would be inadequate to the job anyway. The usual agency is not oriented to the real problems of the poor, and the poor generally do not seek its services. Treatment personnel, drawn from the middle class, are not in tune with the clients and find it difficult to work with them. There is a special need for integration of any treatment program into the local institutions, i.e., the schools and courts, and this generally is not done.

Another problem is that in this type of neighborhood the impact of treatment may be compromised by the stigma of being a patient. At the same time, the understanding and knowledge of the mental health practitioner is valuable, and it is primarily a new approach that is needed. One theory (held also by the staff at Baker's Dozen) is that the best kinds of prevention and therapy are those which can be done in the normal social context of the youth—that is, within the schools, the work, or the natural groups of the community.

In addition, the services must be realistically accessible. For instance, at Baker's Dozen a variety of services are offered because there are so few facilities in the neighborhood. The services are free, as the clients have no money. Baker's Dozen has no authority in the sense that the police or schools have authority, and so it must attract and hold boys and girls by the opportunity for change, for friendships, for the activities that it offers. It must be open the hours that it is needed, not just 9—5 on weekdays. Therefore its schedule is extended to evenings and weekends.

Aides, the term used for the young indigenous workers, were recruited and selected through a process of "screening in" rather than "screening out." Signs, encouraging people to apply, were put up in a wide variety of places including bars and laundromats. Radio and TV news announcements were made. Applicants were considered with characteristics that would ordinarily bar them from employment. Only a fifth-grade education was required and this only so that reading would be possible. No previous work experience was necessary. Most jobs call for a clean police record, but this was not required here. It was essential, however, that no court action be pending which would interrupt the training. As to personal characteristics, the only requirements were that applicants be free of serious physical or mental problems and communicable diseases. Psychological testing was used to identify gaps and problems and was referred to again later when an evaluation of the training was made.

Applicants were encouraged from low socioeconomic groups and from families with low incomes. Five men and four women were selected, all of whom had lived within five blocks of the Center. They ranged in age from 17 to 21. Several had dropped out of school around the seventh grade;

one had completed high school. The reading level ranged from a minimum of fifth grade to a maximum level of 11th grade. One young man was dropped because of legal problems.

The eight trainees were subdivided into high- and low-risk groups, four in each. High-risk youths were described as deprived youths who had had a series of police and criminal involvements, some emotional or delinquency problems, and those who may have spent time in an institution for an offense. They read at a minimal fifth-grade level, dropped out of school early, worked only at odd jobs, and never worked longer than 3 months at any given job. The low-risk youths were defined as deprived youths who had no police record, who continued in school until family and poverty circumstances forced them out. They worked at menial jobs but for longer periods than did the high-risk group. The average number of siblings for the aides as a group was five. All the aides chosen had multiple social problems and were so accustomed to rejection, failure, and defeat that they had to be convinced that all this was true. They suspected that "there must be a catch to it somewhere."

Recruits were numerous, and the rate of completion throughout this project and others run by the Institute for Youth Studies was very high. The staff reports that over 150 multiproblem youths have been trained in Institute for Youth Studies projects and that the dropout rate has been less than 1 percent.[2] One aide selected for the Baker's Dozen project was dropped as he had to serve a prison term, and at this writing he had still not returned to the project. This points up how strong the holding power of the project has been as many of these youths would have undoubtedly been in police trouble and perhaps given stiffer sentences due to their histories of past offenses. In this and other ways they might have been prevented from continuing in the project had they not exercised extreme caution in order to be able to participate.

Applicants were seen in groups during the selection process. Every effort was made not to impose unnecessary barriers that would cause people to drop out. Even so, one aide said at a later date that he had arrived at the Center and found instructions to go to Freedman's Hospital for a physical. As he didn't have busfare, he almost quit until a staff member organized rides for the women and encouraged the men to walk there together, thus solving the problem.

The initial training period lasted 3 months. When it was completed, a graduation was held that was the first such ceremony most of them had ever attended and marked for many the longest period of employment to date. The aides were given a stipend of $20 a week during the training period; this jumped to $75 a week at the end of that time. Presently they are earning $80 a week, and increases are written into the budget. They are considered GS-2 level ($4,108), and provision has been made that they will move up to Government Service levels 3 and 4. The District of Columbia Health Department has written job descriptions and positions

---

[2] These aides are working in schools, settlement houses, and children's institution recreational centers throughout the city.

into their budget, and this new type of position will be continued after the initial demonstration phase has ended. An exciting part of the program has been the development of new careers and the additional resource for manpower in mental health.

Training Program for the Aides

Major training goals were:

1. Development in these youths of the necessary motivation, identity, values, and capabilities for maximally utilizing the offered training.
2. Learning the basic personal, social, and interpersonal skills, attitudes, and knowledge which would help them successfully cope with and solve group, client, and personal problems.
3. Learning specialized skills for their roles in mental health.
4. Developing flexibility of attitude, role, and viewpoint.

Training was designed in three parts which ran concurrently—core group, specialty workshop, and on-the-job training. These were continued after the initial 3-month training period and comprise the vehicle for inservice training which continues throughout the program.

Core Group

This is the basic group which meets several hours a week and is led by the same professional staff person. It provides a place where a variety of issues can be raised and day-to-day problems of work can be discussed. The group itself provides a laboratory for group interaction and management techniques. Work throughout the training program is done primarily with the entire group. It has been found that this makes possible greater participation on the part of the aides as they have the support of their peers.

The level of anxiety among the aides was high due to the new demands made upon them, and the group was found to be effective in dealing with this in a way that allowed for maximum change. It gave each aide a group to move with in his transition from an unemployed school dropout to a semi-professional. This is very important because these young people, drawn away from familiar patterns and attitudes, often feel very isolated. They have helped each other to correct the distorted views they have held as a result of their background. They have learned new ways of solving problems, often by applying the new techniques to problems that come up in the core group. The leader is a visible example of how to lead a group; what he does is more likely to be influential than anything said in a lecture.

The trainees and the staff have had some difficulty in establishing the role of the aides. For instance, such questions arise as to how much the aides should have to say in policy decisions. How much responsibility should they have? The core group was used to define an appropriate job identification. Initially, the aides wondered, "Should I be like the Man or myself." Although they were encouraged to absorb attitudes and techniques, they were discouraged from becoming carbon copies of the staff as it was hoped that a new type of professional, comfortable with lower class behavior and at the same time able to meet middle-class demands, would emerge. Since it was highly desirable that they remain in touch with and empathic to the lower-class group from which they came, this was encouraged. Their observations about the shortcomings of professional techniques were encouraged. The staff had to learn to stand the criticism and separate the useful information from the aggressive attack.

The aides were also encouraged to examine their own backgrounds. With the help of their leader they developed a very perceptive paper, "What It Means To Be Really Poor." This was an outgrowth of their examination of the process of adolescence and the difficulties of living in a slum. They began to acquire some perspective and to sort out what could be done. In their paper they comment that when you are poor you know only your own troubles and your own neighborhood.[3] If you are failing in school you do not have the time to ponder what it is about American education that makes it difficult for the lower income student to achieve scholastically. Nor do you have the energy to do something about the situation.

In the core group, methods of social action are discussed, and the aides have been encouraged to participate in community groups. They have attended schoolboard meetings and Senate hearings. They have been encouraged by the staff to speak up regardless of whether or not other groups in the community find their opinions embarrassing. A prominent issue for these trainees have been that of discrimination. All are expected to have opinions and to act accordingly. They are expected to act responsibly and knowledgeably. Early in the IYS training programs there was discussion as to whether trainees should attend community meetings as observers. This was found to be confusing and tended to weaken the program and was abandoned. A major problem of these young people has been their attitude of defeated, resigned acceptance of an unsatisfactory status quo, and group action protest methods have been helpful in showing them ways to achieve improvement.

The issues discussed are varied. At one core meeting questions were raised about vacation hours, a secretary's attitude, and what to do about a letter received from an invalid old lady who wanted a Christmas basket. (Although this is not a routine agency service, the group had already called her and taken up a collection.) They also discussed whether or not an aide, despite provocation, should ever hit one of the children in his group. Other issues, such as the use of the credit union, are raised by the leader. The staff reports that a great deal of information taken for granted by middle-class workers has to be discussed with the aides in order to be sure that they clearly understand both their rights and their obligations.

---

[3] "What It Means To Be Really Poor." Baker's Dozen aides and Lonnie Mitchell, Ph.D. Baker's Dozen Youth Center, Washington, D.C., unpublished paper.

The job of the leader of the core group is a difficult one. The young people are angry, suspicious, distrustful, vulnerable, hopeful, sensitive, brutally realistic, and terribly unrealistic all at the same time. There is a gap that must be spanned. Neither side wants to be compromised. The leader must be comfortable with authority and know when to turn responsibility over to the group. He must act as a liaison with the staff. He must interpret the staff to aides and vice versa. He must be a good and knowledgeable teacher. The group will scrutinize him and be critical as he represents the people trying to remake them. He is the personification of the professional. All staff working with the aides must be able to handle passivity without becoming dictatorial. If the leader or other staff members become anxious about group inactivity or lack of response, the group's confidence in their own ability will be undermined. A good example of this occurred in an interview with the group. After an initial explanation of the broad questions to be discussed, the group was utterly unresponsive. The leader then restated the issues. The group remained unresponsive. Then upon questioning they said that they found the second explanation insulting because it made them look stupid. Upon hearing that a response is looked for as evidence of understanding, they said that that was "middle class" and asked who wants to "react and commit themselves." The staff reported that complaints about the program and lack of response were common manifestations of anxiety and feelings of noninvolvement in the program.

The staff reports also that they have found a rather strict approach as opposed to a permissive one most effective. Rules are strict, but anything is open to discussion. Aides are docked for being late even if it is a small amount. Hours are checked. A great deal is asked of the aides in terms of meeting professional standards. The aides by and large have been able to do this. On the other hand, the project has not discharged aides for some issues, angry episodes, minor police violations, etc., that would be sufficient grounds for dismissal in some agencies. The fact that the finances are administered through a university has made its employment standards binding on the aides and has imposed stricter rules than the staff would have wished. These, however, have been subject to appeal.

The aides are interested in the process of becoming a professional. Most of them have now grasped the concept of the steps leading to a profession and have either gotten tutoring or resumed special classes in school. They now see that it is not magic which makes a person a doctor, a psychologist, or a social worker, but a process pursued step by step. The program in general and the staff personally have given support to any interest in further education on the part of the aides. One boy audits classes in psychology at Howard. They are also encouraged to continually relate the more academic work in their training to their own lives. The aides have commented on this issue in their paper:[4] "The learning environment of the slum child is dismal. He is often emotionally disturbed. It is a mistake to urge such a child to get an education because it will help

---

[4] "What It Means To Be Really Poor."

him to get a good job and allow him to leave the slums. The most promising motivation for a child in the culture of the poor is the acquisition of knowledge as an end in itself and for its own sake." The irony is that, having found a good job, the aides have found their own educations too limited to allow them sure access to better jobs. One young woman, married and with two children, would like to be a social worker. She is young but would have to complete high school and go on to college, and remedial work takes more time than original schooling did as it must be done around the demands of other responsibilities. This, coupled with the lack of money, poses almost insurmountable problems despite her intelligence and abilities.

Specialty Workshops

The aides were given didactic work on such subjects as interviewing, history taking, record keeping, group observations, psychological testing, etc. The classes resemble college survey courses in style. They sought to provide an overview. Needless to say, the aides needed a great many background issues filled in. The staff operated by giving talks and lectures and utilizing extensive questioning and give-and-take to be certain that the information was being understood and absorbed. The aides often brought up questions about such things as the effects of LSD, alcoholism, etc. The staff talked about issues reported in the newspaper and tried to keep stimulating the group but tried at the same time not to overwhelm the group. The investigators report that it was necessary to keep a current tone to the work because the group as a whole had such a negative feeling about schoolwork that initially they found it almost intolerable. The problem of even sitting still was difficult for some to manage. They had felt so out of touch with previous teachers, so attacked and so unsuccessful, that it posed a difficult teaching task to the staff to create an atmosphere which could foster their learning. Efforts were made also to pace the work so that the aides would learn answers to problems that arose in their groups so the practical significance of the theory would be visible.

On-the-Job Training

Many visits to community agencies were also part of the training. The group visited Congress, the juvenile court, Junior Village (a children's residential home), St. Elizabeths Hospital (a psychiatric facility), and other social institutions. They saw many films on mental health and child development. They interviewed members of the neighborhood for ideas about community needs, and they learned the rudiments of research methods.

Throughout the training it was intended that the aides would learn to become more sensitive to interpersonal feelings. They report an awareness of a considerable change in how much they perceive of one another's feelings. They cite this as a problem in the training as sometimes they feel awkward and ill-equipped to deal with this. This problem is familiar to anyone who has experienced similar training. Although any staff member would talk to any aide who sought his help, there has also been a group psychotherapy program for the aides. This makes it possible for issues inappropriate to other meetings to be referred back to that group. The same psychiatrist has met with the group since their entrance into the program. He feels, as does the rest of the staff, that the aides have overcome some, but not all, of their initial difficulty in talking about their feelings—an idea quite alien to their way of life. They were, as a group, much more comfortable with activity and movement than with verbal modes of expression.

There is a fear that you can be manipulated when people know your feelings. The aides talk about "gritting," which means maintaining silence as a way of controlling a situation and still remaining technically non-obstructive. The staff has learned to call the aides on such tactics and has earned the respect of the aides to the extent that they have done this. The psychiatrist who meets with the group makes no administrative decisions about them because it was hoped that this would further a therapeutic atmosphere and provide one place where the aides could speak without fear of losing their jobs. At times of acute personal stress the aides have been referred to other psychiatrists in the community. The group meets at Baker's Dozen, and it is considered part of their program and is compulsory.

Basically the aides were trained to carry out specific duties and to fill certain roles. These included:

1. Be group leader, helper, and planner for 10 children in each of two groups.
2. Participate with the psychologist, psychiatrist, or social worker in developing structured therapeutic programs for their groups.
3. Observe and record individual and group behavior.
4. Conduct interviews with group members and provide information to the professional staff for feedback and quality-control purposes.
5. Escort groups on trips and tours.
6. Participate in individual and group supervision.
7. Attend staff conferences.
8. Write progress reports and keep records of daily observations on the children with whom they work.

The Groups Led by the Aides

Each aide is responsible for two activity groups. Activities are structured to provide ego-strengthening and therapeutic benefits and include recreation and cultural, social, and community activities. A major purpose is to raise the behavioral standards of the children involved. A strong emphasis is placed on the concept of the aide as a good figure for the group to identify with and on the use of the aide's management to establish beneficial controls over the children. The aides seek to reduce symptoms, lessen police contacts, and improve the social functioning of the children. The children, who are from the area around the Center, had school problems, difficulties with the police, defiant attitudes toward authority, and many symptoms of social and personal disorganization. Referrals were accepted from the juvenile courts, public schools, the Urban League, and other agencies. The age range was 12–16. Both boys and girls were accepted. Youths excluded were those who were being committed to an institution as a result of court action, those in need of immediate hospitalization, and mental defectives whose difficulties posed certain management problems in an outpatient setting. In addition, the aides ran dances and open houses to bring children into the Center and interest them in the program. This further tended to bring in natural groupings of children. Although these children were not unusual in the community and not technically referred, they had many of the same characteristics as those who were. This points up the degree of social disorganization in the community when so many multiproblem children can be found by simply dipping into the community. Speaking of one such child an aide said, "When I say he gave the secretary a hard time, I mean he pulled a gun on her."

The emphasis is on work with the teenager rather than the parent. The aides know from their own experiences that work with the parents would be less fruitful than work with the children. They feel a positive non-parent-connected relationship is helpful to these adolescents. They are only too well aware of the hostility and rejection in the home situations of many of their group members. They point out that these young people would be on the streets if they were not at the Center. The importance of "someplace where nobody yells at you" is underestimated in the aides' opinion. Neither the aides nor the group members see this as a patient-therapist relationship. They see it as working together toward getting along, and planning activities. The aides are rather permissive but have certain taboos, such as not allowing the boys to play the "dozens."[5] They usually try to control fighting by manifesting their disapproval. They also have learned that withholding privileges helps, but by and large they feel that as the boys stay with the groups these problems diminish by themselves. They have more difficulty when they themselves are attacked because the old patterns of self-defense come into conflict with their newly found professional approach.

The groups are designed to improve the coping skills of the teenagers and to help them towards more positive attitudes. At times the group seems to repeat past experiences of the youngsters—for instance, when

---

[5] "Playing the Dozens"—the act of talking about another person's parent with the intent of hurting the person's feelings. Foul and abusive language is often used. "The dozens"—a term used for the act of "playing the dozens." Definition from "A Dictionary of Local Terms and Expressions" edited by Mitchell, Lonnie, Ph.D. (Definitions primarily contributed by Baker's Dozen aides.)

they visit Washington museums, etc. However, one finds on closer examination that although all of these children have been herded through on educational tours, rarely has someone discussed it all with them in terms they could understand and helped them with it. When necessary the aides intercede with other agencies such as the schools. Contact is made and maintained with the young people even when they leave the group. The adolescents sometimes seek intense contact with the aides and the aides have neither discouraged nor encouraged this, but accept it. One little girl used to show up at an aide's apartment on Sunday just to say hello and then leave. The aides lend money if asked, and all have been asked. They try a variety of approaches and are not bound by tradition.

The aides comment that the predominant motif in the boys' groups is that of aggression and sex. Sex is the predominant concern for the adolescent girls' groups. All the aides agreed that the girls in this neighborhood "get wise" too young. By ages 11 to 12 they are too seductive, too stimulated. Many of the girls will become illegitimately pregnant. The aides stress that this tends to further trap the girl who wishes to escape the ghetto. "Theft, murder, fornication, desertion are so much a part of their lives that they become indifferent to what would shock other people."[6] The aides see in their group members the patterns of impulsive living for the moment, and they try to help their group members find other ways of living. They talk to their groups. One aide, herself pregnant, has been asked "how it feels to be pregnant." All of the women aides find such issues under discussion, and they meet them openly and honestly and try to give guidance. They are in close contact with the context of the questions and can answer them more appropriately than someone from another background. Although the planned programs are developed by the teenagers and include such activities as movies, parties, cooking, makeup, etc., depending on the sex of the group, doubtless the informal activity and discussions are also valuable.

The aides try to foster a feeling of concern among their group members and to combat the feelings of helplessness, isolation, and indifference so common among their group members.

Since Baker's Dozen also serves as a training placement for social group and caseworkers and psychologists, the aides' intimate knowledge of the culture is passed on to professionals in many ways. In their training program, the aides have developed a book of slang vocabulary phrases common to the area. They have included street talk, homosexual jargon, drug-addict talk, and prison terms. Publication is being considered at this time. In addition, a series of radio programs was written by the aides and presented over a period of months. They discussed their training program, their perspective on the community, their ideas on why children misbehave, and other topics.[7]

---

[6] "What It Means To Be Really Poor."

[7] Radio program series: "The Nonprofessional Youth in the Community." Station WOL, Washington, D.C., November 1965–February 1966.

Research

Research data are being collected utilizing the self-reports of the aides and projective measures and observations by others of the aides in both experimental and natural situations. The program is being studied in terms of such issues as staff roles and decision-making procedures. Crises are being noted and followed by the research staff. Records are being kept on attendance of both aides and group members. Job performance ratings on the aides, background data on the social situation of the aides, their families, etc., are being kept. Periodic evaluations are added to the initial comprehensive personal evaluation. The aides are asked for indications of their self-image and their self-esteem. Their patterns of behavior (as seen in such things as impulse control), their levels of aspiration, values, anxieties, and other issues are being noted and measured.

Other Issues

The entire issue under discussion—of the effectiveness of the indigenous worker due to his close understanding of his group's culture—leads to a discussion as to whether middle-class people, the professionals, can themselves be effective with the aides. The staff report that this is entirely possible but that certain conditions are essential. It is essential that the staff understand the realities of life in the slum. They must understand the obstacles that have been presented the aides. They must understand the ways in which the aides have not been included in the mainstream of opportunity. They must understand the emphasis placed upon money. At Baker's Dozen the aides are all Negro; the staff is primarily Negro. The staff and aides see the bonds and differences not primarily in terms of color, however, but in terms of class background. All staff, regardless of race, must be able to tolerate hostile remarks about the white community. In this area of the city the problems faced by the residents are brought about both by being poor and being Negro, and both factors have to be considered. On the other hand, the middle-class professional provides these aides with a glimpse of a life they hadn't really seen firsthand before. One aide said he couldn't wait to leave "this lousy area" and that his ambition was to be successful enough to buy a "house next to Dr. . . .and put a little cast iron black boy out front and paint it white . . .," the best thing of all being he would know it would still be there in the morning. This also highlights one of the problems of the program. The job requires that the aides not move out of the area for the duration of the program, and they are chafed by this restriction. They have gotten a good job and they want to move out. They do accept it as a realistic requirement but vow to move as soon as possible. Therefore it is reasonable to assume that they will leave this area. It has been an interesting aspect, and one now being studied, that these aides had lived in the area and were known by many people. They have provided a visible model for other young people as long as they have lived in the area. The effect on those who knew them and on the area is being assessed.

Although many issues have to be dealt with sensitively, the aides have been found to have a far higher tolerance for frustration than predicted. With guidance, the number of severe disruptions has been few. The non-verbal nature of the group makes it difficult for staff. The aides tend to greet each new topic with silence. They also tend to cast the staff in the role of boss. Then, too, the very process of helping people to a new view of themselves makes the leader vulnerable to their new strength. For instance, the aides have learned the power of group activity through their study of the civil rights movement. Now they are aware that if they become seriously dissatisfied they can quit en masse and jeopardize the program and the leader.

The aides cite money as a major asset of the program. The importance to them of the opportunity for a decent job has been tremendous. They are deeply concerned about future work. They question whether or not they will actually be able to get jobs in other similar settings. They still feel as though the system is closed to them. Many of them are not deeply committed to human relations work, although they would probably continue in it if a future existed for them there. All feel the program has changed their lives. They are strongly attached to the staff in the program and are loyal to the agency.

Results

The most impressive finding is that young people such as these can be trained as aides and can do the work successfully. Although levels of efficiency vary, all have been working at an acceptable level. An effective training program has been developed and has been found to motivate and hold the young people. Despite their youth, and many are in need of employment at an age far younger than most professionals reach a job, they are able to handle the responsibility. The aides have served as a bridge between the professionals and the people being served and have served themselves as well.

The staff reports that major changes seen in the aides can be accounted for by having steady, meaningful employment which has enabled them to support themselves and to stabilize their lives. Marked personality change has not occurred, but social adjustment has improved markedly. Both the high- and low-risk groups performed well and, with the exception of one boy who dropped out early owing to trouble with the police, there were no essential differences. However, many of these people have histories of difficulty that follow them. For instance, the one dropout would have returned, but because he was in prison he fell behind in payments set by a previous paternity suit and was put back in jail.

Despite the fact that the backgrounds of the aides were similar to those of their clients, they seemed to see the problems clearly and to want to help the kids get out of patterns that would lead to trouble. The staff found that the aides could cope with many difficult situations and that, with the supervision provided them, they could perform many functions.

In a program with a strong rehabilitative design like this, one has to search out the needs of the aides and provide opportunities to fill these needs during the period of training. Staff must be tolerant and capable. The aides say that their neighborhood is slowly getting better. It is obvious that it still needs improving. The mental health of anyone living in such an area is inevitably impaired. The awareness that much needs to be done has not always sharpened the understanding of how to do it. The staff at Baker's Dozen and the Institute for Youth Studies are finding a way.

Research Grant: MH 14837
Dates of Interviews: Jan. 31 and Feb. 3, 7, 8, 10, and 17, 1967.

References:
Denham, W., Felsenfeld, Naomi, and Walker, W. *The neighborhood worker, a new resource for community change.* A monograph on training and utilization. Institute for Youth Studies, Howard University, Washington, D.C., May 1966.
Klein, W., Denham, W., MacLennan, Beryce, and Fishman, J. *Training nonprofessional workers for human services.* A manual of organization and process. Institute for Youth Studies, Howard University, Washington, D.C., May 1966.
Klein, W., Walker, W., Levine, Myrna, MacLennan, Beryce, and Fishman, J. *Leadership in the training of human service aides:* First report on the counseling intern program. Institute for Youth Studies, Howard University, Washington, D.C., 1965–66.
Mitchell, L. Psychotherapy with the culturally and economically deprived youth. Paper read at annual convention of the American Psychological Association, New York, 1966.
Mitchell, L. *Training for community mental health aides as leaders of child and adolescent therapeutic activity groups.* Institute for Youth Studies, Howard University, Washington, D.C., May, 1966.
Mitchell, L. (Ed.) *A dictionarry of local terms and expressions.* The Baker's Dozen Community Mental Health Center for Adolescents: Institute for Youth Studies, Howard University, Washington, D.C., 1967.
Mitchell, L., and Fishman, J. Mental health for the poor—the use of trained problem youth in a neighborhood treatment program for children and adolescents. Paper read at 122d annual meeting of the American Psychiatric Association, Atlantic City, May 1966.
Training for new careers. President's Committee on Juvenile Delinquency and Youth Crime. June 1965.
"What It Means To Be Really Poor." Baker's Dozen Community Mental Health Center aides and Mitchell, L. Mimeographed paper, 1966.

Behavioral Consequences of Alienation

Investigator:
Melvin Seeman, Ph.D.
University of California
Los Angeles, Calif.

Prepared by:
Antoinette Gattozzi

Although it is probably true that there never has been a human community without its critics, the case against modern industrial society may be unique in history for the intellectual sophistication and emotional appeal of its arguments. Distinguished scholars such as Arendt, Marcuse, Fromm, and Mills have formulated the radical critique for our own time. The critique has an illustrious history, moreover, with main roots in the 19th-century writings of Durkheim, Weber, and Marx. The works in this genre now form a more or less cohesive body of literature known as mass society theory. The mass society has been criticized in many particulars, but the common judgment spanning the decades is that a mass society is, on the whole, an unhealthy one. Indeed, mass society analysts have been aptly called the pathologists of contemporary industrial societies.

Alienation is the dominant theme in mass society analysis. Alienation is regarded as the psychological effect generated by the structural forms that define a mass society and, in turn, it is considered to be the primary cause of a multitude of personal ills and social evils. The pivotal role assigned to the alienation concept can be made clear by outlining the central thesis of the mass society literature. The thesis is essentially composed of three elements—a historically oriented view of contemporary social forms, the concept of alienation, and judgments about the quality of contemporary life.

A mass society is defined by its structural features, which are the forms inherent in the historical developments of democratization, urbanization, and industrialization. It is a society in which most major institutions are designed to deal with people in the aggregate without distinguishing among individuals or small groups of individuals. "Mass" refers not to large size or huge numbers per se, but to the enlargement of the scale of social forms. Thus national governments, nationwide corporations, transportation and communication systems regularly make decisions that affect whole populations. Mass culture, mass production, mass consumption supplant the natural heterogeneity of the people. Pressures for technical efficiency and rational control lead to the bureaucratization of organizations: community is lost. Geographical mobility displaces stability. Kinship ties are attenuated: anonymity and impersonality come to characterize relations among people.

Mass society theorists have argued that alienation is fostered among the members of a society with these structural features. The alienated man suffers incalculable losses of many personal satisfactions as an individual human being. He is, as a consequence, especially vulnerable to mental and emotional disturbances. Further, a society in which there are large numbers of alienated men has little cohesiveness and organic integrity. A mass society may be beset, for example, by such social evils as widespread political passivity, ethnic and racial prejudices, and wildcat strikes of industrial workers.

This capsule statement of the mass society theory does not do justice to the persuasiveness of the formulations, but it does suggest the seriousness of the charges made. There is no doubt that these ideas and assertions, particularly the concept of alienation, have persisted because they are intellectually and emotionally seductive to many thoughtful people. Yet the literature of mass society theory tends to be discursive and rhetorical, and the use of the crucial alienation concept rather more exhortatory than analytical. As a result Prof. Melvin Seeman has noted, "the debate concerning alienation has often remained sterile, however valid the critique of society and however proper and humane the values involved." Professor Seeman has been trying to clarify the terms of that debate and to derive some specific propositions about alienation that would lend themselves to systematic testing.

The task began in 1959 with the publication of a conceptual paper in which Professor Seeman suggested that the various connotations of alienation could be distilled into five related but separate ideas.[1] In defining these ideas, he drew upon the social learning theory of Julian B. Rotter, a theory that Professor Seeman thinks has much in common with the alienative notion of powerlessness and its consequences. These five varieties of alienation, then, were defined in terms of an individual's expectations and his values.

- Powerlessness. The person who experiences a sense of powerlessness expects that forces outside himself control his personal and social rewards. He has little expectancy that his own behavior can be efficacious in gaining these rewards.
- Meaninglessness. The individual regards social affairs as incomprehensible. Therefore, he has little expectancy that he can predict the outcome of social events.
- Normlessness. The individual believes that he is not bound by conventional standards of conduct in the pursuit of his goals. Normlessness, on the contrary, implies a high expectancy that socially unapproved means must be used to achieve these goals.
- Value isolation. The individual rejects the values of society. He assigns low value to the goals and behaviors that are highly valued by most other members of his society.

---

[1] Since that time, Professor Seeman has added a sixth form of alienation, social isolation, which he defines as an individual's low expectancy for social acceptance, as reflected, for example, in the feelings of loneliness and exclusion experienced by members of minority groups.

• Self-estrangement. While this idea has taken a number of definitional forms, the one in which it is perhaps most easily grasped is this: To be self-estranged is to be engaged in activities that are not rewarding in themselves. This is self-estrangement in the classic Marxian sense of alienated labor. In social learning terms, the self-estranged person is continuously engaged in activities he does not value highly.

Professor Seeman has noted that the obverse of these alienative forms — order and trust, consensus and commitment, integrity and engagement — represent humanistic values that are highly esteemed by democratic societies. Thus, to the extent alienation is engendered in a society such as ours in the United States, it exerts profoundly detrimental effects on individual lives and threatens to make a mockery of our most cherished values. The crucial questions, of course, are whether or not the social forms of our modern industrial society really do spawn alienation among individual Americans and, if so, whether or not alienation has the behavioral consequences that mass society theory would predict.

It is the second question that has chiefly interested Professor Seeman. In a series of empirical studies carried out over the last 10 years, he has looked at two forms of alienation, powerlessness and self-estrangement, and has sought to discover whether an individual's level of alienation is related to his behavior in certain circumscribed areas.

Powerlessness and Learning

As noted above, Professor Seeman utilized certain constructs from a theory of social learning in his explication of alienation. The similarities between this theory and the mass society view of the behavioral consequences of an individual's powerlessness are quite striking.

The social learning theory formulated by J. B. Rotter holds that a person's behavior is significantly influenced by two factors and by the situation in which they occur or are embedded. It depends on his expectancy that the behavior will lead to a successful outcome and on the value he places on that outcome. Moreover, the theory distinguishes between internal and external control of rewards. Dr. Rotter and his associates have postulated that, in laboratory experiments in learning, subjects will not do as well when they perceive their success as being dependent on chance or luck or on the experimenter's control of the situation as when they believe that their own skill can decide the outcome. (A number of investigations have since shown that this is indeed true.) Similarly, mass society analysts have contended that the individual living in a contemporary industrial society, believing that he is powerless to determine the successful outcome of his social behaviors, turns away from political activities; his sense of powerlessness makes him indifferent to and a poor learner of political information and of other knowledge relevant to his social functioning.

74

"Thus," Professor Seeman has commented, "the idea of powerlessness extends downward, as it were, in its potential for reorganizing the relatively 'microscopic' studies of laboratory learning ... But the idea of powerlessness also extends upward in its significance, being an integral element in sociological descriptions of 'macroscopic' concerns: The occurrence of mass movements, the conditions of political democracy, and the like."

The first of a series of controlled studies testing the relation between powerlessness and learning was conducted by Professor Seeman and a colleague, John W. Evans, among the patients in 10 tuberculosis sanitariums in Ohio. Their hypothesis was that a patient's sense of powerlessness influenced what he had learned about tuberculosis. They predicted that high powerlessness would be associated with poor learning.

A total of 86 white male subjects were selected from a much larger sample and grouped into 43 pairs closely matched for age, income, education, length of hospitalization, estimated discharge time and, most important, hospital experience—each individual in a pair lived on the same ward of a hospital and was exposed to the same routines and staff care. They differed, of course, in their positions on the powerlessness scale.

The scale consisted of forced-choice items designed to reveal an individual's expectancies for personal control.[2] Most items referred to sociopolitical expectancies. For example, the patients were asked to choose, on the basis of personal belief, between these two statements: "The average citizen can have an influence on the way the government is run," and "This world is run by the few people in power and there is not much the little guy can do about it." The scores of the total sample were divided at the mean of the distribution into "low" and "high" alienation. Each pair of matched patients, then, included an "unalienated" and an "alienated" person.

The investigators also needed a measure of each patient's knowledge about tuberculosis. This they obtained by a standard true-false information test based on one used by the National Tuberculosis Association. Then, to get an idea of the extent to which a patient's objective knowledge was manifested in his ward behavior, the staff was asked a number of questions about the behavior of individual patients. Two questions were pertinent: How good is this patient's understanding of his illness, and of the disease generally? This gave the investigators a measure of what they called reputed knowledge. Finally, they obtained from each patient a measure of his subjective knowledge; that is, an indication of how satisfied he felt with the knowledge about tuberculosis that he possessed. These latter two measures were taken solely to help shed light on the researcher's central inquiry, which concerned the postulated relationship between an individual's expectancies for control and his objective knowledge about an event—tuberculosis—that strongly affected his life career.

---

[2] The alienation measure used in this and the other studies reported here was adapted from the I—E Scale (internal-external control) developed by Professor J. B. Rotter and the late Professor Shephard Liverant at the Ohio State University. The I—E Scale has been extensively tested and refined and shows satisfactory reliability.

The results confirmed the prediction: Alienated patients scored lower on the information test than did unalienated patients. The difference between the two groups was small but statistically significant. The investigators showed that the difference in knowledge about tuberculosis did not reflect any consistent differences in intelligence among individuals in the two groups.

Staff evaluation of a subject's knowledge, so-called reputed knowledge, was in line with the main finding. Patients high in alienation were judged by the staff to be less well informed about tuberculosis than patients relatively lower in alienation. No significant correlation was found between subjective knowledge and alienation, but an interesting interaction was discovered between ward stratification and alienation. The relatively more controlled environments (controlled by the physician in charge) drew fewer responses indicating dissatisfaction from the unalienated than from the alienated patients. The researchers had predicted that the opposite would be the case—that those who felt a greater mastery would resent the tight control exerted in the highly stratified ward. They offered one possible interpretation of this finding. A highly stratified environment is not congenial to the transmission of knowledge and it could be, they suggested, that on such wards the alienated patients actively sought and gained more knowledge than alienated patients were inclined to do. In a less controlled ward setting, knowledge may be acquired more passively, and thus be equally available to those willing to seek it (the unalienated) and those for whom knowledge presumably has little value and, therefore, is not worth any effort to attain (the alienated). This interpretation was modestly substantiated when the investigators compared objective knowledge scores of the unalienated and alienated groups on the two different kinds of wards. There was less difference between the group scores if patients resided on a low-stratification ward than if they lived on a highly stratified ward.

The results of this study, then, provided a reasonably satisfactory demonstration of an association between powerlessness and learning. At least two questions were left open, however. Was the relatively poor learning shown by the more alienated patients the product of their greater sense of powerlessness or did their powerlessness come from possessing little knowledge? Second, information from only one domain of information was tested—the control-relevant domain of tuberculosis information; would the more alienated patients have made an equally poor showing in any other area of knowledge, which might suggest a general withdrawal of their interest in learning? The design of Professor Seeman's next study provided ways to look into these questions.

The next study was carried out among the young male inmates of an Ohio reformatory. The choice of setting was particularly apt. "It is possible to conceive of the reformatory and its associated training apparatus as a vast learning mechanism," Professor Seeman pointed out, "but one in which the essential features of powerlessness dominate institutional life—where, for example, paroles are denied and inmates left in ignorance of the reasons, and where the inmate culture is a response to the more or less total threat to personal control."

The alienation scale used in this study was like the one used with the tuberculosis patients. Once again the scores were divided at the mean of distribution so that the subjects could be described as high or low in alienation. The tests of learning were quite different. This time Professor Seeman tested for new learning rather than measure prior knowledge. To do so, the group of 85 men (none having less than an IQ of 100 or a ninth-grade education) was presented with 24 items of information about correction. A third of these items dealt with the reformatory, a third were concerned with parole matters, and a third dealt with long-range opportunities. The items were compiled from documents not readily available to the men and presumably represented new information.

The men were presented with this material twice in one session. In order to insure that each item would be read, the investigator first asked them to mark off how interested they were in each item; moments after this task was completed, the men were given the items arranged in a multiple-choice-test format which they were asked to complete. The latter constituted their learning scores, for it tested how much of the material they had retained.

The investigator found that men low in alienation achieved significantly better recall of the parole items than did men high in alienation. There was no statistically significant difference between the alienation groups in the recall of the two other kinds of information.

Professor Seeman also made an estimate of the value each man placed on the conventional norms of the reformatory by compiling the number of merit commendations each had earned from prison authorities. Differences in powerlessness were found to be unrelated to learning among inmates who had earned no merits, but high or low powerlessness made a significant difference in learning among men who had earned one or more merits. The highest correlation between alienation and the learning of parole items appeared when low powerlessness was accompanied by a degree of commitment to the values of rehabilitation (as symbolized by the earning of merits). Thus, as Rotter's social learning theory would suggest, the combination of high expectation for personal control and high evaluation of the goals in question was most revealing of the association between alienation and learning.

Merit commendations were an indication of the men's behavior in the reformatory; Professor Seeman also obtained some indication of their behavior outside the reformatory, prior to confinement. Although age and IQ were found to be unrelated to learning scores, continuation beyond the ninth grade and achievement relative to capacity were relevant. A man's willingness to stay in school and to achieve in accordance with his capacity correlated well with both low powerlessness and good learning of parole material. "The most interesting feature of these results," Professor Seeman commented, "lies in the fact that the inmate's learning of corrections-relevant material (the parole information) is related not only to his generalized expectancies for control but to his behavior—both outside the prison and inside it—which presumably reflects such expectancies."

This investigation went a long way towards clarifying the relations between behavior and alienation in the powerlessness sense of low expectancy for control. It yielded a clear demonstration of an association between learning and alienation. More, the findings suggested some limits of this association—it appears only in the learning of control-relevant information—and revealed the fact that some behavioral concomitants of alienation may be found outside the sphere of learning. These two important additions to the body of evidence about alienation were explored in depth in the third study of this series. The study was made in Sweden; Professor Seeman carried out a number of related investigations in Sweden, which gave him an opportunity to examine the cross-cultural validity of alienation effects on learning and other behaviors. The study to be described next was conducted among some 300 students at Lund University; the other studies will be discussed below in different contexts.

The basic design was similar to that of the other investigations. Students were judged to be high or low in alienation on the basis of their scores on the powerlessness scale, and each student's knowledge in one or the other of two domains of information was tested. One was the domain of cultural knowledge and the other was that of nuclear weapons (for a small subsample, political information was also tested). All tests were equal in difficulty. Professor Seeman predicted that high alienation would be associated with poor scores on the nuclear (or political) test, but alienation would be irrelevant to scores on the cultural test. In other words, he hypothesized that alienation would affect learning differentially, as was suggested by the results of the reformatory study, and that the acquisition of control-relevant information is the specific learning most affected by one's relative sense of mastery or powerlessness.

Another alienation proposition was tested in this work. Prior to the initiation of the study, each student had completed a short version of the alienation scale, and these scores were in hand when the study proper got under way. For the study proper, then, most students received a cultural or a nuclear test and a long version of the alienation scale by mail, along with a covering letter and return envelope. Professor Seeman was interested in those who delayed returning the tests or failed to do so altogether, that is, those who showed avoidance behavior. He predicted that high alienation would be associated with late or nonreturns among the group that got the nuclear test but that no such association would appear among those getting the cultural test. This, he suggested, would allow for a "microdemonstration" of the proposition that powerlessness leads to avoidance behavior—"micro-" because what was involved was "the small world of everyday tasks, like responding to an inquiry from the university."

The results concerning alienation and control-relevant learning confirmed the prediction: High alienation, especially for women, correlated with poor knowledge of nuclear weapons or political affairs, but alienation, high or low, showed no associations with cultural knowledge, poor or good.

The data did not reveal so clearcut an answer to the question about avoidance behavior and alienation. The results tended to confirm the prediction—that is, alienated students were slower to return and more often failed to return the packet of tests if they had gotten a nuclear test than if they had received a cultural test—but did not reach statistical significance. There was, in fact, an astonishingly high rate of return (85 percent) before followup letters were sent out, which might be attributable to the fact that in Sweden there are strong, though informal, pressures to cooperate in social research.

This study showed that the proposition concerning the effects of powerlessness on differential learning holds in the domain of sociopolitical information and that it is valid for college-age students of another culture. Taken together, the three studies of alienation and powerlessness convincingly demonstrated the applicability of this proposition to a range of information domains and to different populations of people. In so doing, Professor Seeman's work greatly strengthened the empirical basis of the proposition's credibility and its usefulness in other social research. For example, its applicability to a sensitive and vital area of American life, the education of young children, was recently demonstrated by James S. Coleman and co-authors in their report, *Equality of Educational Opportunity*.[3] Professor Seeman has cited the relevant passage: "* * * a pupil factor which appears to have a stronger relationship to achievement than do all the 'school' factors taken together is the extent to which an individual feels that he has some control over his destiny." To the degree the proposition linking high alienation and poor learning is valid in other areas as well, it bears important implications for those trying to increase public understanding of international political issues, say, or those responsible for public health information campaigns about alcoholism, for instance, or the value of prenatal care.

The Role of Organizational Ties

Mass society theorists have made an important recommendation in their writings. They have repeatedly asserted that organizational ties must be established by the individual in order for him to have an effective mediator vis-a-vis the mass-scale institutions that surround him. This theme is sounded throughout the mass society literature, from Durkheim to Mills; although Mills, in *The Power Elite*, expressed doubts about the efficacy of mediating organizations in our time because they, too, as he saw them, had begun to assume mass-scale qualities.

---

[3] U.S. Government Printing Office. Washington, D.C. 1966.

Perhaps the most familiar example of a mediating organization is a labor union, and mass society theory would predict that union membership mitigates a worker's sense of alienation. To test this, Professor Seeman and a colleague, Arthur G. Neal, formulated a concrete hypothesis that could be examined in an empirical manner. The hypothesis: "We expected members of a work-based formal organization to exhibit less powerlessness than individuals without an organization to speak for them in the crucial area of occupation."

The setting for the study designed to examine this hypothesis was Columbus, Ohio, where the investigators assembled a random sample of adult male subjects from the city directory. Mail questionnaires were used to gather necessary information about each man's union membership and his sense of powerlessness. In addition, each was asked to answer questions about his experience of occupational mobility and to complete a scale designed to determine his attitudes towards mobility. These latter measures were needed, the researchers noted, because several studies had shown mobility and mastery (the obverse of powerlessness) to be related. Finally, subjects also received the well-known anomie scale, developed by Leo Srole, which can be interpreted as measuring generalized despair. This was included because the investigators wanted to find out if nonmembership was associated with other forms of alienation in addition to powerlessness.

Through the use of personal interviews done after the returns were in, the investigators checked the possibility that more alienated than unalienated men would have delayed or not bothered at all to comply with the mailed requests. They found this was not the case: Neither late return nor nonreturn correlated with high alienation. The investigators received replies from slightly more than 600 men (57 percent of the original sample). The occupational statuses of the respondents ranged from high-level executives to unemployed manual workers. Analyses of the data yielded the following results.

First, the basic prediction was confirmed. Compared to the group of organized workers, the group of unorganized workers felt themselves to be more powerless. This finding held when the variables of occupational status and income were controlled. When the mobility variables were taken into account, on the other hand, the investigators did find some interesting interactions.

When the groups of organized and unorganized men were separated into manual and nonmanual workers, the investigators found the same strong association between high powerlessness and nonmembership among the manual workers, regardless of mobility history or attitude. The picture was different among non-manual workers. For this group, a mobility attitude of nonstriving reversed the effect. Thus, among the mobility-oriented white-collar workers, the unorganized were higher in powerlessness than the organized (as expected), but it was the organized workers who were higher in powerlessness than the unorganized in the group of nonstriving white-collar workers. These data enabled the researchers to add a useful refinement to the thesis about organizational ties: It is particularly applicable to workers committed to mobility.

Second, no consistent relation emerged between membership or nonmembership and anomie, although unorganized workers tended to be only slightly higher in anomie than organized workers. By implication, anomie and powerlessness were not found to be strongly and systematically related either. This negative evidence was welcome on two counts. First, it supported the investigators' assumptions that their hypothesis was a relatively specific one—i.e., membership or nonmembership was linked to the powerlessness form of alienation—and second, it was suggested that powerlessness, as they defined and measured it, was a satisfactorily specific form of alienation that excluded more generalized feelings of hopelessness.

Although low powerlessness was clearly shown to be associated with organizational membership, the fact by itself does not support the mass society thesis regarding mediating organizations. One may wonder, as the investigators did, whether membership leads to low alienation or vice versa. The researchers were able to make a start toward the answer by obtaining data on the union situation (open or closed shop, maintenance-of-membership contracts, and the like) in the firms where their respondents worked. While conceding that their findings had to be regarded as only tentative, they concluded that both options were valid. In other words, the mass society argument about membership ameliorating the alienative effects of social structures was not inconsistent with the evidence; alternately, the data also provided support for the interpretation that workers low in alienation may be motivated, by virtue of their expectancy for personal control, to join organizations which are vehicles for the exercise of control in the work sphere.

The proposition concerning the ameliorative effects of organizational ties was directly tested in one other population. This was a large random sample, some 550 men, of the work force of Malmö, Sweden. Professor Seeman worked intensively with this group; in addition to the data required for the mediation thesis, he gathered many other kinds of information pertaining to alienation and its putative effects on behavior and attitudes. Much of what he discovered will be described below in the section on alienated labor. Two aspects of this omnibus Swedish work are relevant at this point of the report, the evidence concerning the mediation thesis and the data demonstrating anew, in the context of the mediation thesis, the relation between powerlessness and learning.

In Malmö, as in Columbus, high powerlessness and poor knowledge of political affairs were found to be associated in the group of unorganized workers, manual and nonmanual; there was no such association to be seen among the organized workers. The same pattern held when such pertinent variables as education, income, and occupational prestige were controlled. Moreover, there was a modest connection between degree of involvement and both powerlessness and learning: Workers who were little involved in their organizations scored higher in powerlessness and lower in political knowledge than did those who were more involved.

Thus, in two disparate cultural settings, men who were members of a work organization experienced less personal powerlessness in the socio-political arena than did their unorganized fellow workers. The evidence gathered in the two studies was consistent with the mass society thesis assigning a meliorative role to such organizations. More investigations are needed, however, to determine how much a worker's sense of powerlessness is minimized by his membership in a work organization as opposed to how much his sense of his ability to influence conditions that affect him leads him to join the organization in the first place.

Alienation in Work

The world of work occupies a prominent place in mass society theory, which devotes much attention to alienated labor. An alienated worker is defined as one who does work that is not intrinsically rewarding to him. He does it because he feels he must, not because he gains personal satisfaction in the activity. To engage in such work regularly, then, is to experience a variety of self-estrangement. Mass society and Marxian theorists have contended that the existence of an alienated labor force is itself responsible for a plethora of social problems. The deleterious effects are seen to be so pervasive and profound, in fact, that Marx and others have argued that many of the social ills of modern industrial societies could be made to disappear if only the alienation of labor were ended.

As expressed in the mass society literature, the consequences of alienated labor include attitudinal effects such as powerlessness and normlessness as well as behavioral effects such as minimal political participation, racial and ethnic hostility, and the substitution of extrinsic goals (job status, for example) for unattainable intrinsic satisfactions. Professor Seeman has characterized this theme of the mass society literature as the generalization thesis. He has begun to test its validity in separate investigations carried out in Sweden, France, and the United States. The Swedish study has been completed and it can be reported in full.

A random sample of the male work force of Malmö constituted the study population. Data were obtained through personal interviews with the workers. The basic measure—whether or not a worker felt alienated from his work—was obtained by reference to a work alienation index, which was developed by factor analysis of the responses to pertinent questions. The scale finally developed by this method was composed of seven items, for example, "Is your job too simple to bring out your best abilities, or not?" The investigator also obtained measures of powerlessness, ethnic and racical prejudice, anomie, political knowledge, orientation to experts, and mobility orientation. According to the mass society generalization thesis, a man who is alienated from his work feels powerless, hostile to "others," and anomic; he is rather ignorant of political affairs, tending to leave them in the hands of experts, and strives for the extrinsic rewards that status confers.

Reasonable though this thesis may sound, the analyses of the data yielded very little support for it. Work alienation was *not* found to be related to any of the theoretical outcomes in a statistically significant manner, although some of the outcomes did relate to one another—for example, high powerlessness was associated with scanty political knowledge and high expert orientation and with racial hostility. Even when variables such as age, income, occupation, and the like were controlled, no clear-cut associations with work alienation emerged. Further, when considering solely the question of how much control a worker felt he exerted in his work process—supposedly the quintessential condition of alienated labor—the associations to the postulated effects were similarly minimal. The conclusion to be drawn from these results, then, was that the attitudinal and behavioral consequences repeatedly attributed to alienation in work simply do not reflect the reality as it exists in Sweden.

An obvious question that arises is whether Sweden, after all, should not be considered an exceptional case because of its homogeneous population, its long history of peace and of social and economic stability. To answer this question, Professor Seeman undertook to perform essentially similar studies of alienation in work in France and the United States. These, too, are highly industrialized societies, but their political and social histories differ markedly from Sweden's and are different from one another as well.

Results from these two studies are not yet available. Preliminary analyses suggest, however, that neither the French nor the American situation differs from the Swedish in terms of the consequences of alienated labor. On the other hand, it appears that the relation between high powerlessness and low political knowledge will be found in both the French and American populations, as will additional validation of the mediation thesis. (The study in Los Angeles should also help illuminate the uniquely American racial situation. In addition to interviewing some 500 adult male white subjects, the investigator assembled a subsample of some 270 Negro workers. It should be instructive to see how the data collected from the white workers compare to those gathered in the Negro subgroup.) When the results from all three countries are available, the generalization thesis of mass society theory will have received a substantial test.

Even if alienated labor does not produce the adverse personal and social outcomes that have been imputed to it, it remains a source of concern. "For one thing," Professor Seeman has noted, "work life absorbs a major portion of the day, and an ethical stance concerning it must come to terms with that fact, regardless of any other consequences of alienated labor. For another, it is reasonable to argue either that the outcomes we have treated constitute an insufficient list (the data say little about the quality of family life, for example) or that the consequences will reveal themselves in a longer-term, cumulative way—for example, in revolutions or in the irregular outbursts of a wildcat strike."

Nor can it be assumed that men alienated from their daily work are indifferent to the fact. The sort of data required to examine the generalization thesis did not touch on such matters. It cannot be said, therefore, whether or not the worker detests his work and is angry at himself for doing it. All that the data do allow us to say, Professor Seeman has pointed out, is that "people can work out fairly effective adjustments to varied kinds of work, *if* by 'effective' we simply mean leading a work life that has little generalized effect on the standard forms of hating, striving, withdrawing, and complaining reviewed here." Thus, although the predictions implicit in the mass society generalization thesis may ultimately prove to be invalid, the ideological indictment of industrial forms that breed alienation in work is a separate issue and one still most worthy of attention.

The concept of alienation bears on some of the most urgent problems confronting our society. Yet the resounding rhetoric in which discussions of alienation are often couched makes it too easy for many people to dismiss the ideas along with the words as baseless pessimism. Professor Seeman's concern as a scientist has been to help turn "the parable of alienation into a proposition," or rather a series of propositions that can be accepted, rejected, or amended on the basis of deductions drawn from evidence methodically gathered in controlled but real situations. As a result of his work, we begin to see that the "pessimism" of the mass society radical critique is not, in fact, groundless.

Much more research on problems involving alienation needs to be carried out before we know just how valid the critique is and, more constructively, how much insight into man's social behaviors can be gained through explorations of the alienation concept. Professor Seeman recently outlined a general program of research to be done in this area and enumerated several studies he thought would be useful. In that paper, which will be a chapter in a book to be published by the Russell Sage Foundation, the investigator also described the unique challenges that such research makes on social scientists.

"The fact remains," Professor Seeman concluded, "that there *were* concentration camps and genocide, that there *are* now widely disrespected qualities in American life—including a widely disrespected war, at the moment—and that there *will* be further urban violence born of frustrated hopes. That kind of past, present, and future create a special tension for the sociologist interested in the problem of alienation. It is the tension between keeping a craft that is worthy of the name, and at the same time making sociological investigation practically and morally relevant. The danger on the craft side is that the work deteriorates into a kind of alienation in itself—bound by technical rules, limited in vision, devoid of personal involvement, and largely oriented to careers. The danger on the side of relevance is that this deteriorates, too—into a subtle anti-intellectualism that is impatient with any thing but the immediate; or into a kind of self-indulgence that emphasizes stance over analysis, so that what becomes crucial is one's identification (as radical, as realist, as humanist, or whatever). My hope is that the secularization of work on alienation can continue to be achieved while avoiding both these dangers—which is to say that clarity and demonstration can be successfully wedded to scope and human concern."

Research Grant: MH 10460
Date of Interview: October 1968

References:

Neal, A. G.; and Seeman, S. Organizations and powerlessness: A test of the mediation hypothesis. *American Sociological Review,* 29:216–226, 1964.

Seeman, M. On the meaning of alienation. *American Sociological Review,* 24:783-791, 1959.

——Alienation and social learning in a reformatory. *American Journal of Sociology,* 69:270–284, 1963.

——Alienation, membership, and political knowledge: A comparative study. *Public Opinion Quarterly,* 30:353–367, 1966.

——Status and identity: The problem of inauthenticity. *Pacific Sociological Review,* 9:67–73, 1966.

——Powerlessness and knowledge: A comparative study of alienation and learning. *Sociometry,* 30:105–123; 1967.

——On the personal consequences of alienation in work. *American Sociological Review,* 32:273–285, 1967.

——Alienation and engagement. Chapter for a forthcoming publication to be published under the auspices of the Russell Sage Foundation (edited by A. Campbell and P. E. Converse).

Seeman, M.; and Evans, J. W. Alienation and learning in a hospital setting. *American Sociological Review,* 27:772–782, 1962.

Note.—In addition to NIMH grant support, the investigator's research has been aided by grants from the University of California and The Swedish Social Science Research Council.

Alternatives to Violence

Investigator:
Saul Bernstein, Ph.D.
Boston University
Boston, Mass.

Prepared by:
Clarissa Wittenberg

The unruly issues of riots, slums, and racial problems are now of major importance. Our state of information is extremely limited, and major decisions are often made on the basis of scant knowledge. Saul Bernstein, a professor of social group work at Boston University, has completed two extensive interview studies to explore these and related issues. His focus has been on our most alienated young people, those who are minority group members and who are living in slums. Initially interested in delinquency and its contemporary forms, he then turned to the impact of the explosive events of the 1960's.

Twice in the mid-1960's Professor Bernstein traveled to nine major American cities to talk to people working closely with teenagers in the ghettos, as well as with some of the youngsters themselves. In the first study, completed in 1963,[1] he found that many of the young people in this country live in terrible housing in slums, are blocked educationally, cannot get jobs, are undermined by family problems, and are caught up in destructive cycles with new babies being born into new one-parent families. Many of these young people are bitter and intensely cynical, and feel hostile and destructive towards this country. Many engage in delinquent acts and are in trouble with the police. These young people do not feel encouraged by the new legislative landmarks which are designed to secure their rights. If anything, many felt more impatient and intolerant of existing inequities than ever before. Many felt that this country had let them down. Mr. Bernstein concluded that many agencies working in the slums were doing good work but against great obstacles, and he especially singles out the street workers as of great importance in reaching these alienated young people.

In the mid-1960's this country was torn by riots and stunned particularly by the Watts riot. Many people were puzzled and shocked because progress had been made in civil rights legislation and the antipoverty program had begun. The civil rights movement at that time was also strong and tasting the fruits of success. It was at this time that the second study was planned to determine if any of the socially approved forces had touched the alienated youth with the same force as had the riots. An

---

[1] Supported by grants from the Duncan Russell Memorial Delinquency Committee of the United Community Services of Metropolitan Boston and the Permanent Charity Fund of Boston.

exploration of the role of these young people in the riots was also planned.

During both studies the investigator visited Boston, Chicago, Cleveland, Detroit, Los Angeles, New York, Philadelphia, and Washington, D.C. The second study done in 1965–66 substituted Rochester, N.Y., for San Francisco. At that time Rochester had had riots and San Francisco had not. The design in both studies called for the location of major social agencies working with young people in the slums, and to interview staff in each of these agencies. In addition to interviews with staff, the young people themselves were interviewed whenever possible. In some cases, staff members were themselves indigenous workers and very representative of the ghetto population. In both studies, the cities were selected because they had large numbers of hostile, alienated young people and because agencies in these cities had long experience in work with young people. The focus was on the poor, including members of minority groups: Negroes, Mexican-Americans, Puerto Ricans, and poor whites.

In the study done in 1965–66, the investigator visited nine cities. He held interviews with 289 people. Most of those interviewed were staff members at various levels of responsibility in agencies active in slum areas. In most cities there were interviews with officials of the Human Relations Commission or its local equivalent. Police, particularly those dealing with juveniles, were included. Educators were seen. Staff members of various poverty programs and of community planning councils were included. Representatives of such Federal agencies as the Office of Juvenile Delinquency and Youth Development, and various research groups, were interviewed. Experimental agencies, such as Mobilization for Youth and Haryou-Act in New York, and the Cleveland Community Action for Youth, were included, as were new training programs such as Manpower in Rochester. Limited time of the second study and the inaccessibility of the young people themselves prevented more than a small number of interviews with really alienated young people themselves. A number of representatives of militant groups, such as Saul Alinsky's Industrial Areas Foundation, were interviewed. All interviews took place between December 1965 and June 1966. In many cases group interviews were held.

This technique resulted in a broad and detailed series of observations of experts and young people about some of the major events of the mid-1960's. While events have been occurring at rapid speed in this area, this study provides a valuable cross section of opinion at that time. The investigator acknowledges that the research is limited by several factors. Obviously, not all alienated youth come into contact with such agencies and the experts interviewed may have some biases. The study is treated as documentary rather than as "hard" research.

The major question of the study was to find if we as a society had found any way other than riots to touch the alienated young person and help him change his status. There is also great concern about the role of the ghetto youth in these massive riots. Although many things have occurred to correct injustices and open up opportunities, it is still questionable if they have made sufficient impact. The study was designed to increase our information about how these young people feel about riots, about legislative landmarks, protest marches, desegregated schools, "black" schools, etc.

The first study (in 1963) showed that there are many people caught in our slums in very destructive patterns. Some changes in patterns of delinquent gangs have occurred. The highly structured large gangs appear to have diminished, although not to have disappeared. Smaller groups referred to as clusters tend to predominate now. Although it may be reassuring to see the disappearance of the highly visible signs of gangs, such as matching leather jackets or gang graffiti on walls, this may be due to the accumulated pressure brought to bear on visible gangs, rather than to their lack of strength. The gangs may have "learned the game." Although rumbles on a large scale have decreased, "snagging" or "Japping" was commonly mentioned. In this form of fighting, a lookout watches the regular movements of one or two members of an antagonistic gang. When it is established that a suitable place will be passed by the victim at a predictable time, about six of the aggressors go home, wash, shave, put on good suits, and then saunter towards that spot. They are careful to go in pairs and not to show in any way by their behavior what is planned. When the victim comes along, they give him a bad beating and then go casually home to change clothes. In some places the ritual was different so as not to risk their good clothes. Clothing is very important in the gang psychology. Another form of gang fighting mentioned is the "fair one." Here a representative of each group fights without weapons or assistance. This, however, calls for a high level of discipline which is rarely achieved. This is relatively infrequent as the fighters are in a very tense, public, and vulnerable position as well.

Most of the aggressive incidents occur between groups with the same ethnic or racial background, although in some places even the most confined ghetto population is quite mobile and there are some incidents where groups have traveled to other areas for conflict.

The study revealed that although these bitter, hostile young people would seem ripe recruits for militant or protest groups that relatively few had joined. The Black Muslims, for example, had little to offer in terms of meeting concrete needs, such as jobs. The NAACP methods often seem too slow and removed to be attractive to these young people. However, some young people, generally the less hostile ones, have joined NAACP. In Boston it was reported that a small number of white gang members were recruited by the American Nazi Party.

The first study also examined the role of the "street worker." Agencies in slum areas have found that "detached" workers can move into the environment of the young people and reach them in a way no office-bound worker could do. They provide a link between agencies and some young people who have lost contact with all legitimate agencies or social groups. Street workers vary; some have master's degrees, some have not yet finished high school. Most have undergraduate degrees. Some have delinquent or prison backgrounds and some are from very stable middle-class backgrounds. As a group they tend to be very active and not attracted by a 9 to 5 life. Most are deeply involved in helping people find themselves and achieve some success. They tend to be not well accepted into any one professional group. They are "lonely" professionals. Agencies have a hard time retaining street workers, and the demands of the job are very grueling, so most workers tend to be in their twenties or thirties. Job opportunity tends to be limited in terms of opportunity for advancement and increased income. These issues are important as more and more innovative agencies designed to serve the ghetto population depend heavily upon the services of the street worker. Social work is considered the nearest profession. Mr. Bernstein comments that street work, which has been estimated to cost about $200 to $600 annually for each youngster, is little enough to pay for work which genuinely reaches them and often their families.

After examining patterns and services and the state of some very alienated young people in the first study, the investigator turned to what was happening and what alternatives there might be to the violence occurring in our cities. An early task was the division of the various riots and incidents into broad categories. In the mid-1960's riots occurred that were the result of spontaneous events, e.g., the riot in Boston following a dance which excluded large numbers of young people who could not be accommodated. Other riots were between racial or ethnic groups, such as the incident sometimes called Watts II on March 15, 1966, between Mexican-Americans and Negroes. However, violence within the ghetto itself was the most serious and disturbing type. At that time Negroes were primarily involved, although some episodes were thought to have had their beginnings in the tensions of Puerto Ricans or Mexican-Americans. Despite much "get whitey" talk and the destruction of white-owned businesses, the aggression at the time of the study was largely confined to slum areas. White men were injured primarily as they came into the riot area in an official capacity, such as happened with police or firemen. Threats to burn and loot white areas did not materialize.

To realize the magnitude of the riots of the mid-1960's a review of the McCone Commission figures is valuable. Although Watts was the most memorable riot of that period, many others occurred. Many, many people

McCone Commission Report summary of riots occurring in 1964:

City	Date	Killed	Injured	Arrests	Stores Damaged
New York........	July 18-23.....	1	144	519	541
Rochester........	July 24-25.....	4	350	976	204
Jersey City.......	Aug. 2-4	0	46	52	71
Paterson.........	Aug. 11-13	0	8	65	20
Elizabeth	Aug. 11-13.....	0	6	18	17
Chicago	Aug. 16-17	0	57	80	2
Dixmoor (Phila.) ..	Aug. 28-30	0	341	774	225

were injured, many arrested, and some killed. To make the figures more dramatic, it must be remembered that only a small fraction of those involved were arrested or noted in official statistics. It is speculated, too, that many more who never took part still tacitly supported the rioting.

All of these occurred between July 18 and August 30, a 6-week period. Five dead, a total of 952 injured, 2,484 arrested, and 1,080 stores damaged. Despite all this, the riot in Watts overshadowed the rest. It began on August 11, 1965, a Wednesday, and ended the following Tuesday, August 17. It was estimated that at times as many as ten thousand Negroes participated. This, however, was still only 2 percent of the population living in the riot area. The size of the riot area was an incredible 46.5 square miles. The dead totaled 34, the injured 1,032, arrests 3,952, and damage was estimated at about $40 million. Only one public building was destroyed and only 14 damaged or burned. This is an interesting issue, as these buildings, while not attractive to looters, do symbolize the dominant "establishment." Although there is always present the explanation of riots being a spontaneous mass protest where people get out of control while attempting to express a protest against degrading living conditions, this explanation fails to account for the control exhibited in some areas and the relative immunity given, for instance, to schools, normally a target for vandals. Rioters in Watts were also observed stopping at traffic lights and driving with caution. Examples were given during the study interviews of looters apologizing when bumping into each other. There was considerable evidence as well that riots may be provoked or related to specific incidents or situations rather than emerging spontaneously from the blue.

Some situations were cited as definite causes of riots. For example, Garfield Park in Chicago, a predominantly Negro area, had a fire station with an all-white staff until after the riot when it was integrated. The California vote defeating Proposition 14, an open-housing ordinance, was considered an irritant in Watts. The inadequate public transportation in Los Angeles was also cited. A man looking for work in Los Angeles who lived in Watts might have to spend several hours on a bus and pay a round trip cost of almost a dollar. Budd Schulberg, who later established a Writer's Workshop in Watts, told of seeing a group on a street in Watts. A 6-month-old baby had died. The mother's grief was intensified by the bitter knowledge that the prompt arrival of an ambulance and a hospital closer than the County General might have saved her child. In April of 1966 there was still no public hospital in Watts, and Los Angeles voters later rejected a bond issue to construct one.

Others interviewed told of comments by law enforcement officers that were irritants. Particularly cited were "abrasive" remarks by Los Angeles Police Commissioner Parker. A comment he had made in 1958, that Negroes committed 11 times the major crimes as other races, was still remembered with bitterness by Negroes in that area.

The rigidity of the Boston School Committee about *de facto* segregation was considered an outrage. Even the withholding of State funds for education, because of the unwillingness of the Boston School Committee to prepare and put into effect adequate measures for the desegregation of public schools, did not produce significant change in 1966. Elections for posts on the School Committee, which produced large votes for the most intransigent members and defeat for the ones in favor of desegregation, added to the affront to the Negroes.

Heat, "the long hot summer," adds to the tensions and problems of crowded living and may bring a state of irritability that is explosive.

Accidents can trigger incidents. A firetruck on an emergency call hit a Negro woman and killed her. Since the fire station involved was all-white and in a Negro area and already the source of tension, the rumor spread that the killing was on purpose.

The presence or absence of social controls is an important element. In Philadelphia, at the "Wall" of the Girard College, a crisis was described which was headed off on at least one occasion by the strong activity of the Human Relations Commission which marshalled clergymen, probation officers, police, street workers, and others to help keep the gang members who were gathering under control. Other types of social control are punitive and may work temporarily but appear to be self-defeating.

For instance the mayor of a riot-torn area in Illinois said he would meet with Negro ministers but not with "violators or demonstrators." Participation in riots was justification for being sent eviction notices if participants lived in public housing. In other places parents in public housing were very concerned about involvement of their children in any kind of a protest for fear it would lead to the family being evicted. Officials of some cities had considered the legality of cutting people off public welfare or un-employment compensation. The assumption is that those who are arrested are guilty and were more active in rioting than those who were not arrested, which may not necessarily be true. These measures, such as eviction, are punishment beyond that established for criminal acts and make life worse for those affected. The accessibility of public officials to those in the ghettos is very important and can reduce the impulse to riot.

Role of the Alienated Young Person in the Riots

Those interviewed in this study described considerable activity by the young people in the ghettos. They looted, burned, and fought the police. Some were members of gangs, although a more frequent pattern was for small cliques to riot together. These were units of three to five youngsters. The older teenagers rather than the younger, and boys rather than girls, predominated. It was the general finding that these young people *did not plan* the riots. Many of the young people who took part were in their twenties or thirties. Strong feelings were expressed by ghetto youth against the middle-class Negroes who attempted to stop the riots. One group of teenagers in Rochester articulated this antagonism, claiming that middle-class Negroes thought that the white reaction to the riot would hurt them. These same young people were bitter that many better-off Negros moved out of the bad areas and then abandoned all responsibility for them. The investigator notes that, despite the concern for the ghetto problems shown by middle-class Negroes interviewed in this study, there is great resentment towards them by those still in the ghetto.

A wide range of feelings was expressed about the riots. Some young people admitted that they enjoyed them. Others said they were dangerous and foolish. Some felt that they are essential to attract attention to the ghettos. One comment was, "It is better to spill blood in Watts than in Viet Nam." There is little doubt that the riots give people in the ghetto a sense of community and power. In Los Angeles it was said that participation in the riots became a status symbol, and many felt good to have been a part of it. Many spoke of the dangers of being shot, hurt, or arrested. Young people in Boston spoke of envying Watts and yet did not speak of riots in their own area. Detroit and Washington seemed calmer than other cities, yet both had riots later. At the time of the study, the riots seemed very remote and unrelated to the Puerto Ricans and Mexican-Americans interviewed.

There is tremendous complexity in the reactions to riots. The impact of the experience itself and its realities, such as food shortage, jail, etc., bring about additional factors that become added to those present prior to the riots. The mass news media and many civic leaders add interpretations and give reasons, and these all become incorporated into the discussion. The reasons given after a riot may be quite different from the motivations of the riot period itself. Still, an overwhelming certainty was that for the people in this study the reality of the unbearable living conditions and the profound feeling of helplessness was a major factor in every riot.

Agency Activity During Riots

Street workers who had established influential relationships with young people on the streets were able to make major contributions. In Garfield Park, Chicago, the workers were able to persuade the young people they knew to leave the riot area. In other cases the street workers were able to enlist gang leaders in the effort to keep their friends out of the riot activity. Several agencies took young people away from the areas to lessen the opportunity for involvement. During the Watts riot the staff of the Special Service for Groups took food to desperate areas. Later, when it was considered unsafe for whites to enter the area, the Negro staff carried on.

All of the cities need more street workers in the rough areas. The street worker is seen by the militant Negro as a threat because of his commitment to nonviolence. Mr. Bernstein quotes a letter sent in plain envelope to three street workers at Lawndale Neighborhood Services of Chicago Youth Centers:

"Grettings Brother:
"Have you ever considered WHY the GREAT WHITE FATHER is continuing to spend MORE money on the various street work pro-

grams throughout the entire country and especially in the BLACK GHETTOS. Also why the GREAT WHITE FATHER is expanding these programs to include community organizations. If you are aware of the current struggle being waged by Black Americans to be recognized as human beings in the so-called 'land of the free and home of the brave,' it is not difficult to arrive at the most logical answer as to why WHITEY is expanding the program.

"The white man wants to contain our people, to keep them from rebelling against living in slum housing, receiving poor education, and thus the worst jobs, if any at all. The people who run America do not want the Afro-American to know who he is, to have an identity, to know of his glorious past, and the prospects of an even richer future if they can get Charlie off their backs.

"Today there is a fierce battle being waged for the minds of the youth of America, especially Black Youth. For young people are invariably more idealistic than older people, and thus are not likely to go for as much bull—as older people. Thus, it is principally the Black Youth who fought the police during the riots of last summer, age range from 14 to 19 years old.

"Because Mister Charlie pays your salary the same as he pays me, ask yourself, if the real—breaks out here, what will be my ROLE? If your wife and children are in the streets during a riot, the BIG WHITE COP will *crack their heads* just like any Negro's head. MY BROTHER, what will you do with your group? Will it be a, 'cool it, baby, they ain't done nothin' to us,' or will it be a 'defend yourselves, brothers'? Things are bound to get worse all over. The War on Poverty is a farce, a throwing of crumbs to the poor, both black and white, to stem the tide of rebellion.

"Every Afro-American street worker has a very important role to play in the coming days ahead. In the language of the street, you can teach the young brothers and sisters to be proud to be BLACK. You can help destroy the often subconscious inferiority complex that exists in many of our ghetto youth. BROTHER, it is a question of whether or not you will truly be a BLACK MAN who cares above all else about the hopes and aspirations of his people. The choice is yours to make and I have confidence that you will not be a SELL-OUT. The fight is ours and we cannot afford to not be victorious.

Your Soul Brother"

In addition to the efforts of the street workers, some agencies were able to make and keep active telephone contact with clients in the affected areas. This is an especially good technique for verifying or defusing rumors.

A common feeling among Negroes, even those who would work to prevent a riot, is that no Negro can totally regret that riots have occurred. Although many people suffer and there is a trauma involved, there are definite gains in terms of community awakening. There is heightened sensitivity on the part of police and politicians to their handling. Whites have a range of reactions from dedication, to eradicating the basic wrongs, to buying guns. Riots in some situations increased communication and in others intensified the polarization.

Participation in the Civil Rights Movement

The civil rights movement in this context is described as a broad combination of legislation, organizations, public opinion, and activities aimed to extend all civil rights to those who have been deprived of them. The means are many, including marches, demonstrations, sit-ins, boycotts, political pressure, etc. In the early 1960's many white people were involved as well as members of minority groups. At the time of the study some militant groups of Negroes had given up on the civil rights movement as an effective force. However, they must also be included here because of their actual and potential impact on alienated youth. The civil rights movement has been concerned with human rights as well as strictly civil rights and often includes a strong appeal to decency as well as to law enforcement.

Little participation in civil rights activity on the part of alienated youth was discovered by this study. One group of boys in Chicago had helped to promote a large meeting to collect food and money to be sent to Negroes who had been cut off from welfare. This had occurred when they had registered to vote in a Southern community. Some other participation took place largely through agencies. For instance, Mobilization for Youth in New York took a large number of ghetto residents to Washington for the March on Washington in 1963. By and large, participation was limited and almost accidental. If a protest march went through their neighborhood, they might join in. The young people in the civil rights movement have been those whose motivations and aspirations have been more clearly defined than those of the young people here under study. By and large, the young people who are most alienated are also bitter and less likely to participate in a civil rights movement. They are quicker to strike out, more hostile to the police, and less disciplined. Some groups would even discourage their participation so as not to jeopardize their cause or inflame a sensitive situation. The more quick-tempered prefer to work at things in a more direct way. The staff at Haryou-Act in Harlem described a group that was concerned about the lack of toilets at a playground. They then got publicity for the problem by urinating in cups at the playground. They did get the toilets. Many of the most alienated young people did not even really understand the civil rights movement. Many in

94

the North thought it was only for ' colored people in the South." The delayed results of the civil rights movement are not attractive to them. This group has had little experience with altruism and cannot believe that anyone does anything for a reason other than his own gain.

It was clear from the interviews that the nonviolent theme is not compatible with the impulses of the angry young men in the ghetto. They feel a strong need to retaliate. Although many situations have been corrected legally, the problems still exist in an extremely frustrating form. For instance, these young men know that legally many restaurants are open to them and that stores cannot refuse to serve them. They also know that they will be ill-received or self-conscious if they venture out of home territory. Their clothing or their hairdos will mark them as different. They see the stores and do not have the money to patronize them. The jobs that are available to them pay so little that often they do not materially advance their ability to have the things they so desire. They see the quick financial rewards that come from illicit operations. They resent having to "break their backs" to earn a legitimate salary and yet know that "their backs" are all they have to offer due to their poor educations.

This study showed that the civil rights movement has to a certain extent increased the awareness of the average minority group member of the discrimination that he suffers. The need for an increase in black pride and a self-respecting racial identity is crucial. There is still the question as to whether any attempt to revive dignity can be totally successful without significant changes being made in the slums and in employment, and in general acceptance and respect on the part of the dominant community.

At the time of the study, the heroes of the civil rights movement were little known to ghetto youth. The Reverend Martin Luther King, Jr., known to everyone since his death, was relatively little known by ghetto youth in most cities, although he had been widely honored in this country and abroad. Malcolm X was an authentic object of hero worship. During the riot in Harlem in 1964, youth were quoted as chanting: "We want Malcolm X." Many knew Cassius Clay whom they admired for his boxing skill. Feelings were mixed regarding his lack of humility. In Roxbury, the Boston Celtics were highly regarded by the Negro youngsters.

The special emphasis on the concept of "black" or "Afro-American," with its repudiation of slavery and its labels, is congenial to the most alienated persons in the ghettos. The concept of Black superiority is welcome to them. However, this study showed that, despite the compatibility of the concept, few of the young people joined the movements; most remained as isolated as before from the larger society.

Puerto Ricans and Mexican-Americans have been much less involved than Negroes in the civil rights activities. The reality of Puerto Rico as a place and the recognizable and respected culture helps them tolerate the problems here. This is true of Mexicans as well. The emergence of the new Black African countries is important but very remote to most American

Negroes. While the Puerto Rican can and does return to Puerto Rico, the average American Negro does not go to Africa, and, if he does, he may feel more alienated and foreign than in the United States. Although the militants have revived or made ties to Africa, by and large the American Negro feels that, good or bad, this is his country.

Antipoverty Programs

The War on Poverty generated a great many programs to attempt to attack serious problems. Of those specifically designed to help adolescents, perhaps Job Corps and Neighborhood Youth Corps are most pertinent.

Job Corps Camps were set up away from slum areas. They offered healthy environments, good food, remedial education, and job training. This might have been beneficial for these particularly unequipped and hostile young people, except that a few things were wrong. The publicity was attractive, but the delays in processing applications caused people to become discouraged. The location of the camps away from home surroundings made some uneasy. The similarity for some youth of being sent away to training school was too marked. Agencies which did send young men had a hard time finding out what happened to them. Information was rarely sent to the referring agency when a young man dropped out or was asked to leave. So, for a variety of reasons, the Job Corps did not make a noticeable mark on alienated youth in the cities studied.

The Neighborhood Youth Corps included programs of jobs for school dropouts, special intensive summer job programs, and activities for in-school youth. Social agencies, government offices, and industry participated as work stations. Youth whose families had incomes at the poverty level were acceptable. Usually assignments were for about 20 to 24 hours a week for those who were out of school and less for those in school. The pay rate was about $1.25. A common complaint was that this rate was too low. Many participants regarded the assignment as work and not training and felt that it was not enough money. Delays in issuing checks and other such problems lowered motivation to stay on in some cases. Even the "poverty" label was offensive to some. After 6 months those out of school had to resume some type of educational program or be dropped.

The Neighborhood Youth Corps was most successful where the policy was clear and counseling was an integral part of the program. The nature of the work assigned and its potential benefit to the young person were also important. Most members valued the opportunity to use business machines and other skilled types of jobs much more than the menial jobs usually available to them.

Agencies which employed these young people found that their early employment phase was often difficult. A combination of patience, understanding, and firmness was needed to deal with absences, unexplained lateness, or early leaving. Some young people were in agencies whose staff

96

understood the hair styles or dress of the youth and the identity issues involved, but also felt these posed a barrier to later employment. Language and attitudes about authority also caused problems. The way that each issue was handled was important in each case. The youth had to be accepted as they were at the beginning, and later the realities of the employment market were introduced.

Local programs were developed in various cities with the approval of the local antipoverty organization. Mr. Bernstein reports on a few that seemed successful or interesting.

Chicago—STREETS (Socialization, Training, Education, and Employment Technical Services)

This was a cooperative venture by the Chicago Boys' Clubs, the Chicago Youth Centers, Chicago Federation of Settlements and Neighborhood Centers, and the YMCA. The purposes in general were to enable disadvantaged youth to function better in relation to requirements of our society. Other goals were to make fuller use of social welfare and other systems, to help the youth move toward adequate education, satisfying jobs, healthy marriages, and so on. The neighborhoods selected for service were among those designated by the Chicago Committee on Urban Opportunity as having the greatest poverty and related problems.

The main feature of STREETS was the hiring of neighborhood adults and youth to help in the work of the agency. The youth worked primarily with younger children. Those with leadership quality were sought. The adults, called neighborhood aides, shared, with the professional staff, in the supervision of the youth, called program aides. The aides also benefited from the agencies' programs as well as promoting them for others. The program was set up in units designed to serve 1,500 youths. These were eight units and a staff of 488 to serve 12,000. Those interviewed were enthusiastic about the program although some aides did not achieve the level originally set for them. The respondents felt that great success had been achieved in some areas. They felt that some aides learned to give up antisocial acts, assumed great responsibility for children, and returned to school. They also carried over to their own peer group what they had learned.

Central to this success was the familiarity of the agencies involved with the neighborhoods and clientele. They already had skill in working with alienated youth and this made their commitment to the most difficult of the young people more durable. They seem to have a good sense of the types of jobs aides can perform, and, in general, the program incorporates the advantages of using indigenous workers. Aides received salaries of about $45 for a 30-hour week.

Detroit—SWEEP (Summer Weekend Evening Emergency Program)

This is a summer weekend program conducted by the Neighborhood Service Organization in high delinquency and poverty areas, in cooperation with the Youth Bureau of the Police Department, with schools, universities, museums, and others. It was for girls and boys, ages 12 to 17, referred by schools and other agencies or people because they were drop-outs or were having difficulty. There was also concern that these young people might present problems during the "long hot summer."

The active program was well attended. In addition to group meetings and home visits, the program took children horseback riding, to Detroit Lions' practice, to the Tigers' games, and to many other interesting places in the area. Street workers and teachers made up most of the program staff. The youngsters were asked to write their evaluation of the program, too, and were positive about the experience. Again with this program, as with the one just described, the experience of the parent agencies was important, and the worker's skills and orientation were of vital importance to the success. The weakest part of the program is its temporary and limited nature. When summer ends, the stresses and deprivations continue, and young people live with and react to them all year. The choice here is between a successful fragment or nothing at all.

Los Angeles—ESCAPE STRING (Education in Service Careers and Employment—and Service Toward Redirection of Impressionable Neighborhood Groups)

A major objective is to help predelinquent youth, and another is to help low-income Negro and Mexican-American youth of academic promise to continue their education with the help of salaries paid for work with this agency. A team of professionals contacted gangs and their families, and then the college students from similar low-income families were assigned to work with them. Professionals supervised the college students. A very satisfactory aspect was the involvement of the students in the agency. As the program went on, if any of the college students were interested in social work, everything possible was done to assist them in attending a graduate school of social work. The staff felt that in some cases the experience gave some college students the motivation to stay in college. The young people helped also benefited. Again, the long experience in this field of the parent agency was important.

Los Angeles had many other programs:

The South Central Volunteer Bureau recruited volunteers for work in ghetto areas. It was very active in helping get food and supplies into the Watts area during the riot. It was felt that many volunteers benefited from this experience.

The Neighborhood Adult Participation Aides worked with a wide variety of agencies to allow them to extend their services into areas that normally would not be offered. Homemaking services or foster father activities were two examples.

The Los Angeles Human Relations Commission had a number of projects. They hired some militant young Negroes to be a link between them and the community. It was felt that this helped in preventing trouble in their areas.

The Los Angeles County Civil Service instituted a program to employ poverty youth in 30 types of civil service jobs as aides. They also searched for other types of employment. Testing and orientation were given prior to employment. Role playing and movies were used to help educate and prepare the young people. Psychiatric consultation was used when necessary and monthly employment followup was done where necessary.

Travelers Aid gave special help to newcomers to the Watts area. Money was available to help with interim crises. Public assistance was not available here until residency requirements were met. Help was given with school problems, medical care, legal difficulties, mental illness, etc. Aides from the previously mentioned Neighborhood Adult Participation program were extensively used.

Rochester, New York State Division of Employment: Special Youth Project; Manpower; and City-County Youth Board: Youth and Work Project.

The focus for these three related programs was employment of poverty-level youth and appropriate training and job experience for them. The State Employment Service had "outreach" programs to recruit youth in streets, bars, pool halls, etc. Some workers could speak Spanish so that Cubans and Puerto Ricans could be reached. Contacts were followed up if office appointments were not kept.

The Manpower Section was a training program run by the Board of Education and the Employment Service. It offered remedial programs, counseling, and primarily vocational training.

The Youth and Work Program was for girls and boys 16–18 years old. Those who were least likely to find satisfactory jobs and most likely to get into trouble were selected. Odd jobs in the program office were used for diagnostic purposes. Then some of the young people were given individual assignments. Others were given group assignments with group discussion first, and then were interviewed for jobs or received more training.

Many other programs were examined during this study. One conclusion was that the experience of local groups well grounded in work with this population was very important. The locally shaped programs were characterized by flexibility and imaginative use of existing agencies and facilities. It was a general consensus that morale was high on these programs and the most discouraging feature was their time-limited existence in some cases. These programs were, by and large, well able to attract the number of young people they were designed to serve. Young people did want jobs and training. The participants felt that the jobs they obtained had the value of being hopeful examples for others in their neighborhoods.

However, these programs, it was stressed by those interviewed, did not basically change the ghetto. The stresses that unemployment cause, and the increasing problems caused by automation, would take far larger and more potent projects to combat.

Racial Feelings

This study discloses the feelings that have become more pronounced as time has passed. At the time of this study the issue of Black Identity and

Black Pride was well in evidence in the ghetto. The study showed that despite the riots of that period the anti-white feeling was not as high as might have been expected. The Black Militants influenced directly only a small part of the ghetto population, although the climate of hate that they preached was moving in that direction. An awakening of many young people to the racial inequities was described. Even the most successful young people in our city slums are finding that they cannot love anyone who helps to keep them down. The anger is high and the chances that it will erupt against a policeman or some other symbol of their oppression is very great.

The study showed that a key problem is in their own identity. The tremendous necessity to reach back and find a cultural history that can bolster respect has led many to study Africa. Others are searching for Negro achievements in more recent slavery and post-slavery periods. A difficulty here is that many Negroes who are tremendously accomplished have achieved this by "doing it Whitey's way" which causes many Negroes to classify them as "Uncle Toms." The solid achievement of even accomplishing that is often lost in this issue. Despite the fact that this study showed that many "successful" Negroes who have achieved middle-class status are very interested and concerned about what happens in the ghetto, this concern is not believed or recognized for the most part. Undoubtedly this is one of the reasons that the civil rights groups are unable to enlist more basic support. The Urban League and the NAACP are often characterized as "Uncle Tom" associations.

Mexican-Americans and Puerto Ricans were beginning in 1965 to show signs that they, too, would organize and ferment to achieve more opportunity. In some parts of the country their conditions are the worst possible. A particular problem is the language issue. Schools have been unable or unwilling to fully meet the complication of having Spanish be a primary language for this group and still helping them to learn the necessary English to compete successfully here. This is a major problem. In 1966 there were about eight hundred thousand Mexican-Americans in Los Angeles County alone. The struggle of the National Farm Workers' Association to get higher wages and better conditions for grape workers was beginning at the time of this study. It has subsequently become more of a political issue. In 1968 one California congressman passed out grapes with a sign that indicated one should enjoy the "forbidden fruit," and he received many packages back from congressmen in other States who did not wish to anger constituents or labor groups by being seen to accept them.

One Mexican-American group of about 50 members walked out of a Federal Equal Opportunities Conference because they were not represented on the commission that planned the conference. A large group held a banquet to celebrate this act.

Though in some ways the problems resemble those of the Negroes, there is a more marked resemblance to the patterns experienced by other immigrant groups. This study and the one in 1963 showed that the youth seem to be between two cultures. It was the impression at this time that they felt superior to the Mexicans and inferior to the Anglos. This causes the classic pattern of family tension and lack of respect for the parents and the old ways. Gang formation is a common way to deal with this and was attractive to those unfortunate enough to remain in the slums.

The Puerto Ricans are in a similar but different situation. In New York in 1964, figures show that Puerto Ricans were even poorer as a group than Negroes. They share with Negroes high rates of public assistance cases, large families, high unemployment, excessive interest rates for loans, etc. They share language and cultural tension with the Mexican-Americans. They, however, seem to have considerable pride in being from Puerto Rico and this is a definite plus, just as the island is a retreat and a refuge for them from life on the mainland.

The Puerto Rican Community Development Project is a comprehensive plan and program for meeting a wide range of needs. It was financed by antipoverty funds and was built upon existing programs.

Conclusions

By 1965 the apathy had coalesced into anger. The conditions in the slums and the state of day-to-day life proved too provocative and unyielding. The methods of protest were too tame and unsatisfying to the needs of the ghetto resident. The alienated young person living in the slums and feeling he had so little to lose was immersed in this atmosphere. The release felt by many who had been pent up was stronger than the prohibitions. Although mixed feelings about the riots are common, the pride at turning their image from "shiftless" to dangerous was welcome for many Negroes. It is definitely more manly to be dangerous in this country than it is to be "shiftless and lazy." Whereas the civil rights movement was able to achieve change in the South and the new laws were making changes, the latter were not of sufficient measure to make a difference in the ghettos of the North. The riots undoubtedly hurt the Negro communities involved—they have suffered real loss, food scarcity, and loss of sustaining businesses. But the gains are real also and unfortunately are often more visible than the gains of slower, more moderate methods. Politicians and policemen, for instance, have become more conscious of ghetto problems and their explosive potential.

Whites, too, have suffered. All have suffered. The investigator found that during this study it was virtually impossible to limit the time spent on this subject with any respondent as the feelings flowed in such an intense and meaningful way.

A warning has come out of this study not to lump minority groups together. Specificity and tailoring to meet conditions in individual areas have been successful. Other suggestions are that intergroup contact should be fostered. Conference, tutoring programs, training programs are all valuable if they contain meaningful contact between ethnic groups. Goals which are yielding of fairly quick success win alienated young people into organized campaigns faster than more abstract goals.

The study suggests that the formation of overall city poverty agencies may be unwise. It was found that they tend to generate problems that get in the way of their own work. The investigator suggests that perhaps it is better for local agencies to deal directly with Federal officials for anti-poverty funds. Another point is that funding is important to agencies and must be given a firm enough and long term enough basis to make it viable. This study revealed that many agencies are forced to curtail and limit their involvements due to fear of cutbacks or loss of funds. There is the concern that programs begun and dropped can arouse more antagonism than those never started. Many agencies have to devote themselves mainly to keeping alive.

Further, the investigator urges that the real serious nature of the problem of the ghettos be faced. He recognizes that a realistic appraisal of economic and social network that causes slums and its tremendous human toll be faced. Varied programs are needed. This study clearly shows that no one type of program will reach all. Even if at times the cost may be high, such programs must still be supported. The difficulty and, at the same time, the ease of predicting riots is thought-provoking. In 1969 some politicians and civil rights leaders are predicting that our major riots are over, but this is hardly assured, and, if it were, the human cost of our racial problems and the loss of any of our young people would still be too high. The commitment has been made in this country many times and in many ways and needs now to be made a reality.

The investigator suggests that many legislative and other steps are needed to combat poverty. The guaranteed annual income is suggested as one idea that might be successful. Cooperative housing might overcome the need for large investments on the part of poor people and give them a chance at ownership rather than at being renters. Street work and social agencies have a strong chance at helping touch alienated youth. The pride in racial identity needs to be supported, but not the hate messages that sometimes accompany it. Indigenous workers recruited from an area to serve an area are also particularly successful, and these positions provide employment for those who might otherwise be unemployed, which is also valuable. Birth control information is often sought in the slums and should be made available. The cities need to improve on services to the deprived areas and so on. Primarily, tolerance must be found for the forward and then backward and forward again patterns of work in this area.

This study suggests that education in the slums is a complex issue and an important one. While the need for technical education exists and is important in preparing young people for our mechanized society, the assumption should not be made that this type of education is all that is needed in the slums. Many students need assistance, educationally and financially, to achieve their potential. Many more could attend college. Programs with liberal admission policies, even preferential admissions, etc., need to be developed.

The investigator also postulates that, if each large firm undertook to hire and train some of these deprived young people, the effect would be striking.

As has been previously mentioned, community service positions utilizing indigenous workers can fill some important needs in our society. Almost all large community institutions, such as hospitals, schools, and social agencies need help. The presently alienated, almost wasted young person could provide the manpower needed for better operation in all these community institutions. Training is the key in both private and government programs for effectively teaching and employing these young people.

A major mistake would be to underestimate the forces that keep slums as slums and keep minority groups in them. The solutions to these problems are extremely complex. One conviction of the investigator is that the poor should be consulted and involved with programs, even though this may at times make progress slower and more complicated.

Research Grant: MH 11396
Dates of Interview: September 1968

References:

Bernstein, S. *Youth on the Streets, Work with Alienated Youth Groups.* New York: Association Press, 1964. 160 pp.
Alternatives to Violence, Alienated Youth and Riots, Race and Poverty. New York: Association Press, 1967. 192 pp.
Schulberg, B. *From the Ashes.* New York: New American Library, 1967. 275 pp.

Child Development Counselors: Lessons From Their Training and Use

Project Director:
Reginald S. Lourie, M.D.
Children's Hospital
Washington, D.C.

Prepared by:
Herbert Yahraes

A pilot project for training a new type of mental health worker, a child development counselor who would make a frontline effort to intercept emotional disability before it could take hold, is now complete and the results are being evaluated. Because the lessons being drawn should be useful in other programs to develop unconventional manpower sources.

The reasoning behind the project ran like this:

In the typical well-baby clinic, the pediatrician and the nurse can give only a short time to each mother and child. This has generally proved sufficient for noting signs of physical illness and of irregularities in physical development and for being concerned with preventive approaches in general. But it is hardly sufficient in most clinics for noting and counseling about signs of emotional maladjustment in the child or of maternal attitudes likely to lead to such maladjustment. If the clinic staff could include a person whose main concern was the normal emotional and psychological development of the child, the clinic might be better able to head off crippling problems. Well-baby clinics, in short, might better fulfill their mission of bolstering the mental as well as the physical well-being of the children passing through them.

Since the traditional mental health disciplines—including medicine, psychology, nursing, and social work—cannot meet even the existing demands on them, however, where are these new workers to come from?

An earlier pilot project conceived by Dr. Margaret Rioch, a psychologist, had found a new manpower supply in mature, intelligent mothers with a keen interest in the community and a desire to serve. The project had demonstrated that such women could be trained for counseling adolescents and adults in mental health clinics and other centers, and that a variety of agencies and institutions were eager to employ them.

Wouldn't it be possible to take another group of such women and train them—again over a 2-year period, half time—for a new profession, child development counseling? And couldn't they then contribute significantly to a highly important but relatively neglected part of the mental health campaign—preventive approaches in the earliest years of life?

104

To answer such questions, Dr. Reginald S. Lourie, chief of the department of psychiatry of the Children's Hospital, Washington, D.C., and medical director of the affiliated Hillcrest Children's Center, undertook to direct an Institute-financed training program for child development counselors. The project was sponsored both by the research foundation of the hospital and by the Bureau of Maternal and Child Health of the District of Columbia's Department of Public Health. Dr. Samuel Schwartz, the Bureau's chief, was codirector with Dr. Lourie. Through most of the project, Dr. Rioch, who had directed the earlier program and stimulated the thinking in this one, served as training director, and Margaret Stolzenbach, a graduate of that program, was her executive assistant and coordinator. The evaluation phase is being conducted by Dr. Stuart E. Golann, of the University of Maryland and the American Psychological Association.

The training centers were, in the main, the well-baby clinics of the District of Columbia Department of Public Health and the one at the hospital. The project directors felt, however, that child development counselors probably could be highly useful at nursery schools, day-care centers, and almost anywhere else that mothers and young children are found, so the trainees were made acquainted with a variety of institutions. Most of the instruction was carried on in the pediatric and psychiatric facilities of the hospital. The teachers included two dozen authorities—many from the staffs of the sponsoring institutions but a number from outside—in such fields as psychiatry, psychology, child development, family and child therapy, social anthropology, and psychiatric social work.

The Trainees and the Program

To recruit trainees, staff members discussed the project's hopes and plans with each of about 50 persons who were leaders in the community or represented such organizations as PTA's, women's clubs, community service agencies, and college alumnae groups. This was done by telephone. Descriptions of the projects were then mailed to interested organizations so they could be posted, read at meetings, or published in newsletters. Stipends of $1,000 per year were offered trainees. Women requesting application blanks were given a preliminary telephone interview that served, among other purposes, to correct misunderstandings about the project and to emphasize the uncertain future of applicants selected for training.

Out of the 101 women who completed their applications, eight were finally selected. All eight—on the basis of autobiographies, interviews, and group discussions with members of the training staff—rated high in intelligence, perceptiveness, self-awareness, integrity, and emotional maturity. Says Dr. Lourie: "We ended with bright, warm, flexible, empathic, verbal women who were interested in others and intellectually curious."

The women chosen ranged in age from about 35 to about 50. All but one were white, though it had been hoped that about half would be

Negro, because in Washington the well-baby clinics serve a primarily Negro population. (A second Negro woman had been recruited, but she withdrew before the training began.) All were mothers, though their children were either grown or well along in school, and all were participating in community activities. Five were college graduates, including one woman with a master's degree, and the others had had at least 2 years of college. Most of the husbands were professional people.

Preceding the start of training, in February 1964, the staff made arrangements with American University to grant credits toward either a bachelor's or a master's degree. It was reasoned that the counselors would always be working alongside professional people and that these, presumably, would be interested in their academic backgrounds. Also, it was hoped, academic recognition for a new type of health-field professional might eventually be developed.

The training program was divided into four semesters which were spread, college-style, over a 2-year period. The trainees worked half time. They had the following weekly schedule during the first semester:

• Three hours of lectures on the physiological, sociological, and psychological aspects of child development.

• A 2-hour seminar on personality development.

• Four hours of practical classroom work dealing with clinical case histories—from well-baby and other types of clinics—in order to learn the kinds of problems that arise and how to handle them.

• Half a day at a well-baby clinic, generally one of the 12 operated by the District of Columbia Department of Public Health and known officially as Maternal and Child Health Clinics. For two weeks the trainees observed clinical routine by accompanying an assigned family through all the clinic procedures, including a home visit by a public health nurse. Then for two weeks they took routine case histories of mothers selected by the clinic staff. After that, clinic staffs were asked to refer to trainees those mothers who expressed interest in discussing problems at greater length than staff-time permitted. The trainees were urged to invite additional interviews with these mothers and to spend unscheduled time in informal waiting room contacts.

• An hour of counseling, at a well-baby clinic, under the immediate supervision of a member of the training program's staff.

• A conference with staff members, primarily to give the trainees an opportunity to discuss their work and to ask questions and to give the staff an opportunity to gauge progress.

For the second and third semesters, the fieldwork was expanded to include one full day a week at a well-baby clinic and half a day in a suburban nursery school, where the trainees could observe the behavior of children—and the attitudes of their mothers—who were growing up in a privileged section of the metropolitan area. The trainees also visited a variety of other agencies to learn the kinds of helping resources available and the problems facing them. Lectures and observational work during the second semester dealt with the following topics, among others: psychological and psychiatric examinations, pediatric consultation, the child's early development, mental retardation, speech and hearing, nutrition, nursery school orientation, child rearing, and planned parenthood. Classroom work during the third semester included 4 hours of lecture-discussion seminars covering child-rearing practices, family interaction, psychodynamics, the psychosocial effects of illness, and techniques of parent-teacher consultation.

During the fourth and last semester, six of the trainees continued to spend a day a week at a well-baby clinic, while the other two worked in a maternity clinic, supervised by an obstetrician. The trainees also spent one day a week working with one of a number of other organizations—neighborhood centers, a mental health clinic, the Family and Child Service Agency, the District of Columbia Day Care Association, the Jewish Social Service Agency, and the Prince Georges County, Md., Maternal and Child Health Clinic.

Course work during this final term included 3 hours a week on "The Process of Child Development." The first half of the course was given in the maternity wards at D.C. General Hospital, where trainees observed newborn babies, talked with the mothers, and participated in a seminar with nurses assigned to the maternity section. Later, at the Children's Hospital, children up to 6 months of age were observed intensively. Then children between the ages of 1 and 2 years were studied. Ward observations were supplemented by lectures and films.

Among their other activities, the trainees attended a course on adolescence given at Howard University School of Social Work; sat in on diagnostic sessions at the Department of Psychiatry of the Children's Hospital; attended lectures in the pediatric-psychiatric training program of the same hospital; and observed a number of interviews between therapists and patients at the Clinical Center, National Institutes of Health.

Major Problems Encountered

In the disadvantaged areas served by most of the Washington well-baby stations, many of the mothers were uninterested in talking with the trainees. They wanted mainly to get through with the pediatrician and the nurse and to get away from the usually crowded clinic. The many who did want to talk generally presented urgent problems of their own—the need for a place to live, for clothes, for legal aid in marital problems, for help with a delinquent older child.

The trainees felt obliged to offer this pressingly needed assistance, usually with the aid of community agencies the mothers had not known about or had been afraid to try, because it was the humane thing to do. In addition, particularly during the early part of the training, when the women often wondered if they were being really useful, it gave them a sense of accomplishment. Sometimes the help with the urgent practical problems opened the way to do something about the basic principles of preventive mental health work centered on the child—to try to get across the idea, notably, that the way a youngster is tended, talked to, and played with will affect his future emotional well-being and his ability to learn. Generally such efforts had to be neglected or abandoned, however, because the mothers visited the clinics infrequently. A few did make and keep special appointments with the trainees.

During the latter part of the training program, the counselors reported greater success in directing the interviews to the field of child development and in dealing with problems directly concerned with the children. Included were problems of nutrition, shyness, destructive behavior, nervous habits, and slowness. Information that the mothers would not otherwise have had on such matters was made available. A report on the project's fourth semester notes that "there seemed to be more counseling and less social work."

During this semester, in the course of their work at the well-baby and maternity clinics, the trainees talked with 450 mothers for a total of 662 interviews. This was an average of about 83 interviews per trainee, and of about six per working day at the clinic. Most of the interviews lasted between 15 and 40 minutes, but some ran more than an hour. About three-fourths of the mothers interviewed had been referred by the clinic doctor; most of the others had been approached directly by the trainee in the clinic waiting room. Some 300 of the mothers were seen only once.

Dr. Lourie points out that even when the main concern had to be the compelling problems of everyday life, the trainees were actually doing preventive work with the child. For if they could help take care of the mother's needs, she in turn would take better care of the baby's. The goal of the training program, though, had been different. In short, the well-baby clinics, with only sporadic family contact available, proved less than ideal for providing the counselors-in-training with experience in the kind of preventive counseling it had been envisaged they would do and for which their other work was preparing them.

A second important problem had to do with the attitudes of the other people working in the clinics. The Department of Public Health had joined with the project's training staff to explain to the clinic personnel the concept of preventive work by a child-development counselor. The results varied considerably, the project reports, ranging from eager acceptance at one end to open resistance at the other, with indifference in the middle. Resistance and noncooperation tend to be met whenener a new group of "manpower multipliers" is proposed for the health field, Dr. Lourie notes. The fundamental cause is the tendency of professional workers to view the new group as a threat to the standards of their profession—the academic degree, the length of training, the other requisites they themselves have met.

All the trainees reported they could work effectively only when the clinic pediatrician—and preferably the nurse also—understood and accepted the program's aims, was willing to make referrals to the counselor, and could give her consultation time. These requirements were not always met, particularly in the early part of the program.

As trainees and clinic staff got to know one another, the resistance generally gave way to cooperation. Three pediatricians became especially interested in the program, so the well-baby clinics they directed were the ones used during the fourth semester. At the end of this term they and the director of the maternity clinic were asked to rate the counseling service from the standpoint of usefulness; all rated it as significant or potentially significant. They were also asked to rate the individual counselors on such items as ability to observe child with discretion, understanding of child, ability to function usefully with patients as individuals, and behavior as a professional person. Out of a total of 48 ratings for the eight trainees, only three ratings fell as low as satisfactory; all the others were good or excellent.

Perhaps significantly, it was not until this last semester that the pediatricians still in the program felt able to score all the trainees on all the individual items.

The Post-Training Experience

Contrary to expectations, the District's well-baby clinics had no jobs for the counselors at the end of the training period, in January 1966. Project officials explain that in spite of improved relationships, there were people at administrative levels not yet ready to accept the concept of counselors trained as these had been. A defensive attitude by the traditional professions may be only part of the explanation, these officials think; another part may be a conviction that the preventive approach to mental illness is impractical—as it often seemed to be, in the atmosphere of the clinics, even to the trainees themselves.

Seven of the graduates took half-time positions with another Health Department activity, a community mental health program, and the eighth went to work for the well-baby clinic at the Children's Hospital. Several of the half-time workers took on another part-time job—with a mental health clinic, the Jewish Social Service Agency, or the National Capital Day Care Association.

The seven counselors in the community mental health program had been hired to do preventive work, they thought, but the pressure to help the children who were already emotionally ill, and their parents, was so great that preventive action had to be postponed. "It's like firefighting," Dr. Lourie remarks. "If you fireproofed the buildings, you wouldn't have so many fires. But you can't stop fighting fires in order to do the fireproofing. Though we did not expect our trainees to have to fight fires, they did apparently make good emergency firemen."

As part of the project's evaluation process, which is continuing, the counselors' supervisors and fellow workers were interviewed about 3 months after the graduates had been on the job. Those interviewed included pediatricians, psychiatrists, public health doctors, public health nurses, social workers, and teachers. Virtually all said that they were pleased with the ability and the performance of the new workers, and that they considered the women to be examples of a potentially significant manpower source. The counselor employed by the well-baby clinic was reported by the clinic's director to have been trained "better than the

109

pediatrician to help with the hundreds of patients who don't need a psychiatrist." This supervisor also reported: "She does better than young doctors. I'm continually delighted she's here."

The women themselves had a different story. Interviews and job diaries showed them discouraged and dissatisfied, uncertain both about what they could do and what they were expected to do. The first few weeks or months on a job are almost sure to be an upsetting period for any recently trained person, Dr. Golann remarks, even if the trainee has a traditional degree and is working in a chosen, and traditional, field. But these child development counselors had been trained in a new field, they did not possess universally recognized credentials, and, worst, most of them were working in fields different from the one for which they had been trained.

Salaries, too, were a disappointment. In the eyes of graduates and of the project staff as well, the Civil Service ranked the new counselors too low. Further, it distinguished between those with a college degree, whom it placed in GS-7 classification, and those without a degree, whom it placed in GS-5, though the training for child development counselor had been the same for everyone. This meant that a counselor going to work for a District of Columbia agency could expect to start at an annual salary ranging from about $6,500 if she had a degree to about $5,500 if she did not.

The child development counselors have dealt with their dissatisfactions in various ways:

• After some months, two of the eight left their positions and enrolled at Howard University to earn a master's degree in social work, one of them studying full time and the other part time. They knew they would have to repeat much of the work already covered, but, says Dr. Lourie, "They felt the need for a label that everybody understands. In training new categories of manpower the identity problem is a prime one."

• The counselor at the well-baby clinic has stopped working in the hope of finding a position in which she feels more useful. In spite of the praise from the clinic's director, she didn't feel needed.

• One woman moved to New York City with her husband and has taken a job with an adoption agency. She counsels both the mothers who have adopted a child and the natural mothers.

• Three counselors are still with the community mental health program but, having received on-the-job training, work mainly with troubled adults.

• The eighth counselor left her part-time job with the mental health program and is employed full-time by the National Capital Day Care Association, where she works with mothers, teachers, and children. Of all the women in the training program, she comes closest to carrying out the project's intention—that the counselors try to head off potential problems and remedy incipient ones. Dr. Lourie is hopeful that through the work of this Association, which plans to develop additional centers for babies and their parents, more appropriate placements for some of the other counselors will be found.

Summing Up

The project has demonstrated, members of the training staff conclude, that it is possible to train mature, selected women in 2 years, half time, to do a satisfactory job as mental health counselors having a specialty in child development. At the end of the program the eight women could counsel effectively with mothers of young children.

The project has been less successful in fitting the counselors into the existing system of health agencies. By and large, the trainees are doing useful work in the general field of mental health, but it is not the kind of work for which they had been trained. Dr. Lourie thinks this situation may well change as the new community health programs develop and new centers for parents and children evolve into developmental centers.

Some of the Lessons Drawn by Project Officials

Very early in the planning of any program looking to the development of a new type of mental health personnel, the professional people—including personnel officers—of the agencies in which the trainees will work should be drawn into it. They can help ease the annoying everyday problems, such as shortage of space, that arise when an additional service is injected into established routines. More important, they can be exposed to the concepts of mental health counseling and to the potential value of the trainees in putting them into practice. The understanding and acceptance of these concepts, even by professionally trained health and welfare personnel, reports one member of the project's staff, and the willingness to cooperate with new types of manpower cannot be taken for granted. Says another: "Even more time must be spent educating the existing professionals than the trainees themselves." Included in the educational program, he reports, should be the professional associations that set the standards for the fields in which the new counselors will be working in part.

Dr. Lourie adds that if agencies and institutions experiencing manpower shortages—shortages especially of intelligent, sensitive, mature people—would analyze their needs, they would find almost certainly that a large part of them could be met by women like those selected for training in the pilot project. "The question is whether existing institutions are flexible enough to use people like this once they have been trained. The women in our program are eager to be useful; but they also want to learn, and they will not stay long in positions which do not allow them to use their capacities."

To insure the best use of people trained in nontraditional ways, plans for their employment should be carefully made well in advance, preferably at the same time that the training program itself is planned.

It is speculated that most of the Negro women who would have been eligible for training were already working and could not afford to undertake the program. If more Negro women are to be recruited for programs such as this one (and it may very well be that more of the mothers at the clinics would have sought the counsel of Negro trainees), stipends large enough to support them probably will be necessary, along with a guarantee of employment at the end of training.

Except on a superficial level and with limited objectives, preventive mental health work probably cannot be carried on in well-baby clinics such as the ones, serving a disadvantaged population, used for the field-training program in Washington. The attitudes and problems of the mothers, along with crowded conditions and the lack of cooperation of some regular clinic staff members, worked against the Washington project. "This is not to say that the child development counselors couldn't and didn't make a useful contribution there," Dr. Lourie observes. "They were trained hopefully to make a better one."

If he were starting over again, the director of this project would still want to train child development counselors, but he would envisage putting them to work in a different setting—day-care centers that accepted children from infancy onward. He hopes such centers will become part of the public school system. If differences in learning abilities, beyond those set by heredity, are determined to a large extent when a child is very young, perhaps mainly during the first 18 months, says Dr. Lourie, why not get the educators interested in the child far earlier than at present? Educators, welfare workers, and health people should collaborate in our lowest socioeconomic neighborhoods, he believes, to provide continuing services from birth on up into the school years as we now know them. In such a program the child development counselor could do her most effective work.

Research Grant: MH 8322
Date of Interview: May 18, 1967

References:

Golann, S. E. Initial findings of the follow-up study of child development counselors. 1966. Mimeographed.
Louire, R. S., Rioch, Margaret J., and Schwartz, S. The concept of a training program for child development counselors. 1966. Manuscript.
Rioch, Margaret J., Elkes, Charmian, and Flint, A. A. Pilot project in training mental health counselors. Public Health Service Publication No. 1254. Washington, Superintendent of Documents, U.S. Government Printing Office.

Operation Hope:
Educating New Leaders

Director:
A. Paul Parks
Operation Hope
Los Angeles, California

Prepared by:
Gay Luce

At a time when the voices of despair are registering with ominous clarity, a small project in Los Angeles is offering an antidote to the ugly waste of young people in urban ghettos. Operation Hope is an experimental training program in which 20 young men and women from Central and East Los Angeles are being helped through college, and encouraged to acquire the skills and credentials that may make them the new leaders in mental health professions such as social work. The program provides a monthly stipend of $200, the *sine qua non,* which combined with part-time job income, permits the participants to study. Moreover, the three staff social workers, Director of Research, Administrative Assistant, and outside consultants of Operation Hope provide special courses, legal and psychological counseling, and assistance during financial and family crises. These young people from the ghettos are likely to revitalize the mental health professions, at a time when welfare and social workers are often seen as middle-class visitors, as outsiders who are ineffectual and hated by ghetto residents, and who seem incapable of devising programs that will attack the consequences of poverty and crowding.

No neat formulae can be offered for selecting and educating ghetto residents, but the program evolved by Operation Hope offers a guideline that could be adapted to any city location. The impact of this program cannot be measured by statistics, since only a few participants have been funded, but the school performance and careers of its trainees will be noticed in the next decade as these people become poverty lawyers, teachers, and mental health workers in the neighborhoods they know well.

Background

It is shocking to discover that close to one out of every six Americans lives in a poverty pocket, an island of hopelessness surrounded by affluence. Innercity ghettos do not communicate with the "outside world";

113

however, the young, who have grown up in an era of television, have seen the widely advertised wealth and "opportunity" that lies only a few miles away. For them it is as distant as Hawaii. These street-wise young people, who are old by 21, know all the discrepancies between promise and actuality. They know that the promise of free education, of job opportunity, of legal equality differs from the actuality they experience. They know that the ostensibly free clinic is a place where they are rudely treated, and where a sick man may suffer for many hours in a waiting line. If they are black or brown, they know they may be sent to jail while a white Anglo is set free for the identical offense. They may know of jobs, yet in a city like Los Angeles they cannot get to them because they do not own cars and there is virtually no public transportation. Many of these students are bright and do well in grammar school, but by high school they drop out as they begin to be inundated with financial and family problems. If they are spunky they are likely to be pushed out.

Traditionally, the people who have tried to help have been sincere and hardworking social workers, people who still come from comfortable middle-class backgrounds and merely visit the ghetto, escaping to a clean quiet home each night. Despite their good intentions, social workers are inevitably seen as transient visitors, and hated by the people they aim to help. They are viewed as spies and purse wardens who enforce moralistic rules which have no relevance. At an early age many children conclude that the caseworker is merely snooping when he asks questions, ferreting out some misdemeanor or technicality that means the family will not get money. The familiar stipulation that welfare recipients would receive no money if an able-bodied man were in the house has created deceptions and family disruptions that have warped the lives of entire generations. The tragedy is typified by a girl in the program who fought and hated her mother throughout her life, and only later discovered that her father had been driven from the house by the welfare act, not by her mother. By that time she and her mother were permanently estranged.

Under pressure and without outlet, despair, passivity, and withdrawal into multisubstance use, such as alcohol and dangerous drugs, are the inevitable concomitants of a life with ramified health problems, and perpetual family crises. Hundreds of thousands of potentially bright and creative youngsters are being warped and wasted. Ghetto existence cannot be patched. Today, ghetto youth live in an ironic vortex of history, marked by the threat of population growth, the exodus of middle-class families to the suburbs, inflation, and war. Ironically, the pressure is on the young, themselves, to rebuild or create the institutions that will readmit the poor into the mainstream of American life, a life of decency and opportunity. Nobody else can do the job.

Considerable institutional and social changes must be constructed before this portion of the American people can participate in its own future. At present there are no institutions that can fully supply city ghettos with the most basic necessities — good housing, health care, and education. The need is for change in institutions, policies or social organizations as they now exist. In a dynamic society institutions should change to meet changing needs. The question that faces our society is how to revitalize our institutions so that they maintain health and well-being. It seems improbable that these institutions can be fashioned by people who live far from the ghettos, and who know the problems only by reading. The hope for constructive institutional changes emanates from within. Operation Hope was evolved to select potential leaders, and give these young people the instruments for institutional change, supplying them with the education that is the key to social participation. It is hoped that this program may lead to changes in the selection of personnel for the mental health fields.

History

Mr. A. Paul Parks, the originator and guiding spirit of Operation Hope, came to Los Angeles with the conviction that his profession of social work needed to be revitalized. An Easterner with a varied work experience, he had extensive experience in the field of drug addiction. He had conducted educational seminars for community physicians on the social implications of drug abuse. Like many of his associates, he began to see that drug addiction and other major social problems could not be treated as if they were local "infections" that could be diagnosed and cured on an individual basis. The traditional medical approach is rarely relevant in the attempt to counter drug abuse. Drugs of all varieties have been the escape of people whose lives are intolerable throughout the centuries and in all countries of the world. Life is indeed unendurable for the very poor and no amount of patching can alter the fundamental trap or the isolation in which the poor, and particularly the black and brown minorities, now live. Neither preachment nor punishment can eradicate the alcoholism and drug use and other consequences of a degrading mode of living in a dishonoring environment.

The helping professions have not always given credence to the fact that human behavior is adaptive and learned. This implies that each community participates in shaping the lives of its citizens and their behavior. In actuality, social work like many other helping professions has often used its power and position to label behavior — an approach which does not produce the techniques that contribute to healthy reactions or change. In gaining status as a profession, social work in some settings has also moved further away from the people it originally set out to work with.

In the early 1960's, social work groups were seeking new solutions to ferment in the ghetto, by recruiting and training local young people for social work. Mr. Parks moved West to join an agency known as Special Service for Groups, Inc., at a time when it was training gang leaders from Watts and East Los Angeles as social workers' aides. He arrived in Los Angeles on a hot August day in 1965, one day after general discontent

115

had combined with heat of summer in the destructive insurrection that came to be known as the Watts riots.

Watts is a remnant of a real estate tract in South Central Los Angeles, but the action that America remembers occurred west of Watts in an area housing some 400,000 people, 300,000 of them black. These people have no access to the resources of the larger city. Poor, they lack transportation, and are unable to work outside their neighborhood. Thus, in their out-of-the-way enclave, they remain invisible to the affluent majority. Here, on a hot night a small incident with the police generated rumors and crowds that slowly swelled into a populace-police battle culminating in the deaths of 34 persons and the destruction of millions of dollars in property. Watts became the predictive symbol, reminding Americans that poverty and racial oppression were hidden in the affluence, and that the problems of huge groups of American people were being neglected. The "Watts riot" announced that this double state could not exist any longer. Two years later Boyle Heights became the center for the development of new solutions, the headquarters for what is now Operation Hope.

Location and Staff

Roughly two miles from the modern Civic Center of downtown Los Angeles is an old barrio — Boyle Heights. With the adjacent neighborhoods of East Los Angeles and City Terrace, it houses about 180,000 people of whom 135,000 have Spanish surnames. Boyle Heights is bounded by freeways, an area of 150 blocks through which many waves of immigration have passed. Like a port of entry to the city, it has received successive waves of Russians, Serbians, Italians, Jews, Mexicans, and others. At present Spanish is the major language and many of the older Mexican-Americans carry on the traditions of their mother country. In the ghettos and barrios of South, Central, and East Los Angeles few new homes have been built for 20 years, but as middle-income people fled to the suburbs, black and brown people took their place. It is in the center of this multi-lingual ghetto that Operation Hope was established in 1968, setting up offices in a few rented rooms.

The four staff offices, the large anteroom and classroom were carefully chosen, for these are not only the working headquarters of Operation Hope, but the center of all activities, seminars, and consultations, the one meeting ground for its many disparate participants. The rooms are spacious and friendly, containing the bulletin boards of events, duplicating equipment, and an incipient reference library for students.

Mr. Parks drew together a staff as varied in completion and background as the students he would seek out. It had to be a group of exceptionally experienced and committed people, because the entire staff would include only five people, and they could anticipate working around the clock, in every conceivable exigency. The staff all had extensive social work experience, and each person came from a different part of the country as well as different ethnic backgrounds. They are supplemented by consultants and instructors.

In philosophy the staff agreed. They had all personally seen the failure of the medical model of social work. They had, themselves, been trained to act as professional social physicians who would diagnose a needy client's problems and try to repair them in the manner of setting a broken bone. Since the ills almost inevitably lie in the complex social environment, not the individual, the medical approach to social work is extremely frustrating. The staff, therefore, felt that a new approach was essential that the people should be selected for the helping professions, out of ghetto areas, not the middle class, with the hope that these indigenous people would invoke needed social and institutional changes. Fortunately, one member of the staff has long been a resident in the neighborhood, and is known among many people in Boyle Heights. It is rare for a project to have on tap a person who is familiar with the history and problems of the people just outside the door.

Many Los Angeles people from wealthy neighborhoods have visited Mexico, but have not heard of Boyle Heights only a few miles away. They would feel as out of place there, as in a foreign country. It is a distance and contrast that cannot be overemphasized, for Los Angeles sprawls over an area of about 400 square miles. Among its eight million people, some epitomize the wealthiest in suburban living, while close to a million represent the most hopeless isolation of poverty. The facade of poverty in Los Angeles is prettier than that of Eastern cities because there are houses and trees, but the isolation is more exaggerated because people who do not own cars cannot leave their neighborhoods. Beaches, museums, plays, and concerts, taken for granted by middle-class youth, cannot be reached without some form of transportation. It is worth repeating that jobs and schools are similarly out of reach for those who cannot afford cars. Thus, the misleading facade of small white houses and palm trees belies a greater isolation and deeper abandonment than the visual filth of a New York City "slum."

Most of the institutions that might change the viscious cycle of mental illness and misery that takes place in the ghetto are also too far away. The people who make the decisions allocating money and setting up basic requirements for housing, health, and education are far removed from the realities of the poor, particularly the poor minorities, the blacks, Chicanos (the current local term for socially active Mexican-Americans) of the West and Indians throughout the country. Middle-income Americans hear statistics about Government budgets and visualize free, tax-supported education that is available to all, as well as free clinics in hospitals, that make medical care accessible to everyone. The services are available on paper. If they are to be made a reality for the people who need them, it will happen when ghetto people themselves, have the education and credentials to attain positions of authority. As all the great voices from the depths of ghetto life have tried to explain, the forces of jungle survival bruise and also strengthen a person, thus creating an individual for whom the games of middle-class education are particularly difficult. The very people who must lead ghetto improvements are therefore not easy to mould; they have needs that are not easily met.

117

Recruiting the Model Trainee

In discussions with a community psychiatrist, a psychologist, and social workers, Mr. Parks and his staff had evolved a profile of desirable traits – a checklist that might be used in interviewing prospective trainees. They wanted youngsters who were dissatisfied, but not passively disgruntled; students who wished to bring about change, yet who had attractive personalities. They needed young people with fire who wanted to learn rather than destroy; people with a sense of justice and motivation. How did one find a young man in the ghetto with fire and talent who had not been too embittered, beaten, legally entangled, mentally warped, or addicted to drugs? The young people had to have developed the strength to survive in the ghetto. They had to be people who knew how to fight, were wise to every con, and canny in the brutal realities of their own neighborhoods. At the same time, they were going to be asked to incorporate a new style of living, adopt a genteel manner, and survive in another world of middle-class college life, learning the subtleties of bureaucracy, and the language of the affluent world. They had to be people who could survive in both life styles simultaneously. These qualities should strike the reader as remarkable, given the environment from which the trainees were sought. It is astonishing that people with such qualifications were actually found. Most of them had been in trouble with the law. Some had been involved with drugs. Any youngster with the spirit and independence of mind to become a leader was automatically too spirited to be considered desirable by teachers and educational authorities. Yet, it was precisely the school "troublemakers," the questioners, fighters, activists, who were the objects of the search.

The Operation Hope staff began their quest by asking for referrals from social workers and teachers. After the Watts riot, Central Los Angeles was inundated with community programs. Nonetheless, when the staff looked for applicants from the Educational Clearinghouses, from schools, social agencies, or ethnic organizations, these agencies could not produce a single person to fit the criteria. In general, schools and agencies were antagonistic to the aggressiveness and spirit that would qualify a student, and in the end they did not help at all.

Not many social workers or teachers actually live in Boyle Heights or other ghetto areas. The ghetto's daily rhythm begins with an immigration and ends with an exodus. From the arrival of milkmen in the morning, the police, the teachers, storekeepers, bankers, and social workers flow into the area. In mid-afternoon, when the teachers begin driving to their homes 20 and 30 miles away, the exodus begins. In this ebb and flow, the teacher or social worker is, in fact, a stranger, a visitor, who does not know the families of the children he teaches or people he tries to help.

After six months of searching the network of social agencies and the neighborhoods, the staff of Operation Hope had to change its initial image of a potential leader and the means of finding him. Many of the young people with leadership qualities had been so emotionally damaged and brutalized during childhood that they could not remain sensitive to other people. Often they were withdrawn and suspicious. The staff began to look at the habits of potential candidates, seeking people who had spent time helping others. Ultimately they did find anomalous people, a man from Watts who was teaching youngsters by coaching them in sports, a girl who had worked with Head Start. After interviewing some 60 people, four prospective students were found, and through them a gravepine was begun that finally attracted some 200 others. The kinds of students who had unbroken spirits, who wished to help others, and could use their anger at social injustice for constructive change were to be found on street corners, in picket lines or community demonstrations, not in welfare agencies.

After months of recruiting, the staff found 33 qualified applicants, but they had funds for only 20. They selected the people who seemed to have the rarest combination of qualities, leadership ability, and sensitivity to other people. Now they were asking these students to hold their anger and their action in abeyance, to take on a middle-class life style, and to postpone their effective action until - perhaps seven or eight years later - they had their credentials. It meant a long-term commitment to an educational program, postponing rewards, and suppressing many of their normal feelings. At a time when many of the disgruntled youth of the United States had given up hope of working through institutions, these students were asked to gamble on the hope that they could later constructively change conditions through the instruments of the establishment. This is some measure of the remarkable men and women who have been chosen to participate. To them, indeed, the program seemed unreal at first. As one man said,

> "At first, I thought you people were from Mars, then I decided you were the 'fuzz' trying to find out what minority people were doing. Right now I do not know what your bag is because I know nobody gives a person money to go to school, but it's a groovy program, and I am making B's for the first time in my life."

The Colleges

Originally, the staff had planned to pick 20 trainees and supply them with money enough to graduate from a State or city college, while offering them special courses in social sciences and remedial work. It was soon apparent that the tax-supported schools were not amenable to these students despite their facilities. Theoretically, California offers virtually free education for all qualified residents. Actually, the State colleges charge about $150 a year and some fees are over $200, an amount that is formidable to these students. In addition, books cost as much as $125 a year. State universities charge $775 per year plus special fees and books.

Most of the ghetto youngsters have missed classes in order to work, or have dropped out of high school in discouragement; one girl dropped out of high school two weeks before graduation, and nobody in her school acted to get her a diploma. Many others have been flunked out for questioning the teacher or expressing opinions. Since the State universities

119

admit only from those students in the top 12 percent of the high school graduates, while the State colleges accept students from the top third, most ghetto students could not qualify, however innately intelligent they were. State colleges may admit 2 percent of incoming classes as members of minority groups and another 2 percent who show promise despite low test scores. On the other hand community colleges take anyone with a high school diploma. A few of the trainees had already entered local two-year colleges on their own, but the administrative bureaucracy was so frustrating that after two-and-a-half years one student had never had the opportunity to discuss his curriculum with an advisor. He had taken endless courses and yet had not fulfilled the requirements to graduate. Another student had piled up 30 course credits without completing any of the basic courses to graduate. At the larger schools, the State colleges, the coldness and rigidity of the administration made the students feel they were not wanted. The unfamiliar routine of application forms and interviews resemble social welfare agencies. As one student had said about bureaucracy, "The place is designed to frustrate you. By the time you explain what your problem is to a number of people, answer endless questions regarding why you had the problem, fill out endless papers – and the waiting is awful – you will be told you will be seen at such and such time by Mr. so and so, and you wait some more."

It was finally necessary for the Operation Hope staff to negotiate scholarships for their trainees at small private institutions, and the students were finally placed at Occidental College, Pepperdine, Whittier, Marymount, USC, and other schools around the metropolitan area. The students had to be helped through high school equivalency exams, the red-tape of application forms and transcripts, and enrollment. They needed additional funds for books, and continuous emotional support. One college administrative official told Operation Hope staff: "We will consider applicants from your program as long as you are available to give support. From our experience minority students will not use school counselors within the institution."

The process of educating young men and women may seem a straightforward matter of funding and organization but it is a subtle and ramified undertaking. Unless helped with all the exigencies of survival, with living needs, books, and emergencies, the student would have to be absorbed by the all-demanding hustle to exist. Although studying may ultimately liberate the student, the first impact is one of extreme tension. Students have to survive not only at home, but in a new environment that is hostile, on a campus whose very philosophy is antagonistic to them. For instance, Chicano students are affronted to find that their hero, Cesar Chavez, is considered a communist agitator by many students, and the black students are amazed to learn that the charismatic Malcolm X is considered merely a criminal by middle-class whites. This is tantamount to sending a devout Christian among people who call Jesus a communist provocateur. On campus the values, dress, language, and social life are all unfamiliar and somewhat threatening. Moreover, the average college student is still partly a child, involved and dependent upon his family, while the ghetto student has been a street-wise adult for some years, depending upon his wits, often supporting or helping to support a family. For the white middle-class student, college may be a slight strain, a first venture away from the comfortable family enclaves. For the ghetto student it is another country, one in which he is scorned because he does not know the school game, a world in which he feels he hostility and cruelty of people who have been comfortable all their lives.

One gifted student in Operation Hope commented that money to facilitate college was the most important contribution any project could have made to his life. No other Federal program operates precisely this way. Still, in attempting to help these students through college, the Operation Hope experience emphasizes how wide is the breach between rich and poor in America today.

Operation Hope

The staff and directors' offices at Operation Hope are open at all times for students, and a "hot line" telephone is maintained at night and on weekends. At least one staff member is always available to help with psychiatric emergencies, health problems, draft exigencies, or legal problems. If a staff member vanishes for several hours, or remains at his office until late at night, it usually means that a student is in a crisis. These students acquired adult problems before they entered college. One 21-year-old, for example, needed medical and legal counseling concerning divorce and the death of his 2-year-old child. Draft counseling is another important need. Since most of the men have jobs and families, they cannot finance the 30 hours of course time that would qualify them for student deferments. Thus, consultations and appeals to local draft boards are necessary staff functions. These students also need advice about courses, professors, and examinations. They require coaching in the techniques of studying, paper writing, and exam taking. All of these areas are routinely part of staff guidance.

These students had been so intellectually and emotionally starved that they devoured attention. None of them had enjoyed the kinds of family or social contacts that would develop intellectual curiosity. Indeed, most of them had such battered images of themselves they were afraid to ask questions in college classes. Many of them needed someone with whom they could discuss the Viet Nam War, the tax system, the meaning of the moon shot, or racial discrimination. One student who began the program with a poor self-image, put it this way: "Now I can question, but I lack power, I've learned how to conform enough to get by . . . ." The staff, who are black, white, and Chicano, are by turns the surrogate parents, doctors, lawyers, philosophers, and companions to whom the students can turn.

Since students live in perpetual crisis, staff members know there will never be a weekend without its emergency, no night without a call from a panicked student. The services of Operation Hope span the gamut from counseling and financial assistance to aid in getting things done. This may mean calling a medical doctor, getting a family welfare check expedited, or getting a family member admitted into a hospital. Any middle-class person takes for granted that he can lift a telephone to accomplish such things, but these needs can become major crises for the ghetto person. The students needed these reality services, as well as step-by-step advice on how to dress, how to behave at an interview, and lessons in the social amenities, the things white students take for granted. They needed lessons in speech, training in group speaking. Many of them needed to learn how to write, to organize papers and express their ideas clearly. Because the campus atmosphere is cold and unfamiliar, the one comfortable place where all the participants could meet has been at classes offered by Operation Hope.

Campus lectures, particularly in the social sciences, have frustrated and angered these students. Often the courses seemed irrelevant or instructors offered opinions that sounded incredibly naive to the ears of these experienced, old-young men and women.

One of the important needs of the students was a sense of ethnic identification and history, and a forum where they could freely raise questions about universal social ideas. Courses in black or Chicano history are often badly taught in colleges. Indeed, these courses often are taught with a condescending point of view that insults the student who is attempting to learn about his own heritage. Consequently, such courses have been taught at the Operation Hope headquarters. During the fall semester of 1970, June Moore of the UCLA School of Social Work, taught a course on the history and philosophy of social work institutions in the United States. The informality of such classes permits the students to interact with each other and with teachers in informal discussion and comradery that is lacking in most of their lives.

Involuntarily most of these students are loners. During the seven-eight years when they are holding jobs and also studying, they are under unusual strain. They need the staff help in homemaking, in finding an apartment, buying a car or filing insurance. Many of them have debts, often from the illegal claims of door-to-door salesmen.

The small "Hope" offices, with their modest library and open doors, provide a kind of home base for these students where they can "rap" with the staff, and admit their real feelings, or ask for help. It is the only such place in their lives. Not at home, at friends' houses, nor in school or clinics can they find support and assistance.

By contrast with the impersonal, bureaucratic schools, and institutions, the staff has an open-door policy which means nobody is ever too busy to see a student when he drops in. There is never a wait. Since the students are the point of the program, staff members are always on hand to help out, to talk, and to provide coffee and a snack. Students rely on this support particularly during exam periods, or when a term paper is due.

Living as they do, in two very separate life styles, the students are under extreme tension. As one Chicano put it, "This project is great but, man, am I having problems. For the first time I am learning to think, I listen and try to figure out what's being said. I'm so excited about hearing people, but I'm bored with my family. I'm finding my girlfriend a drag, we can't talk anymore. And the guys I know, well I haven't seen them in weeks. Man, is this lonely."

For ghetto students in the middle-class colleges the strain of a double life is continuous. There is an internal price they pay for living in two worlds. Part of the price may be in terms of physical tensions, anxieties, or general loss of self-confidence. Realistically, life is a daily struggle. In order to study, the ghetto student leads a tired and lonely life. As one man from Watts described his schedule, he attends school in the morning, works afternoons, sleeps in the early evenings, and studies all night, after his family goes to bed. He has no time or energy for close personal relationships. The stress is such that he must keep his feelings under control at all times. It is not surprising that he has a stomach ulcer. Many of the students in the project suffer from psychosomatic ailments although they are very young. Some have hives, or colitis, ulcers, or hypertension. A few suffer from insomnia, panic, and nightmares. When a student leaves the personal and familiar world of the barrio for the college environment, he leaves his status and sense of acceptance, and must adapt to a highly impersonal structure. He must be careful in his dress, guarded in his manner and speech. When he leaves campus he again returns to a wife (or a woman may return to a husband) whose standards and outlook are the antithesis of all that the campus represents.

To the average student on campus, the ghetto student seems of a different breed. Tough, street-wise, analytical, many of them have experienced jails, and brutalities that the other students have only read about. They have suffered hunger, exhaustion, and have seen their friends turn to alcohol or drugs. They have had to use cunning and muscle to survive. An affluent youngster arrives in college certain that theft and alcoholism are signs of weakness, inferiority. Neither students nor their teachers realize that the crimes they deplore may be the vehicles of survival in the ghetto. The kid who doesn't survive that jungle does not get to enter a project that will help him through college. A person who has not used his cunning to survive will ultimately despair, entering the no-mans-land of inertia and drugs. A ghetto student who seems angry, suppressed, cynical, and hard can only be understood if his armor of hostility and suspicion are also understood; young people who have lived in the ghetto or barrio for 20 years have developed defenses that allow them to cope with drug users, police harrassment, with rejections by schools, social agencies and hospitals. Most of them have needed to devise a hard surface, never revealing their feelings to anyone, never trusting anyone, always analyzing a situation for possible traps. Since they have had to hustle for money all their lives, they may be busy trying to beat the welfare system, or avoiding someone else's con game. Typically, as children, some of the students have been shifted from one foster home to another, in the manner of one girl whose mother was declared mentally incompetent. At age 5 she recalled being put to bed in a relative's house where, as she hugged the pillow, she found a gun. For her, school was a relief from washing, cooking, cleaning, and being beaten with a belt buckle arbitrarily. At 14, she and a friend were put in jail for stealing. Another girl was abandoned at the age of 14 and left alone in an apartment. In order not to be evicted she rented rooms, but when she tried to go on welfare to raise the rent money, the caseworker told her to throw a rent party and charge admission which could be used to pay the month's rent. Two weeks before high school graduation the girl quit school and worked at odd jobs for six years before anyone suggested that she had a good mind and might go to college. To the son of a migrant worker, an avid reader in a large family, the possibility of a college education seemed like the wildest of dreams as he worked in the fields year after year, missing months of school.

To classmates or outsiders these students might seem cool and brusque, with an appearance of self-confidence. Actually, they often live in a state of conflict that is bordering on panic. They know that they must be many times as strong, intelligent, and controlled as their peers in school, and that they are expected to endure and prevail in a manner that would be impossible for many adults. Raised by television, these students have a sophistication that is underestimated by their peers. They know a good deal about the way they look to the other side, and they are familiar with the comforts of most Americans, with the social work jargon in which ghetto disadvantages are discussed, and they realize that they are put down for qualities that are really the product of their environment. They must survive in two worlds, and are expected to be idealistic when they are surrounded by despair and futility and to be willing to give some part of their lives to change a society that would not ordinarily give them a chance.

By adolescence most ghetto children have given up. They see no alternatives and no future. In the southern section of Central Los Angeles they are likely to turn to alcohol, while the eastern section they would more likely use drugs. Many youngsters between 15 and 25 try or actually do commit suicide. There is nobody to help them. Their families are disrupted. Teachers who have taught in these neighborhoods for 20 years, but who live elsewhere, do not even know the parents of their students. As one black student explained, high school students are never told that they have possibilities of further education. Typically, one student stated, "Nobody ever told me I was college material." One very able athlete, with honor roll marks, wasted two years after high school not knowing that he could have attended a tax-supported college without paying thousands of dollars. Scholarship offers had been made through his high school because of his athletic ability, but he had never been informed by his advisors. Another girl wasted six years in dead-end jobs because she similarly did not know college was even a remote possibility. Isolated from the information that every middle-income person takes for granted, and misled by their own schools, the best of these youngsters have a bitter tale to tell. By age 24 many of them say they feel 50. On a college campus this is no advantage.

Impact

The first most important impact of Operation Hope was the fact that the students were sticking out their difficult academic programs. Previously, when faced with crises they had withdrawn from college. In this project, bolstered by the staff, they weathered continual crises and managed to go on studying. Even success was not without conflict. One girl who had, with considerable help made a C in English, remarked, "Well, I guess this means I've given up. I'm conforming, the fight is over. I've entered the system – what can I possibly do to make anything better for myself or anybody else. I did what the instructor wanted and I passed; he wasn't the least interested in what I am, what I feel, or what I want."

The students' marks have steadily improved and several begun to be eloquent spokesmen, writing reasoned essays on the issues close to their hearts. Drug abuse is a topic on which these students have more than usual understanding while the illegality of the drugs generates the crime for which they are punished, it seems clear to them that there is little concern for actually helping addicts; there are no adequate medical or community-based programs available. One of the students wrote:

> "How rational would it be to appoint a doctor as a judge in a court of law? It would seem that this wouldn't be very rational at all, for although he might know medicine he would be quite unfamiliar with the mechanics of law. Taken in this light the question is raised: Why are administrators and law enforcement officials considered to be more knowledgeable in the area of a medical and social problem such as drug addiction?"

The participants are impressive people. Selected for qualities of leadership, they also have displayed considerable aesthetic talents. Many of them write excellent poetry, sing, and paint. Candid and cynical, they are at the same time deep and more idealistic. Although the men and women supported by the project have come from different homes, their stories are painfully similar. Most of them come from families on relief. In grade school they were demeaned by their teachers. They were often absent from school, and were arrested at an early age for some theft such as gouging nickles from a parking meter or for gang fighting. By 17 the "average" young man had been in a house of correction, may have gotten a girlfriend pregnant and have had to marry, spending a year or so washing cars or doing clean-up work in a factory. By age 20, they could see themselves at a dead end, with the odds stacked against them. Yet they had intense intellectual curiosity, and some inner stature that was not altered by the meanness of life around them. As one girl remarked:

> "A long time ago I made up my mind I would rather die than to treat people as I had been treated. I knew what it meant to be disliked for nothing and always used. I suppose having compassion has been the only thing that has saved me from hating the world."

One Chicano student recalls being "busted" on a marijuana charge. When he appeared in court he was sent to jail, while a white kid on the identical charge was released. "Jail is a school where you learn many things." His experience in the army taught him yet more about discrimination as he watched some episodes of mistreatment of the Vietnamese. Now, on his return, he had a mission, to create changes, and as a beginning he has been tutoring kids in an East Los Angeles Parole Center. His own image of his past life was succinctly expressed in a newspaper essay he wrote:

> "I cannot help but bring up a thought that would enter my mind every once in a while in jail. I would picture myself as a person trying to learn how to swim (cope with every day life problems) in a deep, dark, cold sea (the Barrio), and finding myself submerging because of my inability to swim. Along comes a lifeguard (institution: rehabilitation) and pulls me up on the platform (institution) and shows me how to swim (rehabilitates me) and simply throws me back into the deep, dark, cold sea (Barrio) with little knowledge as to whether I had developed the ability to swim. . . ."

Although many of the students in the program came from disrupted or nonexistent families, a few have shown the stability that comes from tacit family support. A student from Watts, who has watched his friends deteriorate along the route of drugs and apathy, somehow manages to study while his family sleeps. He is lucky enough to have a family that is together. He also manages to continue athletics, coaching younger children in school subjects and basketball. He manages to live without close friends, without a confidante or wife, without time for himself. He works in the afternoon, sleeps until midnight, studies until dawn, and goes to school in the morning. When he finally has his credentials he wants to become a poverty lawyer. He has every reason a man could have to play an escape from the poor, enclosed, drugged, hopeless world in which his life has been lived – but he is not content to do as many others have, to get his skills, "go make his pile" and separate himself. Another student who intends to be a lawyer, commented, "I don't look for big hopes anymore but I've learned I can do something and I'm not going to stop fighting."

These are the people who can provide community mental health services, legal aid and instruction from within their communities. These are the new people who are needed in the mental health professions. The attitude of these students offers some measure of the urgent need for change. One girl in the program, who had been quite upset, was asked whether she would like to see a campus psychiatrist.

> "For what? I have had two of those, a psychiatrist and a social worker. One told me I had problems with authority when I was late for an appointment, so I came early the next time and was told I was too anxious. When I got the social worker, I tried to be exactly on time and you know what she told me? I was compulsive. How do you win with that kind of closed system? The only thing I could do is drop dead. They had no awareness that I had no car, had to beg a ride most of the time, and had no money all of the time."

Another student told a conference of mental health professions and social workers, "You mean well, but you really can't help with the kind of problems we have."

126

Colleges and professional schools could alter this impasse by training low-income people and by developing techniques for working with the poor, instead of sending emissaries by day to help the poor adjust to being poor. By drawing professionals from within poor communities, social work and the mental health professions might promote community activity, participation in city planning, in education, and in the establishment of agencies for health care and housing. Such participation would enhance a constructive process of change that is a matter of ethics as much as money.

It has been estimated that some 200,000 youngsters who are in the top of the U.S. population (judged by ability) will never acquire the means to go to college. These are the potential leaders who could rage the real war against poverty. Operation Hope began with the idea that the selection and training of young leaders from the ghetto would offer a model for recruiting and educating a new kind of personnel in social work professions. These would be people who could inject the energy of personal involvement and reality understanding into helping professions such as social work.

In its short existence, Operation Hope has already shown that there are potential leaders within the ghetto, whose ideals and intellect could make them the agents of peaceful social change. The education of such people is difficult because it must compensate for so much: the students' lack of family, confidence, gamesmanship, academic skills, medical, psychological, and legal aid – in addition to money. No program to aid and educate potential young talents from the ghetto can realistically meet these needs, nor leave them to the universities and colleges. The ghetto environment so rapidly destroys trust and normal human emotions that the Operation Hope staff has begun to see that its program should begin with high school students. No person can cope with life and death crises in his family day after day and yet devote himself to learning, yet this is what is expected of the ghetto student. As early as possible, students should be relieved of some of the reality conflicts. In addition, paucity of funds leaves huge gaps in their education; unlike many of their peers they never had the opportunity to relate to man's universal problems through visual art, drama, or music. Most of these students have seen little of the world outside their neighborhoods. Yet, as periodic analyses show, they are aware of the culture outside, and as their education has made them more perceptive, self-confident, and articulate, they are creating art of their own.

This program while only a miniscule experiment in the overall context of America today, has shown that a remarkable transformation can be made. It has helped to liberate a new kind of student. Because they have experienced more of life than most men of 50 when they arrive in college, these "youths" are not passive intellectuals. They approach the arts and social sciences with a personal sense of involvement and judgment. They do not merely accept; they question. If they are old in outlook, their minds are capacious. Their brains are young. They have vitality, compassion, motivation. The result is a kind of genius, a combination of wisdom and brightness, a depth that is not often found. Trivia will not distract them, nor will minor hardships present obstacles. They have a highly developed sense of justice, and an eagerness for history, and indeed, at 23 and 24, they resemble the idealistic young men of the American Revolution who, at the same age, were writing the Declaration of Independence and attempting to fashion a constitution. The qualities that have been elicited in these men and women include a kind of idealistic willingness to gamble on the future. Many young people have given up, and feel that the establishment will not permit changes for the benefit of the left-out Americans. The participants of Operation Hope have no certainty that change is possible, but they have committed themselves to try. With their nascent social genius they may indeed transform the helping professions from ineffectual stopgap procedures, to a realistic confrontation of the social problems behind individual ills. They may infuse new creativity and strength into the mental health professions by entering as a new kind of professional — one who is fearless rather than cowed, analytical rather than sentimental, one who is undeluded about the detailed nature of the ghetto and incapable of forgetting its manner of shaping people. Unlike many social workers in today's professional schools, these people will be able to function in the poorest levels of society as well as among middle-class professionals. They will be able to offer the kind of innovation that stems from understanding where one started and what one's ends are. If their affluent classmates are currently unsure of where they are going, these students are seizing their intellectual honing as a liberation, for this is the only way out of the real hopelessness in which they have lived. The template offered by Operation Hope is there to be extended and copied throughout the country.

Training Grant: MH 11513
Dates of Interviews: September and October 1970

Factors That Influence
the Child's Mental Health

You are the bows from which your children as living arrows are sent forth.

—Kahlil Gibran

Childhood Influences Upon Intelligence, Personality, and Mental Health

Investigators:
Jean W. MacFarlane, Ph.D.
John A. Clausen, Ph.D.
Institute of Human Development
University of California
Berkeley, California

Prepared by:
Herbert Yahraes

Introduction and Summary

The usual way of studying how the circumstances of childhood affect the characteristics of adulthood is to start with the grown person and try to work back. So-called longitudinal studies, though, begin with the child. Three of these, directed by the Institute of Human Development of the University of California, Berkeley, and supported recently with NIMH help, are now approximately 40 years old and probably offer the richest collection of data ever assembled on human beings over a long period.

The projects have attempted to answer such questions as:

• Do personality and intelligence change during the years or remain constant? To what extent are they related to a person's very early experiences?

• How is the mental health of an adult related to his life at home and to other influences during childhood and adolescence?

• What factors contribute to an adult's attitudes, achievement, psychological health?

In the beginning each study had its own set of objectives:

The Guidance Study was primarily interested in personality development. It began studying its subjects as infants. There were 252 of them—every third child born in Berkeley over an 18-month period beginning January 1928. The children were weighed, measured, tested, interviewed, and observed at various times through their eighteenth year. Special attention was given to their life at home during the preschool years. Information about them was obtained also from their parents, brothers and sisters, teachers, and classmates. At 30, when they were rearing children of their own, 167 of them were studied again. (The project got its name from one of the original objectives: to learn whether or not psychological guidance offered to parents would lead to better mental health for their children as adults.) The project's director until recently was Jean Walker MacFarlane, Ph.D., who is now Professor of Psychology and Research Psychologist, emeritus, at the Institute of Human Development and is still working on the study. The present director is Marjorie P. Honzik, Ph. D., Research Psychologist and Lecturer in Psychology.

The Berkeley Growth Study, which also began in 1928, has been particularly interested in physical and mental growth. Its original sample comprised 61 healthy hospital-born babies, who were studied while they were still in the hospital and then every month until they were 15 months old. After that, they were studied every 3 months until they were 3 years old, then every 6 months until they were 18. They were examined and interviewed again when they were 21, 26, and 36 years old. The sample now numbers 54. The project's director is Nancy Bayley, Ph.D., research psychologist.

The Oakland Growth Study has been concerned with the effect of adolesence—the physical and psychological changes occurring then, and the accompanying attitudes and behavior—upon later life. The study began in 1931 with the fifth grade pupils of five oakland, California, schools who would be entering the same junior high school. There were 200 of these. They were studied intensively—through measurements, tests, observation, self-reports. ratings by classmates and teachers, and other means—through the six years of junior and senior high school. At graduation, 165 were still in the group. Follow-up studies made 15, 20, and 26 years later have reached as many as 123. The study began under the direction of Harold E. Jones, Ph.D., and Herbert R. Stolz, M.D. Its director since 1960 has been John A. Clausen, Ph.D., professor of sociology and research sociologist.

Almost all of the subjects were white. In the Guidance Study, though, 3 percent were Negro, a proportion representative of the community's Negro population in 1928. Though all socioeconomic levels were represented, the families of the subjects were predominantly middle class.

In some respects—in anthropometrics, intelligence tests, certain personality measures—the three studies overlapped, making it possible for one set of findings to be compared to another. In some of the analyses now being made, data from more than one study are used. All the subjects, it is planned, will be followed through life, with the principal research interest from now on being factors connected with the aging process.

Of the many conclusions reported since the project began, two early ones were especially important because they upset long-held beliefs. The IQ does not remain constant, the Guidance and the Berkeley Growth Studies soon demonstrated. And bottle-feeding is not necessarily inferior to breast-feeding; in fact, the Guidance Study found, if the mother has little warmth of personality, bottle-feeding is superior to breast-feeding.

The information collected during the four decades of this research is, of course, voluminous and detailed. That gathered by the Guidance Study alone—the most extensive in scope of all long-range studies of this nature in the country—has been described by authorities as "an extraordinary mass of data." For this reason, a considerable amount of material—in particular, much of that obtained during the most recent follow-ups—is still being analyzed.

This report is concerned with the most recent findings (roughly, those of the past five years), which have a number of implications for mental health. For example, findings of the Berkeley Growth Study indicate that the level of intelligence continues to rise until at least the age of 36. This was true for persons with relatively low IQ's as well as for those with relatively high IQ's, and for persons from all socioeconomic levels. The results suggest that, on the average, adults reach their peak of mental ability at a later age than has often been supposed. This age for the group under study will be determined in future follow-ups. But the work already bears out what individuals often discover for themselves: people from whatever level retain for many years the basic brainpower to learn new ways, new skills. The study also points to a number of environmental factors in very early life—parental attitudes among them—that seem to influence a person's IQ for years afterward and perhaps permanently. When knowledge of these factors is widely held and applied, the mental competency of our population can be expected to rise.

By studying the same people over such long periods, the investigators have also been able to demonstrate that the mental well-being of adults—those in their thirties, at any rate—is related to certain childhood characteristics and even to events during infancy. Those people who came down with psychosomatic ailments in adulthood, or became mentally ill, or showed other evidence of psychological trouble had been reporting worse than average adjustments to life even as 11-year-olds. And when these individuals were less than 2 years old, their families had shown more than average amount of disturbance. One of the investigators reports that a major factor in the onset of psychosomatic illness. (which may include to some extent almost all illness) seems to be a tendency toward depression reaching far back into childhood.

Looking into the records of their subjects as children, the investigators have also identified certain characteristics held in common by those who later took up smoking and continued to smoke. And the person most likely to become a problem drinker, preliminary evidence suggests, could have been spotted while he was still in high school.

Most of the recent findings should be useful in detecting children who need special help if they are able to realize their intellectual potential and be able to lead a satisfying life. But the Guidance Study staff warns that in predicting at 18 a person's psychological health at 30 it is easy to overemphasize the effect of traumatic experiences and of the youngster's response to them. Many of the most stable young adults were those for whom the staff had forecast a poor outcome. Disturbing experiences and behavior during adolescence had apparently been, in these cases, maturing. Dr. MacFarlane concludes that pediatricians and other doctors should look for strengths in children and not just pathology.

On the other hand, many of the Guidance Study youngsters who had been highly popular in high school failed to live up to their potential—by the age of 30, anyway—and were puzzled and dissatisfied, perhaps because life had been too easy for them or because they had poured their adolescent energies into maintaining an image of success.

Some of the other findings covered in the following sections are summed up here:

• Certain personality traits become established early and persist. The child who at five was either reserved and shy or expressive and gay tended to show the same characteristics at 16. The child who was either reactive and explosive or calm and phlegmatic at five was likely to be the same at 16.

• Personality is correlated with intelligence, at least in the case of boys. Adolescent boys with high IQ's were generally described as friendly, social, and independent—as they had been since the age of four. There was a positive relationship between these characteristics and the IQ in the case of girls, too, but it was not statistically significant. Men of high intelligence were less likely than men of low intelligence to be hostile, self-pitying, or impatient.

• Frequently the effects of a given environmental circumstance are quite different for one sex than for the other (as they are for subjects with different temperaments). The differences are found in the development of both intelligence and personality.

• The speed of development during childhood, which presumably is determined by both genetic and environmental factors, seems to influence personality characteristics into adulthood. The early talkers (generally those who had received more than the usual amount of parental attention during infancy) were more introspective as adults, perhaps because language rather than action had always been for them the favored response pattern. Boys who matured early had an easier time during adolescence, a higher income at 30, and a strong tendency to conform.

How the Early Environment Affects Intellectual Development

A child's experiences during his very early years seem to affect the level of his intelligence for at least many years afterward. The main conclusions on this subject, summarized here, stem from analyses either by Honzik and her associates in the Guidance Study or by Bayley and her associates in the Berkeley Growth Study.

Socioeconomic conditions. The socioeconomic level of the parents was unrelated to the intelligence of their children during the first 18 or 24 months. But after that, and particularly after the age of five years, the relationship became fairly strong: in general, the lower the parents' status when the child was young, the lower the children's intelligence as measured by mental tests. This was true through at least the age of 18, which is as far as this part of the analysis has gone.

Family income during the early preschool years was significantly related to the children's scores on mental tests at most points up through the age of 15. At the age of 30, it was significantly related to the sons' scores but not the daughters'. Superior play facilities during early childhood were also related to the IQ scores later on.

Parental attitudes toward education. Both boys and girls whose parents had expressed concern when the children were babies that they get a good education were likely to make higher IQ scores at all ages through 30 than the children of parents who had shown little or no concern. Boys were motivated by their mothers' concern; girls, by their fathers'.

Parents' marital adjustment. When the home atmosphere very early in life had been one of parental harmony, or at least of lack of conflict, a girl's mental test performance—but not a boy's—was likely to be significantly better right on up into adulthood.

Maternal characteristics. Mothers who appeared worrisome, tense, highly active, and energetic had children who were more likely than other children to score high on mental tests through the age of 30. The child's need for tactual, auditory, and visual stimulation, Honzik notes, are best met in the family where the mother is responsive and actively concerned with the infant's welfare, even to the point of being worrisome about him. A genetic factor may be at work, too, for the worrisome mother tended also to be the better educated mother, and educational level in this sample, the investigators think, was evidence of native ability as well as of stimulation during childhood.

For the boys, the one best predictor of test performance during the period between 8 and 18 was the closeness of the mother-son relationship as rated at 21 months. Apparently, it is verbal competence that is fostered by a close relationship. For at 18, a boy's verbal IQ was much more likely to be high if the early relationship had been close; his performance IQ was unaffected. At 30, when the test was for performance, not verbal ability, there was no correlation.

Boys whose mothers were anxious, irritable, strict, and punitive toward them during their first few years tended to have IQ's below average during the school years and even as adults. Maternal love or lack of it seemed to have no effect on the mental test scores of girls. But mothers judged to be instrusive—forever meddling in the child's activities—had daughters whose IQ ratings through adolescence tended to be low.

Paternal characteristics. A girl's intellectual development was likely to be increased when, during babyhood, her father had a close, warm relationship with both his wife and with her. It was the father's interest in his daughter, rather than his expression of affection for her, that seemed to count. The father-daughter relationship apparently influenced IQ scores from the age of seven through adolescence. During the preschool years, the relationship between mother and daughter was the more influential.

Childhood IQ and adult success. In the case of men the IQ through childhood and adolescence is roughly a good indication of their success— conventionally judged—as an adult. On the basis of the number of years they had gone to school and on the kind of jobs they held at the age of 30, the men seemed to be achieving "pretty much in accord with their mental abilities." This was not true of the women. But then, Bayley points out, women in general have different educational and occupational goals than men. As a group the women who classified themselves as house-wives had had, all their lives, higher IQ's than the women who were working for pay.

The influence of sex. As noted in the findings above, certain factors that influenced the IQ's of boys had little or no influence on the IQ's of girls, and vice versa. Bayley suggests there is a genetic difference between the sexes in the ability to resist certain environmental influences or to recover from them. "Boys," she adds, "appear to be less able than girls to recover from hostile, rejecting treatment; but they may also profit more, in the long run, from understanding loving acceptance." There also seems to be, Honzik reports, a sex difference in the rate of mental growth. The parents' education showed an increasing correlation with the children's IQ's between 21 months and 15 years, but it became significant for girls by the age of three; for boys, not until five. When there were boys and girls in the same family, this difference still held. The relationship between socio-economic status and IQ also became significant for girls earlier than for boys. Girls' abilities, Honzik suggests, develop earlier.

The home environment in later years. The family situation was assessed each year until the children were 16. In general, the relationships between a given factor, such as parental warmth, on the one hand, and mental development on the other were less—if they were present at all—than they had been during early childhood. In other words, the family situation when the child is very young influences mental development more strongly than the situation later on, when out-of-family influences in-crease.

The Course of the IQ as People Grow Older

After the 1964 follow-up of members of the Berkeley Growth Study, Bayley began analyzing the IQ's of the subjects at that time, when they were 36 years old, in relation to some of the earlier IQ's—those shown at the ages of 16, 18, 21, and 26 years. She finds that until the age of 36, at least, the intelligence level tends to rise.

This is particularly true with the verbal scale of the test, which meas-ures the extent of a person's vocabulary and information, his ability to comprehend, and other factors heavily dependent on his capacity to understand and use words. On this scale, all the subjects, show an increase in score with age, between 16 and 36, though the rate of increase is slowing down.

On the performance scale of the intelligence test, there is a slight decline after 26. The men score the same at 36 as at 26, but the women score lower. This scale deals with the ability to perceive patterns, to visualize the whole from some of its parts, and to manipulate objects in a logical way.

As a group, Bayley points out, the subjects in the study have had a better socioeconomic background than average and have scored above average in the mental tests. However, the group does include several persons whose scores during childhood were quite low, and these persons, too, have continued to grow in intelligence.

The person with the lowest IQ was a man whose ratings were in the low 60's from the time he was 5 until 16. After that they went up, and at 36 reached 80. His performance IQ then was 92; his verbal IQ, 72. He had not learned to read until after he was 21.

Bayley concludes that the intellectual potential of the people in her study remain unimpaired through 36 years and that "in the attainment of information and word knowledge their intelligence is continuing to increase." She finds some evidence—the lowered speed with which the women in general completed some of the tests on the performance scale— consistent with the findings of other investigators that advancing age is accompanied by loss of speed in learning. However, she points out that other investigators have found evidence also that loss of speed is often compensated for by an increase in knowledge and skill.

As people grow older, this investigator believes, they probably show increasing resistance to learning new techniques and new ways of organizing knowledge, but the extent to which these resistances are overcome may be matters of motivation and opportunity, rather than of intelligence.

She points to two men in the study who went back to school in their thirties, after a decade in other employment, one to become a lawyer and the other a doctor. Both have started their new careers "with bright prospects of success." She concludes that motivation and drive and ample time, rather than a small variation in intelligence, seem to be "the important determiners for much of learning in adults."

Do smart babies become smart children and smart adults?

Not necessarily.

Bayley and some of her associates have been analyzing the correlations between mental test scores in infancy (the average of several scores at 10 to 12 months) with test scores at 24 ages, running from 1 month to 36 years. For the first 2 or 3 years the relationships are close; then they fall off rapidly. From 4 years on, there is very little relationship, particularly in the case of the boys.

The investigators have also developed "precocity scores" in order to observe how the precocious infants fared later on. These scores are based on the ages at which a child first put a block together, first noticed a pellet on the table, first said a syllable that had meaning for adults, and so on. There are 115 items in all.

So far the analysis has been completed only for the vocabulary or vocalization factor, comprising seven items or steps that the normal child generally completes between the ages of 8 and 15 months. These include expressing emotions with distinctive sounds and, later on, saying words. During the first 3 years of life, the higher the score on this factor, the higher the IQ, for both sexes. Then the boys' correlations drop sharply and in most cases become negative, meaning that the higher the score on the vocalization factor, the lower the IQ. For the girls, however, the correlations remain high: in their case vocal precocity as a baby is a prediction of high IQ as children and as adults.

Intelligence as Related to Behavior and Personality

The follow-up of the people in the Berkeley Growth Study when they were 36 included a detailed personality assessment made on the basis of the 100-item Block Q-sort. (In a Q-sort, characteristics noted during an interview are given numerical weight by scoring each item on a scale. The interviewer thus can say that the given quality was absent, present to a very high degree, or present to one of the several degrees in between. In this study the transcribed interviews were Q-sorted by the interviewer and by two clinical psychologists.) Bayley has now analyzed the findings and compared them with the scores made on IQ tests during the same follow-up.

The men who had been scored high on such items as impatient, negativistic, self-pitying, and hostile were found to be those who in general had the lowest IQ's. The men described as critical, introspective, socially perceptive, and having wide interests were those in general with the highest IQ's. Little or no relationship was found between IQ scores on the one hand, and on the other hand, characteristics described as either distant and avoiding or warm, calm, and gregarious.

"The men in this sample with high intelligence," Bayley reports, "are best characterized as introspective, thoughtful, and concerned with problems, meanings and values; they are men who are perceptive and have a wide range of interests. The least intelligent are most often found to be impatient, prone to vent their hostilities and to project them onto others."

The correlations between the women's IQ's and various personality attributes are much weaker but similar in pattern. Again it is the thoughtful, insightful person with wide interests who is more likely to score high on the IQ tests. Women described as bland, conventional, or anxious are much less likely to rate high on the tests; so are women described as cheerful, poised, and gregarious.

Another measure of personality styles and psychological attitudes administered during this follow-up was the California Psychological Inventory, a questionnaire designed to measure such characteristics as sociability, self-acceptance, sense of well-being, tolerance, and responsibility. It has 17 scales. Bayley has compared the scores made on each of these at the age of 36 with the IQ scores at that age and also at 16, 18, 21, and 26 years.

Certain of these characteristics appear to be significantly associated with a high order of intelligence at all the ages studied. For men, the clearest and most consistent associations with IQ's are socialization (referring to social maturity, integrity, rectitude); the ability to make a good impression; potential for achievement, whether by conforming with the group or acting independently; and intellectual efficiency. For women, the

138

clearest and most consistent associations are with tolerance, potential for achievement by acting independently, and flexibility.

Ratings on self-acceptance and self-control, qualities usually associated with mental health, were not significantly related to intelligence in either men or women.

When Bayley used the scores on the subscales of the intelligence test, she found some other provocative patterns. Little or no sex difference appeared in the correlations between scores on the verbal-academic scales of the IQ tests and the ratings for achievement potential, intellectual efficiency, and interest in intellectual pursuits. But the other scales pointed to marked differences. With men but not with women, for example, the score on the picture-completion test correlated strongly with the score on socialization; with women but not with men it correlated with flexibility. Scores on the object-assembly test correlated with flexibility, achievement potential, and intellectual efficiency with the women but not with the men. The highest scores in arithmetic were made by the women rating highest in feminine qualities and by the men rating lowest in them. The highest scores in the digit-span test were made by the men ranking high in sociability, well-being, and interest in making a good impression and by the women ranking low in these characteristics.

In short, for this small sample at least, there seems to be a relationship between intellectual processes and personality as manifested in various social attitudes, interests, and motivations. The relationship remains fairly stable over the years between 16 and 36, but differs both with the nature of the intellectual process and with the personality characteristic being considered. It often differs widely between the sexes as well.

In the case of males, the investigators have also found some relations between mental test scores throughout the 36-year period and the behavior and personality characteristics of the subjects during their first three years. Boys who were calm, responding, and happy, and who were active after 15 months rather than before, were more likely than the others to have high IQ's (determined in this case only from the verbal scale). Girls showed no clear pattern.

With females through the years, considerably fewer significant correlations between IQ scores and personality ratings were noted than for males. Bayley suggests that a girl's intellectual potential is less affected than a man's by social and emotional factors. A girl comes into life physiologically tougher, it has been shown; perhaps she is by nature psychologically tougher as well.

Psychological Mechanisms and the IQ

After the subjects in the Oakland Growth Study had been interviewed at 37, Norma Haan, a psychologist, rated them for the presence of coping and defense mechanisms. Among the coping mechanisms she includes objectivity, logical analysis, empathy, sublimation, and tolerance of ambiguity. Among the defense mechanisms are repression, doubt and

139

indecision, and denial of facts and feelings that would be unpleasant or self-threatening to acknowledge. The coping and defense mechanisms are counterparts. For example, the coping partner of denial, says Haan, is concentration—the ability to set aside disturbing feelings or thoughts in order to get on with necessary tasks at hand.

In general, the adults who tended to make use of coping rather than defense mechanisms had the highest IQ's. Further, they were the persons whose IQ's between adolescence and adulthood were most likely to have risen. Coping, the investigator suggests, leads to the development of one's intelligence; defensiveness interferes with one's intelligence as well as one's effectiveness.

Persistence of Personality Traits

Dr. Wanda C. Bronson, a psychologist, has begun to analyze the attitudes and characteristics of subjects in the Guidance Study to learn if these become set very early or change with the years.

Between the ages of 5 and 16, the period covered by the analysis so far, she finds two persistent "behavioral dimensions." One is behavior characterized at one end of the dimension as reserved, somber, shy, and at the other end as expressive, gay, socially easy. The second dimension is a contrast between reactive, explosive, resistive behavior at one end—calm, phlegmatic, compliant behavior at the other end.

If a child was either reserved (somber, shy) or expressive (gay, socially easy) at the age of five, he was likely to be the same at 16. If he was either reactive (explosive, resistive) or calm (phlegmatic, compliant) at five, he was likely to be the same at 16.

The reserved individual tended also to be introspective and, to a lesser extent, anxious and socially withdrawn. In early childhood, he was likely to be inactive and a poor eater; at 16, uncertain and uncompetitive. The expressive boy was the extrovert. Girls showed only one marked difference from the boys on this behavior measure. The reserved girl tended to be cautious and unadventurous at all ages whereas the reserved boy was cautious and unadventurous only between the ages of 8 and 10.

In the case of the other behavior grouping, the reactive and explosive boy tended also to be emotionally unstable, quarrelsome, and complaining. In adolescence but not earlier he was also likely to be rated active and adventurous. Girls showed some differences. The correlation between reactiveness and emotional instability was not significantly strong except during early childhood; the correlations between reactiveness and the activity level, strong between the ages of 8 and 13. The reactive girls tended to be finicky about their food at all ages and to be exhibitionistic at 16.

Both of these attitude patterns—reserve v. expressiveness and reactivity v. placidity—describe characteristics that the individual brings with him to every situation and that affect the environment's impact upon him. An expressive child, for example, would be more ready to initiate or be drawn into an intensive relation with his mother than a withdrawn child. A reactive child, more than a placid one, would be affected by an anxious, intrusive mother.

To what extent and through the mediation of what mechanisms these persistent personality traits are inherited, affected by the environment, and developed in the interaction between heredity and environment is not clear. Bronson does find that the children tend to take after the parent of the same sex and to reject or be unaffected by the characteristics of the other parent. Expressive boys, for example, tended to have fathers of expressive and even aggressive temperament; expressive girls, mothers of the same type. More information on this question is expected to come from an analysis of the children of the subjects in the study.

In another of the Berkeley studies, the boys with the loving mothers— these were the boys most likely to have high IQ's later on—tended as babies to be happy, inactive, and slow. Beginning about the age of 4, though, these boys were consistently rated as independent, social, and friendly.

Personality as Related to Speed of Development

Some of the personality traits noted in preceding sections seem to be related to the rate at which the people developed—began talking, began walking, reached adolescence. The early talkers, Dr. MacFarlane reports, tended to be the late walkers. And those who matured late, as indicated by the age they reached pubescence, differed considerably in some respects during adolescence and young adulthood from those who matured early. This was true of boys in particular.

As an example of how the rate of physical development in youth can influence a person's life for years afterward, this investigator tells of two boys who differed mainly in speed of maturation. The early maturer (who reached adult sexual status before he was 13) excelled in athletics and enjoyed the accompanying rewards. He showed interest in girls at 13 and they in him. The late maturer (who reached adult sexual status after he was 17) avoided girls, and they him, till he was 20. The first boy got a summer job at 14; the second went to Boy Scout camp. After college, the early maturer joined a firm in another city, married, and by 30 had reached a responsible position that takes him and his family to all parts of the world. The late maturer married a girl he had known since grade school, got a promising job with her father's help, and established a home in the neighborhood where they had been born and raised. At 30 he had yet to reach the administrative level in his firm. "I'm too young, they tell me," he reported. "I've always been too young."

Though the details differ from person to person, the early maturing male has been found by the Guidance Study to have an easier time during adolescence and to show more confidence both then and later. This was to have been expected, MacFarlane thinks, because the boy who matured early was also likely to have begun early getting into things and exploring the environment. His interests were outward because there's where the excitement lay. On the other hand, the late maturer was typically the early talker, an introverted fellow who was apparently more fascinated from the start by thinking processes than by action.

At 30, the early maturer was likely to have advanced farther in his work than the late maturer, more likely to be married, and likely to have more children.

Findings by Dr. Mary Cover Jones, Professor of Education, emeritus, from her study of a different sample—early and late maturing boys in the Oakland Growth Study—confirm those results, add some interesting details, and carry the comparison a little farther along. At 33, the men who had matured early rated significantly higher in both sociability and responsibility. They were also more conventional in their attitudes and thinking. Five years later the differences were less marked, but the man who had matured early still appeared to be more assured and somewhat less fearful, and also less insightful and independent. More of the early maturing men have attained executive, status-conferring vocational goals.

The boy who most rapidly approaches physical manhood, Jones suggests, is the one who is first recognized by the adult community and who therefore is most likely to take on—if he doesn't have them already—the personality traits likely to be most valued by that community. Dr. Harvey Peskin, a psychologist, thinks the difference found in both studies may well have a deep psychological basis. The early maturer, he suggests, is less prepared for the changes of adolescence. So he may experience them as less tolerable and therefore less acceptable. He flees, therefore, into adulthood and makes an early and rewarding commitment to the values of his culture. So he is "naturally" more sociable and conforming. On the other hand, the late maturer, not having to deal with the hormonal-inspired drives till later, has more time to look around, expand his skills, and develop a variety of psychological mechanisms for regulating crises. So when puberty comes, he tolerates it better and has less need of outside supports and rewards. This would explain his greater insightfulness.

Here again an apparent sex difference has been found. Girls who reached maturity early, MacFarlane reports, were usually less confident as adults. In school they seem to have felt out of things. These girls are described by Mary Jones, on the basis of observational ratings, as "socially disadvantaged." However, their responses on the Thematic Apperception Test and their self-report scores indicate adequate self-concepts.

Dr. Louis Stewart adds this finding: Among males, at least, the firstborn tends to mature earlier than an only child or a lastborn child. This psychologist thinks the earlier maturation is somehow associated with the events attendant on the arrival of a new baby, for when a mother was pregnant with her second child, and for a year or two after its birth, the firstborn showed an unusual spurt in growth. Numerous experiments with animals and some studies of people show that stimulation in infancy, even painful stimulation, makes for growth, and separation from the mother appears to be an important form of such stimulation. The mother's pregnancy and the arrival of a new child, the investigator suggests, constitute painful, development-spurring stimulation for the firstborn.

142

Incidentally, other work on birth order by Dr. William T. Smelser, also a psychologist, throws new light on the recurrent finding that firstborn children get more education than those born last. In two-child families where both children are of the same sex, Smelser finds, there is no significant difference in the number of years they go to school. But where one child is a boy and the other is a girl, the firstborn, of whichever sex, goes to school significantly longer. And there is a greater proportion of these cross-sex (girl-boy or boy-girl) families. In studying the effects of birth order on years of schooling, then, it is important to ascertain not only a person's birth position but also the sex of the child next to him.

Early talkers v. late. Analyzing the records of men in the Guidance Study, Dr. Kenwood Bartelme finds that the early talkers and the late show significant personality difference both as children and as adults. The same findings seem to apply to women, too, but in a less clear-cut fashion.

The early talkers were taken to be those who had said at least five words before they were 12 months old; the late talkers, those who had not done so until after 15 months. The boys in this second group talked well enough once they got started, but they had a different personality style.

Through adolescence, at least, the early talkers were on the restrained and somber side. Their IQ's were consistently higher than those of the later talkers but largely because of the difference in scores on the verbal factor tests. In high school, the early talkers were known as eggheads; at 30, they still valued intellectual matters and were inclined to intellectualize about a subject, even to the point of splitting hairs, They were also at 30 more practical, prudent, and conservative. The late talkers were active, relatively uninhibited, and even rebellious. "The late-talker," Bartelme remarks, "is the social nonconformist."

The middle group, who began talking between 12 and 15 months, turned out to be the most conventional.

Why one person starts talking exceptionally early and another exceptionally late, even in the same family, is not known, but Bartelme has found one environmental difference. The early talker had received more than the usual amount of attention from his parents, particularly from his mother; the mother, in fact, had seemed to be more involved with him during infancy than with her husband.

Predicting Adult Psychological Health

When the subjects of one of the longitudinal studies (Oakland Growth) were 36, Stewart divided a sample of them into three groups:

1. Those with psychosomatic disorders. Of the 20 afflicted persons in this group, most had either stomach ulcer or hypertension. The others suffered from migraine headaches, spastic colitis, asthma, or arthritis.

2. Those with behavioral maladjustments. Two of the 21 persons here were alcoholic, six had had repeated divorces, another six had failed to make a satisfactory social adjustment, and seven had been treated for mental illness.

143

3. Those who were symptom-free: 25.

Then he went back to the data showing the social and emotional adjustments of these individuals when they had been adolescents. (The data came from the University of California Social and Adjustment Inventory, which had been administered each year between 11 and 17.) He found some important differences.

The people with psychosomatic ailments as adults were reporting a poorer-than-average adjustment to life when they were only 11 years old, which was from 15 to 20 years before the diagnosis of the illness. On scales measuring such characteristics as attitudes toward family, feelings about their own worth, and ability to get along with other people, these persons had rated themselves toward the low end. So had the individuals with behavioral maladjustments as adults. During late adolescence, however, the scores on family and social adjustment had improved among the psychosomatic group but not among the behavioral maladjustment group. During the same period, those who were later to be afflicted with a psychosomatic disorder also expressed a number of vague physical complaints.

Members of the psychosomatic group had been marked, too, by an underlying tendency toward depression, as indicated by feelings of worthlessness, lack of energy, sleep disturbance, and the loss—actual or feared—of parental attention and love. On all such traits there had been during adolescence highly significant differences between the psychosomatic group and the normal. The group with behavioral maladjustments had fallen in between. The results suggest to Stewart that a basic depressive tendency is an important factor in the onset of psychosomatic disorder. And he is inclined to agree with some other investigators that virtually all illness is caused by psychic as well as somatic factors.

To try to find the basis of the maladjustments noted during adolescence, Stewart is now analyzing the records of another study (Guidance) which go back to infancy. His preliminary findings confirm that adults with psychosomatic ailments or with psychological problems worse than usual had been poorly adjusted adolescents. Further, the new findings indicate that (1) members of both groups came from families where, very early in the children's life, there had been more disturbance, and less satisfaction and security, than usual; (2) members of both groups tended to be those who had matured either very early or very late.

This second finding does not imply that early and late maturers are inevitably bound for trouble. The processes associated with either extreme of the maturation rate do seem to produce not only differences in personality, as noted earlier, but also a higher than average potential for illness and psychological difficulties. Stewart is now trying to find early family and childhood patterns that distinguish the two groups—the ill and the maladjusted. He is also looking for childhood factors that distinguish people with one type of ailment from those with another.

In related work, Drs. Norman Livson and Harvey Peskin have been trying to determine which, if any, specific characteristics of a child, displayed at which particular age, can be used to predict his psychological health as an adult. The subjects were 64 young adults, from the Guidance Study, who had been rated for psychological health at 30 by comparing their scores on a personality appraisal with theoretically ideal scores. (The ideal scores were a composite of those made by four clinical psychologists as they attempted to define a fully healthy person.) The adults' ratings were then compared with their ratings as children, from the ages of five through 16, on numerous behavior and personality scales.

High scores on certain characteristics during the years from 11 to 13, but only during those years, were found to be significantly related to adult psychological health. The healthiest men were those who as boys of 11-13 had been relatively extroverted, cheerful, relaxed, and expressive, and relatively immune to irritability. The women had been relatively independent, confident, and inquiring—and had shown a hearty attitude toward food.

The 11-13 age period proved significant, the investigators speculate, because it encompassed the transitional period from elementary school to junior high. Now once again, as when he had left the family to enter school, the child had to take an important step toward maturity. "The demands and opportunities of the junior high school, for both boys and girls," the investigators suggest, "may represent so profound a difference from elementary school as to constitute a qualitatively new experience. The manner in which the child responds to the transition—actively inviting or passively withdrawing from the new experience—tells us something about how healthy an adult he will be."

The psychological health of these subjects will be assessed again during the 40-year follow-up. The investigators plan also to look for factors in the family environment during childhood that may portend good or poor psychological health in later life.

Children Who Turned Out Better or Worse Than Expected

Because of the work reported in the preceding section and of the research under way at Berkeley and other centers, the investigators think we shall be better able to predict while a person is still in school the probable state of his mental health as an adult—and, if the outlook is poor, to take steps to alter it. They emphasize, however, that the relationships reported are based on group averages and that in every group studied there were individuals who did not conform.

More than 20 years ago, when the children in the Guidance Study were 18, MacFarlane and her associates made predictions about them as adults —their personalities, their success in marriage and work, their ability to cope with the problems of life: in short, their mental health. Though the investigators had had few scientific guides, they were surprised by the results of the analysis after the subjects were followed up at the age of 30. In many cases, the predictions turned out to have been wrong. The reasons ought to be helpful for parents, teachers, doctors, and everyone else associated with children.

Many of the most mature adults—integrated, competent, clear about their values, and accepting of themselves and others—were found to have been those who as youngsters had been faced with difficult situations and whose characteristic responses had seemed to compound their problems. They included chronic rebels who had been expelled from school, Mac-Farlane reports, highly intelligent students who were nevertheless academic failures, children filled with hostility, and unhappy, withdrawn schizoids. But the behavior regarded by the investigators as disruptive to growth and maturity seemed in these cases to have led directly or indirectly to adult strength. One of the former rebels recalled that he had desperately needed approval "even if it was from kids as maladjusted as I was." To maintain his rebel status, he said, he had had to commit all of his intelligence and stamina, a circumstance he believed had contributed to his adult strength in tackling difficult problems. "I hope my children find less wasteful ways to mature," he remarked, "—but who knows?"

Close to half of the subjects fell into the group for whom crippled or inadequate personalities had been predicted. But as adults almost all of them were better than had been expected, and some of them far better.

One man, for example, held back three times in elementary school, had not graduated from high school until he was 21. His IQ over the years had averaged less than 100. He had shown little interest in studies, school activities, or people. The school had not recommended that he go to college. The staff thought he'd always be a misfit, a sideliner. But 12 years later he was a talented environmental designer, a good father, and an active worker in community affairs. "Obviously," says MacFarlane, "his tested IQ's were no measure of his true ability."

One girl, who early was suspicious of and even hostile to members of the study staff, lived with a rejecting mother and a poorly adjusted aunt. She hated home and she hated school, partly because of her poor clothes. To escape, she married while still in high school a boy as erratic and immature as she. They soon separated. At 30, with the investigators dreading the impending interview, in came a personable, well-groomed, gracious woman with two buoyant but well-mannered children. She had married again and was living a stable, contented life.

Why were the predictions wrong in such cases?

For one thing, MacFarlane answers, the investigators gave too much weight to the troublesome and pathogenic elements in a child's life—quite naturally, in view of the studies that have traced neuroses and psychoses to such elements—and too little weight to the healthful, maturity-inducing elements. (The latter were present even in the case of the girl who sought escape through marriage at 17. She always remembered that another aunt had given her affection and happiness—had helped her plant seeds that grew into flowers, had given her a kitten to love, had taught her to bake, and one year had been able to help her buy clothes "so I could finally risk being friendly.")

The investigators also overestimated the durability of certain "undesirable" behaviors and attitudes shown habitually over a long period. These frequently turned out to have been devices for achieving some desired

146

end. As an example, MacFarlane cites hurt feelings, in both boys and girls, as "a very successful parent-manipulation tool." In changed situations, such early useful devices lost their effectiveness, and the big majority of the young people then dropped or modified them, sometimes not without difficulty. With a number of girls, the game of getting their feelings hurt was carried over into marriage.

Sometimes the undesirable but long-continued patterns were converted, to the investigators' surprise, into almost the opposite characteristics. For example, it was predicted that overdependent boys with energetic and dominant mothers would pick wives like the mothers and continue the pattern of overdependence. Instead, nearly all such boys chose girls who were lacking in confidence. The boys thus won themselves a role as the proud male protector and giver of support, and in this role, says the investigator, they thrived.

Along the same line, a number of those in the study who were socially inept and insecure as children and adolescents became, again to everyone's surprise, highly successful salesmen. Looking back, MacFarlane sees this as a quite natural transformation. The boys did not have easy, intimate relationships growing up because they did not have them at home. As adults they still fear intimate relationships but have an unconscious desire for social intercourse. Selling gives them the needed contacts without the feared intimacy. (She could be wrong, she adds. The director of sales training for a large firm told her he deliberately picked shy people, because they would concentrate on selling the product instead of themselves.)

One man, who is remembered with special pride, is the highly successful manager of a large business concern. Years ago he had been a shy little boy without friends. Though he had dropped in from time to time to see members of the Guidance Study Staff, his communications had often been limited to hello and goodbye. After high school he enlisted and, since he had taken some shop courses, he was asked to help with the building and repair work at his Army post. First he was flattered that anyone should think he could do anything; then he was proud that he could actually do it. After his service, he went to business school, where he got all A's, as compared to C's in high school. Now he says the most interesting part of his job is to give people "something to do that is a little harder than what they have done or think they can do—but not something they would fail at—and then to watch them expand. Nothing is more exciting to me than to see people get confidence"—which he himself had lacked for so long.

A number of other subjects had had similar experiences. They did not achieve "ego identity"—did not find themselves—until they had been forced into or been given an opportunity to take on a responsible role that gave them the sense of worth they had missed at home. Often these people did not find this new and satisfying role until they had left both their childhood homes and their home towns.

147

"Don't give up on our present generation of adolescents," MacFarlane urges. "Many of ours came through bad times and developed into mature, stable adults in spite of our fears."

In a speech before The American Academy of Pediatrics recently, the investigator quoted comments made spontaneously by a number of the Guidance Study subjects at 30. Some examples:

"When I was confused and worried, the Institute was the only place I could talk out loud to myself and find out what I thought and felt."

"I sensed your respect for me, even when I knew I wasn't acting very sensibly and knew you wouldn't have had respect for me if there wasn't something there to respect because, believe me, I can tell a phony in a split second—because at times I'm a phony myself."

"You asked questions, you listened, but you were the only grown-ups who didn't give advice. You helped me to ferret things out for myself, to make my own decisions. I try to carry this on in the raising of my children."

The investigator then pled with the doctors to take a similar role with their patients. "You pediatricians are the only professional group," she said, "that can furnish continuity and interest over the long age-span of growth from babyhood to maturity, provided, of course, you have the temperament to be sympathetically interested in the vagaries of the human struggle for competence and maturity. Provided, too, you can accept the fact that you can't play God or believe you know all the answers, because one thing we have learned is how little we know. Provided, too, that you can train yourselves to look for strengths in individuals and their situations and not just for pathology. If you don't furnish this function, what professional will? If teaching departments don't incite interest, who will?"

About 20 percent of the cases turned out worse than expected. These included many of the persons who as children and adolescents had had easy, confidence-inducing lives, free of severe strains and marked by academic, social, or athletic success. Prominent among these were a high proportion of the men who had been outstanding athletes in high school and of the women who as girls had been pretty and exceptionally popular. At 30, many of these people had failed to live up to their potentialities and were puzzled and discontented.

MacFarlane gives several possible explanations. Early success may have led to unreal expectations and to a draining of energies into maintaining an image. It may have sidetracked the development of patterns and attitudes that would have made adult life more rewarding. Perhaps there wasn't enough stress in these youngsters' lives to foster development. She thinks some of the people in this group will work free from their dissatisfactions as young adults and will yet live up to their predictions for them; others will go through live wondering what happened and where they slipped.

About 30 percent of the people turned out as predicted. Among the two main groups here were the overcontrolled, who had built a psychological shield against the dangers to be found in other people and in life in general. As young adults they still had the shield. It seems to have protected them, MacFarlane reports, but it also—by denying them access to many kinds of learning experience—has impoverished them. The second main group includes the youngsters who had been subjected to marked variability in family treatment, being handled indulgently one day and slapped down the next. Neither as adolescents nor young adults had they developed stable patterns of behavior. Of the nine adults in this study who were found to be compulsive drinkers at the age of 30, all but one came from this group. Perhaps significantly, the compulsive drinkers had manifested physical vulnerability, too—acute allergies, beginning in infancy.

The Effects of Guidance

The parents of half of the children in the Guidance Study were encouraged to turn to the staff psychologists for discussion of problems whenever they wished. Many did so. Through these discussions, they were helped to a better understanding not only of their children's behaviors and attitudes but also of their own and their spouses'. The control families were not intensively interviewed and discussions were avoided or kept to a minimum. The subjects in the guidance and control groups—the children who have grown up and become parents themselves—are now being compared in order to help explain why they grew up to be the kind of parents they are and have the kind of children they have.

So far, only hard fact has emerged: The group whose parents received little or no opportunity for discussion of interpersonal relations and children's problems has had about four times as many divorces as the guidance group. Dr. Ann Stout, the psychologist who is handling the parent-child study, finds other evidence pointing to the conclusion that when parents are encouraged to discuss family problems with professional workers, their children tend as adults to have more flexible qualities and a better ability to cope with situations. As she puts it, the guidance seems to have tempered some of the negative factors influencing the children's development. For example, there are persons in both groups who were ebullient as youngsters but who for some reason, at some point, took on a rather depressive attitude. They are not getting the satisfaction out of life that they should. However, the depressive subjects in the guidance group show more resilience than those in the control group, and a tendency to find more satisfaction.

Antecedents of Smoking

In 1964 the report to the United States Surgeon General on "Smoking and Health" stated that "While rebellion may play a role in the initiation of smoking, perhaps an important one, there is not much evidence for it. Claims in the literature are at best based on circumstantial suggestive evidence, linked to conclusions by a chain of questionable assumptions." Since then, Stewart and Livson, using data from the Guidance and Oakland Growth Studies, have turned up evidence that cigarette smokers actually are more rebellious than nonsmokers and that this greater degree of rebelliousness is part of the smoker's personality long before he starts smoking. It appears even during the earliest years of school. In a separate study using a different methodology, Clausen finds that the youngsters who became smokers tended to be less controlled and more aggressive than the others and to differ also in other important traits and in their backgrounds. The nonsmoking boys had a stronger drive to get ahead, and they still have it as adults.

To measure rebelliousness, Stewart and Livson used the teachers' ratings on the children's behavior in school and on their attitude toward school and, where the ratings were not available, grades on conduct. A "resistance to authority" measure, taken during four years of high school, was also available for those subjects from the Oakland Growth Study. This was the average of independent ratings made by three staff members after observing the students in a variety of social situations.

From ages five to 15, the persons who later became smokers were found to show more evidence of rebellious attitudes. For all the subjects studied, the difference was clearest during the sixth and seventh grades, when it was statistically significant for each of the two groups and for both girls and boys. For those subjects related on "resistance to authority," the difference continued to be significant through high school.

As adults, too, the smokers—who comprised about 55 percent of the 160 subjects studied during their early 30's—were rated more rebellious. The measure this time was a scale intended to show the degree to which a person conforms to the mores of our society. (Bankers have been found to rate at the top of this measure, which is socialization scale of the California Psychological Inventory; juvenile delinquents and criminals rate at the bottom.) The nonsmokers scored significantly higher than the smokers: the finding could have occurred by chance one time in 100 in the case of women, and one time in 1000 in the case of the men.

So what? The investigators respond that smoking and adolescent rebellion against authority have long been linked in popular thought and that this study provides evidence they actually are linked. If this is so, the investigators continue, an antismoking campaign based upon authoritative pronouncements has little chance of success: a more subtle strategy is required.

Stewart and Livson refer to a handful of recent studies that have used a measure (the Psychopathic Deviate Scale of the Minnesota Multiphasic Personality Inventory) very similar to the one employed in this investigation to rate rebelliousness in adults. These studies have found significantly higher scores among (a) people addicted either to alcohol or narcotics, (b) smokers in a psychiatric outpatient population, and (c) smokers in two samples of male college students. The Berkeley investigators suggest that smoking is an addiction, sharing with the other addictions a common origin in some underlying resentment of authority and being, like the other addictions, not an isolated habit but an expression of "pervasive personality tendencies."

In a second study of the antecedents of smoking, Clausen sent a questionnaire about smoking habits to all subjects in the Oakland Growth Study when they were about 40 years old, received answers from 123, and then searched for personality and background factors—as recorded during adolescence—that might differentiate between those who took up smoking and those who did not, and between heavy and light smokers.

Perhaps the clearest finding, Clausen reports, is that the adolescents who did not become smokers were more controlled in high school, more oriented to adult values, relatively unaggressive, and modest in their views of themselves. The boys were seen as well-adjusted and creative and as having a strong desire to achieve; in senior high they enjoyed prestige and popularity. The girls who did not take up smoking were rated as conventional, unassuming, calm, serious, and self-sufficient. Though well-adjusted, they were less popular than the girls who became smokers.

As a partial, quite incomplete, explanation of these differences, Clausen finds that the boys and girls who matured later than the others were more likely to start smoking and continue. Though there is no direct link between biology and smoking, the investigator hypothesizes, the person who finds himself lagging behind the gang in physical maturity may turn to smoking as a sign that he, too, is growing up.

Clausen also finds differences in the characteristics of the mothers of smokers and nonsmokers. The mothers of the boys who remained non-smokers had been rated as effective, nonneurotic women—significantly less talkative and more clearheaded and cheerful than the mothers of the other boys. The mothers of the girls who remained nonsmokers showed an accepting rather than a critical attitude.

The actual smoking habits of the parents strongly influenced those of the girls, but not of the boys. Among those girls with at least one parent who smoked, a fourth eventually became very heavy smokers and only a fifth did not smoke at all. When neither parent smoked, scarcely any of the girls became very heavy smokers and nearly half never smoked.

Lack of poise would be an important antecedent of smoking, Clausen had thought, but this turned out to be incorrect, especially among the girls. The girls who remained nonsmokers were rated less poised and socially skilled than the others and at the same time more unaffected and more composed.

On the basis of intensive interviews, averaging 12 hours in length, the adults show many of the same personality traits that characterized them as adolescents. The nonsmoking men still have a stronger drive for achievement and are more effective. They are in tighter control of themselves, less self-indulgent, and more self-satisfied. Though the nonsmokers were rated significantly less assertive in adolescence, as adults they are slightly more assertive than the smokers, Probably this change has occurred, Clausen thinks, because most of the nonsmokers have experienced a considerable measure of occupational success. Moderate smokers have done nearly as well, but heavy smokers much less well. Among the women, nonsmokers remain more conforming. They are also rated more fearful and more likely to manifest guilt than are women who become smokers.

The questionnaire relating to current smoking has now been sent to subjects of all these studies. A monograph reporting findings will deal not only with antecedents and correlates of smoking but also with comparisons between addicted smokers and those able to give up or cut down on tobacco use.

Antecedents of Drinking

As another example of using a longitudinal study to answer questions almost impossible to answer in any other way, Mary Jones has been studying the personalities of drinkers and nondrinkers. Her question was: Do personality characteristics associated with a given drinking pattern show up early in life, before the pattern has been established? The tentative answer is that they do.

In the work to date, 68 men and 70 women in the Oakland Growth Study were classified according to their drinking habits and their reasons for drinking. The subjects were in their middle forties. Then their personalities were assessed, through the use of California Q Set, for three age levels: junior high school, senior high school, and adulthood.

More than half of the behavioral items that differentiated problem drinkers from moderate drinkers (typically, a drink or two before dinner, three or four at a party) and abstainers in adulthood were found to have differentiated them also in junior high school. For example, the men problem drinkers, compared with the other men studied, were found to be rebellious, self-indulgent, gregarious, unpredictable, and disorganized. They were less dependable, less considerate, less fastidious, and less moralistic. As junior high students, these men had been marked by the same characteristics. And they had been more concerned than the others to demonstrate their masculinity. Behavior during the junior high school years proved to be a better predictor of adult drinking patterns than behavior during later adolescence.

On the rating that distinguished the three groups both as adults and junior high students, the men who were problem drinkers as adults usually stood at one end of the scale, the abstainers at the other, and the moderate drinkers in between.

Preliminary findings indicate that women problem drinkers resemble their male counterparts in respect to instability, unpredictableness and impulsiveness. However, they tend to be introversive and more marked by feelings of depression, self-doubt, and distrust than the men.

Looking Ahead

When the longitudinal studies began at Berkeley, there was little documented knowledge about factors that helped shape intelligence, personality, and mental health from childhood onward. Now there is a good deal, thanks not only to these pioneering investigations but also to numerous other studies undertaken more recently.

Because of man's complexity and the great variety of the influences pressing upon him, much remains to be learned—a statement that may always be true. But the body of our knowledge is being steadily increased.

152

Among the continuing investigations at Berkeley, two seem especially important: the attempt to identify those factors in infancy and childhood that predispose to psychosomatic illness and psychological maladjustment, and the attempt to ferret out the influence of heredity on certain abilities, and characteristics.

Other important work under way includes research on:

• The relationship of physical factors, such as body build, to specific types of intellectual function, such as mathematical ability.

• The ethical, religious, political, and other values held by a person's family as he grew up; the values he took with him into marriage; the values that now dominate his home.

• What difference it makes if one parent is the disciplinarian rather than the other, or both.

• The value of the Rorschach test, which was administered to Guidance Study members for 7 years during adolescence and again at 30, in predicting psychological health.

• The relationship between a person's interest and satisfactions during childhood to his personality and psychological health as an adult.

Staff members are also busy fitting together and interpreting the findings so that these can be of the widest use. Important books coming up include (1) "Ways of Personality Development: Continuity and Change from Adolescence to Adulthood," by Jack Block and Norma Haan, which uses data from both the Oakland Growth and the Guidance studies; (2) "Children of the Depression," an analysis by Dr. Glen H. Elder, Jr., of the immediate and long-term effects of the depression on the subjects in the Oakland Growth Study; and (3) "The Course of Human Development," a collection of major papers from, and new essays about three studies, edited by Drs. Mary Jones, Bayley, Honzik, and MacFarlane. Also Dr. Clausen is working on a major "life careers" monograph based on information from the Oakland Growth Study. It seeks to answer: What are the major influences upon a person's performance in the most salient roles of adulthood—those of worker, spouse, parent and community participant?

In the near future, Berkeley's Institute of Human Development hopes to establish a program of Intergenerational Studies of Development and Aging that will use the people who have been participating in the present studies—the original subjects, their surviving parents, and the subjects' children. The questions to be investigated include the patterns and processes of aging, the heritability of traits and abilities, and the similarities and differences in family patterns and styles of life from one generation to another.

Research Grants: MH 6238, 8135, 5300
Date of Interviews: April 1967

153

References:

Bayley, N. The life span as a frame of reference in psychological research. *Vita Humana*, 6:125, 1963.

Bayley, N. Consistency of maternal and child behaviors in the Berkeley Growth Study. *Vita Humana*, 7:73, 1964.

Bayley, N. Research in child development: a longitudinal perspective. *Merrill Palmer Quarterly of Behavior and Development*, 11:3, 1965.

Bayley, N. Age-trends in mental scores: ages 16 to 36 years. Paper for American Psychological Association, 1966.

Bayley, N. Learning in adulthood: the role of intelligence. In: *Analyses of Concept Learning*. New York: Academic Press, 1966.

Bayley, N. Cognition. Paper for University of West Virginia Conference on Theory and Methods of Research and Aging, 1967.

Bayley, N. Behavioral correlates of mental growth: birth to 36 years. Paper for American Psychological Association, 1967.

Bayley, N. and Schaefer, E. S. Correlations of maternal and child behaviors with the development of mental abilities: data from the Berkeley Growth Study. Monographs of the Society for Research in Child Development, 29(6):1-80, 1964.

Bronson, W. C. Early antecedents of emotional expressiveness and reactivity control. *Child Development*, 37:793-810, 1966.

Bronson, W. C. Central orientations: a study of behavior organization from childhood to adolescence. *Child Development*, 37:1, 1966.

Cameron, J.; Livson, N.; and Bayley, N. Infant vocalizations and their relationship to mature intelligence. *Science*, 157:3786, 1967.

Clausen, J. A. Adolescent antecedents of cigarette smoking: data from Oakland Growth Study. *Social Science and Medicine*, 1:4, 1968.

Haan, N. Proposed model of ego functioning: coping and defense mechanisms in relationship to IQ change. *Psychological Monographs: General and Applied*, 77:8, 1963.

Honzik, M. P. A. sex difference in the age of onset of the parent-child resemblance in intelligence. *Journal of Educational Psychology*, 54:5, 1963.

Honzik, M. P. The environment and mental growth from 21 months to 30 years. Paper for International Congress of Psychology, 1966.

Honzik, M. P. Environmental correlates of mental growth: prediction from the family setting at 21 months. *Child Development*, 38:337-363, 1967.

Jones, M. C. Psychological correlates of somatic development. *Child Development*, 36:4, 1965.

Jones, M. C. Personality correlates and antecedents of drinking patterns in adult males. *Journal of Consulting and Clinical Psychology*, 32:1, 1968.

Livson, N., and Peskin, H. The prediction of adult psychological health in a longitudinal study. *Journal of Abnormal Psychology*, 72:509-518, 1967.

MacFarlane, J. From infancy to adulthood. *Childhood Education*, 39:336-342, 1963.

MacFarlane, J. Perspectives on personality consistency and change from the Guidance Study. *Vita Humana*, 7:115, 1964.

MacFarlane, J. The dilemmas of adolescents. Paper for American Academy of Pediatrics, 1967.

Peskin, H. Pubertal onset and ego functioning: a psychoanalytic approach. *Journal of Abnormal Psychology*, 72:1-15, 1967.

Stewart, L., and Livson, N. Smoking and rebelliousness: a longitudinal study from childhood to maturity. *Journal of Consulting Psychology*, 30:325-329, 1966.

154

An Anthropological Investigation of Child-Rearing Practices and Adult Personality

Investigator:
John W. M. Whiting, Ph.D.
Harvard University
Cambridge, Mass.

Co-contributor:
Shulamith M. Gunders

Prepared by:
Herbert Yahraes

John W. M. Whiting and fellow workers at Harvard and elsewhere have searched the world over for more information on some of the forces that turn a child—born with the same potentialities, on the average, as other children—into an adult typical of the society in which he has been reared.

The research is a study of certain child-rearing practices and their effect upon adult personalities and behavior. But it differs from most other studies having the same objective. These other investigations generally assume that parents, in bringing up children, have theories as to what is good and bad for a child's development and that these theories are influenced by unconscious motives and anxieties. The work of Dr. Whiting and his group, on the other hand, is based on the idea that differences in child-rearing practices are imposed by differences in certain aspects of the physical and social environment.

A good deal of evidence has been collected in support of the Whiting group's idea. Much of it comes from analyses of data collected by other anthropologists in earlier studies, but the results are supported by more recent field investigations, of which the most important is the Six-Culture Study directed by Dr. Whiting, Irvin L. Child of Yale, and William W. Lambert of Cornell. For this work, six pairs of anthropologists spent a year observing child-rearing practices in six widely different cultures: a Gusii community in Kenya, Africa; a Mextec Indian community in the state of Oaxaca, Mexico; a community of Tarongans in the Philippines; a village of Okinawans; a neighborhood of families of the Rajput caste in

155

the province of Uttar Pradesh, India; and a group of New England families in a village identified as "Orchard Town." The fieldwork, done in the mid-1950's, was financed by the Ford Foundation; the analysis of the results, partly completed, is being supported by Dr. Whiting's grant from the institute.

John Whiting is professor of social anthropology at Harvard; his co-principal investigator, who is also his wife, Dr. Beatrice B. Whiting, is a lecturer in the same department. They plan to spend a year in Africa directing field studies to add to and verify the most important of the observations and interpretations made by themselves and their fellow workers.

"Our aim," John Whiting explains, "is to investigate the process by which a child learns the moral rules of his society in such a way that he will not deviate from them even when the probabilities of his getting caught are minimal—in other words, the inculcation of self-control."

He believes a high degree of self-control may have a variety of causes, among them (a) an exaggerated and paranoid fear of others, (b) belief in an all-seeing and all-powerful God who is concerned with the moral behavior of mankind, and (c) effective training for the parental role. The investigators are particularly interested in this third cause and have given it the bulk of their attention. By "training" they do not mean a series of instructions and examples specifically intended to help fit a girl to carry out a woman's role, or a boy a man's; they mean, most of all, the process by which a child identifies with an adult and, therefore, consciously and unconsciously, tries to be like him, and they also mean the characteristics of a society that affect this process.

The work suggests how differences in certain child-rearing customs lead to differences in certain adult characteristics. It throws light on the process of learning, and in doing so points to what may be a fundamental cause of much juvenile delinquency. "Many of the casualties in our mental hospitals and jails," says Whiting, "probably would have been spared if we had had a better understanding of the complex process of socialization." That's what he is trying to provide.

The investigators' main findings and conjectures are summarized below and presented in more detail in later sections of this report.

A Summary of the Results

1. Cross-cultural surveys offer a support for John Whiting's basic hypothesis—that status envy is a prime force in the development for personality. A child most envies the person who can withhold the resources he values most highly, the hypothesis says, and therefore, he tries to identify with this person. In monogamous societies where the father is home, a male child generally identifies with the father. But where the father is not home, and particularly in societies where mother and child sleep together —and the father elsewhere—during a long post partum sex taboo, a boy's primary identification may well be feminine. The evidence for this is

found in (*a*) the results of various tests for cross-sex identity; (*b*) a display of "hypermasculinity"—a bending over backward to prove themselves men—among certain groups of boys from father-absent or father-weak homes; (*c*) the practice of strenuous male puberty rites—considered a type of brainwashing—in societies whose household structure and other factors would lead to the prediction that a boy's identification would be with women. The investigators believe that these findings may explain much of the aberrant behavior in our own society.

2. Most monogamous societies rated high on an index of guilt; most polygynous societies, low. John Whiting believes that in a monogamous household, a boy is more likely to develop a conscience based on his father's, and that a man's conscience is stronger and more unforgiving than a woman's.

3. Training against aggression tends to be most severe in families where the household comprises not only parents and children but also a number of their kinfolk. The investigators believe that severe training stems from the desire of the adults to steer clear of unpleasantness likely to arise from the children's fights.

4. Training for independence, too, appears to be related to household structure. As measured by early weaning and by reduced contact between mother and child, it is found most often in nuclear households—those comprised of the father, the mother, and the children. Such training, Whiting thinks, probably (*a*) leads a child to grow up with the urge to be successful and (*b*) is necessary to enable a couple to establish their home.

5. Evidence is offered that the type of task assigned a young child— under 10—affects his personality. The most responsible children in the six-culture study were those who had to take care of younger children, and this babysitting job seemed to be related to the amount of outside work the mother had to do.

6. Everywhere in the six-culture study, boys were rougher than girls and wandered farther from home, and girls rated higher on a responsibility measure. Girls were more responsible than boys (and women in general show more sensitivity than men), Beatrice Whiting surmises, because they were more often assigned the care of younger children.

7. A probable link is reported, too, between the kind of tasks assigned a child and the kind of supernatural power the culture believes in. Societies where a child's work is to care for children or cattle, with the results of failure being immediate and dramatic and punishment severe, tend also to be societies where the supernaturals punish a person here and now. Where the main tasks are household chores and schoolwork, there is a tendency to believe in supernaturals who punish only in an afterlife.

8. Some evidence is found that polygyny arises from a long post partum sex taboo, and that the taboo in turn is related to a diet so poor that the mother fears to conceive until the nursing child has been weaned, which may not be for several years.

9. Certain kinds of stress during infancy—including inoculation, circumcision, and periodic separation from the mother during the first days of life—appear to be related to adult stature. In societies practicing

these kinds of stress, the average adult is significantly taller than in other societies. The investigators hope to learn whether or not psychological differences also occur—as they do in rats.

The investigators emphasize that the findings summarized here are based almost entirely on studies of cultures, many of them primitive, other than our own, but there is evidence that some of the conclusions—especially concerning the effect of the father's absence—apply here, too. Study of other cultures is an essential means of discovering universal truths about personality and behavior.

Status Envy as the Unconscious Motivation for Behavior

The most important mechanism shaping the development of a child's conscience—or, in psychoanalytic terms, superego—and an important factor in his behavior throughout life, John Whiting believes, is status envy. According to this hypothesis, the child envies the person who withholds resources from him or deprives him of them. The child thereupon seeks to identify himself with this person; that is, tries to learn to act like this person so that he, too, can become a controller of resources.

Resources include food, water, love, power, freedom from pain—anything somebody wants. Every society has a status system under which persons at a certain level have privileged access to resources while persons at another level do not. The conditions for status envy arise even during infancy, for no matter how everloving a parent may wish to be, there are times when he or she must withhold something the baby wants.

As Whiting views it, the oedipal situation, so prominent in psychoanalytic theory, is merely a special case of the status envy hypothesis. Under the psychoanalytic interpretation, the boy child vies with his father for the mother's love; under Whiting's interpretation, the boy child simply envies his mother—and therefore, identifies with her for a time—because she can dispense to other persons a resource, love, he wants for himself.

The more a child envies the status of another with respect to the control of a given resource, Whiting believes, the more he will practice that role—openly perhaps, but certainly covertly, meaning that he will indulge in a fantasy in which he sees himself as the envied person controlling and consuming the valued resources of which he has been deprived. It is this fantasy of being someone other than himself that Whiting defines as identification. As a simple example, when a child wants to stay up late, but his parents make him go to bed, he may say to himself, "I wish I were grown up. Perhaps if I acted as they do, I would be." And he thinks about grownup behavior as he goes to sleep.

Further, the child will tend to manipulate resources as his parents have manipulated them with him; for instance, if he has been given resources when he had a special need for them—such as solace when he was hurt and assurance when he was frightened—he will respond the same way to his fellows when they are hurt or frightened. The child also will tend to respond to the naughty behavior of others as his parents have responded

158

to his; and, having taken on the parents' role through status envy, he will punish himself as well as others.

In some cultures the investigators suspect a strong tendency for a child to identify with his mother during at least the early years. Depending on who controls which resources, however, he may well identify with both parents. If, for example, the mother has primary control of food and love whereas the father controls the power to administer or to withhold physical punishment, the theory predicts that the child will identify with both parents but with respect to different resources. He will take after his mother with respect to love and affection; after his father with respect to power and authority.

All cultures have rules concerning status that differ considerably from the desires of a growing child. For instance, a child is supposed to act neither like a baby nor a grownup; a boy is not supposed to be a sissy, nor a girl a tomboy. Hence the desire to play certain roles of envied statuses may lie latent for years. "It has often been noted," Whiting observes, "that a mother will frequently respond to her first child exactly as her own mother had treated her, even though she is not aware of practicing such behavior, and, in fact, may even have vociferously sworn that she was going to bring up her children differently. This suggests that covert practice of envied roles may often be disguised and unconscious."

The idea that children identify with the persons close to them who control valued resources is not new, but John Whiting has done more than anyone else to seek confirmatory evidence and has supplied the name by which the hypothesis is now generally known.

The Problem of a Conflict Over Sex Identity

Development of the status-envy hypothesis has pushed Whiting into fascinating speculations for which he has tried to find a solid basis in the child-training arrangements and the behavior characteristics of numerous cultures, including some in the United States.

The speculations so far have centered on cross-sex identity. If a mother has had control of all the resources a young boy values, Whiting's theory says he will envy her status and try to perform her role. Part of the behavior that he seeks to emulate, though, is sex-typed and forbidden. "Such a boy finds himself in dire conflict," the investigator says. "He may practice feminine-role behavior despite the sanctions against it, or, if the sanctions are too compelling, inhibit his impulses to perform such behavior. The theory predicts, however, that he would continue to practice covertly and would thus have a feminine self-image."

As a test of these views, the investigators analyzed sleeping arrangement in a sample of 64 societies. If a boy sleeps alone with his mother during his first years, covering the nursing period, the reasoning went, he will come to consider her as all-important and, because she sometimes withholds resources, as the person to be envied. So his primary identification, or the type acquired during infancy, will be feminine. If he then, after weaning, enters a world in which men are obviously the important persons, able to bestow or to withhold the most valued resources, the boy's secondary identification, acquired during childhood, will be masculine.

In such a case, the reasoning continued, the boy's conflict over sex identity should be especially severe, so severe, in fact, that society would step in to resolve it and assure him beyond any doubt of his masculinity. This would be done through elaborate male initiation rites at puberty, including circumcision and tests of strength and endurance—all serving, in the investigators' words, "to brainwash the primary feminine identity and to establish firmly the secondary male identity."

Native theory is offered in support of this interpretation. Most societies having male initiation rites, the investigators report, have one word referring to all women and uninitiated boys and another word referring only to initiated males. In these societies a boy is born twice; first into woman-child status and then, at puberty, into the status of manhood.

From the sample studied, 13 societies were found to have such rites. In all 13, mother and infant slept together and alone. (For the most part, these were polygynous societies, with a long post partum sex taboo. When a wife had a nursing baby, the father slept in another wife's house or in the men's quarters.) And 12 of the 13 were patrilocal societies, in which the domestic unit comprises a group of closely related male and a group of unrelated females brought in from other villages as wives; in such societies prestige and power are clearly vested in the men.

There are numerous cases, however, where the secondary as well as the primary identification should be feminine because the child not only sleeps alone with his mother during infancy but also grows up in a matrilocal world, controlled by his mother, his aunts, and his maternal grandmother. Such a society, the investigators reasoned, should give a man some means to act out, symbolically at least, the female role, and they found such a means in the custom known as the couvade. Under this custom, during the period just preceding or following the birth of a child, the husband takes to bed, fasts or limits himself to certain foods, undergoes a purification ceremony, and in general accepts the same attention as his wife.

Childbirth epitomizes the uniquely feminine part of a woman's role. "When a man attempts to participate in the birth of his child by closely imitating the behavior of his wife," say the researchers, "this should be a good index of his wish to act out the feminine role and thus symbolically to be in part a woman."

The Harvard anthropologists found the couvade a common practice in 12 societies in their sample. In 10 of these, mother and infant slept together, and in nine, because of the matrilocal residence pattern, women even after the nursing period controlled the resources most valued by a growing child.

"Masculine Protest" Behavior and the Absent Father

In another test of the theory, a husband-and-wife team from Harvard, Robert L. and Ruth H. Munroe, recently studied the Black Carib of

British Honduras. This group springs from escaped Negro slaves who assimilated the culture of the natives, the Island Carib, of St. Vincent, in the Caribbean, and then spread over the coastline of the Gulf of Honduras, in Central America.

As practiced by the Black Carib, the couvade involves a number of restrictions on the father's ordinary behavior, among them taboos on fishing and on extramarital intercourse. If the restrictions are violated, the Carib believes that the new born infant will get sick. But some fathers, the intensive-couvade group, observe many taboos; others, the weak-couvade group, only a few. The approximately 50 fathers studied fell about evenly into the two groups.

The investigators hypothesized that the groups had been brought up differently; specifically, that the intensive-couvade males had been under stronger female influence. This turned out to be correct: during the first 3 years of life the intensive-couvade group had spent more than twice as much time as the others in a household whose only adults were women.

But were these men really more feminine, psychologically, than the others? Cross-sex identity is a tricky thing to measure, but Whiting and some fellow workers had attempted to do it earlier—and successfully, they think—with the so-called magic man test. In this test, the subject is told to suppose that he can be anybody he wishes and is then asked who he would most like to be—a father, a mother, a son, a daughter, and so on. Then he is asked to make further choices. American males brought up in the usual household, with both father and mother attending to them from infancy, tend to choose all the male statuses first; American females, all the female statuses. But the earlier study had found that among youngsters with good reason to envy the status of the opposite sex, a number did make some cross-sex choices. Among the Black Carib, the Munroes found, males who practiced an intensive couvade chose to be a mother, a daughter, or a baby girl significantly more often than males who observed the couvade only weakly.

The Munroes also used the Semantic Differential Test, in which the subject is given a number of scales having contrasting adjectives at each end, like good and bad, fast and slow, and strong and weak, and is asked to use the scales to describe various persons. The men who observed the couvade most strongly tended to rate themselves on these scales the same way they rated women.

There were still other discriminating factors. Black Carib men and women show certain linguistic differences; men, for example, tend to use a different word than women for "yesterday." Asked to translate from English to Carib, the intensive couvade men used female words significantly more often than the other men. Further, when their wives were pregnant, the intensive couvade men experienced many more pregnancy symptoms than the others. Male pregnancy symptoms, which have been found in all societies where they have been asked about, are believed by these investigators to have the same psychological implications as the couvade itself.

161

If all this seems a little beside the point, it may be recalled that numerous investigators have found links between family conditions and juvenile delinquency. The Harvard group is now offering evidence that the specific problem is the mother-present, father-absent or father-weak household structure during the first years of life, because in such a home a boy originally identifies with women and then later on may go overboard to prove his masculinity. This cross-cultural research may, then, explain an underlying cause of much juvenile delinquency, alcoholism, and other aberrant behavior.

Beatrice Whiting puts the matter this way:

If during the first 2 or 3 years of life a child is constantly with his mother and infrequently sees, and is handled by, his father, he will identify strongly with his mother and not with his father; in short, if he is a boy he will have a cross-sex identification. If, later, in life, he is involved in a world in which men are perceived to be more prestigeful and powerful than women, he will be thrown into conflict. He will develop a strong need to reject his underlying female identity. This may lead to an overdetermined attempt to prove his masculinity, manifested by a preoccupation with physical strength and athletic prowess, or attempts to demonstrate daring and valor, or behavior that is violent and aggressive.

A boy's attempt to prove his masculinity has been used to explain the high rate of juvenile delinquency among Negroes in lower-class neighborhoods. John Whiting points in particularly to a study concluding that the Negro juvenile gang member rejects femininity in every form—"and he sees it in women and in effeminate men, in laws and morals and religion, in schools and occupational striving."[1] And a study of the correlates of crime in 48 societies found that lack or limitation of opportunity for young boys to form an identification with their fathers was associated with a higher frequency of theft, assault, rape, murder, and other crimes.[2]

The new developments by the Harvard group are the elaboration of the status-envy hypothesis as an explanation of masculine-protest behavior and the finding of such behavior, linked with father-missing households, during field studies. As one important example, the Munroes found it among the Black Carib. The men who practiced the couvade most intensively were described by the people of the town as braver men, heavier drinkers, and more frequent cursers than the others. "In the day-to-day situation," the investigators report, "the intensive-couvade men were prototypes of the rugged male."

Carrying their work to the United States, the Munroes then examined the exhaustive records of 200 men whose wives had given birth at a Boston hospital. The records were exhaustive because they were part of the comprehensive, long-time perinatal study—an inquiry into early conditions associated with later defects—sponsored by the National Institute of Neurological Diseases and Blindness. The men were white and from a variety of racial stocks and socioeconomic levels. Forty percent of the

---

[1] Rohrer, J. H., and Edmonson, M. S. "The Eighth Generation." New York: Harper, 1960.

[2] Bacon, Margaret K., Child, I. K., and Barry, H., III. A cross-cultural study of correlates of crime. *J. Abnorm. Soc. Psychol.*, 1963, 66.

husbands reported that they had experienced common pregnancy symptoms—for example, nausea, vomiting, toothache, and food cravings. About 30 of these men and their wives were studied, as were a group similar in size and general characteristics except that the husbands had had no pregnancy symptoms.

The men who had had symptoms, the team reports, tended to respond more like females, as compared with the other men, on a number of measures—on the way they completed a drawing, for example, on their preferences in television programs, and on their attitudes toward children. The men with symptoms had been happier about the coming event, and they usually spent more time feeding, bathing, and caring for their children than the other men. But on a scale dealing with typically female activities, such as cooking, washing dishes, and setting the table, the symptomatology group reported significantly less participation than the others. This indicated, the investigators believe, a shift toward hyper-masculinity in the case of activities clearly associated with the other sex.

But the payoff is this. The men were asked if, during their early years, their fathers had been gone from home, permanently or for long periods of time. In many cases they had been, because of divorce, death, or jobs that had taken them out of town. The men with pregnancy symptoms had experienced a significantly greater loss in this respect than the others.

In sum, male pregnancy symptoms have been linked by the Munroes to cross-sex identity in two widely different cultures. This suggests to the investigators and their Harvard associates that these symptoms may eventually prove to be a widely usable measure of a man's identification with the opposite sex. If so, the Harvard group's attempt to prove or disprove the idea that a person's primary identification is with the adult who controls the resources he most wants in early childhood would be considerably eased. This is because the results of tests to uncover a person's primary identification are hard to verify. The presence or absence of pregnancy symptoms in adult males would be a welcome check on the other tests and hopefully could even serve alone.

Several investigators elsewhere have compared the families of Norwegian sailors, gone from home, often for 2 years or more, with families in which the fathers were present. The mothers in the sailor families were found to lay greater stress on obedience—instead of happiness and self-realization—than the other mothers. And the boys tended to be infantile and dependent and to behave in overly masculine ways. John Whiting hopes to learn someday what happens to these boys. He would not be surprised if, during adolescence, they become sailors themselves. Sailing is an occupation suitable for a man who places a high value on obedience, he says; further, on an extended voyage, it permits a man to engage in certain work—such as cleaning one's quarters and sewing—associated with the female role. And Whiting suspects that during their first voyage these boys may have to undergo a rather severe initiation ceremony—analogous to the male puberty rites in many primitive societies, particularly those where a young child has unusual opportunity to identify with females.

The idea that the puberty rites serve to strengthen a boy's masculine identification will be checked in the field during the Whitings' African year. The rites—held in what anthropologists call bush schools, remote from the settlement—continue for days and even weeks and can be extremely exhausting physically and psychologically. In one reported case, the young men returning to their village were at first unable to recognize its inhabitants. Whiting proposes to administer a number of psychological tests to candidates shortly before the initiation ceremonies, and then again afterward. He expects to find a number of cross-sex identifications the first time; very few, if any, the second.

In addition to household structure during infancy, this research group emphasizes, prominent elements affecting adult personality are the relative importance of the sexes as a child grows up and the personal attributes a culture values most highly. Among people in the lower socioeconomic levels in the United States, the Whitings note, the growing boy is likely to perceive men as clearly the more powerful and the more to be envied; so if his primary identification is feminine, his conflict should be unusually severe. But among the middle and upper classes, male dominance is less clear, so the conflict for a boy who has made an initial feminine identification may be small. Beatrice Whiting refers to a study of college boys who spent the first 2 years of their lives with their mothers, their fathers being overseas in World War II.[3] These boys were found to have feminine attributes but to be neither anxious nor defensive about them. The suggested reason is that academic and intellectual circles place a high value on sensitivity, aesthetic interests, verbal ability, and certain other characteristics usually considered more typical of the female than the male.

Answers must still be sought to the following questions, as listed by John Whiting and a former associate, Roger V. Burton, now at NIMH:

Are there times when the absence of a father is more critical than at other times?

How long does it take for a child to establish identity?

How do the effects of a weak father compare with those of an absent father?

What is the effect of an absent father on the development of a girl?

Violence and Aggression in the Six Cultures

Further support for the status-envy idea comes from Beatrice Whiting's recent analysis of violence among the societies covered in the six-culture study. Two of these societies—the Gusii tribe of Kenya, Africa, and members of the Rajput caste in Uttar Pradesh, India—were found to have, as compared with the other four, an unusual amount of violence. The men in the Rajput sample of a few dozen families had been involved in 59

---

[3]Carlsmith, Karolyn Kuckenberg. Effect of early father absence on scholastic aptitude. Ph.D. dissertation, 1963, Harvard.

court cases, 17 of them concerning incidents that had taken a violent turn, leading in three instances to homicide. The Gusii sample—most of whose men had been involved in at least one court case—remembered seven instances of violence between men they could name and numerous others involving men they could not name. The other societies, in contrast, reported very few if any such instances. Among the Okinawans, the study's fieldworkers commented upon "the absence of crime and the low incidence of quarrels, disputes, and brawls." The Mixtecans seemed to fear aggression; children were told that if they became angry and then ate, they would die. In Luzon, the Philippines, there was a good deal of quarreling but scarcely any physical violence. In "Orchard Town," New England, as in these other cultures, assault and homicide cases involving the people studied or anyone they knew by name were exceedingly rare.

Besides the impression that the Rajputs and the Gusii were unusually aggressive, something else differentiated them from the people in the other four cultures. In neither of the aggressive groups was it customary for husband and wife to work, play, eat, or even—in the sense of occupying the same room—sleep together.

Most of the Gusii in the sample studied are polygynous. The huts they build for each of their wives have a special section, with its own entrance, for the exclusive use of the husband. The husband either rotates among these huts or sleeps in a special house, which he may share with his unmarried sons who have undergone the puberty rites. He seldom, if ever, visits a wife with a nursing baby.

Among the Rajputs, the men of a household sleep in a separate structure. When a husband visits his wife, they go to an unused room, or, more likely, a deserted part of the courtyard, within whose walls the wife spends most of her young married life, along with her female in-laws. After a child is born, the husband is not supposed to visit his wife for 2 or 3 years, a taboo which is by no means universally observed.

In both of these cultures, then, the world of the infant is largely a women's world. For his first several years, the young child sees his father only infrequently. But when he is able to move beyond the immediate circle of his mother, the child begins to perceive that the really important people are the men. "The Rajput 3-year-old must notice that the women get down on the floor and cover their heads every time a male enters the courtyard," notes Beatrice Whiting. "The hungry 3-year-old in Nyansongo (the Gusii community) must have looked with longing at the basket of food prepared for his father. He must have learned that his father has a private world in his special room or house. He knows that when he is older he will sleep with his brothers and his father, and will be initiated with other boys in a ceremony from which all women are excluded." Hence it is in the Rajput and Gusii cultures that the status-envy theory would predict protest masculinity, and it is in these two cultures that it seems to be most evident, as indicated by the extent of physical violence. "For the little boys brought up in the other four societies," the investigator observes, "the problem of male control in the world of the 3- to 6-year-olds in not theoretically relevant, as they have already had a chance to identify with males. They have seen men and women interact in intimate settings since birth. Moreover, even if they have made a strong feminine identification, there will be less conflict later in life since the importance of men and women will be more nearly equal and the contrast between the behavior and personal profiles of the sexes will be less."

The Mormons, the Texans, and the Zuni

Status envy and cross-sex identity presumably apply to girls as well as boys but have been little tested with them. In one of the very few studies including tests of both sexes, John Whiting and a group of associates observed members of three different cultures living close to one another in western New Mexico—Mormons, homesteaders from Texas, and Zuni Indians. The fieldwork, part of a larger investigation supported by the Rockefeller Foundation, was done in 1950 but the analysis was completed only recently.

The children given the magic-man test were in grades three to six. Among the Mormon girls, 23 percent chose to be males—reflecting, the investigators report, the relatively high status of men among Mormons. Among the Zuni boys, 10 percent chose to be girls, reflecting the relatively high status of women among the Zuni. There were no cross-sex choices by the Texas children, which came as no surprise because Texan men and women were regarded by the investigators as having relatively equal status.

The effect of cross-sex identification among some of the Mormon girls—assuming of course that the magic-man test is a valid indicator of it—is not known. But there is some evidence from studies of lower-class families by other investigators that girls brought up in mother-child households become more dominant and aggressive than girls reared in households where both the father and the mother are present. Perhaps this is the result of a secondary identification, Beatrice Whiting suggests, arising from the perception that men in lower-class neighborhoods clearly have more power than women. Or perhaps it is the result of a primary identification with a mother who has some masculine characteristics because, without a man, she has to fend for herself.

In any event, the New Mexico study offers interesting examples of the relationship between the structure of a family and the way children are brought up.

The Zuni, as one main instance, emphasized rigid training for the control of aggression. Was this because of some innate love of harmony? Not at all, the investigators say, after a look into history. The Zuni originally lived in single-family houses but by 1300 these had been replaced by the great pueblos, perhaps because of invading Apaches. Crowded living conditions and, especially, the requirement that several women share in the running of the household, led to an emphasis on harmony. In a worldwide sample of 30 societies, 92 percent of those with extended families—this is, households comprising not only parents and children but also a variety of relatives—rated above the median in the

166

severity with which aggressive manisfestations by the children were punished. Only 22 percent of the nuclear family households—parents and children—were equally severe. Punishment for aggression, John Whiting believes, is directly tied in with the desire of adult kinfolk, by blood or marriage, to steer free of squabbles likely to be engendered by their children's fights.

This view gains strength from a recent analysis (by Leigh Minturn, University of Illinois, and William Lambert, Cornell) of the data concerning the mothers in the six-culture study. All the mothers show some concern for the quarrels of their children, but the Mixtec mothers are the most concerned, and the New England mothers the least.

The adults in the Mixtec sample, the investigators observe, are highly interdependent, with many close kinship ties. Brothers and their families generally live around a common courtyard, where the children play; relatives look to one another for help with their work and for financial assistance. Consequently, the Mixtec mothers teach their children to be unaggressive. Physical punishment is used to punish aggression more commonly than it is used for any other type of behavior. Sometimes, to prevent fights, children are even kept home from school. One result is that Mixtec adults are unaggressive and unusually slow to take offense.

The New England families, on the other hand, are the only group whose members are not living next door to relatives and whose livelihood does not depend upon the support of their neighbors. This means that they can ignore their neighbors if they cannot get along with them; it also means they have no claims of kinship to cement relationships in case they do want to be friends with their neighbors. Under these circumstances, a mother is likely to tell her child to go play with somebody else if he can't get along with the children next door; she also seems reluctant to complain to her neighbors on behalf of her children.

The investigators emphasize that New England mothers punish children if they instigate aggression or if they attack younger children even though provoked. More than any other group of mothers in the study, they are concerned that children learn the rules of "fair fighting" and the occasions that justify retaliation.

As another example of the influence of household structure upon child training practices, the homesteaders from Texas, in the earlier study, exerted early and strong pressure for self-reliance and independence—pressure, say the investigators, that does not spring from an innate desire for their children to be successful but is related, like the Zuni and Mixtec training against aggression, to living conditions. In the Texans' case, events had brought a swing away from the extended family, a feature of Great Britain in Elizabethan times. The male head of this extended family had been in full control, and child-rearing practices had included relatively late weaning, at two years, and swaddling, which hampered movement. "Dependence was more valued than independence," the investigators observe, "and obedience was strictly demanded."

But this type of family fell upon hard times in America, where, because of the problems of the new environment, achievement came to be valued and patriarchal authority was challenged. The major concern of the Texan parent, in contrast to that of the Elizabethan, is that the child may be excessively dependent.

This difference between the Elizabethan and the Texan families is apparently not unique. In a sample of 30 cultures, the median age for the beginning of independence training—as judged by the time when there is reduced contact between mother and child—was found in nuclear households to be 18 months; for all other households it is 30 months. One of the factors believed to figure most importantly in independence training is time of weaning. A survey of the information about 52 societies the world over found that weaning began at less than a year in only two, the Chamarros and the Marquesans, of the South Pacific. Among the Texan mothers studied, the average age was less than 9 months. (The Zuni mothers weaned at the age of 2 or 3; the Mormon mothers, earlier than the Zuni but later than the Texan.) With respect to child-rearing practices that promote a strong drive for success, the investigators report, these Texan homesteaders are extreme.

John Whiting and his co-workers consider the Mormons an especially interesting case. Historically these people had retained the patriarchal features of the Elizabethan family but adopted polygyny and the mother-child household. Closely correlated with polygyny the world over is the post patrum sex taboo, and this was so with the Mormons. Although definite evidence is lacking, the anthropologists think the Mormons probably adopted another feature usually found in polygynous mother-child households, the practice of mother and infant sleeping in the same bed.

Under such conditions, Whiting and other authorities have theorized in recent years, the mother unconsciously redirects her sexual interest toward her child during the period of the post partum taboo. Then, in compensation, and in line with the universal taboo against incest, she joins with the father in a strong effort to control the boy's sexual impulses during childhood and adolescence.

If this is so, then sex training should be most severe in societies where mother and child sleep together. To test this hypothesis, 18 cultures were surveyed. Ten of these were found to be above the median in the severity with which sex behavior is punished in later childhood, and eight of these ten have the exclusive mother-child sleeping arrangement. In the eight cases where the father and mother sleep together and the infant sleeps elsewhere, sex training was found to be severe in only two.

The Mormons, of course, when this study was made, had long since adopted the standard American independent family structure and nuclear household. But some of the older practices still held: notably, the research team reports, the mothers had a warm, seductive relationship with their children (but worked to severely control sexual impulses and behavior in later childhood and adolescence). The dominant value in this culture was virtue, as it was harmony in the Zuni culture, and success in the Texan. And these values showed up when children were asked what they most wanted to be. The Texas children most wanted to be successful, and the

168

Mormon to be good, kind, or happy. The most popular Zuni choice was to be a man or woman, or, simply, a Zuni.

However, the investigators thought that the Mormons' change in social structure should be accompanied by a shift from virtue to success as the dominant value and along with this, more emphasis on independence and less on the control of sex. Considerable evidence was found that the Mormons studied in New Mexico were indeed moving in this direction: one-third of the sample could not be distinguished from the Texans in their child-rearing practices. The investigators predict that "in another generation the Mormon and Texan family structure and value system will be indistinguishable."

Monogamy, Economic Progress, Sin, and Guilt

In John Whiting's view, as the preceding section may have made clear, the association between monogamous societies and material progress is not happenstance but rooted in child-rearing practice. A new baby is taken into bed with his parents, and sooner or later the father says: "Why don't you wean that baby and get him started?" So there is an early pressure upon the child toward growing up, Whiting remarks, and this leads to a strong pressure toward achievement. In the polygynous society, on the other hand, there is no reason for the child to be weaned early. And, being in a happy state, why should he struggle for achievement? Contrary to a common notion, the relative lack of economic progress in polygynous societies—which include the great majority of those in Africa and many of those in the Middle East—has nothing to do with the cost of multiple wives, either in the bride price paid to acquire them or in the time, energy, or substance spent to keep them. "In polygynous societies, by and large," says Whiting, "wives are an economic asset, and a man can hardly afford not to have more than one."

Children in monogamous, nuclear-household societies, as compared with those in polygynous societies, tend to grow up not only with different ideas about the value of material progress but also, Whiting believes, with a different type of superego, or conscience. As the investigator explains his idea, a man's role calls for him to be strict and unforgiving; a man says: "A rule is a rule." But a woman's rule calls for her to be aware of contingencies and to exercise forgiveness; a woman says: "It all depends." So the male conscience is more strict than the female, and the child who acquires his conscience primarily through identification with a male finds it less easy to forgive himself than the child who acquires it primarily through identification with a female. The child whose primary identification has been with his father should, therefore, have more guilt feelings than the other child.

If this is so, Whiting goes on, people in monogamous societies, where the father plays a much stronger role early in a child's life, should have stronger guilt feelings than those in polygynous societies. To test this idea, the investigator grouped 28 societies by household structure and rated each one on an index of guilt, which was the extent to which a sick person

169

blames himself for his sickness. Whiting and Child had developed the index years before because self-recrimination as a response to illness seemed "a probably useful index of the degree to which guilt feelings are strong and widely generalized."

The results were as predicted: Most monogamous societies rated high on this index of guilt; most polygynous societies rated low. Further, the proportion of monogamous societies having high guilt levels was greater among those with nuclear household structure than among those with extended household structure, as might be expected because in the latter a child is likely to have a greater opportunity to identify with women. And among polygynous societies, the proportion was higher where the father lived with his wives and children in the same household than where mother and children lived by themselves.

In monogamous societies, then, as Whiting sees it, social control is achieved largely through the development of a strong—or male—conscience, which gives one a sense of guilt and a readiness to accept responsibility for one's actions. But throughout the world he finds two other independent systems at work to keep behavior within bounds. One is sorcery, whose believers are convinced that antisocial behavior will be punished by the magical power of others. Another is a sense of sin, or the belief that badness will be punished by a supernatural power.

As for belief in sorcery, the investigator finds that it tends to occur in societies where mother and child sleep together, and the father elsewhere, and where there is severe punishment for sexual behavior in childhood. This combination of circumstances, he believes, produces anxiety about sexual impulses, and the anxiety leads to a paranoid fear—very apparent in societies having a strong belief in sorcery—of retaliation from other humans.

As for a sense of sin, Whiting says that "the gods seem to reflect the parental treatment of children." He points to cross-cultural surveys by himself and others indicating that where children are relatively neglected during infancy—by not being fed as soon as hungry, for example—and punished severely for aggression in later years, the society typically dreads punishment by gods or ghosts; where the parents are more benevolent, the gods tend to be also.

Whiting is speaking in general terms. He believes that more than one of the systems—paranoid fear of retaliation by humans, dread of punishment by the gods, and a sense of guilt and personal responsibility—can act on one individual at the same time. But he also believes that one or another system will tend to be emphasized in a given culture, depending upon the child-rearing practices of that culture.

An Inquiry Into the Origin of Polygyny

Some of the basic determinants of personality appear to be related to the household structure, and the Whitings think that the household structure in turn—as suggested in the examples of the Zuni, the Mormons, and

170

the Texan homesteaders—is related to the environment. Recently John Whiting found himself trying to demonstrate this in the matter of polygyny, an inquiry beginning with the chance observation at Harvard's Laboratory of Human Development that societies practicing circumcision, generally as a part of male initiation rites, are not evenly distributed. Most of them are found in the tropics, but the records show none for the tropical regions of South America.

As noted earlier, male initiation rites occur most frequently in societies where mother and child sleep together and where a boy, therefore, according to the status-envy theory, may acquire a primary feminine identification. In turn, the mother-child sleeping arrangement occurs most often in societies with a long post partum sex taboo, and this taboo tends to be associated with polygyny. It leads to polygyny, Whiting suspects, rather than the other way around. But what leads to the taboo?

The tribesmen themselves generally explain that if a lactating woman has sexual intercourse, her milk will become sour or thin and her baby will get sick. The real explanation, Whiting conjectures, lies in the nursing mother's conscious or unconscious dread that she will conceive again and thereby endanger the life of the child she is nursing. There would be good reason for this dread if the mother was on such a poor diet that pregnancy would reduce the already low protein value of her milk below the danger point.

Combing through the records of diets the world over, Whiting found that the long sex taboo was found most frequently among societies with a diet low in protein, and that these low-protein societies were found most frequently in the rainy tropics, where the climate is conducive to the growing of low-protein root and fruit crops. The investigator assumes that a diet based largely upon such crops probably leads to a high incidence of a protein deficiency disease, kwashiorkor. Aware of this, at some level of consciousness, a mother avoids getting pregnant while she is lactating. And when she avoids it by abstinence, the husband is led to seek another wife. Thus Whiting—while emphasizing that his assessments of climate, nutrition, and health in many cases had to be crude—traces a connection between polygyny and climate. As to the polygynous societies in the South American tropics, he suggests that many of them practice abortion rather than abstinence as a means of child-spacing.

The Effect of Chores Upon Character

Analyzing the reports of the fieldworkers in the six-culture study, Beatrice Whiting finds further evidence to support her husband's thesis that child-rearing practices, and therefore personality, depend to an important extent upon certain fundamental characteristics of a society.

One of the important variables, the analysis suggests, is the kind of tasks a child is expected to do. The most responsible, from the standpoint of recognizing that something needed to be done and doing something, were those who were expected to take care of their younger brothers and sisters or of cousins. This babysitting chore seemed to be related, in turn, to the amount of work a woman was supposed to do outside the house. The highest ratings for responsibility went to the Gusii children of Nyansongo, in Kenya, and the Mixtecan children of Juxtlahuaca, Mexico. And in both these cultures the women had to be away from the house much of the day.

The children given the lowest ratings for responsibility were those of Khalapur, India, where baby tending was a common chore but the mothers were always home, and Orchard Town in New England, where the commonest chores were household tasks and the mothers did not ordinarily work outside the home while the children were young.

No matter what the culture, girls were scored higher on responsibility and nurturance than boys. If a young child was poking a knife at another youngster, for example, or needed help in crossing a road, it was an older sister who was more likely than an older brother to notice what was going on and take action. Such responsibility is a matter of training, Beatrice Whiting thinks, and has a lifelong influence. Specifically, in the six-culture study, it was found that children who were assigned the care of younger brothers and sisters at an early age were more nurturant and responsible about all younger children. Since girls are assigned this task more frequently than boys, it is not surprising that they score higher in both nurturance and responsibility.

This investigator finds other behavioral differences between girls and boys that hold true for all six cultures and can probably be considered universal sex differences. Boys are more aggressive; in spite of radical differences in the way they are brought up, the boys of all the cultures strike other persons more frequently and engage in more rough play than the girls. They are also more mobile. In the six cultures, little boys wander farther from home than little girls, and older boys stay away from home much more during the day than older girls. Mrs. Whiting is not sure whether or not the higher mobility of boys may be ascribed to differences in the way parents treat the two sexes. In all six cultures, the girls are assigned more household chores, so the girls must spend more time at home. Still, little boys may just naturally be more difficult to keep boxed in.

Differences in the chores assigned to the children may result not only in some of the personality differences between the sexes, Beatrice Whiting believes, but also in some of the differences in how societies view the supernatural. Her reasoning goes like this. If the chores involve for the most part the care of children or animals, the consequences of failure will be immediate and obvious. If a baby is left untended, for example, he may put noxious things in his mouth or fall and hurt himself; if cattle are left untended, they may get into the corn and eat an important part of the coming year's food. In contrast, the importance of getting the dishes washed or the house cleaned is less clear because results of failure are less dramatic. Household tasks must seem arbitrary as compared with baby-sitting or cattle tending, and schoolwork—whose importance must be taken largely on faith—must seem even more arbitrary. Mrs. Whiting believes that a child's view of the tasks and of the rewards and punishment associated with it will be generalized to his view of the nature of the world order, and this world view will be reflected in religious beliefs. Consequently, if children perceive their tasks as arbitrary, with major reward or punishment absent or remote, as in the case of schoolwork, the members of the society will tend to believe in a future life where rewards and punishments are handed out for the deeds done or not during this one. But if children know that failure to perform a task will be punished at once, the society is likely to believe that punishment by supernatural beings is meted out now rather than in a future life.

Two surveys of cultures believing that supernatural beings are concerned with the moral behavior of man give results viewed by the investigator as supporting these ideas. The first survey dealt with the effects of schools. Five of the 26 societies in this sample have schools, and all five believe in a future life where rewards and punishments are handed out for behavior in the present life. Of the 21 societies without schools, 14 do not believe in punishment in the future life. The second survey dealt with the effect of cattle raising. Thirteen of the 36 cultures in the sample are cattle-raising societies, and 12 of these believe that punishment by the supernatural is immediate. Half of the 22 societies that do not raise cattle believe that punishment by the supernaturals comes now; the other half, in a future life. "But certainly when we are dealing with such complex subjects," John Whiting remarks, "more factors are involved than the ones we've been chiefly concerned with."

Beatrice Whiting thinks there may well be a critical age—from about 3 to about 8—for the influence of task assignment. Her own research has dealt with children under 10. Older children have been inculcated with such values as cleanliness and orderliness, she observes, and they are better able to understand future goals; so household tasks and schoolwork will seem less arbitrary.

If certain facets of personality are indeed related to task assignment, Mrs. Whiting points out, one should expect to find wide personality differences within a society, particularly one like ours where the assignments show wide variations. Children who grow up in large families and have to help care for younger children; children whose tasks are obviously related to the economic welfare of the family, as in families with farms or grocery stores; and children in households where the mother works and where the children's failure to do the household chores results in chaos— all these should be different from children whose chores seem arbitrary and are frequently left undone and where such failure often goes unpunished, as was the case with the youngsters of Orchard Town.

The Relation Between Stress During Infancy and Adult Characteristics

Laboratory studies have shown that animals, particularly rats, subjected to an unusual amount of stimulation during infancy grow up better able to cope with stress, whether physiological or psychological, and to be significantly larger, too. The animals develop faster and they learn faster.

John Whiting and several members of his group—in particular, Thomas K. Landauer, now at Stanford, and Shulamith M. Gunders, now at Bar-Ilan University, Israel—have been much interested in learning whether or not the same thing applies to human beings, and why. If so, the implications might be tremendous. The findings might even point to a way of strengthening psychological health for a lifetime through a simple procedure during infancy.

The inquiry began as the narrowest of sidelines to the Harvard group's main efforts. It was undertaken because the chance to compare laboratory findings with the findings of "natural experiments," as contained in the reports on a number of cultures known to expose infants to certain stressful practices, seemed too good to pass up.

The stimulation found effective in animals has included exposure to cold and to electric shock, painful manipulations, and supposedly gentle handling—lifting the infant from the cage, stroking it for a few minutes, and then returning it. Apparently all such stimulation has a lasting effect on the endocrine gland system. Landauer and Whiting, leafing through the material on scores of societies, noted many practices that might be considered stressful to the human infant—among them, exposure to extreme heat or cold, the administration of emetics or enemas, scraping the skin with a shell or other sharp object, and tight swaddling. Then they compared the average height of adults in the societies engaging in these practices with that of adults in other societies.

Significant differences were found when children under the age of 2 were exposed to either one of two main classes of stress: (1) Piercing, which includes circumcision, inoculation, and piercing the nose, lips, or ears to receive an ornament, and (2) molding, which includes shaping the head and stretching the arms or legs, usually for cosmetic purposes. Out of 66 societies, the men in those that practiced either molding or piercing were more than two inches taller on the average than the men in the other societies. This relationship between infant stress and adult stature was found in every major geographical region and apparently was not influenced by either diet or climate. It held true for both women and men.

Further evidence comes from comparing two groups of individuals in the Fels Growth Study, which was begun in the late 1920's by the Fels Research Institute, Yellow Springs, Ohio, and is continuing. The aim is to learn what factors have helped shape the physiological and psychological characteristics of the 150 persons being studied. When the children were being selected for this work, John Whiting notes, the practice of early inoculation—before the age of 2—was just being introduced. So, as it happened, some of the children in the Fels group were inoculated early; others, not till they were much closer to school age. The Harvard team recently analyzed the records of these two groups and found that the individuals who had been inoculated before the age of 2 are now, as adults, significantly taller than would have been predicted from information on the stature of their parents.

174

Shulamith Gunders then took another look at the reports of the laboratory experiments with animals and noted that in every case, in order for the stress, or stimulation, to be applied, the infant animal had been separated from its mother. Perhaps, she reasoned, the crucial factor was to be found in this separation. For each of 75 societies scattered over the world she worked out a separation score on the basis of information about the baby and its mother during the first 2 weeks after birth—whether or not, for example, the baby was nursed by the mother, slept with his mother, and was extensively handled by people other than his mother.

Dr. Gunders' hunch proved out. In societies with high separation scores, meaning that mother and infant were separated comparatively often during the first 2 weeks, the average height of adult males was 65.8 inches; in the other societies it was 63.7 inches. (Males were used because the figures for them were more often available, but much the same difference was found for females.) As in the first survey, this difference was statistically significant at the .001 level; the likelihood that it had occurred by chance was 1 in 1,000.

The correlation between mother-infant separation and adult height held good whether or not a society subjected the young child to a physically painful type of stress. But where both types of experience occurred—separation from the mother, which is presumed to be stressful, and either piercing or molding—the difference in adult stature was especially marked. In societies whose infants were not stressed in either manner the average male height was 62.9 inches; it was 65.9 inches where the infants were stressed in both ways.

Recent work elsewhere with rats, the Harvard group notes, supports the notion that periodic separation from the mother during early infancy is stressful. In this research the crucial factor apparently was not the separation itself but the accompanying drop in body temperature (about 4 degrees C.) when the infant rats were exposed to room temperature. Exposing the rats to low temperature in the presence of the mother produced the same effects as removing them from the mother. Separating them from the mother under conditions—in an incubator—designed to maintain the body temperature produced no effect.

Physical stress and periodic separation from the mother in early infancy lead not only to taller men and women, John Whiting found, but also to an earlier start of menstruation. In a sample of 50 societies, the average age at menarche in those societies whose child-rearing practices include neither form of stress is 14 years; where one of these forms occur, the average is 13 years, 6 months; where both forms occur, it is 12 years, 9 months. Incidentally, no evidence at all was found to bear out "the folk belief that girls in the tropics mature early." So far as age at menstruation is concerned, neither diet nor closeness to the equator could be found to make any difference.

Dr. Gunders now wondered if there might not be a relationship between recent increases in height in a number of countries—including the United States and Japan—and the growing tendency over the last few decades to have babies born in hospitals, where they are separated from their mother more frequently than they would be at home. She has been trying to answer this finding among the Israelis who emigrated from Yemen. Before the move, a baby was usually born at home and spent the first several weeks with the mother, on her bed, during which time the mother was freed of all household duties. After their arrival in Israel, however, Yemenite women were gradually prevailed upon to give birth in maternity wards, where a baby is generally brought to his mother only at 4-hour intervals and only during the daytime. Dr. Gunders has started a long-term study of 300 Yemenites, born in Israel between 1950 and 1957, about half of them in maternity centers and the rest at home, where they were cared for during the first weeks in the traditional way. So far the investigator has analyzed the weight data for the first 4 years. At the age of 1 month the homeborn children were slightly heavier than the hospital-born, but the difference was not statistically significant. At the age of 1 year, the average hospital-born child was 363 grams heavier than the child born at home, and by the age of 4 this difference had increased to 1,097 grams or about 2½ pounds. Dr. Gunders believes she has ruled out all possible reasons for this highly significant weight difference—including possible differences in diet or in mothering—except early stimulation resulting from periodic mother-baby separation during infancy.

The two groups are to be followed through the years and compared on a number of measures. The hope is to learn if early separation, like that customary in most maternity wards, has psychological as well as physical consequences, as it has been shown to have in rats.

John Whiting intends to do a similar study in the United States. He points out that some hospitals now permit mothers to keep their new babies with them most of the time, and he thinks it will be possible to compare these children with those who spend most of their first few days in the usual central nursery. He expects to find both physical and psychological differences.

Research Grant: MH 1096
Date of Interviews: Nov. 1, 1966

References:

Burton, R. V., and Whitting, J. W. M. The absent father and cross-sex identity. *Merrill-Palmer Quart. Behav. Develpm.*, 1961, 7, 2, reprinted as A-277, "The Bobbs-Merrill Reprint in the Social Sciences," Bobbs-Merrill, Indianapolis.
Gunders, Shulamith M., and Whiting, J. W. M. The effects of periodic separation from the mother during infancy upon growth and development. *Congr. Anthrop. & Ethnol. Sci.*, 1964.
Gunders, Shulamith M., and Whiting, J. W. M. Separation from mother during infancy and physical growth—a cross-cultural study. Unpublished manuscript, 1966.
Landauer, T. K., and Whiting, J. W. M. Infantile stimulation and adult nature of human males. *Amer. Antrop.*, 1964, 66, 5.
Minturn, Leigh, and Lambert, W. W. *Mothers of six cultures: Antecedents of child rearing.* New York: John Wiley & Sons, 1964.
Munroe, R. L., Munroe, Ruth H., and Whiting, J. W. M. Structure and sentiment: Evidence from recent studies of the couvade. Amer. Anthrop. Assoc. meeting, 1965.

Whiting, Beatrice B. (Ed.), *Six cultures: Studies of child rearing.* New York: John Wiley & Sons, 1963.
Whiting, Beatrice B. Task assignment and character development. Unpublished manuscript, 1962.
Whiting, Beatrice B. Sex identity conflict and physical violence: A comparative study. *Amer. Anthrop.,* 1965, 67, 6.
Whiting, J. W. M. Socialization process and personality. In Francis L. K. Hsu (Ed.), *Psychological anthropology: approaches to culture and personality.* Homewood, Ill.: The Dorsey Press, 1951.
Whiting, J. W. M. Sorcery, sin, and the superego: A cross-cultural study of some mechanisms of social control. In *Nebraska Symposium on Motivation.* Univ. of Nebr. Press, 1959.
Whiting, J. W. M. Resource, mediation and learning by identification. In Ira Iscoe and H. W. Steven (Eds.) *Personality development in children.* Austin, Tex.: Univ. of Tex. Press, 1960.
Whiting, J. W. M. Effects of climate upon certain cultural practices. In W. Goodenough (Ed.), *Explorations in cultural anthropology.* New York: McGraw Hill, 1964.
Whiting, J. W. M. Menarcheal age and infant stress in humans. In F. A. Beach (Ed.), *Sex and Behavior.* New York: John Wiley & Sons, 1965.
Whiting, J. W. M., Chasdi, Eleanor H., Antonovsky, Helen F., and Ayres, Barbara C. The learning of values. In E. Z. Vogt and Ethel M. Albert (Eds.), *People of Rimrock: a study of values in five cultures.* Cambridge: Harvard Univ. Press, 1966.
Whiting, J. W. M., and Whiting, Beatrice B. Contributions on anthropology to the methods of studying child rearing. In P. H. Mussen (Ed.), *Handbook of research methods in childhood development.* New York: John Wiley & Sons, 1960.

The Effects of Early Experience on a Child's Development

Investigator:
Bettye M. Caldwell, Ph.D.*
Syracuse University
Syracuse, N.Y.

Prepared by:
Herbert Yahraes

A Syracuse research team has studied the learning characteristics of children from 1 month of age to 3 years and hopes to relate these characteristics to certain features of the home environment and also to the children's mental development. To prevent the retardation often seen in children from the lowest socioeconomic level, two types of intervention are being tested: an excellent day-care program beginning when a child is as young as 6 months and a parent-education program that includes a moving picture, produced under the grant, showing mothers what a baby can do and how his family can help him develop interests and skills. Early results indicate that about half the children under 6 months respond to conditioning procedures, that the day-care project quickly leads to some increase in IQ's and that IQ increases also occur among babies living in homes rated high on a stimulation inventory.

When children are very young, one group will perform much the same as another on developmental tests, regardless of social or racial origin. Beginning somewhere between 18 months and 2 years, however, the curve representing the performance of children from the lowest socioeconomic level begins to drop and from then on these children as a group score significantly lower than other children on measures of ability and achievement.

Commenting upon these findings by a number of investigators, a New York State research team points out that evidently something happens, or fails to happen, during a critical period early in life to stunt the intellectual development of disadvantaged children. Consequently, they enter school with a handicap many of them can never overcome.

Why the difference? What happens or doesn't happen? How can the situation be changed?

The answers are being sought in a many-angled research program undertaken by Dr. Bettye M. Caldwell, professor of child development and education at Syracuse University, and Dr. Julius B. Richmond, dean of the

*Now at the Center for Early Development and Education, University of Arkansas, Little Rock, Arkansas

178

College of Medicine and chairman of the Department of Pediatrics, Upstate Medical Center, State University of New York. If the answers can be found, these investigators point out, they can be used to develop more effectively one of the Nation's most vital resources, the intelligence of its people, and at the same time to promote mental health by combating an important source of dissatisfaction with one's self and with society.

One branch of the program seeks information on how the learning process develops between the first month and the third year of life and how differences in development are influenced by differences in the pattern of family care. Concurrently the investigators are testing one proposed means of preventing deficits in learning ability. This is through a program of "massive intervention," as Dr. Caldwell describes it, in the form of excellent care 5 days a week in the research group's children's center.

The day-care project, made possible by a grant from the Children's Bureau, differs substantially from most other enrichment programs for deprived children in these respects:

1. The project sets the minimum age for admittance at 6 months instead of the usual 3 or 4 years. This is because the investigators are convinced that sensitivity to enrichment declines with age. "The very early years represent a crucial period for the prevention of learning deficits," they report. "Instead of devising methods of reversing the decline, it would be wiser and perhaps more economical to devise ways of blocking the process of decline before it has begun to alter the organism's adaptive capacity."

2. The project offers "programmed care" by a staff of teachers and nurses far larger, in proportion to the number of children, than usual: one adult to about every four children. The goal is to help each child become as aware as possible of the world around him, eager to participate in it, and confident that what he does will have some impact on it.

Preliminary findings suggest that this particular form of manipulating the environment does influence the learning process. Approximately 30 children who had attended the center for at least 3 months showed an average IQ gain of six points. When these children entered the program, they ranged in age from 15 to 32 months and their IQ's averaged about 103; on the retest, the IQ's averaged about 109.

There is no strictly comparable control group at this time. However, the investigators do have test results at 6, 12, 18, and 24 months for 23 children, also from the lowest socioeconomic level, who did not participate in the day-care program. At 6 months, these children's IQ averaged almost 120. At each retest from then on it dropped; at 24 months it was about 100.

Behind the day-care program lies the conviction that low-income families often do not provide the stimulation that even a very young child needs if he is to develop fully his capacities for perceiving and reasoning. But there may be another approach to the problem—parental education. To test this possiblity the investigators have made a moving picture, "How Babies Learn," which will be shown to some of the mothers of the children being studied but not to others. The mothers who see it will be encouraged to discuss the ideas presented and to ask questions. Perhaps these mothers will then provide a more stimulating atmosphere for their children, the investigators reason, and if they do, it may be possible to measure the results as the study proceeds. Such intervention will be far less expensive than the day-care program; of course, the question is whether or not it will be effective.

The study on infant learning follows a child until he is at least 3 years old. It keeps tabs on his physical and mental development, puts him through experimental procedures from the very beginning in an effort to study his patterns of learning, and closely observes his physical and social environment. Where this environment rates high in stimulation value, a preliminary analysis shows, a baby's IQ increases between the ages of 6 and 12 months; where the stimulation value is low, the baby's IQ is likely to drop.

The project now includes 50 families, some white and some Negro, most of them living in public housing. Soon, under the plan, it will add 50 babies from families living in university-operated housing for married students. The new families, too, will have meager incomes, but their social and economic backgrounds and outlooks presumably will differ considerably from those of the families now in the study. The idea is to look for differences both within and between the two groups on a number of matters believed to affect a young child's learning ability.

Each group will be divided three ways so that two levels of manipulation—day-care and parental education—can be tested, and the children in these subgroups compared with those who are merely tested and observed.

Studying the Learning Patterns of Infants

Not all children are motivated to learn by exactly the same procedures. Promise one child a nickel for doing something, Dr. Caldwell points out, and he does it; promise another child a nickel, and he doesn't stir. One child may be crushed by a spanking; another gets up and says, "Ha-ha-ha—you didn't hurt me." A mother who resolves to have infinite patience and never to use punishment may easily stick to her resolutions with a docile child; she may be tempted to abandon them, however, after a different child for the third time has deposited a bowel movement on the living room or supermarket floor.

Apparently, says the investigator, each child has a certain learning pattern which results from the interaction between his inherited characteristics and the way he has been dealt with since birth and which differs at least slightly from the patterns of other children. To test this idea, the researchers are studying each child's behavior in an array of learning situations. "Assuming that a child does have a particular pattern," Dr. Caldwell observes, "it may well influence what he does on developmental measures, such as the Cattell Infant Intelligence Scale and the Griffiths Test of Mental Development. For example, if a child is very sensitive to

180

social reinforcements and happens to be examined by someone who is friendly and smiling and full of encouragement, the child is likely to give his very best performance. But a child who regards smiles and praise as almost an intrusion on his own efforts to solve a problem may well respond negatively in the same situation and thus not reveal his true capabilities."

In this study the early learning situations are conditioning procedures, which are applied for the first time when the child is a month old (and has been brought to the well-baby clinic at the Children's Center). It is now known that some children condition during early infancy and some do not; what the Syracuse group wants to find out is the relationship between early conditionability and later learning. It also wants to relate the findings from the conditioning tests to such matters as the home environment and the parents' ideas about molding a child's behavior.

In the first procedure, the researcher holds a yellow disk where the baby can see it and simultaneously squirts a little air at the baby's face. The baby blinks. After a few trials, some babies become conditioned: they have learned to blink whenever they see the yellow disk, whether or not it is accompanied by a puff of air. Some of the others will learn to associate the two stimuli when they are next tested, at 2 months.

At 3 months, when sounds begin to be important, the psychologist in charge of this part of the research—Stanley Moldovan—changes the conditioning technique and uses a tone to signal that the baby's foot will be tickled. Again, some babies after only a few trials will flare the toes, or curl them, or move the foot—without being ticked—as soon as they hear the bell. Some of the others become conditioned this way the second time around, when they are 5 months old, and some do not.

Preliminary findings—concerned with about 35 of the babies now in the study, all from families low on the socioeconomic scale—show that:

• About half the babies tested at any given age can be conditioned.

• Most of those conditioned to respond to a visual stimulus, the yellow disk, at 1 month can be conditioned to respond at 2 months. And most of those conditioned to respond to an auditory stimulus, the tone, at 3 months can be conditioned to respond at 5 months.

• But there seems to be no connection between a baby's readiness to be conditioned to a visual stimulus at 1 and 2 months and his readiness to be conditioned to an auditory stimulus at 3 and 5 months.

Among older children, some are known to acquire information more readily through their eyes; others, through their ears. The Syracuse findings may be an indication that the same division—into what some investigators call "visiles" and "audiles"—holds true very early in life.

Usually when an investigator applies conditioning techniques to very young children, he is interested mainly in learning whether children of a given age can be conditioned in a given way. The present work, though, is directed toward learning what relationships may exist between early conditionability and later behavior. For example, will children who can be conditioned early turn out to be relatively quick learners later on? Will there be any connection between early conditionability and later IQ? Between early conditionability and socioeconomic background?

The answer to that question on the effect of social class will be no, it is believed, because conditionability very early in life is probably determined by the biological characteristics of the child and not by what has been happening to him. Babies from middle-class families tested by Moldovan for another Upstate Medical Center research project showed much the same conditioning pattern as those in the most recent work. By the time children are a year or so old, however, differences related to socio-economic class—or, perhaps more accurately, to differences in the patterns of parental care—are expected to appear.

The procedures using visual and auditory signals are classical or Pavlovian conditioning, in which one stimulus comes to be associated with another. The Syracuse group is also studying the children's response to operant conditioning, in which behavior is shaped by the giving or with-holding of rewards or punishments. Here, too, little is known either about the factors influencing conditionability in children or about a possible relationship between conditionability and later learning.

The first operant procedure tries to influence a baby's vocalization rate at the age of 4 months. As Dr. Lois Henning, the psychologist in charge, explains, infants between the ages of 3 and 5 months babble a good deal even when no one is around. This is spontaneous vocalization. After about 5 months, the child tends to limit his babbling to those occasions when there is someone to notice it—and to reward him for it with smiles and talk and play—all of which constitute, in the terms of learning theory, "social reinforcement."

There is some evidence that babies from middle-class families are rewarded more often for their cooing and babbling and attempts at talking than babies lower down on the socioeconomic scale. And this is one of the reasons, it is theorized, that babies in the first group get a headstart verbally and reach school age considerably better equipped to benefit from the formal educational process.

The Syracuse group asks whether or not there are marked differences at 4 months in the capacity of children to raise their vocalization rate in response to social reinforcement. If differences do exist, are they mainly between classes or among individuals regardless of class? Do the results at 4 months predict anything about verbal ability and learning ability later on? If accurate predictions can be made about these abilities, what happens when there is some sort of intervention early in the child's life—specifically, parental education by way of the moving picture the research group has prepared, or exposure of the child to the enriched environment of the day-care program?

To establish a baseline, the baby's vocalizations are recorded for a few minutes as he rests in a quite room. The experimenter is present and in the baby's sight but makes no response to his babbling. During the con-ditioning period, the investigator smiles at the baby whenever he babbles and gives him a warm "yes, yes" and a friendly pat on the tummy. This is the kind of reinforcement, the research team believes, that operates in the

182

natural environment of children and may have a critical role in the development of their vocal behavior and of language.

There are no answers yet. Some of the babies—again, about half—do increase their rate of vocalization; the others show no response to the social reinforcement. The investigators think that responsiveness may well be environmental—that the baby who responds in the laboratory situation is the one whose mother talks to him a good deal when he talks, so he learns earlier than the others to use vocal behavior to accomplish social ends.

Whether or not a child is conditioned, the investigators have a measure of his spontaneous vocalization. They will try to relate this, also, to his use of language later on.

Dr. Caldwell and Dr. Henning want to learn, in addition, if this type of conditioning would be a useful training device in enrichment programs for underprivileged children. So they are using it with a few of the infants in the day-care program, making a systematic effort to increase their vocal behavior in the belief that language development may thereby be facilitated.

From the time a child is half a year old, most of the early-learning experiments involve an apparatus that can be programmed to give him one of several kinds of rewards (a bar of music, a trinket, a bit of food, a voice saying, "uh-huh, uh-huh, very good, that was fine, do it again") in return for pressing the correct lever or pattern of levers. The levers can be distinguished by their position or by the size or color of their identifying symbol—for example, dots. The point here is to study differences in the rates of learning and the effects of a given reward and then to learn whether or not these differences are related to the children's backgrounds and to performance on IQ and other tests.

In related work, Moldovan recently found a difference in the reward-seeking behavior of boys and girls when the reward was a toy and when there was a delay between the time of the currect response and the presentation of the reward. Both boys and girls would start out by experimenting with the three levers of the apparatus until there was a payoff. Then the boys would continue to experiment until they had found the correct lever. The girls, on the other hand, would try to follow the same pattern that had led them to the reward in the first place. Each girl had her own pattern—"her own superstitious way"—of trying to get at the reward, and eventually, through a series of modifications, she would make the pattern pay off. The investigator cites this as evidence of differences in the ways people learn. In this case something associated with the sex of the children made a difference; in the work going on, additional factors may show up.

Studying the Stimulation Value of the Home

Four times a year a public health nurse on the staff of the Children's Center visits each family in the infant learning study and evaluates it on the basis of Dr. Caldwell's "Inventory of Home Stimulation." The inventory contains 72 items, all of which grew from certain assumptions by Dr. Caldwell—based on her own experience, on research by other investigators, and on expert opinion—about the conditions that foster a child's development.

The development of a young child, Dr. Caldwell assumes, is fostered by:

1. A relatively high frequency of adult contact involving a relatively small number of adults (the mother, the father, and, when the mother is away, one of not more than three regular substitutes).

2. The provision of a social learning environment that both stimulates the child and responds to him. (For example, the mother reads to the child at least three times a week, responds to him verbally when he vocalizes, tells him the names of things and people, encourages developmental advances such as waving bye-bye and saying his name, and supplies toys that challenge him to develop new skills. She gives these toys added value in his eyes by demonstrating her own interest in them.)

3. An optimal level of need gratification, defined as sufficiently prompt attention to the child's needs so that the young organism is not overwhelmed, but not so prompt or complete that budding attempts to meet his needs himself are aborted or extinguished.

4. A positive emotional climate—an interpersonal situation through which the child learns to trust others and himself. (For example, during the visit of the public health nurse, the mother spontaneously praises the child's qualities or behavior, does not shout at him or express annoyance with him, caresses him at least once, and reports that no more than one instance of physical punishment occurred during the preceding week.)

5. An environment that contains few unnecessary restrictions on the child's early exploratory attempts. (The child is kept in playpen or jump chair no more than an hour a day, is taken promptly from his crib when he awakens from a nap, is not slapped or spanked for spilling or spitting food or drink.)

6. The provision of rich and varied cultural experiences. (The investigator is interested in learning, for example, whether or not the child eats at least one meal a day with his parents, is taken into a grocery store at least once a week, goes on an outing with his family at least every other week, is taken to church by a member of the family twice a month or more.)

7. A physical environment containing modulated amounts and varieties of sensory experience. (For instance, the house is not overly noisy and is neither dark nor monotonously decorated, and the family has at least one pet, one house-plant, and 10 books.)

8. Access to certain kinds of play materials. For a child under 1 year, these include a cuddly toy; items, like beads and blocks, that go in and out of a receptacle; a push or pull toy; a fit-together toy, and one or two cloth or cardboard books. For a child between 1 and 2 years of age they include a child-size table and chair, a ride toy such as a scooter or kiddy car, large blocks or boards, bang and hammer toys, access to a record player and to

184

children's records. For a child between 2 and 3 years of age, they include simple wooden or heavy rubber puzzles, medium-size wheel toys; role-playing toys, such as those used in playing at being a cowboy or a mother; and at least 20 children's books.

A home's stimulation score is the total number of items checked "yes" by the nurse as the result of her observations during the visit and her talk with the mother.

The Home Stimulation Inventory, Dr. Caldwell notes, is an experimental technique. There is yet no proof that any of the items comprising it can influence a child's development. However, a recent comparison of stimulation scores and of changes on the Cattell Infant Intelligence Scale between 6 and 12 months showed that positive IQ changes had occurred in children from homes earning high scores and that negative changes were the general pattern in children from low-score homes. Several years from now the investigators will know more about the impact of this variable. They expect to be able to say, by looking back at what each child had in his home environment at various periods, which items and groups of items are the most sensitive indicators of developmental progress in later years.

The Effect of Parental Theories About How To Influence Behavior

In a second approach to assessing the family environment, the research team is studying each mother's ideas about the most effective ways of shaping the behavior of her child. These ideas, the investigators point out, represent a mother's theory of how children learn, and it would be helpful to know whether or not one theory has greater effect than another on the learning ability of a young child. It would be helpful to know also whether or not there is any difference between social classes in the prevalence of a given theory.

The research team has prepared lists of behaviors characteristic of many children—one list each for 1-year-olds, 2-year-olds, and 3-year-olds. Among the 45 behaviors listed for 1-year-olds are, for example, climbs out of bed after being put to bed, pokes finger or object into an electrical outlet, imitates words or sounds, and acts afraid in the doctor's office. The mother is asked in each case whether she would encourage or discourage the behavior—provided it made any difference to her at all—and how she would go about doing so.

Dr. Caldwell describes the courses open to the mother as:

1. *Manipualtion of privileges and tangibles.*—The mother can give the child a cookie, for example, take him on a trip, let him stay up late—or she can refuse to do so.

2. *Manipulation of maternal emotional responses.*—The mother can kiss the child, smile at him, thank him, frown or glare at him or become upset, or make no response at all.

3. *Manipulation of child's emotional state.*—The mother can enhance the child's esteem by praising him, undermine it by ridicule or by forcing an apology, undermine it through a scolding, or undermine it by physical

punishment—either mild, like a swat on the bottom, or severe, like a spanking.

4. *Manipulation of input.*—The mother can point to herself, her husband, or another child as a model of behavior for the child to imitate. Or she can provide a verbal explanation of why he should behave in a given manner. Or she can demonstrate what he should do.

5. *Manipulation of the environment.*—The mother can establish a schedule to include, for instance, putting the child to bed at the same time every day. Or she can change things—for example, placing a plant out of reach if the child picks it leaves—so that an unwanted behavior cannot occur. She can also get at the cause of an unwanted behavior and correct it.

6. *Mandate.*—The mother can tell a child—through a simple command or through insistence or threat—what to do or not to do.

The Syracuse group thinks that all these ways can be effective but that the skillful mother probably uses Nos. 4 and 5 more than the others. The investigators expect to find positive manipulations, such as granting privileges and giving praise, more commonly used by middle-class than by lower-class mothers. If so, Dr. Caldwell notes, the middle-class mother would have the support of learning theory, which says that rewarding a desired response is a far more powerful way of shaping behavior than punishing an undesired one.

"Maybe only 50 percent, or even considerably less, of the way a child develops can be influenced by his environment, no matter what this environment is or what is done to improve it," Dr. Caldwell remarks. "But environment is the only thing you can do something about; and to do it as effectively as possible, you have to understand what factors in it are most influential." Parental theories about how to shape a child's behavior, she suspects, will prove to be among the important factors.

Some Maternal Behavior Factors That Influence Development

In a related study,[1] the same investigators have been concerned with learning how a child's early experiences influence his social and personality development. The two dozen children in this study are all from low-income families, so any differences reflect differences between families rather than between social classes. Among the data now available are the reults of developmental tests given the children at approximately 6-month intervals during the first 2 years of life and ratings covering a broad range of maternal behavior as observed at intervals running from 3 to 6 months.

The investigators find that those children have reached a higher developmental level whose mothers:

1. Gave them more warmth and affection (the influence of these qualities was not clear until the tests at 18 months).

---

[1] MH 0852, "Infancy Experiences and Early Child Development," Julius B. Richmond, M.D., principal investigator.

2. Specifically expressed a desire that their children do well in school (the influence of this "maternal need for achievement" was seen at 12 months and persisted).

3. Showed an ability to plan for the care of their children and to respond adaptively to the suggestions of child-care authorities.

4. Maintained physical order in the home.

The number of cases is small, the investigators point out, but the findings are what might have been expected. Also, they support the idea that the value of a given home as a child-rearing environment cannot be determined alone from knowledge of the family's socioeconomic status.

A Movie To Help the Child by Educating His Parents

The actors in the moving picture, "How Babies Learn," are children being studied by the Syracuse group, plus their mothers or caretakers and other family members. They are unrehearsed. The narrator is Dr. Caldwell. "You would be amazed," she says in discussing the film, "at how many people regard the first year of life as a vegetative period when all you have to do is feed the baby, change him, keep him quiet, and let him sleep well. The experiences during the first year, however, may well be the most crucial learning encounters that the child ever has."

As the picture opens, the narrator makes two main points: Here are some things a baby does in his first year; and here are some ways you can help make it possible for him to develop his mind and his skills.

A baby can suck, react to light, hold on tightly to something placed in his hand, move his head when placed face down, and make other responses to his environment, the movie points out. Perhaps his most powerful tool in adjusting to the environment and adjusting it to him is his ability to cry. The message of the cry is not very precise, so the mother has to try something; then if the baby doesn't stop crying, she has to try something else. "If he does stop," the narrator says, "the mother has probably interpreted the message correctly. For the baby, this makes possible a very simple but important type of learning. The baby learns that when he cries, something happens."

Commenting on this point, Dr. Caldwell says that the first step in a learning situation is to realize that what one does makes some difference. One of the few things a baby can do is cry. If he does it and gets no response, the result is "a step on the road to apathy." He doesn't have the adult's capacity to tolerate frustration and delay, and he soon quits trying.

Before long, the narrator goes on, the baby may learn that a smile brings more love and attention, and perhaps accomplishes more, than a cry ever could.

As the baby gets his eyes under reasonable control, he begins to look at everything about him. But gradually he becomes more particular. The thing that seems to have the most appeal is someone else's face, especially if that face looks back.

187

By 6 months of age, the movie demonstrates, babies are interested in almost anything. A grasped object is almost certain to be put into the mouth. Holding two objects is difficult, not only because the hands have difficulty but also because the attention is in short supply; holding three objects is almost impossible. And when the mothers hides one object under a pillow, the baby shows no further interest in it.

Between 6 and 9 months, however, important changes take place. Nine-month-old twins are shown sitting up, balancing themselves easily while they examine their environment. They handle objects and taste them. When the rattle is hidden, the little girl goes after it: "She has learned from experience that things hidden are still there." Handling two things at once is now easier; when one is dropped, the eyes—but not always the hands—follow it. The boy twin crawls, pursuing toys or people that interest him. His twin has not yet begun to crawl. But here is a 10-month girl who can crawl and who spends much time pulling herself to a standing position. And here is an 11-month-old girl who walks while holding her mother's hand, or the furniture, and can even grab a toy while she is on her feet.

A number of other instances are given of how behavior changes as the baby develops. "Perhaps this description of infant learning has sounded as though it all occurred automatically, as though it all came from within," says the narrator. "Nothing, of course, could be further from the facts. At every step in the process the people who are important to the baby play a major role. From his parents, his brothers and sisters, his grandparents, and interested friends must come the stimulation necessary to develop fully his ability to learn. Little things can make a big difference. Consider something as apparently insignificant as the position into which the baby is habitually placed during its waking hours. He stays put wherever he is put down. If kept on his back, and if no people are in sight, he may well have a monotonous view. (The film shows a baby who has nothing to look at except a blank ceiling.) Until he can turn himself over and look around for something interesting, his seeing and looking can be given an assist by putting him down on his stomach part of the time. From this position he can practice some of the movements he needs to master before being able to crawl or walk and can choose what he wants to look at to some extent. Mother's face is far more interesting than the ceiling. Or he can be propped in a comfortable position and permitted to examine his surroundings. In this position he can see and can also use his hands to practice reaching and holding.

"During the first half year or so," the narrator continues, "we know that the baby needs people and he needs a variety of experiences to help him learn. But some time between 6 months and a year he seems to need something else: he needs special people. Not just anybody will do anymore. In particular, he seems to need his mother. For some reason, babies reared without this special attachment do not seem to learn as well."

The film shows a 10-month-old girl responding uncertainly and reluctantly to the smile and outstretched arms of a stranger. But when the mother beckons, the baby's face lights up and she crawls joyously to her.

Now another 10-month-old girl, who has not seen her mother for 3 months, appears on the screen. She is thin and looks frightened. Though she goes from one stranger to another with little hesitation, she does not respond enthusiastically to any of them. She passively accepts whatever happens. When a cookie is handed to her, she reaches for it. But when it falls to the floor, the least bit out of reach, she does not try to get it. When a toy is hidden, she shows no interest in finding it. She can stand, but her balance is poor. "In such cases," says the narrator, "if the separation from the mother does not last too long, or if a substitute can be arranged who will give the baby a lot of tender, loving care, the learning deficit associated with prolonged separation of a baby from its mother can usually be corrected."

The movie emphasizes the importance of other people in the process of learning to talk. Long before a baby can learn to talk, the narrator remarks, he must be talked to—must hear sounds made in relation to objects in his environment and in relation to his own needs. Parents often say that older children will teach the baby how to talk, but this apparently is not so. Second and later-born children are, on the whole, slower to learn to talk than the firstborn. "From the standpoint of learning language," the narrator says, "there seems to be no effective substitute for the experience of being talked to by loving and attentive adults."

Play materials can help a baby to learn shapes and colors and to improve the coordination between eyes and hands. But the materials need not be fancy or expensive. Empty food cartons supply a variety of colors, textures, and shapes. Old magazines have pictures that encourage a baby to improve his perceptual skills and to use his developing powers of speech. And nothing could be better than mother's pots and pans: "Such sounds and tastes and such a sense of being involved with objects that have meaning for the whole family!"

As the film shows a baby playing happily with pots and pans, the narrator continues: "Thus in their everyday routines, parents can nourish the learning careers of their babies. In humble but significant activities, parents can help their babies learn to learn."

The little things, the small personal touches, the narrator emphasizes, are the ways that enable a baby not only to grow but also to thrive—"stopping to talk to or smile at the baby while working; playfully encouraging him to try new things; helping him to achieve new and more mature postures; helping him muster the courage to take those first steps, and helping him back up, and reassuring him when he tumbles. By such participation and encouragement the parents invite the baby to move on to a higher level."

Prints of the movie, which has been praised by pediatricians and other child health workers, are now in such demand that the investigators, in the interest of saving the time of everyone concerned, have turned the picture over to the New York University Film Library, New York City, for sale or rent to interested groups.

An Enrichment Experiment With Very Young Children

All but one or two of the 24 youngsters in the day-care program are also in the infant-learning study. When a child in this study reaches the age of 6 months, he is given priority for admission to the day program should a vacancy occur. Those now in the program range in age from 6 months to almost 3 years and are described by Dr. Caldwell as "extremely high-risk children for whom some environmental enrichment is essential if developmental decline is to be prevented."

As an example, she tells about Alberta, who was a sluggish and apathetic child of 10 months when taken into the day-care project at the urging of a public health nurse who had been helping the family for years. Alberta's mother is retarded, presumably as the result of cerebral anoxia, or loss of the brain's oxygen supply, sustained as a baby when her head was caught between the railings of her crib. The mother, who is unmarried, also has a 6-year-old son, and he, too, is retarded, although there is no record or evidence of biological defects.

For a while, Alberta's mother treated her much like a doll, cuddling and rocking her for hours on end. When the girl was about 3 months old, however, the mother seemed to lose interest and began keeping her in a crib in a darkened room most of the day, supposedly to protect her from the extreme hyperactivity and destructiveness of her brother. At 6 months the public health nurse reported that the child seemed to be drifting downward. At 8 months, when the girl was given developmental tests at the Children's Center, the investigator recalls, "It was as though she had a veil over her face and wanted to keep the environment out."

In this situation were all the ingredients for producing culturally determined mental retardation: a disorganized family, a dearth of perceptual and cognitive stimulation, and emotional deprivation abruptly following emotional support. And there was a strong suspicion that the brother's history had contained the same ingredients.

"Perhaps unfortunately," Dr. Caldwell observes, "there is no literacy test for motherhood. We say that mothering is essential and imply that any mothering will do. We seem to assume that anything that sustains life is adequate during the first few years, and we have been very timid about trying to change the environment of very young children. Yet not all parents are qualified to provide even the basic essentials of physical and psychological care."

In the case of older children, Dr. Caldwell continues, society often steps in to help shape lives. In fact, to provide a richer environment for learning, society forces all children over 6 years of age into an institution, the public school system. But much of a child's ability to learn, insofar as this is influenced by the environment, seems to have been shaped long before he was 6. The IQ differences between deprived and privileged children

190

show up in the second and third years. So the time to provide an enriched environment, Dr. Caldwell reasons, begins when the child is about 6 months old.

The day-care program at the Children's Center is thus "an exercise in circumvention rather than in remediation." It is trying to prevent the deceleration in the rate of development that seems to occur in many deprived children very early; it is also trying to maximize each child's potential.

The children in the program are divided into three groups: those from 6 months to about 18 months; those from about 18 months ("when they are walking and showing some interest in toilet training") to about 2½ years; and those older than 2½. Under the original plan a child left the program when he was 3 years old, but the investigators have now obtained financial support—from the Children's Bureau (Child Welfare Research and Demonstration Grant D—156R—enabling them to keep him another year or two. With the additional support they hope also to compare the effectiveness of the present program with that of a day-care center admitting children no younger than 3 years of age. A program for infants and toddlers is much more expensive than one for older children, Dr. Caldwell points out; she thinks it is also much more effective, but she would like some hard-and-fast evidence.

With the children in the youngest group, the emphasis is on individual attention. At least once a day for at least a few minutes, each baby receives the undivided attention of one of the staff members—usually the same one. During these periods the baby is encouraged to reach for, go after, and handle different objects, and he is talked to and stimulated to respond. Whenever he is awake and not in his reclining chair or being held, he is placed on his stomach in order to encourage visual and motor exploration of the environment. The teachers talk slowly and distinctly. They repeat the names of objects as the child plays with them and describe an activity as the child engages in it. Learning games, similar to laboratory tests of visual and auditory discrimination, are played several times a week. Particular attention is given to tasks—for example learning that a reward is hidden under the larger of two blocks—that help a child acquire concepts and the ability to think abstractly.

Children in the older groups receive similar training in sensory discrimination and concept formation, capacities in which children from culturally deprived backgrounds have been found inferior. The children, in small groups, are read to at least once each morning and afternoon. They are given magazines and books and encouraged to look at the pictures and to repeat the names of what they see. Crayons, paint, other artistic media, and musical instruments are made available, as are toys that help a child develop an awareness of color, texture, shape, and sound. There is a well-equipped outdoor play yard. Self-initiated activities are encouraged, for they help in the development of self-confidence; at the same time the children are expected to learn to respond to the house rules.

In this environment, where the adults are friendly and accepting, and the child is encouraged to be curious, to make explorations, and to develop his abilities, even Alberta has made decided progress. After 2 or 3 weeks she became much more responsive. She babbled once in a while and she learned to pull herself up on chairs, and then to walk. Now, after 5 months, she acts most of the time like a normal child. Something happens over the weekends, though, Dr. Caldwell reports. On Friday the girl is outgoing and bouncy; on Monday she is once again apathetic and needs a warmup period of a day or two before responding to either the nursery school workers or the toys. What the end will be the investigators cannot predict. She responds to the environment at the Center but also to the one at home. Perhaps after several years in an enriched environment, Dr. Caldwell observes, Alberta and other such children will have developed the intrinsic strength to sustain themselves no matter what the home atmosphere. This is one of the project's major questions.

*Research Grant:*MH 7649
Related Grant: MH 8542

Date of Interview: June 14, 1966
References:

Caldwell, Bettye M. The effects of infant care. *Review of Child Development Research:* Volume 1. New York: Russell Sage Foundation, 1964.

Caldwell, Bettye M. What is the optimal learning environment for the young child? Presented at annual meeting Amer. Orthopsychiat. Assn., 1965.

Caldwell, Bettye M., and Drachman, R. H. Comparability of three methods of assessing the developmental level of young infants. *Pediatrics,* 1964, July.

Caldwell, Bettye M., and Richmond, J. B. Programmed day care for the very young child—A preliminary report. *J. Marriage and the Family,* 1964, November.

Caldwell, Bettye M., and Richmond, J. B. Social class level and the stimulation potential of the home. Presented at meeting Amer. Psychol. Assn., 1964.

Determinants of Mother-Infant Interaction

Investigator:
Howard A. Moss, Ph.D.
Chief, Section on Parent-Infant Behavior
Child Research, NIMH

Prepared by:
Antoinette Gattozzi

To explore the nature of early experience, a research group directed by Dr. Howard A. Moss is studying parent-infant interaction, especially mother-infant interaction, during the first 3 months of life. The researchers are tracing sequences of maternal and infant behaviors in order to calculate the probability of one action leading to another and to tease out from the total complex the contributions made by parents and those made by the infant. By determining the detailed patterning of the interaction, the investigators may discover how it relates to the child's congenital characteristics and to parents' psychological makeup, their early marital relationship, and parental expectations.

Abundant evidence supports the concept that the nature of early experience exerts profound effects on developmental processes. For example, when Dr. Moss was working at the Fels Research Institute in Yellow Springs, Ohio, he and a colleague, Dr. Jerome Kagan, reported the findings of a child development study conducted there. The study verified that many adult behaviors are rooted in early childhood; moreover, for certain fundamental dimensions of behavior, earliest influences produce the most enduring effects. Ratings of maternal treatment of children from birth to 3 years old were found to be more predictive of later childhood and adult behaviors than were the same assessments made when children were older. Maternal protectiveness up to the age of 3 years, for instance, showed better correlation with a child's passivity behavior during the years 6 through 10 than did protectiveness assessed when the child was actually in the age group 6 through 10 years. Some maternal behaviors, in fact, had a prolonged sleeper effect in that their influence was not discernible until children had reached adulthood.

Drs. Moss and Kagan postulated that the mother's influence is most apparent (and perhaps strongest) during the first years of her infant's life and that her behavior then is more reflective of her own attitudes and values than it is an accommodation to her child's behavior. As the child matures and asserts his individuality, however, he tends increasingly to evoke maternal treatment that is influenced by his unique characteristics. What are the precise timing and behavioral pathways of these dynamic intereffects? How does the child's sex affect his behavior and influence

193

maternal treatment? What are the attitudes that shape the mother's treatment of her infant? Dr. Moss and his associates currently are addressing themselves to such questions, which bear implications for child mental health. Such basic developmental research issues as the evolvement of attachment behavior, the establishment of the prototypic learning frame, the relations between the mother's role in mediating stimulation, and the child's coping style are only meagerly understood. Normative studies such as Dr. Moss is directing are needed to explore these areas so that we may learn how better to help troubled children.

Many of the families that Dr. Moss is studying also are participating in the Child Research Branch's overall longitudinal program, which is designed to yield a multidimensional scheme of early family formation. "For example," Dr. Moss explains, "in the study of married couples, emphasis is placed on the physical quality of the relationship and the degree of affectional contact. In the newborn infant project, special attention is given to congenital differences in skin sensitivity. In the parent-infant project, we can attempt to determine whether children with low tactile thresholds seek or are soothed by greater physical contact with the parents, or if parents with certain needs or experiences have a greater proclivity to handle or caress their infants."

The principal method of research is direct observations, made in the home in two clusters during the infant's first and third months. Each cluster consists of two 3-hour and one 8-hour periods. For the 8-hour stretch, the observer uses a stopwatch and sheets of paper ruled into time-sampling forms that list, separately for mother and infant, 30 different behaviors. Some examples of maternal behavior are: Holds infant close, feeds, stimulates-arouses, imitates, stresses musculature. A few of the infant behaviors are: Cries, fusses, sleeps, is awake and passive, vocalizes, mouths. Every minute, the observer marks the form to show what mother and infant are doing and in what order. Behaviors were selected on the basis of their presumed relevance to aspects of maternal contact or because they reflected the state of the infant. Other researchers have found that the infant's state, or level of arousal, which is a continuum ranging from quiet sleep to agitated crying, is an important influence on the nature and quality of his experience.

During the 3-hour periods, the observer works with a portable keyboard connected to an electrically powered event recorder. Each key represents one of the behaviors. As the keys are depressed, they activate pens in the recorder that leave ink tracings of the coded behaviors on paper. The resulting yards of tracings can be deciphered to produce a detailed description of mother-infant interaction during the period. Both methods are arduous for the observer, demanding maximum attention and concentration coupled with an informal, unobstrusive manner.

About 1,000 hours of observation have been clocked so far, all of them by Dr. Moss. Data collected during the 3-hour periods from a sample of 29 mother-infant pairs are now being analyzed, in part by programming a computer to extract sequences of action from the mass of separate tracings. The time-sampled data from these mother-infant pairs have been compiled and are the basis for the findings discussed below.

Variability.—A strikingly wide range appeared in the amount of time devoted to various behaviors. Great variability was evident at 3 weeks and 3 months, but was more pronounced when the sample was younger. Dr. Moss suggests that, for the infants, later differences in social behavior and learning style—aspects of development that have their genesis in the first weeks of life—are both reflected in and influenced by these revealed differences in behavior. The infant's behavior pattern reflects his unique constitution at the same time as it influences his mother's treatment of him. The squally, fussy child provokes a patern of maternal caretaking quite different from that which the placid, easily soothed infant elicits. Variabilities shown by the mother's behaviors similarly work to differentiate interactional patterns and their developmental products.

Stability.—From 3 weeks to 3 months, marked shifts occurred in most behaviors. At 3 months, infants were less irritable, awake longer, and spent more time smiling, vocalizing, and looking at their mothers than they had at the age of 3 weeks. Compared to the earlier period, mothers devoted less time to feeding and in close physical contact at 3 months, but increased their total attending (nonholding) behavior through social contacts such as talking, smiling, imitating, and generally stimulating the baby. These shifts attest to the enormous rapidity of infant growth and maturity during the first 3 months of life and to the adjustments mothers made, in part in response to the changing infant. The mother's behavior also changes, it seems likely, in accordance with her attitude to the infant, whom she increasingly regards more as a lovable person in her life and less an an animated bundle of total, demanding responsibility.

Sex differences.—Mean scores computed separately for boys and girls revealed several significant differences in both infant and maternal behaviors. These sex differentials also shifted over time: At 3 months, the infant variables showed smaller but persistent sex differences, and maternal variables were not as differentiated by sex as they had been at 3 weeks. The findings augment evidence from other studies of children that, as Dr. Moss puts it, "males are more subject to inconsolable states." Overall, males fussed and cried more and slept less than females. Not unexpectedly, males as a group were held by and attended to more by mothers; mothers also spent more time with boys stressing musculature, and looking at, talking to, and stimulating them. With their mothers, girls interacted more than boys only on such variables as stimulating, feeding, and imitating. Females vocalized substantially more than males at 3 weeks, but not at 3 months when the sex difference in this infant behavior disappeared. Another variable showing an intriguing sex difference was mouthing, which tallied the time an infant mouthed an object (such as his fist or a rattle) other than while feeding. The item represents a level of integrated behavior. At 3 weeks, the mean was 36.8 for boys and 30.6 for girls out of a total of 480 minutes; at 3 months, mean time close to doubled for males (61.2) and nearly quadrupled for females (116.2).

Sex differences in infant behavior and in maternal treatment of infants pose a difficult problem of interpretation. Temperamental differences between sexes date at least from the Garden of Eden, and explanations have been sought for almost as long a time. Probably sex characteristics encode quintessential biological principles. Whatever nature's contribution may one day prove to be, there is no question that societies of men have always embellished the differences. The familiar verse below is part observation, part expectation.

Snips and snails and puppy dog tails
And such are little boys made of.
Sugar and spice and all things nice
And such are little girls made of.

The data from this study accord with the findings of other researchers that demonstrate the very early occurrence of sex differences. The physiological origins and biological functions of these differences are not completely known. There is some evidence that male organisms are generally less viable than female organisms at birth; this would lead to a tendency for males to be either more aroused or more lethargic than females. Further, it is reasonable to assume hormonal differences, perhaps related to the morphological differences. The effects of the routine surgical procedure of circumcision, usually performed within the first week of the male infant's life, are thought not to extend beyond 12 hours.

Parental expectations, cameos of the enveloping society, overlay the infant's biological substrate and contribute to sex differences in behavior. In paradigms, parents encourage their daughter to be complaisant and serene, their son to be staunch and vigorous. The Fels longitudinal study discussed earlier yielded evidence that the child's sex influenced maternal treatment. Mothers were moderately consistent in protecting and accelerating boys but not girls, and much more consistent in restricting girls than boys. Differential effects of maternal treatment on boys and girls were found also. Mothers who were highly protective of a male infant from birth to age 3 years were likely to foster in the child a drive for intellectual mastery, the appearance of such a drive in girls and young women, however, was linked to early maternal hostility.

Parents' modes of treatment also stem from conceptions of their own sex and familial roles. Some of the differences in treatment emanating from these sources were exposed during a procedure conducted by Dr. Moss's research group. Parents were asked to elicit specific behaviors from their 7-week-old infant. In trying to get the baby to smile or vocalize, parents spent more time with females and mothers tried longer than fathers with both sexes. Fathers participated longer than mothers in getting the baby to grab a bell, and they tended to spend a little more time with male infants in this test of motor skill.

Correlations were computed between a score of infant irritability (the total time spent crying and fussing) and a maternal contact score, which was derived by summing the time mothers devoted to holding and attending infants exclusive of behaviors associated with feeding. For the females of the sample, the correlation was positive and significant at 3 weeks and at 3 months, which is to say that these categories of behavior occurred together more often than would be expected by chance. For the subsample of males, the correlation at 3 weeks was positive but not significant, and at 3 months it was negative. This indicates that maternal contact with males—who were, as a group, substantially more irritable than females as a group—was somewhat random in occurrence at 3 weeks and, by the third month, that mothers tended to spend inversely less time with males who exhibited greater irritability.

In terms of the total sample, however, correlations were positive and significant for both periods of time. Such an association suggests a causal relationship. Drawing on these observations and on findings from other studies, the investigators postulate that the infant cry is a potent stimulus shaping maternal behavior. The hypothesis embodies an explanation of the sequence of events between mothers and males as well as the rather different sequence enacted between mothers and females. The investigators' reasoning may be conceptualized as follows.

The mother learns how to care for her infant in a round-the-clock course of trial and error. She regards the cry as a signal for her attention; her responses are as ingenious and varied as she can make them. With practice and experience she learns how best to respond, and attains some degree of success in reducing what is to her the noxious stimulus of the cry and in gratifying her maternal needs. If her infant is a male, she learns by the third month that she often is unable to quiet him. More and more frequently, she may avoid the possibility of failure by not responding at all, or by delaying her response to his cry. If her infant is a girl, however, the mother learns a different lesson. Because her daughter is usually soothed by her attention, the mother feels fairly confident of her ability to succeed and responds consistently to the cry with caretaking activity.

This hypothesis is based on the correlations obtained between infant irritability and maternal contact, and on the finding that males were considerably more irritable than females during both periods of observation, which may imply that males had not been as uniformly soothed as females by maternal contact.

The interpretation provides a way of viewing the first phases of socialization, the gradual but ineluctable process through which an individual is transformed from a relentlessly egocentric newborn into a more or less cooperative member of society. In the beginning, the investigators suggest, the infant arbitrates the pattern of interaction through the powerful stimulus of the cry. As time passes he associates succor and comfort with his mother, and this increases her effectiveness in regulating his behavior. Imperceptibly, the two move toward a juncture

197

beyond which the larger role in determining the interaction shifts to the mother. At this point, socialization may be said to begin.

If this is a valid notion, infants who are usually soothed by the mothers' responses to their cries should be more susceptible to social learning than infants whose mothers do not answer their cries consistently or who are not quieted by maternal care. In the sample under study, the first class of experience corresponds to the females as a group, and the second to the male group. Indeed, this view of one aspect of early socialization is in line with results of other studies and fits the common observation that girls are more sociable than boys.

Psychological Factors in Maternal Treatment

Infant irritability is one important influence shaping mother-infant infant interaction that can be isolated and measured. Parceling out its effects may expose the presence of other influential factors. The researchers derived a measure of maternal responsivity from the data by totaling the amount of maternal contact that was *not* in response to irritability. This tactic uncovered two things. First, it was possible to classify a mother as an over-responder or an under-responder, depending on whether her predicted contact score (based on her infant's irritability) was above or below her actual contact score. Second, even accounting for greater male irritability, mothers were found to have significantly more contact with boys than with girls on such variables as "attends" and "stimulates-arouses;" on the social item "imitates," girls showed the higher mean score. This finding of sex differentiation in maternal treatment also was made when the same type of analysis was done while controlling the amount of time the infant spent in sleep. In this instance, males showed higher mean scores on the variables "stresses musculature" and "stimulates-arouses," and females scored higher again on "imitates." Thus, sex differences in maternal treatment that stemmed from mothers were discovered by controlling the effects of sleep and irritability, the salient aspects of the infant state.

The investigators are seeking antecedents that might link to this finding in the data they have gathered from parents. In addition, parents of 23 infant subjects had been extensively interviewed long before their baby's birth for the Branch study of early marriage. Two variables relating to potential parenthood that were extracted from this latter material have proved germane to the mother-infant study: "Acceptance of nurturant role" and "degree baby seen in positive sense" are prematernal variables that may be predictive of maternal responsivity.

The researchers also have located tentative links between a woman's maternal behavior and her childhood and early family experiences. The maternal behavioral composites of affectionate contact and responsivity appear to be related to a woman's recalled attitude toward the emergence of her secondary sex characteristics and the degree of identification she had with her father. Further substantive details like these, delineating

198

continuities in attitudes that structure maternal behavior, may be found by the current search for relationships between early marriage and mother-infant variables. The investigators are similarly analyzing the data collected by the researchers who studied their infant subjects as newborns; here they are looking for relationships between an infant's congenital behavior and the behavior displayed in that infant's interaction with parents. Meanwhile, Dr. Moss and his associates have begun another study with a larger sample of parent-infant pairs. They hope to replicate the findings of the first study, and to follow sequences of action with greater refinement.

Dr. Moss is also interested in the mother's role in mediating stimulation for her infant. Past studies have accumulated evidence indicating that infants have a need for stimulation, and that its quantity and quality are influential along many channels of development. Too much or too little, too intense, chaotic, or monotonous stimulation, as uniquely experienced by the individual infant, may have deleterious effects. Clearly, mothers play a central role in balancing stimulation for their infants as they arouse or quiet them and regulate their autonomically generated stimulation. In the mother-infant pairs studied, mothers offered male infants greater amounts of motor stimulation. At the same time, as one possible interpretation of the data suggests, males were experiencing heightened levels of internal and self-stimulation. If this pattern is found again in the new study, its meaning and implications will warrant further exploration.

Dr. Moss believes that apart from survival, coping with stimulation is the infant's consuming developmental task. In this context, a mother's part in mediating stimulation is a fundamental task for her. Studies of parent-infant interaction may demonstrate how different mothers handle stimulation for their infants, how differences in infants affect the stimulation balance, and what relations exist between the kind of stimulus dependency established and later developmental configurations of social behavior and learning style.

Intramural: NIMH
Date of Interview: Mar. 23, 1966

References:

Kagan, J., & Moss, H. A. The stability of passive and dependent behavior from childhood through adulthood. *Child Develpm.,* 1960, 31, 577-591.

Kagan, J., & Moss, H. A. *Birth to maturity: A study in psychological development.* New York: John Wiley, 1962.

Moss, H. A. Methodological issues in studying mother-infant interaction. *Amer. J. Orthopsychiat.,* 1965, 35 (3), 482-486.

Moss, H. A. Coping behavior, the need for stimulation, and normal development. *Merrill-Palmer Quart. Behav. Developm.,* 1965, 11, 171-179.

Moss, H. A. Sex, age, and state as determinants of mother-infant interaction. *Merrill-Palmer Quart. Behav. Developm.,* in press.

Moss, H. A., & Kagan, J. Stability of achievement and recognition seeking behaviors from early childhood through adulthood. *J. abnorm. soc. Psychol.,* 1961, 62, 504-513.

Moss, H. A., & Kagan, J. Report on personality consistency and change from the Fels Longitudinal Study. *Vita hum., Basel,* 1964, 7, 127-138.

Studying the Infant-Mother Relationship For Clues to the Causes of Aberrant Development

Investigator:
Nahman H. Greenberg, M.D.
University of Illinois College of Medicine
Chicago, Ill.

Prepared by:
Herbert Yahraes

Through an intensive study of physiological patterns during infancy and of the interaction between infants and their mothers, a University of Illinois psychiatrist is seeking hard and fast information about the origins of emotional difficulties and psychosomatic illness. The investigator is Nahman H. Greenberg, M.D., director of the Child Development Clinical and Research Unit at the University's College of Medicine, Chicago.

Dr. Greenberg points out that a baby's development—and, according to psychoanalytic theory, its emotional health in later life as well—is profoundly affected by the quality of its mother's love. The investigator wants to find out how this love operates, so he focuses not only on how a mother feels or says she feels but also on what she does. Certain types of maternal activity, he believes, either satisfy or fail to satisfy certain of the infant's biological needs and may influence either for better or worse the infant's developing social relationships. Consequently, if mothers' actions and infants' responses, and vice versa, are cataloged and analyzed, eventually it should be possible to relate a given pattern of action-and-response in infancy to a given type of disturbance in later childhood and perhaps in adult life. The relationships can be established, of course, only by such long-term studies as the investigator has embarked upon.

In one part of his program, Dr. Greenberg is determining how various kinds of activity on the part of an infant affect its physiological state as shown by respiration, heart rate, body motility, and body tonicity. This information will provide a baseline for measuring the effect of the mother's behavior upon these same characteristics.

The babies being studied this way include a so-called normative group, born to the wives of medical and dental students at the university, and an institutional group born to unwed mothers—mainly white girls, of all socioeconomic levels—and living in a foundling home.

The measurements are made in the nursery of Dr. Greenberg's psychophysiology laboratory for at least an hour at a time as the baby sleeps, tosses, plays, smiles, cries, or does whatever else comes naturally. By pushing a button, an observer indicates—on the magnetic tape which is recording the measurements—the kind of activity going on at a particular time. Moving picture cameras, one for closeups and one for distant views, are available for filming all or part of a session. At one point in each observation period the experimenter introduces a "sensory event" and notes the results. This point occurs when the baby fusses because he is hungry, and the "sensory event" consists of attempts to pacify him in various ways.

The ways in which mothers and babies interact are observed and filmed in the same laboratory. In addition, the mothers are studied through psychiatric interviews and psychological tests.

The institutional group of babies was added to the research plan so that infants who were all being reared under the same conditions and, of course, in the absence of their natural mothers, could be compared with the others. Through a data collection system at the foundling home, the investigator receives a 24-hour-a-day record on tape showing for each baby when it moved, cried, and was lifted from the crib. He also receives a filmed record—made by preset cameras at various times—of the activity of the aides caring for the babies.

In a second part of the research, the investigator is concerned with infants—and their mothers—in whom developmental disorders are already apparent. Several of these babies have appeared in the so-called normative group; the others—there are now 45 in all—have been referred to him over a 2-year period from the university's department of pediatrics and the well-baby clinics of the Infant Welfare Society of Chicago. When Dr. Greenberg first saw them, they ranged in age from 3 to 23 months. All had been raised in their own families. They were not mentally retarded nor did they have neurological defects.

Among the symptoms of abnormal development were disorders described in general as hypermotility, including head-rolling, body swaying, and some forms of self-injury, mainly head-banging, nutritional anemia, pica and other feeding disorders, and failure to thrive.

As Dr. Greenberg points out, it is generally impossible for an investigator who is stuydying disturbed adolescents or adults to dig back and get accurate data about their infancy. But given an infant showing a developmental disorder, it may well be possible to find out what has gone wrong so far in his very short life, and then perhaps to correct it or at least to set up warning signs for other families and physicians.

"The effort is to work back and reconstruct the developmental history," Dr. Greenberg explains, "and learn what the mothers did to get something like body-rocking or head-banging, or eating plaster off the wall, or refusing to take anything but a bottle and developing an anemia as the result." As a major part of this effort, the investigator and his associates observe and record the behavior of mother and baby during extended visits to the laboratory nursery. The researchers are particularly interested in the mother-baby relationship at feeding time and the baby's behavior during what would ordinarily be a period of mild stress, when the mother leaves him alone and then a stranger comes in.

Preliminary Findings

The rationale of this research program and the findings to date are presented in some detail in the succeeding sections. The main findings may be summarized as follows:

1. At 1 month of age, the institutional babies observed during a pilot study could be pacified more easily than the others and, unlike the others, equally well by any of the methods used. Pacification brought a greater change in their heart rate. At 2 months, the institutional babies had gained only half as much weight as the others. These differences seem traceable to the amount of stimulation provided in the foundling home.

2. On the average, the institutional babies were handled—for feeding, bathing, and all other purposes—only about 90 minutes a day. Nevertheless, the institutional environment is less uniform than had been expected, for some babies were found to get considerably more attention than others. (The differences are going into the babies' records, and an effort will be made to study their effect.)

3. The abnormal behavior of the infants with developmental disorders appears to arise from serious disruptions in the infant-mother relationship, and these disruptions apparently occur because the mother is emotionally disturbed. For the most part, the mothers are considered to be either psychotic or borderline. "Commonly there has been severe trauma in their own lives," the investigator reports, "and they identify with the baby in terms of their own traumatic childhood and mothering."

4. Most of the infants with developmental problems show an abnormality in the way they pacify themselves. Finger-sucking is uncommon, and many of the infants have developed an aversion to bottles. To reduce tension, the investigator reports, these infants tend to engage in hypermotility, such as head-rolling or body-swaying.

5. In their relations with these infants, the mothers appear to be either detached and neglectful or overstimulating and harsh. When the mothers feed their babies, they show little or no tenderness. Some of the same mothers, though, handle their infants for inordinately long periods of time. Their behavior in this respect, the investigator reports, overstimulates the infant and is inappropriate to its needs.

6. Separated from their mothers, these babies do not show the typical response of sobbing or crying. In the hospital, away from "psychotoxic" influences, the babies tend to improve quickly.

7. Most of the mothers are resistant to initial attempts with psychotherapy.

8. There is nothing to indicate so far whether or not the developmental problems and the disturbed infant-mother relationship will affect

personality and emotional health later in life. The investigator believes that they will.

9. The great majority of the infants in the atypical group come from families at the lower socioeconomic levels. The investigator hopes to check reports that the pattern of disturbance among infants from families at the higher levels is different.

The Interactions of Mother and Infant

Dr. Greenberg defines psychosomatic differentiation, his field of study, as the process of growth by which individual psychophysiological patterns develop. This process is most vulnerable to outside influences at the stage of least differentiation, and this stage—with respect to the influences of mothering—begins at birth. Because the mother in large part creates the infant's sensory environment, it is she who most strongly influences the developmental process. But the investigator points out that the infant itself, through its inborn propensities, may influence both the amount and type of maternal behavior. An infant who sleeps most of the day can be expected to influence a mother's behavior differently from an infant who has been irritable—in the sense of being peculiarly susceptible to stimuli—since birth.

In studying an infant's heart rate, muscle tension, and other measures of physiological activity, and how these are affected by the mother, the researchers distinguish six basic behavioral states or degrees of internal tension: Sleeping, drowsy, awake-inactive, awake-active, fussy, and crying. To a great extent, the investigator explains, a mother can regulate these states through such activities as feeding, holding, talking to, and smiling at her baby. A particular activity by the mother calls into use and helps develop a particular sensorimotor mechanism in the infant. In other words, mother and infant are two psychophysiological systems, which interact through specific mechanisms of stimulation and pacification. As these mechanisms come into play, there is a change in the degree of the infant's internal tension, and of the mother's as well.

A mother reacts to the different behavioral states in different ways, and one mother's reaction to a given state may differ from another's. In one case, for example, Dr. Greenberg found that the mother tended to avoid her baby when it reached the crying state, but when the baby was quiet, would begin talking to and playing with it to the point of overstimulation. At least party because of the mother's way of reacting, the investigator believes, the baby developed a serious nutritional disorder and gave evidence—for instance, by showing greater distress than normal when the mother left the room—of emotional difficulties.

Requirements for Normal Development

As Dr. Greenberg sees it, an infant's responses to its mother's stimulation have two functions. In the first place, they satisfy needs. Sucking, for

203

example, is necessary to satisfy the need for nutrition; visual sensations are necessary if the visual apparatus is to mature and serve the infant's normal needs to recognize those close to him and then to explore and to learn. In the second place, the infant's responses serve to pacify and soothe him. Up to a point, sucking—even when no food is being received—serves as a normal pacifier or a way of reducing tension. The same is true of movements of arms, legs, body.

For development to proceed normally, the investigator hypothesizes, the infant's feeding experiences must be such that the organism remains in equilibrium. On the one hand, the organism must be sufficiently aroused by the mother's actions to respond to sensory stimuli; on the other hand, the amount of tension generated must stay within bounds. When the equilibrium is upset, a variety of behavior distortions may arise—among them, insufficient sucking, hyperirritability associated with feeding, regurgitation, a fearful avoidance of food, and aversion to dietary change.

A mother who does not establish a warm relationship with her infant through feeding, the investigator goes on, may attempt to engage him through visual interactions such as smiling, or through excessive body stimulation in the form of rocking and carrying. In either case, the stimuli the infant receives are probably insufficiently diversified for the best possible development for his nervous system.

Unable to cope naturally with the feeding situation, a mother may also withdraw from the infant and avoid any but the most necessary contact. In this case, lacking appropriate levels of stimulation from outside, the infant becomes irritable and excited and may turn to various techniques of stimulating or pacifying himself. In the earliest months, Dr. Greenberg reports, he may engage in excessive sucking, particularly of his hands. Later on he may turn to body-rocking, head-rolling, or other rhythmic motor activity—all in the interest of ameliorating tension.

In sum, under this hypothesis, when the mother's behavior impairs or overtaxes the normal sensorimotor routes for satisfying needs, the infant uses certain of his developing functions maladaptively—that is, for tension reduction. As the individual develops, Dr. Greenberg believes, he will outgrow a particular maladaptation but, if stressful conditions continue take on another. Thus the infant with a developmental disorder such as head-banging may become, unless his distress is removed, the child or adult with a character problem, a psychosomatic illness, a psychosis, or some other impairment.

The investigator emphasizes that he has no evidence that an infant who bangs his head, bites his hand, eats dirt, or shows other developmental abnormalities is more likely than other infants to be headed toward severe emotional difficulties later on. Dr. Greenberg merely hypothesizes that this is so. He believes that only a longitudinal study—one that follows an infant through the years rather than one that tries to look back from later life to infancy—can say for sure.

"Hopefully," he says, "we may begin to develop objective means of describing psychophysiological development and look at some factors in maternal behavior influencing them. We shall be learning more about the characteristics of the 'dark age' of infancy so that our notions about health and disease in terms of this period of life will be based upon objective data."

Troubled Mothers

The mothers of the infants with development problems—and particularly the mothers whose babies rolled their heads or manifested disturbed motility in other ways—were found to have difficulty in managing their aggressive impulses. In response to an infant's display of vigor, Dr. Greenberg reports, these mothers tended to show hostility and at times to engage in almost assaultive activity. Further, if a baby tried to suck a hand or a thumb, the mother would draw it away, often rather roughly. At feeding time the mothers tended to act in an impersonal, get-the-job-done manner described as "institutional." But sometimes they went to the opposite extreme and strove to attract the infant's attention to themselves by facial gestures and excessive handling.

Could it be that such mothers just don't know how to handle babies?

"Most of these mothers come from the lower socioeconomic levels," Dr. Greenberg answers, "so there may be an educational factor involved. But I don't know that to be a good mother requires formal education; I think it requires an adequate personality." Most of the 45 mothers in the group studied so far have been found to have major emotional disturbances. They are usually irritable, distant, neglectful, depressed, and markedly anxious, the investigator finds. They go from one crisis to another.

Troubled Children

When the mother of a normal infant leaves him alone in the laboratory's nursery and then a stranger comes in, the investigator's films show, the child is apt to cry or sob for a while. Not so an infant with developmental problems. Such a child either continues to do whatever he has been doing, without any sign of acknowledging the separation; or he retreats, or sits or lies motionless, or begins body-rocking; or he engages in extreme crying and cannot be comforted by being held, played with, or even fed. The crying in the last situation is not weeping, Dr. Greenberg observes, but straightforward shrieking.

Unlike most children who have been raised at home, however, these babies with developmental problems apparently reach the age of 8 or 9 months without having established object specificity, meaning the ability to show a preference for one or more of the persons around them. When one of these infants has to be separated from his mother in order to be hospitalized, he generally accepts the ward and cheers up more quickly than other babies. In Dr. Greenberg's words, these infants have a gregariousness that lacks definition and singularity, with the result that everybody becomes an acquaintance but no one a solid friend. Whether or not such a state, with its portent of trouble later on, will continue remains to be seen.

The most marked symptom in several of the children is pica, a craving for unnatural foods. This has become a public health problem of some size, according to Dr. Greenberg, because the afflicted babies often eat paint-covered plaster and then develop lead poisoning, which affects the central nervous system and may result in convulsions and death. (In an attempt to find the lead-eaters early enough, teams of doctors and nurses are going into homes in some parts of Chicago and collecting urine samples for analysis.)

Pica children apparently feel deprived and hungry, but just what happens in the mother-infant relationship to give rise to their condition, says Dr. Greenberg, is not yet clear. Interestingly, the films taken in the laboratory nursery do indicate that the mothers of pica babies—in contrast to most of the other mothers—act normally in the feeding situation.

The investigators have encountered even worse problems. One of the first children referred to Dr. Greenberg, for example, had been admitted to the University of Illinois Hospital at the age of 7 months with a common trouble, failure to thrive. "She was quiet and somewhat detached and withdrawn," Dr. Greenberg reports, "and frequently nodded her head in the typical movements of *spasmus nutans* (head-rolling). She turned away from the observers, although she was attentive to auditory and visual stimuli. She showed no reactions of pleasure, and we were unable to make her smile. She sucked eagerly when she was held and fed, but was interested only in the bottle and paid no attention to the feeder's face."[1]

Moving pictures made in the laboratory nursery indicated that Betty was getting a fantastic type of attention. On one occasion, for example, the mother reached into the crib, pulled Betty's fingers from her mouth and began kneading the baby's face and head almost as if they were dough or clay. Betty began fussing. The mother explained that she was accustomed to rubbing the baby's face and body for hours at a time "to build her up."

Betty soon gained weight in the hospital and improved in other ways. She became curious and responsive, smiled, reached for toys and people. Her head-nodding stopped within a week-and-a-half.

After Betty was discharged, the mother brought her back several times so that the team could continue to study the mother-infant relationship and try to help the mother with her own emotional problems. When she complained of brutality to Betty by the people they were living with, the doctors and their staff even helped the family move into a separate apartment. A month later, however, Betty was returned to the hospital in a coma and died of a fractured skull.

Since then, several other battered babies, among those admitted to the hospital, have been added to Dr. Greenberg's cases. Brutality to infants is

---

[1] Greenberg, N. H. Origins of head-rolling (spasmus nutans) during early infancy. *Psychosom. Med.*, 1964, 26, 2.

more common than generally realized, and its impact on mental health in later years may well be shown—through studies like Dr. Greenberg's—to be grievous. The investigator calls attention to suggestions that schizophrenics have experienced not only harshness during infancy but also physical cruelty.

Treatment

If we know how emotional disorders originate, perhaps we can step in to prevent them or at least to shorten the treatment and make its effects more enduring. And the logical approach in cases like those under study, where physical symptoms point to psychological problems, Dr. Greenberg believes, is to try to restore the babies' normal developmental channels by removing the pathogenic factors in the infant-mother relationship.

Many of the mothers in this particular study, though, show no conscious concern for their babies and therefore resist therapy for themselves. About the only thing psychotherapy has accomplished so far, Dr. Greenberg finds, is to help some of the mothers get through periods of extreme anxiety. If the study clearly demonstrates that certain maternal responses are harmful, he hopes eventually to let mothers see in moving pictures how they are reacting to their babies' needs. Then perhaps the point can be made that certain aspects of their behavior are not ideal.

When the infants are removed from what the investigator terms their psychotoxic environment, many improve quickly. The most dramatic results occur in babies only a few months old who have feeding disorders. Within a week after they have been hospitalized, these babies often stop regurgitating, begin eating normally, and gain in weight. Further, they show less withdrawal and apathy and more curiosity and social responsiveness.

Among the unanswered questions: How long will the improvement last? Why do some of the babies, particularly those with motility disorders, show no substantial change in the new environment?

Dr. Greenberg points to another aspect of the situation: some mothers subconsciously do not want their children to become completely well— they *need* sick babies.

Institutional vs. Family Babies

In preliminary work several years ago, Dr. Greenberg found decided differences between institutional babies from the foundling home, and family babies being reared by their own parents. One difference lay in the babies' responses to pacification attempts when they were in distress. The institutional babies as a group were easier to pacify than the others, and at one month of age could be pacified equally well by any of three techniques—feeding them, giving them a nipple pacifier, or holding them in a sitting position in their cribs. The family babies, on the other hand, could be smoothed much more easily by either of the first two methods than the third. As the babies were pacified, their heart rates dropped, but the heart rates dropped considerably lower among the institutional babies.

These findings indicate, the investigator suggests, that family babies may organize their response patterns earlier—that is, show a preference among pacification attempts earlier. In addition the findings may indicate that the babies raised in the nursery (1) are more sensitive than the others to pacification efforts, and (2) have less effective feedback mechanisms for controlling the heart rate. The increased sensitivity could be explained by the conditions of sensory restriction under which infants are being raised. In this study the attention given a nursery baby—for feeding, bathing, and all other purposes—was always less than 2 hours, and sometimes as little as an hour and a quarter, in a 24-hour day. The aides rarely sang or spoke to the infants, and the feedings—for which nipples with large holes were used—were often very rapid.

Another difference was in weight. Even though the institutional babies were on a more than adequate diet and were getting excellent pediatric care, by the end of the first 2 months they had gained only half as much as the other babies. Dr. Greenberg believes that this difference, too, is attributable to the restricted sensory environment of the nursery infants.

At this point there is no evidence to suggest that the observed differences are permanent or that they have implications for personality development. In the matter of weight, in fact, there is evidence—given the investigator by a number of adoptive mothers—that institutional babies quickly catch up after they have been adopted. The findings do indicate to Dr. Greenberg that the nature and the extent of the opportunities for communication between the infant and its surroundings can affect physiological function and behavioral activity in infancy.

This earlier work is being repeated and extended with the groups of infants now under study.

For the Future

In order to study the frequency of developmental problems, the research group is sending pediatric checklists to each mother who delivers at the University of Illinois Hospital. The lists enable her to describe quickly virtually all aspects of her baby's behavior. Lists go out at 3, 8, and 18 months, and many of the mothers check and return them. If the baby's behavior appears to be abnormal, the mother is asked to bring him in for a checkup, and she may then be invited to participate in the study being conducted by Dr. Greenberg.

In still another effort to get precise information about the conditions leading to emotional disturbance, Dr. Greenberg's team is beginning to survey 2,000 babies a year born to families using the well-baby clinics of the Infant Welfare Society. Dr. Greenberg explains that the society sponsors one of the few child guidance centers in Chicago that treat emotionally disturbed children of preschool age. Eventually a few of the babies being surveyed will develop emotional disorders and be referred to this center for treatment. Then the research group will be able to look for a relationship between the circumstances of infancy and the types of emotional disturbance that develop—or, as the investigator sums it up, who gets what.

Most of the babies now under study because they have developmental disorders come from families at the lower socioeconomic levels. Would babies from other types of families show the same troubles? Dr. Greenberg doesn't know, but talks with other psychiatrists and with pediatricians have given him the impression that babies from middle and upper middle-class families have a much lower incidence of feeding problems and of hypermotility. Developmental disorders in these babies seem to be related somehow to sleep disturbances. Sometime in the future the investigator hopes to check this point by studying infants from Chicago's North Shore, where most of the residents are professional people.

Adopted Children

Studies in child guidance clinics and mental hospitals indicate that adopted children have a higher incidence of a variety of psychiatric problems, but these studies generally have not taken into account either the age of adoption or the time that may have been spent in an institution before adoption. Dr. Greenberg believes both factors to be critical. The babies in his institutional group, to be followed through the years, will all have been adopted at the same age of 2 months. Eventually he hopes to compare their emotional well-being not only with that of the normative group, but also with that of some of the children from the foundling home who were adopted just a few days after birth. In the case of the 2-month group, he also hopes to throw light on a largely unexplored area, the nature of the parent-child relationships in adoptive families.

Research Grant: MH 5527
Career Program Development Award: K3-MH 13, 984
Date of Interview: June 5, 1964

References:
Greenberg, N. H. Studies in psychosomatic differentiation during infancy. *Arch. gen. Psychiat.,* 1962, 7, 389.
Greenberg, N. H. Origins of head-rolling (spasmus nutans) during early infancy. *Psychosom. Med.,* 1964, 26, 2.
Greenberg, N. H. Developmental effects of stimulation during early infancy. *Ann. N.Y. Acad. Sci., in press,* 1965.
Greenberg, N. H., Cekan, P., & Loesch, J. G. Some cardiac rate and behavioral characteristics of sucking in the neonate. Presented at annual meetings Amer. Psychosomat. Soc., Atlantic City, 1963.
Greenberg, N. H., & Loesch, J. G. Celiac disease. Draft, 1963.

Greenberg, N. H., & Loesch, J. G. A comparative study of some behavioral and physiological activities in nursery and family-reared infants during the first 2 months of infancy. Presented at annual meeting Amer. Orthopsychiat. Assn. Chicago, 1960.

Greenberg, N. H., Loesch, J. G., & Lipgar, R. Preliminary observations on symptom-formation during infancy. Draft, 1964.

How the Child Separates From the Mother

Investigator:
Margaret S. Mahler, M.D.
Masters Children's Center
New York, N.Y.

Prepared by:
Herbert Yahraes

Several times a week, a number of young mothers in the Greenwich Village section of New York City spend a morning or an afternoon in an old brownstone house on Horatio Street. Their children play or sleep. The mothers care for them as usual, talk to one another, or read. All the while they are being closely observed by a research team, and the mothers know it. The young women who serve as playroom teachers are actually trained observers, and one of them slips out every half hour to dictate a report on the activities and attitudes of one of the mothers and her child. Other observers, out of sight, make notes from booths. Even the room where the diapers are changed has an observation window.

Never before, it is believed, have normal mothers and normal children been studied so intensively over the period in which the investigators are interested—from the age of about 5 months to the end of the third year. The findings are expected to increase our understanding of why some children become schizophrenic or show other signs of emotional disturbance and to improve our ability to prevent such developments.

The brownstone house is the home of the Masters Children's Center, an organization for the study and treatment of disturbed children and the study of normal children. Dr. Margaret S. Mahler, the internationally known children's psychoanalyst who directs the center's research program (and is clinical professor of psychiatry at Albert Einstein College of Medicine), believes that the roots of much childhood mental illness are to be found in the relations between mother and child during the period, beginning when the child is about 5 months old, in which their initial oneness begins to slowly come apart. Dr. Mahler calls this the separation-individuation phase of child development, meaning the phase in which the child gradually separates from his extremely close, symbiotic union with his mother and comes to recognize himself as an individual. In the investigator's words this is the period in which the child hatches from the symbiotic membrane and becomes as individuated toddler. If something goes wrong with the hatching process, Dr. Mahler theorizes, emotional problems develop; if something goes *very* wrong, the problems may be severe and in extreme cases may lead to the type of schizophrenia she has described as *symbiotic child psychosis*.

It was through her work with psychotic children that Dr. Mahler became aware of the importance of this period of development. In many cases of symbiotic child psychosis, the symptoms could be explained, it seemed to her, only by supposing that the child for some reason had not successfully come through the hatching process and was trying frantically to regain union with his mother.

But just what had gone wrong? And when? And might it have been prevented?

She found she could offer only theoretical answers, because this period of child development had never been studied intensively enough to provide a detailed description of what happens normally. To help supply the needed information, some of the staff of the Masters Children's Center made a pilot study of mothers and children and reported that in the normal course of events the separation-individuation phase apparently comprises four major parts. In each of these the child is developing both physically and psychologically; in each he is called upon to accomplish certain tasks.

The current study was undertaken in 1963 to verify these findings and to set forth in detail the mother-child relationship and the child's behavior patterns that are characteristic of each subphase. Heading the staff assisting Dr. Mahler and Dr. John McDevitt, a psychoanalyst, and Dr. Kitty LaPerriere, a psychologist. The information is collected by observing mother and child at the Center, interviewing the mother every week, making a long, informal visit to the home every 2 months, and occasionally observing father and child. The babies are tested periodically, and moving pictures of mother-child interaction are made both at the Center and in the home.

The families in the study, all of whom live within walking distance of the Center, are described as middle class and Protestant; most of the fathers and many of the mothers are college graduates. The mothers are happy to participate in the research, Dr. Mahler reports, because the Center provides excellently equipped playrooms for their youngsters and emotional support to themselves, and because the mothers like to feel that they and their children are serving the cause of mental health. The Center is open to them 3 days a week; most of them come in for two or three mornings or afternoons. By the time the project ends, in 1968, more than 40 children and their mothers, half of them in the course of the less-detailed pilot study, will have been observed during the separation-individuation process.

One of the objectives of the research is to point to the danger signals in each phase of that process—the indications that child and mother are not successfully coping with the problems natural to a given stage of development and that they are, consequently, storing up problems for later stages. It is hoped that the children now under study can be compared with one another at various periods, into adulthood. Some of the children appear to be proceeding through the separation-individuation phase more successfully than others, and a variety of at least temporary problems are being encountered. A long-term follow-up, the investigators explain, would be

212

the best possible way of establishing a link between certain events or patterns in this phase and the quality of mental health in later life.

As discussed later, the investigators think they have already spotted a few of the danger signals. The chief general conclusion emerging from the work so far is that the child's psychological development depends in large measure upon the "emotional availability" of the mother. In all phases of the separation-individuation process, he needs to be sure of her interest and love.

The Roots of Childhood Schizophrenia

Discussing her earlier work with psychotic children and their mothers, Dr. Mahler recalls an experiment by another investigator, in which chick embryos and newly hatched chicks were pricked with a pin. The chicks that had hatched showed only infinitesimal damage but those still in the shell developed major anatomical defects.

"The lesson is applicable to the child's psychological development," Dr. Mahler observes. "There is a natural timetable for the maturation and development of the controlling, steering, integrating part of the personality, the ego. The earlier in life that this timetable is interrupted, the more detrimental to the total personality." From her previous research, the investigator believes that in childhood schizophrenia the timetable has been interrupted very early, either before or not long after the beginning of the separation-individuation process.

Because of disturbed or insensitive mothers, some of the children who later developed schizophrenia had suffered numerous and severe frustrations and emotional trauma during the first few months of life. At one extreme there was the depressed mother who could show no sign of affection for her daughter. At the other extreme there was the smothering and overwhelmingly affectionate mother who constantly overstimulated her son and showed no comprehension of his need to experience life at his own pace.

But Dr. Mahler found just as many cases of childhood psychosis in which the mother had been of at least average competence and devotion. In some of these cases the child had shown such an extreme vulnerability—had behaved so abnormally almost from birth—that not even the most favorable environmental situation, the investigator is convinced, could have prevented psychosis. In such cases, she says the vulnerability is "seemingly intrinsic," or congenital.

Whether the disposition to childhood schizophrenia is innate or acquired, Dr. Mahler believes that the core of the problem is the same: an inability on the part of the child to use the mother as a "beacon of orientation." She points out that an infant's mental apparatus is too undeveloped to organize and act upon the stimuli he receives from within and without; hence his survival depends upon his mother. His psychological development also depends upon her. Even after he has passed the completely helpless stage, he looks to her for guidance and strength in a world that can be terrifyingly—as well as enticingly—strange.

In the type of childhood schizophrenia described as *autism,* Dr. Mahler theorizes that the baby's personality development has failed to move beyond (or else has regressed to) the "normal autistic phase" of development. During this phase, lasting from birth until sometime in the second month, the infant seems completely unaware of any distinction between himself and the world around him. The most conspicuous symptom of the autistic child, says Dr. Mahler, is his apparently complete failure to perceive his mother as a living being who represents the outside world and serves as a beacon and guide. Mothers say: "I never could reach my baby. . . ." "He never greeted me when I entered, he never cried or even noticed when I left the room. . . ." "She never made any personal appeal for help at any time." Such a child seeks refuge in an "autistic shell," the investigator believes, because he apparently has experienced reality—and even his mother—as an intolerable source of irritation; he has defended himself by warding off reality and withdrawing into an utterly constricted, deanimated world.

In symbiotic child psychosis, according to Dr. Mahler's theory, the trouble with the baby's personality development arises at a later stage and results from an imbalance between the rates at which the child is maturing physically and emotionally.

As the investigator explains it, a maturational spurt puts the normal toddler, in his second year, in the position of relatively advanced physical independence. But in some cases his emotional development seems to lag far behind. Physically, in such a case, he is able to move away from his mother; emotionally he is not. So he is bewildered and panicky. Minor frustrations common to the early part of the separation-individuation phase bring extreme reactions. He may give up walking for months because of a fall. Typically, the break with reality is triggered by some event—such as enrollment in nursery school, the birth of a sibling, hospitalization—that makes him fear loss of or separation from his mother and throws him into a panic he cannot handle. In his hallucinations he appears to be trying to restore the delusion of an earlier period that he and his mother are one. Since constant panic is unbearable, the child retreats into "secondary autism" and cuts himself off from the world. Though his behavior is then like that seen in autism, says Dr. Mahler, successful treatment depends upon realizing that his personality has developed further, to a stage in the process by which a child separates from his mother. The goal of therapy, she believes, is to enable the mother and the child to reestablish the symbiotic tie, and then to help them move forward through the separation-individuation phase.

During the earlier research, Dr. Mahler and her associates were able to achieve this goal in about half of the dozen child-and-mother cases treated (four of the others withdrew from treatment against professional advice). The therapist saw mother and child together—several times a week and for as long as 2 hours at a time. The therapist's first task, the investigator explains, was to make her presence felt—to allow the child to experience it as something positive without having to acknowledge her existence as a person. Gradually her presence became a soothing phenomenon, and the

214

child felt more comfortable with it than without it. Then the child came to use the therapist as an extension of himself—a tool to reach something, a soft platform to learn against. Eventually he allowed her to meet his needs more actively—to feed him, to play with him.

"The theory is that the therapist represents a mothering *principle*, not a distinct human object," Dr. Mahler says. "The situation seems to be comparable to that stage in development when the baby dimly recognizes that ministrations relieving distress come from outside himself. It is likely that the therapist's comforting presence helps to ameliorate some of the child's intense aggression and destructiveness and, therefore, reduces the level of anxiety." Gradually, and in the face of considerable resentment at having to relate to her preschooler as to an infant, the mother was led into the kind of relationship with the child that had been established by the therapist.

The present research, with normal children and their mothers, was undertaken both to check Dr. Mahler's ideas about the critical importance of the separation-individuation phase and to help establish—as an aid to workers in the field of child mental health—the normal course of events during that period.

Stages of Development

From the work to date, Dr. Mahler offers the following picture of a child's development following the "normal autistic phase" of the first few weeks of life.

Beginning about the second month and continuing into the fifth, the infant is in the *symbiotic phase.* The boundaries between himself and his mother still tend to merge but he seems to be dimly aware—particularly when he is being fed, changed, or actively cared for in other ways—that his needs are being met by something outside of himself.

By the fifth or sixth month, the infant seems to recognize that the object through which his gratifications are provided and his discomfort relieved is his mother. When her face is near, he tries to touch and investigate it; he watches her play peek-a-boo and then plays it himself. This is the beginning of the *separation-individuation phase,* the subject of the current research.

The first 4 to 6 months of this stage are found to comprise a fairly distinct subphase which Dr. Mahler labels *differentiation.* It is marked not only by explorations of the mother's face and mouth and hair but also by a turning to the outside world for pleasure and stimulation. The infant looks beyond nearby objects. He takes a more active interest in toys. He finds pleasure in using his whole body. He begins to creep, climb, and stand up. He makes progress in coordinating the use of eyes, hands, and mouth. During this period the children at the Center were seen to be active for a longer time and to be more vivacious when their mothers were close. They showed a distinct preference for playing at their mothers' feet.

215

Beginning as early as the 10th month and as late as the 12th comes the subphase described as *practicing* during which the child takes delight in trying out his new skills, particularly his ability to get around by himself. Eager to explore his environment, he crawls or walks farther and farther from his mother's feet and often becomes so absorbed in his own activities that for long periods of time he seems to be oblivious to his mother's presence.

The infant's dominant mood during this practicing period, the investigator reports, is elation. As another authority on children has expressed it, the toddler is now beginning his "love affair with the world." There is such wonderment to be explored that he often disregards bumps, falls, and other frustrations. Sometimes at the Center he slips out of the infant room, where his mother is sitting, and makes his way into the adjacent toddler room which is equipped with toys and apparatus for the older children. But in the midst of his investigations he stops as if suddenly aware that something is wrong and goes back rapidly to his mother, only to venture forth again a little later.

A child during this phase seems to need periodic physical contact with his mother. "We see babies crawling to the mother, righting themselves on her leg or touching her in other ways," says Dr. Mahler, "or just standing and leaning against her for 'emotional refueling.' Even a wilting, fatigued infant perks up in a very short time upon such contact."

The Period of "Rapprochement"

At 18 months, or a little earlier or later, the child gradually passes into a stage when he is more subdued and even a little troubled. He has been acting during the practicing period as though he were omnipotent and the world were his for the taking. Now, Dr. Mahler reports, it dawns on him that he has to cope with the world as an individual who is very small, relatively helpless, separate, and lonely. Watching him in the playroom, the investigators notice that he is no longer either relatively unaware of his mother or unmindful of frustrations. And they interpret some of his expressions as indicating surprise at finding himself a separate being. For example, says Dr. Mahler, when he hurts himelf he looks perplexed because his mother is not—instantly and automatically—with him. As the toddler realizes his physical ability to move away from his mother, he generally seems to have a great need for her to share every new skill and experience. The observers' notes and the moving pictures show that children during this third stage of the separation-individuation process are continually concerned with their mothers' whereabouts.

Those watching a youngster week after week report than in this phase of development the toddler's pleasure in functioning on his own is proportionate to his success in eliciting his mother's interest and participation in his activities. When the mother leaves the room the child—sometimes only by a fleeting expression of sadness or anxiety, sometimes by a tantrum—displays unhappiness. Sometimes he goes and stands by or climbs onto *her* chair, taking it over for a while as a substitute for her. He does not easily accpet physical contact with people who offer themselves as substitutes. Because of this behavior, Dr. Mahler calls this third stage the period of *rapprochement.* For most of the youngsters studied, it is a time when individuation proceeds rapidly, but separation is resisted strongly. It is a period that is conducive to misunderstandings between mother and child. Some mothers cannot accept the child's demandingness, cannot understand why a toddler who is obviously more capable and independent than he was a few months ago during the practicing period, must now insist upon her sharing every aspect of his life.

As the investigator explains it, the child needs his mother's active emotional support at this time in order to prevent serious injury to his self-esteem. He has had inklings that he is not really the omnipotent being he had fancied himself. If he can count on backing from his mother, he comes gradually to accept this fact and to pour his energy into normal psychological development. "If the mother is quietly available," Dr. Mahler says, "if she shares the toddling adventurer's exploits, playfully reciprocates and thus helps his attempts at individuation, the relationship between mother and toddler progresses to the point where verbal communication takes over. Emotional participation that the toddler can count upon seems to facilitate the rich unfolding of his thought processes.

"The less emotionally available the mother has become," The investigator reports, "the more insistently and even desperately the toddler attempts to woo her." He won't accept comforting from anyone else; he can't seem to lose himself in play. If emotional supplies are not forthcoming, he seeks substitutes in eating and sucking. He also turns to such aggressive behavior as throwing things and hitting people. All this may drain so much of the energy available for development, Dr. Mahler theorizes, as to hamper psychological growth.

One sign of an unusual degree of conflict in the youngster, the investigator believes, is a more than average amount of "shadowing"–that is, keeping the mother in his sight even in the midst of play, and at other times following her around. Another sign is an exaggerated use of the game of darting away in order to provoke the mother into pursuing him and scooping him up. Both types of behavior have been observed in some of the children under study. Other children have shown a third danger signal–severe and protracted "separation anxiety" when the mother leaves the room.

The Final Subphase of Separation Individuation

The fourth subphase begins about the end of the second year and continues well into and sometimes all the way through the third year. It is a complex stage which the researchers describe as "the period in which object constancy is attained." They mean by this that during the final phase of the separation-individuation process the child develops the ability to retain mental representations of himself and his mother as distinctly separate individuals. When she is absent, the investigators explain, he can picture her as being away from him and also as returning to him; her continual physical presence becomes less imperative.

As an indication that this stage has begun, the child makes his way to the toddler room for prolonged periods and accepts the nursery teacher as a partial substitute for his mother. For example, he takes food from her and he gladly joins with her in play. But under many circumstances—including aggression by or against another child, weariness, a bump, soiled diapers—he calls for his mother and seeks her out. And if he is in that kind of emotional state he will insistently demand her when someone else enters the room, perhaps the opening door evokes the anticipation of the mother's appearance, the research team suggests, or perhaps the stress of having to cope with an additional, less familiar person makes the need for mother more acute.

The child shows an increasing interest both in his playmates and in adults other than his mother. He is mildly or moderately negativistic, showing resistance quite often to the demands of adults—a characteristic, remarks Dr. Mahler, that seems essential for the development of a sense of identity. He begins to develop an awareness of time, commonly absent in the schizophrenic child. Along with it he shows an increased ability to endure separation and delays. Concepts like "later" and "tomorrow"—generally first associated with the activities of his mother—come to be used as well as understood.

Crises arise in this period, Dr. Mahler reports, when the mother cannot accept the child's negativistic behavior and his more or less frequent display of "primary process" type of thinking, manifested in primitive, illogical talk and actions, and seen at its most extreme in schizophrenics. This kind of thinking is common among youngsters during this period, says Dr. Mahler, but even some apparently normal mothers are unable to deal with it calmly and help the child progress to the rational "secondary process." One mother, for example, found fault with her youngster for eating well at Grandma's but poorly at home. Angered, the child told her, "I eat you up. Then I spit you out. Then I put you in the garbage pail." The mother was hurt, angry, and disturbed. She and the youngster bickered for an hour. Finally the girl said, "Then I put you back together again." It would have been more conducive to emotional health, Dr. Mahler observes, had the mother said at the very beginning something like: "Now you know you are just being angry at Mommie. Maybe I shouldn't have said anything about how well you eat at Grandma's. Anyway, you know very well that nobody eats people and puts them in garbage pails."

Bridging the communicative gap between the child's world and the adult's, says the investigator, requires the deciphering of the child's primary-process language and actions, playing along with them, and gradually offering him more logical expressions and more realistic solutions to his problems. Fortunately, most mothers do this. To find and help those who don't, Dr. Mahler and her associates believe, would be one of the ways to help reduce the incidence of emotional disorders.

Variations in Behavior

The types of behavior characteristic of one subphase are not limited to it. In other periods, though, says the research team, either they are seen less frequently or they are less important to the particular developmental tasks with which the child is dealing. For example, a joyful exploration of the world is characteristic of the second, or practicing, subphase but of course occurs during the rapprochement period as well. Its occurrence during that period, though, is less significant than the behavior by which the child is working through the job of finding himself an individual, separate from his mother, yet renewing on a more advanced emotional level his bond to her (rapprochement).

Again, during the final subphase, even a youngster who has been eagerly coming to the toddler room for a long time may suddenly start clinging to his mother when she leaves for the infant room, where mothers are encouraged to stay. Or he may let her go but keep running back and forth, as he did for a time months earlier.

Nor does every child follow the pattern most characteristic of a particular stage. For some children in the rapprochement period, the need to assert separateness over-shadows the need to establish closeness. While one child seeks out his mother with every new toy or activity in order to engage her attention and participation, the researchers report, another child may be primarily engaged in making sure that this very thing does not happen. He will hold a toy in his hand, look at his mother, and veer off to seek out a different adult, or to remain by himself. This is most likely to be so if his mother has been overprotective and intrusive; in this case it is she, rather than the child, who becomes the "shadower."

The Mother's Influence

The research is documenting what most mothers know—that different children do not proceed through a given development stage either at the same rate or in the same way. And it is uncovering evidence that the mothers themselves influence the pattern.

Early during the first stage of the separation-individuation process, for example, Bernie showed great interest in locomotion and would persistently try to crawl and to pull himself up. Stuart, on the other hand, usually just lay on the floor and looked; though obviously interested in the things and the people around him, he made little effort to get to them. Constitutional factors may have been at work, say the investigators, but so were the attitudes of the mothers. Bernie's mother often appeared listless and apathetic during the earliest months but cheered up—and encouraged the boy—when he began moving around. Stuart's mother, though, liked to keep him close. Instead of encouraging him to shift for himself, she met all his needs so promptly that he never had to exert himself to get what he wanted. On the developmental tests when they first came to the center,

Bernie and Stuart rated about the same. A few years later, however, Stuart did not do nearly so well as Bernie.

Two sisters, Ann and Susan, are offered as particularly good illustrations of the strength of the maternal influence during the separation-individuation phase.

When Ann was 9 months old, she was often observed sitting at her mother's feet, looking up at her and patiently begging for attention. She got very little of it and in consequence, the investigators say, had little psychic energy for investing in the activities normal to the next, or practicing, subphase. She would make only brief forays from her mother; her "love affair with the world" was subdued and of unusually short duration. Throughout the final subphase, Ann was an unhappy little girl who could not easily endure physical separation from her mother, did not get along well with other adults and children, yet showed little joy when the mother returned after brief, everyday separations. In one camera-recorded scene, she has a tantrum when her mother starts to leave the room; the child insists on going along but then gives up and just stands there, suffering. Finally she regresses by retiring to the play area for the youngest babies. She turns her back on the other people and is clearly hurt and angry.

Like a few of the other children in the study, Ann is described as already vulnerable—already in trouble. The investigators believe that these vulnerable children, unless further environmental experience amply compensates, may well develop emotional problems rooted in the unmet needs and unaccomplished tasks of the separation-individuation phase. After the present study has been completed, the researchers hope to predict what types of problems are likely to develop in a given child under given circumstances and then to keep in touch with each family for some years.

With Susan, Ann's younger sister, the mother had mellowed even though she was the same somewhat aloof, self-centered person. At the center, every so often she would put the baby down and bury herself in the newspaper. But Susan was a more outward-going and determined baby than Ann, and when she wanted her mother's attention, she knew how to go about getting it. In one scene, she tugs at her mother's dress, beseeches her with her eyes, and finally starts to pull herself up to her mother's knee. The viewer can almost hear the mother say, "Oh, the heck with it," as she puts the paper aside and lovingly picks up the baby. In a later subphase, Susan looks distressed when her mother leaves the room but, unlike her sister, soon turns happily to playing with the other adults and children. She is joyful when her mother comes back. A child who has a good relationship with her mother, Dr. Mahler emphasizes, shows relatively little separation anxiety.

The difference between Ann's experiences and Susan's, the investigators suggest, may have had a genetic basis, since the younger girl was able to command the mother's attention and draw upon and be secure in her love while the other was not. But they believe that Ann's progress through this critical period would have been less stormy with a mother more attuned to the child's emotional needs.

With Genie, Danny, and Matthew—three children of Mrs. A., all of whom have been studied at the center—the similarities have been more striking than the differences. All three have been conspicuously motor minded. They undoubtedly had an inborn motor proclivity, says Dr. Mahler, but they also had a powerful secondary impetus: the mother's great interest in having them become independent as soon as possible. The incessant crawling, climbing, seesaw balancing, and such activities were not only pleasant in themselves but also brought the mother's approval. Particularly in Genie's case, the investigator believes that the hyperactivity probably served another purpose as well: it seemed to make up for an unmet need arising from the mother's tendency to ward off physical closeness and cuddling.

"The research has clearly established," Dr. Mahler reports in summing up the work so far, "that the emotional availability of the mother is necessary for the optimal unfolding of the child's innate potentialities." This is so, she explains, because the child, throughout the process of separating from the mother, is emotionally so dependent upon her. If he is left markedly uncertain about her emotional availability, signs of potential trouble are seen.

Dr. Mahler adds that the research also points to the sturdiness and adaptive capacity of the normal toddler. "Even against considerable odds," she remarks, "he is usually able to extract from his mother the necessary emotional supplies."

When the current work has been completed, the investigators expect to write a detailed description of mother-child interactions during each part of the separation-individuation phase and to list and explain the danger signs—those behaviors and attitudes believed to warn of impending emotional trouble for the child unless corrected.

Research Grants: MH 8238, MH 3353
Date of Interview: Mar. 17, 1966

References:

Mahler, Margaret S. Thoughts about development and individuation. *Psychoanal. Stud. Child,* 1963, 18.

Mahler, Margaret S. On early infantile psychosis: the symbiotic and autistic syndromes. *J. Amer. Acad. Child Psychiat.,* 1965, 4, 4.

Mahler, Margaret S. On the significance of the normal separation-individuation phase. *Drives, Affects, Behav.,* 1965, 2.

Mahler, Margaret S. On the development of basic moods, and the depressive effect. In Solnit, Schur & Loewenstein (Eds.), *Heinz Hartmann Festschrift.* New York: International Universities Press, 1966.

Mahler, Margaret S., Furer, M., & Settlage, C. FF. Severe emotional disturbances in childhood; psychosis. In *American handbook of psychiatry.* New York: Basic Books, 1959.

Mahler, Margaret S., & Laperriere, Kitty. Mother-child interaction during separation individuation. *Psychoanal. Quart.,* 1965, 34.

Early Social Development In Children

Investigator:
Richard Q. Bell, Ph.D.,
Chief, Infant Development Section
Child Research Branch, NIMH

Prepared by:
Antoinette Gattozzi

Most psychologists would agree that social behavior develops out of the interplay between the individual and his environment. From birth to early childhood the most significant elements of the individual's environment are probably his parents. The relationship between child and parents, once thought to fit a simple stimulus-response paradigm, generally is regarded today as a complex interaction whose nature is affected by both child and parents. The contributions of each coalesce with great subtlety and become more and more difficult to distinguish as the relationship moves through time. In a research program designed to circumvent this difficulty, Dr. Richard Q. Bell and his associates are looking for newborn behavior characteristics that are precursors of social development at the preschool age. The investigators are studying infants before they begin to interact with parents, then observing the subjects' social behavior when they reach the age of 2½ years.

Dr. Bell became interested in the direction of effects at work in parent-infant interaction through research he did some time ago with Dr. Earl S. Schaeffer of the NIMH Laboratory of Psychology. The two scientists devised a questionnaire to compare attitudes of mothers of mentally normal and abnormal children. Attitude patterns of mothers of schizophrenic children could not be distinguished from those of mothers whose children were mentally retarded because of brain damage or other birth defects. Dr. Bell inferred that the same factor—reaction to the child's condition—might be the significant one. This line of reasoning led him to questions about the child's effect on the parent and to the search for congenital characteristics.

Increasingly in recent years, clinicians have postulated that factors contributing to temperament differences among individuals may be present at birth, and that these early differences may be implicated in the later development of mental illnesses. No clear evidence has been found, however, that indicates what these factors are or how they are deleterious. The investigators' efforts to identify congenital contributions to social development, although not directly concerned with etiological problems, may show how to begin to answer such questions.

222

Two aspects of behavioral development were of special interest to the investigators—the child's tendency to stay near adults and his ability to cope with sudden, unexpected changes in the environment. Attachment to adults, in a sense, is the binding force of the parent-child interaction as well as its most important product. The mother may have no task of greater consequence during the first few months of her infant's life than to make her presence and actions important to him. Both attachment to adults and coping ability are highly salient features of human behavior, the development of which can be observed and measured in very young children. Moreover, these behaviors show a wide range of variability in any random sample of children. "They are fundamental dimensions of normal development," Dr. Bell notes, "and they find a prominent place in descriptions of both normal and aberrant personalities."

The research proceeded in two parallel projects. In one, the scientists observed neonates to record characteristics of individual infants before cultural forces had begun to shape them. These children were studied again when they reached preschool age. In the other project, the investigators observed the play of preschool children to detect patterns of social attachment and coping ability. Questionnaires were used in both projects. Each mother of a newborn subject filled in a questionnaire about her infant's behavior when he was 1 month old, then completed the same questionnaire when he was about 2½ years old. Mothers of the preschool children not studied as newborns completed the same questionnaire; that is, each recalled her child's behavior as an infant. Dr. Bell's design of the research included both prospective observations and retrospective questionnaires because he hoped to demonstrate how the two approaches might be combined in a longitudinal study to accelerate data analysis. This is another of Dr. Bell's research interests; it is a central concern in difficult, time-consuming longitudinal studies.

The major outcome of the program to date is the tentative identification of a congenital behavior syndrome, a pattern of newborn behavior that is linked to a pattern of social behavior at age 2½ years. The investigators found that a newborn male who shows high formula consumption relative to birth weight, whose respiration is rapid, and whose mother describes him as restless and hard to soothe at age 1 month, will be, at the age of 2½ years, relatively nonsocial. He will be rather disinterested in other children and relatively independent of adults.

Research results also include, in brief, the discovery of biological consequences associated with birth order and sex, the identification of biological effects of family size and structure on preschool social behavior, and the establishment of a tentative link between patterns of preschool social behavior and styles of cognition at age 6 years.

The Study of Newborns

Newborn infants are notably difficult subjects to study. In the welter of behavior they exhibit, many items are affected by temporary conditions of this period. Above all, change in the newborn is swift. To get meaningful and replicable results, factors known to affect neonate behavior transiently either must be accounted for or their effects eliminated from the data. Elements that change rapidly have to be avoided. Dr. Bell comments: "As an uncivilized human being the newborn is intriguing theoretically, while being at the same time one of the most difficult subjects as far as abstracting stable measurements is concerned."

Many past studies of newborns reported conflicting or inconclusive results because they failed to isolate influential variables. Dr. Bell compiled the following list of factors to be controlled in studies of infants and young children. It reveals how demanding such research is, especially studies carried out during the first hundred hours of life.

1. *State of arousal.*—There is a continuum of arousal that ranges from quiet sleep at one end to the excitation of robust crying at the other end. The infant's position along the quiescent range of the continuum is particularly difficult to judge, yet his arousal state clearly affects his behavior.

2. *Complications of pregnancy and delivery.*—These exert many effects, depending on their severity. In this connection it is worth noting that complications are significantly fewer the higher the socioeconomic level, and that males are more subject to complications than females.

3. *Parity.*—Evidence exists both documenting certain transient congenital differences between first- and later-born children and hinting at the possibility of lasting differences. For example, first-borns have been shown to have higher levels of L-lactic acid and 17-hydroxycorticosteroids during the first few days of life.

4. *Analgesics and anesthetics.*—These effects may originate in the prenatal or postnatal periods. Barbiturate medication give predelivery, for instance, has a pronounced dampening effect on the newborn's feeding adequacy and attention to visual stimuli up to the fourth day of life. A mother who is breast feeding and on sedation may pass residual sedation to her infant.

5. *Age and sex.*—There are key parameters in themselves, as well as factors that interact with others.

Over a period of 2 years, the investigators studied a total of 75 infants in the nursery of Suburban Hospital in Bethesda, Md. All infants were white, full-term, and free of complications of pregnancy and birth, so far as their records indicated. They came from families of various socio-economic backgrounds, and none was a first child. Observations were made on the third and fourth days of life—as far as possible from the confounding conditions concomitant with birth and as close as possible to the time infants were to be taken home. Among the measures the researchers obtained were rate and regularity of respiration, mouth movements, eye movements behind closed lids during sleep, rate and pattern of non-nutritive sucking (on a sterile nipple stuffed with cotton and offered just before regular feeding), rapidity and vigor of response to interruption of feeding, amount of time and height to which an infant raised his head while prone, tactile sensitivity, and various body dimensions. Of the 40 neonate characteristics measured, the investigators were interested only in those that showed wide range across infants and stability within individual infants, or those linked to known factors such as sex or parity. Stability was judged by the consistency of the measure from test to retest.

Interaction between sex and type of feeding.—Measures were made of the prone head reaction (PHR), which is presumed to be a correlate of muscle strength. The infant was placed supine for 55 seconds, then turned to the prone position. A soft rubber device was held near the infant's head to measure how high the chin was lifted during the next 60 seconds. On the basis of past studies, the researchers expected males to show higher PHR scores than females, indicating greater muscle strength in males. They also expected that PHR would correlate negatively with skin sensitivity, which was being tested separately.

Results were no more than suggestive concerning the hypothesis of greater muscle strength in males, and the data relating muscle strength to skin sensitivity also were inconclusive. Although the association was in the expected direction—the greater the muscle strength, the lower the sensitivity of the skin—correlations did not reach significance.

Perhaps the most valuable result of the PHR measurements was the discovery of a transient interaction between sex and type of feeding. On the first round of measurements, breast-fed males and bottle-fed females scored the highest PHR values; 13 hours later, at the time of the second observation cycle, this phenomenon receded and males scored generally higher than females regardless of the way they were fed.

The investigators found the same interaction between sex and type of feeding in their study of tactile sensitivity. This was not unexpected in view of the relation, even though it is of low order, between muscle strength and skin sensitivity. Unlike the experience with the PHR measures, however, the effect of the interaction did not disappear on retest. Breast-fed males and bottle-fed females still showed less skin sensitivity. These results confirmed the finding that type of feeding can interact with sex to produce an effect during the neonate period; the interaction affects, at least, PHR and skin sensitivity. Studies of newborns that unknowingly sampled different proportions of breast-fed males and bottle-fed females could encounter contradictory data.

Yet another surprising effect related to type of feeding was noted. After infants were handled for body measurements, breast-fed babies became and remained more active than bottle-fed infants. Dr. Bell offered two possible explanations. An electrolytic difference between the two kinds of milk may differentially affect arousal centers; or perhaps a breast-fed infant is more responsive to handling because he is usually more hungry than one fed by bottle. This may occur because his mother's milk is low in volume or late in starting.

Relation of skin sensitivity and arousal characteristics.—The original impetus behind the study of skin sensitivity was to search for sex differences. There is evidence that adult females have greater skin sensitivity than adult males. Such reports contributed to a hypothesis developed from observations of primitive human societies. The hypothesis is that males are equipped congenitally with greater muscle strength and higher tactile thresholds than females in order to fulfill the adult male role of gross motility in space and low response to pain. The principal adult female role, on the other hand, is the place-bound care of offspring, a role enhanced, according to the hypothesis, by the female's lesser muscle strength and higher skin sensitivity.

Investigations of newborn skin sensitivity have not been able to gather definitive evidence demonstrating a sex difference. It is still not known, therefore, to what extent the greater skin sensitivity of adult females is a congenital attribute and in what degree it is culturally induced. To discover how nature and nurture interact, scientists must isolate and measure each influence separately.

The investigators tried three different kinds of skin stimuli: Removal of a covering blanket, a fine jet of air, and application of the nylon points of an instrument known as an aesthesiometer. The first two of the three tests confirmed the hypothesis; their results pointed to greater skin sensitivity in females than in males. Females were more sensitive to stimulation of the abdomen, for example, than were males. The interaction of sex and type of feeding was found in the trials using the aesthesiometer.

The procedure with the aesthesiometer followed this form. As the infant slept, one of a set of increasingly thick nylon filaments was pressed against the heel of the left foot until the filament bent, at which point the pressure being exerted was exactly known. When the pressure of a filament elicited a response—anything from the flexing of two toes to mass body movement—the value was recorded as threshold. The procedure was followed three to five times during a sleep cycle (the infants slept right through the tests), and the final score was the mean of the individual trials.

As noted above, the tactile sensitivity data showed sex differences in some tests and on some subjects but not others, and the question of congenital sex differences in skin sensitivity could not be settled. However, two consistent relations appeared that opened an avenue for follow-up studies. Skin sensitivity scores were found to relate to other characteristics of the infants. Newborns with low skin sensitivity showed a low level of arousal as indicated by respiration characteristics while asleep and by slow response to interruption of sucking. Thus the data contributed to one of the research program's preliminary goals, the description of newborn behavior patterns that might be related to later behavior patterns.

Effects associated with sex and parity.—It became obvious early in the course of the newborn study that precise location of an infant's position on the arousal continuum was essential to clarify other variables. Arousal levels were monitored by subjective measures when the infant was awake and by respiration counts when asleep. The investigators were not entirely satisfied with the subjective measures and their use made replication of the study by others hard to do. To find out whether an objective measure of arousal might be used instead, Dr. George M. Weller undertook a separate study of infants' galvanic skin response. (Dr. Weller was a Ph. D.

candidate working at the Child Research Branch at the time. He is now on the faculty of Temple University in Philadelphia.)

Forty newborn infants from the nursery of the U.S. Naval Hospital Medical Center in Bethesda were the subjects. They were screened to exclude any with prenatal or perinatal complications. Only bottle-fed infants were chosen, and both first- and later-born were included. Skin conductance was measured by an electrode disc taped to the bottom of each foot. Activity was observed by Dr. Weller and recorded on a manual counter. Some items in the activity inventory were agitated crying, head movements, arm and hand movements, movements of the eyes behind closed lids, and no movement. These items defined six states of arousal ranging from deep sleep to marked agitation. Visual counts of respirations were made and then galvanic response was measured.

Dr. Weller found conductance and activity levels positively correlated more strongly in the waking than sleeping states; respiration, too, after special statistical treatment of the data, showed a positive correlation with conductance. The results indicated that galvanic skin response might be used as an objective measure of infant arousal levels. Dr. Weller also discovered that females and later-born infants showed consistently higher skin conductance and displayed higher levels of activity than their counterparts. He cautioned that before any implications may be drawn, the findings must first be confirmed (the finding on females has since been located in data from another study), and then shown to extend beyond the first days of life. Nevertheless, the study found the first unequivocal evidence of congenital differences between males and females and between first- and later-born infants. Because differences in conductance are associated with differences in maturation during this very early period, it can be said that females and later-borns are congenitally more mature than their counterparts up to the fourth day of life.

The results may be pertinent to the question of how nature and nurture interact. Girls are treated differently from boys by their parents; second- and later-born children not only experience the company of siblings absent from a first-born's early months of life, they also get different treatment from parents now versed in child rearing. These cultural differences frequently are cited to explain the persistent and often very obvious differences in social behavior between males and females and between first- and later-born children. Dr. Weller's findings indicate that biological factors may play a role in these differences.

Stable characteristics of newborns.—In the end, the voluminous data accumulated in the newborn study were analyzed to extract items that were stable from test to retest. Respiration rate during sleep and tactile sensitivity as measured by the aesthesiometer were the most stable characteristics. One other measure readily available from hospital records proved very stable; this was the amount of formula consumed by bottle-fed infants. Sucking patterns, total crying in response to sucking interruption, and PHR were next in order in stability. Borderline stability was shown by measures of respiration variability, pattern of crying, and reaction time in response to sucking interruption. It seems doubtful that many measures of arousal level and spontaneous skeletal muscle movements will be useful in studies of differences among newborns because of the instability of individual scores on these items.

The Study of Preschool Children

The preliminary study of preschool social behavior began with separate samples of 2-year-old boys and girls for whom no newborn data were available, and continued adding subjects as the children completed the 1 month of study and the investigators sharpened their methods. Children selected for these preliminary studies were second- or later-borns. Each mother completed a questionnaire that asked her to recall her child's behavior as an infant. From this questionnaire the researchers drew up "clusters" of infant behavior characteristics. These recalled characteristics were then related to clusters of preschool behavior displayed by the children. The analysis gave the investigators their first leads to the newborn and preschool relations they might find when they followed up the newborn subjects.

Later, when the children who were studied as newborns were near the age of 2½ years, they were brought to the nursery school daily in groups of six or seven of the same sex. Just as in the preliminary studies, they were studied at play by two teachers who participated in their activities and by two observers seated behind a one-way vision window. None knew what newborn factors had been singled out for possible relations to the behavior they watched. The observers counted and timed aspects of play and the teachers rated the children on such items as amount of physical contact initiated with teachers, ability to be soothed by teachers when upset, and relations with peers. Boys and girls displayed different patterns of play, an observation made by many other students of child behavior. Girls were more aware of others than boys and were more shy with strange adults. Boys were more interested in toys than people. Girls seemed more mature than boys in speech development and motor coordination.

Maternal recall as a mediator variable. — Dr. Bell devised a complex series of analyses employing maternal recall as a mediator variable to link the prospective and retrospective data and test the feasibility of this method of accelerated longitudinal analysis. The series began, as noted above, with the first samples of the preschool study by testing for relationships between sets of measures made by observing a child's behavior in nursery school and sets derived from the mother's retrospective report of his infancy. The comparison yielded the first potential relations between infancy and preschool behavior.

The next analysis used questionnaires completed when their infants were 1 month of age by mothers of subjects studied as newborns. Sets of items located on these were tested for relationships with sets from the (same) questionnaire retrospectively completed by mothers of preschool subjects not studied as newborns. In this way, the questionnaire itself was validated and measures were located in the 1-month questionnaires that could be related to measures made in newborn observations.

A third analysis located relations between sets of newborn measures and sets of items from questionnaires completed at age 1 month. The final step was to test for relations between newborn and preschool characteristics in a common sample. One set of newborn characteristics does appear to be associated with a set of preschool social characteristics. This is the congenital behavior syndrome in males discussed earlier in this report. It traces continuity between newborn behavior and social responsiveness; no clear relations have been found yet between newborn characteristics and later coping ability. The findings that led to the description of the congenital behavior syndrome currently are being prepared for publication, along with a report of relations found between all measures. The latter analyses do not rely on mediator variables such as maternal report or an index of family size and structure. This index, in addition to its potentiality as a mediator variable, was found to be related to aspects of dependency behavior.

Effects of family size and structure.—An arresting feature of behavior had appeared in the preliminary sample of preschoolers. Boys from large families with short intervals between children were consistently higher than other boys on the rating of teacher contact. Mrs. Mary F. Waldrop, director of the nursery school and one of the teachers, explored this observation. She noted studies of young animals made elsewhere that reported an offspring's need for maternal physical contact. Other researchers showed that a child deprived of protective adult support will increase his dependency behavior when he does have contact with adults. These reports suggested to Mrs. Waldrop that a child has a need for physical contact with a mother (or a mother substitute such as a female teacher) and that if the need is not met, he increases his efforts to achieve physical contact. A mother of many children closely spaced cannot always be available to any one child; indeed, other investigators have found that mothers of many children tend to become unconcerned about the younger ones. With these clues, Mrs. Waldrop began an analysis to test the hypothesis that preschool boys from large families would show more contact-seeking behavior with a female teacher than boys of the same age from smaller families. Further, by using some information about maternal availability in the home, she hoped to get a lead on whether a large family was associated with low-maternal availability.

The first step was to quantify the size and structure of a child's family in an index of family size and density (FSD) composed of four weighted factors. These were number of children, timespan between the child and his next younger sibling, timespan between the child and his next older sibling, and average timespan between all births. The higher the FSD index, the larger and more dense was the family into which the child was born.

An FSD index was computed for each of 44 boys and compared with the rating given him on the behavior "child initiated contact with female teacher." The postulated relation emerged. Moreover, a prediction based

229

on an alternative hypothesis was not supported. The behavior could not be explained by a child's greater experience of social contacts because of the number of siblings he had: There was no correlation between FSD and the rating "friendliness with peers."

A significant negative correlation was found between FSD and a rating made in the child's home of maternal initiation of contact. This finding raised the possibility that low-maternal availability in large, dense families may be a factor in the heightened contact-seeking behavior of children born into these families.

Are there other factors that might cause such a child to seek more contact with adults than do other children? Phrasing the question in the investigators' terms, are such children congenitally different from children born into small, low-density families?

To answer this question, Mrs. Waldrop turned to the analysis of a different set of data that had just become available. This was a sample of boys and girls for whom both newborn and nursery school measures were available. From the newborn data the investigator constructed a lethargy score for each child. It was obtained by adding the infant's ranks on (1) suck rate, the number of sucks counted during 8 minutes of non-nutritive sucking; (2) total crying, the number of cries during 60 seconds following removal of nipple; and (3) reaction time to nipple removal. The higher the score, according to the theory, the more lethargic and ineffectual as a feeder was the infant.

A significant positive correlation appeared between newborn lethargy and preschool contact seeking. The higher the lethargy score, the greater the amount of contact seeking. Another correlation tended to substantiate these findings. The higher the FSD index, the less was the child's ability to defend himself against the aggression of peers. These results were indicative of a distinct newborn behavior pattern in children born into large, dense families. The pattern is characterized as lethargy and is predictive of heightened contact-seeking behavior at the age of 2½ years.

By looking at the results of the two FSD studies together, it is possible to say that children born into large, dense families will tend at the preschool age to be dependent in this one sense. One component of the tendency is biological, a congenital pattern of lethargy, and the other may be social, low-maternal availability.

In one way these findings simply take a place in the large body of evidence detailing the risk of deleterious effects on children born into families with many siblings closely spaced. Other researchers have shown, for example, that rates of prematurity, maldevelopment, and mental deficiency increase with an increase in parity, especially after the third and fourth child. Infant mortality was found to be highest when the birth interval was less than 2 years; poor physical status and low IQ scores have been associated with an increase in family size. One epidemiological study discovered a strong correlation between paranoia and the presence of a sibling less than 2 years older.

In another way, however, the findings add a critical new idea to the study of family effects on child development. Most investigators have

230

assumed that the controlling factor was social class because large family size has been associated repeatedly with low socioeconomic status. But Mrs. Waldrop found no relation in her sample between FSD and a widely used index of the father's occupational-educational level. The results indicate, then, that families on the higher socioeconomic levels, if they are large and dense, are not exempt from the consequence of later children being more lethargic and less effectual feeders than their siblings. It might be well to note explicitly that these findings apply to large numbers of subjects, but not necessarily to an individual child in any one family.

The immediate value of this part of the program lies in the success of its unique methodology. The investigators demonstrated how to relate prospective and restrospective data. Their experience leads them to believe that mediator variables in addition to maternal report and FSD—for instance, social class—might be used to link newborn and preschool behavior in longitudinal and cross-sectional samples.

Dr. Bell and his colleagues plan to complete the data analyses of the newborn-preschool measures already in hand, and to make behavioral measures of infants born to couples studied in early marriage by other investigators of the Child Research Branch. They are also raising new questions about early social development. Does social responsiveness vary in infants as young as 3 or 4 months? What are the effects on mothers of specific newborn characteristics? In particular, how does a restless, hard-to-quiet infant affect the patterning and quality of his mother's care and peculiarly shape the initial opportunities of learning? Are there any characteristics of sleep during the first months of life associated with the congenital behavior syndrome? Having located some beginning and end points, the researchers now would like to trace processes involved in the transition.

The observations and ratings made in the nursery school also were employed to test another hypothesis, one relating social behavior to later cognitive development. Although this research question was not part of the original program goal, the necessary data were there so the investigators took the opportunity to use them in a new departure.

Social behavior and cognitive style.—Earlier studies of cognitive style had found that a maternal attitude fostering independence and interaction with the environment was associated with nonverbal skills; maternal fostering of dependence tended to develop a child's verbal abilities. A child's style of dependency has been related to another aspect of cognition, the way disparate objects are described and grouped. Two of investigators. Dr. Frank A. Pedersen and Paul H. Wender (the latter is working currently in the NIMH Laboratory of Clinical Psychology) wanted to see if the social behavior measures of preschool children were predictive of the children's cognitive functioning at age 6.

The investigators gave tests of cognition to a group of 6-year-old boys, graduates of the first nursery school sample. One test was the Wechsler Intelligence Scale for Children, which measures verbal and nonverbal abilities. Another was a new sorting test designed to elicit a child's style of categorizing. (It was devised by Dr. Irving Sigel, of the Merrill-Palmer

231

Institute.) The third was the Children's Embedded Figures Test, which measures the ability to extract a relevant item from an irrelevant surrounding field. It tests perceptual aspects of cognition and is thought to index an individual's dependence on context in acts of perception and judgment. In a series of studies that has extended over several years, Dr. Herman A. Witkin, of the State University of New York, has shown that those who are good at picking out the figure embedded in the surrounding field (field independent) tend to be socially autonomous and to take an active, analytical view of their world. Field-dependent subjects, conversely, are likely to be socially dependent and to see their world in diffuse, global terms.

Each boy's performance on these tasks was compared with his ratings on four different kinds of behavior reflecting dependence or autonomy, measured when he attended the nursery school: Contact seeking, attention seeking, orality (thumb sucking, mouthing), and sustained, directed activity. These were the findings:

- More contact-oriented, attention-seeking boys in the preschool period showed lower nonverbal IQ's at age 6 years than did boys not high on those preschool ratings. Those who had high ratings on sustained, directed activity in the nursery school were high on nonverbal IQ's at the later age.
- Boys rated high on contact seeking and orality in the earlier study were, at 6 years of age, high on the use of the categorization response that reflects the global approach.
- Those high on sustained, directed activity in the nursery school were more likely than the others to use a superordinate concept in their categorizations (recognizing, for example, that a saw and a pair of pliers were both tools), a style the investigators suggest is a high order of abstraction for 6-year-olds.

Results of the Children's Embedded Figures Test correlated significantly only with the early measures of orality, but all associations were in the predicted direction.

The investigators concluded that preschool dependency behavior is indeed predictive of certain kinds of cognitive functioning at age 6 years. Theirs is the first report of these relationships at so early an age.

On the basis of the data available to them, Drs. Pedersen and Wender were not prepared to say just what social or biological factors might be involved in the relation between social behavior and cognitive style. They were able, however, to rule out the influence of socioeconomic class. In their sample, family socioeconomic levels were not decisive relative to the differences in cognition displayed by the boys. Perhaps maternal or paternal attitudes are primarily mediating factors, as earlier studies indicate; or perhaps, as the investigators suggest, congenital factors make important contributions.

They made this suggestion after carrying the study one step further. Dr. Wender took a close look at the family reports of four boys who were extreme on social and cognitive measures, hoping to turn up some plausible leads on the parental characteristics differentiating the boys' polar positions. Not only did definite patterns fail to emerge, on the contrary, the boys came from remarkably diverse backgrounds. The investigators know that their review of the families is not reason to discount the influence of parental characteristics on the social-cognitive developmental axis. For one thing, their family information was based largely on contacts with mothers and did not include data for an analysis of paternal effects. For another, current learning theory suggests the importance of specific patterns and timing of rewards; this area of the children's background was unknown to the investigators. Still, the failure of the data to yield clues implicating parental characteristics calls into question hypotheses about the effect on cognition of maternal variables such as affection and neglect. An alternate hypothesis worth considering, the investigators say, is that "congenital differences in children generate the relationships between social behavior and cognitive functioning."

Intramural: NIMH
Date of Interviews: Mar. 24, 1966

References:

Accelerated Longitudinal Studies

Bell, R. Q. An experimental test of the accelerated longitudinal approach. *Child Developm.,* 1954, 25, 281-286.

Bell, R. Q. Retrospective and prospective views of early personality development. *Merrill-Palmer Quart. Behav. Developm.,* 1960, 6, 131-144.

Effects of Children on Parents

Bell, R. Q. The effect on the family of a limitation in coping ability in the child: a research approach and a finding. *Merrill-Palmer Quart. Behav. Developm.,* 1964, 10, 129-142.

Bell, R. Q. The problem of direction of effects in studies of parents and children. Paper presented at the Conference on Research Methodology in Parent-Child Interaction, held under auspices of the Department of Pediatrics, Upstate Medical Center, State University of New York, Syracuse, N.Y., October 1964.

Newborns

Bell, R. Q. Some factors to be controlled in studies of the behavior of newborns. *Biologia Neonatorum,* 1963, 5, 200-214.

Bell, R. Q. Level of arousal in breast-fed and bottle-fed human newborns. *Psychosom, Med.,* 1966, 28, 177-180.

Bell, R. Q., & Costello, N. S. Three tests for sex differences in tactile sensitivity in the newborn. *Biologia Neonatorum,* 1964, 7, 335-347.

Bell, R. Q., & Darling, J. F. The prone head reaction in the human neonate: relation with sex and tactile sensitivity. *Child Developm.,* 1965, 36, 943-949.

Weller, G. M., & Bell, R. Q. Basal skin conductance and neonatal state. *Child Developm.,* 1965, 36, 647-657.

Relation of Newborn and Preschool Behavior

Waldrop, M. F., & Bell, R. Q. Relation of preschool dependency behavior to family size and density. *Child Developm.,* 1964, 35, 1187-1195.

Waldrop, M. F., & Bell, R. Q. Effects of family size and density on newborn characteristics. *Amer. J. Orthopsychiat.,* 1966, 36, 544-550.

233

Social Behavior and Cognitive Functioning

Pedersen, F. A., & Wender, P. H. Early social correlates of cognitive functioning in young children. Paper presented at the Society for Research in Child Development, Minneapolis, March 1965.

Family Communication and Child Development

Investigator:
Fred L. Strodtbeck, Ph. D.
University of Chicago
Chicago, Ill.

Prepared by:
Herbert Yahraes

In the give and take of family discussions an investigator supported by the National Institute of Mental Health is seeking information on factors that influence the development of a young person's intelligence and personality.

Dr. Fred L. Strodtbeck and his research group at the University of Chicago use what they call the technique of revealed differences to study how members of a family interact. The father, the mother, and one or more teenage children are given copies of a set of questions and asked to respond individually. Some examples:

Should the parents of a 13-year-old girl have any say about who is invited to a party at the girl's house, or should the decision be entirely up to the girl?

A high school junior likes math and would like to take a geometry course but thinks she won't do well. Should she take the course, or should she take a course that she would be more certain of doing well in?

Having a nice personality and being well liked are more essential for success than any particular type of skill. Do you agree?

The families are then asked to talk over those problems—always numerous—on which differences of opinion have been revealed and to try to agree on an answer. At this point the experimenter leaves the room, but the discussions are recorded and later analyzed. Some of the cases on which there was disagreement are discussed by three or more members of the family, some by only two.

Members of the family, the grantee explains, have sized up one another over the years and now have certain expectations of how each will behave. Because of these expectations, a family discussion is likely to bring out typical behavior. Consequently, the discussion, or interaction, is analogous to a sample of blood: Analysis provides clues in the one case as to how the body is functioning, in the other, the family.

The grantee believes that the study of family interactions will get at some of the basic reasons for the ways, healthy or unhealthy, that children adjust to life and go on to influence the adjustment of others, in particular their own children. Findings will be checked, it is planned, when the children in the families studied have become adults.

The judges who listen to the tape recordings of the discussions give each participant a power score. On a given question, for example, if only the father gave a certain response but then, during the discussion, won the others to his way of thinking, he gets four points and the others none. If, instead, the mother and child won the father over to their side, they each get two points and the father none.

The judges also score the participants on such matters as the conviction with which a position was held; the contribution made by each person toward (a) reaching the decision, and (b) preventing and relieving strain during the discussion; self-assurance; and the warmth and understanding shown to each of the other persons.

Among other points considered during the analysis:

• The family's health, or the quality of family relationships, as inferred from how well the family went about reaching consensus on a given problem.

• The family's success in dispelling any tension so that members were free to move on to the next question with a clean slate.

• The masculinity of the father and the femininity of the mother.

High IQ vs. Average IQ Teenagers

In a study nearing completion, the University of Chicago group has used the revealed-difference technique to study families having an adolescent child between 13 and 15 with very high intellectual ability. Five of the children were girls, five were boys. They had IQ's higher than 160.

The controls were classmates of average ability. Their IQ's ranged from 110 to 120. Their fathers had been matched by religion and socioeconomic status with the fathers of the high IQ group.

One of Dr. Strodtbeck's graduate students had theorized, in suggesting the study, that the children with extremely good intellects would tend to be more isolated and withdrawn than the others and would thus make for poorer family relations. But the opposite has proved true: Family health was considerably better and the relations much warmer in the families with a brilliant child. This was not owing solely to the direct contribution of the brilliant child, for when the parents were discussing a problem alone, their warmth and helpfulness were even greater than when the child was present. In the other families, when the father and mother were alone, their relations grew rougher.

The high IQ family, Dr. Strodtbeck reports, has much greater problem-solving abilities. When the parents and the teenager talk with one another, they show greater precision in identifying their differences, and greater clarity in reconciling them. Presumably this is explained in part by the high intelligence of the youngster and perhaps of his parents as well. At the same time, Dr. Strodtbeck believes that growth of intellectual competence is fostered by the kind of warm family relations he finds displayed by the high IQ families in this study.

236

"We think that if a person's high intellectual capacity is to be realized," the grantee says, "he will have to be relatively free of internal concerns, so that he can continue to take in information about the world and to stimulate other people to talk in ways that enable him to learn from them. If a child's family life fulfills his needs, his energy is released for learning more about the outside world. But if he is tied up in neurotic conflicts in his family, he will not have the zest for taking in information from outside."

Recent studies have shown, the grantee notes, that the IQ's of children hospitalized as schizophrenics had started sliding down before the trouble became apparent. "When you're working on an extremely tough problem," he explains, "you just don't have as much energy for encoding information from the world around you."

Using the revealed-difference technique, another investigator has compared parents of children hospitalized for schizophrenia with parents of children hospitalized for tuberculosis. He found, Dr. Strodtbeck reports, that the husbands and wives of the schizophrenic children failed to reconcile their views—after originally giving different answers—five or six times as often as the parents of tubercular children. Dr. Strodtbeck believes that studies underway or planned by his research team will help uncover some of the elements in family relations responsible for such differences.

In addition to the teenagers and their parents in the IQ study, Dr. Strodtbeck's long-term research program embraces half a dozen groups, among them:

1. A number of young men who, with their parents, were first studied by Dr. Strodtbeck in 1952, in New Haven, when they were from 13 to 15 years old. The first study showed that the higher a father's power score, the lower the achievement values expressed by his son. The followup study finds that this effect apparently has a lasting influence. Young men whose fathers scored high in power tend to have chosen, or drifted into, occupations lower than their fathers'. On the other hand, the sons of fathers who were low in power tend to have outpaced them. Though other findings await analysis of the data, the grantee believes that one of them will verify and extend a finding of the IQ study. The New Haven study will show, he believes, that warmth in family interactions relates not only to functioning at higher IQ levels in early adolescence but also to higher accomplishment as an adult.

2. A group of "pathological families"—families with children in their teens who had needed treatment for a behavior problem from 3 to 10 years before the study.

3. A number of two-child families in which the parents are relatively young, about 40 years old when their first child is a high school junior, and a number in which the parents are 10 years older. This study is underway. Among the findings to date: The older parents permit their children to exert more influence than the younger, as measured by the power scores achieved during the family discussions.

The Acquirement of Masculinity and Femininity

The investigators are particularly interested in the processes by which a child takes on masculine or feminine attitudes, since the way a person identifies his sex role can be an important factor in his emotional health throughout life.

Dr. Strodtbeck explains that *masculinity* is taken to imply level headedness under pressure, the ability to strike out effectively when a crisis is at hand, an unwillingness to be involved in trivial concerns, the ability to act considerately and helpfully without the fear of being considered effeminate, and curiosity about what's going on.

On the other hand, *femininity* is taken to include a greater interest in persons than in things, concern for the quality of the relations between persons, the management of a paired relationship—as that between husband and wife—so that the members are complementary rather than competitive, patience in matters involving the welfare of others, and concern and support for members of one's group in time of crisis.

Among the families in the high versus low IQ study, the grantee reports, brilliant children displayed to a relatively high degree characteristics of the role commonly ascribed to the opposite sex. That is, a brilliant boy was judged to be more like his mother than an average boy, but at the same time not any the less like his father. A girl with a high IQ was judged to be more like her father than an average girl, but at the same time not any the less like her mother.

"We believe," says Dr. Strodtbeck, "that the greater warmth of the high IQ families makes it easier for a child to identify with the parent of the opposite sex and to do so without becoming anxious. Thus a child can behave more flexibly."

As evidence for such identification, the study has determined the correlation between the power scores of each of the parents and the lower rating the child has given to himself. The parent whose power is correlated most positively with the child's own sense of potency, the study assumes, will be the parent with whom the child most closely identifies.

The findings:

• Boys with average IQ—slight positive correlation with father's power, negative with mother's.

• Boys with high IQ—positive correlation with mother's power, negative with father's.

• Girls with average IQ—slight positive correlation with mother's power, negative with father's.

• Girls with high IQ—positive correlation with father's power, negative with mother's.

Dr. Strodtbeck emphasizes that these findings are based on a study of only 20 cases. But they make sense, he says, if one of the components of high intelligence is "freedom from phobic avoidance of elements characteristic of the opposite sex culture."

In sum, as this investigator sees it, the development of high intelligence is fostered by, and at the same time contributes to, family warmth and understanding. In such an atmosphere the gifted child is freer both to develop his capabilities and to adopt a broader set of worthwhile attitudes and qualities even though some of these are generally considered characteristic of the opposite sex.

Research Grant: MH 5572

Young People of Normal Mental Health

Investigator:
Daniel Offer, M.D.
Michael Reese Hospital
Chicago, Ill.

Prepared by:
Herbert Yahraes

Psychiatrists try to help sick people become well, but what is *well?* *What* do we mean by *normal mental health?*

Psychiatry has too long neglected this question, says Dr. Roy R. Grinker, Sr., an eminent psychiatrist and director of the Institute for Psychosomatic and Psychiatric Research and Training, Michael Reese Hospital and Medical Center, Chicago. Hence, as one part of a broad research program, members of the Institute's staff have been trying to find some of the answers. Their work is supported by the National Institute of Mental Health.

This report presents highlights of three studies: *First,* a continuing investigation of normal high school students; the work of a team headed by Dr. Daniel Offer, the institute's assistant director; *second,* a study, nearing completion, by Dr. David Marcus and several associates, including Dr. Offer, of what seems to be an important difference between families that do not have a disturbed adolescent child and families that do; *third,* a completed study by Dr. Grinker of a group of normal colleges students.

I. Psychiatry Views the Normal Adolescent

After some years of daily contact with adolescents who were disturbed or delinquent, or both, Dr. Offer decided to take a good look at the other kind, the normal ones—their backgrounds, personalities, viewpoints, worries, and behavior.

In adolescents, he points out, it has been unusually difficult to distinguish health from illness, normal turmoil from pathological process. Even in the case of psychotherapists, ideas about the characteristics making for normality in teenagers have been generally based on memories of a person's own adolescence and observations of his own children. With the understanding to be gained by a systematic study, Dr. Offer reasoned, psychotherapists would have a more valid baseline for judging disturbed teenagers, and families, schools and society in general would be better able to handle problems presented by teenagers and to recognize, prevent, and cope with abnormal behavior.

Dr. Offer is now halfway through an intensive 3-year study of 84 normal adolescents—boys from middle-class families in the Chicago metropolitan area selected from two public high schools during their freshman year.

Among the findings to date:

1. The normal adolescent, like the disturbed one, has feelings of shame, guilt, depression, or anxiety. But he is less afraid to look at himself and to admit his feelings. Psychiatrists would be happy, Dr. Offer remarks, if patients even at the end of therapy were as aware of their problems as these normal boys are of theirs.

2. Many of these atomic-age boys are worried about the same things that boys have worried about for generations—including sex, religion, and money. Only a few are worried about the state of the world. A teenager's three most difficult problems, these boys say, are to do as well educationally and vocationally as his family expects, to control his impulses, and to get along with other people.

3. The boys have a conservative sexual code and, through the sophomore year at least, they behave conservatively. Many of them daydream about a specific girl but do not readily admit it. Five percent go steady; 35 percent group-date only; 35 percent do not date at all. Typically the boys are concerned with how to behave when out with a girl. Most are interested in sports—as a means of displaying masculinity and of sublimating, Dr. Offer believes, both aggressive and sexual impulses.

4. About 20 percent smoke. A few drink.

5. Many of these normal boys—generally when they were only 12 or 13—have performed minor delinquent acts and have associated with delinquents. Twenty-five percent of them, in fact, have been involved with the police over such incidents as stealing from a drugstore, fighting, throwing bottles on highways, or overturning garbage cans. After a boy has been in trouble once or twice, though, he seems to have learned his lesson. He does not make delinquency a pattern. Nevertheless he sympathizes with juvenile delinquents and ascribes their troubles entirely to their parents and to society.

6. These normal teenagers are not inclined to rebel against either their parents or their parents' generation. They see clearly what values their parents hold, and they tend to hold the same ones themselves. When adolescents and parents disagree, it is on such matters as the use of the car and the time to come home at night. The boys find their fathers reliable, their mothers understanding. They feel closer to their mothers and can more easily discuss emotional problems with them.

7. Members of the group express definite ideas about what they are going to do when they have finished school. But they tend to change these ideas as time goes by.

For the most part these findings stem from four 40-minute psychiatric interviews with each boy, spread over a period of a year and a half. Four more such interviews are planned, as are less intensive interviews with the parents. The complete description of these normal adolescents will also take into account teacher ratings, school performance records, and the results of projective testing as other means of getting information about hopes, fears, and anxieties.

How does one pick a normal adolescent? Dr. Offer and his associates did it by going to two high schools in the fall of 1962, one in a suburb just north of Chicago and the other in a suburb just south, and giving several hundred freshmen boys two tests. One was the Self-Image Questionnaire for Adolescent Boys, developed by Dr. Offer and an associate, Dr. Melvin Sabshin, now head of the Department of Psychiatry of the University of Illinois College of Medicine; the other, the Bell Adjustment Inventory. Each comprised a number of scales, or subtests, and each scale was intended to measure one aspect of how the boy regarded himself or his world. Taken all together, the grantee believes, they provided a good picture of a boy's ability—in terms of his emotional adjustment—to meet his problems.

Of the boys tested, Dr. Offer selected the 114—about a third of the total—whose scores on all the subtests had been closest to the average. Thus he eliminated the boys who scored highest (and were, presumably, extremely well adjusted) and those who scored lowest. He also eliminated those who scored much higher than average in some areas and much lower than average in others. So in this study the normal adolescent is what Dr. Offer calls the *modal*, or average adolescent.

After making his selections, the investigator checked with the school authorities and found that 3 of the boys were serious behavior problems (in a randomly chosen group of the same size, 15 would have been). These were dropped from the study. A few boys declined to participate and a number moved.

Dr. Offer emphasizes that most of the boys being studied come from families at one or another level of the middle class. About 10 percent come from stable, working-class families, as would be expected from the proportion of such families in the population represented, and about 7 percent are Negroes, as again would be expected. Presumably the study's findings would hold true for middle-class communities in any metro- politan area.

None of these well-adjusted boys has lost a parent because of divorce, only three because of separation, only two because of death: in sum, only 6 percent come from disrupted homes. This compares with 9 percent of the general population of teenagers (aged 18) in the two communities studied and with 45 percent of the delinquent adolescents studied by another investigator.

More than half of the selected group are either the oldest or the only child in the family—a striking statistic, says Dr. Offer, but one that may only reflect the tendency of families to move to the suburbs when the first child is ready for school.

It developed also that the group had its share of honor students—12 percent—during the freshman year, but no failures.

When Dr. Offer was organizing his project, some of his associates doubted that it could succeed. Normal teenagers, they argued, would never show up for appointments with a psychiatrist—they'd feel disgraced.

As a matter of fact, more than half of the group did miss their appointments during the early months and had to be scheduled again. This proportion has now dropped to one-fifth, which the investigator considers good, because the interviews are held after school hours and frequently involve two round trips for the parent who does the driving.

Teenagers are extremely egotistical, Dr. Offer notes. They participate in the project because someone is interested in learning what they—and not adults—think about teenagers and the world. Teenagers are also extremely altruistic. They participate because they have been told that in the long run the project will help other teenagers.

What does he think of these normal youngsters? "Oh my!" the psychiatrist says, "They're tremendous!"

II. Teen-Agers in Trouble: A Communications Breakdown?

Parents requesting psychiatric help for an adolescent child, psychiatrists at Michael Reese observed over a 3-year period, complain most frequently about:

1. Delinquent behavior, ranging from assault and major theft to isolated incidences of vandalism in school.

2. Difficulty in making and keeping friends.

3. Inability to adjust to school situations.

4. Inability on the part of the parents to "manage" the adolescent.

The adolescents, on the other hand, most frequently complain that their parents do not understand them; hence their problems. Their second most frequent complaint is that they do not understand their parents.

The investigators asked themselves: In a family where the teenagers are apparently normal, have the parents and youngsters been understanding each other better than in a family where a teenager is disturbed?

Twenty middle-class families were studied, each intact and each including at least two adolescents ranging in age from 14 to 19 and in good physical health. Half the families were classified as normal, or non-disturbed: no member had, or had had, any obvious emotional trouble. The other half were classifed as disturbed: one of the adolescents had been hospitalized for psychiatric reasons, the diagnosis in five cases was schizophrenia and in five cases character disorders that had led to such actions as car stealing, assaulting parents, and, in the case of one girl, becoming pregnant.

Then the Q-sort technique was used to obtain from each adolescent both a description of himself and an account of how he thought his mother would describe him. Similarly, each mother described her son both as she would have liked him to be and as the thought he would describe himself.

Analysis of the data leads to these principal findings:

1. In normal families, mothers and children were in good communication. An adolescent understood his mother's expectations for him and was able in turn to convey his own viewpoints to his mother.

243

2. In disturbed families, the patient and the mother were in poor communication. The lines between the other disturbed adolescent and the mother were open but not to the same extent as in undisturbed families.

In general, it has been the experience at Michael Reese that the mother of a disturbed child explains that the child is rebellious toward her ideas—an explanation that the Michael Reese psychiatrists are inclined to disbelieve. In describing behavior as rebellious, they suggest, perhaps a mother is excessively suspicious or distrustful. Or perhaps she has been making inappropriate demands on the adolescent. Or perhaps, as in this study, the lines of communications have broken down: the adolescent has not known where the parent stood and the parent has not known where the adolescent stood.

Lack of communication, the investigators report, may apply particularly to adolescents who are delinquent but not psychotic. In the present study, in any event, such teenagers said they had been trying through their behavior to force open the communications at home, particularly with their mothers.

III. Normality in Young College Men

Several years ago, as part of a research project on how the body responds when emotions are repressed, Dr. Grinker had occasion to study 65 normal young men. They were freshmen at George Williams College in Chicago where the basic goal is "to provide professional education for Christian leadership, primarily for Young Men's Christian Associations," but where "men and women of all faiths and races who seek to prepare themselves in a Christian atmosphere. . ." are welcomed.

About half the group had been selected as normal on the basis of various personality tests; the others were judged normal on the basis of a psychiatric interview and answers to an extensive questionnaire.

After interviewing the selected students, Dr. Grinker's findings were startling. "Here was a type of young man I had not met before in my role of psychiatrist and rarely in my personal life," he reported. "On the surface they were free from psychotic, neurotic, or disabling personality traits. It seemed that I had encountered some mentally 'healthy' men who presented a unique opportunity for study." As the investigation continued he came to feel that the entire student body enjoyed unusual health.

Typically the healthy young men in the study came from small- or medium-sized Midwestern cities. Their fathers were semiskilled or white-collar workers earning a little more than $5,000. The parents had been loving but strict. Family quarrels, if any, had been generally over money. The boys had gone to work early. They had loved sports. They had had rigorous training in religion.

Factors emphasized by Dr. Grinker as having contributed to the boy's mental health include:
1. Sound physical health from birth onward.
2. Average rather than high intelligence.

3. Warm relationship with both parents.

4. Parental agreement about bringing up children—including the setting of definite and understood limitations on behavior.

5. Reasonable and consistent punishment.

6. Sound early religious training.

7. Part-time jobs when young.

8. Strong identification with the father.

9. A viewpoint (picked up at home, at church, in boys' clubs, at the Y.M.C.A.) that sees the world as calling for action, not introspection: a person *does* something about problems.

10. Ideals centered on doing the job well, doing good, being liked, achieving contentment and sociability, and succeeding at what one chooses to do rather than striving for either social or economic prestige.

The investigator divided his healthy young men into three groups—the very well adjusted, the fairly well adjusted, and the marginally adjusted—and then studied differences in their background and behavior. In general, the parents of the very well adjusted group had more often been in agreement about their children's unbringing, had more openly expressed their affection for each other, and had shown a less rigid concern over such problems as dating, smoking, and drinking. The mothers had been warmer, closer, and more relaxed, and more of the fathers had given all the love the students recalled having wanted. The very well adjusted individuals had done better in school and had been more active socially during adolescence. They were more specific than the others about what they wanted to do—go into Y.M.C.A. work, most of them—after college. They were less frequently anxious, embarrassed, or depressed. When they were angered they tended to speak out- the marginally adjusted ones, to keep quiet.

Even members of the very well adjusted group have had and do have problems. Dr. Grinker reports, "Like anyone living, they have had conflicts, established defenses, and have had to sacrifice potential assets in the process of adjustment." He notes in particular a narrowed range of interests and a tendency toward some anxiety about failing. But in general they and the others who were studied work and play well, cope realistically with experiences that rouse them emotionally, and have had warm, human relationships with parents, teachers, friends, and girls. They also feel good, and have hopes for the future—among them, "doing the best I can."

When he describes these young men to social and professional groups, Dr. Grinker is often told, "Those boys are sick; they have no ambition," He disagrees because he thinks "doing the best I can" *is* an ambition.

Intense commitment to change, the investigator says, may in itself be one of the elements in neurosis-building. Neither the men in this study nor their parents have shown much interest in moving fast; they go ahead at a pace that does not overstrain. They are not creative, not explorative; to many persons they might appear dull. But Dr. Grinker believes that they and people like them give our society "a solid steady core of stability."

The investigator observes that what he considers mental health or normality in these young men is of one type and that research among many kinds of populations is necessary to delineate other types and find what they have in common.

Research Grant: MH 4870

References:
Grinker, Roy R., Sr. (with the collaboration of Roy R. Grinker, Jr., and John Timberlake). "Mentally healthy" young males (homoclites). *Archives of General Psychiatry*, 6(6), 1962.
Offer, Daniel and Sabshin, Melvin. The psychiatrist and the normal adolescent. *Archives of General Psychiatry*, 9 (5), 1963.
Offer, Daniel, Sabshin, Melvin, and Marcus, David. Clinical evaluation of normal adolescents. Presented to American Psychiatric Association, May 1964. *American Journal of Psychiatry*, 121(9), 1965.

The Impact of Visual Media on Personality

Investigator:
Albert Bandura, Ph. D.
Stanford University
Palo Alto, Calif.

Prepared by:
Clarissa Wittenberg

One of the fundamental means by which human behavior is acquired and modified involves vicarious learning. Both children and adults learn modes and standards to a great extent by observing the behavior of others. A great deal of attention has been focused in this country upon the television industry as this fact has become more and more apparent. In addition to television, motion pictures, books, and other reading material are visual media effective in producing vicarious, as opposed to directly experienced, learning. The variety represented by television alone demonstrates the difficulty of making simple judgments about the effect on the viewer. The variations in viewers and the surrounding circumstances in which they see the television again points out the complexity. The most insistent public focus on TV has been with regard to violence and its part in the violence observed in our society. An investigation of violence per se seems less likely to yield information on the underlying process of influence than is the study of the visual media with regard to its impact on learning in general. Dr. Albert Bandura has spent over ten years studying the effects of such media upon children and adults in a variety of situations. His work yields the definite finding that such media are powerful methods of teaching and important sources of influence, but that many lessons may be taught and they may not be the obvious ones. It becomes obvious that the environment in which the media is viewed is very important.

This research has demonstrated the stimulation of aggressive behavior by the viewing of aggressive acts on a screen. Variables have then been explored with attention given to the characteristics of the model and the attributes of the observer, and the consequences accompanying the demonstrated patterns of behavior. The difference between acquisition and spontaneous performance of aggressive acts has been examined. Further research has been done with the use of the visual media as therapeutic tools to relieve longstanding and serious phobias and to improve the social adjustment of withdrawn children. The common thread throughout the research of Doctor Bandura and his associates is the concept of observational learning and the effectivity of the modeling process.

247

Doctor Bandura states that research bearing on modeling processes demonstrates that, unlike the relatively slow process of trial-and-error learning, patterns of behavior are rapidly acquired observationally in large segments or in their entirety. The extent of this form of learning can be seen in children's play when they reproduce parental behavior, including the appropriate mannerisms, voice inflections, and attitudes. This process in a more general way is referred to as "identification."

Doctor Bandura became involved in this subject in 1958 when he conducted with Richard Walters, research on the family conditions which gave rise to extreme aggression in children. The focus was the adolescent from the "good home" who became antisocial and delinquent. Although a great deal of research had been done about the effects of poor and adverse family and social conditions, not much had been done to explain the reasons why affluent young men were becoming delinquent and antisocial. Families were selected who looked well integrated and socially well adjusted, but whose children were being followed by the probation department in the San Francisco area. A matched control group was also interviewed. Two central factors emerged. Many parents of the delinquent boys were models for antisocial attitudes and aggressive behavior despite their smooth social exterior. A second pattern was that the parents, especially the fathers, often would not permit aggression towards themselves but would encourage and reward their son in fights outside the family or defend the boy's right to "raise–." In sharp contrast, the non-delinquent boys were encouraged more to defend themselves with their ideas or in the nonphysical spheres. Aggression of a physical type was consistently discouraged through nonpunitive means in these families. These boys, who were not on probation, had been taught through example and precept a different way of solving their interpersonal problems than the aggressive boys.

Another incident occurred that dramatized the influence of demonstration or modeling. In 1961 the San Francisco Chronicle reported that a boy had been seriously knifed during a reenactment of switchblade fight the boys had seen the previous evening on a televised rerun of the James Dean movie, *Rebel Without a Cause*. This was a vivid illustration of the imitation of film stimulation and stirred considerable speculation. The form of the aggression had been so clearly shaped by the film that it gave rise to the idea that aggression viewed through pictorial media may be influential in shaping the form of aggression when the person is in a provocative situation. The importance of the visual media in stimulation or instigating aggression also became a focus on this research.

Transmission of Aggression

One set of experiments was designed in 1961 to determine the extent to which aggression could be transmitted to children through exposure to aggressive adult models. In this early experiment children observed an adult who exhibited relatively unusual forms of physical and verbal

248

aggression towards a large inflated plastic "Bobo" doll. A second group watched a very subdued and inhibited model. The control group saw no model at all. Half the children in each experimental condition saw models of the same sex and half observed the opposite sex. Later the children were mildly frustrated by having toys restricted for their use and then their behavior was recorded in a new situation where they could behave either aggressively or nonaggressively. The results showed that exposure to aggressive models heightened the children's aggressive responses to subsequent frustration in new settings in which the model was absent.

In 1963 this investigation was extended by Bandura, Ross and Ross. The effects of real life models and filmed models were compared. The children in this project, as well as in many of these studies, were drawn from the Stanford University Nursery School. In this study they ranged from 35 to 69 months of age, with a mean age of 52 months. There were 48 boys and 48 girls who took part. Two adults, a male and a female, served as models. A female experimenter conducted the study with all of the children. A "Bobo" doll was again used as the subject of aggression.

One group of children observed real models in the room with them, behaving aggressively toward the doll. A second group saw a film of the same models performing the same acts. A third group saw a cartoon of an aggressive figure. The control group was not exposed to any of these stimulations. Again half of the children saw models of their same sex. These children had previously been rated in terms of their normal aggressive behavior by their nursery school teachers and they were matched to the control group on this basis.

The children who saw the real life aggression were asked into a room and invited to join a game. The child was shown a table with a variety of activities. The model also worked at a small table doing tinker toys. Then the model turned to the "Bobo" doll and kicked it about the room, sat on it and punched it in the head, pummeled it, and hit it with a mallet among other things. The sequence of acts was repeated three times and was accompanied by verbally aggressive comments such as "Sock him in the nose * * *," "hit him down * * *," "Pow." These acts were not those usually performed spontaneously by children with a "Bobo" doll. Although the doll is designed to be hit, the usual play involves poking it or trying to knock it over rather than "beating it up." The main interest of the research was not whether the children hit the doll but whether they adopted the unusual modes of aggression demonstrated by the adults.

The movie sequence was identical except it was presented on film.

The cartoon sequence was presented in a TV console and the experimenter introduced it as a color TV cartoon program. A film was then presented of a female model costumed as a cat performing against a brightly colored and fantastic setting. A title and a picture of a stage introduced the production. The cat figure then performed the same acts with the "Bobo" doll. Music was played accompanying the film.

Following the exposure, the children were tested for the amount of imitative and nonimitative aggression in a different experimental setting without the presence of models.

In order to clearly differentiate the exposure and test situations, subjects were tested for the amount of imitative learning in a different experimental room which was set off from the main nursery school building.

The children, both control and experimental groups, were mildly frustrated before they were brought to the test room by having the children begin to play with attractive toys and then being told that they were the experimenter's best toys and that she was saving them. The children were then taken to the testing room and the experimenter stayed with them, but did paperwork off to one side.

The testing room contained a variety of toys, some of which could be used for imitative or nonimitative aggressive acts, and others which tend to elicit predominantly nonaggressive forms of behavior. The aggressively oriented toys included a "Bobo" doll, a mallet and pegboard, dart guns, etc. The others included a tea set, crayons and paper, a ball, two dolls, etc. Play material was also arranged in such a way as to eliminate any variations in behavior due to mere placement.

The subject spent 20 minutes in the testing room during which time he was observed through a one-way mirror and his behavior was rated. The 20-minute session was divided into 5-second intervals, and so a subject was scored 240 times. The judges reached high levels of reliability in their scoring. The following response measures were obtained; imitative aggression; partially imitative responses; mallet aggression; sitting on "Bobo" doll; nonimitative aggression; aggressive gunplay.

Results

Exposure to aggressive models increased the probability that subjects will respond aggressively when instigated on later occasions. Further analysis shows that subjects who viewed the real life models do not differ from those who viewed the filmed or TV models in total aggressiveness, but all three experimental groups expressed significantly more nonimitative aggressive behavior than the control subjects.

The exposure to aggressive models is a highly effective method for shaping subjects' aggressive responses. Experimental subjects displayed a high level of imitative physical and verbally aggressive acts whereas control subjects rarely behaved in these novel aggressive ways. Thus exposure to aggressive models not only reduced children's inhibitions over aggressive behavior that they had previously learned, but also taught them new ways of aggressing.

A prediction had been made that imitation is positively related to the reality cues of the model and this was only partially supported. While subjects who observed the real-life aggressive models exhibited significantly more imitative aggression than subjects who viewed the cartoon model, the live and film, and the film and cartoon models increased nonimitative aggression in the children to the same degree. Data indicated that of the three experimental conditions, *exposure to humans on film portraying aggression was the most influential in eliciting and shaping aggressive behavior.*

The Effect of the Sex of the Model

The boys exhibited more total aggression than girls, more imitative aggression, more aggressive gunplay and more nonimitative aggressive behavior. The girls, for instance, were more likely to sit on a "Bobo" doll and refrain from punching it.

Subjects who were exposed to male models as compared to female models expressed significantly more aggressive gunplay. The most marked differences in aggressive gunplay were, however, found between the girls who had been exposed to the female model and males who had observed the male model. The girls who saw the female model tended to reproduce more partially imitative acts than the boys who saw the male model and were more likely to reproduce the larger actions.

The sex of the child and the sex of the model have an effect upon the degree of influence of the models, and this influence is determined in part by the sex appropriateness of the model's behavior.

Another section of this experiment dealt with the possibility of cathartic action upon the viewing of aggressive film material. The subjects were first frustrated and then provided with an opportunity to view an aggressive film following which their overt or fantasied aggression was measured. Many parents and educators encourage hyperaggressive children to participate in aggressive recreational activities, to view highly aggressive TV programs, and to be aggressive in therapeutic settings in order to "discharge" their aggression. Bandura's work and the work of other investigators demonstrate that the provision of aggressive models and the inadvertent reinforcement of aggression which occurs in these situations act to encourage aggressive tendencies rather than dissipating them. On the other hand, providing aggressive children with examples of alternative, constructive ways of coping with frustration can be very successful in helping them modify their destructive behavior patterns. Already frustrated children show more aggressive behavior after viewing live or filmed aggression than do frustrated children who are not shown a film. The filmed aggression *does not* fill their need, nor does it diminish their aggressive tendencies.

The view that social learning of aggression through exposure to aggressive film content is adopted by only deviant children, also finds little support in Doctor Bandura's research. The children who participated in this experiment were all considered normal; yet 88 percent of the subjects in the "Real-Life" and in the "Human Film" condition, and 79 percent of those in the "Cartoon" condition, exhibited varying degrees of imitative aggressive behavior. In assessing the possible influence of televised stimulation on behavior, it is important to distinguish between learning and overt performance. Although children may learn whole patterns of behavior by watching TV, they do not ordinarily perform indiscriminately the behavior of televised characters, even those who they regard as highly attractive. The responses of the parents appear to be very important in discouraging overt imitation. The investigators stress that the behavior is learned, however, even if parental disapproval inhibits it being performed and it may be elicited on future occasions. Indeed, recent research demonstrations show that children will not exhibit disapproved aggression in the presence of the prohibitive adult, but that they are inclined to perform such behavior when the disapproving adult is absent.

Children who had been previously rated as more aggressive than the others by their teachers did not differ in their aggressive reactions in the experimental setting.

The investigators have formulated a theory of social learning of aggression (Bandura and Walters, 1959) that would suggest that most of the responses utilized to hurt or injure others, such as kicking or hitting, were learned as exploratory asocial acts. For instance, the infant who learns to control his legs and kick is exercising and exploring his own movements, but not being aggressive. When frustrated, however, he may call on this response as one that can express his intense feelings, and then the kicking becomes involved in social interaction. On the basis of this theory, it would be predicted that the aggressive responses acquired imitatively, while not necessarily for aggressive goals in the experimental setting, would be utilized to serve such purposes in other social settings. It would also be predicted that children in the experimental settings would use this behavior aggressively more frequently than children in the control groups.

These previously mentioned experiments were primarily designed to measure the extent to which children learn by observing the aggressive action of adults. A second major question is whether exposure to aggressive models influences the harshness with which people treat others. To study interpersonal expression and aggressive behavior requires studies in which people are provided with opportunities to behave punitively toward another person after viewing aggressive or nonaggressive models. A study conducted in Doctor Bandura's laboratory by Donald Hartman reveals that aggressive models not only foster learning of aggressive behavior, but can also increase interpersonal aggression.

The catharsis hypothesis has generally assumed that viewing aggression reduces aggressive tendencies in observers if they experience anger at the time of exposure, but that it may increase aggression in nonangered viewers. To test this idea, Hartman conducted an experiment that proceeded in the following manner. One group of delinquent adolescents underwent an anger-arousing experience, while a second group had an essentially neutral experience. The boys then observed one of three movies. In the control film two boys engage in an active but cooperative basketball game, whereas in the other two films the boys get into an argument that develops into a fist fight. The instrumental-aggression film focuses on the behavior of the attacker, including his angry facial expressions, flying fists, foot thrusts, and hostile remarks. The pain-cues film focuses almost exclusively on the reactions of the victim as he is pummeled and kicked by his opponent.

Major obstacles arise in the study of interpersonal aggression because a socially significant measure would involve injurious behavior which cannot be used for humane and ethical reasons. This major obstacle has been overcome by several researchers by creating a situation in which one person can administer shocks of differing intensities and durations of his own choosing to another person. However, the electrodes are not connected to the victim so that he in fact does not suffer any pain. After viewing the films, the boys in Hartman's study were provided with opportunities to shock a victim. The intensity and the duration of the shocks administered were recorded.

Boys who had observed either the aggressive acts or the pain-cues films selected significantly higher shock levels, both under angered and nonangered conditions than boys who watched the control film. Moreover, angered viewers behaved more punitively than nonangered viewers following exposure to the aggressive films, a finding that is directly counter to the prediction of the usual catharsis hypothesis. Boys behaved most aggressively when they were angered and witnessed another person beaten severely.

Vicarious Reinforcement and Learning

In 1963 a study was reported by Bandura, Ross and Ross which explored the issue of vicarious reinforcement; that is, the changes in the behavior of observers resulting from witnessing the consequences experienced by others. In this study, nursery school children witnessed a variety of situations. The prime issue was whether or not they viewed an aggressive model being rewarded for his acts. The major finding was that children who witnessed the aggressive model rewarded showed more imitative aggression, and preferred to emulate the successful aggressor than children who observed the aggressive model who was punished. This last group both failed to reproduce his behavior and rejected him as a model. Control over aggression was vicariously transmitted to the boys by the administration of negative responses to the model and to the girls by the presentation of socially incompatible examples of behavior.

Interviews with the children at the completion of the experiment disclosed that although children in the aggression-rewarded conditions voiced disapproval while they watched the acts that they nevertheless emulated his behavior on the basis of its success. The key issue was that they admired the power the model gained over reward resources through his reprehensible behavior. The investigators noted that the children stated that physical aggression and forceful confiscation of the property of others is wrong and they criticized the model for doing it. Therefore, when these same children later copied this type of behavior, they can be expected to experience considerable conflict and discomfort. *They did not resolve this conflict by praising violence, but tended to do it by*

253

criticizing the victim. They viewed the victim as weak or provocative, ungenerous or unsharing, and thereby in a sense "bringing it on himself." In situations where the aggressive model was punished, even when the victim was quite provocative, the victim was not criticized and the aggressor was considered bad. Successful "pay off" of aggression rather than its intrinsic desirability served to stimulate imitation.

The implications of this finding in terms of the attitudinal and behavioral effects of television would indicate that successful hostile aggression would outweigh even the previously established values of right or wrong for the viewer. This study involves only a single aggressive incident that was rewarded or punished. In most televised programs the "bad guys" gain control over important resources and win considerable social and material rewards through aggressive acts, and punishment, if any, is delayed, as Dr. Bandura says, "until the last commercial." Many episodes which are antisocial and "pay off" are viewed before the punishment occurs.

Bandura and his associates find that fear of a punitive or aggressive model is not a necessary factor in identification and adoption of aggressive behavior. The success of the aggressive act rather than the fear of the aggressive agent is seen as more influential. This has relevance to the concept suggested by Freud of "identification with the aggressor," which postulates that a perceived threat by a punitive agent is the primary motivating force in the assumption of aggressive traits.

Social Power, Status and Identification

Although it is often assumed that social behavior is learned and modified through direct reward and punishment of responses, informal observation and studies suggest that the "power" of the individual involved may also be influential. A child who perceives his mother as a prime source of rewards in the family may identify with her rather than with the father who he may see as occupying a subordinate position, and even compete with him for rewards.

A study was devised to set up conditions with nursery school children and female and male models to reproduce possible family constellations of power and reward structures. One of the adults assumed the role of controller of a fabulous collection of toys and offered to go shopping for such highly desirable items as two-wheel bicycles for the children. The other adult served as a competitor, who monopolized the attractive play equipment and left the child out. In a second condition, the child was the recipient of rewards and attention. For half the boys and girls, the male controlled the reward resources simulating a husband-dominant home, and for the remaining children the female model controlled the positive resources as in a wife-dominant home. The two adults exhibited divergent patterns of behavior, and then the imitative behavior of the child was measured.

Models who were seen as having the power to reward elicited twice as much imitative behavior as models who were perceived by the children as possessing no control over the rewarding resources. Power inversions on the part of the male and female models produced cross-sex differences, particularly in girls. It was found a differential readiness existed between boys and girls in the willingness to imitate behavior by an opposite sex model. Boys showed a decided preference for the masculine role, whereas ambivalence and a masculine role preference were widespread among the girls. The investigators suggest that these findings probably reflect both the differential cultural tolerance for cross-sex behavior displayed by males and females, and the privileged status and relatively greater positive reinforcement of masculine role behavior in our society.

The research team further suggests that although failure to develop sex-appropriate behavior has received considerable attention and is often assumed to be established and maintained by concepts of dependency, psychosexual threat and anxiety, external social variables may also be important. For instance, the distribution of the rewarding power within a family may be very important. Although the small child has great contact with this mother he also has ample time to observe his father's behavior. Also children do not adopt "wholesale" the traits of one model. A child exhibits a relatively novel mix of behavior in his own repertoire.

The makeup of the family constellation is also important. This research shows that in a three-person group, for instance, if one person is denied access to rewards, the others may experience negative evaluations of the rewarding model and thereby decrease his impact as a modeling stimulus. The introduction of each new person and his treatment at the hands of the model may produce new shifts in the relationships.

Reinforcement by Self-Approval

People tend to set for themselves certain standards of behavior and respond to their own actions in self-rewarding and self-punishing ways in accordance with their self-imposed demands. This is a major difference in human and animal learning studies. Even children can decide whether their own performance is creditable or not. Speculation about how children develop these internal standards was transformed into an experiment. The children were given the opportunity to observe models performing, and then permitted to evaluate their attainments according to high or low standards and reward themselves accordingly. It was predicted that children tend to adopt the standards of self-reward exhibited by the models they observed, but that children in the control group who saw no model would have no consistent pattern of self-reinforcement. It was also predicted that the subjects would adopt the self-reinforcement patterns of the same sex model to a greater degree than that of a model of the opposite sex. It was also predicted that children would match the self-reinforcement patterns of adult models more closely than those of peers.

This study reported by Bandura and Kupers had a group of boys and girls from a summer recreation program as subjects. It was designed to be an investigation of the transmission of standards of self-reward. The children ranged from 7 to 9 years in age. Adult and child models performed a bowling game in which they adopted either high achievement standards or a low standard for self-reward. On games in which the models attained their standard, they praised themselves and treated themselves to candy; but when their attainments fell short of their adopted standards, they appeared self-critical. Later, the children who had observed, played the same game alone and the scores for which they rewarded themselves were recorded. The control children saw no models at all.

Children who saw no models or who saw models with low standards tended to reward themselves generously following a mediocre attainment. Children, who saw models set high standards for self-rewards, rewarded themselves sparingly and only when they attained a superior performance. This suggests that the behavior of the models is influential in the development of self-control as well as in the transmission of standards for self-rewards. The children tended to match the patterns for rewards set by the adult models more closely than those set by peer models. The results showed that patterns of self-reinforcement can be acquired imitatively through exposure to models, without the subjects themselves being administered any direct differential reinforcement by external agents.

Another study was devised to further examine the formation of personal standards. In the experiment previously described, the children modeled their own standards after those of the model. It was thought that this was partly because the performance scores had little absolute value and therefore the evaluation of the model served as a primary basis for judging what might constitute an inadequate or superior performance. This study was also designed to see if observers would select models who were similar to themselves in ability and reject those who were markedly divergent. It was predicted that subjects would adopt the self-reinforcement standards of the model whose ability or competence was similar to their own. They would disregard the examples of those whose accomplishments were too different from their own and adopt a more reasonable standard for themselves. The investigators hypothesized that even low or merely adequate performances by adults would be highly regarded, and if a child matched or exceeded the performance of an adult that it would raise his own self-esteem. It was hypothesized that children attaining the achievement level of even an inadequate adult would tend to reward themselves highly.

In this study, groups of 80 boys and 80 girls ranging in age from 8 to 11 years were given a series of tasks and then they were either told that they were successful or not. Then they observed a model displaying competent, superior or inferior performance. The superior model adopted an exceedingly high standard for self-reward, and the inferior model set a low one. The children assigned to a control group saw no models at all.

Results showed that children who observed inferior models tended to adopt lower standards for themselves and rewarded themselves more generously than children who were exposed to more competent models with higher standards. Children tended to scale down the achievements of

256

the adults to a lower standard more commensurate with their own abilities.

This experiment also examined whether children's willingness to adhere to high standards is affected by their prior success or failure experiences. Children who have had failure experiences tended to reward themselves less than their successful counterparts, a finding that was most noticeable among children exposed to the inferior model. Control subjects who had experienced failure displayed a higher rate of self-reinforcement at lower levels of performance than did children who experienced past success. The investigators suggest that under some circumstances self-gratification may primarily serve a therapeutic rather than a self-congratulatory function. The same principle is seen when a person "treats" himself to a play or a special dinner to help himself over a difficult experience.

Another finding was that boys and girls differed significantly in the frequency of verbal self-praise, but not in the incidence and magnitude of self-administered material rewards, such as candy. Boys were more generous in commending themselves for equivalent achievements.

Contiguity and Other Factors

It is often assumed that the occurrence of limitative or observational learning is based on the observer experiencing reinforcing consequences. This does not account for the learning of imitative behavior when the observer does not perform the model's responses during the process of acquisition, and where neither rewards nor punishments are given to either model or observer. It is suggested that in these cases a contiguity theory can best account for observational learning. Contiguity means that events or objects in a series or close to each other in time or space become associated. When an observer then witnesses a model exhibit a sequence of responses the observer acquires through the principle of contiguous association of sensory events certain perceptual and symbolic responses that cue other responses even after time has elapsed.

Bandura states that the acquisition of matching responses may take place through contiguity, whereas the reinforcements administered to a model exert their major influence on the performance of imitatively learned responses. Several of Bandura's studies have shown that even children who do not reproduce the aggressive behavior of models were able to describe the behavior in great and accurate detail. When these nonperformers were rewarded they would readily reproduce the modeled behavior. However, these children usually failed to reproduce the entire behavior pattern and this indicates that factors other than exposure to models or contiguity influence response acquisition. It appears that observers attend to models that are most relevant to them. Both prior experience and the distinctive qualities of the modeling example are important in determining the attention paid to it by the observer.

Social behavior is generally highly complex and composed of a large number of different behavior units combined in a particular manner.

Bandura points out that such responses are produced by combinations of previously learned components which themselves may be intricate units. The rate of acquisition of new responses will then be partly determined by the extent to which the necessary components are contained in the repertoire of the observer. For instance, small children may be more able to reproduce motor behavior than verbal behavior.

Learning—Pain, Fear, and Other Emotional States

Studies of vicarious emotional learning show that people develop emotional reactions to certain places, people, or events through observing others undergoing emotional experiences. However, the findings reveal wide individual differences in the degree to which people are affected by the emotional arousal of others. Bandura and Rosenthal reasoned that observers who are easily susceptible to emotional reactions and who are emotionally aroused at the time of exposure to the affective expressions of others will show the strongest emotional learning. To test the hypotheses, adults observed a model performing a task when a buzzer sounds and then the model feigns an expression of pain as though he had been shocked. Throughout this period, the observers' physiological responses were measured to determine the degree to which the formerly neutral buzzer had taken on negative emotional value for the observers as a result of the other person's adverse experiences.

Prior to the emotional conditioning phase of the study, observers experienced different degrees of emotional arousal produced both physiologically and psychologically through the administration of epinephrine, a sympathetic stimulant. Before the study began all subjects completed the Taylor Manifest Anxiety Scale to provide a measure of their general susceptibility to emotional arousal.

The results show that the observer's level of emotional arousal is a significant determinant of vicarious emotional learning. Observers who experienced either very low or very high arousal displayed the weakest vicarious learning of emotional responses, whereas those who were under moderate arousal were affected most. Interviews conducted with the adults after the experiment was completed disclosed that those in the high arousal groups neutralized the emotion-arousing situation by diverting their attention from the model's distressing cues and by conjuring up positive or relaxing thoughts. Further study of these cognitive activities may throw light on how people insulate themselves against the distressing experiences of others. In this experiment some subjects felt extremely empathic with the model and others derived considerable satisfaction from witnessing pain being inflicted upon the model.

Therapeutic Applications of Modeling Procedures

Research in this area has shown the potential of modeling influences for changing people's attitudes, behavior, and even their personal standards of

258

self-evaluation. It is also a potent means of treating powerfully charged patterns such as phobias and fears of long standing. One experiment, reported in 1967 by Bandura, Grusec, and Menlove, treated children who were extremely afraid of dogs. During the course of treatment, the phobic children who observed a bold peer-model handle dogs comfortably and appropriately, lost their fears.

After being referred by their parents, the children were given standardized performance tests, on the basis of which 24 boys and 24 girls, ranging in ages from 3 to 5 years, were selected.

The initial selection test included a graded sequence of tasks which involved increasingly intimate interactions with a dog. Initially, the investigators brought the children into a room where a cocker spaniel was confined in a modified playpen. Later, tasks were required which ranged from walking up to and looking at the dog, to finally climbing into the pen with the dog, petting her, scratching her, and then remaining alone with the dog in the room.

The children were then assigned to one of the following treatments: a modeling-positive-context where a fearless peer model exhibited progressively bold interaction with a dog in the midst of an enjoyable partylike atmosphere; a modeling-neutral-context where the subjects observed the same type of brave behavior modeled, but in a neutral atmosphere; an exposure-no-model condition (here the children saw the dog, but with the model absent); a positive-context group which participated in the party, but were never exposed to either the dog or the model.

The day after the treatment series was completed the children were tested with the experimental animal; then about 1½ hours later, with an unfamiliar white mongrel. The dogs had been tested prior to the experiment, and it was established that they were about the same in terms of activity level and attractiveness. Half the children were tested with the familiar animal first, and then with the unfamiliar white mongrel; for the remainder, the sequence was reversed.

A month later a followup evaluation was done, and the children were again tested to determine the stability of the treatment effects, as manifested by the children's willingness to interact fearlessly with the dogs. The two groups of children who observed the peer model interact fearlessly with the dog, achieved and retained substantial reduction in their fears of dogs. In an effort to minimize the cognitive aspects, all the children were informed that the test animals were harmless. After the experiment was over, the children were told that while most dogs were friendly, before petting an unfamiliar dog they should ask the owner. This was done to reduce indiscriminate acts by the children toward strange dogs.

The effect of the modeling was obvious; the atmosphere, whether partylike or not, had a minor effect, if any.

The investigators speculate that several factors are involved in the extinction or disappearance of the avoidant behavior. One is simply that as the child acquires more information about dogs and about contact with dogs, he becomes less fearful. The nonoccurrence of anticipated adverse

259

consequences to the model, plus the pleasure the model has from contact with the dog, may help extinguish the fear reaction as well.

Treatment of Dog Phobia Through Filmed Modeling

Another experiment was done (Bandura and Menlove, 1968) with children who were seriously fearful of dogs. One group was shown a movie which demonstrated how a single model would display progressively less fearful interactions with a dog, as in the preceding experiment. Another group observed a movie which showed boys and girls of varying ages interacting positively with a variety of dogs of different sizes and dispositions. Children in the control group were shown movies with no canine characters.

Results showed that children who observed approach behavior which resulted in no adverse effects to the model, displayed enduring and generalized reductions in their own concerns about dogs. Controls showed no change. Comparison of the final step achieved (i.e., staying with a dog alone) by children who had seen the single model and those who had seen the movie with many models showed that the latter approach was superior. However, although modeling was equally effective regardless of the severity of the children's phobic behavior, those who manifested a wide variety of fears benefited somewhat less from the multiple modeling technique than children who had fewer fears.

The control children were shown the multiple model film after the main experiment was completed. They were markedly more able to handle dogs after this.

The investigators found here that the symbolic portrayal is less powerful than live demonstrations. A single model seen live is more effective than a single model shown in a movie. However, a movie can be made more powerful by using multiple models and a wider variety of objects than it is usually practical to provide live.

Snake Phobia Project

This project, conducted by Bandura, Blanchard, and Ritter, was carried out with adolescent and adult subjects who were terrified of snakes. In the area of California where Stanford is located, snakes are prevalent enough to seriously limit the life choices of any adult who is severely frightened by snakes. For instance, it would mean he couldn't be in any job where he would be required to inspect houses, read meters, show real estate, do plumbing, or any activity where he might be out of doors or in basements. He would be limited as to the location of his home and be largely unable to participate in many popular local sports, such as hiking or camping.

Fear of snakes is considered by psychologists to be a relatively stable fear and for that reason is often used in laboratory experiments.

The subjects ranged in age from 14 to 60 years of age. Some of the phobias had existed for 15 to 20 years. In the initial phase of the experiment, the participants were administered a behavioral test that measured the strength of their avoidance of snakes. In addition, they completed a comprehensive fear inventory. This inventory was then available for determination later to determine if reduction in anxiety about snakes brought about other changes.

The cases were individually matched on the basis of their avoidance behavior and assigned to one of four conditions. One group participated in a symbolic modeling treatment where they would run for themselves a film depicting young children, adolescents, and adults engaging in progressively more threatening situations and interactions with a large (about 4-feet long) king snake. The subjects were taught to be relaxed during the film. They were told to stop the film when scenes made them anxious, reverse it to the beginning, and watch it over. They were asked to attempt to achieve deep relaxation at the same time. They were to view the threatening scene repeatedly until it was neutralized for them.

The second group, receiving live modeling with guided participation, watched a model handle a snake in increasing proximity until it was wrapped around him. The subjects were then aided in performing with the snake. The model held the snake and had the subject touch it, stroke it, and then gradually hold it until anxieties about contact were gone. Then the subject and the model performed the tasks together until the clients were able to hold the snake in their laps, to let it crawl around, and finally to retrieve it.

The third group received a form of desensitization treatment. Deep relaxation was paired with imagined scenes of interactions with snakes. As in other conditions, the treatment was continued until the clients' anxieties had disappeared or until the maximum time of 6 hours allotted had passed. This time limit was imposed upon all groups.

Subjects in the control condition participated in the behavioral and attitudinal assessments without receiving any intervening treatment.

In the assessment phase, all initial tests were readministered. In order to test the generality of extinction effects, half the clients in each of the conditions were tested with the now familiar brown-striped king snake and then with an unfamiliar crimson-splotched corn snake that appeared strikingly different. The rest of the groups saw the snakes in reverse order.

The subjects were asked to look at, touch, and hold a snake with bare and gloved hands; to remove the snake from its cage, let it loose in the room, and then replace it in the cage; to hold it within 5 inches of their faces, and finally to tolerate the snake in their laps while they held their hands passively at their sides. Before and during these tests clients rated the intensity of their anxiety on scales.

Control subjects remained unchanged in their ability to handle the snake. The subjects who had symbolic modeling and desensitization had substantial reductions in phobic behavior, and *live modeling combined with guided participation proved to be an unusually powerful treatment that eliminated snake phobias in virtually all subjects (92 percent).* The modeling procedures not only extinguished avoidance responses of long standing, but they also neutralized the anxiety-arousing properties of the phobic objects. Both of the modeling treatments achieved marked decrements in anticipatory and performance anxiety. Although subjects who had received desensitization treatment also experienced less emotional arousal when approaching a snake, the magnitude of their fear reduction was significantly less than that shown by their counterparts in the modeling conditions.

It was found that attitude changes toward snakes occurred. The more potent the treatment and the more changed the subjects ability to handle the snake, the greater the positive change in attitude.

In addition, other fears were affected by the removal of the snake phobias. Fear of other issues was relieved in proportion to the potency of the treatments employed. For instance, live modeling with subject participation effected widespread fear reductions, not only related to animal anxieties, but also in relation to a variety of threats involving both interpersonal and nonsocial events. The investigators note that this seems to involve two different processes. The first involves generalization of extinction effects from treated stimuli to related anxiety sources. In other words, being relieved of one serious fear makes a person generally less fearful and more able to cope realistically with other concerns. The second entails positive reinforcement of a sense of capability. Having successfully overcome a phobia that had plagued them for most of their lives, subjects reported new confidence that they could conquer other problems and successfully deal with other anxiety-arousing situations.

A 1-month followup assessment revealed that the beneficial changes produced in behavior, attitudes, and emotional responsiveness were effectively maintained. The clients also displayed evidence that the behavior improvements had been carried over from the therapeutic to the real-life situations. They were able to hike, garden, and even help frightened friends or children overcome fear of snakes.

It is the conviction of these investigators that any type of phobic disorder can be successfully treated by this method with considerable success. Subsequent experiments show that information alone does not contribute to therapeutic change. It was primarily through a combination of demonstration, information, guided performance, and the control over observational experiences that this success was achieved.

Other snake phobia treatment experiments have been done with children as subjects, and these have been equally successful.

A slightly different type of therapeutic program was developed by Robert O'Connor working with Doctor Bandura to improve the social behavior of withdrawn children in a nursery school setting. A group of withdrawn children was shown films of children playing together and having a very good time. Another group, as controls, was shown a movie about Marineland, instead. The group of withdrawn children, who had seen the movie designed to help them overcome their social inhibitions, showed demonstrable improvements in social interactions; those who had seen the other film, showed no change in their behavior.

Conclusions

There is little doubt that filmed or televised images have tremendous power to shape attitudes and behavior. That this deserves investigation can hardly be questioned when we realize the almost universal contemporary exposure to TV. The complexity of the problem and the successful study of TV and movies are best approached by isolating factor after factor, and then painstakingly evaluating the results. These studies are even more striking when it is clear that they, for the most part, deal with the impact of single incidents with relatively little reinforcement, whereas the average commercial-viewing fare is repetitive and often highly glamorized. The multiple violent techniques demonstrated by a wide variety of relatively unpunished people on TV can be expected to be highly effective in teaching, and even in eliciting violent and aggressive behavior in the viewers. On the other hand, there is the same potential for influencing viewers toward positive action and more constructive methods of problem solving. Unfortunately some of the problem-solving forums that are televised, such as the U.N. in critical debates, are repetitious, monotonous, lacking in the pace and focused force of the usual programming, even though there is no denying their importance. Television can contribute to the dissemination of information and be highly influential in developing awareness. However, this research points out that, at times, new information without some guide as to action can arouse increased anxiety. The stream of information about slums and racial tensions without constructive proposals may illustrate this phenomenon.

Since people can imitate more successfully acts that are within their own range, they may imitate the more direct acts rather than the more abstract ones. This is likely to be especially true of children who, for instance, are more likely to have extensive physical vocabularies than verbal ones.

Doctor Bandura's research has dealt with the simpler units of behavior, and he indicates that he feels that more research should be done in terms of subtle factors. Physical violence is not the only kind of destructive act and, perhaps, even more benign than some types of interactions between people. For example, the portrayal of racial prejudice, the dramatizing and romanticizing of poor marital interactions, lying, and cheating may be more important than the number of fist fights and murders that are seen. In addition, Dr. Bandura states:

> "All the laboratory studies that I have reported deal with the immediate impact of a single exposure to aggression on the viewer's attitude and conduct. While the questions about immediate effect have been clarified to some extent, we need much more research on the cumulative impact of television, and the way in which the medium combines with other beneficial or adverse influences in the shaping of people's thoughts and actions."

He also points out that results of recent studies of therapeutic applications of modeling show that such influences can produce generalized and enduring effects.

Another factor is the number of people exposed to essentially the same stimulation. The same visual images are seen by people who ordinarily would not come into contact with the same influences. The cultural spread is much larger than ever before in history. Certainly, an unprecedented audience all over the world witnessed the Apollo 11 walk on the moon.

This body of research points up the fallacies in several popular ideas. One is that violence only affects those who are already violent or deviant and involved in aggression. This has not been borne out. All viewers tend to be affected. Normal children also learn and are encouraged to perform aggressive acts by viewing them under certain circumstances. Another idea is that if parents instill in their children adequate standards of what is right or wrong, the violence they see will "wash over them." It was clearly demonstrated that even where children can label behavior as bad or wrong, if it was successful, they may imitate it and the conflicts would be resolved more often by a reevaluation downward of the worth or the role of the victim. Whether or not the observed aggressive acts are successful becomes more important than the moral value of these aggressive acts.

Perhaps the most prominent idea which has been questioned is that of catharsis. There is no evidence that viewing violence, at least in most forms, dissipates aggressive drives and makes a person more healthy. In fact, it has been demonstrated that a frustrated viewer watching violence would become less inhibited and more likely to act on violent impulses.

The difference of sex roles and the impact of male and female models have been briefly discussed and seem important. Clearly, our society works toward helping girls inhibit aggression and to enhance masculine roles at the same time. The boys are given more latitude towards aggressive expression and less toward the emulation of any feminine traits. Still the effects cannot be oversimplified, as can be seen in the new phenomenon of unisex clothes and the girls who picket, swear, and attack the police; and the boys who embrace nonviolence even to the point of choosing prison over the army. What part in this was played by TV is not fully understood. This is the generation, however, that is often referred to as the "TV generation" and one of the first groups to have been exposed to its influence during the entire span of their lives. Doctor Bandura points out:

> "It is evident that observers do not function as passive videotape recorders which indiscriminately register and store all modeling stimuli encountered in everyday life."

The tremendous prices commanded by advertising time on TV would alone testify to the power that both the industry and the public attribute to it.

Learning often takes place in a neutral setting and even with strict prohibitions, and then acts are later effectively performed. The police recruit learns to shoot on a range, the army enlistee at a camp. Later they shoot people. Undoubtedly parents can have a considerable effect on their children's activities, either by monitoring what is seen or by encouraging or discouraging imitation. This research shows, too, that the learned behavior may still be retained. However, it will take more to break down a parental prohibition if it is firmly expressed on the part of the parent than if no intervention is attempted.

Many issues, such as moral and personal achievement standards, often considered the province of the parent, school, and church are now being directly and powerfully influenced by other sources, such as TV. Certainly, censorship seems a limited answer. It is doubtful, for instance, that merely banishing cigarette commercials from TV would have been as effective as the antismoking campaign has been. It may be that the key lies in the presentation of a broader variety of ideas and more objective information.

Research Grant: MH 5162
Date of Interview: October 1968

References:

Bandura, A. Behavioral modifications through modeling procedures. In: Krasner, L., and Ullmann, L. P., eds. *Research in Behavior Modification.* New York: Holt, Rinehart and Winston, 1965, pp. 310-340.

_____Influence of models' reinforcement contingencies on the acquisition of imitative responses. *Journal of Personality and Social Psychology,* 1 (6): 589-595, 1965.

_____Vicarious processes: a case of no-trial learning. In: Berkowitz, L., ed. *Advances in Experimental Social Psychology.* Vol. II. New York: Academic Press, 1965. pp. 1-55.

_____Role of modeling processes in personality development. *The Young Child: Reviews of Research.* Published by the National Association for the Education of Young Children, Washington, D.C., 1967.

_____A social learning interpretation of psychological dysfunctions. In: London, P., and Rosenhan, D., eds. *Foundations of Abnormal Psychology.* New York: Holt, Rinehart and Winston, 1968, pp. 293-344.

_____Modelling approaches to the modification of phobic disorders. *Ciba Foundation Symposium. The Role of Learning in Psychotherapy.* London: Churchill, 1968, pp. 201-217.

_____*Principles of Behavior Modification.* New York: Holt, Rinehart and Winston, 1969.

_____Social-learning theory of identificatory processes. In: Goslin, D.A., ed. *Handbook of Socialization Theory and Research.* Chicago: Rand McNally, 1969. pp. 213-262.

Bandura, A.; Blanchard, E.B.; and Ritter, B. The relative efficacy of desensitization and modeling approaches for inducing behavioral, affective, and attitudinal changes. *Journal of Personality and Social Psychology,* 1969, in press.

Bandura, A.; Grusec, J.; and Menlove, F. Vicarious extinction of avoidance behavior. *Journal of Personality and Social Psychology,* 5(1): 16-23, 1967.

_____Some social determinants of self-monitoring reinforcement systems. *Journal of Personality and Social Psychology,* 5(4): 449-455, 1967.

Bandura, A., and Harris, M.B. Modification of syntactic style. *Journal of Experimental Child Psychology,* 4: 341-352, 1966.

Bandura, A., and Kupers, C. Transmission of patterns of self-reinforcement through modeling. *Journal of Abnormal and Social Psychology,* 69(1): 1-9, 1964.

Bandura, A., and Menlove, F. Factors determining vicarious extinction of avoidance behavior through symbolic modeling. *Journal of Personality and Social Psychology,* 8(2): 99-108, 1968.

Bandura, A., and McDonald, F. Influence of social reinforcement and the behavior of models in shaping children's moral judgments. *Journal of Abnormal and Social Psychology*, 67(3): 274-281, 1963.

Bandura, A., and Mischel, W. Modification of self-imposed delay of reward through exposure to live and symbolic models. *Journal of Personality and Social Psychology*, 2(5): 648-705, 1965.

Bandura, A., and Perloff, B. Relative efficacy of self-monitored and externally imposed reinforcement systems. *Journal of Personality and Social Psychology*, 7(2): 111-116, 1967.

Bandura, A., and Rosenthal, T.L. Vicarious classical conditioning as function of arousal level. *Journal of Personality and Social Psychology*, 3(1): 54-62. 1966.

Bandura, A.; Ross, D.; and Ross, S. Imitation of film mediated aggressive models. *Journal of Abnormal and Social Psychology*, 66: 3-11, 1963.

Bandura, A.; Ross, D.; and Ross, S.A. Vicarious reinforcement and imitative learning. *Journal of Abnormal and Social Psychology*, 67: 601-607, 1963.

Bandura, A., and Whalen, C.K. Influence of antecedent reinforcement and divergent modeling cues on patterns of self-reward. *Journal of Personality and Social Psychology*, 3(4): 372-382, 1966.

Hartmann, D.P. Influence of symbolically modeled instrumental aggression and pain cues on aggressive behavior. *Journal of Personality and Social Psychology*, 11: 280-288, 1969.

O'Connor, R.D. Modification of social withdrawal through symbolic modeling. *Journal of Applied Behavior Analysis*, 2: 15-22, 1969.

Parental Behavior and The Origins of Schizophernia

Investigator:
Theodore Lidz, M.D.
Yale University School of Medicine
New Haven, Conn.

Prepared by:
Herbert Yahraes

An intensive study of families with a schizophrenic offspring has led Yale investigators to characterize schizophrenia as a deficiency disease. Schizophrenia, they conclude, results from a deficiency in the nurturing supplied by the parents, plus a deficiency in the transmission from parents to child of the basic techniques, particularly those dealing with language, that he needs for adapting himself to the world when he leaves the family.

On the basis of their findings, Drs. Theodore Lidz and Stephen Fleck suggest that schizophrenia may be passed along almost as truly as certain physical characteristics but without any involvement of the genes. Dr. Lidz is professor of psychiatry at the Yale University School of Medicine and a career investigator of the National Institute of Mental Health; Dr. Fleck is professor of psychiatry and public health and psychiatrist-in-chief of the Yale Psychiatric Institute, where the patients were hospitalized.

Many authorities suspect that an inherited biochemical abnormality plays at least some role in schizophrenia. The Yale investigators do not deny that this may be so, but they find no reason to think that it must be so. They believe that schizophrenia can be fully explained on the basis of what happens to a person within his family during the first two decades of his life. In general this depends upon the adequacy of his mother and father to fill their roles as parents, and this in turn is influenced strongly by their experiences as children with their own parents.

In every family studied, at least one of the parents was judged to be seriously disturbed. Many of the other parents were judged to be, if not seriously disturbed, rather difficult and peculiar. Generally the problems of the parents were found to have antedated the marriage.

Dr. Lidz and his associates, principally Dr. Fleck and Alice Cornelison, a research social worker, began their investigations in 1953. They wanted to learn whether or not there was something specific within the family circle that might be responsible for the appearance of schizophrenia in an offspring.

Their interest in the family sprang from the concept of schizophrenia as a condition in which a person fails to achieve a workable integration of his personality by late adolescence or early adult life. Unable to direct himself, he then retreats into asocial ways of living. Characteristically he does so by breaking with the way the people of his culture think and

267

communicate. His failure, the investigators reasoned, might result from failures in the way he had been prepared to take up life as a reasonably independent adult. Since the family is the fundamental training place and the parents the most important influence upon the developing child, an intensive study of family backgrounds appeared essential. Indications from recent studies that schizophrenic patients had grown up in seriously disturbed families reinforced the investigators' line of reasoning.

The research team selected only families in which it could study, in addition to the patient, at least the mother and one brother or sister; almost always the father was available, too. These and other relatives, together with teachers and friends of the patient, and friends and associates of the parents, then and earlier, were interviewed at length in an effort to get an intimate and detailed family picture. No other series of families, the investigators believe, has ever been so thoroughly studied.

Single, specific causative factors have not been found. Schizophrenia developed in the families studied, the investigators conclude, because the parents had failed to carry out the tasks essential to the adequate bringing up of children. The study groups these tasks into three functions: (1) parental nurturance, meaning normal love and care; (2) the proper structuring of the personality, which is achieved through a family structure in which the parents support each other, carry out the roles appropriate to their sex, and respect the boundaries between generations; (3) the transmission of the techniques essential for adaptation to the culture in which the developing human being finds himself. In the families studied, the investigators report, there was a failure to carry out adequately not just one but all three of these functions.

"There is nothing so mysterious about schizophrenia," Dr. Lidz remarks. "It is only mysterious when you go to the back wards of a hospital and see the people who have been there for many years who are just standing rigidly or jabbering to themselves. But if you watch young people coming into the hospital and take your time to get their story, it makes sense. If a person really understood human development, in certain families he would have to start looking for something like schizophrenia even though he had never heard of that condition."

The findings of the present study, the researchers believe, provide ideas both for preventing and treating schizophrenia. There is some indication that they may also lead to a means of predicting in which families schizophrenia is likely to develop.

The sample investigated is small, 17 families, so the researchers point out that validating studies are essential. It is also unrepresentative, since the families could afford care—costing thousands of dollars a year—in an outstanding private mental hospital. All the families except two were rated either upper class or upper middle class, although schizophrenia is more prevalent at the lowest socioeconomic levels. The researchers explain that they wanted to avoid the complexities created by economic distress and related conditions as factors contributing to whatever family deficiencies might be found. As it happened, the series differed from the cases usually studied in that most of the families were intact, but this circumstance, too, the investigators think, helped them clarify the conditions essential for the development of this most common of mental diseases.

The researchers believe that the findings based on the sample studied will stand up. "We've had at least 200 schizophrenic patients at the Yale Psychiatric Institute since the study began," Dr. Fleck reports, "and everything we know about those 200 fits in with what we've learned in our intensive study of the 17."

A recent French study of primarily lower class families is reported to supply at least some evidence that the Yale team's findings are applicable to families at all levels.

When the patients were taken into the study, they were in their teens or twenties. Some had only recently broken down; others had been sick a long time and had been treated in other institutions. They and their families were studied over periods ranging from 4 months to 10 years. In some cases the number of factfinding interviews—in addition to the therapeutic interviews with the patient and, sometimes, other members of the family—ran into the hundreds.

Members of the research team have been publishing their findings in professional journals as the work has progressed. The present report is written as the main study nears its end. It summarizes the principal findings, notes some of the research problems encountered, and discusses work that has grown out of the investigation.

Troubled Marriages: Two General Types

In more than half the families with a schizophrenic offspring, the research team reports, the parents' problems had led to *marital schism*. This is defined as a state of severe chronic disequilibrium and discord, which aggravated the personality troubles of each parent and constantly threatened the marriage. In the other cases the parents' problems had led to *marital skew,* a state in which, though the marriage was not constantly threatened, the more normal parent allowed the psychopathology of the other one to dominate the home and thus distort the child's development.

As an example of schismatic marriage, the investigators discuss a couple they call Mr. and Mrs. Grau,[1] the wife Catholic, the husband bitterly anti-Catholic. Soon after marriage, Mr. Grau informed his wife that the children's religion would never cause trouble because there weren't going to be any children. When, nevertheless, Nancy was born a few years later, he refused—to his wife's distress—to let her be baptized.

Looking back during her late teens, after schizophrenia had set in, this girl could remember no period when her parents had not been fighting openly and threatening to separate. Her recollections corresponded with those of her younger sister, Ellen. At issue besides religion had been Mrs. Grau's child-rearing practices (she was overly protective of Nancy as a

---

[1] All names are fictitious.

young child and then, as the girl grew up, highly intrusive), the proper amount of formal education (at least 4 years of college, asserted Mr. Grau, deriding his wife because she had only two), and a number of other matters. The investigators describe the husband as chronically irritable and paranoidly suspicious. Although his wife had been unusually insecure about motherhood, she might have functioned more adequately, they suggest, had she received at least a reasonable amount of emotional support from her husband.

Mr. and Mrs. Newcomb are presented as one example of the other general type of marriage—skewed. Even though Mrs. Newcomb was exceedingly difficult, she and her husband got along well because he was constantly grateful for her attention and deferrent to her judgment.

When the first child, Jack, was born, the father bathed him because the mother feared she might accidentally drown him. Jack and a younger sister were virtually isolated from other children until they went to school. Then Mrs. Newcomb pestered the teachers with demands that the children's special abilities be recognized. When Jack and his sister quarreled with their mother in later years, Mr. Newcomb's only advice was to do as he did and never oppose her. Jack became psychotic during his freshman year at college.

Whether skewed or schismatic, all the marriages studied had the same general effect: the production of an environment so deleterious to normal development that a person need not look beyond it, the investigators believe, to explain why at least one child in each family became schizophrenic.

Faults in Family Structure

The research group has drawn out the factors considered common to each marriage and of significance in producing the harmful environment. Some of these factors are viewed as deficiencies in the organization or structure of the family; the others, as disturbances in the way the parents, largely unconsciously, conveyed the essential techniques for adaptation.

In matters of family structure the following deficiencies were found:

I. *The Parents Failed To Form a Coalition*

Though husbands and wives have differing roles and functions, the researchers point out, these should interrelate to form a unit in regard to the children.

The father's primary role, as the Yale team sees it (drawing upon the ideas of two Harvard sociologists, Talcott Parsons and Robert F. Bales), is to earn the living and to establish the family's status and its relationship with other families and groups. The mother's primary role is concerned with interactions within the family, including the regulation of tensions and provision for the members' emotional equilibrium.

When a marriage is working properly, each parent supports the other's role, thus providing some of the assurance and strength of other must have to perform it. Further, as the result of this mutual support, the investigators explain, the child's natural tendency to divide the parents and, in fantasy, shove one out in order to have the other for himself—the Oedipus complex of psychoanalytic theory—is naturally frustrated, so the child's development proceeds in the normal direction. He grows up to value marriage and to see it as a union in which each person works for the other's satisfaction as well as his own.

This structural necessity, parental coalition, may often become weakened in normal families, the investigators assert, but in the families investigated it had either collapsed or become critically distorted very early, if indeed it had ever been achieved.

In the schismatic marriages, husbands and wives criticized and devalued each other, thus placing an almost unbearable burden upon the children; for in the natural course of development, Dr. Lidz explains, a child identifies himself with, and models himself upon, the parent of the same sex. The other parent serves as a model, too— of the kind of person with whom the child will seek to unite when he leaves the family. (The transformation of the person he selects into the kind of person he has been unwittingly seeking, Dr. Lidz notes, is more readily achieved "when his perception is blurred by sexual impulsion.")

But it is terribly difficult for a boy to accept his father as a model—in spite of the very strong natural tendency to do so—if the father is constantly being devalued by the mother, whose love the boy seeks. Similar difficulty and confusion arise when a girl hears her mother criticized and disparaged. The trouble is compounded because the parent who normally is a primary or basic love object, or desired source of affection, is constantly tearing down the parent with whom the child identifies.[2]

Even in those families having little overt conflict between husband and wife, the study finds a marked failure of the parents to support each other. Mrs. Newcomb, for example, did not belittle her husband to his face, but she made clear her expectation that Jack would have a brilliant career in art rather than, like his father, a moderately successful one in business. Beyond this, she ran the family. Though the father made the money, he had abdicated the other obligations of his parental role.

II. The Parents Failed to Maintain the Essential Boundaries Between Generations

Generally the failure to maintain the boundary between generations was marked by the effort of one parent—and sometimes both—to satisfy through the child an emotional need not being met by the other parent. In the Nussbaum family, following a bitter and protracted quarrel, the wife

---

[2] Lidz, T. *The Family and Human Adaptation*. New York: International Universities Press, 1963.

held herself aloof from her husband, who then became excessively attentive to their daughter. He would cuddle her until she went to sleep, and would even sleep with her on nights when she woke up and was afraid. This near-incestuous relationship, as the investigators describe it, was broken off by the girl late in adolescence in sudden terror that she was pregnant. A little later she became openly schizophrenic.

Several of the mothers said they lived only for their children. They lived *through* them as well, the study finds, unable to differentiate clearly between their own needs and anxieties and those of their offspring. Such mothers closely supervised the children's activities, fought or sought to fight all their battles, were constantly intruding. Some mothers behaved as though their children were little more than extensions of themselves, living—as at birth—in a symbiotic relationship. One mother, for example, when she needed a laxative, gave her twin sons a laxative also; when the doctor prescribed a sedative for her, she gave it to the boys as well.

Sometimes one parent competed with the child for the other parent's love and attention. In the Lamb family, for example, the husband, resenting from the start his wife's efforts to care for their son, acted less like the boy's father than a jealous older brother. Later he boasted of his athletic record and appeared to want his son to be an athlete, too. But he criticized the boy's efforts and lost his temper over them. Such rivalry, Dr. Lidz comments, leads a boy to stop trying to acquire masculine assets lest they arouse the father's hostility. At the same time Mr. Lamb belittled his son's interests and achievements in other fields. If anyone was going to be encouraged and admired, it had to be the father.

When the generation boundaries are confused, the researchers note, the child's place in the family is disturbed, and energies that should be going into furthering his own development are drained off to provide emotional support to a parent, or to struggle with a rivalry imposed by a parent, or merely to survive. His emotional development is warped; he has difficulty gaining his own identity.

III. *The Parents Failed to Maintain the Sexual Roles Appropriate to Them*

The sex of a child, the investigators assert, is the most decisive factor entering into the formation of the child's—and adult's—personality characteristics. Confusions and dissatisfactions concerning sexual identity can lead not only to perversions but also to neuroses and character defects.[3] In the patients studied such confusions were also found to be part of the complex of problems leading to schizophrenia.

A person takes on the attributes appropriate to his sex, Dr. Lidz points out, not simply by being born a member of that sex but by being confronted with the appropriate expectations from infancy onward and by identifying himself with the appropriate parent.

---

[3] Lidz, T. *The family and Human Adaptation.* Cited earlier.

If the parent of the same sex as the child plays an inappropriate role, the child's development is likely to be warped. In some of the families studied, the role reversals were obvious. One husband mothered the children and took care of the house while his wife ran a business. Another husband went to his law office every day, but it was his wife who actually earned his office rent and the money for all the other bills. Naturally, say the investigators, the children in these families grew up with distorted views of masculinity and femininity.

In most cases the failure to maintain the appropriate sex-linked roles is reported to have been less obvious but just as real. The psychiatrists explain that a girl needs to grow up in the company of a warm, expressive, helpful woman if she is to have the childhood experiences that will enable her to fit easily into a woman's role herself, but the mothers of the schizophrenic girls in this study were found to be distant and cool, toward their daughters at least. A boy, if he is to fit readily into a man's role himself, must grow up in the company of a man strong enough to represent his family to the outside world, to live without being overwhelmed, and to let his family feel his love. But the fathers of the schizophrenic boys in this study tended to be either weak and ineffective as husbands and parents (though usually successful as moneymakers) or else aloof.

The failure of a parent to maintain an appropriate role can usually be traced to that parent's personality problems, the research team reports, but these problems are often aggravated by the other parent. As an example, Mr. Forel married one of three sisters who were openly contemptuous of men. (His wife boasted to her sons that as a teenager she had dated boys mainly for the pleasure of standing them up.) Mrs. Forel laughed at her husband's efforts to make decisions for the family; refused for years—until threatened with divorce and a reduced income—to move to a city where his career would be advanced but where she would be a long way from her sisters; teased him sexually but denied him satisfaction. Of the two sons, the older grew up trying to please his mother and aunts, and women in general, by his effeminate interests; the other grew up clinging to his father and fearing all women. It was the younger child who became schizophrenic.

In this case, the investigators suggest, Mr. Forel may have been sufficiently weak and masochistic to bring trouble upon himself and his children no matter whom he married, but the trouble would have been less severe had he married a more nearly normal woman.

Defective Transmission of Cultural Techniques

Ordinarily the family provides the child not only with the models to follow but also with the fundamental skills and techniques necessary to live as an independent human being. The most important of these are the techniques for communicating with others, mainly through the use of language. The investigators point out that a person must acquire the language of his culture in order *(a)* to think, *(b)* to acquire most of the other techniques, and *(c)* to associate constructively with other people.

In the process of thinking, the researchers explain, an individual uses words to build a symbolic version of the world, which he then manipulates in imaginative trial and error in order to arrive at the most desirable course of action. The extent to which his representation of the world conforms with reality depends importantly upon the meanings of the verbal symbols with which he builds it. Hence his thoughts and actions are deeply influenced by the language he learns.

The schizophrenic patients in the Yale study had all learned English, but they had learned it in environments that provided, in the investigators' words, training in irrationality. Some of the parents were delusional. A man who had made a fortune in business spent most of his spare time isolated in his bedroom reading stock market reports and Eastern theology. He, his wife, and the governess all believed him to be the reincarnation of an Asiatic god, and they brought up the children in the same belief. A mother, writing in her diary after her son was born, confided her hope that she had given birth to the Messiah and for years recorded the family's unhappy life in idealized terms. Another mother believed her telephone was tapped. Mr. Grau preached a world conspiracy of Catholics.

In most cases, however, the parents were simply distorting reality, unconsciously, to meet their own emotional needs. The Lerners pretended to the world at large that Mr. Lerner was a busy and respected lawyer, although in fact virtually all of his clients had fallen away after his partner's death some years before. A father wrote each week from a distant city that he would soon come home. He never appeared, but his wife kept assuring the children for years that daddy would be there "next week". Another mother kept promising lovely trips, but did not keep her promises.

A young patient remarked during the course of a family therapy session that her recent visit home had been marred by her father's nagging. "Your father never nags," the mother snapped, though he had been nagging the daughter just a few minutes before. Later on the patient turned to her mother and said, "I find that I'm often uneasy with you." "If you are," the mother replied, "you're the only person who is." Yet this mother consistently upset almost everyone she talked to at the hospital.

Under such conditions, the research team notes, much of the communication within a family must be unreal, with the result that children come to distrust their own perceptions and to be confused about the meanings of words—and to face, therefore, severe problems in adapting themselves to the real world.

A parent insists that things be perceived in the way the parent needs them to be—"a type of brainwashing," the researchers comment, "that begins in infancy." In order to be accepted by such a parent, a child has to accept the role of the one who is wrong—who is even, perhaps, "crazy."

Imperviousness to the children's emotional needs was also noted. A parent would listen to a child but seemingly not hear him, and would be even more unmindful of messages the child did not put into words. The impervious parent is not rejecting the child, the investigators believe; rather, he is rejecting anything that threatens his own equilibrium. "We feel that many of the parents have a very narrow base of stability, that they are sort of hanging on—limiting their environment so that they can cope with it," the study reports. By so doing, the parents also limit what the child is able to see, perceive, or do, and they create in him despair about the validity of communication.

The conclusion that the patients had been trained in irrationality is based not only on the researchers' own experience with the parents and on the recollections of other members of the family but also on the results of two projective tests—the Rorschach, in which a person tells what he sees in a series of ink blots, and the Thematic Apperception test, in which he tells what he sees in a series of pictures.

Dr. Margaret Singer, a psychologist who made a blind analysis of the parents' responses—made it, that is, without knowing anything about the cases—almost invariably and in considerable detail confirmed the picture that had been built up by direct observation and history taking. As an example, in interpreting Mrs. Newcomb's responses in the Rorschach test, Dr. Singer wrote: "She takes a negativistic viewpoint and kills off meanings by saying that she feels nothing. She keeps conveying that meaning is hardly worth seeking because one cannot find anything likeable or clear, and furthermore, she will not try. She will not talk directly about anything ... At the same time that she blurs meaning-fulness, she creates an aura of being a nice, sweet person ... "

After reading Mrs. Newcomb's responses to the Thematic Apperception Test, the psychologist reported: "She is agonizingly contradictory, and when the tester inquires about an inconsistency, Mrs. Newcomb simply slaps down the examiner and further blurs meaning by stating that the picture does not make any sense ...Nothing about reality seems to please her or seems right, logical, or consistent. Sexuality is among her worst topics. People are both male and female at the same time."

The investigators report a tendency to minimize the extent to which children are exposed by their parents to serious distortions of meanings. "Parents who are borderline schizophrenic or somewhat paranoid," the study says, "are not counted in the statistics of mental illness. A vague and rambling mother who is more or less schizophrenic may obscure meanings to an extent that even a psychiatrist has difficulty in communication with her, but her children have been exposed to her blurrings and inconsistencies of meanings since they were born. A father who is only considered somewhat rigid and overbearing by his business colleagues, at home dominates the behavior and thinking of the family with his paranoid rigidity and distrust. Such circumstances are apt to be more malignant when the deviances are not sufficiently pronounced to be categorized as 'crazy,' or when the distortions of the disturbed parent are accepted by the other parent, or when the parent holds a place of esteem in the community and therefore must be right."

The investigators report that some of the parents also failed to transmit basic nonlinguistic skills. One patient, an artistically gifted young woman, for example, had never learned how to buy and adjust a brassiere, or even how to put on her stockings properly. She had never done any cooking, and she had never shopped in a grocery store.

Skills, customs, and social amenities are picked up not only from parents but also from peers. The young people who developed schizophrenia in the families studied, however, tended to have associated less than usual with other children. Thus, the investigators point out, there had been less chance for eccentricities learned at home to be corrected. Since these eccentricities presumably had helped keep the child apart from his peers, a vicious circle had operated. Most of the patients became overtly psychotic, the study emphasizes, only after leaving their restricted world, bumping into customs and ideas that seemed strange and becoming aware of a confusion—sometimes terrifying—about their roles as men or women. Universities with a good psychiatric staff, Dr. Lidz remarks, expect to find every year, a few months after the start of school, a group of students requiring hospitalization. Detected and treated early, most of these can return to college within a year.

Words, Meanings, and Schizophrenia

In schizophrenia, the investigators believe, the patient alters his representation of reality—a representation built with words—in order to escape from a world that has grown untenable. Faced with conflicts to which he sees no solution, he changes his perception of himself and others and abandons the meanings and logic of his culture. He thus finds room for living and a kind of self-esteem.

This distortion of the thought processes without loss of intelligence potential, according to the investigators, is what distinguishes schizophrenia from other types of mental illness. Generally the distortion occurs in only certain areas of thought. "Provide really good care for patients," says the research team, "and they don't continue looking very schizophrenic."

(One of the patients in this study learned analytic geometry while he was hospitalized; another composed intricate music; a third analyzed the stock market and selected a portfolio of stocks that would have paid off handsomely had the psychiatrist followed his patient's advice.)

The abandonment of meanings, with the consequent distortion of thought, the research group explains, isolates the patient and tends to make his condition self-perpetuating. He no longer tries to match his concepts with those of other people and thus to learn whether or not his concepts are the ones required for living normally.

Why don't other persons facing conflicts that seem insoluble take the schizophrenic's way out? Because they cannot, the investigators suggest. The schizophrenic can take it because he has never attained a firm and useful system of meanings. More than other people, he has encountered serious difficulties in understanding and coping with the situations in which he finds himself. He has never been sure, at least in certain areas of living, just where he stood. He has grown up in an environment where words were used to mask or even deny reality.

Mothers and Mental Health: A Revised View

In general, Dr. Lidz points out, psychoanalytic theory has held that if a child is to be schizophrenic, something must have gone wrong with the mother-child relationship at the very beginning. "We don't go along with that," he says. "In these families, some of the children did not become schizophrenic even though the early mother-child relationship was bad. Others became schizophrenic even though they did not have particularly devastating experiences in early childhood."

The investigators emphasize that the functions of a mother extend over many years and that her ability to carry them out depends upon a variety of emotions, attitudes, skills, and ways of communicating, which have been shaped by her relationships with her own parents and brothers and sisters and with her husband. The first year or so of a child's life is only one of the critical periods. Another occurs when he starts to attend school. His security then depends upon having a firm base at home from which he can move outward, and this base includes a mother who can encourage him to surmount the inevitable difficulties rather than convey her anxieties or her own distrust of the larger world.

Another critical period occurs at puberty. For a child to develop into an emotionally healthy adult, Dr. Lidz holds mothers—and fathers as well—must have the proper attitudes in regard to a child's changing needs over the first two decades of life.

Question: If a mother has trouble getting along with a child who later develops schizophrenia, may not the original difficulty have been caused by some inherent deficiency in the child? The investigators remark that this suggestion is often advanced and that it does seem to hold true with certain autistic children. But no evidence to support it was found in the cases studied. Rather, there seems to have been "a disharmony in the mother-child relationship." The disharmony arose because of the mother's own difficulties, those of her husband, and the problems of the marriage.

Psychiatry has been overemphasizing the role of mothers in the development of schizophrenia, the study suggests, because "the pathological characteristics of some of these mothers make a lasting impression upon the psychiatrists whom they harass," with the result that the psychiatrists tend to generalize from these mothers to all mothers of schizophrenic patients.

Everything considered, women probably do have a more important role than men in the production of schizophrenic children, the investigators suggest. For one thing, women have a greater influence upon children. For another, statistics indicate that schizophrenia develops somewhat later in women than in men. Since women can remain sheltered longer, this may mean that more mentally disorganized women will marry. But in general the investigators believe that it takes two persons to produce a child and two to produce the distortions in family structure and communications that can make a child schizophrenic.

The Parents' Backgrounds

The clinical workers in this study had an unusual experience: they got to know the parents of schizophrenics and in many cases to help them, and they wound up feeling as much sympathy for them as for the patients.

Among the parents were a number of individuals who were pursuing successful careers in the fields of business, industry, education, and the arts. Fifteen of the seventeen families came from the upper socioeconomic classes. As long as relationships with other people were fairly formal, Dr. Lidz explains, even the most peculiar and disturbed of these individuals managed to get along. It was in close relationships, notably those within the family, that the peculiarities became strikingly evident.

These parents had not tried to hurt their children, the research team reports; they had done everything they could to help—everything within their abilities and the limits placed by their own emotional difficulties. "Too often," the team observes, "the psychiatrist forgets his psychiatric understanding when dealing with parents and expects them to have been able to be different from what they were, or to change through reading a book or just because he tells them to behave differently. They, too, are as much bound to their unconscious conflicts as the patients and could not have been other than what they were." [4]

The problems of the parents had been exacerbated but not caused by the marriage. Mrs. Newcomb had grown up feeling unwanted because she was a girl. Her father preached the value of education but refused to let his daughter go to college. He also refused to let her boy friends come into the house. Mrs. Newcomb's mother had made clear her feeling that her own beauty and money had been wasted on an unsatisfactory marriage.

The mother of another boy who developed schizophrenia was schizophrenic herself. She was the daughter of an anxious, overly protective, and confused woman. And this woman, the patient's grandmother, had been permitted to grow up believing herself to be her mother's younger sister. Here was evidence, the researchers point out, of serious pathology across four generations.

In the case of Mrs. Forel, who had been dominated first by her mother and then by two sisters and who, in turn, dominated her husband, the investigators found a pattern of female domination going back to her great-grandmother.

---

[4] Lidz, T., Cornelison, Alice R., Fleck, S., and Terry, Dorothy. The intrafamilial environment of the schizophrenic patient: I. The Father. *Psychiatry*, 1957, 20, 4.

Another mother recalled that her father had been a slave to routine. Every night he would read to her from 7 to 7:45, precisely. He committed suicide when she was 6.

The husbands, too, are reported to have had difficult backgrounds. One man's father had been an alcoholic. Another husband was closely tied, even after years of marriage, to an almost psychotic mother. The father of Mr. Grau, the man who became irrational on the subject of Catholicism, was described as having been stubborn, dominating, and perhaps paranoid. Mr. Newcomb, grateful for any crumb of affection his wife could offer, was an orphan.

"We almost feel," says Dr. Lidz, "that schizophrenia is the end result of cultural deviation increasing gradually over the generations. Then you get two parents who are unable to straighten out each other's distortions—and you end up with a child so deviant that he virtually leaves society."

So what can be done?

"That is essentially what the mental health movement is about," the investigator answers, ". . . to stop this vicious circle of unstable parents having unstable children." Among the approaches, he lists premarital counseling "to try to keep some of these people from getting married"— an effort that is not usually successful—and marital counseling, to help husbands and wives better understand each other and themselves. Another approach is to educate parents about bringing up children. "The parents will still have their emotional problems," he observes, "but they will do better with their children simply because of knowing what to do." He believes there should be more marriage counseling centers and more family planning and well-baby clinics, and wider use made of them.

The Brothers and Sisters

The investigating team had set itself two major questions:

First, what factors in the family environment are responsible for, or contributory to, the development of schizophrenia?

Second, if certain factors in the family environment lead to schizophrenia in a particular child, why are the brothers and sisters not affected?

The answers put forward to the first question have been summarized in preceding sections. The Yale group's belief in their validity is reinforced by the findings, noted below, reported as answers to the second.

1. *Most of the brothers and sisters of the children who became schizophrenic developed serious problems themselves.*

The patients in the study had 24 brothers and sisters. Three of these, investigators found, were also schizophrenic. Seven others were considered to be borderline schizophrenics and eight others to be emotionally disturbed. Only 6 of the 24 were judged to be either adequately or well adjusted, and all but 1 of these, the investigators report, suffered from constricted personalities, marked by limits on their emotional maturity, their perceptiveness, and the use of their intellectual resources.

2. *The children who became schizophrenic had been brought up under circumstances that differed from those affecting their brothers and sisters.*

In half the cases the circumstances were markedly different. One patient, for example, had been conceived during a brief reconciliation between his parents 11 years after his mother—Mrs. Forel—had ended the marriage relationship. He was mothered by his father and an older brother and sister. After Mrs. Forel was injured in an accident, her husband became more subservient to her than ever and she became more openly contemptuous of him. The older children left home when the boy was 6, and the father died when he was 11. Mrs. Forel then went to live with one of her beloved sisters, who forced her to board the child elsewhere. The Forels offered the most dramatic example of changing circumstances, and even children close together in age and of the same sex were found to have been subjected to different influences.

Nancy Grau was caught in the middle of the conflict between her parents, mainly over religion. Ellen, born less than 2 years later, escaped the worst of the battle—partly because Mr. Grau assumed that his wife would not dare let Ellen become a Catholic, and partly because Ellen skillfully avoided situations that she knew, from watching Nancy, would bring down trouble.

Even a pair of identical twins faced different developmental pressures. As the investigators explain it, the mother came to prefer Peter, who had been born first, and to identify him with her envied twin sister, who also had been born first. Through this boy the mother fancied she would live out the dominant, aggressive role to which she had always aspired. The other twin, Philip, came to represent the passive and feminine aspects she despised in herself.

Peter grew up to be grandiose, antisocial, in constant need of admiration, and unconsciously terrified of all women because he viewed them as overpowering and engulfing, like his mother. He struggled with a dilemma common in adolescents who become schizophrenic, the researchers report, in that he was supposed to be a part of his mother—to achieve success in order to complete her life—and at the same time was supposed to be a man. He chose to go to a distant college in order to get away from his mother's seductive behavior. When his mother then turned toward Phil, however, Peter felt betrayed, "and murderous impulses mingled with the incestuous, creating panic." He tried to fill his need for love in a homosexual relationship but lost his partner to another boy.

Philip, on the other hand, early relinquished his mother to Peter, the investigators explain, and thus protected himself from her engulfment and Peter's hostility. This twin, too, tried homosexuality, but in his fantasies he was a girl—and therefore not in competition with his brother—and he wandered about the town in girls' clothing.

Peter became psychotic at college and had to be hospitalized. Philip broke down, too—in part, the investigators explain, because he needed Peter to bear the brunt of the mother's attention—but was successfully treated while living at home.

280

3. As a group, children of the same sex as the child who became schizophrenic were clearly more disturbed than children of the opposite sex.

The nine male patients in the study had eight brothers and six sisters. The only healthy sibling was a sister. The 16 female patients had 7 sisters and 3 brothers. Two of the brothers but only one of the sisters were emotionally stable.

These findings are explained, the investigators believe, by the findings reported earlier—the failure of the parents to maintain their appropriate sex-linked roles. The fathers of the boys formed poor models for their sons; the mothers of the girls, poor models for the daughters. One or more, and commonly all three, of the following reasons were involved: The parent's own serious psychopathology; the parent's unnatural attitude—intrusive, rivalrous, or aloof—toward the child; a parent's loss of worth resulting from the other parent's depreciating attitudes and behavior.

Under the circumstances, the Yale group explains, a child who wanted the approval and affection of the parent of the opposite sex, tried to differentiate himself from, rather than identify himself with, the parent of the same sex. Thus the child lacked a model to follow in order to gain maturity as a man or a woman.

At the same time, the parent of the opposite sex, to whom the child was naturally drawn, produced further confusion by conveying a distorted picture of that sex. Mothers presented sons with a model of women as persons dangerous to males; fathers presented daughters with a model of men as unworthy of or even dangerous to females.

It follows that certain types of family structure and interaction will be more dangerous to a child of one sex than to a child of the other. A mother who cannot establish clear boundaries between herself and the child will interfere more seriously with a boy's development than a girl's. This is because a boy, to achieve a firm masculine identity, must break away more completely than a girl from the initial mother-child symbiosis. Likewise a weak father is worse for a boy than a girl because a boy needs to identify himself with a masculine figure.

On the other hand, a cold and aloof mother does more harm to a girl than to a boy because a girl needs to absorb maternal feelings in order to develop maternal characteristics herself. Likewise a father who dominates and belittles the mother interferes more seriously with a girl's development than a boy's. In this case the girl, seeking her father's affection, must differentiate herself from the woman he finds unsatisfactory instead of pursuing the normal course and endeavoring to emulate the woman he loves.

Published descriptions of the parents of schizophrenic children often seem contradictory, the investigators report, but the contradictions may be reconcilable if the patient's sex is taken into account. "Firm sexual identity—that is, to behave as it is appropriate for a member of one's own sex to behave—is one of the strongest foundations of a stable personality," the study says. "A child who grows up insecure in his essential identity is likely to be in trouble."

In sum, if family conditions are such that one child becomes schizophrenic, this study finds, other children are more likely to be affected deleteriously if they are of the same sex as the patient. Not all the affected children become schizophrenic, because family pressures differ from child to child, and also because the child who becomes schizophrenic often lessens the impact of the parental disturbance upon the other children—by serving as a target, for instance, or as an example of how not to get along.

The Patients Improve

Of the nine male patients in the study, only one is still hospitalized, elsewhere. The others are reported to be fending for themselves, most of them quite well. However, one young man who went back to college after several years of hospitalization and another who is working are not considered very successful patients.

The young women haven't done so well. The investigators don't know why but call attention to a finding by Dr. David Rosenthal of NIMH, that schizophrenia tends to become more chronic in women than men. The research group notes also that five of the eight female patients in the study were rather chronic cases when first hospitalized—"the parents being less alert to their abnormalities or less apt to secure optimal care." Two or three of the young women still have to be hospitalized from time to time.

In the group's judgment, only a few of the patients would be good bets as parents themselves; it is hoped that most of them won't have children.

Implications for Therapy

The investigators believe that they themselves and the doctors associated with them are now better able to treat schizophrenia because the study has made them more aware of the results of family interrelations. The patients' problems and communications have become much more comprehensible. As Dr. Flecks puts it: "We now understand quickly things that before this study might have taken us months to figure out."

As the result of this work and of research elsewhere reaching the same general conclusion that schizophrenics have abnormal family backgrounds, the research team expects to see an increasing emphasis on efforts to change a patient's environment.

The tendency at the Yale Psychiatric Institute has been to keep schizophrenics long enough so that when they leave the hospital they can work and live on their own, away from the families in which they were brought up. But the Institute also tries to change the environment by changing the parents through psychotherapy—individual, family, parents alone, and group. Dr. Lidz believes group therapy, in which parents of schizophrenic

282

children meet together, to be particularly effective. It lessens the parents' feeling of guilt, gets them over the difficult period of adjusting to their child's hospitalization, enables them to see what has gone wrong in other families and therefore what may have gone wrong in their own and what they can try to do about it. Where patients can be hospitalized only a month or so, he points out, group therapy offers virtually the only hope of effecting an environmental change.

On the basis of his experience during the study, Dr. Lidz doubts that any great change can be worked in the things basically wrong with the family. The main hope lies in changing attitudes—those of the parents toward the patient and those of the patient toward the parents. "In the case of the patient," he says, "our main effort is to free him of the obligation to feel and think as he did in the past, in order to satisfy the needs of a disturbed parent or to model himself on that parent." If the patient had been able to see his family truly and to accept its peculiarities without becoming enmeshed in them, Dr. Lidz believes, he would not have become sick.

The psychiatrists who conducted the study say they would now prefer to keep young patients hospitalized a longer rather than a shorter time—"because we have come to realize that the young schizophrenic has a great deal to learn, mainly about how to get along with people. In a way, he now has to go to school—a school for resocialization—and he cannot finish in a couple of months."

In numerous other mental institutions the effort is to get the patient out of the hospital as soon as possible. "You hear it said again and again that if we use drugs, we can get the patients back in the community in a short time and they can get along," the investigators note. "That's true, to an extent. At our general hospital, Yale-New Haven, we are interested in that approach. We feel some things can be modified—perhaps the parents' attitude toward the child and toward each other—so that the patient can go home and get along with outpatient care."

"But here at the Institute we aren't very excited about doing that. We're not interested in keeping patients out of the hospital, nor in sending them back home fast, into what we feel is a pathogenic environment. We're interested in finding out how we can get them to lead reasonably satisfactory lives. And that's a very different goal."

"You see," Dr. Lidz adds, "there are different ways of treating different patients, according to the conditions surrounding them and according to what can be provided for them."

The research group sees another implication in its findings: that psychiatrists should take a different attitude toward the parents and not consider them either malicious or downright rejecting.

Birth and Progress of a Research Project

As a medical student (College of Physicians and Surgeons, Columbia University) and an intern (New Haven Hospital and National Hospital,

London), Theodore Lidz recalls having been particularly interested in birth disorders affecting the central nervous system. These were organic disorders: damage or maldevelopment could be demonstrated or surmised. He became impressed with the idea that schizophrenia was "a different kind of birth disorder."

The idea was strengthened during his psychiatry residency at the Johns Hopkins Hospital, 1938-41, under the late Adolph Meyer, one of America's great psychiatrists. Dr. Lidz helped care for Dr. Meyer's private patients. "I got to know the relatives of the patients quite well," he recalls, "and became impressed how really disturbed many of them were. The more I listened to them, the more certain it appeared that an individual in those families couldn't possibly have grown up to be a stable person. Some of the siblings felt the same way and told me why they thought they were not schizophrenic but the patient was."

Dr. Lidz wrote a paper on five of the patients and their families and was thinking of sending it off for publication when he noticed that the initials of their last names went L, M, N, O, and P. "I thought that if the initials could occur this way by coincidence," he relates, "it could also be coincidence that the families of my schizophrenic patients were disturbed."

So he and his wife—Dr. Ruth Lidz, whom he describes as a congenital psychiatrist, inasmuch as her father was professor of psychiatry at Heidelberg—set out to learn whether or not family environments were worth investigating for their role in the development of schizophrenia. They compared the histories of the latest 50 schizophrenic patients admitted to the Phipps Clinic at the Johns Hopkins with those of the latest 50 manic-depressive patients. Even though the histories were far from complete, the husband-and-wife team found marked differences in the family backgrounds of the two types of patients.

Publication of the findings was delayed 8 years. The first interruption was the war, during which Lidz served as an Army psychiatrist, rising to be a lieutenant colonel and chief of the neuropsychiatric service of the 18th General Hospital. Later, as the Lidzes compared notes with psychiatrist friends who, like themselves, were treating schizophrenia, the observation that schizophrenics come from disturbed families "seemed so obvious that we saw no reason for reporting it." Then they realized that while the finding might be obvious, nothing like it had been published. So in 1949 out came the results of the study the Lidzes had done in 1941.[5]

Dr. Lidz went to New Haven in 1951, determined to undertake the present study if he could find financial support, which he did 2 years later from NIMH. (The other Dr. Lidz went to New Haven, too, mainly as wife and mother and assisting in the study only part time, also maintaining an office at home as a practicing psychiatrist.)

Dr. Fleck, who had worked with Dr. Lidz at the Johns Hopkins Hospital, left his teaching position and part-time practice in Seattle and joined Dr. Lidz at Yale to pursue this study and carry out their ideas on how a

---

[5] Lidz, Ruth W., and Lidz, T. The family environment of schizophrenic patients. *Amer. J. Psychiat.*, 1949, 332-345.

mental hospital should be conducted. Dr. Fleck assumed responsibility for the hospital. Miss Cornelison, a social worker, took the major responsibility for assisting the parents and gaining information about the families. Typically, a research project begins with the formulation of a specific hypothesis and continues with attempts to demonstrate its validity—through experimentation, observation, and other types of study. But Dr. Lidz explains that in this case it seemed wise to start with only a very general hypothesis and to explore the field. "We might have set up the hypothesis that schizophrenia is caused by a certain type of mother, for a number of observations seemed to point in that direction," he says. "But then we should have been studying mothers, and we had reason to suspect that fathers also were important. In the beginning we just had the idea—look, children grow up in families; their thinking has to be determined to a certain extent by what goes on in the family; they need certain kinds of care in the family. We also knew that most, if not all, schizophrenics grow up in disturbed homes. We sought to learn if something in the radius of the family might be responsible."

The investigators had given themselves 5 or 6 years. (As in most such cases, the research job for the senior members of the team was only part time. The first obligation was to run the 44-bed psychiatric hospital. They also taught. The proportion of their time they could give to research was never as much as 50 percent and frequently was much lower.) But the exploration pointed to so many potential sources of trouble that Drs. Lidz and Fleck wondered if they would ever identify the essential ones.

Everywhere they looked they discovered something amiss. Usually both parents were disturbed, but generally one of them more than the other. Some of the patients had lacked proper nurturance during infancy but all of them had lacked it later on. Some of the families had been in an almost constant tempestuous state; others had been relatively though only superficially calm. Communications within families were distorted, though in different ways.

Another problem, in addition to the confusing wealth of material, popped up. As patients selected for the study began improving, they began showing hostility to their parents, and the parents reacted by trying to take them out of the hospital. The team lost several subjects just as it felt it was beginning to know the family. It solved the problem by telling the parents ahead of time what to expect and by providing them with the emotional support they needed.

The investigators had originally dared hope they would find a specific cause of schizophrenia. Instead, to fit their observations, they found it necessary to develop ideas about the structure and functions of the family. "It didn't take us 12 years to collect our material," Dr. Lidz remarks. "Much of the time went in trying to find a way of thinking about it—in trying to develop concepts. We also had to learn a great deal about how families function and the functions of families."

When the parents fail to establish the essential structure and fail to carry out the essential functions, the investigators concluded, schizophrenia can develop in the offspring most affected by the failures. The circumstances leading to these failures, but not the general nature of the failures themselves, differ from family to family.

The exploration, then, has led to the hypothesis that schizophrenia develops as the result of "deficiencies in family organization and functioning as noted in failures of the family's nurturant capacities, structure, and capacities to transmit the essential adaptive techniques."

"The patients in the study had not gained the essentials for existence as independent adults," the investigators sum up. "They had not gained adequate trust in others, confidence in themselves, a stable personality organization and structure, or the linguistic tools they needed in order to think clearly for self-guidance, to understand others, and to relate to others in cooperative endeavors. With such deficits, their integration and adaptation were bound to be highly tenuous."

The research group believes that the case histories of the families studied—and also the histories of other schizophrenics treated by the same investigators—support the hypothesis. But the group recognizes that important questions remain to be answered.

A Study of Sociopaths

If the hypothesis is correct, the group observes, abnormalities in the families of children who are emotionally disturbed but not schizophrenic should differ from those of the families that have been discussed. As a partial check of its findings, therefore, the team instituted a study of individuals described by some psychiatrists as sociopaths and by others as persons with a character disorder. These persons have calloused consciences or, as Dr. Lidz prefers to put it, consciences that operate ineffectually. The behavior of such persons bothers society but not, apparently, themselves.

The investigators looked for sociopaths from families at the upper socio-economic levels—as were most of the families in the schizophrenic study—and found them. By and large the boys had come to the attention of some public agency for auto theft, stealing from stores, or assault; the girls, for sexual delinquency.

The big problem in this phase of the study has been the dropout rate. The parents have cooperated so begrudgingly, in general, that the researchers have not gotten to know that families with anything like the thoroughness desired. However, from a preliminary study of the material now available, the psychiatrists report themselves reasonably sure that the two sets of families do indeed differ. Superficially, at least, the parents of a sociopathic child seem to be marked by these characteristics:

1. An unawareness of what the child has been up to. As an extreme example, one boy sneaked a girl into the house and kept her in his room a week, with his parents completely unaware.

2. A willingness to accept sociopathic behavior until the situation reaches the point where the police, or some other agent of society, steps

in. For example, one mother knew that her boy kept stolen money in the house, but she did nothing because, as she explained, she was afraid of getting him into trouble.

3. A concern with appearances rather than more basic values.
4. Often a disregard of social and ethical values.

One underlying fault in the families of sociopaths, the investigators suspect, may turn out to be that the parents have abdicated authority to the children. This too, would be a breaching of the boundaries between generations, but quite different from the one found to occur in the families of schizophrenics.

A Research Problem: Selecting Families for a Long-Term Study

Drs. Lidz and Fleck would like to test and elaborate their hypothesis about the causes of schizophrenia by closely observing families in which schizophrenia is considered likely to develop. Such a predictive or longitudinal study, they point out, would turn up more nearly accurate information about family interactions during the early lives of the children than even the most painstaking restrospective study, such as the one just ending.

But how do you select the families? If you make a blind start, observing any new families that agree to cooperate, Dr. Lidz points out, you may not get the job done in a lifetime. Figuring the incidence of schizophrenia at something more than 1 percent and figuring 3 children to a family, he notes, you would have to take in about 30 families in order to get 1 likely to have a schizophrenic offspring. "Maybe the more disturbed families would avoid coming into the project," the investigator goes on, "so you could very well study 50 families and not come up with a schizophrenic. If I'm to study families for 15 or 20 years, I need greater assurance that I'm dealing with a high-risk population."

Here Dr. Lidz puts his finger on one of the major problems of clinical research: the comparative slowness with which human beings develop and therefore the length of time that must be given to such studies as the relation between aberrant developmental factors and schizophrenia, or other mental disorders.

Like other investigators facing this problem, Dr. Lidz is looking for a shortcut—in his case, some screening procedure for selecting high-risk families so that the ratio of families studied to families in which schizophrenia develops is not greater than that about 5 to 1. He is hopeful that current work with a test of thought disorders in families that have produced a schizophrenic child will provide the answer.

A Possible Solution: Testing for Disordered Styles of Thinking

The finding that schizophrenic patients had been exposed all their lives to disordered and irrational modes of thinking and communicating within the family gave the research group a number of questions: (1) Is disordered thinking indeed a characteristic of all families producing a schizophrenic offspring? (2) Will a simple test for disordered thinking distinguish these families from normal families? (3) Will it distinguish them from families in which a child develops a psychiatric problem other than schizophrenia? (4) Can families in which schizophrenia is likely to develop be spotted beforehand through such a test?

Recent work by Dr. Margaret Singer, the psychologist who was mentioned earlier, and Dr. Lyman Wynne at the National Institute of Mental Health provides evidence, in addition to that of the Yale group, that the answer to the first question is *yes*. Using projective test material gathered at NIMH and at Yale, those investigators found that disordered thinking in schizophrenic offspring was related to peculiarities in the styles of thinking and communicating of the parents. It proved possible on the basis of the projective tests, all by themselves, to differentiate parents of patients from parents of normal persons. Because the type of peculiarity differed from family to family, it was even possible to say which patient was the offspirng of which parents.

The Yale group meanwhile has been working with a simpler instrument known as the Object Sorting Test. In the first part of this test a person is given something—such as a toy, a dish, a pack of matches—and directed to place it on a table along with whatcver other objects on the table belong with it. Then he is asked why all the objects in a group belong together. This process is repeated a number of times. In the second part of the test the person is shown in succession a number of different groups, all the objects in a given group having something in common—they are all red, for example, or all toys, or all smoking materials. Each time the person is asked why the objects belong together. Everything he says during the test is recorded.

This version of the test is the one developed a dozen years ago by an Australian psychologist, S.H. Lovibond, and used with schizophrenics. The scoring system was based on the idea that in schizophrenic thinking a person is unable to suppress, out of all the material that comes to mind, the unessential irrelevant, and illogical. In the Object Sorting Test, such a person might group a toy cigar and a ball together because both were made of rubber, but he might then add the packet of matches to the group because matches can be used to light cigars. The highest scoring patients—that is, those who most often made inappropriate groupings—were found to be those whose schizophrenia had been rated most severe.

Later, another Australian investigator used the test with parents of schizophrenic patients. He reported that 60 percent of these parents, including at least one parent of each patient, scored high in contrast to only 9 percent of a group of parents who did not have a schizophrenic child.

This was exciting. When Dr. Lidz and his associates repeated the experiment, however, they got much less striking results. Where was the trouble? "We thought we could run it down in 4 months," Dr. Lidz recalls, "but it took 4 years. In the beginning we couldn't say that the people in Australia were wrong because, as we went over our techniques and results, we found where we ourselves might have been wrong. For example, there was a weakness in the control group that might possibly have accounted for the difference. So we kept working, and writing back and forth, and eventually concluded that the investigator down there hadn't run a proper control group and hadn't had anybody check the reliability of his scoring.

"Nevertheless, there was something in it—not as good as he had put it but good enough to be highly interesting to us. When we finally finished, we found that the mothers of schizophrenic patients scored significantly differently on this test from the mothers of controls, but that there was no significant difference between the two groups of fathers.

"Our psychologist kept saying, however, that there really was something wrong with the way the fathers went at this blamed thing and that it wasn't being picked up by this particular scoring method. So then we started working up different scoring methods."

When Dr. Singer demonstrated that the parents of schizophrenics could be identified on the basis of projective tests, Dr. Lidz sent her the records of the Object Sorting Test as administered by the Yale group. She was in California. The tests had been administered in New Haven by other psychologists, and Dr. Singer was aware only of the husband-wife pairings. Nevertheless she identified 80 percent of the couples correctly. On the Object Sorting Test as on projective tests, she reported, the responses of the parents of schizophrenics were marked by the fragmentation and blurring of attention and meaning.

Using Dr. Singer's comments, Dr. Cynthia Wild at Yale has developed a new means of scoring the Object Sorting Test for use by the Yale group and other researchers in studying schizophrenic families. The responses are scored in several categories, of which the first is *An Inability to Maintain a Consistent Attitude to a Task.* The types of responses scored in this category are described as:

1. *Fragmentation of attention.*—This includes the introduction of an extraneous topic (such as a personal experience) or of behavior that interferes with the testing (such as getting up and walking around the room). It also includes "shifts of context of reference," meaning that the subject has a piecemeal approach to the objects within one group and seems to shift fluidly from one frame of reference to another. For instance, when shown a circle of red paper, a red eraser, a red rubber ball, and a red book of matches, he says that the eraser doesn't belong except that it could be used to eradicate anything written on the paper, that the matches could be used to light the paper, and that the ball doesn't belong either except that, like the eraser, it is rubber.

Meticulousness to a peculiar or bizarre degree is also scored. As one example, a subject looks at a group of objects, all of them made of rubber, and points that the toy cigar has a paper band, the eraser contains abrasives, and the sink stopper has a metal handle.

2. *Inability to maintain the role of a subject being tested.*—Here the subject wants to take over the tester's role. He reaches out and adds

289

another object to the group the examiner has place in front of him, or he badgers, criticizes, or lectures the examiner for not following the subject's idea of how the test should be given.

3. *Negativism.*—The subject does not accept the basic assumption of the test that there is some reason why certain of the objects belong together. Asked why a group of round objects go together, for example, he says, "Who says they do!"

The second main category is *Blurring of Meaning.* Here a subject gives the right answer, but adds several others and doesn't indicate which he considers best. Or he gives the right one with an air of extreme uncertainty or qualification. He does not let any response stand. For example, he puts the red ball with the red paper circle and says, "Both reddish and round, and otherwise I don't see any real connection with the other things."

The final main category is *Peculiars.* It includes: (1) *peculiar verbalizations,* such as stilted language and made-up words; and (2) *imprecise referents,* meaning vague statements that could be applied to almost any group of objects—for instance, a subject groups the pieces of silverware because "you use them together."

After satisfying itself that the scoring system was reliable, meaning that clinical psychologists, working independently, tended to arrive at much the same score in each case, the Yale group began applying it widely. One of the first findings pointed to a relationship between scores on the Object Sorting Test and both age and education. There was a tendency for older parents to make higher, or worse, scores. There was a considerably more marked tendency for parents with the least education to make the worst scores.

"In these studies of thinking," Dr. Lidz comments, "people with less than a high school education respond much more poorly than we expected. We believe this can be explained by the ways of thinking they learned. The poorly educated are accustomed to viewing things very concretely, they have difficulty thinking conceptually."

This relationship between test scores and education, the investigator suspects, ties in with the widely reported observation that schizophrenia is most prevalent among people at the lower socioeconomic levels. These people are also the ones with the least education and therefore, Dr. Lidz believes, the ones most likely to have trouble viewing their difficulties in an organized way and teaching their children to think clearly. (Another factor in the greater incidence of schizophrenia at the lower levels, Dr. Lidz points out, probably is the greater incidence of disorganized families.)

The new scoring system has now been applied to the transcripts of approximately 200 parents, including some who had been tested by investigators at the National Institute of Mental Health. For a clear-cut comparison between parents of schizophrenic children and parents of apparently normal children, however, the subjects were matched on education and age, fathers and mothers separately, a process that cut the sample to about 100 individuals.

290

Major findings follow:

1. Of the parents of patients, 75 percent had high scores (above the group's median); of the control group of parents, 31 percent.

2. In 58 percent of the couples with schizophrenic offspring, both parents had high scores. The corresponding figure in the case of the control couples was 12 percent.

3. The two groups were discriminated better when compared on the basis of the total scores for each couple. In the patient-parent group, 79 percent of the couples had *high* scores (as compared with 75 percent of the individuals). In the control group, 82 percent of the couples had *low* scores (as compared with 69 percent of the individuals).

In view of number 3 and of related findings—notably that in control couples where one parent scored high, the other almost invariably scored low—the investigators suggest that a healthier parent may offset the effect of the sicker one, so that the family style of communication is not seriously disturbed.

The question now is: Will the Object Sorting Test differentiate the parents of schizophrenic children from the parents of children having other serious emotional disturbances? Work on this has been started. If the answer is affirmative, mental health researchers will have something they have long needed—a relatively simple technique to provide a first step in screening out families with a high risk of having a schizophrenic child. Those families can then be observed through the years to learn all the circumstances entering into the development of schizophrenia in one of the children.

A Basic Problem in Clinical Research

Dr. Lidz believes that too little research is being done on schizophrenia, apart from studies on biochemical or pharmacological matters. As he states it, the problem is circular. Good clinical research in schizophrenia demands a good facility—that is, a hospital treating psychotic patients—having a stable staff of experienced clinicians. Only under such conditions, he believes, can enough patients be studied intensively and long enough to yield meaningful results. But most experienced clinicians are not prepared to give the bulk of their time to inpatient service and research, and most inpatient service would not begin to pay them adequately. Further, not enough people are getting the kind of training—"thorough training, going beyond a couple of years of inpatient experience"—that will enable them to provide really adequate care to psychotic patients.

"What I think we need," Dr. Lidz says, "are more places where people can work cooperatively on a given problem, as here at the Yale Psychiatric Institute. In such a place one gets to know patient after patient in many different situations—not only in individual therapy but in group meetings, for example, in staff meetings, in rounds. The average psychiatrist does not have access to this wealth of information; the average resident is exposed to it for a year or two and then goes off, into private practice."

And the man in private practice who wants to do a clinical study of some condition, the investigator points out, has to work with very few people. Not more than half-a-dozen institutions in this country, says Dr. Lidz, are able to undertake the intensive and long-term clinical research needed if we are to make sizable advances against schizophrenia.

Research Grant: MH 728
Date of Interview: Mar. 22, 1965

References:

Fleck, S. Family dynamics and origin of schizophrenia. *Psychosom. Med.*, 1960, 22, 5.
Fleck, S., Cornelison, Alice, Norton, Nea, & Lidz, T. Interaction between hospital staff and families. *Psychiatry*, 1957, 20, 4.
Fleck, S., Lidz, T., & Cornelison, Alice. Comparison of parent-child relationships of male and female schizophrenic patients. *Arch. Gen. Psychiat.*, 1963, 8.
Fleck, S., Lidz, T., Cornelison, Alice, Schafer, Sarah, & Terry, Dorothy. The intrafamilial environment of the schizophrenic patient. In J.H. Masserman (Ed.), *Individual and familial dynamics.* New York: Grune & Stratton, 1959.
Lidz, T. Schizophrenia and the family. *Psychiatry*, 1958, 21, 1.
Lidz, T. The relevance of family studies to psychoanalytic theory. *J. nerv. ment. Dis.*, 1962, 135, 2.
Lidz, T. *The family and human adaptation. New York: International Universities* Press, 1963.
Lidz, T., Cornelison, Alice, Fleck, S., & Terry, Dorothy. The intrafamilial environment of the schizophrenic patient: I. The father. *Psychiatry*, 1957, 20, 4.
Lidz, T., Cornelison, Alice, Fleck, S., & Terry, Dorothy. The intrafamilial environment of the schizophrenic patient: II. Marital schizm and marital skew. *Amer. J. Psychiat.*, 1957, 114, 3.
Lidz, T., Cornelison, Alice, Terry, Dorothy, & Fleck, S. Intrafamilial environment of the schizophrenic patient: VI. The transmission of irrationality. *A.M.A. Arch. Neurol. Psychiat.*, 1958, 79.
Lidz, T., & Fleck, S. Schizophrenia, human integration, and the role of the family. In D. Jackson, (Ed.), *Etiology of schizophrenia.* New York: Basic Books, 1959.
Lidz, T., & Fleck, S. Family studies and a theory of schizophrenia. Manuscript, 1965.
Lidz, T., & Fleck, S. The mothers of schizophrenic patients. Manuscript, 1965.
Lidz, T., Fleck, S., Alanen, Y., & Cornelison, Alice. Schizophrenic patients and their siblings. *Psychiatry*, 1963, 26, 1.
Lidz, T., Fleck, S., & Cornelison, Alice R. *Schizophrenia and the family.* New York: International Universities Press, 1966. (Monograph series on schizophrenia, No. 7.)
Lidz, T., Fleck, S., Cornelison, Alice, & Terry, Dorothy. The intrafamilial environment of the schizophrenic patient: IV. Parental personalities and family interaction. *Amer. J. Orthopsychiat.*, 1958, 28, 4.
Lidz, T., Schafer, Sarah, Fleck, S., Cornelison, Alice, & Terry, Dorothy. Ego differentiation and schizophrenic symptom formation in identical twins. *J. Amer. Psychoanal. Association*, 1962, 10, 1.
Lidz, T., Wild, Cynthia, Schafer, Sarah, Rosman, Bernice, & Fleck, S. Thought disorders in the parents of schizophrenic patients: a study utilizing the object sorting test. *J. Psychiat. Res.*, 1962, 1.
Rosman, Bernice, Wild, Cynthia, Ricci, Judith, Fleck, S., & Lidz, T. Thought disorders in the parents of schizophrenic patients: a further study utilizing the object sorting test. *J. Psychiat. res.*, 1964, 2(3), 211-221.
Wild, Cynthia, Singer, Margaret, Rosman, Bernice, Ricci, Judith, & Lidz, T. Using the object sorting test on parents of schizophrenic patients. *Arch. Gen. Psychiat.*, 1965, 13(5), 471-476.

The Causes and Treatment of Childhood Schizophrenia

Investigator:
William Goldfarb, M.D., Ph. D.
Henry Ittleson Center for Child Research
New York, N.Y.

Prepared by:
Herbert Yahraes

Research getting at some of the basic problems of childhood schizophrenia—including causes and effective methods of treatment—is being conducted in a mansion high above the Henry Hudson Parkway in the Riverdale section of New York City. The mansion is the Henry Ittleson Center for Child Research, named for the late banker. Twenty-four schizophrenic children, from 6 to 11 years old, live and go to school there. Twenty others come on weekdays for treatment and for classes, which are taught by specially trained teachers of the public school system. The director is Dr. William Goldfarb, a pioneer in coordinating clinical research and the treatment of disturbed youngsters. He is also associate clinical professor of psychiatry at Columbia University.

The Center is making a careful study of schizophrenic children over time, Dr. Goldfarb explains. It wants to see what changes occur not only while the children are at the Center but also after they leave; it hopes to follow them into adulthood. This is believed to be the first study to keep track of schizophrenic children during the process of growth rather than to look back at them after years of treatment.

The first findings of this research program, which began a dozen years ago, are summarized here; some are presented in more detail further on. They are based on observations of children from intact families only, because the investigators are especially interested in how the characteristics of the parents, and the ways in which parents relate to each other and the children can affect the development of mental illness. The children studied come from all socioeconomic levels.

Major Findings and Conclusions

1. The schizophrenic children under study fall in to two main groups, labeled by the investigators as *organic and nonorganic.* Children classified as organic are considered to have brain damage, but this is revealed only by a close examination. Their neurological signs are usually "soft," meaning equivocal. (Psychotic youngsters with obvious neurological defects are excluded and referred to neurological services.) Children

293

classified as nonorganic have no sign of even slight physiological impairment. Of the 129 children studied so far, about two-thirds have been placed in the organic group.

2. The families of the organic or brain-damaged children are of more nearly normal adequacy than the families of the other schizophrenics. An early study found that almost half of the nonorganic schizophrenic children had mothers who were schizophrenic, too. A new study is in process.

3. The symptoms of the organic child do not spring directly from his physiological impairment but from family-child interactions set in motion when he fails to respond quite normally to his environment. The parents' response to this failure is to stimulate him too much or too little, generally the former, or to confuse him. His response stamps him more than ever as different. The cycle continues. The product is a child so confused about himself and the world that he withdraws more or less completely and exhibits other characteristics of the childhood schizophrenic.

4. The symptoms of the nonorganic, or apparently undamaged, child *may* have been influenced by some undiscovered defect. But they appear to be completely explainable as maladaptive reactions to an abnormal environment. This environment, which has been shaped by "parental perplexity" or "parental paralysis," is marked by indecisiveness, insensitivity to the child's needs, bewilderment in the face of unusual behavior, and inability to direct the child. The end, again, is a confused and panic-stricken child whose bizarre behavior, like that of the organic youngster, is a means of coping with his distress.

5. Under residential treatment, both groups of schizophrenic children improve clinically, acquire learning skills, and rate higher on a standard test of intelligence. About three-fourths return to the community. But there is a decided difference in their response to the Center's schooling. A study of 37 children in residence during a recent 3-year period found that all those in the nonorganic group eventually gave at least a normal performance in reading and arithmetic. In the organic group, most of the children improved but reached a peak that was lower than normal and then leveled off. In sum, as emotional disabilities were alleviated, the children became free to use their potentiality for learning, which was at least normal in the nonorganic group but below normal in the organic.

6. For some schizophrenic children, the Center's experimental day treatment program seems to be just as effective as its residential program. These are the children in the organic group. The nonorganic children in the day program do not do nearly so well as those who live at the Center. Presumably this is because the former return every afternoon to a pathogenic family environment.

Dr. Goldfarb points out that the division of schizophrenic children into two broad groups is not yet generally accepted, though evidence of organic impairment in some child patients has been reported by half a dozen other investigators as well.

294

One big impediment to general agreement on the causes and nature of childhood schizophrenia, Dr. Goldfarb believes, is that different investigators use different means of evaluating their patients and different labels for describing the results. To clarify the Center's research techniques and findings, Dr. Goldfarb and his associates are making a moving picture showing some of the children under study and in each case the reasons for classifying the child neurologically as clearly organic, equivocally organic, or clearly nonorganic.

Beyond offering information on the causes of childhood schizophrenia, the Center's findings have important implications for treatment. They strongly indicate, for example, that the majority of schizophrenic children are educable. (Most of the children in the learning study had arrived at the Center without educational accomplishments; almost all had been considered unmanageable by the schools in the community—and most of them uneducable as well.) The study also suggests that day programs for schizophrenic children can be very successful, particularly if limited to children like those found by the Ittleson Center to show signs of neurological impairment. Day programs are far less expensive than residential programs. The average annual cost for a child in residence at the Center is about $8,500 (the bulk of which is met by city, State, and private contributions, these last funneled through the Jewish Board of Guardians, a charitable organization under whose auspices the Center was chartered). In contrast, the average annual cost for a child in the day program is approximately $4,500.

The Ittleson Center has undertaken its long-term study not merely to learn what happens to childhood schizophrenics, but also to test the effects of certain treatment procedures. Among the questions it hopes to answer are: (1) Will treatment directed at correcting a specific problem of a schizophrenic child—for example, lack of self-awareness—make for overall improvement? and (2) Will work to improve communications within the family—which are judged to be abnormal, particularly in the nonorganic cases—result in improvement in the child?

Dr. Goldfarb hopes also to study a group of children who have neurological defects but are emotionally normal. The reason they have not become schizophrenic, he believes, lies in the way they have been handled at home. Detailed information about this would presumably help substantiate the Center's findings about the causes of childhood schizophrenia and increase our ability to take preventive measures.

Three Principal Defects of Schizophrenic Children

The children at the Henry Ittleson Center differ widely in capabilities, behavior, and, the investigators believe, in the causes of their disorder. But they are alike in displaying extreme emotional reactions that combine fear, anger, and disorganized motor response. These reactions—which the investigators consider to be similar to the fear reactions of very early childhood—seem to spring from the children's overwhelming feelings of strangeness about themselves and their world. And these feelings are believed to be rooted in the three major defects that the investigators, originally on the basis of clinical observation alone, found common to all these children.

The first defect lies in the processing of perceptual information. The children have their senses but do not make normal use of them. In particular, they pay little attention to what they see and hear. Some of them when they come to the Center appear to be deaf.

The second big trouble is a deficiency in the child's awareness of self—the absence of a sure sense of a unified and intact body. Most of us grow up and think we have always had that sense, Dr. Goldfarb remarks; actually we achieved it. This defect is manifested in a variety of ways. One child was found talking to her hands as if they were beings quite independent of herself. Another asked if her hands would fall off. Children cutting paper have to be watched, for several have cut into their fingers, unaware that their fingers are part of themselves—and apparently unaware, too, that the pain of a cut finger results from an action by themselves. One child asked to have her head opened because there were men running around in it; a dental examination found a badly decayed tooth. Another child, walking with a counselor, asked: "Is this a long walk? Am I tired? Do my feet hurt? Will my feet hurt?"

Some of the children are not sure whether they are boys or girls, or of their physiological needs. They become agitated when hungry or when under pressure to relieve bladder or bowels. But they have to be told to eat or to go the toilet; they also have to be told to stop eating or to leave the toilet, for they have no sense of when their needs have been met. Such children, unable to find gratification even in satisfying hunger, are uncommon, but it is characteristic of childhood schizophrenics, Dr. Goldfarb notes, to be confused about pleasure as well as pain and to find trouble directing themselves into pleasure-giving activities.

The principal defects noted so far—in self-awareness and in the ability to take in and organize what the senses perceive—lead to a confusion also about space and time. To allay the resulting anxiety, schizophrenic children use a variety of mechanisms, including withdrawal, a seeking for sameness, and a compulsive over-concern with time and place, marked by endless questions about where something is or when some daily event is going to happen.

The third major characteristic of the schizophrenic children studied is a difficulty in communicating with people. Like the other characteristics noted, it occurs universally but in many degrees and forms, ranging from mutism to talking in such a way that the child cannot be fully understood.

Two Groups of Schizophrenics
   Compared With Normal Children

Long observation led Dr. Goldfarb and the other staff psychiatrists to conclude that many of the schizophrenic children—surprisingly many, they thought—had inherent defects. Their view was supported by a neurologist who was not on the Center's staff and who did not know how the children had been tentatively classified. He found that a majority of the first 26 children intensively studied gave evidence of neurologic impairment—54 percent in their examination, 58 percent in their history, 65 percent in either examination or history. The neurologist and the psychiatrist saw eye to eye 8 times out of 10.

The organic and nonorganic groups were then compared with a group of normal children and with each other on the basis of a number of neurological and psychological tests. The findings provide important information about the underlying reasons for the principal defects common to childhood schizophrenics. They also show, the researchers believe, that certain behavioral variations usually considered characteristic of childhood schizophrenics in general are, in fact, most characteristic of the group designated by these investigators as organic.

All three groups of children were found to have the same average sensory acuity—in sight, hearing, and touch. But marked differences appeared in the children's responses to perceptual tests. Some of these tests dealt with the ability to differentiate body cues. Esthesiometer tests, for example, measured the child's ability to discriminate two tactile stimuli presented simultaneously; the finger-location test determined his ability to localize the fingers of his hand (when these, out of his sight, were touched one by one). These abilities, Dr. Goldfarb points out, help make it possible for a person to have a clear image of his body. Other tests measured the ability to discriminate a picture from its background and the ability to form a picture from fragmented parts.

In all these tests the schizophrenic children were markedly inferior to the normals, and in all except the figure-discrimination test the organic group children were markedly inferior to the nonorganic. Evidently, says Dr. Goldfarb, the schizophrenic youngster takes in messages from the environment but doesn't handle them properly—doesn't make normal patterns of them or respond to them normally. So he has no clear consciousness either of himself or of his environment.

The results of the *delayed auditory feedback test* are taken to support that conclusion. In this test a child's voice was returned to him after a delay of 0.16 second. When a normal child heard his voice after the delay, his speech became distinctly different but he recognized his voice and showed no signs of confusion. When the schizophrenic child—of either group—heard his voice, his speech did not change but he did not recognize it as his own. Further, he acted as though confused, restless, and under tension. The investigator concludes that the schizophrenic youngster, since he did not change his speech, was speaking without hearing or, more probably, without listening. This finding supports clinical observations that the schizophrenic child tends to exclude hearing as a means of learning about and dealing with the world around him. The investigator also concludes that the schizophrenic's inability to recognize his own voice shows a limitation in his awareness of himself. The results of this limitation are to be seen in his confusion and restlessness, often amounting to panic, under the conditions of the experiment, and his feelings of strangeness, fear, and rage in everyday life.

Persons with perceptual impairments of the type shown by the schizophrenic children at the Ittleson Center, Dr. Goldfarb observes, might be expected to have impairments also in the higher cognitive processes involved in conceptualization. The tests bear out that expectation. They show that the schizophrenic child *(a)* finds it difficult to differentiate right and left; *(b)* is poorly oriented for time, place, and person; *(c)* has trouble grouping objects by form and color; and *(d)* represents the human body far more primitively than normal children. In all the tests leading to these results, the organic group was significantly worse than the nonorganic.

To measure overall intellectual functioning, the investigators used the Wechsler Intelligence Scale for Children. The schizophrenic children proved to be inferior to the normal children both in total IQ and in each of its components—verbal and performance IQ. More than half of the schizophrenic children but none of the others had IQ's in the retarded range—under 75. More than 90 percent of the normal children but only 23 percent of the schizophrenics showed at least average capacity—IQ's above 90. Marked differences appeared between the two groups of Ittleson Center children. The average IQ of the nonorganic schizophrenics was 92; of the organic, 62 (as compared with 109 for the normal children).

Tests of motor coordination and locomotor balance showed similar variations. On the Lincoln-Oseretsky test, which provides 36 motor tasks, the normal children's average score was 70.1 and the schizophrenic children's 27.9, but the nonorganic group averaged 48; the organic only 17.2. On the railwalking test, the average scores were 60.2 for the normal children and 23.7 for the schizophrenics, but the nonorganic group scored 43.8; the organic, only 13.

Another differentiating measure was the *whirling test,* in which the child stands erect, eyes closed and arms extended parallel to each other, and the examiner applies varying degrees of pressure to turn the child's head, without discomfort. In general contrast to the nonorganic schizophrenic, the organic schizophrenic tended to whirl—that is, to turn his whole body, as long as pressure was applied, in the direction his head was turned. Such a response, not shown by children in the normal group, is considered to indicate immature development of the central nervous system.

The investigators were especially interested in the results of the *auditory startle test.* When normal children, wearing earphones, were subjected to a sudden loud tone, they showed that they were aware of it but not distressed by it. The schizophrenic children gave a wide range of reactions. At one extreme, eight children showed no evidence of hearing the tone at all. At the other extreme, six children showed extreme discomfort. With one exception, all these extreme cases were in the organic group.

Dr. Goldfarb reports that children at the Center who give no evidence of hearing speech or other sounds on one occasion may react with frenzied distress on others, and that such fluctuation between pseudodeafness and distress may be seen in the same child on the same day. The auditory startle test, he believes, indicates that the most marked forms of hypersensitivity and sensory avoidance are linked with organicity rather than nonorganicity. But some measure of sensory avoidance does, he emphasizes, frequently occur among nonorganic schizophrenics.

Measurement of speech and voice characteristics, through techniques developed at the Center, showed distinct differences from one schizophrenic child to another, but not between the two groups. All the schizophrenics had deviances in such matters as volume, pitch, fluency, stress, intonation, and inflection—characteristics that determine a person's ability to get across meanings beyond those in the words themselves. Ordinarily the culture's standards for these characteristics are learned very early in life. Since the schizophrenics had learned them only partly if at all, these children had a way of speaking that isolated them still further from normal activities. Typically the voice was so inexpressive that even when a child's words could be understood, the person talking to him felt shut out and unable to get through.

To sum up, children in both the organic and the nonorganic groups were found to be measurably different from normal children in a number of tests of perception, cognition, and psychomotor functions. In certain cases—notably the delayed auditory feedback test and the measures of communicative ability—the children in the nonorganic group were found to deviate as greatly from the normal as those in the organic group. In general, though, the investigators believe, the results support the conclusion that childhood schizophrenics can be divided into two general clusters—indeed, that such a division is necessary to an understanding of childhood schizophrenia.

"What is currently called schizophrenia," Dr. Goldfarb declares, "is a hodgepodge population that needs subclassification. In mental deficiency it has become increasingly possible to separate out subpopulations on the basis of cause, such as phenylketonuria or severe maternal deprivation. This is likely to be the history of schizophrenia." But in working out a subclassification, he emphasizes, the relationship between the child and his family has to be thoroughly investigated even in those cases where an organic defect is apparent.

Reproductive Complications

The comparison of schizophrenic and normal children has been carried a step farther through a study of their prenatal and perinatal histories—the record of events before and during birth and shortly afterward. In this phase of the research, the investigators studied three groups: (a) 29 children in residential treatment at the Center; (b) 39 brothers and sisters of these children; (c) 34 public school children comparable to the schizophrenic children in ages and backgrounds.

299

The comparison was made on the basis of a "reproductive complications record" listing 83 conditions that had been used by other investigators in studying factors associated with cerebral palsy, mental retardation, and childhood behavior disorders. Many of these conditions are suspected rather than known to be related to fetal damage. A few of the items are listed below. Those in the first three groups were scored *plus* and considered presumptive evidence of reproductive complications. Items in the fourth group, *The Newborn*, were scored either *plus* or *double plus*, generally depending upon the severity of the condition; a *double plus* rating was considered highly significant evidence of reproductive complication.

Historical (+)
    Mother's age over 45
    Abdominal or pelvic X-ray of either parent
    Accidental conception despite using spermicidal contraceptive jelly
Pregnancy (+)
    Total gestation period less than 8 months
    Smoked 20 or more cigarettes daily
    Excessive nausea
    Severe emotional shock
    Any infection
    Endocrine disorder
    Unusual medication
Delivery (+)
    False labor
    First stage of labor more than 24 hours
    Face, brow, breech, or transverse presentation
    Midforceps, high forceps
    Precipitous delivery
    Placenta previa
    Baby held back
The Newborn (+ or ++)
    Cyanosis + or ++
    Weak cry +
    Absent cry ++
    Injuries + or ++
    Jaundice + or ++
    Vomiting + or ++
    Convulsions ++
    Abnormal reflexes ++

When information from all sources—mothers, attending physicians, and hospital records—was used, the schizophrenic children were found to have had more than half again as many reproductive complications on the average as their brothers and sisters and the public school children. The difference in the number of complications, both those rated more significant and those rated less significant, was particularly marked in the case of the boys.

One of the problems in a study like this, the investigators point out, is that data from the mothers of severely disordered children "are inevitably selected and colored by such repressive or distracting influences as guilt, illusory wish fulfillment, or defensive denial." So the investigators place more weight on the analysis of hospital data which had been recorded at the time of observation and without any knowledge of how the infant would turn out. This analysis shows that the average number of reproductive complications is significantly greater for the schizophrenic boys than for their brothers or for the boys in the public school group. Between the schizophrenic girls and the girls in the other groups, however, there is no significant difference.

The sample was small, and the Ittleson Center's children may not be representative of all childhood schizophrenics. Nevertheless, the investigators say, the finding apparently ties in with earlier findings by other researchers that (a) more boys than girls have childhood schizophrenia and (b) more boys than girls are affected by disorders such as cerebral palsy, where brain damage is an undisputed factor, and by mental retardation, where brain damage frequently has a significant role. The investigators note also that the ratio of boys to girls at the Center is about three times as high in the organic group as in the nonorganic.

All in all, this research team is inclined to believe that:

- Cerebral dysfunction as a result of reproductive trauma is more typical of the boy than the girl schizophrenic.
- The higher proportion of boys among schizophrenic children reflects the importance of brain damage as a contributing factor to the adaptive disturbances in these children.

Dr. Goldfarb emphasizes that brain damage, from whatever cause, need not lead to a behavior disorder—and that even when it does, the disorder may well not be childhood schizophrenia. Further, childhood schizophrenia can occur even when the brain seems organically normal. Evidently the experience of the child in his family relationships is also important.

The Families of Schizophrenic Children

Before a child is admitted to the Ittleson Center and then again when he is discharged, a trained observer pays a long visit to the child's family and notes the interactions between mother and father, both as wife and husband and as parents; between parents and children; among the children; and among all the family members. The observer rates the family on 46 aspects of its behavior, including the spontaneity of interactions, the methods used by the parents to exercise control, and the ways in which the children's needs are met. In each case a high score means that the members are acting in a way that reflects and enhances the mental health of the group. The sum of the ratings is called the family adequacy score.

The research group has used this technique to compare the families of 22 children at the Center with those of 22 normal children. The families of the schizophrenic children in the nonorganic group were found to be the least adequate, by far. On the average they scored 158 out of a possible 300. The families of the other schizophrenic children scored 206, and the families of the normal children, 220; the difference between these latter 2 groups was not statistically significant.

The investigators also considered the relationship between the normality scores of the patients and the adequacy scores of the families. (A normality score is the average of the ratings made by the Center's staff in an attempt to express quantitatively how close a child's behavior approaches that of a normal child.) A negative relationship was found: the schizophrenic children from the least adequate families had, on the average, the highest normality scores; the children from the most adequate families had the lowest.

In another phase of the work, the *parental perplexity* displayed by the mothers of schizophrenic children was appraised before anyone knew into which category their children would be placed. As noted earlier, parental perplexity, or paralysis, is taken to include passivity, marked uncertainty, lack of spontaneity, absence of empathy with the child (and, therefore, a lowered awareness of the child's needs), bewilderment or blandness in the face of socially unacceptable or bizarre behavior by the child, and an absence of forthright parental control. With each of the two techniques used to evaluate this quality, the mothers of the children eventually diagnosed as nonorganic were found to be considerably more confused and inadequate than the mothers of the children diagnosed as organic.

Might not the mothers' perplexity be traceable to their children's behavior rather than the other way around? This question has often been answered *yes*, Dr. Goldfarb notes, but the researchers at the Ittleson Center have found that the most bewildered and inadequate mothers are those whose children are in the nonorganic group while the most deviant behavior is displayed by the children in the other group.

"There can be little doubt," the investigator sums up, "that schizophrenic children with evidences of physiological aberration come from the more adequate families, whereas schizophrenic children displaying no evidence of intrinsic physiological aberration come from the least adequate families."

Those very inadequate families—what kind of persons are the parents?

To the casual observer, Dr. Goldfarb answers, they may seem normal enough. They make their way in the world. They do not, commonly, disrupt society. But they have confused the developing child by their paralyzing perplexity about life in general and child rearing in particular. Usually they have offered no rewards or punishments, or have offered them inconsistently. They have failed to define clearly where and when a child is free to move and act, and where and when he is not.

One of the most outlandish symptoms of a schizophrenic girl, for example, was a total lack of sensibility to social requirements. Her mother described the extensive sexual play between the girl and a brother: "I just cry that it should be over," the mother reported, "but I don't say—'Don't do it.' Am I acting the right way?"

Another mother was unable to discipline her boy or express love—or any other emotion—for him. But she showed an approving interest in his abnormal concern with words and numbers. The proper manipulation of words would make him omnipotent, he believed, and 2 plus 2 was any number he wanted it to be.

Another boy had a mother who would stand by helplessly when he threw a tantrum and wrecked a neighborhood store—and a father who would point to a glass of milk, order the boy to "pass the catsup" and, when the boy showed confusion, insist on being obeyed without argument.

Generally, Dr. Goldfarb reports, the parents in these inadequate families have not gratified the child's needs—as for food or a dry diaper—when these needs or cravings were at their most intense; consequently, the child has not developed either a feeling for the rhythm of life or a sense of anticipation and hope.

What about the parents of the children considered to have organic deficiencies?

These parents display inadequacies, too, the investigator answers, but to a lesser degree. Paul's parents are typical. The boy's physical development has been slow, and he has always been clumsy. He finally began walking at 18 months, but often fell and needed help to rise. He took to staring at his feet for long intervals and seemed totally isolated. After the birth of a brother when he was four, Paul began having uncontrollable tantrums. He also began spending hours pulling the window blind, or quietly sucking his fingers. His nursery school teachers reported him "completely un-reachable."

Paul's parents were found to be likable persons, with some fairly common problems. His father, though a successful businessman, tended to deprecate himself and to see Paul as the image of his own weakness. Paul's mother—a sensitive, emotionally open, jolly woman—subconsciously saw Paul's deficiencies as punishment for her premarital sexual experience. Both parents responded to different subconscious motivations in the same way: they put pressure on the boy to do better.

As Dr. Goldfarb explains it, Paul from the start had a limited capacity for finding form and meaning in what he saw and heard, so his environment was more than normally complex and puzzling. The complexity was increased by his parents' efforts to get him to respond. As a way of handling his panic, he finally came to avoid looking and listening.

Communications Between Mother and Child

The Ittleson Center investigators—like others at Yale, the National Institute of Mental Health, and elsewhere—have been impressed by the confused communications in families in which an offspring has developed schizophrenia. To document their observations and provide further information, these researchers have been making moving pictures and tape recordings of visits at the center between mother and child. The observed visits, which last about 20 minutes, are made at the request of the staff. The child does not know his mother is coming. A preliminary analysis of

25 such visits has been concerned principally with the communicational behavior of the mother.

Some of the women made little effort to talk with their children. Others talked a good deal, but in a way that was obviously confusing. One mother, for example, kept saying to her 6-year-old boy, "How are you? How are you doing?" at a time when he was crying and saying that he wanted to go home. At another point, she asked, "What did you have for lunch, Jimmy—ham?" He answered, "Fish." Then she said, "Jimmy, what did you have for lunch, huh?" and he said "Fish." Then she said again, "Tell me, what did you have for lunch, sweetheart?" He stood in front of her and looked at her and said, "Fish." By laying down a barrage of topics, this mother, like some others, discouraged the child from communicating his own feelings.

When the mother of Mary—a child with a great deal of anxiety about her body—greeted her, Mary said, "Finger," and smiled and motioned to her finger. The mother said, "What's that?" Mary replied, "Finger," and smiled broadly. The mother said, "What is it?" Mary answered, "I love finger." The mother made no verbal response. This interchange, the investigators point out, illustrates both the child's deviant means of communicating her need for affection and the mother's failure to do anything to counteract this deviancy or to meet the need. Earlier, Mary's mother had told the Center that she and her husband both had been afraid to touch the child as a baby. "Both of us got up in the night, and one gave her the bottle and one held the baby," the mother said. "I put a handkerchief in his hand to hold the baby's head because I was afraid that if he would touch her with his bare hands, her head would dilapidate."

A common error reducing communicational clarity was found to be discordance between the mother's expression and the child's level of comprehension. For example, a 10-year-old boy greeted his mother with a French word, *combien*. (The investigators learned after the visit that this apparently meaningless word was an error on his part. He had actually had a French lesson that day and had meant to say *"Comment allez-vous?"* in an effort to win his mother's praise.) His mother did not express her puzzlement about *combien,* nor did she insist on an explanation so that he would sound less incoherent. And she missed entirely his natural desire for praise. She said, "Are you speaking French already?" and then, "You couldn't have learned it all in a couple of days. There must still be some left to do." This remark distressed him because he thought she was saying he had not studied his lessons, whereas she was actually using an adult variety of sarcastic humor. He said, "I did really my studies." Eight minutes later, he persisted, "Mommy, how come you said I couldn't learn it all yet?"

Such errors occur also in interchanges between mothers and normal children, the investigator notes, but tend to be much milder. This mother, Jimmy's mother, and a number of others displayed what the investigators describe as *imperviousness:* they failed to recognize, or at least to acknowledge, a child's feelings and meanings.

304

Each mother was given a clarity score, based on an analysis of the transcript of the first few minutes of the visit. In general, the mothers of the 16 children classified as organic scored higher than the others. This findings supports the hypothesis, Dr. Goldfarb notes, that the roots cf childhood schizophrenia, in the cases where there is no neurological impairment, lie in parental failure. The normal mother spends much time explaining novel experiences to a child so that he can grasp them and relate them to previously achieved understandings. She stimulates and guides his psychological development, encouraging some of his responses and discouraging those that are not acceptable. By voice and gesture she stimulates an interest in acoustic and visual experience. She encourages the child to be attentive to her communicational clues, and she is attentive to his. The communicational failures observed during the mother-child visits at the Center suggest to the investigators that many of the mothers, particularly those whose children are neurologically sound, did not successfully carry out such aspects of the maternal role.

Dr. Goldfarb and his associates recognize that the verbal interactions in this study may have been influenced not only by the characteristics of the mothers but also by the setting in which the interactions took place—a visit to a child in an institution. To obtain comparative data, the researchers have now arranged to study mothers who visit their children in an orthopedic hospital.

Treating the Child in a Residential Center

As the result of its clinical observations, its tests, and its study of the families, the Center has developed a treatment program it describes as corrective socialization.

In one way or another, Dr. Goldfarb notes, the child's home environment failed to supply what the child needed in order to perceive and understand reality—that is, to get a true picture of events outside of himself and inside of himself—and to act accordingly. The failure occurred in many cases because the children presented a special challenge to which the parents did not react appropriately. In the other cases the failure resulted from a high degree of parental confusion and paralysis. Whatever the primary cause of the failure, the consequence was "a calamitous and unvarying state of strangeness."

Dr. Goldfarb believes that this feeling of strangeness explains the states of panic often noted among schizophrenic children. "The persistent and overburdening sense of strangeness makes it difficult for the child to cope with what is unfamiliar," he says, "and restricts the likelihood of the kind of satisfying complacency which accompanies the perception of what is familiar." He and his associates call the panic states "primordial" because they are considered to represent elemental reactions to strangeness (in contrast to the panic that can arise from unconscious conflict).

The Center's therapeutic approach has these general goals: To help the schizophrenic child orient himself to the real world and to improve his

305

ability to recognize himself as an individual capable of self-direction—to realize, for example, that this is his hand and that he can throw a ball with it if he wants to. Toward the achievement of these goals, the staff of eight psychiatrists, eight teachers, five social workers, four psychologists, two nurses, and nine child care workers or counselors—including members assigned to the day program—tries in many ways to relieve the child's strangeness and anxiety and to enlarge his range of gratification and pleasure.

The children are given a carefully structured world, having boundaries in space and time that they can come to recognize and hold onto. The Center's large grounds have been marked off into small areas having clearly defined functions—a garden area, a playground area, a bicycle area. (Before the grounds were divided, the children wandered over them aimlessly and anxiously.) Inside, too, the space is carefully delineated in terms of the function it serves, and the children are encouraged to move freely within the bounds appropriate to the current activity. At bedtime, for example, a child may move about his group's bedroom, bathroom, and playroom. At schooltime, he may move about the classroom. Even the most regressed child, Dr. Goldfarb reports, quickly learns the spatial boundaries for any given activity.

The children learn, too, that there are set times for specific activities each day, each week, and each month. Acceptable variants of behavior with respect to time are taught. For example, pajamas are worn to bed at night, clothes must be worn during the day, overclothes are worn outside in winter.

In all talk with the children regarding space and time, the staff tries to be completely clear. The child is told again and again what he is going to do and where and when. He is offered choices, but these are simple—the choice, for instance, between playing in the bedroom or in the playroom. Activities, and communications about activities, are linked as often as possible to rewards; the child is told, for example, "In the morning we dress and then go down for breakfast." The idea is that the reward encourages the development of a sense of anticipation and of the ability to generalize about time—characteristics that the typical schizophrenic child does not have.

"The climate is child-centered in that it responds sensitively to the child's needs," Dr. Goldfarb reports. "However, it is adult-directed in that it is characterized by active, assertive, adult direction, and it is the adult who determines and delineates the environment for the child. The atmosphere thus contrasts sharply with a permissive, nondirective environment. The child is reminded at all times of adult expectations. The whole idea is to correct the child's abnormal ideas and behavior whenever they are expressed, at the moment they are expressed—all day long."

As an example, a staff member found Mary, mentioned earlier as being abnormally anxious about her body, in panic because she had bumped her arm and had seen a slight red bruise appear. "I'll die," Mary cried repeatedly. "I'm going to bleed to death." Reassuring words did no good, so the adult gravely took her arm, bent the elbow gently several times,

306

examined each finger carefully, and finally informed her he was sure he could make the arm better in a few minutes. He asked Mary to watch the red mark get lighter as he patted the arm. She watched eagerly and her tears subsided, but she continued to ask if she would die. The staff member informed her authoritatively that there was absolutely no possibility of her dying from the bruise. As proof, he showed her that the redness was already disappearing. The girl complained that the arm still hurt. In that case, he told her, there was one more thing he could do. He ceremoniously proceeded to put cold water on the injured area. Patting the arm dry, he asked, "Doesn't that feel better now?" Mary looked at her arm and then up at him and said, "Yes," and walked quietly to her classroom.

The recurrent puzzlement, often accompanied by panic, shown by the schizophrenic child reflects an inability to see a relation between the experience to which he is being exposed and some earlier experience. It also reflects, Dr. Goldfarb continues, a desire to see such a relation—to find a pattern and familiarity in his experiences. So an expression of puzzlement in the adult's cue to offer explanations and to help the child evaluate a particular event. "Very much like a parent of an infant," the investigator says, "the staff member uses warmth, affection, comforting, and physical contact to reinforce the learnings involved and to improve the range of pleasure in and tolerance for informational input."

Along with corrective socialization, the Center uses drugs in some cases and individual psychotherapy in virtually all. And it works with the parents in an effort to clear up their own puzzlements and anxieties, and thus enable them to develop a healthful home environment.

Three-fourths of the children, as reported earlier, do return home. Detailed information about their progress awaits an analysis, which is under way, of observations over the last 10 years. However, the Center already knows that most of the children need special help, such as a special school or a special class to maintain them in the community. These findings, then, are indications at once of progress, of problems, and of opportunities.

Day Treatment Versus Residential: Comparison of Results

The day treatment center was opened in 1959 in cooperation with the New York State Department of Mental Hygiene. It is the equivalent of a day hospital. It cares for its children from 9 to 4:30, 5 days a week and 9 months a year. During that time it provides the same kind of detailed, on-the-spot intervention as provided in the residential treatment program. For approximately 20 children, the day center has 3 child psychiatrists, a psychiatric supervisor, and 3 teachers. Caseworkers serve the families as they do those of the other children. Extensive psychological services are provided.

The two types of treatment have been compared by Dr. Goldfarb and his associates on the basis of changes in two groups of children over a

307

3-year period—one group living at the center, the other going there days. Each group had 13 children matched as to sex, age at admission to treatment, neurological diagnosis, and intellectual functioning at admission.

Three of the children in each group were so retarded in intellectual functioning that no full IQ score could be obtained. Two of these in each group were classified as organic, while the classification of the third remained in doubt. On the basis of psychiatric appraisals and the results of tests, these six nonscorable children showed no improvement over the 3-year program, regardless of the treatment program.

Of the other 20 children, 6 in each treatment group were classified as organic and 4 as nonorganic. The following findings pertain to these 20:

- Most of the children classified as organic showed improvement, both as rated by psychiatrists and as indicated by tests of reading achievement and IQ. The extent of the improvement was apparently not influenced by the type of treatment program. In reading, the organic children in the day center went from an average standard score of 96 to one of 129; those in the residential program, from 74 to 132. The day children showed an average IQ of 62 upon admission, reached an average of 74 at the end of the second year, and then dropped to an average of 65 at the end of the third year. Similarly, the organic children in residence went from an average IQ of 66 to one of 80 at the end of the second year, and then dropped to 72. (These drops, after the initial rises, are unexplained.)

- None of the nonorganic children in the day program showed any improvement as rated by psychiatrists. Three of the four in the residential program did show such improvement. The children in each treatment group improved in reading, but those in the residential group far more—from 89 to 182, as compared with from 98 to 137 for the day children. As for the IQ scores, the children in each group started with an average in the upper 80's and gained a few points in the first 2 years. In the third year the average IQ of the residential children shot up to 103, while that of the day children remained 92.

In sum, the bulk of the schizophrenic children who had brain damage, but were sufficiently intact to be scorable on an IQ test, improved to about the same degree whether in the day or the residential program. The nonorganic children, on the other hand, did substantially better in the residential program.

These differences can be explained, the investigators suggest, by differences in the families. The family of the nonorganic child has been a more fundamentally disturbing influence, from which it benefits him to get away completely. But the organic child seems not to need complete separation: he can progress if he is given an educational and environmental experience with which he can cope, and if his family is given professional assistance in contending with his deviancy and meeting his needs.

The most efficient treatment of schizophrenic children, these findings suggest, calls for two types of facilities: One offering a day program for children of the organic type, and one offering long-term impatient treatment for those children whose deviant manifestations are explained to a large extent by psychosocial factors. In making these suggestions, the investigators point out that the samples in this study, which is being repeated, were small and that all the children came from intact families. Other confirmatory studies are urged.

Research Grant: MH 5753
Date of Interview: Dec. 28, 1965

References:

Goldfarb, W. *Childhood Schizophrenia.* Cambridge: Harvard University Press, 1961. Published for the Commonwealth Fund.
Goldfarb, W. The mutual impact of mother and child in childhood schizophrenia. *Amer. J. Orthopsychiat.,* 1961, 31, 4.
Goldfarb, W. Families of schizophrenic children. *Ment. Retard.,* 1962, 39.
Goldfarb, W. Self-awareness in schizophrenic children. *Arch. Gen. Psychiat.,* 1963, 8.
Goldfarb, W. Childhood schizophrenia. *Int. Psychiat. Clinics,* 1964, 1, 4.
Goldfarb, W. Corrective socialization: A rationale for the treatment of schizophrenic children. *Canad. Psychiat. Association J.,* 1965, 10, 6.
Goldfarb, W., & Goldfarb, N. Evaluation of behavioral changes of schizophrenic children in residential treatment. *Amer. J. Psychother.,* 1965, 19, 2.
Goldfarb, W., Goldfarb, N., & Pollack, Ruth C. Treatment of childhood schizophrenia: A 3-year comparison of day and residential treatment. *Arch. Gen. Psychiat.,* 1966, 14.
Goldfarb, W., Levy, D.M., & Meyers, D.I. *The verbal encounter between the schizophrenic child and his mother.* Presented at the 20th Anniversary Meeting of the Psychoanalytic Clinic for Training and Research at Columbia University, 1965. In press, 1966.
Goldfarb, W., & Mintz, I. Schizophrenic child's reactions to time and space. *Arch. Gen. Psychiat.,* 1961, 5.
Goldfarb, W., & Pollack, Ruth C. The childhood schizophrenic's response to schooling in a residential treatment center. *Evaluation of psychiatric treatment.* New York: Grune and Stratton, 1964.
Meyers, D.I., & Goldfarb, W. Studies of perplexity in mothers of schizophrenic children. *Amer. J. Orthopsychiat.,* 1961, 31, 3.
Meyers, D.I. & Goldfarb, W. Psychiatric appraisals of parents and siblings of schizophrenic children. *Amer. J. Psychiat.,* 1962, 118, 10.
Taft, L.T., & Goldfarb, W. Prenatal and perinatal factors in childhood schizophrenia. *Developm. Med. Child Neurol.,* 1964, 6.

Schizophrenia: New Light from the Life Histories and Biochemistry of Siblings and Twins

Investigators:
William Pollin, M.D.
James R. Stabenau, M.D.
Loren Mosher, M.D.
Joe Tupin, M.D.
Axel Hoffer, M.D.
Martin Allen, M.D.
Barbara Scupi, M.S.W.
NIMH

Prepared by:
Maya Pines

When one identical twin become schizophrenic, but the other does not, what in their environment caused the difference? And when both twins become schizophrenic, what in their biochemical make-up predisposed them to it?

By asking provactive questions like these, Dr. William Pollin and his associates at the Section on Twin and Sibling Studies, Adult Psychiatry Branch of NIMH, hope to uncover major pieces of the jigsaw puzzle that is schizophrenia - a disease which accounts for roughly half of all hospitalized mental patients in the world. They are not primarily interested in twins, but in schizophrenia, and for the past six years they have been conducting a series of strictly controlled studies that combine the techniques of psychiatry, genetics, and biochemistry. These studies focus on: (1) the specific family patterns that contribute to triggering schizophrenia in one twin, but not in another, and (2) the underlying biochemical abnormalities that are shared by both twins. Thus, they point the way to two fruitful lines of attack on this widespread disease.

On the biochemical side, they are currently evaluating the possible significance of their most recent finding on 11 pairs of identical twins: the high rate of catecholamines excreted in the urine of both the schizophrenic and the healthy twin. The catecholamines have two important functions: Some of them, particularly norepinephrine (noradrenaline) carry messages to different parts of the brain; and all of them play an

310

essential role in the body's efforts to cope with stress. For this reason, previous reports of high catecholamines in psychiatric conditions had been attributed to the effects of the patients' anxiety. However, stress usually produces other signs as well - for instance, an elevation of adrenal steroids. Yet the healthy twins showed no parallel rise in their adrenal steroids, indicating that the high rate of catecholamine excretion was not solely a response to stress. And, indeed, other analyses in this Lab determined that the amount of catecholamines in both twins was under genetic control. This strongly suggested that overactivity of the catecholamine system did not merely reflect psychosis, but might help to produce it.

The Sibling Studies: Schizophrenia vs. Delinquency

As Dr. Pollin points out, it is very rare in behavioral research to have really well-controlled comparative studies. This represents a serious problem, particularly since there are so few well-anchored, reliable measures of personality or of psychopathology. Psychiatrists can clinically get the impression that a certain kind of life course is very relevant to a psychosis, but trying to nail down the mechanisms involved is extremely difficult.

He began, therefore, by studying siblings, on the theory that children of the same parents would provide a better basis for comparison. He wanted to compare the circumstances that led a child in each of three sets of families to become either schizophrenic, delinquent, or exceptionally well adjusted, while another child in the same family was just normal. "In some ways, delinquency and schizophrenia are polar opposites," he explains. "Schizophrenia is a disease in which inner representations of the external world become completely distorted, resulting in delusions and hallucinations. Delinquency is a pathology in which one's relations to the outer world are disordered. It is the difference between acting in and acting out." However, nonspecific reactions of guilt and shame are present in the families of both.

The research scheme devised by Dr. Pollin together with Drs. James R. Stabenau and Joe Tupin fitted in with the trend towards focusing not solely on the schizophrenic patient, but on the patient and his family as a unit. It involved three groups of five selected families. The ten youngsters in each group were carefully matched for age (between 14 and 18), sex, sibling order, and social class. All were Protestant. All were being raised by their biological parents. Both parents and both siblings in each family participated in all phases of the research. The five schizophrenics ("S" indexes) had been diagnosed as schizophrenic by at least two psychiatrists and had suffered from hallucinations, marked paranoid delusions, or marked regression for 6 months to 9 years. The five delinquents ("D" indexes) were referred by legal agencies; they had been charged with car theft, promiscuity, or running away. The exceptionally well-adjusted youngsters ("N" indexes) had been nominated by the staffs of a local junior college and high school for their outstanding academic work and/or personality adjustment and peer relationships. With the exception of the S indexes, all were seen during outpatient visits, and all participants, including the 15 normal control siblings, were interviewed and tested at length.

From the outset, very different patterns emerged among the three sets of families - patterns which appeared to antedate the symptoms of psychological disturbance in S and D families. Among the D families, for instance, all relationships were unstable. There were no fixed roles or responsibilities for anyone, and it was uncertain who would be the father, who the mother, who would dominate or be the leader at any time. By contrast, the S parents seemed locked in a rigid relationship to each other and to their children. It was a kind of stalemate. On the other hand, the N parents seemed flexible, empathic, and able to complement one another. On tests of communication and clear thinking, such as the Object Sorting Test and the Revealed Differences Test, both the S and D families did poorly compared to the N families.

The family histories of the three groups revealed even more striking differences. In nearly every S or D family (but not in the N families), a major crisis, spontaneously characterized by the family as "the worst time," had occurred when the index child was between 6 months and 3 years of age, usually reaching its peak at about the time he was 18 months old. "One of the important consequences of this differing incidence of family crisis appeared to be its potential for serving as the origin of a negative identity in a child through identification with a depressed, guilty, and anxious mother," wrote Drs. Stabenau and Pollin. "In addition, the disruptiveness of the family life at that time further served to reduce the sense of internal security for the index child."

During these earliest years, too, the parents in the S group often viewed the child who later became schizophrenic as either physically or psychologically "damaged." (Few of the non-schizophrenic children were considered defective in this fashion.) And nearly all the children who later became either S or D had younger siblings born within their first two years, while few of the controls did.

But why did schizophrenic symptoms develop in one group, and delinquent symptoms in another, when both suffered from early family crises? The researchers point to differing family life styles and, in the case of delinquents, to an additional crisis: the sudden collapse of the role of the father, just before the child began to act out. Depending on the timing of this change, one child within the family would become delinquent while the other would not. In one case, for example, a father who had kept his drinking under control slipped over the edge and became an alcoholic. In another, the father developed Parkinsonism. A third father lost his job. The appearance of delinquency nearly always followed a severe loss of self-esteem on the part of the father, usually when the index child was in his teens. The delinquent then seemed to identify with what he saw as an ineffectual, failing father.

Instability of this kind was unknown in the families of the schizophrenics in this sample, where the fathers were employed and generally in good health. Here symptoms often seemed to follow major separations from a parent, close sibling or grandparent. Often the mother scrutinized the index child's activities with phobic concern about where he was and with whom he played, fearing harm at play or his being killed in the streets. This resulted in depriving him of the freedom to explore the world around him - a freedom granted within broad limits to N children, and given almost recklessly to D children. Typically, the index child's life style was, and had been, extremely constricted.

In addition to differences such as these in the patterns of family relationships, existing evidence of a genetic factor in schizophrenia suggests that certain organic factors must have been present in the S families, though not in the others.

An Intensive Study of Identical Twins Discordant for Schizophrenia

As long as the subjects were genetically different, these findings had limited generalizability because inherited traits might account for most of the differences between them. In 1962, Drs. Pollin and Stabenau determined to repeat their study - this time, with identical twins. One-egg twins, they believed, would represent "the optimal controlled sample," in which not only genetic factors but also social, ethnic, chronological and psychological variables were matched to a degree not attainable in other ways.

Twins have been studied with great interest ever since antiquity. The ancients who believed in astrology were intrigued by the fact that twins born at almost the same time could have contrasting life histories. To explain this divergence, they decided that major changes in the configuration of the heavenly bodies must have occurred precisely in the interval between the births of Twin 1 and Twin 2. This meant that if they could locate identical twins with differing life histories and find out the moment of their birth, they could pinpoint the limits of major astronomical periods. Therefore, they actively sought out and studied such twins. But it was only in the 19th century, with Francis Galton, that the classical twin method came into use as a method of measuring the relative contributions of heredity and environment to a specific illness or other condition.

Since monozygotic (MZ) or identical twins are genetically alike, but dizygotic (DZ) or fraternal twins are genetically no more similar than any other siblings, the degree of concordance between twins of both types is meaningful. If 40 out of 50 pairs of MZ twins are concordant for an illness, but only 10 out of 50 pairs of DZ twins are so concordant, the difference between these two figures is a measure of the genetic contribution to the illness. However, this assumes that the environment of MZ twins could be considered to have been constant - a major flaw in the method, according to Dr. Pollin.

"We set out differently," he explains. "We did not try to evaluate the relative importance of the genetic factor, but to ignore it, in the sense that it was controlled for both. We were thus in an optimal position to study the non-genetic factors involved." It took very extensive recruiting through hospitals, university psychiatric departments, and other sources to find enough pairs of identical twins in which one was healthy but the other was adjudged clearly schizophrenic by five psychiatrists, and in which both parents were willing to come to Bethesda to be studied for two or three weeks at the NIH Clinical Center, together with both twins. But finally 16 such families were brought to the Center and evaluated, together with 9 control families.

Having at least these key members of the family present is "almost essential if one hopes to obtain a meaningful historical reconstruction concerning the differential experiences of the two twins," declare the researchers. "Much of the more important data concerns the mother's pregnancy and the birth and first years of life of the twins, facts known only to the parents. In the absence of prolonged psychoanalytic relationship with the parents, such material appears to be most accessible via a family-focused evaluation situation in which four family members are constantly supplementing, stimulating, and correcting the material that each recollects and presents." Besides, they could be given complete psychiatric, psychological, and biological work-ups, including tests of blood, urine, and chromosomes and some 25 different psychological tests. The twins' zygesity was determined by investigating 28 blood-group factors, as well as fingerprints and 10 anatomical features. Over 30 different collaborating investigators participated in the study.

The schizophrenic twin was admitted to an inpatient ward. If actively psychotic at the time of the study, in most cases he received lengthy treatment at the Clinical Center at no cost to the family. The other members of his family stayed in a physically identical ward on another floor. The nonschizophrenic twin was often interested in being evaluated because he wanted to find out his chances of remaining healthy.

Ever since Dr. Franz Kallmann described his genetic theory of schizophrenia in the 1940's and stated that the concordance rate for schizophrenia was approximately 80 percent - that if one identical twin became schizophrenic, his co-twin was likely to develop the same symptoms in 80 percent of the cases - these figures have stuck in the public mind, producing great fear among affected families. However in 1963, after a careful study of 16 pairs of MZ twins in which one was schizophrenic, the Finnish investigator Pekka Tienari reported that none of the co-twins was affected. Previous studies had traced twins through mental hospitals; Tienari started out with parish records of twin births and followed them up. This may have accounted for some of the difference in results, since the overburdened families of *two* schizophrenic patients would be more likely to have them committed to a mental hospital than the families of one. A larger study by Einar Kringlen in Norway followed up all the twins born in a given area during a given decade and found the concordance rate for MZ twins to be 38 percent, substantially lower than any reported before 1960.

Like the Scandinavian work, Dr. Pollin's current analysis suggests that instead of being concordant for schizophrenia in 80 percent of the cases, MZ twins are actually *discordant* for the illness in approximately 75 percent of cases. Even at the time of his earliest twin studies, he was able to reassure the healthy twins about their prospects, and while all members of the family found the study stressful, in most cases the healthy twins left the Center with their fears lessened.

These figures focused interest, once again, on the psychodynamic factors involved in schizophrenia. Tienari had noted that the twins who were psychologically more submissive were the ones to develop schizophrenia in all but one of his 16 cases. Kallmann and others had made similar observations. The NIMH study of twins essentially confirms this insight, and also explains how and why the environment of the stricken twin differed from that of the healthier twin, almost from the time of conception.

In a detailed report on the first five families studied in 1964, Drs. Pollin, Stabenau, and Tupin described "a consistent pattern of historical events and related familial attitudes" which distinguished the index from his healthy co-twin:

1) The twin who later became schizophrenic weighed less at birth.

2) He was perceived by his parents, particularly by his mother, as vulnerable, and his survival was thought to be imperiled.

3) He was the focus of more worry, involvement, and attention than his co-twin.

4) He developed somewhat more slowly.

5) He tended to perform less successfully, and to be perceived as the less competent and weaker of the twins.

6) He tended to be the more docile and more compliant of the two, was less independent, and had difficulty in achieving any degree of autonomy and separateness.

7) These relative differences tended to be persistent and unchanging.

This pattern resulted in part from constitutional differences, and in part from "a rigidly 'imprinted' role expectation, initiated at birth, determined by the constitutional differences, and subsequently reinforced by minor differences in development," the authors report. They see it as largely the result of a self-fulfilling prophecy.

In all five instances, the mother had a strong conscious fear of death concerning the index twin and/or herself, immediately after his birth. In two of these cases there was a brief period of legitimate concern about the index twin's survival, as he remained in the hospital for several days after his co-twin was taken home. In another, however, the mother would not accept the pediatrician's assurance that both twins were fine and that the smaller one, because of her size, would necessarily feed more slowly and take less formula - she had a phobic anxiety that the smaller twin would die if she did not feed her as frequently and as much as the other.

These worries led the parents to concentrate their efforts on the smaller twin. In each of the five families, the mother felt that the smaller twin "needed her more." When she fed both twins, she fed the smaller one first. If only one could be breast-fed, it would be the smaller one. In two instances, the mothers reporting pinching and slapping the smaller twin and using cold water on him to keep him awake so he would eat more.

Once established, this pattern persisted as the twins grew up. "The smaller twin would receive extra praise for things taken for granted in the larger one," the researchers report. "He would receive additional help with schoolwork, and would be less expected to dress himself or take responsibility for personal needs or household chores." The bigger twins were always a bit more successful in school and social life. They played the leader role and made all the decisions. They were also less docile and "good." Only the healthy twins had episodes of active rebellion or acting out. One, for example, engaged in violent controversies with his father, in which the index twin never participated. The index twins never showed non-compliance; if they expressed it at all, it was passively, in such a way that the parents could rationalize it as just another symptom of their disability.

Since the twins appeared identical in so many ways, "the needs of all concerned to find distinguishing identities for them led to a sharpening and highlighting of such initial differences," note Drs. Pollin, Stabenau, and Tupin. They reflect that if the healthy twins had not been present for nearly constant comparison, the parents might not have perceived the index twins as so weak or vulnerable, but might have accepted them as normal. Their anxiety and intense involvement with the smaller twin often led the parents to ambivalent feelings towards him. They tended to project the negative side of their self-image onto this smaller twin more often than on the larger one.

This general pattern tended to hold true as the study progressed. In a report on 11 families with MZ twins discordant for schizophrenia in 1965, the authors declared that each of the 11 index twins was the smaller one at birth. The difference in birth weights ranged from 1/2 ounce to 1 pound 12 ounces. This lower weight "appears to reflect some lower level of anatomic development and/or differentiation, and consequently, a lesser physiological competence and stability present at birth," they reported. The index twins also had a marked preponderance of such problems as cyanosis, infantile colic, feeding difficulties, burns, multiple fractures, and severe illnesses which knocked them flat for months at a time. Their parents recalled that these smaller twins had "worried more," cried more, been more "fussy," and seemed more sensitive. Almost without exception, and from earliest childhood, the index twins were described as more dependent, more submissive, more fearful, more compliant, and more constricted than their heavier co-twins.

To help refresh their memories, the parents were asked to bring in whatever pictures or home movies they had available. ("It seems all families have large numbers of pictures in shoe boxes," says Dr. Pollin. "They may never have put the pictures into albums, but they have them.") Nevertheless, there remained the problem of retrospective distortion. To alleviate it, a social worker lived with the families in their homes a couple of days, then went to see as many relatives, doctors, teachers, and friends as possible, accumulating up to 25 interviews per family to get a more objective view of the past. Often she found that many of those who knew the family recalled the bigger twin as an easier child to deal with. Almost from birth, the smaller twin actually had quite a different life course - as he must have had a different, less favorable intrauterine experience.

It is quite normal for one twin to be smaller than the other at birth. Thus, many parents fall into the pattern described above because of realistic concern for a vulnerable child. However, they change this pattern after the child gains in strength and maturity. It is only in certain cases, when parents are too troubled or rigid to modify their picture of the weaker twin, that the pattern becomes potentially dangerous. Apparently something about the weaker twin's situation resonates with a particular problem in these parents' lives, relighting an intense, unresolved conflict. No matter how much the pediatrician may reassure them, they remain consumed with anxiety about the child. On the other hand, they find dealing with the stronger twin an easy task - a distinct relief. In this way the twins experience different models of parental behavior, and have increasingly divergent experiences.

In a later report (1967), Drs. Pollin and Stabenau discuss two additional sets of identical twins in which, surprisingly, the twin who became schizophrenic did not weigh less at birth. They find it very significant that, despite a favorable start, these children suffered from specific stresses which reversed their relative position and, in effect, made them weaker than the lighter twin. In one of these cases, the index twin had turned blue from cyanosis because of poisoning from a defective heater next to her bed and had been taken to a hospital, near death, while her co-twin, who slept in another part of the room, suffered only minor effects. In the other, the twin who was heavier at birth nearly died from a severe case of Rocky Mountain spotted fever at age 3 and 1/2, after which there was great concern regarding his health and survival.

Thus, whether it began before birth - through differences in fetal positioning and consequent crowding, differences in fetal circulation, or other factors that produced relative physiological incompetence - or through accident in early childhood, life presented very different experiences to these "identical" twins. Between the ages of 2 and 6, the stronger twin was usually the more verbal and the more independent. From 6 to adolescence, the weaker twin often became increasingly dependent on his healthier co-twin - who simultaneously began to turn to others for friendship. In late adolescence and early adulthood, the healthy twin moved further towards individuality and heterosexual relationships. This accentuated a sense of loneliness and despair in the weaker twin.

"Often, disorganization, withdrawal, and schizophrenic symptomatology develop in the lighter birth weight twin at just this time, i.e., when the heavier, more differentiated twin is making a sudden spurt in the development of an individual identity and the establishment of heterosexual and genital level of personality organization," write Stabenau and Pollin. To the index twin, the world had always appeared more threatening - and its stresses mounted all around him as he grew up.

317

The Veterans' Study: 15,000 Pairs of Twins Discordant for Schizophrenia

In 1967, the Medical Follow-Up Agency of the National Academy of Sciences-National Research Council made available to researchers its national registry of all the pairs of white male twins born between 1917 and 1927 who served in the Armed Forces during World War II or the Korean War. It was a list drawn from the 54,000 pairs of twins born during that decade. It excluded 23,000 pairs of twins who did not serve in the Armed Forces at all, as well as 15,000 pairs in which only one twin served. This left 15,930 pairs of twins healthy enough for both to have passed the physical and mental tests leading to induction into the service.

The records of these men yielded a wealth of information that could be fed into computer tape: Induction physical examinations; inpatient and outpatient hospital and clinic diagnoses during their period of services; VA hospital diagnoses after they left the service; and diagnoses based on responses to a questionnaire. They were between 38 and 48 years old in 1965, after a follow-up period averaging 18 to 20 years.

Among these 15,930 pairs of twins, Drs. Pollin, Martin G. Allen, Axel Hoffer, and their associates found 338 pairs in which one or both twins had been diagnosed as schizophrenic at some time after entry to active duty. In some cases their zygosity was unknown, but 226 pairs could be identified as identical (MZ) or fraternal (DZ) twins. Among the 80 MZ pairs, 11, or 13.8 percent, were concordant for schizophrenia. Among the 146 DZ pairs, only 6, or 4.1 percent, were concordant for the disease. The concordance rate for schizophrenia was thus 3.3 times greater among MZ pairs than among DZ pairs. By contrast, the concordance rate for neurosis was almost the same in both kinds of twins - 10.7 percent for MZ pairs as compared to 7.1 percent for DZ pairs.

A re-analysis of 18 earlier major twin studies showed a similar ratio in all but one instance, suggesting "the presence of a genetic factor in the pathogenesis of schizophrenia, and its relative absence in psychoneurosis," report the researchers. "However, since approximately 85 percent of affected MZ pairs in the NRC sample are discordant for schizophrenia, the role of the suggested genetic factor appears to be a limited one."

This large sample of twins also allowed Drs. Allen and Pollin, to their own surprise, to cast doubt on one of the most widely accepted notions of the psychodynamic determinants of schizophrenia in analytic theory: the "diffuse ego boundary" hypothesis. This holds that schizophrenia is due to a "confusion of identity" resulting from weak ego boundaries, and that such problems are greater in twins, especially MZ twins. Therefore, MZ twins could be expected to have a higher incidence of schizophrenia than DZ twins, and all twins would be expected to have a higher incidence of it than the general population. However, neither proved to be the case. The incidence of schizophrenia in the total sample of 31,818 male veteran twins was only 1.14 percent, close to the proportion in the general population. And the incidence of the disease among MZ twins was only .97 percent, compared to 1.22 percent in DZ twins. The authors point out that though these figures do not support the "diffuse ego boundary"

318

hypothesis, they do not actually refute it, either, since possibly other factors unique to twin personality development might offset whatever ego boundary defects exist.

The Transmission of Schizophrenia

"It is very easy, in work with family dynamics, to say, Aha, *this* is the difference in the behavior of the mother and father that leads to schizophrenia - *these* are the schizophrenia-producing characteristics of parents. However, that is not the way we think of it right now," warns Dr. Pollin. Parental factors are only one among a variety of etiologic factors that may play a role in lowering resistance to the disease or triggering it, he explains.

For years there has been an ideological struggle between psychiatrists who believe that schizophrenia results from some genetic, biochemical impairment, and those who believe it comes from faulty child-rearing. Dr. Pollin sees a great need to integrate both points of view.

So far there is no definitive evidence that parental behavior is the predominant factor, he points out. Whether or not it is a necessary factor cannot be determined until enough prospective studies have been completed. Much of the disturbance seen in the parents of schizophrenics may be secondary to the disease, rather than a cause of it. All that can be said with assurance so far is that certain family patterns seem to accompany schizophrenia. However, these patterns cannot be blamed for the disease. It may be that there was some defect in the child from the beginning - a defect we do not yet know how to recognize or define.

Nor are the patterns of family interaction that Dr. Pollin described the only possible ones in the development of schizophrenia. They may represent only one of several different patterns leading to the same effect. By choosing to work only with families in which both parents and both twins were willing and able to come to the NIH Clinical Center for an extended period of time, he narrowly limited his sample. As he makes clear, the incidence of schizophrenia tends to be high among broken families and those with a great deal of strife and schizms - the very kind he had eliminated from his study. "We dealt with families where over-involvement with a child and over-protectiveness were more likely to be a factor," he notes. "If we had not required the families to participate, we might have found other patterns, centered on more overt types of rejection."

Illnesses can be passed from one person to another in many different ways. They can be transmitted by a microbe, as in bacterial infection; genetically, as in phenylketonuria; socially, in the sense that poor, socially backward slum families live in conditions that are likely to produce a high incidence of TB; or by various combinations of these factors.

To understand the transmission of schizophrenia, it helps to look at other illnesses, Dr. Pollin believes. He particularly likes the model developed by two English researchers to explain the incidence of a very different illness: congenital dislocation of the hip.

319

Though much simpler and more concrete, congenital dislocation of the hip clearly has genetic as well as environmental factors, as does schizophrenia. It runs in families, with identical twins concordant for it in 40 percent of cases. Yet the majority of twin pairs are discordant for the disease. Drs. Cedric O. Carter and John A. Wilkinson of the Medical Genetics Unit, British Research Council, were able to tease apart the various factors involved.

They found, first of all, that certain aspects of the anatomy of the hip joint were controlled by heredity. If the hip joint is visualized as a kind of modified ball and socket, the shape of the socket — its depth, and the size of its roof — is the key to a good fit. Obviously, the shallower the socket and the shorter its roof, the easier for the head of the thigh bone (the ball in it) to pop out. Yet this shape was determined by a genetic factor. Thus, a genetic factor produced an anatomical predisposition for the illness.

Next, investigating the fact the dislocation of the hip was eight or nine times more frequent among girls than among boys, they found a generalized laxness in all the joints of female infants, which they traced to a flow of hormones from the endocrine glands of girl babies just before birth. These hormones temporarily loosened the infants' connective tissues.

The condition was also much more common among children born by breech presentation, which bent their legs in a position that favored the thigh bone's popping out. The custom of swaddling had similar effects, mis-directing pressure on the baby's legs; this accounted for the high rate of dislocation of the hip among certain American Indian tribes.

Among the Chinese in Hong Kong, on the other hand, dislocation of the hip was rare. The researchers traced this to the custom of carrying infants in a back sling which, far from loosening the hip joint, tended to push the ball back into the socket.

When twins were discordant for the illness, it often turned out that one twin had been carried in a back sling, while the other had not; one had been swaddled, and the other had not; or else, being of different sexes, they had had different levels of hormones at birth. With MZ twins, the most common difference was their manner of birth: because of the intrauterine mechanics involved, one would be born by breech presentation, while the other was not.

Though the differences between schizophrenia and congenital dislocation of the hip are obvious, Dr. Pollin believes one can draw some cautious but useful analogies between the two illnesses. In both cases, there are many different pathways which lead to the same abnormal structure. The development of the human ego, like that of the hip joint, can be impeded by genetic factors, intrauterine mechanisms, environment in early infancy, social customs, accidents, or various combinations thereof.

It should also be noted that "schizophrenia" is a shorthand word for various forms of mental illness, he points out. When Eugen Bleuler introduced it in 1911, he used the plural: "The Group of Schizophrenias." It is still generally believed that schizophrenia includes several different, though overlapping, disease entities. Eventually, when the total picture

320

becomes clearer, several different patterns of family interaction and bio-chemical characteristics may be recognized as leading to different forms of schizophrenia.

The Possibility of Prevention

The fact that the majority of twins with the genotype for schizophrenia do not become schizophrenic shows that some kind of intervention is possible: Most life experiences do not lead to the development of schizophrenia. "However, so far we don't even know what specific biochemical changes take place at the time of the psychotic break," points out Dr. Pollin. "Nor do we understand why LSD, in microamounts, can cause a break with reality and a florid psychotic reaction. We are still fumbling in the dark — as though we were trying to treat heart disease without understanding the basic mechanism of the heart."

Within ten years, our knowledge of the factors that contribute to a high risk of schizophrenia should be at about the same level as our present knowledge of the various factors that contribute to a coronary, Dr. Pollin speculates. He hopes that it will then be possible to state with some certainty which combinations of factors represent a risk high enough to warrant the use of preventive drugs, or which factors in early childhood need to be modified.

"If you understand the specific steps that lead to a disease, you can approach its therapy and prevention from a rational point of view," he says. "But our treatment of schizophrenia has been quite the opposite – all entirely empirical or accidental. People have stumbled on methods of treatment. The tranquilizers were found during a search for a new type of anti-histamine. If one depends on such accidents, the odds against finding the most rational treatment and prevention measures are very bad. We must define more precisely the specific factors that contribute to a high risk."

Dr. Pollin cites the work of Dr. Sarnoff Mednick, Professor of Psychology, New York School for Social Research, New York, New York, with children of schizophrenic mothers as an example of the kind of studies which offers the best hope of finding clues to prevention. The children of schizophrenic mothers are a high-risk population. Dr. Mednick expects that, out of his first series of 200 children, at least 30 will become schizophrenic within 15 or 20 years. However, instead of having to depend on their relatives' memories, he will have a complete record of the children's pre-illness characteristics and of the conditions under which they were raised. This will allow him to see what differentiates the children who become sick from those who stay healthy. So far, Dr. Mednick's results fit in very well with Dr. Pollin's for he has found a clear correlation between the development of schizophrenia and the kind of pregnancy and birth difficulties which might have caused damage to the patient's central nervous system either before or during birth. Given a genetic predisposition to schizophrenia, such insults to the central nervous system might well be the factor that triggers the disease.

321

For the past three years, Drs. Pollin, M. Allen, and D. Cohen have been carrying out a prospective study of their own to better understand the development of personality characteristics and family relationships which - when accompanied by other factors – might play a role in producing schizophrenia. However, unlike Dr. Mednick, they do not anticipate any cases of schizophrenia among their subjects. They are simply studying the origins of certain patterns in the early life of twins. Having contacted obstetricians in the Washington area about women who expected multiple births, they asked the parents' cooperation and then did prenatal interviews in the parents' homes. One of the psychiatrists in the section was present at the time of each multiple delivery. If the twins were identical, the researchers kept careful records of exactly how the twins differed at birth, how the birth process itself varied, the neurological findings on each, and their behavior in the nursery. They followed up the twins regularly, first every few weeks, then every few months at home, and from time to time the twins were brought to the NIH Clinical Center for extensive tests and films.

"We wanted to define exactly when the differences between identical twins became consistent. We found that one of them became more dominant, more skillful with objects, more comfortable with strangers, less fearful, at a very early age," declares Dr. Pollin. "Our first group of twins, 10 pairs, is now between 2 and 3 years old, and we are collecting our second sample of 10. We hope that by the time they are 5 years old we will be able to pull together some useful generalizations."

Biochemical Abnormalities that May Predispose to Schizophrenia

Recent studies by Dr. Pollin have singled out abnormalities in the catecholamine system as a genetically determined factor which may contribute to the development of schizophrenia – and perhaps to other psychoses. In Leningrad, in the summer of 1970, he reported his preliminary findings on 19 pairs of identical twins, of whom 11 were discordant for schizophrenia, 4 were concordant (both schizophrenic), and 4 were normal controls. All were inpatients at the NIH Clinical Center in Bethesda, where their diets were similar and samples for nearly all pairs of twins were obtained on the same day.

Each identical twin excreted nearly the same amount of catecholamines as his co-twin. The following catecholamines were analyzed: Dopamine (the precursor from which norepinephrine and epinephrine are manufactured); norepinephrine; epinephrine; normetanephrine; metanephrine; and VMA. The intraclass correlation coefficients – which measure the extent to which intrapair similarity in identical twins is greater than the similarity between persons who are not genetically related - were high and statistically significant at values that ranged from $<.05$ to $<.001$, indicating that the levels of these substances were under a significant degree of genetic control.

The similarity remained even when one identical twin was schizophrenic and the other was not. For the 11 discordant MZ pairs of twins, the intraclass correlation coefficients were +.79 for norepinephrine, +.77 for dopamine, +.62 for normetanephrine, and +.80 for metanephrine. "The degree of genetic control present is not submerged or obscured by the presence or absence of schizophrenia," reported Dr. Pollin. "It is especially high for norepinephrine and dopamine."

This was particularly interesting by comparison with the MZ twins' discordant production of adrenal steroids. The catecholamines play two important roles in the body: (1) Some of them (norepinephreine and dopamine, those most clearly under genetic control) act as neurotransmitters in the central nervous system, e.g., norepinephrine in the hypothalamus, the area where emotional activities are integrated with higher abstract activities, and (2) All of them are known to rise in response to stress. However, they usually rise together with other responses by the adrenal glands. Yet in this case, the healthy MZ twins did not show any abnormally high level of 17-OH steroids; only their schizophrenic co-twins did. Thus, the high levels of catecholamines in both twins could not be attributed entirely to the stress of the immediate situation. In Dr. Pollin's hypothesis, they may represent one of the underlying factors that predispose to schizophrenia.

Researchers have long thought that it would make sense if some of the steps leading to serious psychopathology were located in the system that responds to stress. For if one is stressed and becomes anxious, beyond a certain point this anxiety can itself reduce, rather than increase, one's ability to cope with stress. As one's ability to cope with stress decreases, the external threat appears greater, leading to a greater response, and eventually to a pathological spiral.

A man who sees a lion come charging at him responds with a sudden rush of epinephrine (also called adrenaline) and other catecholamines. This brings about many physiological changes. His blood is massively shunted from other parts of the body into the muscular system, equipping him to run twice as fast as he otherwise could. His energy is mobilized for either fight or flight. Useful and adaptive as this response may be to a caveman who often faces dangers requiring physical prowess, it becomes self-defeating in our society, where the threats are more complex, subtle, and chronic. Studies in Dr. Pollin's Lab have shown that high levels of circulating epinephrine lead to a constriction of the perceptual field – they make one see less. Again, the ability to focus on a wild animal to the exclusion of everything else might prove quite useful in a jungle, but in a complex situation it would be better to increase one's ability to make subtle abstract distinctions – the kind of ability which is impaired by high levels of epinephrine. These high levels of epinephrine also diminish the precision of man's reaction to stress, leading him to over-react in increasingly non-productive ways. In this fashion they can produce the stage of exhaustion described by Hans Seyle, in which all ability to adapt to stress is lost.

It is therefore quite possible that the hyper-secretion of catecholamines impedes the development of the ability to cope with stress, and thus leads to schizophrenia. This might be one of the mechanisms involved, together with the non-genetic factors discussed above. In cases of discordance among MZ twins, perhaps one of the twins develops techniques to cope with the hypothetically higher level of catecholamines, while the other does not; then, as a result of his larger number of successes, he develops in normal fashion. Meanwhile his less successful co-twin becomes increasingly dependent, submissive, and constricted, and in the absence of certain kinds of intervention from family or friends, the direction of his development may become irreversible.

Many interesting and important leads tend to implicate the catecholamines in mental illness, Dr. Pollin points out. For instance, most drugs that are able to cause an artificial psychosis are methylated derivatives of amines. Thus, mescaline is a methylated derivative of dopamine. Methionine, one of the essential amino acids, is believed to be essential specifically because it supplies the methyle group, a very common group which plays an important role in body chemistry. And it was shown in this Lab nine years ago that when large quantities of methionine are administered to schizophrenic patients, some of these patients will suffer a severe exacerabation of their psychosis. (This is one of the few biochemical findings about schizophrenia on which there is general agreement.) This leads to the hypothesis that some abnormal, methylated metabolites of the catecholamines are formed in the body of certain persons because of a genetically determined fault; that one of these metabolites is chemically similar to a psychotomimetic drug; and that this metabolite – perhaps a methylated derivative of epinephrine – causes the psychotic symptoms. However, this remains to be proved.

Another lead comes from Parkinsonism. One of the side effects of all effective anti-psychotic drugs known to date is that they produce tremors similar to Parkinsonism. It was originally believed that these tremors and rigidity were an allergic response to the drugs. But it has now been shown that if anti-psychotic drugs are given in high enough dosage, some 95 percent of all patients will develop Parkinsonism. The biochemical basis of Parkinsonism has recently been established – it is a deficiency of dopamine, which among other things serves an essential neurotransmitter role in the basal ganglia, the part of the brain associated with motor activity. So Parkinsonism implies a lower level of dopamine. A lower level of dopamine implies a lower level of all the catecholamines, since in the body dopamine is the substance from which the other catecholamines are derived. The drug L-Dopa treats Parkinsonism by increasing the level of dopamine. Interestingly, it has had ill effects on some schizophrenic patients. In the past two years it has been used on a fair number of these patients, not to treat their illness, but to treat the severe Parkinsonism-like symptoms developed by some 2 or 3 percent of schizophrenics as a result of high dosages of thorazine. In a significant number of cases, L-Dopa exacerbated the psychosis. This, once again, seems to indicate that increased levels of dopamine and other catecholamines help to produce the symptoms of schizophrenia.

If indeed an inherited biochemical fault involving high levels of catecholamines predisposes certain persons to schizophrenia, it is a fault that might become manifest only if the system were working at high pressure – which brings one right back to the intrauterine experiences and family factors with which Dr. Pollin began.

"There is something unfortunately seductive about biochemical work," notes Dr. Pollin, an analyst who does not find the analytic and biochemical approaches conflicting, but complementary. "At least it can be quantified! We have fascinating life histories about our twins, each one a novella, but presenting it in a hard, precise way is infinitely more difficult."

He points out that whether the research is approached from the angle of biochemistry or that of family patterns, two issues remain unclear:

1) Can his findings be replicated with a larger sample? and

2) Which of his findings are specific to schizophrenia, rather than to all psychoses?

His next study will try to get at these issues. From the large pool of twins made available by the NAS-NRC, he hopes to select four matched groups of twins: one group of twins who are discordant for schizophrenia, another who are discordant for depression, a third who are discordant for severe neurosis, and another who are normal. Each group will consist of about 20 pairs of twins. Through extensive biochemical and psychological comparisons of these four groups, Dr. Pollin hopes to determine which factors are specific to schizophrenia, and which are common to all severe psychopathology.

Research Grant: Intramural
Date of Interviews: December 1970, January 1971

References:

Allen, M., and Pollin, W. Schizophrenia in twins and the diffuse ego boundary hypothesis. *American Journal of Psychiatry,* 127 (4):437-443, 1970.

Hoffer, A. and Pollin, W. Schizophrenia in the NAS-NRC panel of 15,909 veteran twin pairs. *Archives of General Psychiatry,* 23:469-477, 1970.

Mosher, L., Pollin, W., and Stabenau, J. R. Identical twins discordant for schizophrenia: Neurological findings. In press, *Archives of General Psychiatry.*

Mosher, L., Pollin, W., and Stabenau, J. Families with identical twins discordant for schizophrenia: Some relationships between identification, thinking styles, psychopathology and dominance-submissiveness. *British Journal of Psychiatry,* 118:29-42, 1971.

Pollin, W. The unique contribution of twin studies to the elucidation of non-genetic factors in personality development and psychopathogenesis. *Acta Genetic Medicae et Gemellogie,* 19 (1-2):299-303, 1970.

Pollin, W. and Stabenau, J. Biological, psychological and historical differences in a series of monozygotic twins discordant for schizophrenia. In Kety, S. S., and Rosenthal, D. (eds.). *The Transmission of Schizophrenia* London, Pergamon Press Ltd., 317-332, 1968.

Pollin, W. Possible genetic factor related to psychosis. For presentation May 7, 1971, Annual Meeting of the American Psychiatric Association, Washington, D.C.

Pollin, W. A new approach to the use of twin study data in studies of the pathogenesis of schizophrenia and neurosis. In Kaplan, A. (ed.). *Genetic Factors in Schizophrenia.* To be published by Chas. C. Thomas Press.

Pollin, W., Allen, M. G., Hoffer, A., Stabenau, J. R., and Hrubec, Z. Psychopathology in 15,909 pairs of veteran twins: Evidence for genetic factor in the pathogenesis of schizophrenia and its relevative absence in psychoneurosis. *American Journal of Psychiatry,* 126, #5:597-611, 1969.

Stabenau, J. R. and Pollin, W. Early characteristics of monozygotic twins discordant for schizophrenia. *Archives of General Psychiatry.,* 17:723-734, 1967.

Stabenau, J. R. and Pollin, W. Maturity at birth and adult protein bound iodine, *Nature,* 215:996-997, 1967.

Stabenau, J. R. and Pollin, W. Comparative life history differences of families of schizophrenics, delinquents, and "normals." *American Journal of Psychiatry,* 124:11, 1968.

Stabenau, J. R., Pollin, W., and Mosher, L. A study of monozygotic twins discordant for schizophrenia: Some biologic variables. *Archives of General Psychiatry,* 20:145-158, 1969.

Stabenau, J. R., Tupin, J., Wener, M., and Pollin, W. A comparative study of families of schizophrenics, delinquents, and normals. *Psychiatry,* 28(1):45-59, 1965.

Advances in Diagnosis and Treatment

We shall do so much in the years to come,
But what have we done today?
We shall give our gold in a princely sum,
But what did we give today?

—Nixon Waterman

Why Adolescents Kill Themselves

Investigator:
Joseph D. Teicher, M.D.
University of Southern California
School of Medicine
Los Angeles, Calif.

Prepared by:
Gay Luce

Using interviews and psychological tests, a research team has compared 50 adolescents after an attempted suicide, with unsuicidal peers of the same age, sex, and background. Although economic privation, broken homes, and disciplinary problems were found in the control group—the sequence and timing of events occurred at a different phase in the development of the child. The profile of the suicidal adolescent includes longstanding problems with family, a stage of escalation during adolescence, and a final stage of alienation—a chain reaction that dissolves the adolescent's closest personal bonds. Given detailed biographical knowledge of an adolescent, this study indicates that it should be possible to pick out the youth in danger, for adolescent suicide is not irrational but overdetermined by sequences of life events occurring in critical periods.

Background

Adolescent suicide is horrifying, unthinkable, and a little unreal to most adults, for we tend to be complacent about the troubles of the young. To the modern adults, *Romeo and Juliet* may seem only a story. Yet many adolescents cling to one another in similar love, with the desperation of a last hope in a lonely world. A modern Juliet is likely to be a frightened and pregnant little girl: the boy is likely to be rejected, and both may feel totally alone.

Literary descriptions of childhood suicide seem bizarre, yet they resemble modern case histories. In Thomas Hardy's *Jude the Obscure,* the restless wanderings and misery of unmarried parents overcome an unwanted oldest boy. When he hears that yet another unwanted baby is coming, he kills himself and the other children. It is not that such events don't happen, but we are reluctant to believe them.

In 1965, Jacobziner estimated that there were 60,000 attempted suicides among young people under age 20 in the United States each year.

Adolescence can be a particularly lonely and difficult period, a time of biological upheaval and social change. A person is expected to emerge from the safety and dependency of childhood into responsible maturity. Even healthy and happy adolescents become moody and oscillate between passions and depressions in a manner that the older people around them rarely understand. Most adolescents have fantasies about killing themselves in moments of rage and frustration or when they feel totally isolated from their families and friends. This is not surprising. Who has not imagined, with some glee, the remorse his parents would feel if he killed himself? Between such imaginings and the act lies the world of pathological events that Doctor Teicher and his associates have begun to define.

Statistics portray great misery among a large population of adolescents. Suicide ranks as the fourth most frequent cause of death for young people 15—19 years old. Fortunately, the vast number of attempted suicides in this age group are thwarted. An estimate of 60,000 suicide attempts a year may seem exaggerated, but hospital admissions offer a convincingly sad picture. In 1960, for instance, at New York's Bellevue Hospital attempted suicide was the reason for admitting 10 percent of the child and adolescent patients. At Kings County Hospital in Brooklyn, 13 out of every 100 children who came to the hospital had attempted or threatened suicide. Each month, the huge Los Angeles County-U.S.C. Medical Center admits about seven patients between 14 and 18 who have attempted to kill themselves; over 80 a year.

The Attempted Suicides

There has been a general tendency to dismiss a suicide attempt in an adolescent as an impulsive act stemming from a temporary crisis or depression. Perhaps it is soothing to believe that someone so young with "life ahead of him" could not have intended to kill himself. He could not have considered that he might die. On the contrary, Doctor Teicher and his associates at the Medical Center of the University of Southern California have found many adolescents who attempted to take their lives more than once. At first they may have used the drastic move as a threat to draw attention to their problems. Instead, it generally made matters worse. After an escalation of long-standing problems and loss of any meaningful relations, many concluded that death was really the only solution to unsolvable, unbearable, and chronic problems.

Beginning with Freud around 1920, many keen minds in the development of psychiatry have wrestled with the problem of adolescent suicide, but inferences drawn from a few cases or psychological studies did not indicate how to predict a suicide from outside circumstances. In the fall of 1964, the investigator and his associates began to study the life situations of adolescents who attempted suicide, comparing them with control adolescents matched for age, race, sex, and family income—control adolescents who had never attempted suicide. Quite a few interesting patterns have been drawn from this study of 50 young people who

330

attempted suicide. All were between 14 and 18. None of them was mentally retarded or obviously pregnant. All had been brought into the Los Angeles County-U.S.C. Medical Center sometime between September 1964 and May 1965 because of their suicide attempt.

At least one parent, usually the mother, was studied as well. For comparison there was a control group of 32 youngsters and their parents. Three-quarters of the attempted suicides were girls. On the average the suicidal adolescents were around 16 years old. They were white, Mexican, Negro, Protestant, Catholic, and Jewish.

Procedure: Charts of Life Events

The procedure called for an interview with the adolescent patient within 24 to 48 hours after the suicide attempt. The parent or parents were also interviewed. Then, the suicidal youngster's therapy sessions in the hospital were taped and transcribed for further analysis.

Two biographies were elicited from structured interviews. There was the parent's version of his child's history, and there was the adolescent's version of his own life. On the basis of the case histories, a life history chart was constructed for each suicide attempter and his matched control. This was done by constructing a chronology (in parallel) on a vertical continuum that depicted all the experiences of the adolescent from birth until the suicide attempt. These graphic charts show residential moves, school changes, the beginnings of various behavioral problems, separation, divorce, or remarriage of the parents, and deaths in the family. The charts were put in a sequence that displayed how the events tended to pile up at a particular point in the adolescent's life. This indicated how the crises had accumulated during the adolescent's life.

What events distinguished those who attempted suicide from those who did not? A simple comparison of events in the lives of the control group and the suicide-attempters might not show that there was a very pronounced difference. The investigators discerned a distinct process leading to progressively deeper unhappiness and pessimism. The suicide-attempters went through a sequence that led to progressive isolation from the important people in his life. The control adolescents did not. The process can be summarized in three stages: The suicide-attempters all had a long-standing history of problems from chidlhood into adolescence. There was also a period in which problems seemed to escalate, usually at the very beginning of adolescence. Moreover, the problems mounted in a manner that seemed to exceed those of peers and friends. Finally, came a phase characterized by a "chain reaction dissolution of any remaining meaningful social relationships." This isolation occurred in the days and weeks preceding the suicide attempt.

Sequential Analysis of Life Events

The advantage of looking at things sequentially can be demonstrated by comparing the two groups. For instance, the life histories of the suicide-attempters showed that 72 percent of them came from broken homes, yet 53 percent of the control group also came from broken homes. Former studies of suicide have emphasized the fact that there were more broken homes among suicide attempters than "control" adolescents. However, none of these studies examined the broken homes of comparison groups. If one looked only at the incidence of broken homes and severed parental relations, there is no great difference between suicidal youths and comparable nonsuicidal youths. However, by looking at the chronological biographies of these two groups, the grantees have seen that the relevance of a broken home depends upon *when* the instability occurred in the child's development.

Critical Phase

Although 72 percent of the suicide-attempters and 53 percent of the control adolescents came from broken homes, the timing of divorce and remarriage was different. In the suicidal group 58 percent of the parents remarried, but only one-fourth of the control parents remarried. More-over, these control parents managed to remarry very early in the child's life and remained married. The parents of the suicidal adolescent either remarried quite a bit later in his life, or, if they remarried early, they were subsequently divorced and remarried several times again.

The chronological mapping of biographies shows that the suicidal adolescents had parents who were divorced, separated, or remarried after the onset of adolescence. By contrast, the control families experienced change earlier, if at all. Instability in the home apparently had a differential effect depending upon the age of the child. Both groups experienced the instability of a broken home, but the nonsuicidal adolescents had a stable homelife during their last 5 years, while the suicidal youths had experienced instability then. As the investigators have written:[1]

"This is particularly significant, not only because divorce, separation, or the acquisition of a stepparent is stressful and disruptive event per se, but also because it occurs during a particularly stressful life time in the life cycle, i.e., adolescence."

A great many people who have written about suicide have implied that the loss of a parent in childhood might cause depression and perhaps suicidal feelings later in life. This study would not bear out such a conclusion, since the control group also experienced parental loss in childhood. Perhaps it is not loss of a parent in childhood that predisposes a

---

[1] Jacobs, J., and Teicher, J. D. Broken homes and social isolation in attempted suicides of adolescents. *International Journal of Social Psychiatry*, 13(2):146, 1967.

person to depression and suicide in later life. Loss of a love object, as the grantee has remarked, is an important aspect of the process. But loss must be viewed as a part of the process, and particular attention must be paid to the time when it occurred. Most of the adolescents began their maelstrom descent toward suicide after a long period of alienation from parents. One 14-year-old who had tried to commit suicide twice was asked why. She replied, "It's my mother."[2]

Asked what her mother did, she answered, "We just don't get along. We haven't for 3 years. Before that we were like sisters and then it seems like since she divorced my stepfather it started a lot of trouble."

This girl enjoyed being in the hospital and did not want to return home. It is particularly poignant that she wanted to be committed to a State mental hospital rather than return home. Many of the young suicide attempters described their alienation from parents as a process in which either the mother or father would nag them, would cut them off from their friends, would disapprove of their favorite friends, and thus made it difficult for them to have relationships outside the home, at the same time making life very difficult for them within the home. This was their version.

The Broken Romance

Typically, many of these adolescents had fallen in love and formed very possessive and exclusive romantic relationships. This actually isolated them even more. A girl and boy would concentrate so intensely on one another that they tended to cut off all their friends. Then, if the romance failed, they would feel hopeless, lost and despairing.

At the time of the interviews none of the adolescents in the control group was ending a romance, but a number of the "suicidal adolescents" had just broken a romance. Moreover, five of these girls were either pregnant or feared that they were pregnant. As the biographies revealed, pregnancy inevitably led to a great sense of isolation. These girls withdrew and were rejected by their boyfriends. Usually, they were also rejected by their parents at this time when they most needed support. The suicidal adolescents were really in a state of depression compared with their counterparts, and, indeed, as the grantees point out, this seemed to have been prompted by their real experiences in life.

The Way They Saw It

Only 38 percent of the suicidal youngsters considered their childhood to have been happy. But about 94 percent of the control group considered

---

[2] Unpublished transcript.

childhood to have been a happy time for them. In describing the biographies, the investigators wrote:[3]

"Judging from the verbatim accounts of the suicide-attempters in the interviews as well as the suicide notes left by them, and notes written by other adolescents outside our sample, the decision to suicide was the result of a rational, decision-making process. However, the choice of death is not based on a desire to die. They would, if they could, choose to live. Death, in a sense, is not chosen at all but results from the progressive failure of adaptive techniques to cope with the problems of living, where "the problem" is the maintenance of meaningful social relationships. In short, the potential suicide felt he had no choice, i.e., death is necessary. It is from this recognition of necessity that his sense of freedom stems and immediately preceding the act itself there is often a feeling of well-being, a cessation of all cares. This is evidenced in the matter-of-fact presentation found in suicide notes."

Profile of Problems: Disruption at Home and Discipline

Early in childhood or adolescence the suicidal youngsters usually experienced the break-up of their home. In some cases this meant the institutionalization of the child or a family member. Many of them were placed in foster homes or left with relatives. Many of them changed schools and residences frequently. Many of these families were very poor. In some cases, the parents also had been depressed and had attempted suicide. A sizable percent of the suicidal youngsters had either a parent, relative, or close friend who had attempted suicide. Seventy-two percent had one or both of their natural parents away from home, either because of divorce, separation, or death. Most of those living with stepparents felt they didn't like the stepparent. A great many had a parent who was married several times. In about 62 percent of the cases both parents were working. Half of these families lived on less than $3,600 per year. The background is one of poverty, instability, and unhappiness.

The specific period just preceding a suicide is characterized by a vicious spiral of events. It may begin when a parent feels unable to cope with some behavior in his or her adolescent. The parent begins to nag and use severe disciplinary procedures to prevent the youngster from going out. He may resort to physical punishment. Parents of the suicidal adolescents felt that their children would get into less trouble if they were watched more closely. Therefore, they would question them about their activities and whereabouts. Because the adolescent's trust in his parent somehow depended upon dignity and the maintenance of a certain amount of privacy, questioning set up a vicious circle of mistrust. From the point of

---

[3] Jacobs, J., and Teicher, J.D. Broken homes and social isolation in attempted suicides, of adolescents. *International Journal of Social Psychiatry*, 13(2): 148, 1967.

view of the adolescents (as revealed on a rating scale), withholding privileges, fussing, nagging, and whipping were considered the worst disciplinary techniques. The suicidal adolescents and their nonsuicidal counterparts agreed on this rating. At the same time, some of the adolescents felt they would gladly forego undesirable behavior, and their parents should have helped them to discourage this behavior. When the parents didn't intervene, the young people took it as a sign of rejection.

As the parent-child situation got worse, the parents grew frustrated, and the adolescent felt that his parents couldn't understand and were punishing him inappropriately. The biographies revealed that this impasse led to the adolescent's rebellion or withdrawal. This stage of deterioration usually led to a breakdown of communication between parent and child, in which the youth's withdrawal was a consequence. Essentially, both parent and adolescent would give up and stop trying to communicate.

Many suicidal adolescents said that they got into the habit of lying and would simply withdraw into their rooms, or withdraw into themselves in order to avoid their parents and conflict.

School

A third of the adolescents who had attempted suicide were out of school at the time. Either they were ill because of pregnancy or because of an earlier suicide attempt. An astonishing number had already attempted suicide in the past. A quarter of these suicidal adolescents had been out of school because they were acting up in class, had shown some emotional instability, or had been involved in fights. Half of them had been truant from school during the last 5 years because of lack of interest or active distaste.

To Whom Do You Turn in Time of Trouble?

When asked to whom they turned when they were in trouble, a quarter of the suicidal adolescents said there was no one to turn to. None of the control adolescents felt such isolation. The pathos and the loneliness of the suicidal adolescent is very dramatically shown in some of the figures. Of the 46 percent who reported their suicide attempt to other people, less than half reported it to their parents. Almost two-thirds of them talked to people other than family members. This is particularly significant since 88 percent of the suicide attempts occurred at home, very often with the parents in the next room. In every instance, the lack of communication between family and the child and lack of communication with peers was a very important factor in the period leading to suicide. On interview, these suicidal adolescents conveyed the despairing sense that death was the only solution, there was no other way out. Consider these excerpts from a letter by a 17-year-old Negro boy to his father. This note was written the evening before he made his second suicide attempt:

"Dear Father, I am addressing you these few lines to let you know that I am fine and everybody else is and I hope you are the same.

335

Daddy, I understand that I let you down and I let Mother down in the same way when I did that little old thing [the suicide attempt] that Wednesday night. Daddy, I am sorry if I really upset you, but Daddy after I got back I realized how sad and bad you felt when I came back to California.—I had lost my best girl the week before I did that. I had a fight because some dude tried to take advantage of her when I sped to the store, so I came back and I heard a lot of noise like bumping so I run in and there he is trying to rape my girl, my best one too.—Daddy I tried as hard as I could to make it cheerful, but it does get sad. Daddy I am up by myself. I've been up all night trying to write you something to cheer you up, because I could see your heart breaking when you first asked Sam's wife if they would have room and that Sunday Dad, it was hard but I fought the tears that burned my eyes as we drove off and Daddy part of my sickness when I had taken an overdose I did just want to sleep myself away because I missed you Dad.

"But when I left I felt like I had killed something inside of you and I knew you hated to see me go, and I hated to go, but Daddy, well, I kind of missed Mother after I had seen her. I miss you and remember what you said, 'settle down', but Daddy I tried so hard so I went and bought some sleeping pills and took them so both of you could feel the same thing."[4]

When an adolescent has retreated from family problems into a love affair, and then the romance breaks up or culminates in pregnancy, then there is even more isolation than before. A girl is especially alone if her boyfriend disappears and she has already alienated other friends. Parents often become disillusioned and give up at the time their child needs help the most. In a letter to her former boyfriend, a desperate young girl showed the lengths to which she would go for a social relationship and a solution to the problem of pregnancy. She wrote on the night of a suicide attempt. A short excerpt indicates the tragic sense of rejection and isolation.

"Dear Bill, I want you and I to get an understanding about certain things because I think you got the wrong impression of me * * * and believe me it hurt. I knew all the time you were hinting to me I was too young, didn't know nothing about life, but you were wrong. I know a whole lot about life. I'm ashamed of the things I know to be so young. I couldn't tell you this personally, 'cuz I couldn't face what you might have said and I sure it would have hurt my feelings badly. I'm two months pregnant by you. You don't have to admit it, I don't care. You may say anything you like. You don't have to worry about any trouble. It would be a disgrace for me to let people know I threw myself on you knowing you didn't care or feel anyway toward me. Don't worry, no one will ever know my child's father. I will never mention you to him or her whichever it be."[5]

---

[4] Teicher, J. D., and Jacobs, J. Adolescents who attempt suicide: Preliminary findings. *American Journal of Psychiatry*, 122(11):5, May 1966.

[5] Teicher, J. D., and Jacobs, J. Adolescents who attempt suicide. *American Journal of Psychiatry*, 122(11), 1966.

Parents and Physicians: Surprised

Despite the history of increasing problems, the families were inevitably hurt and surprised by the suicide attempt. Parents and physicians who had seen the adolescents would say "it was so unexpected." Actually, some 46 percent of the suicide-attempters had visited their physicians at some time before the attempt. Over half had been treated for some physical or mental disturbance during the prior 5 years. A third had some serious physical complaint, and a third of them had some family member who was sick or had been hospitalized. In screening the adolescents to be included in this study, Doctor Teicher and his associates examined over 100. In the first 30 they found 11 with duodenal ulcers.

In spite of the long history of problems, however, the physician and mothers acted surprised by the suicide attempts. While perhaps expressing some guilt, the mothers would deny that there was anything in the home situation that would cause a suicide. The very people who were closest to the suicide-attempters apparently failed to see the progression of social isolation: the problems with parents, with poverty, broken romances, excommunication from school or peers, especially in the instance of pregnancy. Since these are problems that most people would be reticent to discuss with others, adolescents in such predicaments are especially isolated.

After a period of not communicating, their first suicide attempt came as a surprise to parents, friends, and schoolmates. The physicans who saw them just after the attempt had been taken off guard perhaps because suicidal people are not easily distinguished from others with severe problems. There seem to be no simple and convenient ways of anticipating a suicidal attempt. No litmus test can determine who is a potential suicide. Clearly a major reason that suicidal attempts are not warded off is lack of communication of the real feelings. The true biography of the unhappy person was not known by anybody around him.

Profiles for Prevention

Adolescence is a time of sufficient duress for parents and youngsters as new behavioral problems arise. Moreover, many of the suicidal youngsters in the Los Angeles study also had illness or mental illness in their family during the preceding 5 years. Doctor Teicher and his associates feel that various sets of events must be considered in anticipating suicide. Among them are such factors as economic status, geographic mobility, and the divorce rate in the home. These alone do not predict suicide. However, these events seem to occur at particular times in the adolescent's life and the timing may be critical. Along with an escalation of behavioral problems, a youth who is isolated from family and peers may be in danger of trying suicide.

It should not be surprising to learn that their parents also had unhappy histories. The mothers often got married only because they were pregnant.

337

Some had illegitimate children. Quite a few suffered depression and were depressed after giving birth. This was particularly notable among the mothers of the *boys* who had attempted suicide. Many had illegitimate children or had been forced into marriage because of pregnancy. Seventy percent of them were separated or divorced, a good number of them after short-lived marriages of convenience. Needless to say, a huge percentage had suffered from economic deprivation.

Male Suicide

The number of suicides and suicide attempts among girls far outweighs the number of attempts among boys; and this has been associated with broken romances, rejection, and unwanted pregnancy. In attempting to understand the male suicide attempts, Doctor Teicher and Dr. N.L. Margolin did a special study of 13 of the boys in their group. They were interviewed by one of the authors after their suicide attempt. Identical questionnaires about parent-child relationships and school, about adjustment to peer groups and career aspirations were given to the boys and their parents. Both took a battery of psychological tests in addition.

The boys in the control group also came from broken homes. Many had both parents working and relatives living with the family. However, the vignettes of the suicidal boys differed in that they showed a repeated sequence of events which the authors summarize in this order: They had, first of all, a mother who was angry, depressed, or withdrawn, both before and after pregnancy. Generally it was an unwanted pregnancy. Then, there was the loss of some very significant person or persons in the patient's early life, usually the loss of the father. There was also a reversal of roles with the mother. At the time of the suicide attempt it had seemed to the boy that the mother (or his mother-surrogate) was also going to leave his life forever. During the boy's period of distress his mother was preoccupied with her own depression, up to the time of her son's suicide attempt.

An 18-year-old Mexican-American boy is typical. His mother never wanted him. She became very overprotective until he was about age 12. At age 5 his semi-alcoholic father left the home. At this point he and his mother began to shift around from house to house, mostly living with his grandmother. After the divorce he began to get headaches. His mother thought he missed his father. He always felt rejected, and he made depressed statements such as: "I wish I hadn't been born." Then at the age of 15 he was rejected by a girl. This left him emotionally fractured. He would get into romances where he was inevitably hurt and depressed. His mother felt she had never been shown any love or affection by her own family, and she was a chronically depressed person. She explained that, as she was getting older, she had been dating two men. One was a rather selfish man who overlooked her son. She broke up with him. Her boy was then 17 years old.

"I was a very blind and stupid woman. I didn't realize what I was doing to Tom, how sensitive and emotional he was. Well, time went by and Tom started to go to parties and dating, not too often, but he had started to have friendships on the outside. Soon after I met someone at work from the same department and we got along real well. He was divorced also. He has a family of three to support, so we have quite a lot in common. The man moved in. He liked my son and went out of his way to cultivate him, but apparently things went along very well until Tom started to complain that since Sam had moved in with us he was nothing around the house just in my way, that I didn't love him any more, but that was not true."[6]

In a pleading letter to the doctor she asked what he could do to undo the damage she had done her son at an early age. Here was the tragic pattern of events—the unhappy circumstances around his birth, the divorce, his father's withdrawal, infantile identification with the mother, frequent moves, repeated loss of peer relationships, the clinging to an angry and depressed mother, and, finally, the threatened loss of his mother to a new man. Case after case revealed this kind of dependency and frustration in the first years of life. In 11 cases the fathers were physically absent from the home. In eight instances the father had left home before the child was 6 years old. Almost all of these boys were prevented from being children. They were thrust into the role of helping their mothers either because they were the oldest or the only child. In each case there was also a sense of loss on the part of the child, either because the mother and father had just recently separated, because the mother had a serious illness, or because a stepfather had just recently left home. In one instance, the mother had just recently married, and the boy had been left by his girl friend.

"On the basis of our data we find that the male adolescent suicide attempt seems to have its origins in the mother-child relationships of infancy. Most importantly, these relationships revealed not only early deprivation, but chronic repeated separation threat or object loss. This state of affairs leads to continued, intense, archaic identification with the mother. The lack of a masculine image in the experience of these boys together with the ambivalence of the mothers prevents any working through of the Oedipal phase of development."[7]

A helpless and dependent child needs his mother and cannot "allow" her to be bad. He then blames himself for anything wrong in the environment, which allows him to soak up the badness, as it were, making things around him all right. The investigators suggest that this situation eventually creates a self-destructive pattern.

"The early and repeated separation trauma resulting in disturbances in early ego and superego development lay the foundation for later pathological identification, and leave their marks on character

---

[6] Margolin, N. L., and Teicher, J. D. Thirteen adolescent male suicide attempts. *Journal of the American Academy of Child Psychiatry,* 7(2):301, 1968.
[7] Op. cit. p. 312.

formation and personality development. As the child enters adolescence, the conflicts over separation intensify due to a number of concurrent reasons, all of which essentially have to do with the biological and psychological need to be autonomous from the mother. The adolescent male tries to defend himself against feelings of his helplessness in many ways. He may regress to feelings of omnipotence and pseudoindependence and seek challenging, dangerous situations such as reckless driving, motor-cycling, etc. He may act out antisocially as a defense to prevent loss of identity. However, it seems that these defensive attempts cannot be maintained when actual separation from the mother is threatened. This threat can occur in the form of the mother's withdrawing because of her depression, her becoming interested in a new husband, etc. Also significant is the breakup of the adolescent's romance, i.e., experiencing the loss of a mother surrogate. When the mother becomes depressed and suicidal, the adolescent perceives rightly that his very existence is a burden upon her. He acts as if he were saying, 'If I destroy the bad part of myself, then mother will live to care for me.'

"Internally, ego regression with splitting occurs. The split-off part of the ego, representing the bad self, is rejected and persecuted by the parts of the ego and superego identified with the rejecting suicidal mother. *This identification is of great significance in the suicidal adolescents.* Freud (1923) states that the ego, feeling hated and unprotected by the superego, will let itself die, a situation that is similar to the anxiety in infantile separation from the mother."[8]

In these 13 cases, the boys professed to love their nagging and ambivalent mothers. They did not necessarily feel they were loved, but because of an infantile dependence, the mother's depression, anger, withdrawal, and disapproval had a very devasting effect upon them. In many instances, the mother also had suicidal thoughts, and the boys identified with their mother's depressed and suicidal state. Interestingly enough, the suicidal girls described their mothers in uniformly glowing and idealized terms and denied any flaws, despite the fact that their mothers were often very hostile.

"The suicide attempt is an overdetermined symptom and whether it is an attention-getting or an attempt to die it is always serious. It is an effort to solve a chronic problem, living; a plea for help; an expression of rage and hostility; and at times a symbolic reunion with the pre-Oedipal mother or father."[9]

Therapy

In many ways the therapist in the hospital has proven to be the lifeline of these youngsters. He maintains his contact with the suicide attempters from the beginning of consultation until final rehabilitation or referral.

---

[8] Op. cit. pp. 312–313.
[9] Teicher, J. D. The treatment of the suicidal adolescent—the lifeline approach. *Proceedings of the IV World Congress of Psychiatry*, p. 749, Madrid, September 1966. Excerpta Medica International Congress Series No. 150.

When they are first brought to the hospital they are shaken, anxious, depressed, insecure, guilty, and apprehensive because of the anger and hurt that they've caused. They feel terribly alone, and this is probably their worst agony. Usually the mother has been angry and sometimes guilty; her next reaction is usually hostile and she will defend herself with great denial. The father, or more usually the stepfather, would consider the suicide attempt a bother and show little concern. Doctor Teicher recommends that suicidal adolescents should be hospitalized, if only briefly, and placed in a ward where there are other adolescent patients to offer warmth, support, and understanding. In many instances the patients of this study didn't want to leave the hospital, and they would cling to the staff and other patients. Adolescents will often talk about the precipitating events, such as their parents' refusal to let them go out, or a broken romance. The rejection by a boyfriend or a girlfriend is a most common precipitating factor, but this would be taken in stride as an unhappy experience if there had been some positive experiences earlier in life. The role of the therapist as seen by the investigators is that of a person who provides understanding and love. Slowly the therapist can guide a young person to cope with his conflicts and communicate with his family. Meanwhile he offers support and is always available so that the adolescent doesn't feel so lonely and isolated.

From this study one may clearly see that youth, itself, is no antidote to a hostile environment. The old myth that all suicide attempts are impulsive and irrational is forever banished, and in this study one can see how an accumulation of adverse factors at a critical period shapes the biographical profile of the potential adolescent suicide. This profile might be used in further studies to predict and prevent suicide attempts.

This brief research has already shown that no simple correlations between life events can predict suicidal despair in a young person. Yet young people—in shockingly vast numbers—are miserable enough, and lonely enough that they are brought to hospitals by the tens of thousands each year, after attempting to kill themselves, often in a room right next to their parents.

Further research in this area has implications beyond suicide prevention. The development of biographical profiles may yield techniques whereby informed doctors, social workers, and school personnel might spot the precarious young person in time to obtain therapy for him. However, the import of this research is broader in its implications. It begins to fold back the curtains upon the circumstances and the timing that weaken an individual to the stresses of life and alienate him from all of those who might help him. The chain of misery seems to pass from one generation to the next, and in each case privation plays its part. Moreover, the relations of family members show a psychodynamics that produces instability and separation instead of cohesion and mutual help. Adolescence can be an especially creative and exciting time of life. In this particular era, adolescents are having an ever-increasing impact upon society—they have changed the entire genre of popular music, for example—but exceedingly great numbers of adolescents are having the opposite experience. Suicide prevention studies among the most unhappy of these people may give considerable insight into what it takes to deflect an entire life from misery toward productiveness and participation.

Research Grant: MH 1432
Date of Interview: September 1968

References:

Jacobs, J., and Teicher, J. D. Broken homes and social isolation in attempted suicides of adolescents. *International Journal of Social Psychiatry,* 13(2):140–149, 1967.

Jacobziner, H. Attempted suicide in adolescence, *Journal of the American Medical Association,* 191(7):11–14, 1965.

Margolin, N. L., and Teicher, J. D. Thirteen adolescent male suicide attempts. *Journal of Child Psychiatry,* 7(2):296–314, April 1968.

Teicher, J. D. The treatment of the suicidal adolescent—the lifeline approach. *Proceedings of the IV World Congress of Psychiatry,* Madrid, September 1966. Excerpta Medica International Congress Series No. 150.

Teicher, J. D., and Jacobs, J. Adolescents who attempt suicide: preliminary findings. *American Journal of Psychiatry,* 122(11): May 1966.

_____The physician and the adolescent suicide attempter. *Journal of School Health,* 36(9):406–415, November 1966.

Studies of Child Abuse and Infant Accidents

Investigator:
Elizabeth Elmer, M.S.S.
Assistant Professor of Social Case Work
School of Medicine
University of Pittsburgh
Pittsburgh, Pennsylvania

Co-Investigators:
Grace Gregg, M.D.
Byron Wright, M.A.
John B. Reinhart, M.D.

Contributors:
Thomas McHenry, M.D.
Bertram Girdony, M.D.
Paul Geisel, Ph.D.

Prepared by:
Clarissa Wittenberg

Historically, the terrible toll taken by childhood illness and industrial accidents overshadowed the risk of children being injured by their parents. At one time children were believed to be in the grip of the devil because they had been conceived in sin, and harsh punishment was thought necessary to save them. Parents "owned" children and almost any punishment was considered legitimate. As our concepts of child development have become more sophisticated and our understanding of learning and discipline has advanced, harsh punishment has become less and less acceptable. Consequently the parent who beats his child is an object of censure. Today, we hold parents responsible for the well-being of children, and, therefore, the malnourished and medically neglected child becomes a subject of concern. Recognition that parents do abuse their children has grown, and hospitals and doctors are increasingly aware of the problem. Studies have been done to help define the problem and its dimensions, and to record the effects of abuse on children.

Children's Hospital of Pittsburgh is located in a large low-income district of the inner city and, like many other city hospitals, has an active emergency ward where many injured children are brought. Some of these children have multiple bone injuries. Early in the 1960's the staff began to systematically study the possibility of abuse in these cases. A research team headed by Miss Elizabeth Elmer began, in 1962, a study of 50 families with children suffering from bone injuries who had been admitted

343

to the hospital over the previous 13 years. This was a follow-up study to determine what happened to these children after their initial admission to the hospital. A second study followed which focused on infant accidents, and compared infants and families where accidental injury had occurred with those where neglect or abuse was present.

The problem of diagnosing abuse was attacked in the first study. Cases were selected for the follow-up study on the basis of their hospital admission record. Although abuse is a complicated subject involving both social and medical problems, the criterion of multiple bone injuries was selected for the purpose of a less controversial diagnosis. The family history was then examined and the families judged to be either abusive or nonabusive; those who could not be placed clearly in either group were considered unclassified.

The first study showed clearly that these children are in serious jeopardy, that many die and many become severely retarded and/or crippled and spend their lives in institutions. The first Study of Fifty Families resulted in an examination of what constitutes abuse. An examination of the "failure to thrive" child was begun and the role of accidental injuries noted. The second study focused on small babies not yet capable of getting into trouble on their own, thus illuminating the role of the parents in such accidents.

Both studies resulted in an examination of the theories and accepted ideas surrounding this issue. For instance, the working mother, commonly felt to contribute to child abuse, did not appear to be important. Neither were these children typically abused by extramarital partners or non-related figures; there was no "wicked stepmother" syndrome. While many parents were found to have serious emotional problems, few were mistreating the children for bizarre or extemely sadistic reasons. These children were rarely abused "coldly." Few of the parents were "bad" parents and total failures; most stayed with their families and eventually exhibited some success with their children. Neither did the parents typically injure all of their children. Abuse has been found to be a phenomenon related to the child-bearing period of the mother, and often the mother has been uninformed about contraception.

THE FIFTY FAMILY STUDY

A radiologist and a pediatrician selected 50 former patients for the study. Basic criteria included:

(1) Injured bones, revealed by x-ray film, indicating the occurrence of more than one traumatic episode, in conjunction with –

(2) Absence of clinical bone disease that might account for the condition.

(3) A history of assault or gross neglect, or the absence of a history showing convincingly that the injuries were accidental or attributable to an unusually traumatic delivery. A small group of children do suffer undiagnosed fractures at birth.

344

The Final group was equally divided between male and female subjects, of whom 36 were white and 14 Negro. This racial distribution approximated that of the hospital's clientele. A number of the children had come to the hospital for other complaints, and bone injuries had been discovered in the course of routine examinations.

The majority of subjects had been young babies at the time of their admission. Seventeen were under 3 months of age when multiple injuries were found. Nine were between 3 and 9 months of age. This is in contrast to the curve for childhood accidents where the incidence rate for accidents is minimal below the age of 9 months. It then begins a sharp climb, reaching a peak between 2 and 3 years when it begins to level off.

Fewer than 50 families were actually interviewed — due to deaths, institutional placements, and refusals. Only families who still had their children were interviewed. Six families refused to cooperate. Thirty-one of the children in the original group, plus two siblings found to have bone injuries, added up to a total of 33 children studied and 31 mothers interviewed. Seven were foster mothers and one an adoptive mother. Essentially the families were told that the object of the study was to examine the hospital's treatment of patients, and an attempt was made to avoid focusing on the suspected episodes of abuse in order to minimize suspicion and distortion. It is of interest that the noncooperative parents were in general better educated than the rest of the group. They may have been more suspicious of the hospital's motives or more guilty about their own behavior.

Information was accumulated from hospital records, current examinations, home visits, and interviews with the mothers. It was initially anticipated that the fathers would not be available for interviews. Fathers were not interviewed formally, and it was felt that potentially information from the fathers would have been of value.

Each of the children was given a current examination which included a complete pediatric evaluation, psychological testing, a psychiatric interview, a hearing test, and an x-ray survey of skull, long bones, chest, pelvis, and spine—with special attention to the sites of old bone injuries.

On the basis of all this information, the children were divided into three groups. Twenty-two were considered abused, four nonabused, and seven unclassified. Nonabused children were those whose early bone injuries had a plausible explanation other than assault by an adult. If agreement could not be reached as to the cause of the injury, the child was considered unclassified. For example, one such child had a record of birth injuries and a hospital admission at 3 months with fresh fractures, but no account could be obtained of abuse or accident. Unclassified families, then, while not labeled abusive cannot be considered nonabusive either.

Almost all of the families struggled to live on low incomes. Most had less than a high school education and correspondingly few job opportunities. In most cases the families had three or four children. About a quarter of the families in this study were on welfare; however, none of the nonabusive families was. The families lived in substandard, but not the worst, housing. Most lived in private dwellings or apartments, but none in trailers or rooming houses. Many of the families kept their homes in fairly good condition and the mothers tended to be good housekeepers. Physical squalor was not characteristic of this group.

The study families, particularly the abusive ones, suffered from marital stress. Many couples had been separated and reconciled many times without coming to any real resolution of their problems or differences. The abusive families tended to have more quarreling and drinking than the others. Several abusive mothers expressed fear of their husbands, and the investigators thought that in general their fear was well justified. One father, for instance, had a prison record for murder; another was observed to blow cigarette ashes in his baby's eyes and then to knock the child's head against a post. It is possible that mothers with poor self-control tend to be attracted to men with similar problems, or that the mothers want the fathers to appear in a bad light so as to appear sympathetic by comparison.

For disciplinary measures most of these families relied on physical means of control. Whipping and spanking were the most commonly used methods of discipline; scolding, withdrawal of privileges, shaming, and shaking were also common. Reasoning with a child or avoidance of the conflict were methods almost never used. *These parents tended to see even small infants as needing discipline and as consciously and deliberately misbehaving.* It was rare for anyone other than the mother, or the mother and the father together, to discipline a child — and very unusual for the father to deal with the children by himself.

The nonabusive families tended to use a few types of punishments consistently, while some of the abusive families used a broad range of disciplinary measures that they were searching for some effective way to manage their children.

Mothers who abused their children felt very negatively toward the child who had been injured. It is not known if they felt this way about all their children or only the one who was abused. In one exceptional case, the mother expressed sympathy for the child who had been abused by her husband.

The abusive mothers appeared to have more emotional problems of greater severity than the nonabusive ones. Depression was common with about half of the abusive mothers troubled by difficulties in eating or sleeping and having a tendency toward crying spells. The nonabusive mothers, in general, had fewer and milder symptoms.

Several of the abusive mothers admitted to uncontrollable actions in the past — including physical aggression against other women; sexual promiscuity; and secret, compulsive spending. These mothers, who themselves had serious problems of control, admitted being afraid of their husbands as well. By their own reports, more of the abusive mothers than the nonabusive were easily irritated.

The abusive mothers were lonely people, often with no place to escape from the pressures of home and children. In many cases they had poor relationships with their own parents. There were no friends or relatives to help. It was noted that the mothers actively discouraged friendships, and did not join even relatively impersonal groups such as the PTA.

Child abuse is a family affair, however, and regardless of the identity of the abuser, the rest of the family participates. The other parent is involved by virtue of lack of interference or tacit approval. In many cases siblings may have injured the child, but again the responsibility must rest with the parents. The family dynamics are important in these situations.

The following case history illustrates the type of family problems that surround child abuse:

A 19-year old mother brought a three-month-old baby, her third, into the hospital. The baby was wearing a cast, and his weight including that of the cast was 10 pounds. He had had a birth weight of 5 pounds, 3 ounces. His x-ray showed that he had an old fracture of the skull, an injury to his shoulder, fracture of the left arm, multiple injuries to knees, ankles, and long bones of both legs. In addition, he had a bulging fontanel suggesting subdural hematoma.

The mother expressed her horror that every time she picked up the baby he appeared to have something else wrong with him. The child had been in another hospital at six weeks of age when he had been injured falling off a bed onto a concrete floor. When the emergency room doctor saw the baby, he wanted the police called as he thought it obvious that the child had been beaten. The baby needed two subdural taps at that time.

The mother's explanation was that she had put the baby in the middle of a double bed while she went to another room to wash his crib. A 14-month-old sibling was in the room with the baby. She heard a thump and thought toys had been dropped, and then ran to find the baby on the floor. She assumed that he had "scooted off" the bed. The father was critical of the mother for not watching the baby.

The mother had been a favorite child and had attended church faithfully. Her family had had ambitions for her to get a good education. At sixteen, however, she became pregnant and was disowned by her parents. The minister of her church was also very critical of her. The baby was born after a six-month gestation period and died after three days. During this crisis the mother was alone as none of her family came to see her. She married the father, and became pregnant again and had a little boy. When he was three months old, she became pregnant again and delivered the baby who was the patient. This added up to three births within 22 months. Two children had been premature. In addition, her parents separated and blamed their troubles upon her "disgrace."

The Children

Most of the children were quite young at the time of their first admission to the hospital. This study has shown that many children die or suffer grave and irreversible damage, but also that some children survive

347

this early abuse, and reach a phase where their parents can successfully care for them and they can attain a reasonably good physical condition.

Eight of the 50 children had died by the time of this study. Most had been under five months of age at the time of death; two had been slain by their mothers. Five children were in State institutions for the retarded. Many, who were in basically good health, had scars or deformities, but considering that they had been at the point of death and had suffered very serious injuries they were quite well-recovered. One child was suffering from malnutrition, and several had organic brain defects. A large number of children were observed to show signs of upper motor neurone disease, as manifested by hyperactive tendon reflexes as well as abnormal plantar reflexes. A few children had signs of cranial nerve involvement manifested by strabismus and nystagmus. These signs appeared to be related to injury in all of the children born at full term, except in the case of one who was jaundiced at birth and had had convulsions prior to the injury.

In the premature children with signs of neurological damage, the effect of prematurity itself cannot be discounted. Only two of the prematures were known to have had head trauma and symptomatic convulsions. In one child, prematurity was the only known condition that could account for central nervous system damage. The abused children had twice the incidence of neurological signs as was true of the rest of the group.

The investigators found that two of the children had been injured in substitute homes. In one case the substitute home was arranged through an informal agreement between the natural and the foster parents, and in the other an adoption agency chose the home for an infant who was born out of wedlock. The latter child was subsequently moved to another foster home. In all, 11 children in the study were moved to substitute homes for their own protection, following the abusive incidents.

Birth

Histories were obtained from the mother, and other available sources such as hospital records. *It was found that about a third of the children weighed less than 5.5 pounds at birth, indicating prematurity.* As the national figure for prematurity is 8 percent, the percentage in this study is extraordinarily high. It is known that birth weight varies by race and by socioecnomic status. The national rates are 7 percent prematurity for whites and 12 percent for nonwhites. In this study, however, the higher percentages of low birth weight occurred among the white families: 8 of the 24 white and only 2 of the 8 Negro children had birth weights of less than 5.5 pounds. Although the significance of the large number of premature babies is not known, one possible explanation is that premature infants, because of their incomplete development at birth, are more vulnerable to bone injuries than full-term infants. A pediatric radiologist, Dr. John Caffey, is of the opinion that there is more vulnerability in the first few weeks. The bones of a premature baby may be injured even with normal handling, for instance, during diapering. However, when chronological age plus the number of weeks of prematurity equals nine months, Dr. Caffey observes that vulnerability to bone injury becomes that of any full-term newborn.

The median age of the premature children in this study was 11 months at the time of hospital admission. This would indicate that their injuries were not due to immature bone development, but to other factors. Of the 21 abused children whose birth weight was known, seven were premature; none of the nonabused children were premature. It is known that premature babies are more difficult to care for than full-term ones; they may be more irritable and cry more due to their immature nervous systems. The mothers may be more apprehensive about picking them up because they are so tiny. In addition, the emergency situation that so often surrounds premature birth may be a serious strain on an already easily upset mother. Preparations for births are often incomplete when a premature baby arrives, and for a family with only marginal resources the strain can be severe.

Negroes, who often had extended families or else lived in overcrowded housing where other women were available, seemed to cope with the strains of prematurity better, with relatively fewer combinations of prematurity and abuse.

There is another issue, too, that must be considered: the more subtle problem of the mother's condition during pregnancy. A woman who is unhappy about herself, her marriage, her pregnancy, or her other children may take inadequate care of herself or be too overwhelmed to obtain help. In many cases these mothers may not even seek prenatal care.

Other questions arise: For instance, what causes one family to zealously protect, or even overprotect, a premature infant, and another family to abuse such an infant. Why, if a couple with abusive tendencies has other children, is the premature child selected for abuse?

Conditions at Time of Original Admission

At the time of admission to the hospital there was no difference between the chief complaints of the abused children and the others. The majority were brought to the hospital because of limitation of motion or pain in an extremity. The next most common complaint was convulsions, then "failure to thrive," and gastric symptoms. Convulsions and subdural hematomas, physical conditions that are often associated with brain damage, were diagnosed in eight children upon admission. Surgical procedures connected with subdural hematomas were necessary in seven cases. Two other children required orthopedic surgery due to bone injuries. One-third of the group had previous hospital admissions.

Records of growth show that poor growth and abuse are not always associated. However, many of the children showed an improvement in appetite and growth while they were in the hospital.

349

Condition at Time of Study

Retardation

Forty-five percent of the entire study group had IQs under 80. Twelve of the 22 abused children and none of the nonabused children fell in this low IQ group. This is more striking when one realizes that this group does not include five of the original children who were placed in State institutions for the retarded. Only children still at home were included in the study. The investigators stress that they have no way of knowing what was cause and what was effect in this relationship between abuse and retardation. Neurological impairment is important in retardation, and many of these children showed such signs. In addition, many had histories of poor early growth, a condition thought to be associated with later mental retardation.

Speech problems, which are often associated with both emotional difficulties and mental retardation, were found in this study to be more closely related to mental retardation than to emotional problems.

Emotional Characteristics

The abused children had marked difficulty in impulse control as compared with others in the study. Many of the children, regardless of their classification, had poor self-concepts. Even the nonabused children had suffered serious injuries, pain, and traumatic experiences at an early age. Most had scars or physical deformities. It is not difficult to understand that they might view themselves poorly or feel inferior, especially if the parents had not been able to help them in a sensitive way.

Eight of the abused children had difficulty in controlling anger, and either had outbursts, of rage or serious inhibition of negative feelings, manifested by very apathetic responses.

General Functioning

The abused children who remained in the same environments had a substantially greater number of problems than the nonabused children. Eight of these were retarded. The unclassified children had more general problems than the abused children who had been moved to foster homes. Seven children, whose physical development had been poor at the time of hospital admission and who had been moved from the home, had achieved an average level by the time of the study. To emphasize the importance of the home environment, two children who remained in the same poor homes showed average development on admission but below average development at the time of the study.

350

Families at the Time of Abuse

The abusive families by and large lived in far more difficult circumstances than did the nonabusive families. However, all these families had often lived under stress, and for some reason abuse was not a constant process. Rather, it breaks out and then abates. In many cases, the sex or ordinal position of the abused child had a special significance for the abusive parent. One child was a second girl, as her mother had been, and both were family scapegoats. In another family, the two girls were severely abused by the mother, but never the boys.

The birth of a sibling less than one year before or nine months after the incident of abuse was found to be important. Nine of the abusive mothers were pregnant at the time of the abused child's hospital admission, one abusive mother had miscarried just before the child was admitted, and two others had borne an infant other than the patient during the year prior to admission. In only one of the other 11 families, unclassified and nonabusive taken together, was there an interval of less than one year between the injured child's admission and the birth of a sibling.

The investigators found that the connection between abuse and the burdens of pregnancy and child-rearing is clear and important. They cite the theories of Bibring, who identified pregnancy as a biologically determined maturational crisis that is not always resolved with the birth of the baby, but usually continues for some time, even in the most auspicious circumstances. The investigators point out that *these families abuse their children primarily during the child-bearing phase of marriage.* Later they appear to cope in a better fashion. *It was found that those families who had successfully begun to use contraception were able to recover from their previous strain and to stop venting their feelings of frustration and rage upon their children.*

Several of the mothers who were abusive were quite disturbed, and some were under psychiatric care. In three cases the fathers were clearly very disturbed or antisocial.

Substitute Care

A change in environment often saves the life of a child who has been assaulted. Still, some children were abused while in foster care. It was found that foster parents who voluntarily took children who were injured, neurotic, or retarded often had an unhealthy need to have children who were excessively dependent upon them. Furthermore, while much good can be accomplished, even the best foster or adoptive parents cannot undo irrevocable damage already done to the child.

Some foster children, due to their previous abuse, have severe difficulties even after the original crisis is resolved. These are troubled children and symptoms can appear long after the original trauma. In addition, the protective care so helpful in the beginning can cause rebellion later if the foster parents are unable to modify their methods in accordance with the changing developmental needs of the growing child. However, most of the children in placement showed marked improvement in their physical health.

INFANT ACCIDENT STUDY

The majority of the abused children in the Fifty Families Study had been brought to the hospital as accident victims even though their injuries were caused by assault. A few innocent parents of children suffering authentic accidents had unfortunately been suspected and sometimes accused of abuse. The masquerading of abuse as an accident and the reverse was possible because neither phenomenon was clearly understood. The investigators decided to study infant accidents, including abuse, to try to pinpoint the characteristics distinguishing one from the other.

Subjects were infants under 13 months of age who had been brought to Children's Hospital for x-ray following an impact accident or abusive incident. Since the younger the baby the more important the role of the caretaker, it was felt that this study would yield information about parental maltreatment and neglect, and not be complicated by the considerations of the normal accidents of the active toddler. One hundred and one children were seen, both inpatients and outpatients. Various issues were explored: for instance, the difference between families of abused or neglected children and those suffering accidents, with or without injury. The differences between retarded children who had been abused and retarded children who had not were also studied, with special attention to the mothering received by each group.

Abuse was suspected if the families' explanation of the injuries were not adequate, or if abuse was reported, or if more than one injury was present. Initial assessments were made of family stress. Pregnancy and very small children were considered stressful. The family was considered to be under strain, too, if either parent had a close relationship with another adult who was unrelated to the child. This issue was considered and observed because of a number of mass media reports of abuse involving step-parents of paramours. As in the first study, this did not turn out to be an important issue.

The family was also considered under stress if the baby had developmental problems such as a significant deviation in growth, language, motor or social development, or such troubles as feeding difficulties or excessive crying.

All of these issues are important as parental reports are heavily influenced by anxiety, guilt, and concern when a child is brought to a hospital. An accurate report of the precipitating incident is hard to obtain. It is necessary to look at the entire family structure to find the clues that differentiate the abusive family. When abuse is suspected, deficiencies and deviance will usually be found in other aspects of family life. This study focused upon family structure, interpersonal relationships, and child care practices, in order to illuminate these differentiating issues. Because the children were so young, the mother was considered the principal caretaker and her interaction with the baby was carefully examined. In order to assess the mother-baby relationship, the pair were observed – and also the mother was interviewed and asked to fill out questionnaires. The observations were felt to be of particular importance, as the mother's habitual behavior with the child is likely to be beyond her awareness and ability to report. The observations provided data to supplement and correct the information gained through the other methods.

Many issues involved with mothering were examined in addition to the traditional ones of providing food, shelter, and medical attention. The stimulation given the baby, the verbal responsiveness, the quality of play, and the ability of the mother to assess the changing needs of the child were all considered. As in the previous study, a high number of retarded children in this group was noted and some important observations about their mothers were made.

Attempts to have an equal number of boys and girls, white and non-white, were unsuccessful as the potential subjects did not fall this way. Most of the children presented for x-ray were white females. Black female babies rarely appeared and, in addition, it was more difficult to enlist the cooperation of the nonwhite families in the research. All social classes were represented, but the majority of the families were in the lower classes.

Although a few families had refused to participate in the first study, the refusal rate was even higher in the second. It was suspected that the increased public awareness of child abuse and the outcry and pressure that had been building up made some parents less cooperative. Also, even parents of accidentally injured babies experience great guilt leading to unwillingness to discuss the event. In the Infant Accident Study, it was found very difficult to keep the allegedly abusive parents as subjects. They rarely refused outright to come to an appointment or to allow a home visit, but they failed to appear or were away from home at the specified time.

Neglect played an important role, and several families who could not be considered abusive were still considered deficient in their care of their children based on observations made during the study. Some parents, for instance, left their children without competent babysitters when they were absent for prolonged periods of time, or failed to obtain needed medical care despite repeated and careful instructions as to the needs of the child.

The final study group consisted of 100 cases, 78 of which were followed through all phases of the study and 22 in which families participated in the initial and final procedures, with only a mailed questionnaire in the interim. One of the mothers had two children in the study, making the total number of children included 101.

The methods included initial screeening of x-rays, several home interviews with the mothers, and observations of the mothers in examination, feeding, and teaching situations. A questionnaire was mailed, and several pediatric and developmental evaluations were made. In several situations the mother was put under mild stress. In one instance, where she was asked to teach her baby to stack a series of blocks, the task was generally too advanced for the child so as to determine her reaction when frustrated by the baby. In another, she was asked to fill out a questionnaire when accompanied by the baby, to learn about her attitude when she was intent on another task. Four of the research persons saw each baby and family, and they were seen in as many situations as was practical.

The babies were evaluated twice in the first two years of life, a time of extremely rapid growth and development. This allowed for observations of the effect of the environment in a way not possible at later stages of life. Effects of poor parental care are obvious very soon during these early stages.

Of the 101 babies, brought to the hospital, only 10 were entirely without signs or symptoms. These 10 had been brought to the hospital for examination and reassurance, that despite a potentially injurious event, no injury had occurred. The other 91 babies displayed a range of conditions from mild bruising to symptoms related to the central nervous system, such as momentary unconsciousness with or without vomitting, seizures, paralysis, and coma. The proportion of abused children without symptoms was roughly equal to the proportion of nonabused.

In addition to x-ray examinations of the site of the presumed injury, 21 x-ray surveys of the entire skeleton were performed. Ten of these were part of a diagnostic work-up for failure to thrive, the rest because multiple injuries were suspected. Eighty-two children had no evidence of fracture, 12 had a single recent fracture, and 7 had multiple fractures. The proportion of children with multiple fractures was much greater among the abused than the nonabused children. It was thought that if skeletal surveys had been universally performed, they might have disclosed other unsuspected, clinically unimportant fractures, which would have helped to evaluate the quality of child care. However, it is difficult to justify x-ray examinations without symptoms of injury.

Twenty-four children were judged to be abused, or to be both abused and neglected. Ten children were thought to be neglected only. There were 67 nonabused, non-neglected children. All initial judgments concerning abuse and nonabuse were reevaluated at the end of the one-year study.

The research was focused on the effect of abuse on the growing infant. The main areas of investigation included mental and motor development, behavioral characteristics, health status, and physical growth. The baby was seen as being affected by at least two kinds of factors – those that are relatively unchangeable, such as conditions at birth, and those that are influenced by the caretaker. It was hypothesized that the abusive group, in comparison to the nonabuse group, would show more stress, less support, and greater authoritarianism.

As required by State law, when abuse was found, reports were made to the Child Welfare Services and the parents were informed. Reports were made on eight children. A few other families were already known to the

Child Welfare Services when they came into the study. In several cases, the mothers had named their husbands as the abuser and had separated from them. Two mothers overtly rejected the children whom they had mistreated, and the study personnel helped them arrange for placement away from home. The protective agency removed eight children from their own homes.

Because it is often observed that sick children are irritable and difficult to care for, it was noted whether or not the child had an acute illness at the time of admission. Eighteeen of the babies were sick with gastrointestinal and upper respiratory complaints when brought to the hospital. A few had anemia, and suffered other problems such as eye infections. By and large the babies were not suffering from infections, and the traumatic event was not related to the extra demands and needs of a sick child.

Twenty-four of the babies were admitted to the hospital, eleven of these for protection while further investigation of the family condition was carried out. Thirteen needed hospital medical-surgical care, some for incidental medical problems and some for injuries resulting from the accident or abuse.

The "failure to thrive" babies were studied from several standpoints. For some, metabolic and endocrine studies were done with inconclusive results. This condition, defined as occurring when a child has weight and height below the third percentile for his age and sex, is not well understood. Rarely are these children seen because of trauma; characteristically, the mother who brings them in is full of concern because a child has not reached the expected developmental landmarks. Often she is anxious because her child is not growing and will assert strongly that she feeds her baby well.

Home interviews in this study did substantiate that some of these mothers fed their babies adequately. Medical opinion is growing that this entity belongs with others where psychological phenomena and physical development interact pathologically, as in anorexia nervosa or infantile marasmus. Studies at Johns Hopkins Hospital have indicated that the problem lay in the hypothalmic area and that it was reversible without any hormonal or chemical treatment when the child was placed in a hospital, a relatively nurturing environment. It was postulated that emotional disturbance in these children may have had an adverse effect upon the release of the pituitary tropic hormone via the central nervous system. In the Infant Accident Study, "failure to thrive" babies whose environment was changed tended to achieve normal growth,but rarely normal development.

Initial Pediatric Evaluation

Upon initial evaluation, 54 — or slightly over half the children — were found to have either no medical problems or only the insignificant ones expected during the first year of life. Two-thirds of the abused children, however had serious health problems. Slightly fewer than half the babies had a number of actual and/or potential health problems including prematurity, moderate or high perinatal stress scores, significant medical problems, and histories of acute illness. Children in the abused group had a disproportionately greater number of health problems per child than the nonabused children.

The abused group was also distinguished initially from the nonabused by their poor physical growth. In part their retarded growth was probably due to prematurity (9 or 37 percent were premature by birth weight, gestation, or both), but even giving credit for weeks of prematurity did not bring them to normal level.

An estimate of how well the child was cared for in general was judged by the manner in which baby appointments and immunizations were attended to by the caretaker. Nineteen had not been seen regularly, if at all. Twenty-eight of the mothers had not kept their babies' immunization schedule up-to-date, and some babies had not received any immunizations at all. Most of the faulty child care was concentrated in the abused group. However, upon questioning it was found that 92 percent of all the mothers were able to recognize symptoms of poor health in their children and to find suitable medical services for them when they became ill.

Thirteen babies were considered poorly dressed, dirty, or ill-kempt when they were brought for their pediatric visit. The number of abused children in this category was much greater than the number of nonabused.

Accidents Versus Abuse - Initial Findings

Eighty-eight caretakers gave an accident history. *Twelve abused children were among those with credible accident histories, an overlap that illustrates the complexity of diagnosis in these cases.* Thirteen other children either had totally unexplained injuries or they were x-rayed because of suspected abuse, but no injuries were found; none of these had an accident history.

The assumption was made that adequate protection by the caretakers could completely abolish true accidents. The investigators realized, however, that this is unlikely and even undesirable, as a child reared in such a protective environment might have many other problems.

Three-fifths of the accidents were termed "active" because the baby's motor activity was an important contributing factor. Active accidents were subdivided into three categories: "open field" in which the babies propelled themselves into danger — for example, falling down the stairs when a gate had been left open; falls from appropriate furniture, such as couches or dressing tables; and falls from inappropriate furniture, such as the tops of washing machines - caused for instance, when a baby in an infant seat wiggles and the seat slides off the slippery top of the washing machine. It was thought that most of the active accidents might have been prevented by the use of built-in safety devices, such as belts to confine babies on dressing tables.

356

Passive accidents were those in which the baby's contribution was minor and the responsibility of the caretaker greater. Subdivisions of passive accidents included babies dropped by their caretakers, those suffering "Act of God" events, such as being hit by a stray baseball, and those who were admittedly assaulted by another person.

The accidents were described, then the abused group was compared to the nonabused, non-neglected children who had suffered accidents. Points of comparison, in addition to general health and injuries already mentioned, were behavioral characteristics, age, and ordinal position. The families were compared as to social class, stress at the time of the incident, and health of the mothers.

The only infants who differed behaviorally were the babies who had active, open-field accidents. They were predominantly negative in mood, not distractible, and moderately or highly active. This combination of traits can be seen to result in babies who are difficult to protect from harm. By contrast, the other subjects, including the abused children, were positive in mood, easily distracted, and moderately active. The babies represented in the "open field" accidents were also the oldest (median age, 42 weeks) and, therefore, their motor development was more advanced.

Most of the babies in the accident group, active or passive, were only children in their families, while on the average the abused child was the second child. This suggest that parents of a first child are not as aware of potential hazards as they might be, and also indicates that in abuse cases – in addition to evaluation of the stress of having several small children - the possibility should be considered that one small child might injure another.

Ninety-two percent of the abusive parents were identified with Class V (low) according to the Hollingshead Two-Factor Index. Forty-eight percent of the nonabusive, nonneglectful families studied fell in this class.

Regardless of the type of injurious event, the mothers typically had special stress added to chronic factors of strain. The abusive mothers mentioned baby irritability generally and the other more often mentioned disrupted schedules, fatigue, etc. Over 50 percent of the mothers of abused children had significant health problems, for example, mental retardation, emotional difficulties, seizures, and heart disease. Such major health conditions were found in only 20 percent of the nonabusive mothers.

In attempting to determine the quality of the mother-child relationship, the investigators studied the caretaking process. This process makes manifest much about the mother's interaction with the child and gives some measure of her general ability to function. The ability of the mother to monitor the environment for her helpless baby changes in relationship to many things. The mother, of course, operates within her own milieu and class structure, and this partially defines good mothering for her. The events that occur, the health and stability of the mother, the abilities she is potentially able to bring to bear to help her child, and her ability to perceive accurately his needs all affect her care of the child. Her degree of affection as well as her convictions about child rearing also enter in.

357

Undoubtedly, too, the resources of the mother to provide support, affection, and aid for her are crucial.

Stress is seen as a major issue in child abuse, the caretaker being under insupportable stress in most such situations. In the case of the accidents, it has been noted that most of the mothers were reacting to stress in varying degrees – the abusive mothers, however, were under greater stress, had less support, and fewer personal resources. The interrelationship of stress, support, and the ability to cope can be seen as a continuum.

It must be remembered that the early years of child rearing are heavily demanding. Little money is available, and many young people are unprepared to become parents. Shifts occur in families even when children are desired and planned for, and greater strain is felt with unwanted babies. The investigators view most young families as being at a point of lowest tolerance for stress at a time when they are subjected to the highest stress during the years when children are being born. However, it must be realized that what constitutes stress for one individual can be handled by another. Unfortunately, some types of chronic stress are brought on by poverty, which rarely permits growth or learning and usually undermines a family's ability to function. The investigators were most interested in everyday stress, as opposed to extraordinary or emergency stress, because they felt that chronic stress was of key importance in child abuse.

The demographic data about the abusive families was a documentation of the degree of chronic stress. Almost half the abused children were black, and most of the combined abuse and neglect occurred among the black families. Because of the larger numbers of children with comparatively few fathers in these homes, the families fall into a group known to be especially vulnerable to many kinds of stress. According to socioeconomic status, all the families in the combined abuse and neglect group are classified in the two lowest classes of the Hollingshead scale of social position.

There were ten families that were considered neglectful but not abusive, and it was found that in some ways they resembled both the abusive and nonabusive families.

The nine families demonstrating abuse but not neglect were predominantly lower class, with two members of the middle and upper classes; the ten families showing neglect alone included four classes from Class I, the highest of Hollingshead's classifications. One of these families was classified as neglectful because they habitually left the baby in the company of an active 30-month old sibling without adult supervision. Another family was called neglectful because their child was encouraged to perform physical feats distinctly beyond his limited ability, such as hanging from the pantry shelf by his fingers.

An assessment was made of the medical condition of the child and the mother's reaction to it. It was found that of the ten "neglect only" mothers, eight showed only slight reactions to medical problems. The mothers of the abused children reported feeling great stress due to their babies' medical conditions. The focus of these mothers on their babies'

358

health was seen by the investigators as being realistic in view of the extremely poor health of these children.

There was one group of 24 women, primarily made up of black mothers, who were unusually bland or under-reacting to medical problems in both themselves and their children. One such mother had noted an abnormality in her baby's eye for more than a week, but hadn't sought medical advice about it. The investigators had several ideas, but no definite answers to explain this attitude. A middle-class mother, they believe, tends to emphasize her attentiveness to her child whether or not it is warranted. This is not always the case with the lower socioeconomic class mother. The investigators also note that many of the "upper reactors" were poorly educated and suggest that perhaps they did not really understand the potential hazard of some of the conditions. However, seven of the "under-reactors" belonged to middle- and upper-class groups and were well educated. An analysis of the "under reactors" by social class showed no significant class association. It is also suggested that the apparent apathy may be a defense against implied criticism and intrusion by the outsider or a way of coping with what would otherwise be overwhelming anxiety. It may also indicate a true indifference or a general state of apathy which includes, but is not limited to, the child.

The type of stimulus perceived as stressful and the reaction to it are highly individualized matters. To avoid imposing any preconceived hierarchy of stress, the investigators inquired what had happened to the mothers or their families since conception for the index child. The events divided naturally into Hill's four categories: physical difficulties, separations from persons or possessions, accession events such as a new person moving into the house, and social disgrace. The mothers' reactions were dichotomized as 1) mild or non-existent, or 2) strong. The number of stress events and associated reactions were combined to yield a total score for each individual. Mothers in each group were ranked and the groups compared.

In general, recent events were given highest stress ratings by the mothers. Acute conditions were reported as more stressful than chronic ones, and events involving the immediate family as more stressful than those involving extended family or friends. The proportion of mothers reporting no stress whatsoever was greater among the neglectful than the nondeviant, and only 4 percent of the abusive reported no stress.

Accidents, moves, and physical illness were the greatest sources of stress for the abusive mothers; also, prominent among the accidents were attacks upon the mothers by others. Several women reported having been beaten by their husbands. One abusive mother claimed to have been raped on her way to the hospital with her baby. Although the report seemed questionable, it was similar to others in its preoccupation with violence, either factual or fantasized.

A common source of stress for the abusive and other families was a change of residence. Typically the family moved during the woman's pregnancy to obtain more room. In both the abusive and nondeviant

359

groups, the moves in late months of pregnancy resulted in strain on the mothers and at times brought on premature deliveries.

Illness was often reported and sometimes – especially in the group of abusive mothers – reported not as chronic conditions, but related to pregnancy for the index child. The abusive mothers felt very strained by the pregnancy of the child in question and ranked pregnancy as a higher stress even than deaths.

According to the physician's rankings of physical disorders associated with pregnancy, the abusive mothers who reported the most stress actually had the least, thus indicating a higher psychological sensitivity. Six of the abusive mothers who reported difficult pregnancies were caring for other young babies when they were pregnant and, also, had fewer people available to help them.

Potential support factors included a satisfactory male relationship: the presence of a man in the house – whether spouse, common-law partner, or father; a continuous association with a male during pregnancy; help from the man in relation to the baby; a stable source of income; a continuous source of medical care; participation in religious activities and involvement with neighborhood activities. The abusive families and the others differed significantly in the amount of support available. The abusive families had the least support.

Statistically significant factors were continuous association with the father during pregnancy and help from a male – whether husband, father, or friend - in relation to the baby. The current presence of a male in the home on a stable basis did not appear to be a significant positive factor; nor was marital stress a significant negative factor. During pregnancy the help of the father appeared to be mainly psychological, but once the baby arrived the mother received more support when some male did something concrete to assist in the care of the baby.

The effects of race on stress and support were assessed. When support was low, black mothers reported significantly more medical stress than white mothers; they suffered more physical problems than the whites. The white mothers, however, reported significantly more social stress when support was low. This comparison would seem to reflect the perception of the woman, white or black, as she viewed herself in relation to her peer group.

The mothers were scored for general negative and positive reactions to their babies, and several trends appeared. The abusive mothers tended toward extreme reactions, judging the babies to be either all good or all bad, while the non-abusive parents saw their children more realistically as both pleasing and annoying. The abusive mothers were relatively silent with regard to their children's development. Fifteen of the 19 abused children showed early signs of retardation.

360

It was predicted that the abusive mothers would use harsher methods of punishment and would have less interest in teaching their children than the other mothers. The results were not so clear cut.

Forty-one percent of all the mothers used some form of physical punishment with babies less than 6 months old, usually slapping the hands or the buttocks. At 9 months, physical punishment intensified. By 24 months, 87 percent of all the mothers were using this method of physical punishment at least part of the time.

The type of behavior punished varied with social class. Mothers in the two highest classes punished principally for aggressive acts; middle-class mothers for activity, dangerous or otherwise; and lower-class mothers, for conduct such as excessive demands, disobedience, or crying. Generally the abusive mothers, most of whom were lower class, punished for unacceptable conduct. Across all groups, girls were consistently punished earlier: by the age of 9 months, 31 percent of the girls, but only 5 percent of the boys were being punished; by 18 months, the figures rose to 70 percent and 50 percent for the girls and boys, respectively.

The investigators had become aware that most mothers are extremely sensitive to their babies' aggressive acts against them as mothers. When asked how they would respond if their infants struck them or spat upon them, the overwhelming majority of the mothers of babies 6 months of age or older said they would retaliate in kind, ". . .to show him that he is *not* to do that kind of thing." Three mothers of babies who were less than 6 months of age also said the same. Eighty percent of the abusive and 63 percent of the nondeviant mothers said they would hit back against infant aggression.

Regardless of their social class, most mothers asserted that a baby should know right from wrong by the age of 12 months, and one-third of the mothers specified 6 months. This belief implies a common lack of realistic information about infant development and when babies learn concepts of right and wrong. These mothers also perceived the babies as having "tempers" and other directed feelings at a much younger age than is actually possible.

The mothers involved in this study usually discriminated very little between discipline and teaching. When asked how they would attempt to teach the baby some new behavior representing a real learning effort for him, they most frequently responded in terms of scolding or spanking to get him to learn after first giving verbal instructions. The investigators feel that infants are punished physically more often than is realized. When it is common practice to strike babies, however lightly, with the goal of teaching them, the laws of probability indicate that some babies are going to be struck too hard and that some will be injured.

Values Related to Mothering

The mothers were questioned as to their expectations concerning the child. The majority preferred their babies to be "good"; that is, respectful, grateful, obedient, and not rebellious. These were the particular goals of the abusive and neglectful mothers; they were not interested in creativity, etc.

There were varied opinions among them as to what constituted an "ideal mother." All the abusive and the neglectful mothers mentioned keeping the baby clean and giving him material things. A few mentioned the importance of being a "proper" woman. They described the ideal woman in negative terms as somebody who does not run around or sit at bars. The abusive group often described the ideal father in terms of discipline or financial support. Several women said that the ideal father should not beat the mother.

Quite a few mothers felt that affection should be restrained: that there is danger in being too affectionate toward babies. This trait was more marked in the abusive and the neglectful mothers.

The index of values related to mothering clearly and significantly distinguished between the abusive and the nonabusive groups, correctly classifying 77 percent of all the families. Among the abusive mothers, emphasis was placed on cleanliness and materialistic values. They tended to perceive themselves and their husbands in stereotyped roles, a perception suggesting difficulties in forming and maintaining close relationships. Their fear of showing too much affection toward their babies was another manifestation of the same difficulty. These characteristics, together with the common need to have an obedient, compliant baby, established the abusive mothers as more authoritarian than the nonabusive women.

The Baby

The contribution of the baby to the mother-child relationship is extremely important. A smiling baby who is responsive may keep even a detached mother involved. While many types of behavior are important, it was decided that four behavioral characteristics would be examined: mood, level of activity, approach or the way the baby related to a new person or new object, and distractibility. These characteristics were studied during the initial and the final pediatric examinations.

Among all the children the distribution of positive and negative mood showed a decided difference according to sex and developmental age. Regardless of their developmental age, half the boys were positive, half negative. The girls were strikingly negative when developmentally young but became positive as they matured. Abused boys were markedly negative compared to their nonabused peers. Abused girls were more positive than nonabused girls; however, the abused females as a group were developmentally older than the nonabused.

362

Eight abused children, four boys and four girls, were separated from their parents by the time of the second testing. All were predominantly negative in mood. According to the study data, this seemed associated less with their removal from home and more with the mood to be expected from the above findings. The four negative boys were similar in mood to the majority of abused males, while three of the negative girls were developmentally young and thus apt to be more negative.

The factors of sex, age, and abuse which affect predominant mood need considerably more study before the interrelationships will become clear. Nevertheless, these findings suggest that boys and girls may indeed respond to abuse in quite different ways.

It was not possible to find associations between mental development and behavioral patterns. Some of the children were advanced developmentally, some at age level, and some retarded. Some in each group were positive in mood and could be distracted.

Distractibility depends upon whether or not a child can be intrigued away from something he is doing, especially if it is a hazardous activity. In this case, it is a positive quality, as opposed to hyperactive distractibility which interferes with concentrated learning.

All of the babies who were positive in mood and distractibility were positive in approach; that is, interested or curious or pleased at meeting new people and new things. Among the nonabused children who had negative or mixed scores on mood and distractibility, a racial difference occurred on the approach scores. The whites of both sexes were predominantly positive in approach, while the blacks of both sexes were predominantly negative. The investigators noted that the examining doctor was a white woman and wondered if this could be a factor influencing these results.

Activity levels did not distinguish between abused and nonabused children. The babies who were both abused and neglected were low in approach and play behavior and high in negative activity. The "abused only" or "neglect only" had wider repertoires of behavior. However, of the "neglected-only" children, a large proportion either remained high or became high in activity. It was observed that the mothers were largely ineffectual in controlling their children; they tended to pile on command-after-command while the children became more anxious, active, and difficult. The ability of these mothers to limit the activity of their children, who seemed to be in special need of help in controlling or directing their activities, seemed very meager.

Observations of Interaction

The mothers were observed with their babies during a feeding period at home and in a teaching situation in the pediatrician's office. It was learned that mothers vary considerably in their perceptions of what is dangerous to their babies. While the mothers were in the doctor's office, the babies were often attracted to the doctor's kit containing instruments. Most

363

mothers did not permit their children to handle these, yet failed to see the danger in the sharp corner of a drawer that the children loved to pull out. The examining table was also a danger, as mothers often turned away while their babies who were lying on it waited to be dressed.

The actions of each baby and mother were tallied and analyzed according to content, mode, and context. Mothers of retarded children concentrated on feeding them and behaved more positively toward the child as the baby ate. They did not talk spontaneously to the child as much as the mothers of non-retarded children. The investigators believed that this reflected the mother's concern that the child eat rather than play or socialize. There was an overwhelming tendency for mothers of retarded *abused* children to show low verbal response to the babies' vocalizations, but an opposite trend was shown by mothers of retarded *nonabused* children. The age of the baby was not a factor in the mother's tendency to verbalize when the baby made sounds. Some babies responded to their mothers' speech, others did not, and again this was not related to baby age.

It is probable that an involved mother gives her baby many types of stimulation in addition to the verbal. The verbal response, however, seems to be a good indicator of the total social environment provided for the baby. Mothers with a good education were much more verbally responsive than those with a poor education.

A significant association appeared between mothers who responded verbally and the higher rates of development among these babies. The investigators note that such an association has not previously been reported but they point to several conditions that may affect it. The children of well-educated, intelligent mothers may have superior genetic endowment. Also, babies who have had a great deal of verbal experience do better on tests, which often require ability to follow verbal instructions.

With regard to control, the abusive mothers tended to give their children great latitude until their patience wore thin, when they would abruptly threaten or strike their children. The neglectful mother seemed to burden the child with repetitive commands and threats to which he paid little attention, apparently sensing that the mother did not know how to control him, or for some reason was unable to do so. As he became more active, the mother became more frenetic.

The abusive and neglectful mothers tended to care for the babies, but made neither broader responses nor extra reactions to their children. They tended toward stereotyped responses.

The teaching situation, which was essentially an artificial one, aroused some anxiety. However, the observers of the feeding, who knew the mothers, thought that they behaved much the same as they had in the past. This was substantiated by the significant positive correlations between the feeding and teaching observations with respect to maternal-verbal responses among all cases; mothers of nonretarded children; high social class; and females.

364

Final Evaluation of the Babies

The most important final difference between the abused and the nonabused babies appeared in the scores on the Bayley Mental Scales. There was significantly more retardation among the abused children when compared with the nonabused. The likelihood of retarded mental development among the abused children was greatly increased when they were also judged to be neglected by their parents. The fairly high rate of mental retardation found in all groups of children in this study may mean that the hospital outpatient population is biased in this direction.

The final checkups showed little difference in height and weight increases between the abused and nonabused children. However, this was true largely because one-third of the abused children had been removed from their homes and placed in benign and nurturing homes. All but one showed remarkable catch-up growth. There was a significant association between height and mental development ratings, with retarded mental development occurring more frequently among children below the 10th percentile in height.

In terms of family characteristics, the single factor most strongly related to the mental development ratings was the amount of income per person in the household. The percentage of children within the retarded, normal, and advanced groups coming from families with less than $100 a month per person was 74 percent, 46 percent, and 7 percent respectively. Although abused children more often come from families with low incomes, the relationship between income and mental development was not altered significantly when controlled for the occurrence of abuse. When children with retarded and normal development were combined, 79 percent of the abused and 52 percent of the nonabused children came from low-income families; this represents a statistically significant difference.

Among those with advanced development, the majority of the children were white; among those with slow development, the majority were black.

Although stress was found important, no statistical association between ratings of social stress and ratings of mental development appeared. However, the number of supportive resources for the mother was related to mental development. Among the families of retarded abused children, 69 percent were low in support while only 31 percent of the families of nonabused retarded children had similar low ratings. When stress hits a family with few sources of support and assistance, then the problems become more intense.

The presence of the father is also important. The group who were advanced mentally all had their fathers at home, while only 59 percent of the retarded had fathers living with them. The father was absent in the cases of 64 percent of the retarded children who were abused.

Regarding the probability of retardation, three factors in addition to abuse are important: low monthly income per person, significant physical problems in the baby, and low verbal responsiveness in the mother. When any two of these factors plus abuse was present, 100 percent of the children were retarded. Among children without any of these factors, only 21 percent were retarded.

The second evaluations showed that, remarkably enough, there are children who appear normal despite abuse, and it is also evident that there is a range of intensity in abuse. Some children are subjected to pervasive and long-standing abuse, while for others the abusive incident is isolated in an otherwise favorable environment. *The investigators caution that an overall characterization of the abused child demands both pediatric and family assessment. The physical and mental effects of abuse can be mimicked by other conditions, and also the physical and mental state may not fully expose the abusive atmosphere of the home.*

Diagnosis of Abuse

A crucial factor in the diagnosis of abuse is the willingness of the physician to consider abuse as a possible cause of a child's injuries and to examine him accordingly. Dr. Grace Gregg, a pediatrician and an investigator in this study, points out that a diagnosis of abuse requires a history that fails to explain the injury, the elimination of systemic disease, and an assessment of the type of care that would allow such a condition to develop. "Failure to thrive" children must be looked at with an eye to abuse and neglect. It is important where there are multiple injuries that each be accounted for. Multiple bone injuries are considered a key indication of abusive treatment. It must be remembered, however, that some bone changes do not show up immediately on x-ray and may be hidden until about 12 to 14 days. Furthermore, x-ray can tell the condition of the bones, but not how they were injured nor the motivation of the person responsible for the injury. In some cases a parent can roughly and abruptly grab a child to prevent an injury and accidentally hurt him. However, while this type of accident can happen once, a series of such incidents would be highly suspicious. Also, the idea that siblings can injure infants is unpopular, but must be considered.

Malnutrition is a key indication of abuse or neglect, but evidence of malnutrition is difficult to identify when intake becomes adequate, unless photographs are taken.

Familiarity with the normal injuries of children is indispensable to adequate diagnosis. Superficial injuries above the elbows, shins, and knees that do not resemble dermatologic conditions should be examined to see if they have been caused by rough handling, human bites, cigarette burns, etc. All bones and joints should be examined, not merely those pointed out as injured.

Legal Issues

By June 1967, 52 child abuse reporting laws were in existence in all 50 States, the Virgin Islands, and the District of Columbia. Puerto Rico

366

added a law soon thereafter. In most cases mandatory reporting by medical personnel, occasionally by schools or social workers, and investigation by law enforcement agencies was typical. In some states the professional can be fined or imprisoned if he fails to report a case of child abuse.

At first glance it looks as though the situation has been acknowledged and adequately covered. However, this is far from the case. The Children's Bureau looks upon child abuse reporting laws as case-finding devices. How successful they are for this purpose is difficult to assess. Some problems have, however, been identified. For instance, diagnostic guidelines are not well-drawn. There is the possibility of an inappropriate accusation, perhaps a law suit. Medical training is often limited in terms of teaching the type of social-family assessment that is required in many child abuse cases. This type of case can be tremendously time-consuming and time is a rare commodity in most medical practice.

Another problem is that of confidentiality. The child abuse laws place the child's right to safety above the traditional rights of the patient – in this case, the parent – to protected communications. A social class difference may slant the manner in which a case is treated. For example, in many States hospitals and physicians are required to report a case if an abused child is brought for care. Private doctors, however, are not exposed to the same public attention and might – and do – manage private patients differently. A doctor who reports a patient stands to gain ill-will and lose the family for treatment. He may feel he can give more help by not reporting the case and staying involved as an interested and concerned family doctor. Patients who can afford private care can also "shop" around. They can go to different physicians and the full extent of the child's history of trauma might be hidden in this way.

The goal is not, it must be remembered, merely full reporting. The goal is the protection of the child. The two are related, but not the same.

The investigators feel that professionals who report a family in good faith should be granted immunity in the event of a law suit. Other changes should allow for concern for the other children in the family.

The lack of community placements for such endangered children also make some people reluctant to confront an abusive parent, as it is realized that all too often the child must return home with an even more enraged and abusive parent.

There is considerable question as well, as to whether or not the police should be given responsibility for establishing whether abuse has occurred. In many cases this type of approach with the goal of proving guilt and establishing criminal behavior is unfruitful. As this research has shown, the problem may be subtle; a child may have been left with inadequate supervision or the parent may have shown poor ability to anticipate the child's pattern of activity. The caretakers may be extremely immature or disturbed, and thus cannot be considered directly responsible for injury to the child. Nonetheless the child may be in great jeopardy. But it is questionable whether most police have the orientation, time, or training to investigate these issues.

Prevention is largely ignored, as is appropriate follow-up and assistance, to families in need of community aid. Expanded protective services are much to be desired. Assistance with related problems such as contraception should also be available.

Punishment of the parents or probation, which often means only the most minimal surveillance, rarely accomplishes much toward the most important goal – protection of the child. Punishment for doctors or hospitals may very well be self-defeating and discourage reporting. The most fruitful approach is via education. Physicians need to be sensitized to the issues and hospital procedures need to be changed so as to permit early identification of the endangered child. Referrals to social agencies should be facilitated and child care resources developed. Where a murder or brual attack has taken place, then the police are appropriate; where an overwhelmed mother has a child who continually injures himself due to lack of supervision, another resource such as the help of a trained home-maker might be more appropriate.

Prevention of Child Abuse

To save a child from the serious effects and irremedial damage caused by abuse and neglect, it is necessary to recognize the situation when it occurs. Professionals need to be alert when they notice that young families are having their children too quickly, with no relief between pregnancies. The danger signs of marital strain, poverty, isolation, and overwhelmed mothers need to be heeded. Premature births with indications of family strain should be of great concern; all possible assistance and surveillance should be given these parents. Parents with children showing developmental difficulties should be given similar help.

It is important that education be restructured so that every young woman has some idea how children grow and develop. Classes should be held early in school, possibly at the elementary and junior high level, ensuring that all prospective mothers will be at least basically informed and, if possible, have supervised experience with child care. It cannot be too strongly stressed that far too many women think a young baby is responsible for his acts and can react intellectually like an adult. The whole concept of physical punishment for infants requires re-thinking in the light of knowledge about child development. Again, it must be realized that, despite ideas that physical punishment is a lower-class phenomenon, this practice was found in all classes. And males must be taught the importance of their contribution to the stability of the family and the emotional life of the child.

Education in family planning should be made available if we are to prevent parents from becoming so overwhelmed that they destroy their own children. Appropriate birth control methods should be made easily available. Unwanted children are in grave danger of abuse and all its long-term residual damages.

368

Education of legal personnel, especially that of judges, is necessary. The investigators note that even in cases which represented blatant abuse as manifested by multiple skeletal trauma with central nervous system damage, when they petitioned for removal of the child from the home the authorities were more concerned about the rights of the parents than the welfare of the babies. Some children were returned to the custody of their parents after their fractures had healed and their general condition improved without any assessment of the family at all. The courts do not seem to be truly aware of the risk to the child — that it might not merely be a question of a single meaningless act, but that abuse may constitute an active expression of a wish to be rid of the child. The overwhelming odds against complete recovery from parental abuse seem to escape appropriate attention. The horror of many situations and the intense feelings they arouse may cause some people to try and mend the parent-child relationship in order to wish the whole situation away. It is not always true that the natural parent is best for the child, nor is it true that any parent is better than none. Parents, on the other hand, need not be treated as criminals because they have abused their children. A total assessment of the entire situation and its pressures needs to be made.

One issue, that of community support, demands special attention. As family patterns change and mobility increases, social institutions such as the church lose their strong hold on family life. People who tend to be isolated become even more so. It is probably true that many parents who do not beat their children would also benefit if a neighbor could help them out when they are overwhelmed, or if a network of friendly visitors would somehow fill this void. Volunteers could be used to extend the work of the public health nurses and the hospital clinics to ensure that both mild supervision and help would be available to young mothers. Homemaker services can be extremely important. Community programs and neighborhood associations could also be helpful if the prohibition about interfering or getting involved could somehow be broken down constructively. It is possible that an auxiliary to the police department could be useful.

The interrelationship of poverty, isolation, and too many unplanned-for small children is important. Too often, little is done to reach the very people who are too weak to ask for help. Newspapers and TV, too, often carry only the sensational story and not the steady compilation of data that might enable us to make reforms in our welfare systems, our birth control clinics, hospital regulations, courts, and foster home programs — data that might enable us to prevent such tragedies and save these children.

Research Grant: MH 14739

Date of Interview: June 1969

References:

Caffey, J. Multiple fractures in the long bones of infants suffering from chronic subdural hematoma. *American Journal of Roentgenology*, August 1946.

De Francis, Vincent. *Child Abuse — Preview of a Nationwide Survey.* The Children's Division, American Humane Association, Denver, Colorado, 1963.

Elmer, Elizabeth. "Identification of Abused Children." Children. U.S. Department of Health, Education, and Welfare, 180-184, September-October 1963.

Elmer, Elizabeth. Hazards in determining child abuse. *Child Welfare,* January 1966.

Elmer, Elizabeth. Child abuse: overview of the problem and avenues of attack. Paper presented at the 5th Annual Mental Health Institute, St. Louis, Missouri, July 1966.

Elmer, Elizabeth. Abused children and community resources. *International Journal of Offender Therapy.* 11, 1, 1967.

Elmer, Elizabeth and Gregg, Grace, M.D. Developmental characteristics of abused children. *Pediatrics,* 40; 4(Part 1): 596-602, October 1967.

Elmer, Elizabeth *Children in Jeopardy.* University of Pittsburgh Press, 1967.

Gregg, Grace, M.D. Physician, child-abuse reporting laws; and injured child, psychosocial anatomy of childhood trauma. *Clinical Pediatrics.* Philadelphia, Pennsylvania: J. B. Lippincott Co., December 1968.

Hill, Reuben. Social stresses on the family. *Social Casework,* 39: 139-150, 1958.

Powell, G. F., M.D., Brasel, J. A., M.D., and Blizzard, R. M., M.D. Emotional deprivation and growth retardation simulating idiopathic hypopituitarism: 1 — clinical evaluation of the syndrome. *The New England Journal of Medicine,* 276, 23:1271-1278, June 8, 1967.

Powell, G. F., M.D., Brasel, J. A., M.D., Raiti, S., M.D., and Blizzard, R. M., M.D. Emotional deprivation and growth retardation simulating idiopathic hypopituitarism: II — Endocrinologic Evaluation of the Syndromel. *The Journal of the American Medical Association,* 88:358-362, April 27, 1964.

U.S. Department of Health, Education, and Welfare. The child abuse reporting laws: a tabular view. Washington, D.C., 1966. (Reprinted with revisions in 1968)

370

The Re-Education of Criminals

Investigator:
John M. McKee, Ph. D.
Draper Correctional Institute
Elmore, Ala.

Prepared by:
Herbert Yahraes

Introduction and Summary of Findings

In a sparsely settled agricultural area 25 miles north of Montgomery, Ala., lies a unit of the State's prison system known as Draper Correctional Center. There, some 800 men, more than half of them in their twenties or late teens, are serving sentences ranging up to life for crimes ranging up to murder.

Under the Alabama parole system, an offender is usually considered for parole when he has completed one-third of his term. (Inmates joke about one of their fellows who is serving three life sentences that run consecutively. "When he gets through the first one," the joke goes, "they are going to have a — of a time getting him through the next two." Actually he has served several years and can expect a chance to prove himself in the outside world in a dozen more.) The parole system helps an offender to get a job; it requires, in fact, that he have a job, or an assured place in school, before he is released. And it tries to keep track of him and to counsel him. Nevertheless, it is estimated that from 65 to 70 percent of the general run of parolees fall into criminal ways again and find themselves back in prison.

Among a special group of inmates, however, in a project given impetus by an NIMH grant, a preliminary followup indicates that only about 30 percent of those released have had to come back.

That dramatic cut in the recidivism rate appears to have been achieved, in great part at least, by applying principles of behavioral science to specific educational and social problems of inmates. The basic tool has been programed instruction, under which a person proceeds at his own pace through a given subject, whether it be writing grammatical sentences or building good relations on the job, and wins rewards as he goes along. The project is conducted by a private nonprofit organization, the Rehabilitation Research Foundation, chartered by the State to develop and administer programs of research and training in human development. Offices and most classrooms, all within the gates at Draper, are in a warehouse-type brick building that once served the prison as a cotton mill.

Dr. John M. McKee, the psychologist who conceived the program and who, as executive director of the Foundation, administers it, points out

371

that the participants have been volunteers, so presumably they have been more highly motivated than the nonparticipants to improve themselves and to make good in the outside world. Offsetting this at least to some extent, he believes that many and perhaps most of the students originally wanted only to escape work on the prison farm, or at maintenance jobs, or in the laundry, which serves the entire State prison system.

Besides willingness to volunteer, prospective students usually have had to demonstrate a sixth-grade level of education, which was considered essential if they were to benefit from either academic or vocational training. Beginning in 1968, however, applicants below this level have been accepted and given 20 weeks of individual and group instruction directed toward fitting them for an occupational course. Applicants' criminal records (except in the case of rapists, who were ruled ineligible by the State Board of Corrections because there are women on the Foundation's staff) and their records of behavior in the institution have not in themselves affected admissibility. But priority has gone to men having a reasonable chance of being paroled soon after completion of training.

Doctor McKee traces the genesis of the Draper project to 1959, when he was one of a group of psychologists who dreamed of establishing a center for research in behavior, with emphasis on the application of learning theory. The psychologists were staff members of the Division of Mental Hygiene of the Alabama State Department of Health; their behavior center would be part of the University of Alabama, and one of its many possible research studies would deal with inmates of Alabama prisons. When the group was unable to raise the necessary funds for the whole program, Doctor McKee decided to see what he could do with the correctional project. He felt certain, after several years of directing mental hygiene work in the State's prison system, that if you wanted to pry a man loose from antisocial activities, you had to show him how to become and—more important, to get him to believe that he could become—a self-respecting member of society. Programed instruction, Doctor McKee believed, offered a highly promising way of meeting these requirements.

Draper's warden, John C. Watkins, who had majored in sociology at the University of Alabama and then completed course work for a master's degree from Auburn University, strongly encouraged Doctor McKee and offered to make Draper available as an experimental center if Alabama's Commissioner of Corrections approved. A. Frank Lee, the commissioner, not only approved but also scraped together $3,000 to help finance a trial run of McKee's idea. ("We sold the commissioner," McKee recalls, "by giving him a little programed sequence that quickly taught him how to multiply in his head certain 2-digit numbers by other 2-digit numbers.")

That was in 1961. The following year, NIMH made a grant to expand the work and analyze the results. Institute support, which continued into 1969, went mainly to develop, test, and apply self-instructional programs in the academic and personal-relations fields. The findings were so promising that in 1964 the Office of Education and the Department of

Labor granted funds, under the Manpower Development and Training Act (MDTA), to enroll more inmates and to add vocational subjects. Work programs under the NIMH and MDTA grants have complemented each other.

For the most part, enrollees now spend 8 hours a day in the program. There is considerable variation in how these hours are apportioned. The student whose aim is a high school equivalency certificate, for example, will spend most of his time in academic work. Typically, though, two of the hours are given to basic education courses, including English, remedial reading, and arithmetic, and the rest to vocational training—in the classroom for theory and in the shop for practices. Vocational courses include welding, repair of electrical appliances (including air conditioning and refrigeration systems), barbering, sign writing, and work in an automobile service station.

Among the regular staff members, in addition to Doctor McKee, are Donna M. Seay, a vocational educator who serves as the Foundation's assistant director; four learning managers or supervisors, who in a conventional educational system would be called teachers; five vocational instructors; and three counselors, for guidance to men in the program, for job placement, and for followup.

The staff is augmented by the so-called college corps—junior and senior college students, majoring in sociology, psychology, or education, who join the regular staff during summer vacations or for part of a semester during the school year. Some 50 corpsmen from a dozen colleges and universities in Alabama and neighboring States have worked at Draper, three or four at any given time. They have served as counselors, as aides to the regular instructors, and, perhaps most important, as "peer models"—examples of the fact that a young man can do something worthwhile with his life. "With encouragement from the corpsmen," Doctor McKee reports, "many inmates came to believe for the first time that their lives counted and that they, too, could succeed."

About five "service" corpsmen also are on duty, mainly as assistants to the instructors. They are relatively well-educated inmates who have shown special interest in the project and the desire and ability to work with members of the regular staff and with fellow inmates.

Augmenting the academic and vocational work, the project has set up:

1. *A reading laboratory,* which evaluates and provides help for each student who seems deficient in reading skills. Some of the work—notably, rate-comprehension exercises presented by a variable-speed film projector—is done in groups, but most of it is individual. Each student receives a kit that contains stories and self-graded tests on the content of the stories. Vocabularies are developed through other self-graded exercises. Students are encouraged to spend at least an hour a day outside the laboratory reading any library book of their choice, provided it is not far below their known level of ability.

2. *A seminar program,* which provides the group interaction not present in the programed instruction courses. Group discussion, or seminars, have dealt so far with English composition, poetry

appreciation, human behavior, great books, creative writing, and current events. Most of the leaders have been volunteers from Montgomery recruited by Doctor McKee because of their interest in the subject matter. The program has been so successful in awakening and expanding the prisoner's interests that it will be continued and broadened.

About 100 inmates were enrolled in the Draper project as of mid-1969, bringing the grand total of participants—including a number in the early years who were involved for only short periods—to almost 2,000. Better than 40 percent of the current enrollees are Negroes, a proportion that has more than doubled since the start of the program. Two thirds of the institution's population is white.

Doctor McKee reports the following major findings, most of them based on a followup of 228 graduates of the vocational training program (out of 290 who had been released) from 1 to 3 years after they had left Draper.

• Sixty-eight percent of those released—most of them by parole, the others by completion of their terms—were still free. Of the other 32 percent, almost half had been returned to Draper for technical violations, such as failure to keep in touch with parole authorities, or consorting with known criminals, while the rest had been picked up for new felonies or misdemeanors. This contrasts with the pretraining record of these men: fully 70 percent had been recidivists and only 30 percent had been first offenders. For the State as a whole the recidivism rate was estimated at between 50 and 70 percent.

• Of the 288 men in the followup, about 80 percent had initially gone into jobs directly related to their training and another 10 percent had gone into such jobs later on. The number of employers who hired graduates reached 361, since some graduates changed jobs several times. Two-thirds of those released got jobs through the efforts of the program's job development and placement officers. Only a few graduates—eight out of the 187 for whom this information was available—performed unsatisfactorily in their first jobs.

• The average income of the trainees who have been released—based on follow-up data from 150—is $3,640 a year. Each man pays an estimated average of $546 a year in taxes. Moreover, the public has been relieved of the burden of maintaining the man in prison, estimated at $1,200 per man per year.

• After 200 hours of programed instruction, students have shown an average gain in educational level of 1.4 grades. When this instruction was coupled with a reading improvement course, the gain was 2.5 grades.

• In the hope of getting a certificate of high school equivalency, 178 students have taken the State's General Education Development tests, and all except nine have passed the tests and received the certificate. These students typically had been at the seventh grade level or even below in at least some of their subjects when they enrolled. (Incidentally, evidence of the cash value of a high school education was turned up by a 1967 study of one group of former inmates. Men who had earned a certificate of high school equivalency during their imprisonment were making an average of

374

$349.30 a month; the others were making $279. As compared with pre-imprisonment earnings, the high school equivalency group had added more than $140 a month; the others, less than $40.)

• Thirteen students were accepted by colleges while they were still inmates, and entered the colleges upon parole. Three of these have graduated; the others are still in college. Most of the students have received help from a scholarship loan fund called PACE (Program for Achievement of a College Education), which the Foundation administers. The fund was started in 1962 when the inmates who had taken part in one of the early programed instruction experiments, for which they were paid, donated their earnings to establish it. Since then it has been supported by gifts from outside. Loans to college students, graduates of the Draper program, have ranged from $40 to over $2,000. The fund has had to turn down some requests and meet others only in small part.

To disseminate information about its accomplishments and methods, the Foundation has held four conferences—in Montgomery, Houston (with the University of Houston as cosponsor), New York City (with the Staten Island Mental Health Center as cosponsor), and Berkeley, Calif. (with the University of California as cosponsor). Each was attended by more than 100 persons from correctional institutions, pardon and parole boards, State employment services, State manpower development and training programs, and vocational rehabilitation agencies. More than 2,000 persons have visited the project for first-hand information. A manual on Draper's training methods has been prepared.

Correctional institutions in a number of States—including California, Florida, Georgia, Illinois, Indiana, Nevada, Oklahoma, South Carolina, and Tennessee—have adopted some part of the Draper program, and others have expressed interest in doing so. For lack of funds, Doctor McKee reports, Alabama has not yet been able to extend the program beyond Draper.

Programed Instruction

At the basis of the program is learning theory, or reinforcement theory, which says that if desirable behavior is rewarded and undesirable behavior ignored or punished, a person's behavior will eventually be modified in the desired direction.

"There is no substitute in this world for competence," says Doctor McKee. "And that is what these trainees have lacked all their lives—a feeling of competence. They have failed in every major task they have undertaken, perhaps with good reason: the family may have failed them, or the school. As the warden says, they have even failed in crime, or they wouldn't be here."

Programed instruction, or P.I., is intended to substitute success for failure. As defined by Doctor McKee, it is "an attempt to systematically apply basic principles of learning theory to an individual learning situation." Subject matter is said to be programed when:

1. Its training objectives are behavioral: that is, the learner will be able to *do* something specific.

2. Material is presented in a logical sequence of steps—called *frames* or *exercises*—each small enough to be easily learned.

3. The student is required to respond actively to each step; that is, he is asked to apply information or exercise skills immediately after they are introduced.

4. The learner receives immediate feedback; that is, he is told at once that he is right or wrong. In good P.I. he is almost always right. This explains the behavior-shaping power of P.I., says Doctor McKee, because the knowledge that a response is right is reinforcing to the student: he is encouraged to go ahead. If he is wrong, he is told why and may be referred to a section that helps him over the difficult part. He is asked to correct his answer; then he is moved forward in the program.

A course on sentence structure, for instance, begins by defining *subject* and *predicate* and giving examples. Then it offers a few simple sentences and asks the student to pick out the subject and predicates. It tells him the answers. If he has been right, he goes on to more complex sentences; if wrong, he reviews the definitions and corrects his mistakes before going ahead.

One series of lessons teaches personal hygiene as an important factor in getting and holding a job. Other lessons try to teach desirable work habits and customer-relations attitudes. Here is one unit, or frame, from the customer-relations course for automobile station workers:

Make the first move count.— J. Q. Customer drives into your shop. This is his first visit, and he feels a bit wary. The longer he is left waiting, the more doubtful he becomes. He may even decide that you're not interested in his business and leave.

* * * But no! You're on your toes! You see that no one has made a move to help him. At that particular moment you cannot leave your work, so you call out, "Good morning, sir! Someone will be with you in a moment." He at least knows now that someone is aware of his presence and is hurrying to assist him. The sooner you can approach him, the better.

Put a check mark by the following statements that are *true:*

1. Most customers don't mind waiting. _____
2. If the customer is kept waiting too long, he may leave. _____
3. You should approach the customer as soon as possible. _____
4. Keep the customer waiting for a while to show him how hard everyone is working. _____
5. If it is not possible to approach the customer immediately, tell him that someone will be with him as soon as possible. _____

You scored 100 percent if you checked numbers 2,3, and 5. You realized that most people do not appreciate being kept waiting. Time is important to all of us, and no one likes his time to be wasted. Too, a customer will be more impressed with your attention to *his* needs than he will be with your efforts to fix someone else's car!

If you checked a wrong answer or failed to check the correct answer, go back and correct your answer before continuing.

In the Draper project, a learning area replaces the usual classroom. It is a room with rows of stalls or cubicles, like those found in college library stacks, so that each student has his own, compartmentalized, study space. A dozen or 15 students work in the same area under the eye of a learning manager or supervisor, but no two students are likely to be engaged on the same subject. The supervisor answers questions, offers encouragement, and keeps records.

Programed instruction makes it easy to work with a person at several levels, depending on his need. One student, for example, is relatively far advanced in English, so he is studying it at the eighth grade level. Since he is extremely weak in arithmetic, however, he studies that subject at the fifth grade level.

P.I. materials come either in text form or for use in teaching machines. The machines have advantages. They can automatically skip over material that the student's responses show he already knows, and they can present extra practice sequences when the response indicates these are needed. Further, they can control cheating and can tabulate the number of correct and incorrect responses, thus easing the supervisor's job. The Draper project uses them to some extent but, largely in the interest of economy, has relied mainly on texts, or "software," and feels the results have been good.

In the beginning, the available P.I. courses covered only a few subjects and often lacked what Doctor McKee considered a necessity: self-administered tests that evaluated the subject's knowledge at the start, at various points along the way, and at the end. So the project set to work to develop materials of its own. Some 30 Draper-tested courses covering aspects of such basic subjects as grammar and mathematics, such vocational subjects as electronics, welding, auto mechanics, and bricklaying, and such social relations areas as applying for a job, good job habits, and table manners have resulted; they are on sale through the University of Alabama.

The development of its own courses went hand in hand with the use of existing ones. One of these, used purely because it did exist, was Russian language for beginners. But could this possibly have any value to prison inmates? "Yes indeed, it could and did." answers McKee. "The fellows who took it went back and spouted off a few words in Russian to one another. And when the others asked 'What's that?', our boys said, 'If you went to The School, you'd find out.' Their new knowledge gave them prestige, and that's important."

Some of the students began programing on their own. One day, a few months after the project began, two inmates—call them Ted Jones and Bill Smith—came to McKee and said, "Hello, Doc, take a look at this." McKee looked and saw a sheaf of handwritten instructions and diagrams entitled "A Programed Course in Fingering Movements on the Trumpet.

By Ted Jones and Bill Smith." It had 1,164 frames. Leafing through it, McKee remarked, "Gee, I believe I could take this course and learn to play the trumpet. It even teaches you how to blow through the trumpet. You blow as if you were going to spit a piece of tobacco off your tongue."

"Well," Ted Jones answered, "if you are as smart as the four men we've already put through the program to test it, and at the end could play those three tunes—yeah, if you are as smart as they are, you could learn to play those tunes, too."

"Another year and a day for you," McKee joked back, and went on to encourage Ted and Bill to continue their work, which they did, writing lessons for the clarinet and saxophone and a basic course in music notation (One of the musicians is now in college; the other has been returned to Draper for a parole violation.)

Over the years other inmates have developed courses in personal grooming, etiquette, parts of speech, improving the memory, orientation for new prisoners, and other subjects. One man who was studying technical writing signed up for a half-year course in welding just so he could program lessons in the theory of it. The course in technical writing, incidentally, was dropped after a few years because employers shied away from hiring its graduates. But the welding lessons, like most of the other courses developed by inmates, have become part of the Draper curriculum.

Meanwhile the commercial production of P.I. materials has boomed to such an extent that hundreds of courses are available. The problem at Draper is no longer to develop new courses but to select from the most promising ones at hand. One new program, though, is definitely planned. It will be written with the aid of offenders—in particular, successful and unsuccessful parolees—and will teach *how to succeed on parole.*

Reinforcement

Although programed instruction has its own built-in reinforcement—the lift one gets from finding that an answer is correct (or, if it isn't correct, from learning what was wrong and from being encouraged to go ahead)—the staff at Draper found that the typical inmate got bored after a few weeks. So it has employed a number of tangible rewards to create a motivating environment. For instance, students who complete a course are given points, and enough points win them a Certificate of Achievement. Along with written recommendations, these certificates provide a strong basis for favorable parole consideration. Many former inmates have reported that the certificates also helped them to get jobs.

Now undergoing trial is a "contingency management" plan under which a student contracts at the end of each day's classroom work to complete a certain number of frames the next day. A frame comprises one question and one answer in a programed instruction course. A contract is an agreement, recorded on a form, between the student and the supervisor. The student is free to specify the number of frames he will do provided this is at least equal to his accomplishment during the baseline period at the beginning of the course. The student also agrees to take the tests assigned by the supervisor at the appropriate points in the course. And student and supervisor agree that upon completion of a certain number of frames or of a test the student will be free to take a 15-minute break. (The amount of work to be completed before a break depends upon the total amount for the day as specified in the contract.) The agreement makes it possible for each student to average one break an hour.

The breaks are taken in a room—the "reinforcing event" area—fitted out with a coffeemaker and supplies, newspapers, books, magazines, letter-writing materials, shoe-shining equipment, crossword puzzles, playing cards, checker and chess sets, and a radio.

An experiment that preceded the adoption of this plan involved 16 students. First they worked through a 3-week baseline period having two scheduled breaks per day. Then came 4 weeks managed by the experimenter. During the first two of these weeks he set the performance level at 20 percent higher than the baseline average; during the last 2 weeks, he raised it another 20 percent. Most students achieved these increases.

Then came 2 weeks of self-management, with the students themselves at the end of each day setting the amount of work they would do the following day. In almost every case they agreed to work and did work faster than during the second phase, when the experimenter was calling the pace. Frames completed per hour averaged 61 during the baseline period, 101 during the experimenter-managed period, and 125 during the self-management period.

These increases in work per hour were accompanied by a decrease in the number of hours worked. During the second and third periods, the students were permitted to leave the study area when they had completed the stipulated or agreed-upon number of frames and the appropriate tests. They could go back to the dormitory and rest, work out in the gym, talk to friends, or engage in other free-time activities. Consequently, the number of hours worked per day dropped from slightly more than 5 in the baseline period, to 4.35 in the experimenter-managed period, to 3.4 in the self-management phase. But the total work completed rose from 320 frames in the baseline period, to 405, to 435. The increase in frames completed did not adversely affect test performance.

In sum, the experiment indicates:

1. The knowledge that a reward is waiting spurs students on. This is so whether the work to be done is set by the experimenter or by the student. But when it is set by the student, productivity seems to increase still further.

2. In many cases, permission to leave the experimental area at the completion of the performance contract for the day acted as a more powerful reinforcer than the immediate reward—one or more of the activities available during the 15-minute-break periods. After students were told, part way through the experiment, that they might continue to

study rather than take an earned break, the group as a whole chose continued work as often as it chose immediate relaxation.

In addition to the built-in reinforcement of programed instruction and the extrinsic, tangible rewards offered at Draper, something else is at work. In the process of learning to be a student, Doctor McKee observes, a man learns to enjoy certain intellectual pursuits. He reads the newspapers, he picks up a book, he listens to the news on TV, he carries on an intellectual conversation—his whole world is changing and opening up. He is going from such reinforcers as a party, free time, and points toward a certificate to find intrinsic rewards in the subject matter itself and in the process of his development. This is theory, but you see it working in the lives of all of us.

The attitude adopted by the staff is also a motivating factor, Doctor McKee believes. "We attempt to be firm but not punitive," he says, "helping but not totally permissive, and flexible but not vacillating. By employing positive rather than negative reinforcement whenever possible, an atmosphere had been created that is much different from the hostile, punitive one expected by most inmates."

As an example, he cites his own behavior when he helps administer a test for a high school equivalency certificate. It's a long test, dragging on for several hours. Since the typical inmate's span of attention is short, and since McKee knows from experience that the inmate may say "The—with it" and walk off, the director keeps coming back and showing interest. "How are you doing—any problems?" he'll ask. "I don't tell him any answers," McKee says, "but I get him to say, 'Well, yeah, this part I just took,' or something like that. And I say, 'Well, let me see,' and look at the part and say, 'Yes, you've got some tough questions there. Better go back over what you've been reading and writing to make sure you've got the right answers. I'll be back.' " What I'm trying to do is to maintain alert behavior—keep them sticking with the job and not bugging out.

"That's what they've been doing all their lives—bugging out, escaping. And strangely enough, this escape behavior has been reinforced. Rob a house, forge a check, steal a car—and run away. Girl friend squeezing you in? The job getting you down? Run away.

"Even people in correctional work have been reinforcing such behavior. An inmate will get tired of the work he's been assigned to. Or he'll get tired of the person he's working with. So he starts manipulating a change. He'll tell the classification officer: 'I'm bugging out of this. I need a different job. My supervisor's down on me—I don't know why.' And he'll keep trying and after a while he'll get his change."

From staff interviews with prospective students, McKee suspects that a large proportion of the inmates who volunteered for school were simply running away once again. But he accepted them because in his project there is nowhere to run to, except back to the job they escaped from.

380

A "Second Language"

Doctor McKee emphasizes that with prisoners—and probably any other population, for that matter—programed instruction has to be supplemented by discussion groups and sometimes by individual counseling or teacher-student conferences. The inescapable inadequacy of many P.I. courses, standing by themselves, was brought home to him one day a few years ago when he congratulated a trainee on having made the extraordinarily high grade of 96 in a high-school-level grammar course. The trainee gave a deprecatory smile in response and said: "This here English, Doc, don't give me no trouble nohow." Like many other students, he had learned the rules but wasn't applying them.

The project then tried the seminar approach—trainees meeting in groups with a teacher and working together at speech modification. This was much more successful. As the trainees listened to one another, they learned to detect errors, which they called to the group's attention.

Now the staff is experimenting with what it calls the "second language" approach; that is, teaching standard English by the oral methods used in teaching a foreign language.

In this approach a man's present speech, no matter how poor by conventional standards, is never criticized. It is the one he has picked up as a child, and it is usually quite effective in meeting his needs to communicate with his usual associates. The trainees are simply told that the school wants to give them the ability to use another kind of speech on appropriate occasions, such as when applying for a job or meeting a girl friend's parents. "We all have different levels of speech," points out Sally Roy, a former public school teacher who is now a research associate with the Draper project. "A child of five will speak to his mother one way, to his friends another, and to his teacher a third. We speak one way to the dog and another to the Mayor. The hope is that the trainees will use this different level we are giving them more and more often and that eventually it will become their usual level."

The project got the idea from St. Mary's Dominican College Business School in New Orleans, a basic education center for the Job Corps. In training Negro, Cajun, and other disadvantaged girls to be secretaries, staff members from Draper found, Dominican College was trying not to correct their language but to give them a new one for use on the job. It called the new language "business speech."

In its second-language experiment, the staff at Draper gives extensive drill work on the most common errors noticed during talks with the trainees—errors exemplified by such sentences as "John and me want to go to town," "He don't know no better," and "They is ready to fight." The trainees hear over and over again, on tape, the correctly spoken version of these and hundreds of other examples. They also listen to themselves at frequent intervals. And there is group work, including mock job interviews, some of it recorded by a videotape machine.

Has any employer said, "I can't take this man because he doesn't talk well enough?"

381

"It happened in New Orleans," answers Doctor McKee. "People there said, 'We can't take this girl; she doesn't speak right; she'd give us a bad image.' We don't know whether or not it has happened here. But it seems reasonable to suppose that an employer hires a man on the basis of the total image he casts, including his ability and his self-confidence, and that his speech is part of this image. Even an employer who himself says 'He don't' cannot help being impressed by a man who speaks well. Rehabilitation is a cluster of things, including attitude changes. We think that proper speech is part of the cluster. It is not merely that the man who learns what we are calling a second language has acquired a new skill but that he is enhanced by having done so. People look twice at him and think that he is worth more. He himself has a greater feeling of worth and a sense of belonging."

For the Future

Aided by a new grant from the Department of Labor, Doctor McKee expects to continue the program of education and vocational training and to make more extensive and rigorous followups. He hopes to answer these questions, among others:

• What is the most effective type of training program, as measured by work adjustment and recidivism? Can P.I. simulate real work situations, beyond that of a job interview? Can realistic work-stress conditions be simulated and the means of handling them be transferred to actual job conditions following release?

• What specific barriers, particularly those related to employer attitudes, make it more difficult for the offender to find and hold a job?

• Do released convicts who receive "labor mobility" funds (small grants of Federal money to tide them over until the first paycheck comes in) or Federal bonding assistance, or both, have a better post-release record than those who do not?

• How can an inmate's behavior, not merely during the hours given to the training program but throughout the day, be shaped to conform to desired standards? Involved are *(a)* deciding which kinds of behavior are desirable, because they make for a successful transition from the institution to a job in the community, and which kinds of behavior are undesirable, *(b)* determining the frequency with which each kind of behavior occurs in the sample of men to be studied, and *(c)* selecting, applying, and measuring the effectiveness of measures—among them, probably, certain changes in the attitudes of the custodial staff—to encourage one kind of behavior and discourage another. This, then, is a major, long-term experiment in behavior modification and one that is dear to Doctor McKee's heart.

Research Grant: MH 14990
Date of Interview: December 1968

References:

Clements, C. B., and McKee, J. M. Programed instruction for institutionalized offenders: contingency management and performance contracts. *Psychological Reports,* 22:957-964, 1968.
McKee, J. M. Adult basic education for the disadvantaged: procedures used to raise the basic educational level. Presented to the American Vocational Association, 1966.
McKee, J. M. Programed instruction in the correctional process. Presented at Conference in Manpower Training for Offenders in the Correctional Process, 1968.

Delinquent Gangs: An Answer to the Needs of the Socially Disabled

Investigator:
James F. Short, Jr., Ph.D.*
University of Chicago
Chicago, Ill.

Prepared by:
Herbert Yahraes

Members of juvenile delinquent gangs, according to a theory advanced in an important new study, suffer from a condition described as *social disability*. Much more so than other boys, they grow to school age without the skills needed to meet new situations. Thus they are handicapped both in getting along with teachers and classmates and in learning, and their school experiences in turn make them additionally handicapped for conventional activities later on, including work. In an effort to meet the universal need for relationships with other people, they drift into gang membership.

According to a complementary theory advanced in the same study, participation in a gang's delinquent activities may be likened to playing a game in which most moves bring a slight reward but in which also, at long, irregular intervals, a severe penalty may be exacted. If action is coming up in the gang and a member fails to get into it, he immediately loses what he values most—status. If he does get into it, he is almost sure to win a little prize in the way of higher status and a stronger sense of belonging, and his chances of being seriously penalized through injury or arrest are not, for any one instance, very great. This explanation is termed *the theory of aleatory risks*.

Along with other insights into gang processes and gang members' values, the theories of social disability and aleatory risks have been developed in the course of a study of Chicago street-corner groups, undertaken in 1959 with support from the National Institute of Mental Health and now practically finished.

The research group has been led by Dr. James F. Short, Jr., and Dr. Fred L. Strodtbeck. Dr. Short, a sociologist, is now dean of the graduate

---

*Now at the Department of Sociology, Washington State University, Pullman, Washington.

school at Washington State University, but during the study's fieldwork served at the University of Chicago as a visiting member of the faculty. Dr. Strodtbeck holds appointments at the University of Chicago in the departments of sociology and psychology and is director of the Social Psychology Laboratory. Another major contributor has been Dr. Desmond S. Cartwright, now at the University of Colorado.

The investigators believe their study to be the largest attempt yet made to get information useful in understanding and dealing with teenage delinquent gangs. It grew out of a new program under which college graduates working for the Y.M.C.A. of Metropolitan Chicago hang around with gang members—listening to their talk, going along with them to parties and to encounters with other gangs, encouraging them to take up sports, getting them admitted to ball games, seeing that they are treated for venereal disease, talking them out of stolen cars, putting them in touch with employment programs, and so on. These Y employees, assigned one to a gang and known as *detached workers*, came to be widely accepted and counted upon.

Through weekly interviews with the detached workers, frequent observation of gang activities, talks with the boys themselves, and the administration of various psychological tests, the researchers studied 16 gangs in considerable detail. These gangs, of which 11 were Negro and five white, had 598 members.

For comparison, the researchers studied several hundred boys who lived in the same areas as the gang members but did not belong to gangs. They studied also two Negro and two white groups of middle-class boys, all of them members of Y.M.C.A. Hi-Y clubs; no middle-class gang could be located.

The principal concern was with group motivations and processes—with what makes gangs tick.

The project's major findings are summarized in the numbered paragraphs that follow:

1. *Gang members and other lower-class boys express as high a regard for middle-class standards as do middle-class boys.*

This finding came as a surprise, Dr. Strodtbeck reports, because it ran contrary to the widely accepted theory that juvenile gang delinquency is a reaction against middle-class standards.

The investigators arrived at the finding by using a semantic differential to study values held by the boys. A semantic differential is a set of paired words, opposite in meaning, for learning how people regard a given set of goals or standards. Among the pairs in this case were *good-bad, pleasant-unpleasant,* and *smart-sucker.* Each word in a pair was one end of a seven-point scale. If a boy considered something wholly good, for example, it was given a value of one; wholly bad, a value of seven; just midway between good and bad, a value of four. Among the images rated by the scales were these:

Representative of middle-class standards:
Someone who works for good grades at school.
Someone who likes to read good books.

Someone who saves his money.

Representative of lower-class standards:
Someone who has a steady job washing and greasing cars.
Someone who likes to spend his spare time hanging on the corner with his friends.
Someone who shares his money with his friends.

Descriptive of many boys in delinquent gangs:
Someone who is a good fighter with a tough reputation.
Someone who has good connections to avoid trouble with the law.
Someone who makes easy money by pimping and other illegal hustles.

All boys studied—gang, nongang, and middle-class—evaluated highly the images representing salient features of middle-class style of life. No other images were evaluated more highly.

But lower-class images did get a higher score from lower-class boys than from middle-class boys. And criminal images, though rated low, received higher scores from gang members than from nongang members and higher scores from the latter than from middle-class boys. Further, some evidence was found that gang boys more than others might be inclined to judge participation in illegal activities from the standpoint of whether or not it was smart rather than whether or not it was good.

The boys' ratings of themselves, as they are and as they would like to be, showed that regardless of the group to which a boy belonged he would like to be, on the average, both smarter (meaning less of a sucker) and better.

2. *None of the gangs studied can be characterized as strictly criminal or as being part of a criminal subculture. However, illegal activities were characteristic to some extent of all the gangs.*
The activities of gang members, as reported by the detached workers, were combined into 37 items of behavior. Factor analysis then disclosed the presence of five groups of closely associated activities, some of the groups being more characteristic of certain gangs than of others. The five groups, or factors follow:

(a) *Conflict.* Main items: individual and group fighting, the carrying of concealed weapons, and assault. Though robbery, theft, becoming a public nuisance, and statutory rape also appear in this factor, they are part of other factors as well.

(b) *Stable corner activities.* Characterized by sports, social activities, and gambling. No serious delinquent item is prominent.

(c) A cluster of behaviors difficult to sum up but finally called *stable sex pattern.* Principal items include sexual intercourse, statutory rape, petting, and the buying, selling, and use of alcohol. Holding a job is fairly prominent, too—the only factor in which it is prominent.

(d) Called *retreatist* because the buying, selling, and use of narcotics and marihuana ranked highest among the activities. Only one retreatist gang was found.

(e) *Authority protest.* Principal activities: stealing autos, driving without a license, becoming a public nuisance, drinking, running away from home, playing truant, joyriding.

From the individual scores, the investigators determined the average score of each gang on each factor. Gangs varied most greatly on *(a)*, least on *(e)*.

The ranking of a gang on any one factor was found to correlate positively with its ranking on all the other factors except *(b)*. The higher a gang's score on the conflict factor, for instance, the higher its score on all the others except the one built around sports and social activities.

The six gangs found to engage in the most conflict were all Negro. Three of the four gangs that engaged in the least conflict were also Negro. White gangs ranked significantly higher than Negro only on the "authority protest" factor. The gangs ranking highest in "authority protest" were those engaging least in sports and other activities of *(b)*.

3. *The white community is more concerned than the Negro with the excesses of its young people, and in general controls its young people more effectively. Among the many and complex reasons are the greater economic stability of white communities and the existence of indigenous institutions of established leadership.*

From a statistical study of the relationships among various types of behavior, the investigators find that Negro gang members tend to make no clear distinction between delinquent and conventional behavior. The Negro gang boys participated in such conventionally approved activities as doing the household chores and taking part in organized sports; they also participated in such conventionally disapproved activities as fighting, illicit sexual relations, drug use, and auto theft. In contrast, white gang boys were less inclined to participate in approved activities and were more openly at odds with the adult community, particularly concerning rowdyism, drinking (almost universal), drug use (rare, compared with the situation in Negro gangs), and sexual delinquency. In short, the investigators suggest, delinquency among Negro gang members is part of the total life pattern, and the community appears to accept it as such.

Life in the lower-class Negro areas was found to be organized around such institutions as "quarter parties" (sometimes called "rent parties"), pool halls, and taverns to a greater extent than in comparable white areas. One Negro poolroom that was a hangout for prostitutes and thieves was also a hangout for gang boys. Among the persons present on one occasion was a man who had just escaped from the police, still wearing one handcuff. He was being kidded.

In the white areas, the investigators report, life generally revolved around more conventional institutions—the Catholic Church in particular, ethnic groups, unions, bowling leagues, other organized recreational patterns, and political and "improvement" associations: these last organized in large measure to keep the Negroes out.

Economically and socially, "no white area [was found to be] as disadvantaged as the least disadvantaged Negro area." The Negro gangs came from neighborhoods where the median family income ranged from

387

$3,200 to $5,200: the white gangs came from neighborhoods where it ranged between $6,200 and $6,500. Unemployment was 10.6 percent in the Negro areas; 4.8 percent in the white areas. In the Negro areas, 40 percent of the dwelling units had more than one person per room; in the white areas, 14 percent.

4. *Rating themselves on friendliness, cleanness, smartness, kindness, helpfulness, and goodness, white gang boys produced considerably higher scores than Negro gang boys. With the two middle-class groups, though, the situation was reversed.*

If the Negro gang boys really are so fundamentally disadvantaged as the scores indicate, the investigators believe that "a major modification of the social system" will be needed to change "this negative self-image." the middle-class Negro boy rates himself highly, the study suggests, possibly because he may see himself at the top, looking down, whereas the middle-class white boy may still see steps ahead.

The investigators reached their findings by having the boys in the study compare themselves and their associates with other neighborhood boys on the basis of 42 adjectives. The ratings—*more, the same, less*—were given numerical values and subjected to statistical analysis. By various checks, the researchers satisfied themselves that in making the ratings the boys were actually describing themselves.

Some other findings:

Among Negroes, the higher the socioeconomic status (ranked as follows: middle-class, lower-class, nongang, gang), the higher the boys rated themselves on masculinity. Among whites the opposite was true. What is involved, the investigators suggest, is a cultural difference in the degree to which being manly is a focal concern.

The gang members who saw themselves as *polite, loyal, helpful, smart, clean, obedient,* and *religious*—rather than troublesome, mean, tough, and cool—were also the boys who reported engaging in more delinquent activity than the others. Explanation? Perhaps the boys with the characteristics expressed by those adjectives are the ones who, more than others, hold the group together, the investigators suggest, and frequently are thrown into roles and situations leading to delinquent acts.

5. *Gang members more than the other boys studied seem to suffer from "social disability"—defined as an impairment of the individual capacity to participate constructively in interpersonal relations. Social disability includes anxiety, emotional disturbance, and lack of acceptance of others.*

The boys compared themselves with the members of their groups by means of the semantic differential technique, the measure being the average of the scores on five scales—good-bad, clean-dirty, kind-cruel, fair-unfair, and pleasant-unplesant.

Results: the white middle-class boys evaluated associates significantly higher than themselves; the Negro middle-class boys evaluated themselves markedly higher than their companions. The lower the social level, the more likely a boy was to rate himself as better than his associates.

388

Among lower-class, particularly gang boys, the investigators infer, there exists an underlying dissatisfaction with their peers. Beneath the surface solidarity of the gang, there are signs of mutual frustration and lack of trust. Mental health depends strongly on accepting oneself, and the ability to accept oneself, the investigators note, seems strongly related to the ability to accept others.

The inference about gang boys is apparently bolstered by a personality assessment, which suggests that these boys are less self-assertive than the other boys studied, more reactive to false signals, slightly more neurotic and anxious, less gregarious, and more narcissistic. In sum, they are lacking in qualities that make for helpful relations with others.

As an example of gang boys' insecurity, the study notes that they were much more sensitive than nongang boys to how others were answering questions and performing various tasks; they were more anxious about their own performance as compared with others. Yet gang experience, with its constant challenge to prove such qualities as toughness, smartness, and adeptness with the girls, probably does little to alleviate such insecurity except in the gang itself.

6. *The roots of social disability appear to lie in early family life.*

In considering the causes of delinquency, sociologists and psychologists often emphasize status deprivation. But this is conceived of mainly in occupational and economic terms, the present investigators point out, whereas feelings of self-worth determined by factors not directly connected with job levels and income rates may prove equally relevant.

Observations at an experimental nursery school for lower-class Negro children—conducted at the University of Chicago by Dr. Strodtbeck under an Office of Education grant—suggest that at the age of 4½ years these children are less able than those of middle-class homes to associate with other children without fighting. They seem to have been harshly brought up and to have been cautioned frequently that the world around them is threatening. Further, they are retarded in cognitive development and verbal skills, partly because, the grantee finds, they have lacked stimulation from reading materials and constructive play and partly because they have not been exposed to an atmosphere that rewards good use of language.

Gang boys, the researchers have observed, are relatively ignorant of how to dress for a given occasion, eat in public, or carry on a polite conversation. Their limited social skills are attributed to their narrow social experience not only within the gang but also, and first, within the family.

The family does not equip the child to meet the demands of school, the investigators theorize, and unsatisfactory experiences in school further narrow his opportunities to play roles that will prepare him for getting along with employers and fellow workers and, in general, for dealing with new situations. In contrast, middle-class parents early help their children develop the ability to adjust as the situation requires. "Company" is different from "family," and entertaining the boss teaches approved means of relating to authority as well as something about the requirements of dress and manners.

The study emphasizes that since the family life of the boys was not investigated, there is as yet no proof of the suspected differences. Nevertheless, the lower-class nongang boys did give evidence of having had more opportunities to learn how to get along with people. Roughly 75 percent of them had successfully adjusted to school, as compared with about 50 percent of the gang boys. Also, more nongang boys than gang boys reported having had contact with adults of relatively high status, such as the administrators of youth agencies, clergymen, and employers.

As further evidence that the lower-class nongang boys had stronger family or institutional ties, these boys spent less time in places, including street corners and poolrooms, where there was a high risk of becoming involved in delinquency.

Differences in intelligence, too, are reported as contributing to the social disability of gang boys. The following table shows IQ estimates based on scores on so-called "culture-free" tests—tests that try to minimize the effects of previous training. As the investigators put it, the school and other social institutions reward the bright boy—and the gang boys are handicapped in respect to brightness.

	IQ Estimates		
	Gang	Nongang	Middle class
Negroes	69	74	96.5
Whites	85	91.5	111

7. *One factor in the formation of Chicago's juvenile gangs is the tense, fearful atmosphere of lower-class areas.*

People who live in the same area very long, Dr. Strodtbeck comments, tend to develop attitudes toward one another that respect property rights. But the typical urban Negro family has moved three times within the last year. "At no other time in history," the grantee continues, "has any segment of society been more distinctly jerked away from functioning kinship and social relationship networks. Here in Chicago, Negroes live in perpetual fear of the neighbors. Many a tenement door has three locks on it. The fear is not only that a neighbor may mean harm but also that if trouble comes to him and you are at all close to him, you will be sucked under, too. When resources are so limited they cannot be shared, you find ways of keeping people at a distance. The relevant community stops at the apartment door. It does not take in the building, nor the block, nor extended kin."

The investigators also note a disposition to exploit each situation to one's personal advantage and to assume that every one else will get his, too, if he can.

"The tensions with usurious landlords and the defensiveness before bill collectors, Aid to Dependent Children investigators, police, and other agency representatives," the study reports, "create an atmosphere in which other potentially legitimate sources of support, as well as neighbors,

390

are defined as part of a hostile outgroup. The result is that, for the adolescent, a liaison which is as informal as standing on the corner with other boys comes to be sought particularly because it requires so little formal commitment of exposure."

8. *By engaging in group delinquency, gang members help to satisfy common adolescent needs both for working with and depending upon others and for achieving status.*

Boys are likely to bring to the gang a suspicion of the dependability of human relationships, the study notes, and the gang contributes to this suspicion. Status within the gang is subject to constant challenge, and threat to status may disrupt even close friendships. But the gang does provide a status system in which boys can succeed after they have failed in more conventional settings.

Because adolescence is a period of emancipation from childhood, most teenagers find it difficult to admit and to gratify their dependency needs. This is particularly the case among gang members, who are under pressure, in a culture that values toughness, to shy from anything likely to be interpreted as a sign of personal weakness. But planning and carrying out gang forays and talking about them afterwards—with opportunities to admit to fright and to express appreciation for help—create a strong though temporary bond of loyalty, the study reports, that probably serves to meet dependency needs for a time.

The investigators point out that a gang boy's early decisions to do something illegal are not necessarily a deliberate attempt to develop bonds with other boys: Easy material and aggressive exploits are attractive in themselves. The satisfaction that comes from working with a group may be at the start only a bonus.

9. *Short-run hedonism, or a search for pleasure without regard for the consequences, has often been advanced as an explanation of why gang members participate in seriously delinquent activities. A more valid explanation may be a process that balances the immediate outcome of an action, in terms of the gain in status if one joins the action and the loss if one holds back, against the remote possibility of punishment by the larger society if something goes seriously wrong.*

In putting forth this theory of aleatory risks, or risks strongly affected by a probability process, the investigators conclude that the disposition of gang boys to join the action cannot be explained either by the values they hold or by neurotic or irrational tendencies. Further, the researchers argue, short-run hedonism is not a good explanation because the term implies, wrongly, that an atmosphere of abandon surrounds gang decisions and activities.

As Drs. Strodtbeck and Short see it, in such a loosely organized group as a juvenile gang there tends to be a continuous leakage of status and, therefore, a need for continuously working status-maintaining mechanisms. The boy who participates in a delinquent action wins a slight reward; his status is maintained or even heightened.

To be sure—particularly in the case of fights, since guns and knives are common in lower-class neighborhoods—there is a chance that the action will lead to serious consequences, with some of the participants being hurt, killed, or arrested. But the investigators estimate that not more than a fifth of the cases do have serious consequences to gang members, and they point out that not more than a fifth of the offenses actually committed by gangs studied were known to the police. Hence the risks are likely to appear well worth taking. A boy can avoid all risk by staying aloof, but in that case he suffers a loss of status.

10. *Members of delinquent gangs do not pursue the middle-class goals they espouse because, in part, (a) they don't know how and (b) gang life, which they value, emphasizes behavior incompatible with such pursuit.*

Gang boys can be told how to reach middle-class standards, but the information rarely penetrates to the point where it arouses action. In this respect, Dr. Strodtbeck adds, they are like an inveterate cigarette smoker who is told how he can improve his health.

The investigators believe that the boys mean what they say, both alone and in groups, about such values as getting a job, saving money, getting married. Alone, the boys rate these values highly; in groups, they deride them. In this respect they are like the medical school students who, in another study, were found to speak idealistically about their chosen profession only when alone with the investigator. Contradictory value systems, the study notes, are a mark of modern society, particularly among adolescents.

Gang life, as well as medical school, may be seen as a phase in a person's career. The study explains that no gang boy expects this phase to last forever. The trouble is that involvement in gang life hampers the achievement of values held individually with respect to future phases.

Sex is one example. Among gang boys, as among boys generally, it was found to be a matter of much concern and some anxiety. The pressure of the gang compounds the problem, the investigators explain, because it is harder for gang than for nongang boys to withdraw from sexual competition and excel in some other endeavor. Among the gangs studied, marriage was by no means taboo but "making out" was more highly valued, and the boys who were the gang leaders always had finesse in sexual matters.

Becoming the parent of an illegitimate child apparently does not affect a boy's status one way or the other, and it may actually raise a girl's status. Citing other studies, the investigators observe that the unmarried lower-class Negro girl who becomes pregnant may suppose she has some chance of landing the boy as a husband; in any event, she gets gratifying attention from her female relatives and the social worker. And, Dr. Strodtbeck adds, the financial help she receives from the Aid to Dependent Children program may enable her to pull out and live in slightly more savory surroundings that those at home.

"Both boys and girls," the report concludes, "are caught in a cycle of limited social abilities and other skills. Their disabilities contribute to their worries about status and in this way contribute to involvement in delinquency."

As with sex, so with work. Individually the boys begged the detached workers to help them get jobs, but on the street they bragged about "hustles" of great variety. During one 3-year period, every member of one of the gangs held at least one job, for a time; at the end of the period, not one of the members was employed. The investigators explain that the kind of work such boys can get is generally neither sufficiently well paid nor sufficiently challenging to serve as an acceptable status alternative to the gang. Further, participation in gang activities is not conducive to a good work record, and a good work record is not conducive to participation in gang activities.

One gang member did fall in love with his job as messenger—in part, because it gave him a uniform and a chance to talk to people. He married his girl and began buying furniture and a car. Eventually he was promoted, but the extra money was not enough to meet the credit payments. In addition, the new job kept him from circulating and threatened to expose his limited reading ability. He dropped out of legitimate work and is now a well-paid employee of a group in the numbers racket.

11. *Gang life offers few if any constructive tasks because, in part* (a) *the leaders must choose activities at which most of the members are proficient;* (b) *boys who have found fellowship and other rewards in delinquent activities may find the level of reward in conventional activities too low;* (c) *the leaders know that the easiest way to meet a threat to their status is to engage in delinquent activity.*

Team sports might seem a promising basis for group solidarity, the study notes, but gang boys tend to be aggressively poor losers. The Y.M.C.A. program attempts to get around this handicap by seeing that every team in a tournament gets a trophy—for participation or sportsmanship, if not for winning. The program also appoints influential gang members as "field consultants" at a small salary. Hence, at sports events, consultants from rival gangs know one another and feel bound to some degree to try to keep peace. Without such devices, the study reports, team contests would often erupt into gang warfare.

12. *The fewer the opportunities to which a group is exposed in its own area—for example, recreational centers, counseling agencies, churches, schools, chances to work—the more the group is in trouble with the law.*

Based on interviews concerning "the area where your group hangs out," the study developed *opportunity scores* for each boy studied and for each group. These scores—which reflected the boys' awareness as well as the actual existence of the opportunities—were then compared with the average number of offenses, per group member, known to the police. The table gives the results.

Opportunity Scores versus Delinquent Behavior

Group	Opportunity score	Offenses, per boy, known to police
Negro gangs	9.0	3.14
White gangs	9.3	2.73
Negro lower class	11.0	.47
White lower class	13.7	.31
Negro middle class	15.6	.06
White middle class	20.2	.02

Possibly the most powerful influence against delinquency, Dr. Strodtbeck reports, is the opportunity for a youngster to step into a job as soon as he leaves school. "In Europe," he observes, "when you get out of school, at any level, you can get a job that pays in accordance with the contribution you can make to the production process. You have more trouble doing that here—and more delinquency."

For the Future

The detached worker program, Dr. Strodtbeck reports, has been successfully used to prevent gang fights and is now being experimented with as a gateway to what sociologists call "the opportunity structure." If a boy can become interested in employment, perhaps he can also become interested in going back to school or in getting more education and training some other way. And if the road can be cleared to steady employment for one boy, perhaps he can become a channel through which other boys can be reached. But there are many forces pressing on a gang boy to remain pessimistic about his chances in the larger world.

Research Grant: MH 3301

Reference:

Short, James F., Jr., and Strodtbeck, Fred L. *Group Process and Gang Delinquency.* University of Chicago Press, Chicago, 1965.

Delinquent Girl Gangs

Investigators:
Malcolm W. Klein, Ph. D.
Helen E. Shimota, Ph. D.
University of Southern California
Los Angeles, Calif.

Prepared by:
Gay Luce

Juvenile delinquents, according to court records, account for less than a million offenders in the country. But their impact ramifies, and the social costs of their destructive behavior cannot be evaluated by a head count. A high rate of illegitimacy and a new generation of underprivileged children are among these costs. Because roughly four-fifths of all juvenile arrests are boys, and because their gang activities have been most conspicuous and amenable to study, the preponderance of our information about delinquent gang behavior and background almost omits the part played by girls, an information gap that should be filled if our remedial action programs are to take root.

What is the nature of the delinquent girl gang? How does it influence the boys' gang? Who joins, and how does she differ from her nongang counterparts?

Some answers to these questions have emerged from a study in south central Los Angeles. The neighborhood, 75 percent Negro, was a residential region covering many square miles. Incomes ranged from under $1,000 a year to $10–$15,000. Unlike the congested eastern slum, this was an environment of small houses, duplexes, and apartments, spaced by grass and trees. Less than 2 percent of the adolescent population there belonged to gangs, and the gang membership was often dispersed over a square mile. In the course of an extensive study of gangs and delinquency, the investigators singled out a number of boys' gangs with a membership totaling about 600, and a half dozen or so sister gangs, whose membership amounted to about 150. These were Negroes ranging in age from 12 to 25. Their gangs were in constant metamorphosis, shifting in membership, disbanding, reforming. A rounded picture of these youngsters, their backgrounds, psychometric evaluation, their influence upon one another and opinion of each other was obtained with the help of a variety of Los Angeles agencies, the schools, the police, the juvenile court, and particularly with the aid of special group workers assigned to the gangs by the County Probation Department.

The procedure of collecting information utilized these sources at three levels. In order to search out the interaction and influence of girl and boy gangs upon each other and to determine the nature of these groups, a system of personal interviews was established in which the gang members, detained for a delinquent offense, were asked to describe the role they played, the roles of their associates and of the girls, and to give their own perceptions of the event. These were compared with police records, and with the direct observations of group workers and the study staff. Interestingly enough, the youngsters cooperated well and offered candid descriptions that jibe with the reports of police and group workers.

The half dozen or so girl gangs under scrutiny varied considerably in size, cohesiveness, and activity. One of the larger groups had never met as an organized unit. Another gang concentrated upon making life miserable for schoolmates and fighting girls who were not gang members. The most extreme group indulged in violence, hitchhiking and mugging drivers, robbery, and vandalism. This gang dispersed when many of its members became pregnant, and was succeeded by another gang of 20 younger girls who may be carrying on the tradition.

In the course of the study it became clear that gangs of girls were not as long-lived as boys' gangs. They were indeed dependent units, and with one exception, they all began in relation to a boys' gang. They were characterized by greater turnover in membership, and tended to disband if their brother gang dispersed.

Within the literature on delinquency it has been speculated that sister gangs often play the devil's advocate, inciting violence, starting fights, encouraging greater and grander illegal plans. The findings within the Negro gangs in south central Los Angeles would indicate an opposite effect. By questioning boy-gang members in this area after each incident, it became apparent that girls rarely participated in the planning or action. Frequently, the girl's role was that of an observer on the fringes of theft or assault. When asked how a girl's presence on the scene would influence plans or action, almost half of the boys replied that the accidental presence of girls would have postponed or prevented the event, especially if the plan were a theft. In good measure, the boys' responses were a reflection of a need for esteem. Among the adolescent boys, notably, the girls' opinion weighed heavily, and few of the boys thought they would win respect for attempting an offense and getting caught. In sum, the boy who valued the girls' opinion of him said he would be prevented or delayed in his illegal plan. It seemed that the boys could take chances of being apprehended without worrying about their image, but if a girl actually witnessed the act there would be no way of denying or disclaiming the behavior.

Although the actual pillage and violence perpetrated by these juvenile gangs is probably overdramatized, these are youngsters who disrupt their neighborhoods and schools, use drugs, and destroy more than they construct. They are part of a minority group in an extended ghetto, low in income and high in unemployment. They are a small part of a major social problem under study, a group whom remedial classes and camps, and special resocializing schools can barely hope to help utilize their potential. Perhaps the major burden of their delinquent pattern is borne by the generation beyond their own, for the social cost of their many illegitimate children outweighs the robberies and assaults they conduct today. An understanding of female gangs may indeed make it possible to counteract this trend.

Research Grant: MH 7993
Date of Interview: February 25, 1965

Psychiatric Drugs for Children

Investigator:
Barbara Fish, M.D.
New York University Medical Center
New York, N.Y.

Prepared by:
Herbert Yahraes

An improved method of evaluating the effect of psychiatric drugs on emotionally disturbed children has been developed by the Children's Psychopharmacology Unit of the New York University School of Medicine, Department of Psychiatry, and is being applied to the study of a number of compounds.

The Unit, established in 1961 with the aid of a special grant from the National Institute of Mental Health, is directed by Dr. Barbara Fish, psychiatrist-in-charge of the Children's Service of Bellevue Hospital's psychiatric division.

Dr. Fish and her fellow workers have confirmed that a child's response to a psychiatric drug may be quite different from an adult's. For example, trifluoperazine (Stelazine), a tranquilizer having less sedative action than chlorpromazine, was found to be a stimulating agent when given to retarded schizophrenic children and to be capable, on the basis of preliminary findings, of bringing moderate improvement. The hope is that even more potent agents will be discovered.

To get a trustworthy measure of a drug's effect, the Unit has found it necessary to divide emotionally disturbed children into four general groups and to observe the results of medication in each group. These groups or types, constituting a *clinical typology,* are as follows:

I. Autistic-dysjunctive: severely impaired schizophrenic children.

II. Immature-labile: a borderline group, less severely impaired at present than the children of group I but more severely impaired at present than the children in groups III and IV.

III. Anxious-neurotic: children with predominantly neurotic manifestations. These children show anxiety and feelings of helpless dependence and inadequacy.

IV. Sociopathic-paranoid: children with predominantly sociopathic or paranoid features. These children tend to deny personal responsibility for their feelings and acts; their behavior may be antisocial; they may be overly suspicious.

The children in the first two groups are the most severely disturbed and those in the last two, the least disturbed. The classification is done on the basis of psychiatric interviews. Specially developed rating scales are used to determine the severity of each child's condition before and after treatment.

In one pilot study of children on the psychiatric ward of Bellevue Hospital, the Unit has investigated the effect of chlorpromazine and diphenhydramine on each of the four groups. Chlorpromazine (thorazine) is a widely used tranquilizer; diphenhydramine (benadryl) is an antihistamine that makes some adults sleepy but acts in young children as a mild tranquilizer.

Of the more severly disturbed children—those in groups I and II— 80 percent improved on chlorpromazine and 50 percent on diphenhydramine. None improved when given only a placebo.

However, among the less severely impaired children—those in groups III and IV—the percentage of those who improved on chlorpromazine did not differ significantly from the percentage of those who improved though they received nothing but a placebo. The improvement in several of the chlorpromazine-treated children, however, was more marked. This indicates that a large proportion of the children in groups III and IV get better or worse for reasons having nothing to do with drug action.

To sum up, improvement in the first two groups of children seems to depend primarily upon the effectiveness of the drug being studied and in the second two groups upon such factors as hospitalization, psychotherapy, and special education. If the children in this study had not been classified, chlorpromazine would have appeared effective—that is, better than placebo treatment—for the entire group. In reality it was significantly better only among the severely impaired children.

* * * * *

When drugs are evaluated, the investigators report, children must be matched by age as well as by severity of illness, because some types of treatment are more effective with certain age groups than with others. For example, all the children who improved with diphenhydramine were under 8½ years of age. Older children were not helped by this drug. Again, all those children who improved when receiving only a placebo were more than ten years old. On the other hand, there were children in all age groups who improved with chlorpromazine.

Dr. Fish points that whether or not a particular kind of behavior is abnormal often depends on the age of the child, since behavior appropriate to one age may be immature or markedly deviate if it occurs in an older child. "The simple fact that the child is a growing organism," she observes, "complicates every aspect of the evaluation of psychiatric treatment. . . . One must detect changes produced by therapy in an organism that is already in the process of change."

In a second pilot study, the Children's Psychopharmacology Unit is investigating the effects of trifluoperazine on a number of group I children raning in age from 2 to 6. Trifluoperazine is a tranquilizer used for chronic adult patients. Dr. Fish found several years ago that it increased the alertness and motor drive—and sometimes even the responsiveness and language ability—of severely apathetic, withdrawn, schizophrenic children.

The children selected for the current study showed gross withdrawal and greatly impaired speech. With each child the dose of trifluoperazine was gradually built up to the level at which the drug was doing the most good without causing side effects. With some children the best dose was six times as large as with others. Dr. Fish's team also noticed considerable differences among individuals in the doses of chlorpromazine and diphenhydramine required for best results.

So far only 12 children have been followed in the trifluoperazine study. Four of these have improved on the drug as compared with one in the control group. They show increased alertness and improved language and social ratings. These results, however, are not yet statistically significant.

The investigators are now—
—drawing more children into the study, to make a total of 24;
—trying other potentially stimulating drugs on the children who have not improved on trifluoperazine;
—developing ways to measure changes in alertness, in order to facilitate the rapid screening of compounds.

* * * * *

Dr. Fish estimates that at least 60 percent of severely disturbed children can be moderately improved by presently available drugs. Among children in an outpatient population who were too disturbed to benefit from psychotherapy, drugs enabled one-fourth to go to regular schools and another one-half to participate in group activities and special classes.

Special screening of drugs potentially valuable for disturbed children is essential, the New York University Unit reports, because a drug's action may depend upon the stage of the child's development. This is true in the case of diphenhydramine, but a better known example is phenobarbital, which calms adults but may excite young children. Quite possibly, drugs that are ineffective in adult animals or human beings may prove valuable for children.

The investigators point out that dosages of psychopharmacologic drugs must be determined separately for children and not merely adjusted from adult dosages according to body weight. A dosage that has been scaled down in this manner may be so high for a child as to cause toxic symptoms, or it may be so low as to be ineffective.

Research Grant: MH 4665
Published References:

Fish, Barbara. Drug Therapy in Child Therapy, Psychological Aspects. *Comprehensive Psychiatry,* 1:1, February 1960.
Fish, Barbara. *The Influence of Maturation and Abnormal Development on the Responses of Disturbed Children to Drugs.* Reprinted from proceedings of Third World Congress of Psychiatry, *June 1961.*
Fish, Barbara. *Evaluation of Psychiatric Therapies in Children.* Delivered at the *meeting of the American Psychopathological Association,* February 24, 1962.
Fish, Barbara. *Progress Report to NIMH.* February 1963.
Fish, Barbara and Shapiro, Theodore. *A Typology of Children's Psychiatric Disorders: Its Application to a Controlled Evaluation of Treatment.* Presented at the annual scientific meeting of the Academy of Child Psychiatry, September 1963.

Brief Psychotherapy vs. Drugs: Fitting the Treatment to the Illness

Investigator:
Leon Eisenberg, M.D.*
Johns Hopkins University School of Medicine
Baltimore, Md.

Prepared by:
Herbert Yahraes

Significant findings in the treatment of emotionally disturbed children are reported by a clinical research group at the Johns Hopkins University School of Medicine. The most important result of the work to date, in the view of the group's leader, Dr. Leon Eisenberg, professor of child psychiatry, is its demonstration that effective treatment depends upon accurate diagnosis. The group reports that:

1. Brief psychotherapy—half a dozen sessions—worked a marked improvement in the behavior of disturbed children diagnosed as neurotic.

2. Disturbed children diagnosed as hyperkinetic, or overactive, showed little response to psychotherapy but improved to a significant extent when treated with a stimulating agent. (Such agents have been used for some years with hyperkinetic children; the Johns Hopkins work verifies their effectiveness in a carefully controlled study.)

3. The same stimulating agent markedly improved the behavior of delinquent boys in a training school.

The work suggests that the country's resources for helping disturbed children before they become disturbed adults can be stretched through the wider use in appropriate cases of a short-term course of treatment instead of long-term, intensive psychotherapy.

The research also suggests that certain psychoactive drugs may be useful in the management of institutionalized delinquents. There is at least the possibility that they could make institutionalized youngsters more amenable to training and education and, therefore, less likely to return to antisocial activities.

In current work Dr. Eisenberg and his associates are trying to: (a) Find out how psychoactive drugs work—that is, what functions they affect; (b) find more objective ways of diagnosing disturbed children and measuring the effects of therapy; and (c) provide more information on some of the defects in mental functioning that result in low IQ scores.

---

*Now at the Department of Psychiatry, Massachusetts General Hospital, Boston, Massachusetts

All these studies should lead to improvements in therapy for disturbed children. The investigators hope that the third study will also lead to stronger efforts to prevent reasoning disabilities in children from deprived homes. The recently completed and continuing research of the Hopkins group is presented in more detail in the following sections.

Neurotics and Hyperkinetics

In a project now nearing completion, Dr. Eisenberg undertook to expand the results of earlier work by his group in the Children's Psychiatric Clinic of the Johns Hopkins Hospital. This had shown that disturbed children given a placebo and psychotherapy for 7 weeks were at least as likely to register marked improvement as disturbed children given a tranquilizer and psychotherapy. But the improvement was closely related to the type of disorder. Two-thirds of the neurotic children, but only one-third of the hyperkinetic children, showed substantial gains. Later studies indicated that most hyperkinetics did respond to either of two stimulating agents, dextroamphetamine and methylphenidate.

The investigator describes the neurotic child as shy, introverted, afraid of new situations, inhibited, anxious. Typically the parents complain that he is fearful, won't go out and make friends, can't even be dragged to parties. The hyperkinetic child, in contrast, is distractible and forever on the go. In school he pays attention to every disturbance rather than to the main activities of the class. He does not follow directions. He is often accused of being aggressive because he doesn't keep his hands to himself. His parents complain that they cannot manage him and are afraid he is going to get into serious trouble.

The new project called for both a psychotherapy study with neurotics and a psychopharmacology study with hyperkinetics. Eighty children were selected for each. Ruled out were children whose IQ was less than 80, those who had severe neurological defects, those who were in trouble with the law, or those who were so sick they required institutionalization. "I don't mean you can't treat such patients," Dr. Eisenberg explains. "I mean they were different from the ones in whom we were interested for this particular project. We wanted to define our population carefully."

The children ranged in age from 5 to 13 years. On the basis of parental education, they came from three social classes—middle, lower middle, and lower—but mainly from the first and second of these. The hyperkinetics tended to come from lower social levels than the neurotics and to be younger. Most of the children had been referred to the clinic by the schools and other community agencies; some, by private physicians. In a few cases mothers had called the clinic themselves.

The Value of Brief Psychotherapy

The problem of setting up a control group—untreated persons against whom to compare the treated ones—for the psychotherapy study was particularly difficult. That's because the process of including a person in a study of psychotherapy may in itself be therapeutic. "The moment you talk to a disturbed child and his parents," Dr. Eisenberg points out, "potentially you change them—and if you don't talk to them, you don't know what the child was like at the beginning of the study. Mere questioning may amount to interpretation even when the doctor has not intended to give advice. For example, if the mother says that the child is disobedient and you then ask how she disciplines him, you are implying a connection between his misbehavior and her methods of discipline. You're already giving treatment, so to speak."

The control group in this case was a *consultation-only* group. After the intake process—three sessions of history taking and psychological testing—the parents were told that the child should do well without treatment if certain recommendations were followed. The recommendations were tailored to the case. A mother who was exceptionally harsh or punitive might be advised to let up on the discipline; a mother who was too lenient might be advised to show more firmness. Parents might be given suggestions for improving relations with each other.

The point is that the consultation was limited to one 30-minute period, at the end of which the parents were assured that the child's condition would be checked again after 2 months. (The families in the consultation group were offered treatment after the 8-week period of the study if they wanted it and the doctors thought it desirable.)

In contrast, the experimental group was given *brief psychotherapy,* defined as five additional interviews lasting from 45 minutes to an hour. During these periods the child was seen by a psychiatrist, and one or both parents by a social worker.

After 8 weeks, most of the children had improved, but those in the psychotherapy group significantly more so than the others. This finding was based partly on ratings by the psychiatrists who were treating the children, and such ratings, the grantee points out, may be unintentionally biased. However, the psychiatrists' ratings were confirmed by an independent set of ratings made by the children's teachers, who did not know to which group a child had been assigned. Further, on measures of friendliness and aggresiveness, derived from the mothers' descriptions of the children on a rating instrument known as the Clyde Mood Scale, the children in the psychotherapy group showed a greater change for the better than the others.

The children in the earlier studies who showed improvement were found a year later to be maintaining it. The children in the new study will be followed up, too.

The results of this part of the investigation strengthen Dr. Eisenberg's conviction that psychiatric clinics and psychiatrists in private practice should place considerably more emphasis, in treating disturbed children of the neurotic type, on brief psychotherapy. For one thing, it works. For another, a given clinic or individual psychiatrist can reach more people with it. Further, says the investigator, "Brief psychotherapy makes much more sense to the parents, who in general are grateful for the statement that you will see their child so and so many times instead of the vague, 'Well, it may take a long time.' With brief psychotherapy, there are fewer dropouts."

The results of this form of treatment have not been compared with those of long-term, intensive psychoteraphy, the investigator observes. "But if I were the director of a community agency, with the task of setting up a program for disturbed children that would bring the greatest benefit to the community on a service level," he says, "I would certainly put much more emphasis on brief psychotherapy than has been traditional."

Medicine for Hyperkinetics

In the drug study, 40 of the hyperkinetic children were given either dextroamphetaminé or methylphenidate, commonly used with adult patients as stimulants, and the rest were given a placebo. At the end of the 8-week study period, those who had been receiving a drug were rated both by clinic personnel and by teachers as significantly more improved than the others. As viewed by the mothers, they still scored high in aggressiveness but less than before.

On several objective tests, too, the drug-treated group surpassed the other. One was a discrimination task, in which the children were shown pairs of pictures flashed on a screen in rapid succession and asked to tell which picture in each set was the larger. When the time between the pictures in a set was more than 2 seconds, no change occurred in either group during the course of the study. But at a spacing of 2 seconds the drug-treated group made appreciably fewer errors at the end of the study while the other group showed no change.

The investigators consider a 2-second spacing in this test rather stressful for a child. So the drug takes hold, they think, at the point where performance begins to break down under pressure.

Dr. Eisenberg was especially impressed by the results of the Porteus Maze Test, which calls for the subject to trace his way, with a pencil, through a series of mazes of increasing difficulty. When a child enters a blind alley, he is scored as having failed on that particular maze even though he backs out and continues in the right direction. An impulsive child, then, is likely to end up with a low score. Both groups of hyperkinetic children made poor scores at the beginning of the study. Eight weeks later the placebo group showed no improvement, but the scores of the drug-treated group shot up about 15 points.

Interestingly, the children with the lowest IQ's—all of which were within the normal range—showed the greatest improvement. "Apparently the child who is functioning well," Dr. Eisenberg explains, "isn't going to be driven by the drug to levels of superfunction. But children with relatively low IQ's may have a better potential than the IQ scores indicate. They may not be using it because of their inability to pay attention and to

404

control their motor activity. These are the children who may be helped most, at least in the skills demanded by the maze test."

This reasoning may also explain some of the results of earlier work with emotionally disturbed children in two institutions. In each case, the investigator found a strong trend for the children who had been given a stimulating drug to make fewer mistakes than the others in learning a standard laboratory test. (The children in this preliminary work were not differentiated either by the type of disorder or by IQ scores.)

To test the idea that a stimulating agent improves the learning ability of certain disturbed children by improving their ability to pay attention, Dr. Eisenberg's associate, Dr. C. Keith Conners, has now worked out a way of measuring the latter. The child being tested watches a pattern of lights on a panel and presses a particular light whenever a new pattern appears. He has to keep watching the panel in order to press the right light at the right time. The idea is to learn how many mistakes he will make over a 10-minute period. Once the researchers have baseline rates for disturbed children, they propose to test a variety of psychiatric drugs to learn if the attention span can be favorably altered. If the plan works out, the group will have a way of telling beforehand which kind of drug will affect a given type of child most favorably.

Why should a stimulating agent work with hyperkinetics—children who appear to be already overstimulated? Before answering, Dr. Eisenberg poses a companion question: Why should phenobarbital, a sedative, tend to overexcite children and, often, the elderly? The usual explanation, he goes on, is that interfering with the functions of certain structures of the brain may produce different effects at different stages of development. That is, a given drug has a certain, unchanging pharmacologic effect, but the physiologic expression of this effect depends on the balance among the brain centers, and this balance changes as the brain develops. In the case of stimulating agents, one has to suppose that the drug in some way is improving the inhibitory or control centers of the brains of hyperkinetic children. If scientists can learn how this is done, the search for more effective drugs will be greatly advanced.

Treating Delinquents

Twice within recent years the Hopkins team has gone into a training school and tested the effect of psychoactive drugs on delinquent boys ranging in age from 11 to 17. The first time the team used perphenazine, a tranquilizer. Some of the boys in the study were given the tranquilizer, others a placebo, and the rest nothing. Those who got medicine, whether it was the active drug or the placebo, responded with a substantial improvement in behavior.

"We had altered the social environment," Dr. Eisenberg explains. "All the youngsters wanted to get out, and the medication was something that was supposed to make them better and help them get out sooner. To be in the treatment cottage, where some of the boys were on perphenazine and some on placebo, became a matter of prestige."

The tranquilizer, in other words, had a placebo effect: the boys expected the medicine to make them better and they did get better. In this respect they were just like the boys taking the placebo itself. Failure to allow for such an effect has clouded the results of many a test of new medicines.

When the team returned to the institution, they tested dextro-amphetamine, one of the stimulating agents used successfully with hyperkinetics. The drug was given to some of the boys in each of two cottages and this time the results were quite different. Only the boys receiving the medicine showed a decided improvement in behavior, as rated by houseparents, teachers, and cottage mates. However, there was some improvement among their associates, both those who were untreated and those who received a placebo, and this change may have resulted, the investigators suggest, from a more harmonious atmosphere brought about by the change in the drug-treated boys.

Though the improvement lasted no longer than the treatment, the Johns Hopkins group holds that further research with delinquents along the line it has pioneered is "a compelling social necessity."

"I don't think you can change the symptoms of delinquency merely by medication," Dr. Eisenberg declares. "But if you can diminish a youngster's anger and hostility and aggressiveness so that instead of fighting everything he may be willing to listen to what's said to him, then the ordinary treatment procedures might be more effective."

Putting it another way, medication may lead to improved behavior, and improved behavior may lead to better relationships with houseparents, teachers, and other personnel in a training school, and these better relationships should make possible a more constructive outcome of a boy's training school experience.

So far as Dr. Eisenberg knows, this lead has not been followed up. He points out that most of the facilities for delinquents are not in medical hands and do not have much medical support. Beyond this, when staffs remain underpaid and undertrained, and are hard put, consequently, to work toward the professed goal of reeducation, medicine that might be effective in other circumstances is not likely to do much good.

The investigator doubts that drugs can help the delinquent who remains in his decaying neighborhood and troubled home. Without change in the social circumstances that breed delinquency, he says, the behavior will almost certainly continue. Social rehabilitation is the key to delinquency control; drugs, counseling, and other measures are adjuncts or aids that may be useful and essential—because patterns of antisocial behavior tend to persist—once the environment has been altered.

Tranquilizers

The use of stimulating drugs for hyperkinetics is bound to increase as the result of the recent findings, Dr. Eisenberg believes, while the use of tranquilizing drugs for disturbed children in general should be considerably reduced. He judges that the tranquilizers have been prescribed far too freely in the treatment of children.

No drug is free of hazards, he holds, and no child should be placed on medication unless there is a clear need for it and clear evidence that the chosen medicine is likely to be beneficial. None of his group's three outpatient studies with disturbed children produced evidence of beneficial effects that could be ascribed to the tranquilizers, and he finds little or no evidence in the literature that tranquilizers are of any benefit for the usual child who comes into an outpatient clinic. With the schizophrenic child the story is different.

Diagnosing the Disturbed Child

Because of considerable overlap in types of psychiatrically disturbed children, the John Hopkins group is looking for more objective diagnostic means. Among the numerous measures being studied are the answers to a symptom questionnaire filled out by the parents of the 400 disturbed children treated by the clinic since 1959, when the NIMH began supporting its research. The questionnaire lists 70 symptoms, or types of behavior, and the parent indicates to what extent each of these applies to his child.

Preliminary analysis shows that certain clusters of these symptoms are more characteristic of one type of disturbed child than of the other. Neurotic children register higher on the clusters, or factors, tentatively labeled *inhibited, shy,* and *psychosomatic.* Hyperkinetics register higher on the factors labeled *hyperactive, tantrum behavior, aggressive acting out,* and *sibling rivalry.* The symptoms grouped under the labels *anxious, stubborn, and school problem* seem to apply as much to one type of child as to the other.

In work now going on, the investigators hope to learn if factor scores provide a good diagnostic and prognostic tool and if improvement is related to changes in the scores on particular factors.

Several hundred parents of normal children, approached through PTA's, have filled out the same questionnaire. The researchers wanted to learn if such parents see as many things wrong with their children as the parents who have sought help from the clinic. The answer is that they don't: about 40 of the 70 symptoms were found to have been checked much more frequently for the psychiatric population. Through factor analysis the reseachers expect to come up with a detailed description of how a disturbed child differs from a normal child in terms of behavior as viewed by the parents.

The Thinking Process in Children

The Johns Hopkins group has also undertaken basic research to learn more about the reasoning processes of the developing child and thus to aid in understanding and treating defects in these processes. As Dr. Eisenberg explains it, such work should make it possible in many cases to determine the factors responsible for a low IQ score and do something about them. This phase of the program is the particular interest of Dr. Sonia F. Osler, a psychologist.

Dr. Osler began by testing the ability of normal children to form an idea or concept and by studying the process involved. In the simplest test, the child was shown two pictures at a time, one of a bird and one of something else. The first pair, for example, might show a bluebird and an automobile; the second, a robin and a dog; the third, an airplane and a canary. There was a lever associated with each picture, and the child had to press one of the levers each time. If he pressed the one under the bird picture, he was rewarded with a marble. Sooner or later, most children got the idea that the common denominator or unifying concept was *bird* and pressed the correct lever each time.

In her first study, Dr. Osler presented three concepts—bird, animal, and living thing—to groups of public school children aged 6, 10, and 14 years. Half of the children in each group were of average IQ and half were above average.

Most of the results were predictable. The bird concept proved the easiest to grasp; the living thing concept, the hardest. Older children did better than younger children, and brighter children did better than average children. Interestingly, however, the average and the bright children used different approaches. The average child tended to follow a hit-and-miss process. He would make a random number of mistakes, then begin getting the right answer more frequently, and finally grasp the idea. The brighter children, on the other hand, tended to go along making mistakes and then jump all at once from the random to the perfect level of performance.

The results suggested that while the average child was proceeding blindly on a trial-and-error basis, the brighter one was making guesses or hypotheses and at some point saying, "Ha! Now I see—that's what the answer is!"

To check on this, Dr. Osler devised a test calculated to confuse the hypothesis makers by providing a good deal of irrelevant information. The problem was to get the concept of *two*. One card of a pair might show a dog and a ball; the other, two birds and an automobile. In another pair, one card might show a shoe and a baseball bat; the other, three fire trucks and a cat. In this situation, brightness proved no asset. The higher IQ children, presumably because they had seen and been obliged to discard so many hypotheses, ended up scoring no better than the others.

Next the investigator changed the rules of the game so that right answers were rewarded only one time out of two. This situation bothered both the older children and the brighter children more than the younger children and those of average intelligence—a finding reached by comparing the scores of each group with the scores made when the right answer was rewarded every time. In fact, in some cases age and intelligence proved to be absolute disadvantages; college professors, for example, were stumped by some of the problems handled by the average 6-year-olds. In a test like this, Dr. Eisenberg observes, a person of intelligence and sophistication keeps making hypotheses and discarding them, since none of them rewards him consistently; a 6-year-old thinks less and performs better. The investigator points out that even animals can learn certain types of responses without being rewarded every time.

These results again are taken to indicate that normal children use two approaches in solving problems of the kind presented in these tests. Young children make the responses that a trial-and-error approach leads them to think will pay off at least some of the time. As children grow older, they tend to look for some hypothesis—some rule—that will give them the answer every time. Bright children show the same tendency.

Dr. Osler has these projects under way:

1. An analysis of children's information-processing ability as shown by their responses to a new series of tests in which the amount of irrelevant information is systematically varied. The investigator is learning how much information, of the kinds presented in this research, can be handled by normal children of a given age. She is also learning just where the concept-forming process breaks down when a failure occurs.

2. Comparisons between normal and retarded children and between normal and disturbed children.

3. Comparisons between the normal children studied so far, all of them from good neighborhoods, and children from slum areas. Since other investigators have found that deprived children lag in intellectual development, the Hopkins group expects that the slum-area children will have considerably more difficulty with the tests. This would be an indication either that they had less native ability to form concepts or draw logical inferences, or that for some reason they were hampered in using that ability. The research group believes the second explanation to be the true one. Specifically, they believe that difficulty with the tests could be traced to backgrounds so impoverished that the children had had little experience with materials like those used in the tests—not only in the variety of pictures but also in objects of different sizes, shapes, and colors. If the comparison gives the expected results, the investigators will test their line of reasoning by training some of the slum-area children beforehand to recognize these materials.

Through this phase of the work, in sum, the investigators are looking for evidence that a lag in a child's reasoning ability may be caused by a deficiency in experience instead of in intellect, and can therefore be prevented or corrected.

Service and Research

In discussing the implications of recent findings by his group and others, Dr. Eisenberg stresses two compelling mental health needs: to act more effectively on the basis of what we already know and to make greater efforts to get the answers to what we still do not know.

One thing we already know is that disturbed children are more likely than other children to become disturbed adults; hence it is good preventive psychiatry to reach these children. And child psychiatrists could reach many more of them, the investigator observes, by following the implications of two of the findings reported earlier, as to the value of brief psychotherapy for neurotic disorders in childhood and of psychiatrically supervised treatment for delinquents in an institution.

A clinical study by Dr. Eisenberg a few years ago when he was a consultant to Baltimore's welfare department suggests a third way of making our psychiatric resources go father. At that time he talked with a number of disturbed children from foster homes, discussed each child with the social worker in charge of the case, and made recommendations. These had to do with such matters as advising the foster parents to modify their treatment of the child in some respect, finding a different school, or getting the child interested in such an organization as the Boy Scouts. They did not include psychotherapy, because there was none to be had, or medication.

When the records of the welfare department were checked a year later, those children for whom the recommendations had been carried out were found to have made a much better adjustment than the others. (In the other cases the recommendations had not been carried out for such reasons, generally, as that the caseworker had become overloaded or had been transferred, or that a certain facility was not available in the child's neighborhood.) This study was not so rigorous as one might like, Dr. Eisenberg observes, but it does offer evidence that if psychiatrists are used to enhance the effectiveness of other mental health workers, a greater number of disturbed children can be helped.

Dr. Eisenberg points out that while measures to reach disturbed children are essential, preventive psychiatry will be most effective if it helps correct the conditions that lead to disturbances in children. To this end he holds that psychiatrists must go beyond the clinic and the consulting room and work with other professional people to broaden the availability, or improve the effectiveness, or both, of family planning programs, good health care, decent housing, training for displaced workers, casework services to minimize family breakdown, substitute-care for homeless children, enriched school programs, and the like. Some deprived children manage to grow into functioning adults, he observes, but far too many contribute to statistics on delinquency and disease: "They become premature and inadequate parents themselves, fated to repeat for a succeeding generation the cycle of deprivation."

In spite of research achievements in the last decade or so, Dr. Eisenberg emphasizes, our knowledge about preventing and treating psychiatric illness has serious limitations. For example, we don't know how psychoative drugs work, so we cannot see clearly how to get better ones. We have no completely acceptable system for classifying children's psychiatric disorders—an impediment both in treatment and in research. For a number of reasons—including the placebo effect, the lack of fully reliable techniques for measuring changes in attitudes and personalities, and the possibility that even in double-blind studies the investigator will detect the children who have been receiving the medication—it is extremely difficult to gauge scientifically the worth of a given form of treatment.

Psychiatrists are charged with relieving suffering, Dr. Eisenberg notes, but if they are to do this most effectively psychiatry must acquire additional knowledge and new skills. Hence, though there is an urgent need for more psychiatric service, there is also an urgent need for a heavier investment of psychiatric personnel in research.

Research Grant: MH 2583
Date of Interview: Apr. 14-15, 1965

References:

Conners, C. K., Eisenberg, L., & Sharpe, L. Effects of methylphenidate (Ritalin) on paired-associate learning and Porteus Maze performance in emotionally disturbed children. *J. Consult. Psychol.,* 1964, 28, 1.

Cytryn, L., Gilbert, Anita, & Eisenberg, L. The effectiveness of tranquilizing drugs plus supportive psychotherapy in treating behavior disorders of children: a double-blind study of eighty outpatients. *Amer. J. Orthopsychiat.,* 1960, 30, 1.

Eisenberg, L. *The Strategic Deployment of the Child Psychiatrist in Preventive Psychiatry.* Presented at the World Congress of Psychiatry, Montreal, 1961.

Eisenberg, L. The sins of the fathers: urban decay and social pathology. *Amer. J. Orthopsychiat.,* 1962, 32, 1.

Eisenberg, L. Role of drugs in treating disturbed children. *Children,* 1964, 11, 5.

Eisenberg, L., Conners, C. K., & Sharpe, L. *A Controlled Study of the Differential Application of Outpatient Psychiatric Treatment for Children.* Presented at the Sixth International Congress of Pscyhotherapy, London, 1964.

Eisenberg, L., Gilbert, Anita, Cytryn, L., & Molling, P. A. The effectiveness of psychotherapy alone and in conjunction with perphenazine or placebo in the treatment of neurotic and hyperkinetic children. *Amer. J. Psychiat.,* 1961, 117, 12.

Eisenberg, L., Lachman, R., Molling, P. A., Lockner, A., Mizelle, J. D., & Conners, C. K. A. psychopharmacologic experiment in a training school for delinquent boys. *Amer. J. Orthopsychiat.,* 1963, 33, 3.

Osler, Sonia F., & Shapiro, Sandra L. Studies in concept attainment: IV. The role of partial reinforcement as a function of age and intelligence. *Child Develpm.,* 1964, 35.

New Approaches to the Treatment of Very Young Schizophrenic Children

Investigator:
Marian K. DeMyer, M.D.
Indiana University School of Medicine
Indianapolis, Ind.

Prepared by:
Herbert Yahraes

In a broad-front research attack on early childhood schizophrenia, the Indiana University School of Medicine is searching for causes, collecting information to facilitate diagnosis, and experimenting with promising new ways of treatment.

The program is headed by Dr. Marian K. DeMyer, a children's psychiatrist and director of the medical school's Clinical Research Center for Early Childhood Schizophrenia, housed in the La Rue D. Carter Memorial Hospital, Indianapolis. This hospital contains the State's residential treatment institution for disturbed children.

The children most intensively studied are inpatients at the Center. When admitted they are between 2 and 5 yars old. In general, they cannot get along with adults or other children, fly easily into rage, either do not speak at all or else use language in odd and incomprehensible ways, do not listen to directions, find little pleasure in play, and show a remarkably narrow range of interests. Some of them twirl or rock themselves for long periods; others bite or hit themselves. They often seem unsure of who or what they are.

Some of these children have been diagnosed as *autistic*, a type of childhood schizophrenia marked by a withdrawal from other people; others as *symbiotic*, a type in which the child physically clings to his mother. Because some of the children display, at different times, each of these characteristics, Dr. DeMyer classes them as *symbiotic-autistic*. Still other patients suffer from what Dr. DeMyer labels *chronic undifferentiated schizophrenia*. Their behavior is less abysmally abnormal than that of the autistic and symbiotic children; they have some conversational ability and usually show some conformance to social amenities.

Investigations under way are directed toward:

- presenting detailed descriptions of the behavior of various types of schizophrenic children and of other children with psychiatric disorders;
- learning how, if at all, the preschool schizophrenic child differs biologically from normal children and whether or not the differences are responsible for his illness;

412

- learning whether or not certain influences in the home, notably the personalities of the parents and the way the parents treat the child, contribute to the onset of childhood schizophrenia;
- determining the value of several new approaches to treatment.

So far the Center's research program has led to two results of major importance.

First, out of a group of 149 young psychiatric patients, 51 percent were found to have clearly abnormal electroencephalograms and 15 percent had experienced at least one epileptic-like seizure.

In each instance the proportion would have been higher had borderline cases been counted. The abnormalities would be found in less than 1 percent of any randomly selected normal population.

The patients included neurotics, childhood schizophrenics of all types, and children with a severe but nonpsychotic behavior disorder, marked by such activities as stealing, setting fires, attacking other children and adults, and refusing to get along in school. A high proportion of abnormal EEG's was found among all the patients except the neurotics.

The results are important because they indicate that many children who are mentally ill have a physical impairment of the brain. The possibility that the impairment signals an effect of the illness rather than a cause, Dr. DeMyer observes, cannot yet be ruled out. Current studies of schizophrenic and nonschizophrenic children may turn up clues to the origin of the impairment.

Before the EEG study, Dr. DeMyer had leaned to the psychogenic explanation of most psychiatric illness and had given only superficial consideration to organic factors. "As the result of this study, done in a careful way and using the severest criteria for EEG dysrhythmias," she notes, "I knew that our research program would have to include a careful study of the central nervous system and other biological matters."

Second, conditioning principles similar to those used in training animals—and to those often used, unknowingly, by parents in training their children—have been successfully applied to improving the behavior of severely schizophrenic children and broadening the activities of which they are capable.

Under the Center's new treatment program, called the *semester system,* the child goes through cycles of 5 months at the center and 7 months at home, and the staff works first of all to make him easier to live with. It tries to correct those behaviors the parents have found most disruptive of family life and it instructs the parents how to handle him. In accordance with conditioning theory, desired behavior is rewarded, both with food and with a "social reinforcer" such as praise, and undesired behavior is ignored or is associated with an "aversion stimulus" such as physical restraint.

Proposed by Dr. Don Churchill, children's psychiatrist and the Center's assistant director, the semester system was introduced in the fall of 1965 with the admission of four new patients. In all these cases, after the children had gone home for a 7-month stay, the parents reported they were having much less, if any, difficulty with the particular kinds of

413

behavior they had identified as the most troublesome. The system is now being used with all the Center's inpatients—11 at present.

How many times a child will return for the 5-month hospital cycle remains uncertain. But Dr. Churchill observes that he is not interested merely in improving behavior and has not thrown overboard the psychoanalytic concepts in which he was trained; he just doesn't find these concepts very useful in working with extremely sick children. According to psychoanalytic theory, the therapist establishes a relationship with a mentally ill person and uses this relationship to induce normal behavior. But with most children like those at the Center, Dr. Churchill notes, it has been extremely difficult both to establish a relationship and to effect much improvement. If a certain amount of normal behavior is first trained into such severely ill children, the investigator suggests, they may show more interest in the adults about them, and the therapeutic relationship will follow and be fruitful. In any event, the trained-in normal activities may crowd out at least some of the customary abnormal ones.

As one promising way of training in normal behavior, the Center has been experimenting with a technique for inducing a schizophrenic youngster to imitate specific actions of the therapist. The first results are exciting: two of the most severely sick children have been trained to imitate several hundred simple activities and to say a few dozen words. To Dr. Joseph N. Hingtgen, the psychologist in charge of this work, the preliminary outcome suggests that the schizophrenic process is not completely irreversible—that perhaps even terribly withdrawn children can be brought up to something approaching the normal level.

Dr. Hingtgen emphasizes that he is speaking on the basis of only a few cases—two of his own, and several reported by another psychologist, Dr. O. Ivar Lovaas, who works at the University of California, Los Angeles, and whose ideas have influenced the Indianapolis group. Further, the technique requires such an immense amount of work that only a relatively few children could be helped if it had to be administered professionally. But Dr. Hingtgen finds that it can easily be taught to parents. The basic idea is that normal children, to a great extent, learn by imitating adults. Gravely psychotic children, however, pay no attention to adults and, therefore, fail to imitate. They have to be *trained* to imitate so that they can learn to behave normally. The training can be accomplished through many long and laborious sessions in which the child is rewarded for doing what the therapist—or the parent—does, beginning with such simple activities as holding up a finger. Eventually the child begins to imitate the adult spontaneously, and even to do what the adult requests.

This imitative learning technique fits in nicely with the ideas and practices of the new semester system and, depending on the results of current work, may eventually be tried with all the children at the Center.

More information about the findings noted, together with a brief report of some of the other research of the Indianapolis group, follows.

Abnormal EEG's in Young Psychiatric Patients

The EEG study was part of the research seeking to describe the anatomical, biochemical, and physiological makeup of the preschool schizophrenic child. Among the children tested were 58 diagnosed as autistic, symbiotic, or symbiotic-autistic, 44 with chronic undifferentiated schizophrenia, 37 with a nonpsychotic behavior disorder, 10 as neurotics, and 13 with normal controls. They were from 4 to 10 years old. Since most of the psychiatric patients fought against the test, the EEG's in virtually all the cases were taken after the children had been calmed by a tranquilizer, promazine—given in too small a dose, Dr. DeMyer reports, to affect the pattern of electrical discharges.

As noted earlier, 51 percent of the psychiatric patients were found to have abnormal EEG's, a proportion that would have been slightly higher had the neurotics, only one of whom showed an abnormality, been omitted. All of the normal children had normal EEG's. Among the children with nonpsychotic behavior disorders of the acting-out type and among those with the various types of schizophrenia, there were no significant differences in the proportion of abnormalities; also, the types of abnormalities were the same and were present to about the same extent. Most characteristic was the type of activity described as paroxysmal spike and wave (PSW), which consists of a mixture of synchronous spikes and slow waves. This type appeared in almost two-thirds of the children with abnormal EEG's.

The EEG study, which was directed by two neurologists—Drs. Philip T. White and William DeMyer—in cooperation with the investigator, opens several important questions, including:

1. *What relationship has the central nervous system disorder, demonstrated in half of the psychiatric patients, to the abnormal behavior of these children?*

On the basis of this and previous studies, the investigators answer, it seems established that at least the EEG abnormality labeled PSW has more than a chance relationship to disturbed behavior. This means that in seeking the causes of childhood schizophrenia and other psychiatric disorders, the role of cerebral dysfunction cannot be ignored. But the exact relationship between abnormality and behavior remains to be discovered. One puzzling fact is that most children with epilepsy, who have EEG abnormalities similar to those found in this study, have normal social and intellectual skills and behave normally except during a seizure. In the children with schizophrenia and behavior disorders the EEG abnormalities presumably could be the result of biochemical changes caused by the stress associated with psychiatric illness. But they could also be one aspect of an organic disturbance, congenital or acquired very early in life, directly responsible for the illness.

2. *Why did only about half of the psychiatric patients show abnormal brain waves?*

One possible answer, says the investigator, has to do with the electroencephalographic technique itself, which cannot pick up all abnormalities.

415

Another possibility has to do with the way abnormalities are defined. The Indianapolis study counted only those variations in the EEG that were distinctly different from normal; now the records are being reexamined to determine the effect of taking borderline changes into account. Previous EEG studies of psychiatrically disturbed children. Dr. DeMyer recalls, reported abnormalities in as low as 2 percent of the patients, and in as high as 90 percent. She thinks that biases both in psychiatric diagnosis and in EEG diagnosis explain part of this wide range.

As still another possibility, the sampling may have been inadequate, meaning that many of the records which were normal for the particular hour when they were made might have been abnormal if made at some other time. The investigator points out that even persons with epilepsy often have normal records except when seizures are occurring; perhaps, she reasons, the records of most psychiatric patients would show abnormalities if taken at times of intense anxiety or shortly afterward. A study in which brain waves would be picked up and telemetered to a recording station, by an apparatus worn by the child, throughout a day of usual activity is being planned.

There is the possibility, too, that a number of the children with normal records will show abnormal ones a little later in life.

The Center is preparing a laboratory to get further information about the brain's electrical activity in psychiatric patients by recording cerebral-evoked potentials, meaning the brain's electrical responses to external stimuli—a light, a touch, a sound. The subjects will be schizophrenic children whose EEG's are normal. Normal and retarded children will be tested the same way.

3. *Do the families of patients who show no EEG abnormalities differ significantly from the families of those who do?*

In the EEG study, no attempt was made to evaluate the families. However, a study nearing completion, in which families with a schizophrenic child are being compared with one another and with matched families whose children are normal, should provide an answer. The subject bears upon the genesis of childhood schizophrenia. Another investigator, working with somewhat older children, found that children showing no organic impairment came from more deeply disturbed families than the others, the implication being that in some cases an organic impairment contributes to the onset of schizophrenia, but in other cases—where the family is seriously disturbed—schizophrenia can develop whether or not something is organically wrong.

Dr. DeMyer and her associates have also used the EEG to study the sleep and dream patterns of seven schizophrenic children hospitalized at the Center. Their sleep habits at home, the parents reported, had been extremely erratic. At the Center, though, the staff considered their sleep to be remarkably regular, and the records of brain waves and eye movements during sleep showed that these children spent the same proportion of time in the dreaming stage as normal children. This study, then, finds no evidence to back up the suggestion that patients may hallucinate in the waking state because they have been unable to hallucinate as much as other persons during sleep.

Earlier Experiments in Conditioning

The Center's use of conditioning techniques—with promising results—follows a series of experiments to find ways of getting very sick youngsters to come out of their shells and act more normally toward people and things.

In one of the earlier experiments, directed by Dr. C. B. Ferster, an autistic child would spend an hour or two, every day, in a room containing such fascinating equipment as a pinball machine, an electric train set, a phonograph, a picture viewer, a telephone set, a trained monkey in a cage, and vending machines. Each device could be operated by the child if he put a coin in the proper slot (in the case of the monkey, the coin turned on a light in the cage and the animal went into his act); and the child could get the coins by pressing a key that operated a coin-dispensing machine.

Rats and cats will learn to keep pressing a bar, and pigeons to keep pecking at a disc, if such activity occasionally brings them food. This learning process is known as operant conditioning because it gets the subject to work, or operate, in a desired manner. The same principle held good with the schizophrenic children. They learned that by pressing the key often enough, they would get a coin good for any of the devices, and soon they spent most of their time working for coins and spending them. The most popular devices by far were the candy vending machines.

Dr. Ferster's next question was whether or not the same technique could be used to help the child understand more difficult situations and engage in more complex behavior—an important question because one of the most marked characteristics of schizophrenic children is their extremely narrow range of activity.

In one of the new situations, coins were delivered only when a panel on the dispensing machine was lighted. In another, a device could be operated only if a coin was placed in a slot when the slot was lighted. A more difficult task required the child, if he were to get a coin, to compare two colors or figures or pictures and touch the one that matched a third, which he had been previously trained to touch. Dr. Ferster's question was answered in the affirmative, even the autistic children came to understand and master the new situations, though more slowly than normal children.

To sum up, the study found that children who rarely had taken any account of their environment could soon begin, through the use of conditioning techniques, not only to notice the environment but also—by pressing keys, matching pictures, and dropping coins—to manipulate it. True, the environment was artificial and the behavior needed to control it a little out of the ordinary. But the results were taken to indicate, in these schizophrenic children, "at least the existence of normal processes at a

417

very basic level," with no suggestion of an underlying deficit except in the rate at which the children learned.

The next question was whether or not a similar laboratory situation could be used to teach socially adaptive behavior—specifically, interaction with other children. Normal youngsters in a preschool group are almost constantly interacting: by playing together, for example, grabbing each other's toys, and fighting. But schizophrenic children hold themselves aloof.

In research directed by Dr. Hingtgen, the Center tried to develop cooperative behavior in some of its children. Only two machines were used—the coin dispenser, set to deliver one coin for every 15 presses of the key, and a vending machine offering candy, crackers, and cereal. Six children participated. After each had been trained to operate the machines, they were paired, and for the rest of the experiment both members of a pair went to the laboratory room together.

For a while, each member of a pair, A and B, was free to operate the coin lever at any time. When it was operated by A, a panel behind the lever showed red; when it was operated by B the panel showed green.

Step 2 required a little cooperation because A could operate the lever only when the panel showed red, and B only when it showed green. After one child received a coin, the other child's light was presented. The children learned by trial and error that they had to take turns.

In step 3, the children had to use a two-key panel in another part of the room. One key could be illuminated by a red light; the other by a green. When the red light was on and A pressed the corresponding key, the coin lever showed red; then A could go to work to get a coin.

In the final step, when A pressed the red-light key, the coin lever showed green, and B could operate the machine; when B pressed the green-light key, the light on the coin machine went red for A. Thus A and B had to work for each other by providing the appropriate coin-lever light.

Starting with step 2, the children learned to work for each other in an average of 23 sessions.

To the investigators' surprise, in view of earlier observations of schizophrenic children at play, the youngsters in this particular situation frequently made physical contact with each other. One would lead the other to the correct lever, or one would operate the correct lever by manipulating the other youngster's hand, or one would pull the other away from the coin lever or from the vending machine.

In one session a 4-year-old boy was working at a very low rate. He had to press the coin lever 15 times in order to be rewarded, but he often stopped and began twirling. Since his partner, a 6-year-old girl, could not go to work for her coin until he received his, she began pulling him back to the lever whenever he wandered off. Once she slapped him, and his response rate went up. Another time, a slap set him to crying and he refused to use the machine at all. After a long period, she went over to him, hugged him around the neck and led him back to the lever; his response rate went up. In later sessions, she slapped him at times, hugged him at others.

All the children appeared to be communicating with their partners through vocal and facial expressions, and two of the less seriously disturbed used words—"That's the red light." "That's enough." "Get the coin."

This social interaction, however, did not carry over from the experimental room to life outside. Evidently young schizophrenic children were capable of modifying their usual behavior, but how could the modifications be made to stick?

The next experiment tested the effect of directly rewarding the children for making physical contact with each other. The mechanical devices were not used: an observer simply handed the children a small piece of candy or a bit of a cookie or cracker whenever they performed the desired behavior. In the first stage the children were rewarded whenever one touched the other. The required behavior was made gradually more complex until, in the end, the reward was given only when the child touched the other with both hands and said something, whether comprehensible or not.

This time there was a little more carryover. Parents and ward personnel reported that the children would come up to them once in a while, touch them, and make a sound or two. But this social behavior died out in a few weeks, presumably because it no longer brought the kind of reward that had been used in developing it.

The research group then tackled one phase of an old and basic problem: why the severely schizophrenic child does not respond like a normal child to what he hears and sees. Clinicians are satisfied that he *can* hear and see, in spite of the many indications he may give to the contrary, particularly in the matter of hearing. But sometimes, apparently, he shuts out his perceptions, and other times, apparently, he fails to organize them—at least he does not act upon them in normal fashion. Part of the trouble, some investigators have thought, may be an inability to discriminate among stimuli.

Dr. Hingtgen used an auditory discrimination test with six of the children. First a child would learn that by pressing a lever often enough he would get a coin, which he could use to obtain candy from a vending machine. Then the experimenter fixed the dispenser so that it would drop coins only when music was playing. Like rats, pigeons, and normal children in earlier experiments, the schizophrenics soon learned to work at the dispenser only during periods of music; in other words, they learned to discriminate between music and silence.

The children also showed they could discriminate between speech (the voice of someone reading a story) and silence, and between speech and music. Then the investigators tried single words, in pairs. When a voice said *chalk,* for example, the machine was operating; when the voice said *ball,* it wasn't. Of the six children being tested, all except one learned to distinguish even between words, like *mama* and *apple,* that are rather similar phonetically. Again, though, the learning took longer than with normal children.

If schizophrenic children have this power of auditory discrimination, why don't they use it all the time? Maybe, Dr. Hingtgen ventures, it's a matter of paying attention, and perhaps they pay attention only when they are going to get something—and when that something meets such a basic need as for food.

The researchers were discussing ways of testing this and other possibilities, and of putting the findings to practical use, when Dr. Lovaas, the University of California psychologist mentioned earlier, came to the school of medicine and described some of his work with young schizophrenics. He, too, was using rewards—and punishments, also—but in a nonautomated situation, and with just one adult and a child working together, intensively. He theorized that a schizophrenic child fails to learn because he fails to imitate, and he fails to imitate because he doesn't associate paying attention with reward. Once the child has been taught to pay attention and to imitate, he can start learning on his own.

What was new here was not the general learning-by-imitation concept but its systematic and intensive application to schizophrenic children. One of the aspects that impressed the Indianapolis group was the comparative simplicity of the technique. You present the child with a model, or example, of the type of thing you want him to do. He imitates you. You reward his imitation. This is easier than waiting for the child to perform, more or less accidentally, the behavior you have in mind, then rewarding him for it and going on to shape that behavior by rewarding him for increasingly complex variations. Getting two children to the point where they were touching one another with both hands and saying something required as many as 30 daily sessions of at least an hour each.

But the most hopeful aspect of the learning-by-imitation concept was the possibility that eventually the schizophrenic child would come to imitate spontaneously. As Dr. Churchill puts it: "To teach a child separately every little thing he has to learn in the course of his growing up is patently impossible. But if we can teach a child to imitate others, there is the hope that the learning process will become more automatic—will not stop at the end of the learning session, but continue through the day."

The Indianapolis investigators decided to test the new technique—modified, though, to omit punishment—with some of the children at the Center.

Tommy was first. He was six-and-a-half, a mute child with a very narrow range of behavior. He had been subjected to every available type of therapy, but in 3 years at the Center had shown no significant improvement.

He was taken off the ward, given his own room, and kept there for 20 days. Every morning about 8 o'clock Dr. Hingtgen and Mrs. Susan Coulter, his research assistant, would come in when Tommy got up, and every evening about 8 o'clock they would put him to bed. They were there at least eight of the intervening hours and—so that he would come to associate food and drink with the adults who were asking him to imitate them—gave him all his meals.

The investigators aimed to get three types of imitation. One was imitation in use of body parts—touching two fingers together, for example. Another was imitation in use of objects—from so simple an activity as picking up a pencil to so complicated a one as using scissors to cut out a picture. The third, since Tommy was mute, was imitation of sounds and speech.

Like other seriously schizophrenic children, Tommy generally avoided looking at adults, so the first sessions were rather wearing. The procedure went like this. One of the teachers—Dr. Hingtgen and Mrs. Coulter alternated—would seat Tommy in a chair directly in front of him and say, "Tommy, look here. Clap your hands." And the teacher would clap his own hands. At the beginning, Tommy would not clap his hands. So the teacher would clap his hands for him, to demonstrate what was wanted, and give him a piece of candy or sugar-coated cereal or some other food. The idea was that Tommy could not get out of his chair—he was held in by the teacher's legs if necessary—until he had done what his teacher wanted him to do. Fussing and crying did no good. After 20 minutes or so, Tommy clapped his hands.

When the boy had learned 15 or 20 imitative responses through such a grueling process, he began imitating immediately. For example, Dr. Hingtgen folded his hands in a rather complex fashion, and Tommy, though he had never before seen him do this, did it himself right away.

Sometimes the boy would try doing the same thing over and over, only to find that repetitive responses were not rewarded; so he would stop making them. For the sake of the reward, he learned to watch his teachers very carefully.

Tommy's use of objects had been limited and bizarre. He would busy himself for hours with ritualistic-like activities, such as moving a piece of string back and forth in front of his eyes or tearing paper to bits. Consequently, getting him to imitate the investigators' use of objects was especially difficult. He got around to picking up a pencil and drawing a straight line on a piece of paper only after 3 hours of work—spread over several days, for the sake of everyone's nervous system. But once he drew the straight line, it was easier to get him to draw X's, squares, and circles.

Learning to fold a piece of paper once and then to fold it again took 5 hours.

Getting him to use scissors was a traumatic experience, too. He watched Mrs. Coulter use them and he wanted to hold them but had no idea how. Eventually she used tape to help keep them in place, and in 2 hours she got him to make one little cut in paper. After a number of additional sessions, he was cutting out circles and squares.

Working like that 7 days a week, the investigators would go home "a bit edgy," Dr. Hingtgen recalls, but once the behavior started coming, a session with Tommy was rewarding as well as exhausting.

Getting this mute youngster to make sounds and say words proved to be, as expected, the most difficult part of the process. Since Tommy had no idea what to do with his mouth in order to voice a word, the teachers began by having him imitate the position of the mouth necessary for forming a given sound. In the case of the "ah" sound, for example, Tommy was rewarded at first merely for pointing to his chin and opening his mouth; later he had to make the sound.

To teach him the "P" sound, the teachers brought in a harmonica, which Tommy knew how to use. As he blew it, they would take it away and reward him for continuing to blow. After a long session, he finally came to voice the required sound every time the investigators offered it.

At the end of the 3 weeks, Tommy would say 18 words, imitatively. Some words were very clear—*baby, mama, daddy, puppy*. Some were approximations—*feer* instead of *finger*. He also had more than 150 imitative responses, including standing, running, and jumping, that required him to make use of his body. And he had more than 100 uses of objects.

He was doing all these things only imitatively. But he was imitating consistently and paying consistent attention to the two adults closest to him. At this point, Tommy was returned to the ward, and Dr. Hingtgen and Mrs. Coulter began teaching the learning-by-imitation technique to the nurses and other personnel and to Tommy's parents. The emphasis now was not merely on increasing his imitative repertory, but also on getting him to attach meaning to his various responses, particularly the vocal ones. After 2 more months of morning and afternoon sessions—in the hospital 5 days a week, at home on weekends—Tommy had about 30 words to which he attached meaning. For example, when a teacher pointed to her nose Tommy said *nose*; when she held up a picture of a puppy, he said *puppy*.

Whatever the original cause of early childhood schizophrenia, Dr. Hingtgen believes a youngster persists in his withdrawn attitude and bizarre behavior because he has learned that he can get by without doing anything his parents want. "At home," the investigator points out, "the parents have never been able to command as much from the child as we have because they have not been able to invest so much time. Also, they never think of spending 3 hours trying to get him to hold a pair of scissors, for example, because no normal child requires that long.

"Some authorities have thought that these children really cannot learn, but our idea is that they are very adept at learning how *not* to learn—how not to have to do something." At the beginning of Tommy's training, for example, the boy would giggle or laugh instead of trying to do what had been requested. Then he'd act as if he were going to cry. Then he'd try to fight his way out of the chair, and he might break into real tears. But the investigators would not go away, and they would not cease making their demand, so eventually Tommy would come out with the behavior they wanted. Since Tommy's avoidance behavior, as psychologists call it, was never successful, within 3 weeks he stopped using it.

The same technique has brought similar results in another autistic child, 5-year-old Peggy, who had been even more withdrawn at the beginning than Tommy.

422

Don't the children get tired of the rewards—become literally fed up? Tommy and Peggy did not, although they were eating almost continuously during the 3 weeks of intensive treatment, and each gained about a pound a week. But the rewards were very small; one potato chip would be broken into six or eight pieces.

Then, too, the food reward was coupled with two other reinforcement measures. One was the easing of physical restraint if such restraint had been necessary, as at first it generally had been. The other was *social reinforcement*. Whenever Tommy made the appropriate response, the investigator would say, "Good boy, Tommy"—or hug him, or give him a ride around the room, or just touch him. In an earlier study, the Indianapolis team had tried using social reinforcers alone to improve the behavior of children like Tommy, and the gains had been neither very large nor consistent. But when Tommy and Peggy had finished their intensive treatment, the investigators found it possible to reduce the frequency of the food rewards and count more and more on the social reinforcers alone. "One theory of learning," Dr. Hingtgen observes, "is that all social reinforcers gain their strength by having been initially paired with food and warmth. Hopefully, at some point in the training of these children, social reinforcers—paired only occasionally with food—will be sufficient."

Because only certain behaviors are rewarded—those the adults request and demonstrate—the children do not become automatons, doing everything they see their teachers do. Eventually, it is hoped, the habits they are learning, of paying attention and of doing what is asked and demonstrated, will take hold to such an extent that the children will spontaneously imitate behavior—including speech, play activities, use of household equipment—that normal children imitate. Tommy and Peggy do a little of this now. They also obey some simple instructions even when no demonstration is given.

Dr. Hingtgen throws in a cautioner. Both Tommy and Peggy have been significantly improved but are still a long way from where they should be, considering their ages. So the question is: How far can you take such children through the use of this technique? On the basis of Dr. Lovaas's work, Dr. Hingtgen notes, there is evidence that at least some severely schizophrenic children can be brought into a classroom situation. Whether or not they will ever be normal, no one cay say.

Further, this investigator emphasizes, the technique has been used with probably not more than half a dozen children. "So we don't know yet whether this is a valid technique for all early child schizophrenics," he observes, "or whether those six just happened to be ones that it worked with."

The Indianapolis group, though, has made headway in answering some other questions about the technique. For one thing, its application can be made less strenuous for the teacher than Tommy's case may suggest. Tommy was isolated for 3 weeks and all the shaping of his behavior was done by two persons. Peggy, too, was isolated, but half a dozen persons guided the conditioning process. Dr. Hingtgen now suspects, and will try to confirm, that the same results can be obtained if the child continues to live on the ward instead of being isolated when the conditioning process begins. The investigator also plans to test his idea that the technique, after the intensive preliminary treatment, can be used with two or three children at a time. As he sees it, hospital care might then consist mainly of a series of classes in which the children would learn to imitate various kinds of responses. Sometimes the child would be with a small group; sometimes alone with a therapist or another adult.

In many cases, this investigator believes, it will be good for the parents to come right into the hospital and work with the child on a regular basis, as Tommy's and Peggy's mothers have been doing. "This is a very simple technique," he points out, "and can be taught to anybody: simply rewarding the child at the appropriate time and withholding reward at the appropriate time."

Among the basic questions still to be answered is how many models of behavior a schizophrenic child must be trained to imitate before he begins imitating on his own.

The Semester Program

As noted earlier, the Center now uses conditioning techniques with all its patients in an effort to correct those behaviors in a child that have most upset the family. Though the application is less intensive than the process used with Tommy and Peggy, the techinques are basically the same. While the children are in the hospital, the parents, individually and in groups, are instructed how to take care of them when they come home, as they do for 7 months of the year.

"The predominate experience everywhere in trying to help a young, severely ill child," Dr. Churchill remarks in explaining these rather revolutionary innovations, "has been of working hard and for a long time and then, more often than not, of seeing him transferred to a State institution for the mentally ill or the retarded."

After a child has been a patient at the Center or some comparable place for 2 or 3 years, the psychiatrist continues, the parents "have sort of fallen out of love with him." It is then extremely difficult to get him back into the family again, and this is partly because not very much has been done with either the child or the parents to enable him to live in the home.

"In other words," Dr. Churchill observes, "the emphasis has been on what might be called an all-or-nothing proposition—on curing." A psychoanalytically oriented therapist like himself, he goes on, "has been trained to establish a relationship with a patient and to consider, in line with psychoanalytic theory, what may be going on inside the patient, and why. Even with a very sick youngster it is possible to establish this relationship, to get him attached to you—though this may take a couple of years—and sometimes to work a little improvement. But generally the child still is psychotic."

424

At the Center, where the experience has been typical, he believes, the instances in which these young children have improved sufficiently to return home and to enter a public school have been so few and far between that "we're not sure whether they improved to this extent because of what we did or in spite of what we did."

Now, under the new semester system, the Center has a dual objective: to cure the children, "if they can be cured," and meanwhile to make them easier to live with and to help the families get along with them.

"Family morbidity in these cases is very high," Dr. Churchill notes. "These are families who haven't gone to a restaurant or even out on a family picnic for several years because they cannot manage the sick child. The parents may never go out together because babysitters won't come in. Often the house is stripped, with everything of value kept behind locked doors, and the family is living within bare walls."

In working with the parents, the therapists focus not so much on the emotional conflicts that may have led or contributed to the child's illness but on specific methods of dealing with his most disruptive types of behaviors—methods used by the Center itself while the child is an inpatient. For example, if the child is sitting at the table and throwing food, the parents are instructed to give him a warning. If he throws food again, that's the end of the meal for him and he doesn't eat until the next meal.

This, too, is operant conditioning. It pairs an undesirable behavior, throwing food, with a unpleasant result, removal of food. In the case of a child who begins to wreck a room or a grocery store, the unpleasant result may be simply physical restraint.

Many times, though, the best way to handle unwanted behavior is simply to ignore it. It was failure to do this when the behavior first appeared, Dr. Churchill believes, that may have helped perpetuate it. In other words, even if disturbed behavior has a physiological basis, the first adult response to it may have had a rewarding and thus a strengthening effect.

Sometimes, notably in the case of temper tantrums, there is more than one way of ignoring a behavior, and choosing the effective way requires the parent to consider why the child is acting as he is. For instance, if the child has been using tantrums as a means of compelling an adult to come and do something for him that he should be doing for himself, the effective form of ignoring the tantrum is to stay away. But if the child has been using tantrums to hold off an adult and prevent necessary ministrations, the effective form of ignoring the tantrum is to plow ahead and do what is needed.

Usually it is extremely difficult or impossible to learn whether the abnormal behavior of these young children had its roots in organic trouble or in childhood experiences or, as the psychiatrists and psychologists at the Center are inclined to think, in both.

As an example of the difficulty in tracing the origin of abnormal behaviors, Dr. Churchill tells about 5-year-old Jimmy who socks himself on the head and jaw until he is bruised and his knuckles have calluses.

425

During some 20-minute periods he has been observed to hit himself more than 2,000 times.

After studying Jimmy's history, the psychiatrist first thought that the behavior probably had been *learned,* in the sense that Jimmy had received a lot of attention for it. Adults would step in and hold his hands. Jimmy would hit himself while eating, too, so his parents would hold his hands and feed him. Things got to the point where he was being held most of the time and was refusing to feed himself.

Under treatment at the Center, everything that might be considered to reinforce or reward the hitting behavior was withdrawn, but instead of dying out, as learning theory says should be the case, the behavior continued. There was some improvement, in that Jimmy began feeding himself, but Dr. Churchill noticed a strange correlation: the more the boy ate, the more he also used himself as a punching bag.

Recently the staff tried a different approach—the administration of painful but harmless electric shock, paired with the word *shock,* whenever Jimmy began hitting himself. Within 3 days his hitting behavior, which had been essentially unaltered for 3 years, practically stopped. Further, the investigator reports, this behavior can now be controlled by the word *shock* alone. The boy has become more approachable and is playing with toys, which he had ignored for months.

Some physiological factor is believed to be at least partly involved in Jimmy's trouble.

Sally, another child at the Center, typically withdraws to a corner of the playroom, sits on the floor, and rocks endlessly. All children do a little rocking, Dr. Churchill notes: they find pleasure in the rhythm. Why some schizophrenic children keep it up for hours is not known.

In this connection, Dr. Gerald D. Alpern, a psychologist, calls attention to *blindisms,* the term applied to the repetitive behavior—such as rocking, swaying, and passing the hands back and forth in front of the eyes—seen in many blind children. With much of their external stimulation cut off, these children have turned to themselves for stimulation. Blind youngsters are not mentally ill, but they do obviously have an organic defect: they cannot see. There is a possibility, then, that schizophrenic children who engage in behavior similar to blindisms also have an organic defect. There is also a possibility that blind children who engage most strongly in such behavior have an emotional disturbance as well as an organic defect. This second possibility is now being studied at the University of Indiana Medical School as part of a different research program.

Some of the Center's Other Research Projects

To help pin down the factors contributing to early childhood psychosis, Dr. DeMyer and her associates are comparing in great detail 30 schizophrenic children and their families with 30 normal children and their families. The children are given physical and neurological examinations and are tested psychologically. Samples of blood and urine are analyzed for the presence of abnormal metabolic products. Information about their behavior and growth from birth onward—including eating, sleeping, physical and mental development, and social skills—and about the attitudes, personalities, and life histories of their parents is obtained from an exhaustive series of interviews, covering 13 schedules, with the fathers and mothers.

The investigator points out that the study, like other research on the causes of schizophrenia, looks backward and therefore has to rely for much of its information on what the parents remember and choose to tell. However, it carefully checks the account of one parent against that of the other and it carefully compares all the data about a family in which a child is schizophrenic with all the data about a family that is similar to it except for the absence of schizophrenia.

Besides having to make its observations after the fact, research on the causes of schizophrenia is frequently hampered also by the fallibility of clinical judgment. Drawing upon her own experience, Dr. DeMyer says an investigator is likely to get quite definite impressions about the first families he sees in a study like this and then, unless he is very careful, he tends to see the rest of the families in the light of his early impressions. Dr. DeMyer, trying to be very careful, found that the more schizophrenic children she studied, the wider the range of characteristics she saw in their families.

To minimize the problem of clinical judgment and to permit hundreds of facts about each family to be considered, all data in the current research are given numerical ratings, and the comparisons will be made by a computer.

Tying in with this work on the antecedents of childhood schizophrenia is a recently completed survey of the families of 99 schizophrenic children and 146 disturbed but not psychotic children. These children had been seen at the La Rue Carter Hospital between 1955 and 1963, and the data about their families came from the files. The parents of schizophrenic children, no matter what the type of schizophrenia, were found to be significantly better educated than the other parents (who had about the same amount of schooling as the average Indiana adult) and the fathers held much better jobs.

These findings (a) support the earlier observation by another investigator that parents of autistic children tend to be well educated and successful, and (b) extend this observation to include the parents of schizophrenic children in general. Another interesting and unexplained finding: among the disturbed but nonpsychotic children, broken homes were common; among the schizophrenic children, they were not.

Other research underway by the Indianapolis group includes:
- Observations to test Dr. Churchill's hunch that autistic children at times pay considerably more attention to adults when the adults seem to be paying no attention to the children. In terms of conditioning theory, this would mean that the attention of adults had

427

become negatively reinforcing, and it would have important implications for therapy.

- A variety of studies intended to learn more about, and to describe systematically, the behavior of schizophrenic children. In one of these, a moving picture is made of each child's "behavior day" by filming him for 10 seconds every 5 minutes, from the time he wakes up to the time he goes to sleep. The films will be used to compare the dominant behavioral characteristics of the different types of schizophrenic children and also to study changes in the children from one year to the next. Another study of behavior is concerned with the way autistic children use toys. The first findings show that autistic children, as compared with groups of normal and retarded children, (a) make fewer different uses of a given toy, and (b) spend less time using one toy in combination with another.

- An attempt to develop a quantitative means of measuring the abilities of young schizophrenic children who cannot be tested on standard intelligence tests. In one test being used by the investigator, Dr. Alpern, the youngster is scored on the basis of his failure to carry out certain activities of which he is known to be capable. The reasoning here is that it may be less important to know what a schizophrenic child can do than to know what he won't do. The variability in his "failure score" over time, it is hoped, may be a useful indicator of how well he will respond to treatment.

Research Grant: MH 5154
Date of Interview: Apr. 26, 1966

References:

DeMyer, Marian K., & Ferster, C. B. Teaching new social behavior to schizophrenic children. *J. Child Psychiat.*, 1963, 1, 3.
Ferster, C. B., & DeMyer, Marian K. A method for the experimental analysis of the behavior of autistic children. *Amer. J. Orthopsychiat.*, 1962, 32, 1.
Hingtgen, J. N., Sanders, Beverly J., & DeMyer, Marian K. Shaping cooperative responses in early childhood schizophrenics. Presented at annual meeting of the *Amer. Psychol. Association,* 1963.
Lowe, Lois H. Families of children with early childhood schizophrenia: selected demographic information. *Arch. Gen. Psychiat.*, 1966, 14.
Onheiber, Phyllis, White, P. T., DeMyer, Marian K., & Ottinger, D. R. Sleep and dream patterns of child schizophrenics. *Arch. Gen. Psychiat.*, 1965, 12.
Tilton, J. R., & Ottinger, D. R. Comparison of the toy play behavior of autistic, retarded, and normal children. *Psychol. Rep.*, 1964, 15.
White, P. T., DeMyer, W., & DeMyer, Marian K. EEG abnormalities in early childhood schizophrenia: a double-blind study of psychiatrically disturbed and normal children during promazine sedation. *Amer. J. Psychiat.*, 1964, 120, 10.

An Experiment in Foster Care For Seriously Disturbed Boys

Investigator:
Douglas A. Sargent, M.D.
The Merrill-Palmer Institute
Detroit, Mich.

Prepared by:
Clarissa Wittenberg

Through a special program of foster home placement, a number of seriously disturbed boys who seemed headed for a lifelong series of troubles that would burden the community as well as themselves appear to have been helped toward a relatively normal adolescence.

This program, known as the Detroit Foster Homes Project, so far appears to have been successful even though the boys, neglected by their parents, had previously undergone at least two and as many as nine unsuccessful foster home placements. The community agencies that referred them to the project considered that further placement in the usual type of foster home would be difficult if not impossible.

Persons acquainted with the neglected children in our communities find it hard to be optimistic about their future. But the Detroit program suggests that some of the most troubled and troublesome of these children may be put on the path to a normal life.

The project, which was sponsored and staffed by the Merrill-Palmer Institute of Human Development and Family Life, grew out of concern for the boys who were being returned to the care of the Juvenile Court because they were deemed no longer suitable for foster care. These children were either so aggressive or disturbed as to be difficult to manage, yet foster care was considered the treatment of choice. Until these boys had had the stabilizing opportunity to live in one place with people who cared about them, it was felt, all other forms of assistance would be ineffectual.

Fifteen boys between the ages of 7 and 13 were selected to test two ideas: (1) That the "holding power" of foster homes could be increased to the point where it could sustain the impact of such problem children and thus keep them from detention or reform facilities, and (2) that placement of troubled children in this age group would make it possible for them to adjust and stabilize before the turbulence of adolescence. These boys, 11 of whom were Negro and 4 white, had histories that included chronic anxiety, school failure as well as such behavior as stealing, vandalism, truancy, setting fires, and fighting.

429

Children were not accepted if they showed signs of serious physical illness, brain damage, psychosis, or retardation. One of the boys accepted, however, was suspected of being psychotic and this was later confirmed.

Only a small number of the boys had had a few as two past placements, the number established as a minimum for acceptance by the project. The average number of "official" placements was four. Often a child had also been in numerous unrecorded, "temporary" placements. Besides the placements, many of the children early in life had been shifted from relative to relative. In short, the relationships and living situations of all the boys had been continually disrupted.

One boy, for example, had been deserted by his mother, cared for by his grandmother, and been placed in two temporary homes, all by the time he was a year old. He remained in his next home for 5 years. It was then declared unfit and he was moved. His consequent unhappiness and disorientation made themselves apparent in school, so he was moved again, this time to let him "benefit" from a better, more supportive school program. but he then began to present difficulties in his foster home as well, so he was taken to a community shelter for children. There he was described by the staff psychiatrist as the most disturbed child he had ever seen. He was moved briefly to the Youth Home of the Juvenile Court because his behavior was uncontrollable at the shelter. From there he was admitted to a small children's unit of a psychiatric hospital. After remaining there half a year, he was referred to the project. During his first visit to the office for evaluation, he hid under benches and lockers and refused to speak. He attempted to frustrate an attempt at psychological testing, by trying to stick his hand into the blades of a fan. Incidents or even minor disappointments often set off tantrums of unreasoning rage which lasted as long as an hour. During these he was very destructive and it sometimes took two adults to restrain him. Later on he killed and maimed pets in the foster home.

Another boy came to the attention of the Juvenile Court after three siblings were hospitalized for tuberculosis and a man living in the house with the children and their mother was found to have an active case of the disease. When the juvenile authorities came to investigate, the mother could not be found. Subsequently this boy maintained that if his mother had known they were going to come that day, she would not have let the police take him and that she would try to get him back as soon as she could. This he maintained despite the fact that she rarely visited him and made no attempt to remove him from the detention home. While he was detained there he fought constantly. Obscene or critical comments about mothers were especially likely to trigger his rage. He was academically retarded. He couldn't read. His school record showed that for many years he had often gone to school so tired and hungry he could not study. He acted up in class because he felt it better to be considered bad than stupid.

The other boys' stories were similarly dreary, varying only in detail. In each case social workers had tried to help the family and avoid the breakdown. Most of these attempts were ineffectual. The Juvenile Court had been forced to take custody of the child. In no case was a return to the parents a possible alternative, as their lives were too chaotic. Most of the parents had dropped all contact with the boys. One mother was in a mental hospital and several others had histories of hospitalization for mental illness or alcoholism. All of the families were broken by divorce, separation, death, or the fact that the mother had never been married. One father was in prison. None of the fathers visited their sons. Several mothers themselves had been court wards as children. The occasional visits between these children and their relatives usually were followed by increased anxiety or disturbed behavior in the children.

The extent of family breakdown and its attendant problems was increased by the fact that the boys often came from large families. Ten of these families had from 7 to 14 children. Each child with siblings had siblings in foster care. Rarely had any been placed together. Only six of the boys ever had been able to maintain contact with their siblings.

The Foster Parents

In spite of an intensive campaign and the full cooperation of other agencies, the project found it difficult to find foster parents who met even its rather permissive standards. These required that the foster parents be self-supporting, without obvious mental disorder, be able to read and to value education. Further they were to have some emotional flexibility and the capacity to cooperate with professional workers. (This last point turned out to be of paramount importance.) As it turned out, applicants were eliminated only for such serious reasons as psychosis or marginal financial or occupational status. Only 5 percent of applicants were finally accepted.

In the end, the project reports, it had an acceptable group of foster parents, seriously interested for the most part in what it was trying to do but more like the average foster parent than the ideal—and better so, since this was a demonstration program. A few of the foster parents turned out to have rather serious emotional problems which only became apparent as involvement with the child deepened.

The foster parents ranged in age from 30 to 64, with the average father being 49 and the average mother 44. Ten couples had had only one marriage. Eight had been married 21 years or more. Ten had children of their own, and eight of these couples had children still living at home. Ten of the foster parents came from the South, the others from the urban North. Four had been foster children themselves.

Ten of the families were buying their homes, and two owned their businesses. One father was a professional engineer, and the rest had had long, steady employment in various Detroit factories. Several of the women had had training in practical nursing, beauty parlor work, office machine operation. Several had held long-term domestic positions. One had worked in a factory. Family incomes for the most part were in the vicinity of $6,000.

431

Most of the foster parents had had considerably less than a high school education, a finding that agrees with the results of a preliminary study, by the project directors, showing a low state of literacy to be common among foster parents in general. Because of this low-educational level, project workers used little written material and routinely offered assistance whenever forms had to be filled out. This lack of education became a more obvious handicap when the parents tried to help the child with schoolwork or to communicate with his teacher.

A high degree of community responsibility existed among the foster parents. Several were active in their churches, unions, or neighborhood groups. Most of them were quite involved with their relatives and spent a great deal of time with them.

These people gave a variety of reasons for wanting to be foster parents. Several childless couples said that with a foster child they could feel they had a family. A few other couples said they had worked hard, had achieved substantial income and comfort, and now wanted to do something for an unfortunate child. Several wanted companions for their own children. Some had previously been foster parents and had found it a satisfying experience. Several foster mothers hoped to repeat the highly gratifying experience they had had in caring for their own children. In at least one case the foster mother was lonely and wanted company. At least one couple hoped ultimately to adopt the foster child. Subsequently it became evident that in addition to these overt expectations, there were other needs which led these couples into foster care and not all of these needs were compatible with the job, as it turned out.

Working With the Foster Parents: the First Steps

Through frequent, sometimes daily discussions with individual parents or couples and through group discussions, both before and after the boys had been placed, the staff tried to help the parents understand and cope with the boys' behavior.

Major attention was given to widening the foster parents' range of disciplinary techniques. Because many of the boys had suffered physical abuse and been emotionally hurt by it, spanking was specifically prohibited and help given the parents in developing alternative ways of dealing with undesirable behavior. Particularly encouraged were the anticipation of explosive situations, the avoidance of overstimulation, and the use of words rather than blows as a means of communication.

Many of the foster parents had had an abiding faith in the efficacy of spanking in raising their own children. The project's rule against it created conflict and was not especially successful. Spanking occurred, the project reports. In school, too, spanking or slapping was sometimes resorted to in spite of the project's plea. They conclude that, for a variety of reasons, under the conditions of the project, the occasional use of physical punishment was inevitable.

The project attempted to place the children so that each would be the youngest child in the family to lessen the competition with the family's own children.

Before a boy was actually placed, a caseworker attempted to build a good relationship both with him and with the foster family. Great pains were taken to pace the transition from detention home, etc., to the new foster home according to the needs of the child and foster family. Then, for many days after placement, the caseworker was available almost continually. This was important, the project found, because the parents and the child tended to have a great many questions and worries about each other and to be reluctant to deal with them. Many of these worries were acted out directly by the children, and the caseworker's help was needed to cope with these reactions.

In some of the first cases, the parents had parties for the children when they arrived. But some foster children, it developed, were under so much strain that they could not stand this welcoming ceremony and ran away. So in the later cases, on the advice of the staff, the family's response to the arrival of the foster child was modified and played down.

In general, the best beginnings were in those families that deviated as little as possible from the normal routine and had other children to help ease the strain of fitting into the new neighborhood.

All the boys tested the parents to see if and when they would be rejected. The hardest kind of behavior for some of the parents to deal with was withdrawal. Some of the boys became almost mute, and physically unavailable to their new parents. In other cases, oaths and obscenities were used to test foster parents or to keep them at a distance.

Some of the foster parents asked that the boy be removed from their care. These parents, in general, felt less well prepared for the child and looked upon the caseworker as an investigator checking up on them. The other parents tended to see him as a helper and themselves as part of a team.

The parents who gave up the children seemed to have been most upset by aggression directed against themselves or other family members. They mentioned, for example, "sassing me," "fighting with my son," "defiance," and "cursing and temper."

The parents who kept children, on the other hand, seemed to be more worried about the child's well-being. Typically their concerns focused on such activities as "staying out all night," "backing car into the street (7-year-old)," "walks to swimming pool by himself." It may be that the two groups of parents were not exposed to the same kinds of behavior. Temper tantrums were reported by most of the parents who gave up children but by only a few of the other parents.

Approaches and Techniques

In spite of the insulting and sometimes assaultive behavior exhibited by many of the boys, the project staff made the continuing stability of the foster home one of its key objectives. Trying to hold to this objective became very difficult at times. For example, one child's behavior was occasionally so disturbed—it reached a peak when he killed a neighborhood puppy—that maintaining the placement was, to some degree, a threat to the community.

The easiest action in this case, the project reports, would have been to remove the child. This was avoided, the crisis passed, and the placement has been sustained. There is no certainty that he will not eventually be hospitalized anyway; as the foster mother put it, however, "If he doesn't make it here, he'll never make it."

A foster home placement, the staff points out, demands a great deal of work and devotion from the foster parents and a great deal from the foster child as well. The child, however, cannot begin attempting to modify his own behavior until he has some certainty that people are going to support him and to continue to be concerned about him. Boys like those in the project cannot be expected to increase their trust until they become involved with people who are trustworthy.

The staff recognized, and tried to get foster parents and teachers to recognize, that the boys had suffered real deprivation. The aim was to repair the effects of this, to meet the child's needs at all levels, and at the same time to make appropriate demands on the child.

Each foster home had a variety of crises—among them illness, death, financial difficulty, the mother's going out to work, and the threatened separation of the parents—that endangered its stability. But the crises were often temporary or, in the judgment of the project, not so harmful to the child as moving him would have been. The policy was to scrutinize the health of the home and its members continually but not to move a child without exceptional reasons. There is some evidence to suggest that the involvement of the foster child in coping with these crises was beneficial to him.

In its work with the children and their foster parents, the project used numerous approaches and techniques, the main ones summarized below.

Casework in the home itself was emphasized. —To answer questions as they came up, and to give all the assistance possible, the caseworker visited the foster parents and the child at least once a week—more frequently if the situation warranted. Even when the parents reported having no particular problems or nothing to discuss, the visits were made and—often these were the most fruitful ones.

Originally it had been planned to have the foster parents meet regularly as a group, and this was to have become the key educational medium. However, most parents showed little interest in the planned programs and attended only sporadically. The only programs that were well attended were those planned to recognize the work of the parents, such as the annual dinner. Nor did a group session turn out to be a place to share problems, for these parents, by and large, considered these difficulties to be private property and were often reluctant to discuss them, even with the caseworker.

Psychiatric and other professional help was always available.—Periodic psychiatric interviews were held with the boys. Psychiatric consultation was always available to the caseworkers, whenever an emergency seemed to warrant it. Other specialists in appropriate fields, such as education and psychology, were project consultants and were called upon for help as needed. Beyond this, the actual progress of the project was kept under continued surveillance and modification by the administrative staff and consultants.

Group work services were used for the boys, the general objective of which was to help a boy fit into his new home and neighborhood. Specific aims were to give him healthy experiences with other children, help him attain social skills, especially to learn how to play.

In the beginning boys were added to the group as they were accepted by the project, but the group became unwieldy. To accomplish the therapeutic aims of the group, these boys needed extensive assistance and new carefully selected groups were formed of three or four boys each.

Where there was another young child in the foster home, he was included in the group. Neighborhood friends were invited to share in the group activities which included games, trips, and other recreational activities. Many of the boys, it turned out, had never been to even a store, a bank, or a post office. Several had never been to the city park, Belle Isle, to which the entire city seems to flock in hot weather. Such trips were also used to observe and modify the boy's behavioral troubles.

Special emphasis was given to schooling.—Because parents were not able to keep a child who failed continually in school, and because these children were likely to do so. the project staff—along with the foster parents, if possible—met with the school's administrators and teachers and discussed the boy's problems before a boy was enrolled in a school. It was found that this procedure made for a better relationship between school and parents and helped to save the foster parent from being criticized for the child's behavior or conditions which had developed before he came to their home. Discussions about the boy's needs and the project's ideas about discipline were held with each teacher.

The staff kept in close touch with each school and was ready to help whenever difficulties arose. When a school called for assistance, members of the staff responded at once. Consultants were brought in when advisable. Personal history data and diagnoses of the children were shared with each teacher whenever the project judged this information to be useful. Most of the time this confidence was justified. Sometimes it backfired.

The staff found that the boys tended to do better in highly structured situations, such as a class in arithmetic, than in looser, more informal groupings such as music classes and library and gym sessions. Consequently, when a boy needed a shorter school day in order to survive the strain, these latter were the first classes eliminated.

Efforts were made to have the boys spend as much time as possible with those teachers who were found to be making outstanding contributions. Letters of appreciation were written to teachers and administrators. With the project's cooperation, several of the teachers who were attending university classes wrote reports of their work with the boys.

Tutoring became an important part of the program. —A common problem—and one contributing to behavior difficulties in school—was reading retardation. Even in the third and fourth grades, some of the boys were virtually nonreaders. For all the children having trouble in reading, the project established a therapeutic tutoring program.

The tutors set out to reach the boys by using material familiar to them, including the songs of the Beatles and books of comics. After such an introduction, it was easier to get on with conventional reading material. The sessions were planned to use to the utmost the child's ability to concentrate and comprehend yet keep fatigue to a minimum. Food and other treats were a valuable entree into the confidence of these deprived boys.

Reading became a very important area of achievement, the project reports. Often the boys would want to demonstrate their new reading ability to the caseworker and other adults.

Incidentally, the tutoring sessions were considered a valuable means of helping to meet the difficulties brought on by the summertime closing of the schools. For some of these boys, June meant still another separation from people who had become important to them, and faced them with the rather aimless and formless—and therefore difficult time of summer. Of course, some of the boys simply were glad to get away from school.

Efforts were made to strengthen the boy's sense of identity. —The information available about his background was given to the foster parents, and the healthy ties remaining from his past were nurtured. Attempts were made to fill in the voids in the child's knowledge of his own past.

The project staff initiated contact with the natural parents when they could be located and, in the beginning, in some cases, arranged for them to visit the boys. These visits, it was found, always caused serious difficulty for the boys and in some cases jeopardized the foster home placements. Since it was impossible for these boys to return to their natural parents, and since the foster homes were considered essential to their healthy development, parental visits came to be virtually eliminated. By and large, the staff found, the situation that had led to parental neglect or abuse, and to court action on behalf of these boys had tended to deteriorate rather than improve.

In some cases there was a relative who visited and maintained a constructive interest in the boy. Visits in such cases were encouraged. Occasionally a staff member helped a boy to visit a past foster parent.

The boys were photographed routinely by the psychiatrist, who used this activity as a rapport-building technique. The boys were fascinated by the photographs of themselves—sometimes they were taken alone and sometimes with members of their foster family. The pictures became valued possessions. The pictures were also used as tangible evidence of the project's concern for the child, a concrete demonstration that his person was valued (the photos decorated the project's walls). It also seemed to enhance the child's self-concept.

Another identity strengthening technique was used in the tutoring sessions, though primarily to provide the child with material he would like to read. The tutor would help the child compose a story about himself and then would have it typed for him.

The Outcome of the Program

The project reports the following results:

1. All the boys have received good medical and dental care and are physically well.

2. Thirteen out of fifteen boys remain either in foster homes or have been adopted. Some are enjoying a high degree of security for the first time in their lives.

3. Enuresis, existing in one-half of the boys, has ceased in every case.

4. They are less depressed than they were.

5. Their relationships with people are becoming deeper and more appropriate, although there is still a tendency to try to keep from getting involved.

6. Most are behaving more nearly at a level appropriate to their age. In the beginning, many had a tendency to play with children much younger than themselves—frequently to the despair of the foster parents. One father, for instance, who had hoped for a companionable youngster, found that the boy liked most of all to ride a tricycle or play with the neighborhood small fry. In some cases there are still remnants of such behavior.

7. Fears and anxiety, both conscious and as revealed in the dreams and fantasies of the boys, are less. Those remaining are more realistic. In the beginning, in many cases, violent scenes—peopled with monsters, dismembered persons, and lost children—predominated. Fears of personal or family destruction were common.

8. The boys' attitude toward food has improved. It is less frequently used to assuage anxiety or as a substitute for love. Early in the project, one boy who was offered a piece of cake ate the whole cake, and children offered snacks during a group program or a casework session frequently demanded an entire meal. Another boy, fearful that his foster parents did not love him, feared that he could not have a second helping; another took literally his foster mother's remark, "We don't have a thing in the house to eat," and slipped out to a neighbor's. Still another ate voraciously and became very fat. This boy is now secure enough to be able to diet, has lost 30 pounds, and is proud of the change in his appearance.

9. Antisocial behavior has decreased. From diffuse outbreaks against the community, such as throwing bricks through a school window, they have shifted to more localized acts with a more immediate bearing upon

437

themselves, such a truancy. One boy has stopped stealing even though he had been taught to steal by his mother.

10. In school, some of the boys are still behind the grade level appropriate for their age but all have made progress. One boy had to be sent to a special school but the others are in regular classes. The nonreaders now read.

11. Perhaps the most marked gain has been in verbal facility and spontaneity. This improvement is attributed mainly to the increase in personal security, the lessening of hostility, encouragement of the ability to use words rather than action to express themselves, and the opportunity to talk with friendly people.

12. The boys are less tense and better able to concentrate than when they first came into the project. Then they were inclined to be reckless and physically overactive. They often avoided eye contact or met the eyes defiantly. They either slumped in chairs or were unable to remain seated. Regular interview situations were difficult for them.

13. Contrary to some commonly voiced fears, the boys have not "infected" other children—either those in the foster family or those in the neighborhood. In the case of the boy who killed a puppy, his sadistic behavior with animals has been of concern to the neighbors, but their children, instead of following his lead, tend to reject this behavior and thus to exert a helpful influence upon him. In only one case was there a serious problem between the foster child and the natural child: they fought to such an extent that the mother asked to have the foster child removed. She was concerned also that this boy's stealing would set a bad example for her son. (This is the same parent who wanted a foster child as a companion for her son. This placement was an error in judgment, according to the project.)

Still present in each of these children are the tremendous aftereffects of early deprivation and of repeated separation from parental figures. The children in varying degrees still show signs of hostility, distrust, apprehension, and sadness. Nor has the program been successful in every case. One boy, for example, was sent to a mental hospital. (Later authorities returned him to his natural mother, though she was barely able to care for herself.) One is in a boy's home described as "rather pleasant"; a third is in a treatment-oriented detention facility described as "relatively good."

Nevertheless, most of these "impossible to place" youngsters have become far better able to manage their day-to-day living in a foster home.

The program has demonstrated, its directors submit, that many of the limitations of foster care as a means of helping such children can be overcome through the provision of comprehensive services. It then becomes possible to combine treatment with the advantages of a stable family life and with those which come from living in a community. Thus children who otherwise were likely to have required institutional care were maintained in the community and needed no halfway house to acclimatize them to "civilian life" at the end of their treatment.

Research Grant: R11-MH-1551
Date of Interview: Apr. 6, 1966

References:

Ambinder, W. J. The extent of successive placements among boys in foster homes. *Child Welf.*, July 1965, 397–398.
Ambinder, W. J., & Falik, H. The behaviorally disturbed foster child in school—a preliminary report. Unpublished paper. Detroit Foster Homes Project, 1965.
Ambinder, W. J. & Falik, H. The social acceptance of the behaviorally disturbed boy in his classroom group. Unpublished paper. *J. Sch. Psychol.*
James, Adrienne. Differences between two groups of foster parents. Paper presented at Second Annual Conf. on Foster Care for Emotionally Disturbed Children, Detroit Foster Homes Project, February, 1965.
James, Adrienne. Casework with emotionally disturbed children in foster care. Presented at NCSW, Chicago, 1966.
Mahaffey, Maryann. Progress report of an experiment in foster care for disturbed boys. Paper read at Ohio Welf. Conf., Cincinnati, October, 1965.
Redl, F., & Wineman, D. *The aggressive child.* Glencoe, Ill.: Free Press, 1957.
Sargent, D. A., & Ambinder, W. J. Foster parents techniques of management of preadolescent boys' deviant behavior. *Child Welfare*, February, 1965, 90–94.
Sargent, D. A., Ambinder, W. J., & Fireman, Laura. Verbal abilities and literacy levels required of foster parents. *Child Welfare*, December 1963, 502-503.
Sargent, D. A., Ambinder, W. J., Fireman, Laura, & Wineman, D. Role phenomena and foster care for disturbed children. *Amer. J. Orthopsychiat.*, 1962, 32, 1.
Shiefman, Emma. The Beatles? Yeah! Yeah! Yeah! *The Reading Teacher*, October, 1965.
Shiefman, Emma. A school teacher in a child welfare agency. *Children*, May–June 1966, 116–118.

439

The Role of Learning in the Relapse of Narcotic Addicts

Investigator:
Abraham Wikler M.D.*
Addiction Research Center, NIMH
Lexington, Ky.

Prepared by:
Antoinette A. Gatozzi

The postaddict patient leaves the Lexington hospital free of drugs. He has had the best treatment that medicine knows how to provide. Whether he entered as a Federal prisoner or a voluntary patient, he was carefully and humanely withdrawn from his drug, usually heroin, and received expert aftercare and rehabilitation services. But the grim fact is that the discharged postaddict cannot be given much chance to remain free of drugs. One of three patients is readmitted because he has relapsed to the use of narcotics.

This calculation is based on patient records of the two U.S. Public Health Service hospitals, at Fort Worth, Tex., and Lexington, Ky., that are charged by law to care for narcotic addicts in the United States. Patients are Federal prisoners addicted to narcotic drugs and narcotic addicts who voluntarily enter for treatment. Because of the inherent selectivity of this group, the readmission rate would seem to represent a lower instance of relapse after cure than that which prevails among the postaddict population as a whole. A certain number of relapsed postaddict patients defy accountability as such.

Tragically, some shoot themselves with a fatal overdose of opiates, unknowingly or perhaps suicidally oblivious of their lost tolerance to dosages formerly self-administered. Doubtless there are others who take up using opiates again, stay clear of the law, and do not choose to be withdrawn. Many postaddicts turn to abuse of different drugs, notably barbiturates. A study made 2 years ago of 1,000 consecutive admissions to Lexington found one fourth of the patients physically dependent on barbiturates as well as addicted to a narcotic drug. Although it is difficult to discover the true number of postaddicts who relapse after cure, all observers agree that the rate is high and the problem pressing.

At the Addiction Research Center, a facility of the intramural program of the National Institute of Mental Health, the question of relapse is one of many that researchers are investigating. Understanding why postaddicts relapse after cure depends upon insight into the factors involved in the

---

*Now at the school of Medicine, University of Kentucky Research Foundation, Lexington, Kentucky.

440

initial use and abuse of drugs. More information must be gained about the mechanisms of tolerance, dependence, and the stereotyped withdrawal syndrome that follows abrupt discontinuation of addicting compounds before the question of relapse can be answered definitively.

The classic drugs of addiction are the opiates. Of these, people most often hear of morphine and heroin. Morphine is of great value in the practice of medicine; its prescriptive use by physicians is controlled by law. Heroin is almost identical to morphine in biological activity. Gram for gram, it is two to three times as potent as morphine, which may represent a convenient economy to those who deal criminally in opiates and thereby explain why heroin is the opiate of the majority of narcotic addicts. All heroin is illegal in the United States. An opiate interacts with the cells of an individual's somatic and autonomic nervous systems, profoundly alters the functioning of vital organs and glands, and affects his mood and motivation. Although there is evidence that the phenomenon begins with the first dose, with prolonged use the individual becomes physiologically tolerant to the drug's actions, and the original dose no longer induces the original effects. A very small proportion of those who experience the effects of an opiate over a period of time become dependent on the drug. They feel they must continue using it in order to maintain a sense of well-being, both physical and mental.

Why Do They Relapse?

Addicts call morphine "God's own medicine." Many patients with severe pain who have been given the drug by their physicians would agree with that assessment because the *sine qua non* of an opiate is the capacity to relieve pain. No other compound approaches it in this respect although the search for an equally effective analgesic with lower abuse potentiality has been long and intense. Opiates also possess narcotic, or sleep-producing properties, and for this reason opium derivatives and their synthetic analogs are called narcotic analgesics. Medical scientists do not fully understand how analgesics (from aspirin to morphine) relieve pain. There is still much to learn about pain itself and the influence of emotional factors on the threshold level at which noxious physical stimuli are perceived as pain. The outstanding capacity of the opiates to relieve physical pain and its associative psychic components is probably involved in the postaddict's proclivity to relapse.

Once withdrawn from the drug, the postaddict faces again the personal and social difficulties that formed at least part of the reason why he plunged into drug abuse initially. The narcotic addict's personal problems are thought to center around the expression of aggression and the primary drives of sexual gratification and avoidance of pain. These normal human drives provoke in him sharp, sometimes intolerable anxieties, and he may have abused the drug originally because it led him to a state of dreamy indifference to reality. The social factors that dispose to relapse stem from such handicaps as a truncated education, little or no job experience, racial minority-group status, and a criminal record. These are common features of the backdrop of addiction. All are obstacles to the postaddict's attempts to become productive and responsible.

Other factors in relapse may relate to the physical changes wrought by prolonged use of a narcotic. For months or years the addict surrendered himself many times a day to the pharmacologic thralldom of his drug. It is possible, indeed it now seems likely, that he does not regain his former physical status after the 7–10 days required to detoxify him and the few months in a drug-free environment needed to free him of all obvious signs of addiction. Dr. William R. Martin, director of the Addiction Research Center, is now in the midst of a detailed study of the effects and after-effects of chronic narcotic addiction in man. The classic study done in the mid-1930's by C. K. Himmelsbach, the first director of the Center, showed that as long as 6 months after withdrawal the postaddict is hyper-reactive to some physical stimuli.

Then there is the habit itself, a pattern of behavior that becomes a way of life for the addict, pivoting on the compulsive acquistion and use of the drug. The narcotic habit is embedded in fundamentals of character, social background, and neurophysiological functioning, and breaking it may prove insuperable for many postaddicts. To account in part for this aspect of relapse after cure, a two-factor learning theory has been proposed by Dr. Abraham Wikler. Dr. Wikler is professor of psychiatry at the University of Kentucky College of Medicine and consultant to the Addiction Research Center. For many years he served as chief of the Center's section on experimental neuropsychiatry.

Postaddicts have described experiencing physical symptoms very like those of acute drug abstinence when they return to their home environments many weeks or months after withdrawal. These reports suggested to Dr. Wikler that physical dependence on the narcotic drug might become conditioned during the course of addiction to certain situations in the addict's environment. This conditioning would follow the Pavlovian model, in which a dog came to salivate at the sound of a bell that had rung many times before in temporal contiguity with the presentation of meat powder.

The investigator reasoned that Pavlovian conditioning could occur when the addict failed to get his drug in time to avert the emergence of with-drawal symptoms, which might begin within 3 or 4 hours after the last dose. A conditioned response could be engendered through repeated temporal associations between such sporadic, accidental abstinences and specific environments, for example, a street corner, room, or bar. Thus, even when he had been withdrawn from the drug for some time, when there was, in a sense, no cellular logic for abstinence symptoms, the postaddict's presence in situations of past abstinence might trigger in him physical symptoms that frighteningly mimicked real abstinence.

The second factor that Dr. Wikler hypothesizes in relapse is analogous to the learning theory model of operant conditioning. In this model an individual performs an act spontaneously (he "operates" on his environ-ment) that has a consequence regarded by him as positive or negative. If

442

the consequence is positive and rewarding, the theory holds, it will reinforce the act that preceeded it. That is, the act will be repeated if it culminates in reward often enough. The addict's frequent intermittent bouts of abstinence are totally and dramatically relieved when he does succeed in acquiring and using the drug. Thus, his drug-acquisitory behavior is reinforced again and again by the reward of relief from abstinence symptoms.

Both kinds of conditioned learning may influence behavior in the same individual. Dr. Wikler further postulates that the permanence of this learning is directly related to the amount of effort put into the acquisition of drugs. Here again the investigator took his lead from the reports of former addicts, who often brag among themselves about how hard they "hustled" (almost always criminally) and how good they were at getting their supply when they were "on the street." Dr. Wikler suggests that the status accorded to a successful hustler by addict society is a potent secondary reinforcer of drug-acquisitory behavior. Scheduling of reinforcement and stimulus generalization are other concepts of conditioned learning theory that, Dr. Wikler believes, also are pertinent to the role of learning in relapse after cure.

Addiction and Relapse in Rats

Experiments to test the Pavlovian and operant learning hypotheses were done with rats. The studies involved these basic design elements: Rats that were physically dependent on morphine, a suitable reinforcing agent, methods for conditioning the animals, and testing procedures to determine whether conditioning had occurred.

Rats were made physically dependent on morphine by injecting them with the drug once a day at about 8 a.m. Doses were gradually increased over a period of 6 weeks until the desired high-dose level was reached. The animals then were maintained on this dosage. They were addicted. Control rats were treated similarly, except that their morning injection was an innocuous saline solution. By evening the addict rats' doses were wearing off and they were exhibiting signs of abstinence including "wet-dog shakes." The phrase aptly conveys the rat's movement: A shaking and twitching of trunk and limbs that resemble a wet dog shaking water from itself. Normal rats briefly behave this way after handling. Earlier work by Dr. Wikler and his colleagues had shown that elevated wet-dog frequencies were reliable signs of early abstinence in the chronically addicted rat, roughly paralleling such other abstinence symptoms as loss of weight and low body temperature, increased activity and elimination. Wet-dog shakes may be the murine equivalent of a human abstinence symptom called, in another graphic phrase, "cold turkey." Addicts use it to refer to wave after chilling wave of gooseflesh (medically termed piloerection) and to describe the whole range of symptoms that occurs on abrupt termination of narcotic use.

443

The reinforcing agent had to be an opiate or any other chemical compound that exerted opiate-like effects. Morphine itself was the logical choice. It proved to be unsatisfactory, however, presumably because the quantities required for reinforcing purposes and the methods of delivery to the rats were aversive to the animals. Then the investigators learned of a synthetic drug called etonitazene, which was just being described. Etonitazene produced morphine-like effects in animals. It was shown to be 1,000 times as potent as morphine as an analgesic in the rat. The researchers undertook a series of experiments with this interesting compound to determine if it could serve as the reinforcing agent in conditioning studies.

Their preliminary observations were encouraging. First, they found that rats would drink a dilute water solution of etonitazene without being forced to, that is, without prior water deprivation. Water deprivation had been a complicating but necessary procedure when morphine was tried as the reinforcing agent. If etonitazene were used, water deprivation could be eliminated. Second, drug-treated animals that were abstinent 24-48 hours drank much more water if it contained etonitazene than if it were plain, and abstinent rats consuming etonitazene solution showed lower wet-dog frequencies than those drinking water. It looked as if the greater consumption of etonitazene solution compared to water might have resulted from the drug's power to suppress abstinence discomfort. Further study demonstrated that this was indeed so.

In normal, control rats, fluid consumption was not affected when a solution containing 5 or 10 micrograms of etonitazene per milliliter of water was substituted for plain water. Nor was fluid consumption altered when the substitution was made for animals in a state of morphine intoxication, a period lasting about 7 hours from the time of the single daily drug injection. However, experimental animals showing morphine-abstinence symptoms, which began about the 13th hour after injection and continued until the next morning injection, drank much greater volumes when their fluid was etonitazene solution than when it was water. Moreover, the usual primary abstinence symptoms did not appear when experimental animals in a condition of emerging abstinence were allowed to drink drug solution. The investigators reasoned that etonitazene solution was consumed in greater quantities than water by morphine-abstinent rats because for them—and only for them—it had reinforcing properties, specifically, relief from abstinence discomforts. In sum, etonitazene's various attributes made it an excellent choice for the role of reinforcing agent.

The procedures devised to condition animals were carried out in individual linear mazes. Mazes were constructed so that an animal's access to one or the other end could be blocked. On certain days of the week, from the time of morning injection until 2 p.m., all rats had free run of their mazes and could drink plain water available at either end. From 2 p.m. until the next morning they were allowed access to only one end where, again, they found water to drink at will. The evening routine was altered on other days of the week: From about 8 p.m. until the next morning all rats were confined to the opposite maze end. The fluid available for drinking here was different for each of four subgroups. In every maze, this end also was cued to help the animal discriminate it from the other end. Anise flavor tagged the drinking fluid in the first study; in a replicate study, visual and tactile cues were used instead.

• Drinking water available to one group of morphine-addicted rats contained 10 micrograms of etonitazene in every milliliter of water, a concentration sufficient to relieve abstinence.

• A second group of morphine-addicted rats had no etonitazene in their drinking water. Only the discriminative cues marked this end as different from the other end for them.

• One control group had available for drinking a solution containing half the amount of etonitazene placed in the first addict group's water. The smaller potency reduced the chances of these animals becoming tolerant to, or dependent on the drug.

• A second control group was placed in the same situation as that of the second addict group.

Two basic strategies were behind these rather complicated procedures. First, both groups of addict rats suffered withdrawal symptoms nightly in the mazes; they were conditioned to the mazes as an environment of abstinence. Second, one addict group was conditioned on alternate nights to associate relief from abstinence with the behavior of drinking water (containing etonitazene), tagged with certain cues, while the second addict group was never allowed to relieve abstinence and therefore made no association between relief and the behavior of drinking water (not containing etonitazene), tagged with the same cues. The first group was trained in the operant conditioning model and the second was not.

Conditioning procedures were carried out for 6 consecutive weeks. Animals remained in mazes the following week but were not allowed access to the cued end-compartments. This was a precautionary step to equalize the degrees of addiction of the two experimental subgroups; in case the one that had consumed etonitazene solution every other night during conditioning had acquired a stronger drug-dependence than the subgroup that received only the morphine injections.

Then all injections were halted and animals were returned to their home cages. All drug-treated rats underwent abrupt withdrawal and showed the typical acute abstinence symptoms. Beginning about a week after injections were stopped and continuing at intervals up to several months afterward, the animals were observed in a battery of procedures and relapse tests to determine the effect of training in relation to previous treatment.

Dr. Wikler and his coworker, Frank T. Pescor, a biologist, conducted two complete conditioning studies, retracing each step of treatment, training, and testing. The second study differed somewhat in details from the first, which is the one described above, but the principles of each were identical. The studies yielded comparable results.

The investigators found that wet-dog frequencies of postaddict rats were higher in the mazes than in the home cages long after all other signs of primary abstinence had subsided and postaddict wet-dog frequencies in home cages had returned to the level shown by controls. In some relapse tests, wet-dog frequencies of control rats changed in the same direction as those of postaddict rats, but the amount of change was smaller for controls. Thus, the experiments demonstrated the Pavlovian condition-ability of this abstinence phenomenon in the rat. Considered along with the suggestive clinical reports of former addicts, the experimental evidence supports the hypothesis that abstinence phenomena may be similarly conditioned in man.

Evidence concerning the role of reinforced operant behavior in relapse could not be obtained. During the test period of the study, rats were exposed to both forced drinking of dilute etonitazene water and free-choice drinking of either plain or doped water. According to the hypothesis, those postaddict rats which had learned during training that the doped water alleviated their discomfort (abstinence symptoms) would choose to drink more doped water after cure than would postaddict rats which had not been so trained. The investigators found that, although both postaddict groups drank significantly more doped water than did control rats, there was no difference between the two postaddict groups in the amount of doped water consumed by free choice after withdrawal. Both relapsed after cure, but the investigators could not find any dif-ference between them in the nature of their relapse. Dr. Wikler believes that a test with greater discriminative power than free-choice drinking will have to be devised to expose differences in relapse liability that might exist between the two groups, and thereby to isolate the role of reinforced operant behavior.

The experiment did demonstrate that, regardless of the roles of Pavlovian and operant conditioning, previous addiction itself disposed rats to consume etonitazene solution long after primary withdrawal symptoms had subsided. Dr. Wikler suggests that postaddict rats' greater free-choice consumption of doped water, compared with the amount never-addicted rats chose to drink, may have been due to prolonged aftereffects of ad-diction. The blatant, well-recognized symptoms of primary abstinence in the chronically addicted rat run their course by the third day after abrupt withdrawal, but earlier studies by these investigators had demonstrated so-called secondary abstinence phenomena in the chronically addicted rat, persisting 4–6 months after withdrawal. Moreover, they had found that even 6 months after withdrawal there were minor differences between postaddict and control rats. In the conditioning study, the persistence of elevated wet-dog frequencies long after withdrawal may be regarded as a manifestation of secondary abstinence. The evidence suggests that a long-enduring, subtle homeostatic imbalance in postaddict rats is an important factor in generating relapse after cure. Does protracted abstinence occur in man? When Dr. Martin and his colleagues complete the work mentioned earlier, we shall be able to answer this question with considerably more assurance than is now possible.

The etiology of relapse after cure is certain to involve interactions of both physiological factors, including conditioned learning to a greater or lesser extent. Every promising lead must be followed; until we understand why postaddicts relapse after cure we cannot be sure that the prevailing methods of treating narcotic addiction are truly curative. If postaddict patients are found to experience long-enduring residual aftereffects, for instance, the exact duration and physiological nature of the effects will need to be determined and methods of specific treatment devised. To the extent that conditioning factors are shown to contribute to relapse after cure, extinction procedures would become part of the treatment regimen. Dr. Wikler has speculated about the general outlines of such a program. He points out that extinction of conditioned abstinence phenomena and of reinforced drug-acquisitory behavior require different procedures and should be done separately, beginning with the latter.

Two new drugs would be needed. One would be used with incoming addicted patients during the detoxification phase of treatment. Its qualities would be such that it could be substituted for the opiate patients had been using. On withdrawal, it would not cause the emergence of characteristic heroin or morphine withdrawal phenomena. Then the new drug would be abruptly withdrawn, and the result would be a prolonged but not severe abstinence syndrome. At this point the second new drug would be used. This drug should possess some rewarding properties so that patients would work for it, but it should not be effective in relieving abstinence. In this manner, the usual reward associated with drug-acquisitory behavior would not be forthcoming, and the old conditioned stimulus-response pattern could be steadily weakened.

Dr. Wikler proposes that rewards to condition socially acceptable operant behavior be provided in separate training. Postaddicts might earn money for useful work, which they would be allowed to spend for things they want other than drugs.

Extinction of conditioned physical dependence would begin after this hospital program. It would be carried out in the postaddict's home environment. Surveillance, nonnarcotic drug therapy, and psychotherapy would be used to bolster the postaddict and forestall relapse should conditioned abstinence occur. In this way, the classical (Pavlovian) conditioning factor would gradually be extinguished.

Recent studies made at the Addiction Research Center have provided another possible means of extinguishing conditioned abstinence and drug-seeking behavior. A new synthetic substance—cyclazocine—seems to have especially desirable characteristics. Dr. Wikler thinks that maintenance of postaddict patients on cyclazocine, as proposed by the research group headed by Dr. Martin,[1] would lead to experimental extinction of the

---

[1] Martin, W. R., Gorodetzky, C. W., and McClane, T. K. Treatment of Narcotic Addicts With Cyclazocine. *Clin. Pharmacol., Therap.*, 1966, 7, 455-465.

conditioned abstinence symptoms and drug-acquisitive behavior he postulates are factors in relapse.

Cyclazocine is a narcotic antagonist, a compound that blocks many of an opiate's effects. Like several of the narcotic antagonists known, cyclazocine has analgesic properties; indeed, it possesses many times the analgesic potency of morphine. (It has been found to produce hallucinations in man frequently, however, and this disturbing side effect makes it unacceptable as an analgesic for general clinical use.) Another significant property of many of these agents is that chronic usage does not produce tolerance to their opiate counteractions. This is true of cyclazocine.

The Martin group found that subjects (abstinent postaddict patients) who had been chronically intoxicated and then withdrawn from cyclazocine experienced only mild abstinence symptoms and did not crave more of the substance. Further work demonstrated that, when subjects were taking cyclazocine chronically, even very large doses of morphine failed to produce such customary effects as severe respiratory depression and euphoria. Under these circumstances of cyclazocine premedication, the patients were also protected from developing physical dependence when morphine was chronically administered.

The researchers outlined how cyclazocine might be employed with abstinent narcotic addicts trying to stay free of opiates. The physically dependent addict first must be withdrawn from his drug because cyclazocine precipitates a violent abstinence syndrome in the morphine-dependent patient. Then cyclazocine may be given orally, twice a day, in small doses that are gradually increased to the desired level. The postaddict may be maintained at this level until he is judged to have gained all he can from the treatment; then the agent may be gradually withdrawn. The investigators advised that withdrawal from narcotics and stabilization on cyclazocine be done in a controlled hospital setting. Treatment may continue in an ambulatory setting once the patient has reached the stabilization dose level. Other types of care, provided by psychotherapists and social workers, may then help him build a new life for himself.

While the postaddict patient is maintained on cyclazocine, he would be protected from the euphoria of even large doses of morphine or heroin—taken, perhaps, while on a spree—and from developing physical dependence on opiates again. Cyclazocine maintenance thus would avert two of the pharmacologic actions of opiates believed to be imortant in narcotic addiction. "There may be other benefits," the Martin group added. Referring to Dr. Wikler's work, they concluded: "It is possible that in subjects who attempt to readdict themselves while receiving a narcotic antagonist such as cyclazocine, there may be extinction of conditioned physical dependence and drug-seeking behavior."[2] Clinical trials of cyclazocine in the treatment of postaddicts are currently underway in New York City.

_____

[2] Ibid., p. 464.

448

Intramural: NIMH
Date of Interview: August, 1966

References:

Martin, W. R., Wikler, A., Eades, C. G., and Pescor, F. T. Tolerance to and physical dependence on morphine in rats. *Psychopharmacologia,* 1963, 4, 247-260.

Martin, W. R., Gorodetzky, C. W., and McClane, T. K. Treatment of narcotic addicts with cyclazocine. *Clin. Pharmacol. Therap.,* 1966, 7, 455-465.

Wikler, A. *Opiates and opiate antagonists.* Public Health Monograph No. 52. U.S. Department of Health, Education, and Welfare. Washington, D.C., 1958.

Wikler, A. Conditioning factors in opiate addiction and relapse. In Kassenbaum, G. G. and Wilner, D. M. (eds.), *Narcotics.* New York: McGraw-Hill, 1965.

Wikler, A., and Pescor, F. T. Factors disposing to "relapse" in rats previously addicted to morphine (abs.). *The Pharmacologist,* 1965, 7, 171.

Wikler, A., Martin, W. R., Pescor, F. T., and Eades, C. G. Factors regulating oral consumption of an opioid (etonitazene) by morphine-addicted rats. *Psychopharmacologia,* 1963, 5, 55-76.

Wikler, A., and Pescor, F. T. Classical conditioning of a morphine abstinence phenomenon, reinforcement of opiod-drinking behavior and "relapse" in morphine-addicted rats. *Psychopharmacologia,* 1967, 10, 3, 255-284.

Psychodynamics of Asthmatic Children

Investigators:
Constantine J. Falliers, M.D.
Kenneth Purcell, Ph. D.
William W. Hahn, Ph. D.
Children's Asthma Research Institute and Hospital
Denver, Colo.

Prepared by:
Gay Luce

The Children's Asthma Institute and Hospital is widely known for its multidisciplinary research on asthma, and for outstanding success in treating severely ill children. Partly aided by NIMH, investigators there are studying the manner in which emotions and physiology interact to induce asthmatic episodes. Dr. William W. Hahn has found that asthmatic children tend to withdraw from criticism and to respond to stress with distinctive respiratory and pulse changes. Currently, he is monitoring the sleep of asthmatic children in order to determine what physiological and/or psychological states in sleep are correlated with night attacks. Dr. Kenneth Purcell has devised a system of FM monitoring which will enable the staff to review a child's social reactions in an effort to see the emotional antecedents of acute attacks. Although asthmatic attacks may be triggered by some combination of emotional and allergic circumstances, a new approach has been to scan for biological rhythms that may hold clues to susceptibility. A recent study by Dr. Falliers indicates that there is a 24-hour rhythm in the peak expiratory flow rate—a measure of lung function—in asthmatic children. Furthermore, the timing of hormone therapy alters the timing of this peak.

Innovations in long-distance monitoring by FM radio, and perhaps later by biotelemetry, are opening up new possibilities in understanding how emotions, external conditions, and perhaps body rhythms conspire to produce the crippling symptoms of asthma and how timing may become an effective element in future treatment of the illness.

Background

If asked to make a list of crippling and dreadful illnesses, most people would probably forget asthma. This is odd, because asthma or related allergic illnesses afflict about one out of every 10 Americans. Attacks are both torturing and frightening, yet most people do not consider asthma a particularly serious or dangerous ailment. In point of fact, it causes about

9,000 deaths a year, deaths that are particularly horrible since they arise from strangulation. About 3 million American children suffer from asthma at one time or another; 300,000 have chronic asthma, and many are so severely ill that they do not improve under conventional treatment. They miss from 1 to 3 months of school each year, cannot join in the normal physical activities of their peers, and are retarded in physical growth. Psychologically, these children and their families must learn to cope with a frightful life-and-death emergency that can suddenly strike: A child in an acute attack may gasp for breath and in the failure of his respiratory system, begin to turn blue—sometimes requiring the oxygen equipment of a police department to save his life.

The Children's Asthma Research Institute and Hospital treats about 150 of these youngsters from all over the country. The medical program began in 1939, with the Jewish National Home for Asthmatic Children, and as the need for multidisciplinary research became evident, CARIH was created in 1959, and combined residential and hospital facilities with research. The campus resembles a private boarding school, strewn with small residence quarters, playing fields, and recreational buildings. Inconspicuous among the buildings is a modern hospital and a separate research building. The critically ill children who come to CARIH, for periods of 18–24 months, live with their peers in groups, attend school, and receive an unusual regimen of psychological and medical treatment, and various studies. When they leave, about 80 percent require much less medication than before to help them lead normal lives, and the remainder can lead normal lives with the help of drugs judiciously employed.

The success of CARIH, indeed, points up the very mysterious nature of the illness itself.

In 1966, a group of boys, who had been too ill to walk to school before they came to CARIH, began to play football against teams of healthy children. They not only played: they competed and won. Bedridden children had been transformed into sports competitors. The staff were the first to admit that this transformation was uncanny, and it underscored their problem in understanding the ailment. Were the boys enabled to play football by treatments that caused physiological development? Were they liberated by psychological therapy and the emotional change of being away from home? Was there something generally desirable about the Denver environment? "If we knew for sure," remarked one doctor, "we'd soon have asthma licked."

Psychological Role of the Family

Inevitably, when a child arrives at the institute he enters a totally changed world. He may leave behind a city like New York, with its particular climate and air pollution. There are changes in pollen characteristics, foods, and factors such as the molds that may grow in his basement at home, or household pets, or neighborhood pets. The child is removed from many of the usual physical attributes of his environment that may

451

trigger or contribute to his respiratory troubles. Moreover, he leaves whatever emotional conflicts are engendered by his family. About a third of the children who have come to CARIH have improved so fast, with so little aid from medication, that they were at first called "mircale children." Their improvement suggested that emotional factors may have been singularly important in the acuteness of their illness.

Asthma has long been considered a psychosomatic disease by many investigators. One old and prevailing theory held that asthmatic attacks were the bursting forth of "suppressed crying," and the asthmatic child was supposed to have been unable to express certain emotions. Dr. Kenneth Purcell surveyed the interview responses of CARIH children about the causes of their attacks. A number of them felt that crying precipitated an attack rather than relieving it.

Others thought that laughing or coughing brought on an attack. Thus it appeared that general excitation of the respiratory system was singled out, and it seemed highly likely that these children learned to inhibit crying, coughing, or laughing—precisely in order to avoid an attack. It was the respiratory excitation, not the emotional expression, that they seemed to want to avoid. Suppressed crying might indeed be a learned response. Similarly, excessive mother-child dependency has been cited as a cause of asthma: Does the mother's undue attention elicit the asthma, or is her overprotectiveness inspired by the plight of her asthmatic child? In surveying the literature and evaluating the CARIH patients, Dr. Purcell has been struck with the fact that asthma is by no means homogeneous. Pollens, dust, colds, foods, or climate changes precipitated attacks. Many children have unexplained attacks in sleep, and physical exertion or weather changes were common precipitants. Still, there did seem to be some distinction between the so-called "miracle children" who promptly remitted almost on arrival at CARIH and needed no medication—the intermediate group that could respond to therapy without relying on adrenocorticoid hormones—and the group that absolutely depended for survival upon some hormone therapy. Dr. Purcell postulated that the drug-dependent children may have been more influenced by infection and allergy than the others. Perhaps the rapid remitters were children in whom symptoms had a predominantly emotional basis. On responses to questionnaires, parents of these children seemed to indicate that they had more punitive and authoritarian attitudes than did the parents of the other youngsters. Was family conflict at the bottom of their allergic disease?

One youngster, who had improved remarkably on arrival at CARIH, suffered a terrible attack, suddenly, 6 months later. His family had come for their first visit. However, if the staff had been tempted to conclude that this was a prime example of emotional triggering—they discovered that the family cat had been brought along, and the child was highly allergic to the beast. Thus, the interrelationship of environmental factors had made it difficult to pin down the specific triggers. An ingenious plan, involving 2 years of work and considerable patience, has been devised in order to study the role of the family in asthmatic illness. It was designed to hold environment constant, so that the asthmatic child experienced only one change—the absence or the presence of his family.

Children suffering from chronic asthma in the Denver area were selected for this study. These children are outpatients of CARIH, who have come to the institute for daily tests. After several weeks of evaluation, the families were offered a 2-week paid vacation in a hotel away from home. During this time, the child would be cared for and studied by a surrogate mother from the CARIH staff. This staff member would live at home with the child, with the daily visits to CARIH continuing throughout this period and after the family's return home.

There have been 22 children studied so far. Some have been selected on the conjecture that they would show improvement when their families departed, while others were not suspected of so many emotional factors underlying their illness.

About 70 percent of the youngsters in the emotional group did actually improve when their families were away and showed a resumption of respiratory symptoms when they returned. Only 10 percent of the children whose ailment was judged as less overtly emotional showed change that could be correlated with the presence or absence of the family. Thus, it seems that there are at least two kinds of asthmatic children: those in whom family emotional factors play a role, and those in whom these factors do not seem important. These two groups of children are now being compared on tests of autonomic responses, allergic history, and a variety of other measures. It is, however, too early to remark on the characteristics that distinguish the two groups.

Behavioral Antecedents of the Attack

If there are emotional interactions that precipitate asthmatic attacks, no clear correlation has been found among studies of individual patients. Teams of allergists, psychologists, and pediatricians have concentrated on a few youngsters, obtaining information from the children's schoolteachers, house-parents, physician, and psychotherapist. By converging on all the various aspects of the child's life following an asthma attack, they had hoped to single out the precipitating factors. Invariably there were complications, such as changes in weather or social environment, that made it impossible to construct a convincing link between the attack and the situation that preceded it. Moreover, there was no comprehensive observation of the child's social interactions, excepting when he was in the presence of an adult, and knew it.

Dr. Purcell and his associates decided that a more natural and inclusive mode of observation might be developed by having the children wear FM transmitters. All of their vocalizations, as well as breathing sounds, could then be recorded, and in the event of an asthmatic episode, the antecedent behavior could be heard on tape recordings. This kind of field observation without observers is possible with a miniature radio transmitter, small as a cigarette package, that can be worn on an ordinary belt. It will transmit to receivers in a 200-foot range, all verbalization, whispers, and enough respiratory sounds to signal the audible signs of asthmatic attacks. If a child, so observed, were to have 20 attacks, it would be possible to examine the portions of the recording just preceding, and to compare these with samples taken on other days at the same time. Later, the investigators might be able to re-create situations that led to attacks, substantiating the correlation between behavior and respiratory trouble in the laboratory. One question, however, demanded an answer before such a study could be planned: Would the children become self-conscious and distort their behavior if they knew they were being bugged?

A pilot study now seems to have answered that question. Last year, 16 boys and 10 girls were selected from the adolescent groups as being particularly self-conscious and therefore good to study and test. Half of the youngsters were given live transmitters; the other half were given dummies. They wore these packages for an hour each evening for 10 days, and each child knew whether or not he was really bugged, but had been asked not to tell anybody. At the end of the test, the houseparents were asked to guess which children wore live transmitters and which wore dummy transmitters: Presumably, if the bugged children were behaving differently from those with dummies, it would be apparent to the houseparents, who were interviewed and who had been asked to fill out behavior scales on the test children during different stages in the 10 days.

The 13 children wearing live transmitters gave every evidence of having grown used to the monitoring and of having become oblivious to the transmitter by the third or fourth night. Initially they were markedly self-conscious, but judging from the tape recordings, they began to pay it no heed. Moreover, at the end of the trial, the houseparents did no better than chance in guessing which children wore dummies and which wore live radio transmitters. Behavior differences, if there were any, could not have been very striking. Indeed, the children's own descriptions of their feelings were far more sensitive than were those of their houseparents. Judging from the freedom and spontaneity of their language, the monitoring soon lost any effect on their interactions.

Encouraged by this pilot study, the investigators have contracted with North American Aviation for the development of a campus-wide telemetry system. Beginning in the summer of 1967, the children will be recorded from the end of the schoolday until bedtime. Since transmission is excellent—capturing whispers, wheezes, and other respiratory sounds— the investigators are optimistic about the prospect of comparing the verbal behavior of children with subsequent attacks. They may begin to see whether the premonitory signs of an attack are incited by emotional factors, whether they are more likely at certain intervals, and the technique may be extended later so that physiological changes are simultaneously recorded by telemetry.

Sleep

Mysteriously, out of an apparently untroubled sleep, the asthmatic patient sometimes awakens gasping for air, feeling himself on the verge of suffocation. In some children the frequency of nocturnal attacks is 5–10 times as great as those occurring during the day. The night of sleep has been one phase of the daily round in which CARIH children have been mostly unobserved, but perhaps this span of quiet can reveal how an attack develops and why it occurs when it does. Dr. William W. Hahn has established a sleep-monitoring laboratory, within the research building, with a recording room in which children now sleep through many consecutive nights, while their brain waves, pulse, and respiration are continuously recorded.

Sleep has been found to consist of several stages, each characterized by particular brain wave patterns and physiological changes. A person passes down and up through these different levels of consciousness in a relatively predictable manner throughout the night. Four or five times in the course of a night the progression is repeated, and at each level the sleeper's muscle tone, his arousability, and his psychological experiences appear to be different. At approximately 90-minute intervals the eyes begin moving rapidly, the pulse changes, respiration grows irregular, and if awakened now, most people remember vivid dreams. This rapid-eye-movement stage of sleep has been associated with the gastric secretions of ulcer patients, with attacks of nocturnal angina, and some investigators have wondered whether it may also be associated with asthma. Dr. Hahn has been looking for a possible link between the asthmatic attack and a particular stage of sleep. So far, five children have been studied for a total of 12 nights and some identifiable patterns are beginning to appear.

On nights when a child in the laboratory is experiencing fairly constant wheezing he will be likely to spend very little time in deeper stages of sleep and proportionately more time in the lighter stages. It isn't possible to tell, at this point, whether the child is initially restless, tense, or uncomfortable—and his respiratory distress is a result of this psychophysiological tension. Or does the distress of mild asthma and an impending attack elicit various psychological and physical stresses in the child? During the night it appears that the awareness of discomfort, to the point of waking up and doing something about it, may vary with the stage of sleep. In the laboratory a child with very mild asthma symptoms has awakened from a light stage of dreaming sleep to request a nebulizer (spray medication), yet the same child has continued to sleep for an hour or more, wheezing and showing signs of greater respiratory distress during the other stages of sleep.

Sleep study has a unique advantage for tracking the development of an asthmatic attack. This is the one long period of time when a child will stay still without complaint.

455

Psychophysiological Reactivity in Asthmatic and Normal Children

Two years ago Dr. Hahn and his associates began to find a suggestive difference between asthmatic and normal children in their reactions to mental arithmetic, interference while they were solving problems, and a situation in which they anticipated a mild electric shock. The asthmatic youngsters showed a notably higher heart rate. Careful checking indicated that this was not caused by acclimatization to the Denver altitude, that it could not be attributed to lack of adaptation, nor to medication. The unusual incidence of tachycardia among asthmatic youngsters suggested a possible malfunction within the autonomic nervous system. The investigator speculated that this might be a premonitory signal, the first sign of an abnormal response which might develop into an asthmatic attack were the stress continued.

In a recent study, normal and asthmatic children aged 10–14 were compared as they underwent more severe stresses. The 18 CARIH youngsters were very much improved, had shown virtually no symptoms since shortly after their arrival at the institute, and were taking no regular medication. Their counterparts were 21 healthy youngsters who were Denver residents participating in a summer recreation program. At the outset, each boy was asked to check a list of words that approximated the way he felt most of the time: a quick scanning for attitudes and emotions. Then the youngster was wired for physiological recordings of heart rate, finger and face temperature, finger pulse volume, skin resistance, and respiration. As they lay in the recording room they received four kinds of stimuli—tones, shocks, and two sets of arithmetic problems geared for their age level.

The problem was played to the child by tape recorder, and he was asked to solve it mentally and announce the answer. After each answer, a voice would make some remark which, unknown to the child, was pre-recorded. Following responses to the first set of problems, the remarks were neutral or encouraging. However, during the second batch of problems the child heard increasingly severe criticism. "I wonder if you're really trying—most children your age don't have any trouble with these problems."

After the session the boy was questioned. Did he realize that the voice was a tape recording? Was he aware that ciritcism was part of the experiment? Did he realize that his answers actually had been correct? The questions began with an exploration of his feelings, his reactions to the criticism. Once the child learned that the criticism was a tape-recorded dupe he was usually relieved and more accurate about describing his feelings. In general, the asthmatic children seemed to have been more timid and self-reproachful when they were criticized. They were apt to say that they had gotten angry at themselves, that they felt discouraged and wondered why they were giving wrong answers. The normal youngsters more typically believed that the voice had to be kidding or putting them on. They didn't doubt their ability to compute the problems and tended to be angry at the invisible critic.

456

A close look at their physiological records indicated a curious difference between the asthmatic and normal boys. The asthmatics showed a generally higher heart rate, but their respiration exhibited a curious pattern as the stress mounted. The normal children showed an elevated respiration rate, but the asthmatics reacted by breathing faster up to a point and then, as if this were a kind of ceiling, or as if they exerted control, their respiration became no faster. Slowed expiration is one of the symptoms of an asthmatic attack. It is interesting that the physiological response to criticism resembled, in this manner, the initial stages of the asthmatic attack.

The psychological afterreactions of the asthmatic children, as judged by the checklist of adjectives of mood, showed a preponderance of negative answers when once again they were asked to mark the words that described their usual state of mind. Psychologically, as physiologically, they gave a different response to the stress of adverse criticism in comparison with nonasthmatic peers.

In future studies the investigator will attempt to discover what this difference means. One important possibility is that the emotional reactions of inward anger and nonaggressive self-reproach are stress reactions functionally related to the asthma attack, and not merely a byproduct of the illness. "Although we cannot document a functional or causal relationship, data from the present study illustrate that a complex psychological stimulus initiates emotional and physiological responses in the asthmatic child which differ from those aroused in normal children exposed to the same conditions or stimulation."

Rhythmicity in Physiological Responses and Drug Effects

CARIH children, with all the study, monitoring, and therapy they receive, might seem to lead extremely abnormal lives. Yet for every one of these children, life had never before been so normal. Medically hopeless, always in jeopardy of strangling attacks, these children had lived a more disabling life at home. There, a slight wheezing might be sufficient to bring tension and fear into the whole family. It is clear why the particular symptoms of this disease incur strong psychological repercussions.

At home a child might have to be rescued by the police, or taken to the hospital in an acute attack, stricken, gasping, and turning blue. These episodes sometimes last a few hours, and sometimes linger for as long as 4 days. Special equipment is needed, for the victim's chest would expand, trapping air, his lungs filling with thick mucus. At the CARIH a child in such trouble would immediately receive aid from a pressure-breathing instrument, from chemical sprays to open his bronchial tubes and lungs, and from an instrument designed to remove plugs of mucus from the lungs. He would be attended by calm competent nurses and doctors, at once soothing him and also studying the nature of his attack. To a child who had experienced the emergency measures that all of the children knew, the gamut of laboratory research tests was not particulary imposing.

457

Each of the children was studied along many dimensions throughout his stay. Within the laboratory, the children were exposed to changes in temperature, humidity, barometric pressure, and psychological provocation—in attempts to single out the triggering factor in their allergy. The general finding was never a single factor, but a combination of simultaneous changes that might be very slight. Each child regularly takes tests of pulmonary function during laboratory exercise and controlled climatic changes. Analyses are made of bacteriological samples from the respiratory tracts. Tests of pituitary-adrenal function and immunological factors are continued, along with tests of particular nose sprays used to dilate the bronchial tubes, and studies of the manner in which these dilators may affect the nervous system and catecholamine metabolism. For the child at CARIH, life as a continued object of research is still more normal than was the disabled life of a youngster always on the precipice.

In their efforts to uncover the origins of asthma, and hopefully some unique factor which might be medically countered, the CARIH researchers have taken a new and unusual path. They have been studying one dimension that is usually overlooked in medicine: the periodicity of internal functions and of physiological responses. An almost 24-hour—circadian—fluctuation has been found to be the endogenous characteristic of many organs, cells, and subcellular activity in animals and man. About every 24 hours, body temperature rises to a peak and falls to its nadir, repeating this fluctuation day after day in the normal person. The level of certain adrenal hormones in the blood, or excreted in urine, also shows a roughly 24-hour rhythm. At almost any level, from large body systems down to cell division, rhythm seems to be an important property of the body's organization. The circadian, or almost daily rhythm, is nearly as prominent among certain physiological functions as is the menstrual rhythm. In a manner remotely analogous to the winding of a clock, a person's environment, his regimen of sleep and waking, of meals and social activity, seem to synchronize his multitudinous internal rhythms.

Although new in application to medicine, the relevance of circadian and other biological rhythms has been amply demonstrated by a number of scientists, notably by more than a decade of research on the part of Dr. Franz Halberg and his associates at the University of Minnesota. Not only must the body deliver the right substances to the right places in the correct amounts—but it must do it at the right time. In the case of the victim of Cushing's disease, for instance, a clue in diagnosis is the rise and fall of circulating adrenal steroids, for it is the inverse of a normal rhythm even when the levels remain within the so-called normal range. Phase relationships among body rhythms can also provide meaningful clues to pathology.

Two years ago, Dr. Constantine J. Falliers and Dr. Halberg took a first step in evaluating circadian rhythms in asthmatic and normal children. They compared these two groups of children on certain major body fluctuations as they occurred around the clock.

In January 1966, 19 boys at CARIH—all of them youngsters who were free of symptoms and who required no medication—began to be the focus of special and continuing interest. During the daytime, every 4 hours, they were briefly interrupted by a staff member, and were asked to breathe into a tube as hard and rapidly as they could. This flowmeter measured the number of liters of air they could expel from their lungs each minute. The peak rate of expiratory flow is an indicator of pulmonary function. An asthmatic person, whose respiratory passages are often blocked, may expire too little, too slowly. During stress or an oncoming attack, expiration rate diminishes and air collects in the lungs. Thus a high peak expiratory flow rate is a welcome sign. As these studies were to demonstrate, the peak is not the same at different times of day, even within an individual who is normal. One question that interested the CARIH staff was whether normal and asthmatic children would show their peaks at the same points on the daily round.

In April, and again in May, the boys underwent more than their daily tests. Now, around the clock for 48 hours, they were tested on several physiological changes. Seventeen normal boys of the same age, orphans in Denver institutions, were brought to the institute for scrutiny and comparison. At each age level, the boys lived the same schedule of mealtimes, bedtime, and waking. For a little more than 2 days they were housed in a research wing of the hospital on campus. There they lived in sealed rooms under the constant supervision of nurses. They could not even go to the bathroom unsupervised, since all urine was being collected in 4-hour samples for analysis of 17-hydroxycortiscosteroids.

Beginning at midnight, and every 4 hours thereafter, the boys were briefly interrupted in their sleep or activities for a measure of blood pressure, pulse, a urine sample, and rectal temperature. They were asked to breathe into the expiratory flowmeter, and to estimate when 2 minutes had passed by counting to 120. This ubiquitous little test indicates approximately whether a person senses the passage of time as slow, fast, or indeed as the stopwatch reads. In a relatively predictable fashion, all of these physiological variables and responses change around the 24 hours.

It is, of course, far easier to describe in writing a 48-hour study of 3 dozen youngsters than to confront the actual doing. When measures must be taken at equally spaced intervals, around the clock, and when precision is crucial, staff coordination and exertion is intense. Many staff members volunteered to work on the 2-day marathons, around the clock; an exhausting procedure for all.

Throughout the longitudinal studies as well, it was necessary to chase the boys down promptly every 4 hours, whether they were out playing, roller skating, or swimming. A staff member would have to find them and make them blow into the flowmeter.

The very arduousness of such a study prescribes a very cautious experimental design. There are limits to the endurance of even a mildly sick child, and limits to the energies of the staff. Thus, it is necessary to ascertain beforehand how many samples, at what intervals, are needed to determine the peak of a circadian rhythm, and by what analysis the frequency and peak phase will become clear. A longitudinal study of certain functions could be run for several months with the asthmatic children and one normal child, but measures could only be taken during daytime. Interruption of sleep over several months would not only be likely to alter the rhythms under study, but also to exacerbate the children's symptoms and subject the staff to extreme exhaustion. Thus, within the framework of an unevenly paced longitudinal study containing nightly gaps, short intensive studies were conducted around the clock. By suitable analysis, performed by computer, these could fill in some of the gaps. As Dr. Falliers said of his collaboration, the study could not have been feasible at a small institution without the sophisticated statistical help and the computer analysis offered by the Minnesota laboratory.

In comparing the normal and asthmatic children, the researchers chose to look for the highest daily values—the peak expiratory flow rate, the 4 hours in which adrenal steroids were excreted most, the point of highest pulse or blood pressure, etc. These crests were then plotted on a 24-hour compass, and it was easy to see how the two groups differed or coincided. The normal children, for instance, were close to one another in the distribution of their highest body temperatures, which occurred during afternoon and early evening. The asthmatic children were even more homogeneous, showing their peaks exclusively in the afternoon. Their fastest pulse, however, was more distributed over the day than was the peak heart rate of the normal youngsters. Again, in the excretion of adrenal steroids, the healthy boys showed their peaks between 8 a.m. and 1 p.m., while a few asthmatic children exhibited peaks very early in the morning or in early afternoon. Although a harmonic analysis of the data did indicate some differences between the groups, in the crest phase of their physiological functions, no further conclusions could be drawn from such a preliminary study. Perhaps the asthmatic children as a group showed a little more variability in circadian crests.

On the other hand, the circadian rhythm of peak lung functioning does seem to differ considerably among asthmatic and normal groups. In intensive 48-hour studies, and in longitudinal studies, it has become apparent that there are circadian fluctuations in the peak expiratory flow rate. Healthy children showed crests between 1 and 4 p.m., while the average peak of the asthmatic child occurred around 2 p.m. Here, the healthy children were more heterogeneous and exhibited more individual variation.

Further data, still in analysis, were obtained from May until the end of September 1966. Every other week, the 17 boys and one normal girl in this study underwent 48 hours of round-the-clock study.

Circadian Rhythms in Drug Effects

Adrenal hormones play an important role in the therapy of asthma: sometimes in severe cases cortisone and its analogs are the only medications that make life possible. Judged by available techniques, asthmatic youngsters do not seem to suffer from adrenal insufficiency, and the steroids they take—not for correction of a deficiency but for their potent anti-inflammatory action—have many side effects. One of these appears to be a dampening effect upon growth. These youngsters are usually behind their peers in growth and maturation, although tests at CARIH indicate that they have the normal levels of growth hormone. Some of them have been given anabolic hormones to stimulate growth. Still, the side effects of their lifegiving hormone treatments persist at high dosages. Although the corticosteroid drugs have been available for more than 15 years, no definitive recommendation can yet be made regarding the best time schedule for treatment (e.g., once a day, once every 48 hours, divided doses every 4–6 hours, etc.).

Could side effects be diminished by giving smaller doses at appropriate times? Animal experiments have demonstrated circadian susceptibility rhythms for bacteria, drugs, X-ray, and other stimuli. The treatment that kills an animal at one point on his daily cycle will merely make him sick at another phase. Thus, there is reason to believe that the changing state of the body might enhance or reduce a drug's potency, according to the time it is administered. In June of 1966, Drs. Falliers and Halberg began to study a time factor in the efficacy of hormone treatment. Between June and the end of September, 28 CARIH children were medicated on specific schedules and systematically evaluated for the crest time of their expiratory flow rate. All of the children were sick enough to require hormone medication daily. They were divided into four groups matched as closely as possible for age, sex, home locale, allergies, the amount of hormone they needed, and their expiratory peak flow rates. For 4 months they were maintained on prednisone. One group received it at 1 a.m., another at 7 a.m., another at 1 p.m., and another at 7 p.m. At the end of 4 months it was clear that the timing of the hormone affected the time at which the child now showed his peak expiratory flow rate. These asthmatic children, who had been very similar in their crest phases before the study, now diverged significantly.

Youngsters who received their drug at 1 a.m. began to show their crests almost 2 hours earlier than they had before. Those who received it at 7 a.m. were little changed, but the children who took their drug at 1 p.m. now showed their crests about 6 hours later than they had before. The time of expiratory crest shifted according to the time they received the hormone.

Although this novel finding was not immediately applicable to treatment, it did suggest future possibilities in the scheduling of drugs. The medical staff had the impression that children receiving their medication at 1 a.m. or 7 a.m. were clinically better off than the others. As a result of the study, Dr. Falliers felt that the dosage might possibly be reduced if it were administered in two segments. This procedure is now being tried. However, it is still too early to discover whether the timing of prednisone had any influence on side effects, for these sometimes appear only after many months or even after a drug is discontinued. The youngsters will be monitored for side effects relative to drug timing throughout their stay at

461

CARIH. The feasibility of such long-term surveillance makes the institute an excellent focus for such studies.

A clinical study of about 2-years' duration will be needed before the clinical value of drug scheduling can be determined. This may be a next step, although there are some inherent limitations in the endurance of the children, who are ill, away from home, and undergoing all the trials of growth and of being young. An intermediate study may ascertain whether these kids can function on smaller amounts of steroids, taken in two daily doses.

The implications of this study extended far beyond the treatment of asthma, for steroid hormones are staple medication for many illnesses, whether they be chronic ailments such as arthritis or ulcerative colitis, or an emergency crisis such as pneumonia. The administration of steroids is a delicate matter, as illustrated by the kinds of serious consequences that can follow—the development of diabetes in predisposed persons, or the so-called steroid psychosis. The role of timing in the regulatory action of hormones makes the medical substitution—by regulation from without—a far more complicated manipulation than supplying an artificial limb to an amputee. The exploration of this factor thus has ramifications for helping the victims of a great many illnesses.

The importance of circadian rhythmicity in asthma, and in understanding asthma, may be determined better when round-the-clock studies of physiological functions can be made without disturbing the children—through biotelemetry. In Dr. Purcell's study of vocal and respiratory behavior via FM transmitters worn by the children, there may be a first indication of the value of continuous monitoring. So far, at least, a first look has shown that the asthmatic child may have different timing on specific functions than the normal child. This, in itself, is a clue and an encouragement to continue examining time structure.

Research Grants: MH 10385, 8415, 3269. Also: A 5963 and Ch 5523
Date of Interview: Nov. 23, 1966

References:

Falliers, C. J. Corticosteroids and anabolic hormones for childhood asthma. *Clin. Pediat.*, 1965, 4, 441.
Falliers, C. J., McCann, W. P., Chai, H., Ellis, E., and Yazdi, N. Controlled study of iodotherapy for childhood asthma. *J. Allergy*, 1966, 38, 183.
Halberg, F., and Falliers, C. J. Variability of physiologic circadian crests in groups of children studied "transversely." *J. Pediat.*, 1966, 68, 741.
Hahn, W. W. Autonomic responses of asthmatic children, *Psychosom. Med.*, 1966, 28, 4.
Hahn, W. W., and Clark, J. A. Psychophysiological reactivity of asthmatic children. 1966 preprint.
Jorgensen, J. R., and Falliers, C. J. A rational approach to corticosteroid therapy for asthma in children. *J.A.M.A.*, 1966, 198, 773.
Purcell, K. Critical appraisal of psychosomatic studies. *N. Y. State J. Med.*, 1965, 65, 16.
Purcell, K., and Brady, K. Adaptation to the invasion of privacy: monitoring behavior with a miniature radio transmitter. *Merrill-Palmer Quart. Behav. and Dev.*, 1966, 12, 3.

462

Infant Stimulation as Part of Well Baby Care in a Disadvantaged Area

Investigator:

Margaret F. Gutelius, M.D.
Director
Child Health Center
Comprehensive Health Care Program
Children's Hospital
Washington, D. C.

Prepared by:

Clarissa Wittenberg

Increasingly it has been realized that helping a child "in" must begin very early. People involved with Head Start, a federally sponsored preschool program for disadvantaged children, came quickly to the realization that they were not beginning nearly early enough. Some suggested expanding the schools and preschool programs to even younger groups while others felt very strongly that the young child should be assisted while still in his home. One research program at Children's Hospital in Washington, D.C., has attempted to reach young mothers to help them learn ways of caring for their children and stimulating their intellectual growth so that they will be able to meet with success when they enter school. This program, working with black, unmarried, teenage mothers has shown that many can be helped to provide successfully both well-baby care and the sort of interaction that helps a baby "learn to learn." Results show that babies who have had this combination of well-baby care and infant stimulation have higher developmental I.Q.'s at 6 months of age than babies who have not had this program. This difference continues to show up and to become more pronounced when the babies are compared again at 1 year and 2 years of age.

Almost all of the mothers in the program had ambitions for their children to "go further" than they themselves had done. They wanted their children to be successful in school and do well for themselves in life. This project attempted to help them realize the important first steps in making these dreams come true for their babies. Although in many cases the mothers were quite immature and themselves locked in cycles of poverty and lack of education, most were cooperative and eager to participate in the program.

MOBILE COACH PROJECT

A total of 140 young women expecting their first child were found at city prenatal clinics. The girls selected were black, and between 15 and 19

463

years of age and lived in a specific area surrounding the hospital. They were in their seventh month of pregnancy, of normal intelligence, without chronic physical disease, and without gross emotional pathology. The group was then divided and one section received counseling from the research team and particularly from the public health nurse; the other, the control group, received prenatal and baby care given by city clinics and city health department nurses. The deliveries took place in city hospitals or in private hospitals under contract to the city. After the babies were born, a second screening was done, and only normal babies weighing at least 5 pounds 8 ounces remained in the study. This assured that the experimental and control babies had essentially the same characteristics.

Of the original 140, 95 pairs of mothers and children remained in the final study group. Twelve babies were born prematurely. A typical rate of prematurity for babies born to ghetto mothers is about 12 percent. There were other pregnancies that miscarried or resulted in stillborn babies. The odds are against these babies even in cases such as these where the mothers had obtained prenatal care. After delivery many mothers moved away and a few became uncooperative. Those who moved within a half hour's trip by car were retained. In Washington, this encompasses almost the entire city so that only those who moved to the suburbs or out of the city were lost for this reason. This left 47 mothers and children in the experimental group and 48 in the control group.

A mobile coach brought well-baby care to the door for those in the experimental group. A public health nurse worked with each mother individually to teach her about her baby's development. The mothers were encouraged at each phase of development to respond to their babies' particular needs and to supply a stimulating and protective environment. The mobile coach made possible a very active reaching out and facilitated well baby care. Those in the control group were visited by the city R.N.'s. By and large, the city nurses only followed the babies for two or three months. However, if there were problems it was up to the mother to see that the child got to a well-baby clinic for check-ups. All mothers in the program used Children's Hospital clinics and facilities in emergencies and at times of serious illness.

The orientation of the stimulation program was frankly middle-class and its major goal was success in school for each child. This was a practical test, as schools remain the main way in which children can learn the things they need to know to be successful in our society and to be able to get and hold good jobs. The methods taught the mothers were built upon the concept of protecting and expanding the child's curiosity and developing good verbal skills.

The original plan was to work with the mothers until the child reached 3 years of age and then to assist the families in placing their children in neighborhood Head Start programs. However, Head Start programs have not been extended to 3-year-olds in this neighborhood and therefore only a few of the children have been placed in preschools. Some success in this area has been achieved, however, as one child is attending a Montessori school and four have been considered eligible for scholarships to a good private school in the city. However, it is almost impossible for these mothers to provide transportation and to pay even incidental expenses for private preschool education. The loss of the planned Head Start programs is serious, as it has been demonstrated that it is necessary to keep up a level of stimulation if a child is going to continue to progress and not fall behind.

The Mothers

All of the mothers were between 15 and 19 years of age, unmarried, and pregnant for the first time. They all lived in a 15-census-tract area around Children's Hospital. This area is basically a low-income, black ghetto. It is an area of old rowhouses, old and crowded apartment buildings, a high-crime rate, and many social problems. It was an area highly involved in the riot in 1968. All of the girls had normal intelligence, between 70 and 115 on the Peabody Picture Vocabulary Test, and were without evidence of chronic physical disease or major mental pathology as determined by a short interview with the psychiatrist. They were all willing and able to participate in the program. Almost 70 percent were born and raised in Washington. All of them had finished elementary school, and about 20 percent had finished high school. Most had received average grades in the regular academic curriculum and wished to finish school. Many wanted to take additional training and learn some skill or trade. Very few showed anxiety or depression. About 90 percent were pleased about or at least accepting of the pregnancy. Almost half had known the father for one to three years and more than half expressed love and confidence in him. Most wanted to get married and have one to three more children. None saw adoption as a desirable course for their baby. Most had the assurance of help from the grandmother or other relatives.

The girls lived in crowded households. About a quarter of the girls lived with both parents, but for another half of the group their mother was the head of the house. Over half of both groups had significant contact with their father or another man who had helped to raise them. Sixty-eight percent had an adult male living in the household. Their families' income tended to be at the level for unskilled laborers. However, only three of the girls came from families then on public assistance. Although none of these girls came from the lowest economic level or from the most disorganized families, they were still definitely poor and lived in a marginal way. Although all of the families said they served meat daily, it was found that they lived at a crisis level of food expenditure, spending less than the Department of Agriculture 1962 guidelines for emergency minimum expense. Although a large number of families had life insurance, almost none had health insurance or savings. Most of the girls came from homes that were characterized by good housekeeping, although there were many basically substandard conditions, such as shared kitchens and deteriorated structures. The families, by and large, were struggling to do the best they could. In all of these respects, the mothers and their backgrounds were essentially the same in both the experimental and control groups.

A survey was done prior to the program to determine the child-rearing attitudes of these girls. This covered the entire group. Questions were asked to assess their attitudes about child rearing and to see what they understood of child development.

The first question dealt with the handling of aggression toward the parent. The girls were asked what they would do if at dusk they had to bring a child in from play who then became angry and kicked and hit them. It was found that even mild aggression towards the parents is not tolerated and is usually punished. About 60 percent of the mothers would respond punitively and about half were in favor of spanking in such a case. Some favored explaining why and then spanking.

Another question dealt with the use of punishment for immature behavior during toilet training and was concerned with the acceptance of slow development toward maturity. For a 2-year-old who had a lapse in toilet training most would scold or spank, with scolding preferred. Only one girl would ignore such an incident, whereas most middle-class mothers would do so.

With regard to diet, most felt a rather active controlling role was required rather than a passive one. Almost all of the girls felt that they would coax or make a child eat vegetables rather than simply offering them and then ignoring it.

In the crucial area of verbal development, only 25 percent of the girls would encourage a child to talk when adults were sitting around visiting. Many would permit an answer if the child were spoken to, but a third would prefer the child to be absolutely quiet. Here the girls with the higher I.Q.'s gave significantly different and more positive answers than those with lower scores. This encouragement of speech and the acquisition of early and basic verbal skills, as well as having pleasant associations with speech, is extremely important in the development of communicative skills. The investigators noted here that initially the mothers were pleased with the sounds of their first child and responded naturally with cooing and other sounds. It was found that with help the mothers continued this healthy trend even though it became more difficult when their children became active physically and, in addition, began to bombard them with questions.

When asked what they would do if a child was misbehaving all day long — a question designed to tap the girl's perception of underlying causes of behavior — some girls would look for illness or another reason, such as boredom or unhappiness, while about 50 percent would scold or spank. Here the girls with the lower I.Q.'s gave more positive answers than the others, leading perhaps to the idea that intuition is more important here than intelligence.

Three-fourths of the girls would use praise very sparingly. There was a tendency to inconsistency with regard to discipline among the girls.

The girls, by and large, began with basically warm and motherly attitudes towards children. Almost without exception they expressed and

466

demonstrated love and devotion for their infants during the newborn period. One question with regard to what to do when a child was afraid of the dark elicited interesting answers. About 73 percent would leave a night light on, stay with the child, or make some other sympathetic gesture. Even girls who were generally harsh about discipline seemed to be understanding in this situation.

When asked as expectant mothers what they thought they could do in the first five years of the child's life to help him do well in school, many replied with answers such as "teaching a child obedience," "teaching him honesty," "name and address," "ABC's." Only about a third said "read to him" or other such types of stimulation.

It must be remembered that both experimental and control groups took part in this study, and that the two had essentially the same attitudes and basically were the same in approach to their children.

Prenatal Nursing Activities

The public health nurse associated with the research visited the girls in the experimental group at home and discussed with them many topics. Among these were the issues of diet, their pregnancy, the development of the baby and other things of importance to the girls. Visits were made approximately every two weeks prior to the ninth month of gestation and then each week during the final month. The nurse, Mrs. Marion Brooks, is black as were the girls, and she felt that this helped her to reach them and be accepted by them. She felt that good rapport was developed with all of the girls that she visited, and that most were eager to learn and communicate with her. Her general approach was to be quite definite about methods of child rearing and very supportive of the mother's desire to do well with her baby. Her visits prior to the birth of the baby lasted about one-and-a-half hours each time.

Prior to their deliveries, the mothers were encouraged to prepare for the birth and to plan their care for the child. They were helped to collect bright, colorful pictures for the walls of the baby's room, and the nurse stressed to them the importance of visual, auditory, and tactile stimulation to the young baby.

Well Baby Care

After the birth of the baby, a comprehensive program of well-baby care was begun which included the infant stimulation program. Well-baby care was offered in a dramatic way by taking a mobile coach and a pediatric team directly to the home. One visit was made each month for the first six months and then less frequently until the child reached 3 years. Between each visit the nurse visited to carry on the infant education program. Although there were some technical problems with the use of the coach, parking, etc., it was considered successful, as it demonstrated to the

467

mothers the concern that was felt that their babies receive regular attention. A rather large coach was used with two examining rooms and a toilet, and it was felt that perhaps a smaller coach would have been just as useful. The coach allowed the home examinations to go on in a professional setting and a clean environment and also assured that the staff had a pleasant setting. The use of the coach has now been discontinued as most of the children have now reached 2 years of age.

Medical well-child supervision was planned and administered according to the guidelines of the American Academy of Pediatrics. The program of infant stimulation was developed after an examination of the literature and a study of Caldwell's inventory of Home Stimulation.

After the coach was discontinued a doctor and nurse made home visits via a car. The visits totaled 22 during the three-year period. The children in the comparison group were followed in the regular District of Columbia health clinics, and it was up to mothers to keep appointments and to see that the child received well baby care.

The research families were counseled at each visit of the doctor and nurse on feeding, hygiene, sleep habits and normal growth. Toilet training, feeding problems, temper tantrums, thumb sucking, discipline, and other developmental problems were anticipated and received attention prior to and during the period of their occurrence.

The infants were provided iron and vitamin medication in prophylactic doses from the newborn period through the first three years of life. The mothers were given the home phone numbers of the pediatrician, the nurse, and the director of the project, and were urged to call for advice whenever it was needed. The mothers called often in the early months of their child's life and more infrequently later. When a child was ill, the mother was directed to take him to Children's Hospital, although the project staff treated minor illnesses, such as colds, diarrhea, impetigo, etc.

Group meetings for mothers were held occasionally on Sunday afternoons with the project psychiatrist, nurse, director, and occasional guests to discuss problems in child rearing. It was observed that the interchange of ideas was reassuring to these young mothers and stimulated their interest in the development of their children. In addition to these sessions, social events were arranged. One such outing was to a flower show and another was a swimming party. In addition, there were parties held at each staff member's home. Some of these events took place for mothers only, and some included children. These were designed to provide concrete evidence of the research team's interest in the mothers as well as the babies.

Some of the mothers had a feeling of being singled out and they asked why they were selected while pregnant friends had not been invited to join the program. They were told that it had to do with the timing of their pregnancy, and that the research had to be with young women in the seventh month.

After the babies were born, the mothers were visited by the public health nurse and a carefully designed stimulation program was carried out. It was felt that the very best teaching of the young infant has to be done by the mother who presumably has the strongest relationship, and who can achieve that blend of intimacy, affection, and stimulation that is the key to a responsive baby who is actively able to learn. There is an assumption here that these mothers are less able to do these things than are middle-class mothers. There is also the assumption that these children will be disadvantaged when in school with middle-class children if they are not helped. There is concern on the part of the investigators that these mothers, often overwhelmed as they are, will not see the importance of the type of interaction that produces an open and curious child who is able to learn successfully. The stimulation program was particularly designed to help build the type of verbal-cognitive background that typically occurs in the middle-class home. It is thought that particularly the acquisition of verbal skills depends upon the type of relationships fostered in the early days of a child's life. Intelligence in this study is conceived of as being made up of many abilities, many attributes, and built on many experiences and supported by good physical health.

This program was designed to give the ghetto mother the maximum support and assistance. The public health nurse helped, but did not replace nor displace the mother in her role with her infant. Every effort was made to communicate the value that the research team placed upon her and her infant. Efforts were made to reduce the feeling that only perfunctory care would be available. Many of these girls had so diminished an expectation of assistance that they were slightly suspicious of the program and the quality of care that it offered. The survey on characteristics of the mothers and their attitudes showed a basically positive approach to their children, but one that reflects the pressures of their lives and also their own lack of positive experience in many learning situations. Although middle-class families do not always reflect the most sophisticated ideas about learning and development, they tend at least to have a better idea about these factors and to be more in a position to afford the type of toys and to provide the type of environment where a child can at least explore ways of learning. At this point in time the research personnel were content to try and achieve a little more of the middle-class attitudes towards child rearing.

Throughout the well-baby program and specifically in the stimulation contacts, another message was given indirectly to each mother. It was hoped that by reaching out to her and helping her care for her infant the importance of her task and the value of it would become more obvious to her and that her own early sense of being glad about becoming a mother, and her desire to take good care of her child would be supported and to some degree protected.

469

In both the well-baby and the stimulation programs, as the nurse visited, she observed the mother's behavior with her child and also introduced and discussed various issues. Records were kept via checklists for each visit in the first three years. If the mother was not home, the caretaker, often the grandmother, was seen.

An emphasis was placed on all forms of visual, auditory, tactile, and motor stimulation. The encouragement of exploration, the use of praise, the understanding of normal developmental stages were all important. Avoidance of overstimulation was discussed and protection of the baby from accidents without inhibiting his curiosity. An emphasis was placed on the alleviation of superstition and on assistance to the child in handling his own fears. Normal child development was discussed continuously.

An effort was made to see the mother on each visit, but since many of these mothers either went back to school or were forced to go to work, often the baby was in the care of a relative. When the caretakers were the grandmothers, they were, in general, less receptive to the program than were the mothers. They had already reared children and tended to fall back on ways they had found successful. Also, Mrs. Brooks found that some were quite superstitious, for instance, fearing to let a baby look into a mirror as they believed it caused trouble with teething. It was estimated that on the average a mother was at home with her baby until he was about 15 months of age. Four of the mothers remained with their babies until they were 3 years old. In many cases a good day care center would have given the baby more stimulating care and a better opportunity to have the type of experiences that would help him cope more successfully with school and have a better chance of breaking a cycle of poverty.

The First Year - Stimulation Program

Ten visits were made by the nurse. Each one lasted about 1 hour. The nurse gave the baby toys appropriate to his age. A mobile, a rattle, a small squeeze toy, and plastic cookies on a chain were given to the new baby. Later, at 3 months, a cradle gym, a terry cloth toy; and at 6 months, a cloth book. At 7 months, a plastic hammer and a plastic milk bottle with colorful objects inside were given. A stack toy was chosen for 9 months, and at 1 year, a more advanced cloth book. The nurse in each case explained why the toy was appropriate and, if necessary, showed the mother how to use it. The toys were provided rather than suggested as the investigators knew it was difficult for the mothers to afford extras, and few had cars or time to travel to purchase them. This was consistent with the philosophy of the program to make as much available, as easily as possible, to the young mothers.

The visits varied depending upon the age of the child and the needs of the parents. For instance, at 2 months, the nurse might point out that the child can observe the mobile and takes pleasure in bright objects. She might point out that the baby will stop and listen to soft music or his mother's voice. The mother was told about verbal development. She was helped in observing how the baby begins to speak with throaty sounds and then progresses. The mother would be encouraged to respond to the baby and be told how important that was. Trips out of doors and to new places were encouraged. The development of tactile sense, important all throughout life, was explained. Cuddling, stroking, holding, and kissing were encouraged and the mothers were warned not to hamper a child's movements by more furniture or clothing than what was necessary.

As the need for discipline grew, the mothers were helped to use consistent and patient methods with an emphasis on praise and the understanding that a child's curiosity is valuable and not "bad" behavior. A frequent problem was that the mothers tended to confine or restrict their babies rather than safeguard the environment. The mothers were discouraged from slapping and from continually repeating "no" to their babies.

The Second Year

About 8 hour-long visits were made and special emphasis was put on the mother's talking with her child and encouraging him to speak. The use of books and bedtime stories was stressed. The families were advised to help the child get large muscle exercise and to let him explore, jump, climb, and otherwise be active. Again, as in the well-baby visits, the subject of accident prevention was raised.

The children were given more complicated toys, many of which stressed fine motor coordination, such as wooden beads to string or snap beads. Balls were suggested as a good toy for helping with gross motor development. The nurse also helped the mothers to develop homemade toys and to see that some household items make good playthings.

Although the nurse encouraged water play and mud pies, etc., generally the mothers were uncomfortable and felt such activities were too messy. Generally, the mothers did not want their children to get dirty or to put things the mothers considered dirty in their mouths. The nurse interpreted the need for the child to be free from unnecessary concern about tidiness in order to explore textures and to play in an imaginative and creative way.

The Third Year

Here, there was an increasing emphasis on trips outside the home, on visual motor coordination, and language development. The use of pencils and crayons was encouraged. Discussions with the caretaker or mother emphasized the need to satisfy the child's curiosity, to praise, and reward him frequently, and to admire his achievements. The mothers were encouraged to answer the interminable questions asked and were helped to see that questioning was important to the child and the basis for later intellectual growth. The mothers were told to be honest with their children and to admit it when they didn't know the answers. Consistency in discipline was again stressed.

471

The nurse visited about six times during the third year and each visit lasted about one-and-one-half hours. Dental hygiene was promoted as in the overall well-baby program, and a toothbrush was given the child if he didn't already have one. A small blackboard and chalk and eraser were given at 28 months and a small hardback book at 32 months. A puzzle was given as a farewell present at 3 years.

What Happened to the Mothers

Of the 47 mothers in the experimental group, 17 have married. Out of these 17, five have already had separations occur. In the remaining intact marriages, most of the husbands work at semiskilled jobs, such as barbering, electrical work, etc. It must be remembered that many of the mothers were still dependent upon their families' support and that those who worked generally had low-level jobs. Six of the mothers are receiving public assistance. In one case, the money goes to a grandmother who is caring for the child. Of the experimental mothers, 11 finished high school before delivery and 9 finished after the birth of their child. Twenty-one of the mothers remain ungraduated. Four of these took some further training after delivery and four are still in school. All were encouraged by the research personnel to finish high school.

Nineteen of the 47 experimental mothers have had other children. Fourteen of these had one more child and five had two more. All of these mothers have been given access to birth-control information and devices as part of their maternity care provided by the city. Of the mothers who have had other children, 10 have obtained consistent well-baby care for their additional children.

About one-fourth of the research mothers received both more than $50 a month and fairly frequent visits from the alleged father. Another one-fourth had visits but not money, and the rest either sent small amounts of money and didn't visit or else ignored the entire situation. Not all of the mothers who married wed the father of their first child.

Most of the mothers had enough help from friends or relatives to leave the baby occasionally. A very few were terribly confined. The degree to which they left their babies seemed to depend upon the wishes of the girls. Some were more socially active and felt more hindered by the baby than others. Most were seen to be caring well for their babies and demonstrated love and affection.

Observations of the mothers and babies were made by a psychologist during the physical examinations at 6 months of age. The observer was unaware of the groupings. Results showed that the mothers who had participated in the infant stimulation program were markedly more verbal with their babies than the control mothers. This has not been completely tested out, but appears to be the case as the children grow older.

Most of the mothers seen by the research team were positive about the program and made contacts continually for information, in addition to regular appointments. For the most part, they were receptive to the ideas suggested and eager to learn. By and large, they were able to communicate well with the research personnel.

Early Results — The Babies at 6 Months

Although all the babies started out well at the newborn stage and both groups were comparable, there were differences in the Bayley test in developmental I.Q.'s at 6 months, and at 1 year, and even more pronounced differences at 2 years of age when the experimental children had significantly higher scores than did the controls. In addition, there was significantly less anemia in the experimental group. This was undoubtedly due to the provision of iron and the attention given to the diet of the children during the "out reach" well-baby care. The experimental children, it was found, had also received more meat and had been taken out of doors more often than the control children. Both practices had been encouraged in well-baby checks and by the public health nurse in her stimulation visits. Babies can develop anemia very easily if kept on a basically milk diet since milk has little iron. Their bodies need this substance for growth and development, and unless supplemental iron is given or large amounts of iron rich foods are added, anemia often develops.

At 6 months, there were only four children in the experimental group with hemoglobin levels below 10.0 gms. per 100 ml. Levels below 10.0 gms. are considered anemic, and this is considered one index of general health. There were 14 control children with levels below 10.0 gms. This was a significant difference. In addition, the experimental babies had less skin trouble—primarily diaper rash—than did the others. They had better appetites and less thumb sucking, too. Although it might be predicted that babies in the experimental group would have fewer illnesses, this did not turn out to be the case and patterns in this respect did not differ. Growth patterns were not significantly different in any way either.

The children were also studied intensively physically, anthropomorphically, and in terms of medical history. Again, in most respects, they began the same and continued to be about the same.

In terms of the mothers and their family situations, again many factors were studied, such as crowding, the number of people in the homes, incomes, illnesses, financial resources, diet, and education. The two groups were basically the same, all were overburdened.

More Recent Results

The Stanford-Binet test is used when the children reach 3 years of age, and to date a trend has emerged that gives the experimental children the advantage. This is a statistically significant figure, but not all the children have reached this age. It appears to offer some evidence of the value of the research intervention.

A number of questions are being examined now. A large number of variables have been recorded and a statistical analysis is being conducted with consultation from Arthur Kirsch, Ph.D., who is an Associate Professor of Statistics at George Washington University. To date most variables explored have either been unproductive or both groups have remained very similar, except in terms of the health and development of the infants. A close examination of success in school will be made as these children begin school. No attempt is being made to modify their school experience in any way. The relationship between the mothers and their children will be observed and to a certain extent the relationship of the mothers to subsequent children. It will be important, if positive results are achieved, to find what aspect of the program can be held responsible and to know which aspects really work.

One major problem in this area is the subtlety of the results that are being measured. All of these children, both control and experimental, have received well-baby care, in fact, the D. C. health department R.N.'s who do this also have a certain amount of infant stimulation education that they include in their routine contacts with new mothers. The difference then is one of degree. All the mothers live in crowded homes, all have low incomes, and so on. This similarity in samples, combined with the difficulty in finding sensitive evaluative instruments, means that differences may not be easily seen or documented, even if they exist. There is considerable conviction on the part of the staff that differences exist. Some differences, they feel, are related to the relationship between the mothers and the staff and the enhancement of the mother's self esteem due to her participation in the program. There is a growing awareness that the large social problems that weigh down these families need large and powerful answers to go along with the improvement of infant care in order for differences to be seen. One idea behind working with the mothers, rather than the staff working directly with the child, is to give benefit to subsequent children as well as the child in this research program. Here, again, tremendous pressures make themselves felt. Mothers who participated well and followed directions, who seemed to understand the value of well-baby care and took advantage of it when offered by the mobile coach team still do not always take subsequent children to well-baby clinics in a consistent manner. There is also some concern that, despite pressing social problems and the availability of birth-control information, these young women seem to be on their way to large families. However, it is possible that many want two or three children relatively close together and that having achieved this, they will then exercise an option to limit their families. It is perhaps too early to tell if the idea of birth control has been successfully communicated.

Conclusions

- Early results indicate that young children can be helped to an adequate level of verbal ability through work done with their mothers.
- Relatively uneducated mothers can be assisted to provide a stimulating environment for their children even in overcrowded ghetto homes.
- It is important to work with the mother who is a key figure for the baby, and she may be able to use the same training with subsequent children.
- Well-baby care will be better utilized if taken directly to the home.
- Infant anemia can be wiped out.
- There is a dire lack of preschool facilities.
- There is a desperate need for good day-care centers for infants.
- A nurse who has been given only a small amount of special orientation can be effective in an infant stimulation program.
- Infant stimulation programs should be incorporated into well-baby care.
- Infant stimulation programs and good well-baby care alone may not alter the future of a baby born to a young, poor, black mother living in a poverty area.

This program is in a sense a minimal one—relatively inexpensive, using limited personnel, and the extensive use of a nurse to provide services. It is not a radical departure from the care now generally believed to be desirable. The teaching of the mother makes possible the continuation of the spirit of the program and hopefully will benefit the entire family. It appears that marked changes can be achieved in children through this type of stimulation, and that this is a fruitful approach.

Research Grant: MH 09215
Dates of Interviews: April and September 1970

References:

Brooks, Marion. A stimulation program for young children performed by a Public Health nurse as part of well baby care. Paper presented at the American Nursing Association meeting, 1970, and accepted for publication in the *American Journal of Nursing.*

Caldwell, Bettye. Descriptive evaluations of child development and of developmental settings. *Pediatrics,* Vol. 40, July 1967, No. 1, 46-54.

Gutelius, Margaret, M. Child rearing attitudes of teen-age Negro girls. *American Journal of Public Health,* Vol. 60, No. 1, January 1970, New York, 93-104.

Levenstein, Phyllis, Cognitive growth in preschoolers through stimulation of verbal interaction with mothers. Paper presented at the 46th annual meeting of the American Orthopsychiatric Association, New York, New York, April 1969.

The me nobody knows, Children's voices from the ghetto. Edited by Stephen M. Joseph, Discus Book, Avon Books, 1969, New York, p. 36.

BASIC STUDIES OF
CHILD DEVELOPMENT

Indeed, what is there that does not appear marvelous when it comes to our attention for the first time? How many things, too, are looked upon as quite impossible until they have been effected?

—*Pliny the Elder*

The Development of Intelligence in Babies

Investigator:

Jerome S. Bruner, Ph.D.
Director, The Center for Cognitive Studies
Harvard University
Cambridge, Massachusetts

Prepared by:

Maya Pines

For the past four years, Dr. Jerome S. Bruner has been concerned primarily with the cognitive development of babies: How does the human infant — so helpless and limited at birth — learn to control his environment and himself? How does he grow up intelligent? Although human babies at first appear more stupid than chimpanzees of the same age, by the age of 2 or 3 the normal child has achieved one of the most difficult intellectual feats he may ever perform: he has re-invented the rules of grammar, all by himself, and he has learned to speak. He has also constructed a fairly complex mental model of the world, which allows him to manipulate various aspects of the world in his thoughts and fantasies. And he has learned to mobilize various skill patterns whenever he needs them. Under the guidance of Dr. Bruner, the Center for Cognitive Studies at Harvard is trying to unravel the sources of these formidable achievements.

There are various theories about how children acquire language. In his book, *Verbal Behavior* (1967), Dr. B. F. Skinner claimed that children learn to speak as a result of stimulus-response conditioning. All complicated behavior is learned, he argued; one learns to behave in ordered ways because there is order in the environment. Linguists such as Dr. Noam Chomsky disagreed, suggesting that human beings have an innate competence for language which sets them apart from all other creatures. This innate competence is what allows babies to learn language on the basis of relatively few encounters with words and sentences, they claimed, crediting babies — and mankind — with far more "mind" than most scientists were willing to accept at the time.

Innate Competence

Dr. Bruner and a number of other psychologists in the U.S. and abroad have now gone one step further than Chomsky in emphasizing the importance and activity of the infant's own nervous system. By studying babies well before they learn to speak, these researchers have come to the conclusion that language competence is just one example of an even more significant ability with which infants enter the world: the basic ability to pick up logical rules from mere fragments of evidence, and then use these rules in a variety of combinations. There are programs of action in the human mind right after birth, they believe, not only for language but also for the intelligent use of hands, eyes and tools.

"It's a very different view of man," says Dr. Bruner, "and it's just beginning. People are starting to see that skills of this wide-ranging type couldn't possibly be learned element by element. There must be some kind of predisposition in man to allow babies to pick up so quickly rules that go for such a large number of situations.

Only a few years ago, it was generally believed that newborns could not see more than the differences between light and dark; that during their first three months of life they were so absorbed by their insides that they could hardly react to the outside world; and consequently, that their physical environment had little impact on them — all that mattered was the provision of food and comfort. It now turns out, however, that even on the day of their birth, infants can track a triangle with their eyes. By the time they are 1 month old, they can spot the identity of objects and know when something has been changed. Furthermore, they actively invent rules of theories to explain what they perceive. Even at 3 weeks of age, an infant will have fairly complex hypotheses about the world he has just been born into — and if he is proved wrong, he may burst into tears.

That was exactly what happened at the Center two years ago, during an experiment conducted by a Radcliffe undergraduate, Shelley Rosen-bloom. Researchers there wondered whether babies of 3 to 8 weeks really understood that a person's voice should come from the spot where the person stood — whether babies had the idea of a locus. If so, did these babies also grasp the fact that when the person moved, the sound of his voice should travel along the same path? To what extent had they organized their experience at that age? To find out, it was decided to use stereo speakers that could separate the sound of a voice from its origin. In response to ads in the Harvard Crimson, there is always a procession of babies — mostly the offspring of graduate students — to the Center's lab, where they are made comfortable, given toys, and usually offered something interesting to see or do as part of a psychological experiment, while their mothers look on. This time, the infants were seated in front of a glass partition that separated them from their mothers, whom they could see just two feet away. As long as the speakers were balanced so that the mother's voice seemed to come directly from her, an infant would be quite content. But as soon as the phase relationship between the speakers was changed so that the voice seemed to come from a different spot, the baby would become agitated, look around, or cry — showing that his expectations were thwarted, and that there is powerful information-processing ability in the brains of infants even at that early age. "We now believe that infants have a notion not only of locus, but of path, right from the beginning," says Dr. Bruner. "Then, with experience, it becomes increasingly differentiated. But there is some notion of it right from the start."

The Study of Infancy

The Center's study of infancy has focused on five issues:

1) How the infant achieves voluntary control of behavior in a fashion governed by prediction and anticipation;

2) How visually guided and intelligent manipulative behavior emerges, with emphasis on the transferability and generativeness of skills;

3) How the infant progresses from being a "one-track" enterprise to being able to carry out several activities simultaneously and under the control of an over-rule;

4) How attention develops and its control shifts from external constraints (novelty) to internal constraints (problem-solving); and

5) How pre-linguistic codes develop, particularly in the interaction of the mother and infant.

("Our underlying assumption is that the codes of language, while they may indeed reflect innated patterns, are first primed by a great deal of interactive code-learning of a nonsyntactic type," writes Dr. Bruner. "When certain of these pre-linguistic manifestations are understood, perhaps light will be shed on the deeper question of the nature of language as such.")

In babies' hands, Dr. Bruner believes, lie clues to much of their later development, and he particularly wants to find out how babies learn the value of two-handedness. Nobody, teaches infants this skill, just as nobody teaches them to talk. Yet around the age of 1, a baby will master the "two-handed obstacle box," a simple puzzle devised by the Center to study this process. Seated on his mother's lap, he will suddenly use one hand to push and hold a transparent cover, while the other hand reaches inside the box for a toy.

To Dr. Bruner this is extraordinary, for it shows that the baby has learned to distinguish between the two kinds of grip — the power or "holding" grip, which stabilizes an object, and the precision or "operating" grip, which does the work. Monkeys and apes have developed a precision grip, Dr. Bruner says, but "it is not until one comes to man with his asymmetry that the power grip migrates to one hand (usually the left) and the precision to the other." From then on, he emphasizes, many routines can be devised for holding an object with one hand while working it with the other, leading to the distinctively human use of tools and tool-making.

The experiments at the Center are essentially very simple, but their interpretations are not. Some of these interpretations parallel Noam Chomsky's "transformation" approach to linguistics, which reduces language to basic kernel sentences, each one made up of a noun phrase and a verb phrase. Early in childhood every human being learns the logical rules which allow him to transform these kernels into any possible sentence. Dr. Bruner speculates that when a baby learns to differentiate between the

481

two kinds of manual grip, this foreshadows "the development of topic and comment in human language" — the basic sentence form of subject/predicate, which may be found in all laguages, with no exception whatsoever, and which a baby expresses when he combines a holophrase (a single word or a very short phrase that is used as one word) with another word. Thus, man may be uniquely predisposed, at birth, to reinvent the rules of grammar, to process information, and to develop "clever hands." He is born with a highly complex programing system, the result of millions of years of evolution.

What about disadvantaged children, then — why should they be different, if they are born with the same programing system? "Mind you, you can ruin a child's inheritance, too," warns Dr. Bruner, "with an environment where he acquires helplessness. You can also be trained to be stupid."

Before man's marvellous programing system can be activated for language, for instance, a baby must learn a series of primitive codes - and these require interaction with an adult. "What seems to get established very quickly between infant and parent is some sort of code of mutual expectancy," says Dr. Bruner, "when the adult responds to an initiative on the part of the child, thus converting some feature of the child's spontaneous behavior into a signal." Right from the start, parent and infant are busy communicating through eye-to-eye contact, smiles and sounds. As early as 4 months of age, an infant will smile more to a face that smiles back than to one that does not respond; and if the adult face then stops smiling back, the infant will look away. In some cases, he may even struggle bodily to look away. A child's other attempts at learning can similarly be brought to a halt when his expectancy is thwarted, and things stop making sense.

The Development of Strategies

The prolonged infancy of man has definite functional importance, Dr. Bruner concludes: During that time, the infant is basically developing the strategies that will later be combined for intelligent action — for thought and language, as well as for the manipulation of tools.

One such strategy is "place-holding." The earliest evidence of this can be seen in infants' sucking behavior. As everybody knows, a pacifier will calm a baby. But why? Earlier research had shown that sucking reduces hunger pangs and relieves muscle tension. "Well, but putting electrodes on the temples of babies as they were watching a movie here, we've begun to find out what a pacifier really does," says Dr. Bruner. "One of its principal effects is to cut down scanning eye movements, which cuts down the baby's information intake." At birth, and for a few days thereafter, babies can't cope with more than one activity at a time. When they wish to suck, they close their eyes tightly, to avoid taking in information from the outside. When their eyes are open, they stop sucking. By the age of 3 to 5 weeks, however, they can suck with their eyes open — but as soon as they become really interested in something, the sucking stops. Finally, between the ages of 2 and 4 months, a new strategy appears. Whenever something catches their attention while they are sucking, they stop their usual suctioning and shift to a sort of mouthing which keeps the nipple active, though at a reduced rate. This allows them to pick up where they left off with great ease, once their curiosity has been satisfied. A neat solution to an early problem, "place-holding" of this sort leads to many later skills, both manual and linguistic.

"As I got more into this work on skilled behavior, it became increasingly evident to what extent intention and hypothesis are central to the organization of knowledge and to the filtering of input," declares Dr. Bruner. In his most recent study, "Studies in the Growth of Manual Intelligence in Infancy," which he did with Karlen Lyons and Kenneth Kaye, Dr. Bruner emphasizes the importance of the infants' own programs of action. "When one observes the early behavior of infants — say at the onset of visually guided reaching at around 4 months of age — one is struck by the fact that arousal of intention is the initial reaction to an 'appropriate' stimulus," he writes. "The earliest overt expression of activated intension is not 'trial and error,' but an awkward but recognizable instrumental act that expresses a preadapted program of action."

His movie, "The Intention to Take - The Infancy of Object Capture," illustrates how babies begin with an intention, act out its intended results (or an approximation thereof) and then work backward to the components that will in fact make such results possible. "First, they look at the object," says Dr. Bruner, describing the movie. "They want to take it. It's an intense gazing. Then, as the child's intention gets organized, his lips come forward in what we call an 'A-frame mouth.' Later on, when he takes hold of the object, it will go into his mouth; but already, his whole system is activated, his mouth works. Then his arms come up in an anti-gravitational movement, and up comes that fist." The infants' actions are not yet in the right order for success. "Six weeks later, these actions will seem so well regulated that we'll forget the complexity of even so simple a task. Then they will leap forward to a fully orchestrated act. But the preparation is slow and demanding."

The infants' own intentions, then, are crucial. Of course, some goals can be imposed from outside, and babies can be taught, for instance, to respond to a buzzer in certain ways. Thus, Dr. Hanus Papousek, a Czech psychologist who is now spending a year at the Center, has conditioned newborns to turn their heads sharply to the side at the sound of a buzzer, in order to get milk from a buzzer. "It can be done," says Dr. Bruner, "but it's endless. The babies show so much aversion to this. They're so slow at learning it, you have to present the stimulus hundreds of times."

By contrast, when the infant uses his own initiative, learning often comes with lighning speed. In the Center's lab, a medium-sized room which might be called a baby theater, babies are placed in a well-padded seat facing a blank wall which serves as a screen. Then, with a pacifier in their mouth, they are shown a movie. "We didn't want to condition them to respond to a stimulus," Dr. Bruner explains. "Instead, we wanted to choose something the child does and give it some consequence. Then he is at the controls. So we chose sucking. Would they learn to suck at different speeds in order to produce changes in their environment? And, lo and behold, these little 4-, 5- and 6-week-old infants do learn to suck in longer bursts to produce a clear focus. Or else, if you reverse the conditions so that sucking blurs the picture, they learn to *desist* from sucking on this pacifier. They respond immediately, during the very first session, to changes produced by their own acts."

The movie that the babies watched so eagerly showed an Eskimo mother playing with her child. "It was shot in winter, indoors, and she was constantly involved in little games with him — string games and so on," explains Dr. Bruner. The experiment was devised by a graduate student, Mrs. Ilze Kalnins. When the babies discovered that sucking made the pictures clearer, they cut down their pauses between sucks, stopping only four seconds. On other visits to the lab, when they found that sucking blurred the image, they lengthened the pauses to about eight seconds.

The babies' performance was all the more remarkable because of their inexperience with "place-holding." To bring the picture into focus, they had to suck in longer bursts without looking at the film, then take a quick look before it blurred again.

Curiously, this experiment comes quite close to the kind of operant conditioning pioneered by Dr. Skinner, in which rewards are used to "shape" a child's activity. But Dr. Bruner interprets it quite differently, seeing the babies' rapid learning as the effect of fulfilling their own intentions. Sucking to produce a sharp focus involves quite complex strategies to coordinate looking and sucking. Such strategies come from the inside out, from an innate preadaptation, Dr. Bruner believes. Only after their appearance has been evoked by events can trial and error and reinforcements be of any use.

"What reinforcement is doing, in effect, is locking in that response in a set of alternative responses which in fact works," he writes. "It does not bring into being new responses. For the most part, the children do not *gradually* improve their strategies, but rather increase the skill with which they perform old routines. . . . Two-handed efforts make their appearance abruptly, rather than by some gradual route, and seem to be 'ready' for triggering."

He points to an experiment performed at the Center two years ago with three groups of babies of different ages. The babies were seated in front of a table on which a jingly toy was placed behind a small transparent screen, open at one end. The youngest babies, only 7 months old, simply reached for the toy with the nearest hand and bumped into the screen. After banging on and clawing at the screen for a while, they lost interest and gave up. The next group, the 1-year-olds, began in the same fashion, but then let their hands follow the edge of the screen and reached behind it in a sort of backhand grasp until they got the toy. Only the 18-month-old babies knew right away how to reach the toy efficiently, and did so. Over 16 trials each, none of the babies ever changed his initial strategy; this was the best he was capable of at that stage.

"Trial and error implies the capacity to hold an end constant while varying means," notes Dr. Bruner. "The segments in which this is possible are very short in duration for the child. What thwarts him is distraction, not error." This is why he is so interested in the development of the child's own intentions, and in the kind of "planning control" described by the Russian psychologist, Dr. A. R. Luria, as being located in the frontal lobes. He hopes to study the development of strategies and plans in primates and compare it to that of human infants, so as to gain further insight into this issue.

Studies of Perception and Thinking

The Center for Cognitive Studies came into being in 1960. During its first years of operation, it paid no attention to babies. For Dr. Brunner, too, infant development is a comparatively recent interest. Unlike many other psychologists, who study the same topic for their entire working lives, he has ranged all over the field. And before calling attention to the cognitive growth of infants, he had helped to create interest in four major movements: 1) the so-called "New Look" in perception in the late forties and early fifties; 2) the study of cognitive processes, mostly in adults; 3) educational reform, with emphasis on new curricula; and 4) the study of children's cognitive development. Throughout, he always came back to the same basic questions: How do human beings gather, categorize, store, use and communicate knowledge?

"You can never get a direct test on reality," he says. "You must take scraps and test them against your mental model of the world." In his work on perception, he wanted to learn how people register information through the filter of their own experience. He concluded that the same objects – for example, coins – are perceived differently by different people, in accordance with their values and needs. "Perceptions are highly regulated entry ports," he notes. "An experienced eye will pick up so much more!" In contrast to work that considered perception to be strictly passive, this approach was called "hot" perception, or "the New Look" in perception. It led him to the boundary line between perception and thinking.

Together with other members of the Harvard Cognition Project, he then spent five years studying cognitive processes – "the means whereby organisms achieve, retain and transform information." At the time, this was a major departure from the accepted approach to psychological problems, behaviorism. For roughly 30 years, most positions of prestige in American psychology had gone to people who studied stimuli and responses, bypassing anything that smacked of the "mental."

Spurred on by work in computer simulation and information theory, a few psychologists were beginning to worry about the mind again. Sometimes they called it "the black box." Clearly, the black box had to sort out all the inputs and outputs; but how did it do it? The behaviorists did not even attempt to answer this question, which they considered irrelevant. The members of the Harvard Cognition Project did, as described in

485

Dr. Bruner's book, *A Study of Thinking* (1956). Specifically, they tried to deal with what Dr. Bruner called "one of the simplest and most ubiquitous phenomena of cognition: categorizing or conceptualizing. On closer inspection, it is not so simple. The spirit of the inquiry is descriptive. We have not sought 'explanation' in terms of learning theory, information theory, or personality theory. We have sought to describe and in a small measure to explain what happens when an intelligent human being seeks to sort the environment into significant classes of events so that he may end by treating discriminably different things as equivalents."

"There were some strategy theories I had picked up from John von Neumann," recalls Dr. Bruner. "I wanted to show how, in problem-solving, as in perception, people use strategy for choosing the instances they want to think about. I was arguing that strategy and systematic search efforts are characteristic of all living systems — that there are structures and hypotheses in the mind, and that you're constantly testing them against fragmentary evidence from the environment. You're locked — at the most tragic — you're locked into the structures that are species-specific to you, because that's the way the human nervous system is. But over and beyond that, there is a way in which, through the exercise of initiative on your part, you can turn on your own information, reorder it, and generate hypotheses. The structures in men's minds are productive, generative, just as grammar makes it possible for men to emit any number of utterances."

The Impact of Piaget

The emphasis on strategy in Bruner's work on perception and thought caught the interest of the famous Swiss psychologist, Dr. Jean Piaget. "It was the last thing he expected from an American psychologist," Dr. Bruner notes. "I guess I'm not a very typical American psychologist — at least my colleagues don't think so. I think I'm right in the tradition that started with William James, of pragmatism, and that they're very much in the tradition of Ivan Pavlov! You know — 'we don't have to look inside the organism, there's no structure at all, all the order is outside, and all you do is mirror it.' Well, I take a drastically different view." Drs. Bruner and Piaget first met 16 years ago, when Dr. Piaget came to Boston to give a lecture. And Dr. Bruner was among the first Americans to appreciate the importance of Dr. Piaget's work.

Piaget's monumental studies of child development had been ignored in the U.S. for several decades, until the cognitive movement awakened to their value. In bold strokes, as well as painstaking detail, Piaget had described the growth of human intelligence, from the first day of life until adulthood. He had shown how children construct their own mental models of the world in successive stages, following an invariant sequence, though they may go through the stages at different rates. When a child has experienced enough conflict between reality and his image of it, he changes this image to make it more accurate. Thus, at first a child cannot understand that when water is poured out of a full glass into a wider glass which it fills only half way, the amount of water is unchanged. Being "centered" on only one aspect of reality at a time, he sees that the glass is half empty and says there is "less" water than before. Through a series of experiments, Piaget explored how children develop what he calls "conservation," the understanding that a quantity of water or clay will remain the same, regardless of the shape it takes. As children realize that objects and people have properties that do not depend on their immediate appearance, they become able to deal with symbols. Intelligence consists of such leaps into abstraction — but it depends on a large repertoire of images with which one can visualize certain sequences of cause and effect.

Dr. Bruner devotes considerable space to the contributions of "the Geneva school" in his book, *The Process of Education.* Many of his own papers show a strong Piagetian influence, particularly those in which he discusses the stages in cognitive growth. But eventually he developed differences of opinion with Piaget about how children acquire the notions of conservation and — much more fundamentally — about what produces intellectual growth.

"Mostly we argue about prefixedness," he says. "I found increasingly with Piaget that his notions of interior order were much more prefigures, prefixed than mine. I think this was the thing that caused something of an intellectual rift between us. I think that he misunderstands me more than I misunderstand him. He is too concerned with how the mind just processes things. I told him once, only half-jokingly, that his study of mollusks (conducted when he was only 15) was characteristic of him. His idea was that there was a mollusk, and no matter what that mollusk ate or what that mollusk did, it always turned out to have the same prefigured shell. Piaget's notion of intellectual development is a bit too much like his early conception of the way in which a mollusk grows. As one of his colleagues pointed out when he was here a few weeks ago: What does Piaget need a theory of education for? Either the child hasn't reached the right stage, and there's no point in trying to teach him anything; or he has already reached that stage, and why bother to teach, as he'll learn anyway."

In Dr. Bruner's view, evolution has given man a wide range of possibilities — far wider than Piaget would allow — because man is a cultuer user, and his growth depends largely on the kinds of tools he uses. "I don't believe you can or should separate anthropology from psychology," he declares.

The Center for Cognitive Studies

By 1960, a number of converging trends made the study of cognition seem particularly promising. Some central place was needed to stimulate interdisciplinary research on the subject. With grants from the Carnegie Corporation of New York and other foundations, Dr. Bruner then founded the Center for Cognitive Studies, together with Dr. George A. Miller, a psychologist who was known for his work on psycholinguistics — the study of how cognition and language interact.

487

At first the Center focused on four areas: psycholinguistics, human memory, perception, and the cognitive growth of children. Among its many research fellows and visitors could be found psychologists, philosophers, physicians, linguists, anthropologists, sociologists and cyberneticists. Dr. Bruner was most involved in research on the cognitive growth of children, particularly those between the ages of 9 and 13. A Mobile Laboratory helped him and his associates to do experiments on the development of perception, attention, and judgment in children under controlled conditions, right next to the children's schools.

In the meantime, he had become famous in another field — education. This helped to make it respectable for psychologists to be concerned with the subject. His involvement began when he served as chairman of a conference of scientists, scholars, and educators at Woods Hole, Cape Cod, on better ways to teach science. His resulting report, *The Process of Education (1960),* was the clearest work on curriculum reform at the time, and won him instant fame. It has since been translated into 22 languages and is still being studied by teachers all over the world, particularly the ringing statement — which has been quoted over and over again — that "any subject can be taught effectively in some intellectually honest form to any child at any stage of development."

Although many of Dr. Bruner's ideas have changed since then, he stands by this famous statement, declaring that there is "absolutely no evidence against it." Another dominant theme persists: physics (or math, language, or any other subject) is not something that one "knows about," but something one "knows how to do." It is a way of thinking, rather than a series of facts. Thus, when Dr. Bruner devised a social studies curriculum for the fifth grade, "Man: A Course of Study," he gave 10-year-olds the raw materials with which to act like social scientists and three basic questions to start them off: What is human about human beings? How did they get that way? And how can they be made more so? The materials include films on the life cycle of the salmon, on free-ranging baboons, and on the Netsilik Eskimos, the purest surviving example of traditional Eskimo culture — the kind of authentic records previously available only to college or graduate students. The course has now been adopted by more than 1,500 schools. "Intellectual activity is the same whether at the frontiers of knowledge or in a third-grade classroom," Dr. Bruner wrote in *The Process of Education.* He still believes it passionately. And he is still involved in the creation of new curricula — right now, a new course for adolescents on principles of child development.

At the college level, he proposes a dual curriculum to take advantage of young people's drive to control their environment: On Mondays, Wednesdays and Fridays, students would continue with the essential basic course, such as mathematics or language, in which one step must be taken before another; and on Tuesdays and Thursdays, they would be let loose to govern their own learning in ways as experimental as possible. This would include taking part in budget decisions, teacher evaluation, and related matters — but more than that, it would mean that they could find their

488

own problems to study. Preferably, these should be problems for which no answers yet exist.

Students are usually exposed to only two types of problems, Dr. Bruner points out: those which require analytical thought — e.g., dealing with abstract formulas — and those which require them to do some kind of laboratory exercise. "Both are formulated by the instructor or the text or the manual, and both are important in any science, art, or practical sphere," he says. "But neither is much like problem-finding. This requires the location of incompleteness, anomaly, trouble, inequity contradiction. . . ."

The Growth Sciences

In the mid-sixties, as his studies on children's cognitive growth progressed, Dr. Bruner became increasingly dissatisfied with the age group he had been working with. "We were left with a sharp sense of incompleteness concerning the origins of what we had studied," he noted. He saw that by the age of 3, a repertory of skills is already well developed. Therefore, he began studying younger and younger children.

By 1967, when Dr. George Miller left the Center, the transformation was complete: nearly all the Center's research dealt with the cognitive development of babies, including infants only a few weeks or a few months old. Traditionally, this age period had been neglected because the child seemed so inaccessible between his fifth day of life, when he left the maternity hospital, and his entry into nursery school at 3. Dr. Bruner urged his students to adopt the viewpoint of a naturalist exploring a new species, rather than try to test specific hypotheses derived from a general theory of infant development. "Assume that you are studying the great-chested Jabberwocky," he advised.

In this way, he took a lead in the development of what he calls "the growth sciences," a new composite discipline concentrating on the early years of life. "Just as medical research was organized around concepts of pathology, so today we would do well to organize our efforts anew around the concept of growth," he declared. "Those sciences that can help us understand and nurture human growth — biological, behavioral and social sciences alike — should find ways of joining forces as the growth sciences. Let them then make their knowledge relevant to those who are practitioners of the nurturing of growth: parents, teachers, counselors. It is bizzare that no such organization has yet emerged, though it is plainly on its way."

Research Grant: MH 1324
Dates of Interview: September and October 1970

References:

Bruner, J. S., Goodnow, J. J., and Austin, G. A., *A Study of Thinking.* Wiley, 1956.
Bruner, J. S., Going beyond the information given, in H. Gruber et al. (Eds.) *Contemporary Approaches to Cognition.* Harvard University Press, 1957.

Bruner, J. S., *The Process of Education*. Harvard University Press, 1960. (Paperback edition, Random House Vintage Edition, 1963)

Bruner, J. S., The course of cognitive growth. *American Psychologist*, 1964, 19, 1-15.

Bruner, J. S., Oliver, R. R., Greenfield, P. M., et al, *Studies in Cognitive Growth*, John Wiley & Sons, 1966.

Bruner, J. S., *Toward a Theory of Instruction*. Harvard University Press, 1966. (Paperback edition published in 1968 by W. W. Norton.)

Bruner, J. S., *Processes of Cognitive Growth: Infancy* (Vol. III Heinz Werner Lecture Series). Clark University Press with Barre Publishers, 1968.

Bruner, J. S. and Bruner, B. M., On voluntary action and its hierarchical structure, in A. Koestler and J. R. Smythies (Eds.), *The Albach Symposium 1968*, Beyond Reductionism, New Perspectives in the life sciences. The Hutchinson Publishing Group, Ltd., London 1968.

Bruner, J. S. The growth and structure of skill, in K. J. Connolly (Ed.), *Motor Skills in Infancy*, Ciba Conference, November 1968.

Bruner, J. S., Lyons, K., *The Growth of Human Manual Intelligence:* I. Taking possession of objects, in preparation.

Bruner, J. S., Lyons, K. & Watkins, D., *The Growth of Human Manual Intelligence:* II. Acquisition of complementary two-handedness, in preparation.

Bruner, J. S., Kaye, K., and Lyons, K., *The Growth of Human Manual Intelligence:* III. The development of detour reaching, in preparation.

Bruner, J. S., *The Relevance of Education*, W. W. Norton, 1971, in press.

How Children Learn English

Investigator:
Roger Brown, Ph. D.
Harvard University
Cambridge, Mass.

Prepared by:
Herbert Yahraes

A number of ingenious tests for showing how much a child knows about language have been developed by an NIMH grantee and his associates and are being used by several investigators here and abroad in work with aphasics, children with retarded speech and speech disorders, and children who are deaf.

The grantee is Dr. Roger Brown, professor of social psychology at Harvard University and a leading authority on psycholinguistics, or, as Dr. Brown prefers to call it, the psychology of language.

This investigator himself has collaborated in using the tests to help determine how much language-processing ability has been retained by persons with brain injuries. But his goal is quite different: to learn how normal children acquire grammar. This is important, he points out, because speech is the most characteristic human performance, yet little is known of the mental processes involved in its development.

A child gets his first knowledge of language from the persons close to him, and he tries to imitate what he hears. But by the time he puts words together, he has begun, apparently, to induce a sets of rules for their use. Before the average child is 3, he has somehow developed a basic grammar.

The child's first grammar is not an adult's. It leads to mistakes like *I throwed the ball* and to peculiarities of word usage like *Kitty all gone,* and it is far from complete. However, it does enable a child to put together a very great variety of sentences, most of which he has never heard, and thus to express himself on his own.

Dr. Brown's group is attempting to discover sets of rules that will produce, in the sense that a program for a computer will produce, the sentences that a young child produces. The aim is to get behind the words and the sentences to the machinery that turns them out. Since the appropriate rules would lead to the same product as the child's brain, they might constitute a model of the kind of operations going on in his brain.

Ultimately, therefore, this research may add to knowledge of how the brain works. By elucidating the natural language-learning process and by demonstrating how many children know about language by the time they go to school, the research may also lead to advances in the teaching both of foreign language and of reading.

The investigators use two general techniques: application of grammar tests, particularly in the case of children older than 3; and intensive study of language usage by very young children.

In some of the tests for grammar comprehension, children are given nonsense words and encouraged to use them in speech, with the investigators noting what rules are applied in forming inflections, like the plurals of nouns and the tenses of verbs.

In other tests, children are shown pictures and asked to distinguish between, for example:

The dogs dig and *The dog digs.*

The cup is falling and *The cup will fall.*

The round dish on the table and *The dish on the round table.*

The boy is pushed by the girl and *The girl is pushed by the boy.* (Children under 4, Dr. Brown reports, almost invariably go wrong on this one because, evidently, their grammar contains no passive voice.)

A test may be a simple direction, such as *Put the penny in the glass,* when the glass is standing upside down so that putting the penny *on* it would be simpler.

Dr. Brown and his coworkers have found they can use such tests down to the age of 3 to learn at what point in a child's development the brain processes small grammatical differences of various kinds. Below the age of 3 they have to depend mainly on observation.

* * * * *

In studying a very young child, the investigators visit him frequently and record his and his mother's speech over a several-hour period of normal activity. The transcription of the recording is then analyzed and rules drawn up that seem to match those the child himself has followed in putting together two or more words.

The technique used for this procedure is distributional analysis, in which the words spoken are grouped into syntactical classes (on the basis of where and how frequently they have been used in the sentences and what contexts they have shared with other words). The rules take the form of a computer-like program for generating sentences by selecting words from the groups in a particular order.

The investigators test this program by using it to try to duplicate what the child has already said and by noting how well it predicts the child's new utterances, during later visits, using the same vocabulary. Preliminary work with such programs indicates they do indeed represent the grammar used by a given child at a given stage of development.

The first children studied intensively have been a girl, Anna, who was 18 months old when this phase of the work began (in October 1962) and a boy, Dale, who was then 24 months old. They have been visited every other week.

Anna and Dale are the children of middle-class, well-educated people. The next subjects for intensive study will be a boy and a girl from families considerably lower on the socio-economic scale. Dr. Brown reports that such children lag behind others in every index of speech development because, he thinks, there has been less interplay between mother and child.

492

In addition to collecting more information for a language-learning model, Dr. Brown wants to test this hypothesis about lower-class families and if it is substantiated, try remedial measures.

* * * * *

From the many sentences that a child hears, he somehow extracts the latent structure of the language and for the rest of his life operates in accordance with that structure. Dr. Brown and his associates are "trying to discover the normal progression by which children attain to the rules of English and also trying to understand the learning that is involved."

Some of the clearest evidence that children form construction rules, Dr. Brown observes, lies in the errors children make. So long as a child speaks correctly, it is possible that he says only what he has heard. But when a child from an educated family says "I digged in the yard," or "I saw some sheeps," or "Johnny hurt hisself," it is likely that, instead of imitating, he is applying the rules he has induced. (If *walked*, why not *digged?* If *dogs*, why not *sheeps?* If *myself* and *herself*, why not *hisself?*)

Other evidence comes from some of the tests the researchers have used. For example, a child is shown a picture of a small animal and told, "This is a wug." Then he is shown a picture of two animals and told, "Now there are two of them. There are two ____." The child generally says *wugz*. If the animal is a *bik*, he gives the plural as *biks;* if it is a *niss*, he gives the plural as *nissez*. Thus, even with words he has never heard, he follows the rules he has derived, correctly, for forming and pronouncing plurals.

When a child begins to put words together, generally around the age of 18 months, his utterances are very short—"Anna walk," for example, and "Dale play car." Dr. Brown thinks that this is less a matter of limited memory, since the child may know several hundred words and be able to recall them when needed, than of limited programing ability. During the second year of life, this usually prevents a child from planning sentences of more than two or three words. (Of a dozen children studied by the Harvard group, those about 2 years old had an average span of 2 words, with a range of from 1 to 4; children about 3 years old had an average span of 5 words, with a range of from 1 to 11.)

Even when a mother asks a child to "say what I say," the child reduces the sentences to telegraphese. "Mommy is going to have her soup" becomes "Mommy soup" whether the child is speaking spontaneously (using words heard before, of course) or in immediate imitation of his mother.

In the beginning, Dr. Brown reports, the child probably does not know that in reproducing an adult sentence he cuts it down to the most significant words. More likely he selects these words, mostly nouns and verbs, mainly because of the emphasis placed upon them by the speaker. The same principle holds with polysyllabic words—when they are beyond the child's grasp, he repeats only the stressed syllable.

On the basis of the work done under the NIMH grant and previously, Dr. Brown describes a child's first speech as a systematic reduction of adult speech marked by (1) a short programming limit and (2) selection in favor of stressed elements. Features of the child's grammar can be predicted from the average length of his utterances. The investigators found, for instance, that children whose utterances averaged less than 3.5 words invariably omitted such modal auxiliaries as *will* and *can* and said "I go inside" and "I make a tower." Children who averaged less then 3.2 words per utterance always omitted the forms of the verb *to be* in progressive constructions, saying not "I am going" but "I going."

In helping a child go from telegraphic English to grammatically more complete speech, the investigators note, interplay between mother and child is highly important. For example, Anna's mother says to her, "Anna's going to have her lunch," and the girl, picking out the stressed elements parrots: "Anna lunch." But some day the girl herself ventures, "Anna lunch," and the mother then expands the utterance into the most appropriate simple sentence. In one situation she will say something like, "Yes, Anna is going to have her lunch now;" in another situation, "Yes, Anna has had her lunch." Through many repetitions of this sort, the child learns to express time—and to develop rules applicable to other sentences.

One way to teach a foreign language is to give explicit instruction in the rules of grammar. A newer method, Dr. Brown points out, is to treat the student like a child and have him repeat sentences over and over again. Eventually he is expected to be able to produce new sentences—ones that are somehow implied by those in the practice set. This is essentially what the child does in learning to speak. Hence studies of how the child goes about making his new sentences may contribute to the improvement of foreign-language instruction.

The most important contributions of this study, however, may come from the increased knowledge it provides of normal language development. Arrested or abnormal language development are two of the most prominent symptoms of emotional, mental, or neurological disorders in childhood. Understanding the factors which contribute to normal language development may serve as a guideline for finding the factors which contribute to the erratic speech habits of the emotionally disturbed child.

Research Grant: MH 7088

References:

Brown, R. *The Acquisition of Language.* Presented at 1962 meeting of the Association for Research in Nervous and Mental Diseases.

Brown, R. and Fraser, C. The Acquisition of Syntax. In C. Cofer and B. Musgrave (Eds.), *Verbal Behavior and Learning: Problems and Processes.* McGraw Hill, New York, 1963.

Fraser, C., Bellugi, U., and Brown, R. Control of Grammar in Imitation, Comprehension, and Production. *Journal of Verbal Hearing and Verbal Behavior,* 2:121-135, 1963.

Experiments in How We Learn To Coordinate

Investigator:
Richard M. Held, Ph.D.
Massachusetts Institute of Technology
Cambridge, Mass.

Prepared by:
Herbert Yahraes

A number of authorities on child development have reported in recent years that babies raised in a stimulating environment progress faster than other babies. One of the first experimental tests of this observation was recently made in connection with research to uncover basic mechanisms involved in the development and maintenance of sensorimotor coordination.

Shaping this research program, directed by Richard M. Held, professor of experimental psychology at the Massachusetts Institute of Technology, is the idea that voluntary, self-produced movement, with its accompanying feedback signals to the sensory centers of the brain, is highly important to the growth of the sensorimotor systems. This means, for example, that we can reach for the telephone and, without fumbling, pick it up because we have had a good deal of practice in coordinating messages to the brain from the world around us, messages from the brain to our muscles, and then more messages as the muscles act to change our relationship to the external world.

Dr. Held and his associates have been working in two ways to demonstrate the importance of motor-sensory feedback: They have tampered with its normal operation in adult human beings and in newborn animals, and they have increased its occurrence in babies.

The work with adults has involved, typically, the wearing of prism goggles that make objects a few feet away appear to be displaced 3 or 4 inches—right or left, up or down. People soon compensate for the displacement, it has long been known, and after the goggles have been removed the compensatory effect carries over for a time, now in the form of error. But how is compensation achieved? In a series of experiments, the MIT group has demonstrated that it occurs when what the individual sees is correlated with what he does. If he views his surroundings as he is pushed in a wheelchair instead of as he takes a walk on his own, for instance, or if he holds his hand still as he looks at it, or if it is moved by somebody else and not himself, his brain makes little or no adjustment to the distortion of the visual signals. This work seems to show, then, that compensation depends to an important extent upon the feedback that accompanies voluntary movement.

Other conditions besides active movement together with its sensory feedback will produce some change that may be called adaptation or compensation. This is particularly the case when a person can gain information about the errors he makes while wearing prisms. He can then note his mistakes and very quickly correct them. The MIT researchers believe, however, that this kind of correction involves a rather different sort of process from the one they have been mainly concerned with, which seems applicable to questions about the very early development of sensorimotor control.

Though the experiments with prism goggles may superficially appear rather strange and even bizarre, they are considered quite relevant to a normally occurring process. During growth, Dr. Held explains, head size increases until its linear dimensions become at least one and a half times as large as at birth. As that happens, the distance between the eyes grows, the distance between the ears grows, and other parts of the sensory system change. Because of these anatomical changes, the adult and the young child will have different sensory inputs for the same external conditions. The fact that the adult can handle the same sensorimotor tasks as the child indicates that some adjustment must have taken place. Further, the optical properties of the eyes change, too, in the course of a lifetime, and these changes may require compensation. "In our experiments the changes are abrupt," says the investigator, "while in the natural course of things they are very slow, but we think that some of the factors affecting adaptation are probably the same."

In the work with babies, done under the immediate supervision of a psychologist named Burton White who is particularly interested in child development, the researchers studied several groups of infants who had been born and were being reared in an institution. A control group got the institution's usual care, which was adequate for general health but provided a minimum of handling and other stimulation. Other babies were given 20 minutes' extra handling every day for a month, beginning when they were 6 days old. Up to their fifth month, at least, these handled babies were significantly more visually attentive—shifted their gaze more often from one thing to another—than the controls. But there was no other apparent change.

Another group of babies who had received the extra handling were then given a better-than-usual opportunity to move in their cribs and to look at things more interesting than the monotone ceiling and the white sheets and crib liners. The mattresses were flattened so that the babies, instead of lying in a trough all day, could roll a little and more readily move head, arms, and trunk. Three times a day, for 15 minutes at a time, the babies were placed on their stomachs and the crib liners removed, thus encouraging the children to raise their heads and make other movements in order to watch the ward activities. Interesting objects were hung where the babies could see and swipe at them.

One big change occurred. At the median age of 3 months, these children began to reach for and grasp objects effectively; the control group needed 5 months. The results are what would have been predicted, the investigators point out, from the theory that the development of sensorimotor coordination depends to a great extent upon self-initiated movement and the accompanying feedback to the senses. At least as far as the ability to reach and grasp is concerned, a baby apparently develops faster when he has an opportunity to move and visually interesting surroundings to encourage him to move.

Experiments by Dr. Held and Dr. Alan Hein with cats and by Dr. Held and Joseph A. Bauer, Jr., with monkeys tend to support the same theory. Kittens fitted in infancy with ruffs that prevented them from seeing their paws were unable a few weeks later, when the ruffs had been removed, to guide their paws on the basis of vision. Time after time these kittens would pounce on a slowly swinging ball and miss it. Much the same thing happened with monkeys raised for some weeks in a "holder chair" so constructed that they could use their hands but could not see them. When they were finally allowed to see one hand, they could hardly keep their eyes from it, and the experimenters had difficulty enticing them to reach for food or toys. When the animals did reach, they usually missed. Only when they had seen the hand a long time, from 10 to 20 hours, did they bring the movements under control. Allowed then to see the other hand, the monkeys were just as surprised—and just as unable to control its movements to get what they wanted.

Dr. Held points out that persons who have been blind since birth do achieve sensorimotor coordination. In this case the sensory feedback that accompanies movement is delivered by the senses of touch and hearing. Every once in a while a person long blind recovers his sight and then finds considerable difficulty, for a time, in coordinating what he sees with what he does. He reaches for a cup of coffee and, because he has had no opportunity to maintain motor-visual coordination, upsets it.

Besides increasing our basic knowledge of how the central nervous system operates, the MIT research may have results of immediately practical importance. The work with babies has already provided scientific evidence, the investigators point out, that certain kinds of experience very early in life lead to increased alertness and faster visual-motor development. And authorities on child development believe that the growth of sensorimotor capacities leads to the growth of intellectual capacity. The findings and prospective findings may also throw some light on the development of certain visual disturbances, notably strabismus and amblyopia. The research may have a suggestion, too, for rehabilitation workers. Patients long bedridden lose something of their ability to control the movements of their arms and legs. This is less a matter of muscular weakness, Dr. Held suspects, than a failure to have performed those movements and thus to have obtained the feedback from them—conditions that seem to be important to the maintenance of control.

Voluntary movement and the accompanying sensory feedback are important, the investigator sums up,

—in helping infants develop sensorimotor coordination;

—in helping the central nervous system adjust to the growth of the body; and

—in maintaining normal coordination even in a situation, such as may occur in space, where the incoming signals are distorted.

Compensating for Displaced Sensory Signals

In one of the team's early experiments, subjects sat at a table and looked down at a mirror, which carried the reflection of a diagram. On the table top, some inches below the mirror, lay a sheet of paper. The subjects were asked to take a pencil and to mark with dots on the paper, which they could not see, the positions of the four corners of the diagram. Then they put on prism goggles for a while and, with the mirror removed, looked at their right hands. One group kept the hand motionless; another moved it back and forth; a third group had it moved back and forth by the investigator. Then the prisms were removed and the mirror replaced, and the subjects were asked again to mark the apparent positions of the corners of the diagram. When people compensate for the distortion produced by prisms, the effect lasts for a while after the prisms are removed. In this experiment, consequently, the subjects who had become adapted to the prisms should have marked the corners several inches to one side of the positions originally marked. The only subjects who did mark them this way were those who had moved their hands while wearing the goggles.

The investigators then tried the effect of movement involving the entire body, not just the hands and arms. In a dark room a subject was asked to turn his chair until he was face to face with a target—a slit of light. This showed his ability to judge the direction of a target in reference to himself alone. Then he put on prism goggles, went for a walk of an hour or more, came back, took off the goggles, and was tested again. Invariably he now saw the target as being some distance to the side of where it actually was. This was evidence that while wearing the goggles he had compensated for their distorting effect. But prism-wearing subjects who had taken a ride over the same path in a wheelchair, pushed by someone else, showed little or no adaptation.

Experiments in directional hearing brought analogous results. Normally a person locates the source of a sound because the waves reach one ear, the closer one, a split second before they reach the other. But in this work the subjects, wearing microphones, were exposed to noise from separated sources in a fashion that produced rapidly changing dichotic time differences; that is, differences in time of arrival at the two ears of corresponding acoustic signals. In effect, the apparent source of the sound signals— like that of the visual signals in persons wearing prisms—had been displaced. Subjects who wore the microphones while walking up and down a busy corridor later showed temporary inaccuracies in locating the source of a sound. While wearing the microphones, apparently, they had compensated for the aural distortion. The subjects who had not moved about showed no evidence of such an effect.

These and other experiments seemed to support Dr. Held's idea that adaptation to sensory distortion strongly depends upon the close correlation between signals from the motor nervous system, producing the physical movement, and the consequent feedback signals to the sensory system, showing the results of the movement. Seeking further evidence, he set up an experiment in which the correlation was impaired. The apparatus was a rotating prism arrangement that made a person's hand appear to be moving back and forth even when it was held motionless. When the person moved his hand, therefore, his sensory nervous system presumably could not distinguish between the signals resulting from the actual movement and those resulting from the apparent movement. This hypothesis seemed to be borne out by a test of the subjects' accuracy in reaching for an object after they had been looking through the rotating prisms. Subjects who had not moved their hands (but had had them moved by the experimenter) showed no decline in their accustomed accuracy. But those who had been moving their hands themselves showed much less accuracy than usual: their eye-hand coordination had been temporarily impaired, presumably because the brain had been getting more signals than it could manage. In engineering terms, there had been "noise" in the feedback system.

The investigators have produced the same effect by introducing what Dr. Held calls "inertial noise." In one experiment, for instance, they have had a subject push with his arm against an apparatus that, in spite of his efforts, moves his arm in a direction opposite to the one he wants it to take. The normal relationship between signals to the muscles and the consequent movement of the arm, with the accompanying feedback to the brain, is upset. When wearing prisms in this situation, he compensates significantly less, or not at all.

Further, a recent experiment shows, the compensatory process in completely blocked when there is a delay between the time a subject moves his hand and the time he sees the result of this movement. Ordinarily, the results of movement reach the retina with the speed of light. To introduce a time delay, the investigators built a device enabling a subject to sit at a table and move a control stick hidden from his sight under a mirror on the table. Movement of the control stick actuated potentiometers and these in turn modulated voltages. When these voltages were fed to an oscilloscope they produced movements of the scope trace—a narrow bar 1½ inches long—just like those being made by the hand. The trace was projected onto a ground glass screen, which the subject viewed in the mirror over his hand. In sum, though the subject could not see his hand, he could watch every movement it made. When the voltages were fed directly to the oscilloscope, the image of the movement was perceived instantaneously. In this situation, before-and-after tests showed that a person wearing prism goggles adapted himself to the displacement caused by the goggles. But the voltages could also be fed to magnetic tape and then given to the oscilloscope after a delay. In this case the visual feedback was delayed; the subject did not see the movement until after it had occurred. The investigators found that even delays as small as 270 milliseconds completely eliminated adaptation.

Though efforts to produce and study the effect of still smaller delays are being made, Dr. Held is fairly well satisfied that unless motor-sensory feedback is virtually simultaneous with movement, the brain cannot handle it. Consequently, the nervous system will not adapt itself to the apparent displacement, caused by prisms, of visual signals. This is quite as it should be, the investigator notes. If the feedback signals did not have to be closely coupled with the output signals, the system would sometimes be in chaos trying to decide which of several moving hands was its own.

Dr. Held's work is related to other ongoing research at MIT under the direction of Dr. Hans-Lukas Teuber, chairman of the department of psychology, dealing with the "corollary discharge" and the supposed role of the brain's frontal lobes in controlling it.[1] The corollary discharge theory holds that when the brain calls for movement, some of the signals go not to the muscles concerned but to the appropriate sensory systems. In this way the senses are prepared for the results of the movement. For example, if a person turns his head while looking at an object, the image of this object moves across the retina of his eye just as it would if the object itself were moving. But he perceives that his eyes are moving and not the object; the retinal change has been discounted. And the discounting occurs, Dr. Held postulates, because the sensory feedback (occurring as the result of movement) is matched to the corollary discharge (occurring as the result of the order to move). When the feedback is not matched to the discharge, the movement is perceived in the world outside.

Several investigators have reported recently that adaptation, as measured by the accuracy with which hand and arm reach toward a target after prisms have been worn, may result from a change in the felt position of the parts of the body. Under this view, a person misjudges the location of the target because he no longer accurately feels the position of his reaching arm. But after a series of experiments involving, among other things, the ability of subjects to locate with the unseen right hand various positions taken by the left hand, out of sight under the desk top, the MIT group offers another view.

Before wearing prisms, the subjects, blindfolded, could mark the positions of the left hand fairly accurately; after wearing prisms, they made mistakes of the kind to be expected—marking locations to the right of the actual location, for example, if the prisms had made objects seem displaced to the left. The investigators ask why a person should misreach for his hand following prism adaptation when he doesn't need vision to reach for it accurately—when he can feel his way to it, so to speak.

Dr. Held offers the following hypothesis: In this case, there are actually two different but interacting modes of reaching. One involves the felt

---

[1] "Exploring the Brain's Functions." In Research Project Summaries No. 2, National Institute of Mental Health: Public Health Service Publication No. 1208-2, 1965.

positions of the two arms, but there is no reason for either of the two felt positions to be changed by adaptation, and they probably do not change. The change that occurs lies in the other mode of reaching, which is based upon the matching of arm movements with the orientation of the head. It is reasonable to suppose that adaptation changes the direction of reaching with respect to the orientation of head to target. But in the case considered, perhaps the effect of the change is modified by the influence of the other mode of reaching. Hence a person who has just taken off prisms should make smaller mistakes in reaching for his unseen hand than in reaching for a visible target. The experimental evidence seems to point in this direction.

The Development of Visual Control

A few years ago a research group at the University of California, Riverside, found that when kittens were restrained from walking, they developed marked deficiencies in the visual control of activity. Why? Probably, thought the California group, because the kittens had lacked a variety of visual stimulation. More likely, thought the MIT researchers, because they had lacked visual stimulation correlated with movement.

To get additional facts, Dr. Held and Dr. Alan Hein ran an experiment that has been much admired for its ingenuity. The apparatus was a sort of merry-go-round, with a center post supporting a rotating beam. Attached to one arm of the beam was a kitten, which was able to walk around the post, to jump up, and to turn toward the right and the left. Attached to the other arm was a little box carrying another kitten. Any movements made by the first kitten were transmitted to the box, so that the second kitten made them, too, but passively instead of on its own. The center post and the surrounding circular wall of the apparatus displayed a pattern of stripes, so each kitten received essentially the same visual stimulation.

The pairs of kittens were raised in darkenss till they were 10 weeks old; then they were brought out 3 hours a day for experience in the apparatus. Ten days later the active kittens responded normally to several tests of visual responses. They put out their forepaws to ward off collision when gently lowered toward a surface; blinked at an approaching object; and, when walking on a sheet of glass beneath which appeared a shallow drop to one side and a steep drop to the other, avoided the steep one. The kittens that had been passively moved did not show these responses.

To learn more precisely the conditions influencing visual-motor coordination, Drs. Hein and Held have continued their studies of kittens (financed largely by the National Science Foundation but part of the same general research program supported by NIMH) and recently made a puzzling discovery. Kittens were put through the merry-go-round procedure under both active and passive conditions of movement. But when a kitten moved itself, only its right eye could see, the other being covered by an opaque contact lens, and when the kitten was passively moved, only its left eye could see. The result was an animal with one "active" and one

501

"passive" eye. And the investigators found that when the active eye was open, the kitten could perform normally in the tests of visually controlled behavior; when the passive eye was open, it could not. There was no transfer of information; one eye was disassociated from the other, as if this had been a split-brain study and the connections had actually been severed.

Additional work supports this finding. Kittens were raised so that they could see their forepaws with one eye but not the other. This second eye, though, could see just about everything else, and the animals were free to move. Then the experimenters tested the kittens' ability, first with one eye open and then the other, to reach for and hit an object. This ability was found to be present only when the eye that had always been able to watch the forepaws was open.

"Here is a failure of information to pass with an intact brain," the investigators comment. "It is very surprising." As yet they have no explanation, but they point out that the findings are consistent with the central idea guiding the group's research—that movement and feedback are essential to the development of eye-hand coordination in infants and an important source of the information enabling an adult to correct for sensory distortion.

In work with animals, the investigators are now trying to study what actually happens in the brain under conditions like those used in the experiments. This phase of the research may or may not clear up the puzzle of the disassociated eyes, but at least, Dr. Held believes, it should help identify those parts of the brain essential to the development and maintenance of the ability to direct a visually guided reach and grasp. This is one of the primary abilities enabling man to orient himself to, and get along in, the world around him.

Research Grant: MH 7642
Date of Interview: August, 1966

References:

Efstathiou, Aglaia, Bauer, J., Greene, Martha, and Held, R. Altered reaching following adaptation to optical displacement of the hand. *J. Exp. Psychol.*, 1966, in press.

Held, R. Plasticity in sensory-motor systems. *Scient. American*, 1965, 213, 5.

Held, R. Plasticity in sensorimotor coordination. Paper for XVIII International Congress of Psychology, 1966.

Held, R., Efstathiou, Aglaia, and Greene, Martha. Adaptation to displaced and delayed visual feedback from the hand. *J. Exp. Psychol.*, 1966, 72, 6, 887—891.

Held, R., and Freedman, S. S. Plasticity in human sensorimotor control. *Science*, 1963, 142, 3591.

Held, R., and Hein, A. Movement-produced stimulation in the development of visually guided behavior. *J. Comp. Physiol. Psychol.*, 1963, 56, 5.

White, B. L., and Held, R. Plasticity of sensorimotor development in the human infant. In Judy F. Rosenblith and W. Allinsmith (Eds.), *The causes of behavior: readings in child development and educational psychology.* Boston: Allyn & Bacon, 1966.

Heredity's Effect on Behavior Under Stress

Investigator:
Benson E. Ginsburg, Ph.D.
University of Chicago
Chicago, Ill.

Prepared by:
Herbert Yahraes

A person's experiences during infancy and childhood work powerfully to shape his later attitudes and personality. Indeed, according to psychoanalytic theory, they largely determine the state of his mental health. Looking for scientific proof of this concept, a number of investigators have reported evidence linking mental illness with stressful situations in early life. Animal studies, too, have stressed the importance of early experience. Now comes a geneticist asking that research into the causes of behavior consider more rigorously the effects of heredity. Early experiences may indeed affect later behavior tremendously, reports Benson E. Ginsburg, professor of biology at the University of Chicago. Or, depending upon the genetic situation, they may not affect it at all.

As part of his evidence, this investigator and his students subjected carefully bred mice to certain types of stress during infancy. Some of them, as adults, became significantly more aggressive than usual; others became less aggressive; others showed no effect. The results depended upon the strains to which the mice belonged: that is, upon heredity. In most cases the results depended also upon the time when the stress had been encountered—during all the first 4 weeks of life, or only the first 2, or only the second 2. "All mice," Dr. Ginsburg notes, "are not created equal."

Because work by himself and other researchers shows a strong relationship between an animal's inheritance and certain facets of its behavior, including some abnormal behavior under stress, the investigator believes the same relationship may well hold true in people. If one can select for aggressive strains in rabbits, guinea pigs, dogs, fighting cocks, and bulls, and if equivalent early experience can have differential effects in mice, depending on the genetic background, he asks, why should it be supposed that human beings all respond to a given situation in the same way, regardless of their inheritance? He agrees with psychotherapists that psychological factors are important, but he holds that these must act on a biological substratum—on inherited tendencies and mechanisms.

In recent work with mice, Dr. Ginsburg believes that his research group has uncovered the inherited mechanism responsible for a certain kind of abnormal behavior. Apparently the mechanism lies in a particular cell

503

layer in one structure of the brain, and apparently its manifestations can be treated chemically in certain cases. In some other mice, the same kind of behavior seems to have a different cause and is not affected by the same chemotherapy.

Dr. Ginsburg's work is supported by a grant from the National Institute of Mental Health. His main laboratory animals are highly inbred mice (every individual in a strain essentially an identical twin of every other individual), wolves, coyotes, and dogs.

Stress Mechanism in Mice

The investigator and his group have set out to study differences in behavior among closely related animals, to learn what laws of genetics are followed in the inheritance of these differences, and to determine what body or brain tissues are affected by the differences in heredity and, therefore, give rise to the differences in behavior.

In mice the principal characteristic under study is susceptibility to audiogenic seizures—epilepticlike convulsions induced by the ringing of a bell. The grantee chose this characteristic because: (a) it leads to behavior of an extreme kind, relatively easy, therefore, to identify; (b) it is, like some types of abnormal behavior in human beings, triggered by stress—in this case, sound; (c) it appears only in certain strains of mice and consequently must be under genetic control—a deduction Dr. Ginsburg and an associate, Dr. Starbuck Miller, have demonstrated, through breeding experiments, to be correct.

Some highlights of the findings to date:

1. *Three strains of mice highly susceptible to seizures show a characteristic difference in one tiny area of the brain. It appears to be caused by a difference in either the amount or the activity of one or more closely related enzymes.*

The difference came to light in the course of a meticulous, area-by-area study of activity involving adenosine triphosphate, or ATP. This is the compound supplying most of the energy for biochemical reactions, such as those concerned with moving the muscles, building proteins, and flashing nerve signals. The energy is made available when ATP is broken down in an almost instantaneous reaction involving the enzyme ATP-ase. The investigation centered on this reaction because of an earlier report, which has not yet been verified, that the brains of seizure-prone mice contained less of the enzyme than the brains of other mice.

The Ginsburg group incubated slices of brain tissue in a medium containing ATP or a related compound and then examined them under the microscope for a brown stain produced by one of the chemicals resulting from the breakdown of that compound. The darker the stain, the greater the amount of ATP that had been broken down and, presumably, the greater the amount of ATP-ase (or the greater its activity) in the area of the brain under examination.

504

Of all the areas studied, a difference between seizure-prone and seizure-resistant mice was found in only one—a thin layer of cells in the hippocampus (specifically, the granular cell layer of the dentate fascia), which is one of the oldest parts of the cortex. In the mice susceptible to seizures, this layer stained consistently darker than in the other mice. It also stained darker when triphosphates other than ATP were used in the incubating medium, suggesting that the activity may be caused by other enzymes that break down this class of compounds.

Breeding and other experiments showed that the staining differences were inborn, with two pairs of genes apparently being involved, and did not arise from the seizures themselves. The experiments seemed to show also that whatever led to the staining difference led as well to the seizures, a finding that was given additional support when structural differences were discovered in the cell layer.

In sum, the research group reports, these findings indicate that the epilepticlike seizures of some strains of mice are indeed traceable to an inherited difference most probably involving one small part of the brain. In the test tube, at least, this difference apparently involves a reaction related to energy release. It is conjectured that in the brains of these mice, a certain kind of stress leads to abnormal energy release due to a genetic deficiency in a localized biochemical mechanism.

Whether or not these findings relating to audiogenic seizures in mice can be applied to epilepsy in human beings remains to be determined. Until recently, Dr. Ginsburg notes, little was known of the relationship between seizures in mice and those in people. But electroencephalographic studies by other investigators now indicate that the seizures induced in mice are quite similar to those found in some forms of epilepsy.

2. *The biochemical mechanisms involved in the type of abnormal behavior under study differ from animal to animal, depending upon what genes have been inherited.*

In one strain of seizure-prone mice, the staining reaction, instead of being typical, resembles that found in mice resistant to seizures. (This strain arose, by natural mutation, from a seizure-resistant strain.) Even strains showing the typical ATP-ase reaction differ in other characteristics —for example, the age at which they are most susceptible to seizures and the effect of repeated exposure to noise, which in some strains increases susceptibility.

"A behavior peculiarity," Dr. Ginsburg comments, "can be a kind of stew with a lot of ingredients in it." As further evidence he cites experiments to learn whether or not seizure-prone mice could be chemically protected. Some of them could be. The chemical used was monosodium glutamate, which is closely related to glutamic acid, a compound that appears in the brain and has been widely investigated because of reported findings that it can improve learning ability. Following injections of monosodium glutamate (which also has a common use, to accent the flavor of food), mice of certain strains had fewer and lighter seizures. Mice of other seizure-prone strains, however, were not affected.

3. *Mice that have seizures when exposed to a ringing bell also respond abnormally to a stressful learning situation.*

An ordinary mouse that has learned to run through simple mazes and then is confronted with a maze a little too complex for his learning ability will keep on trying for a while. But a seizure-prone mouse goes to pieces, as evidenced by squeaking and by frantic jumping. An injection, beforehand, of monosodium glutamate will lead to normal behavior, but only if the mouse is from a strain in which the compound will reduce seizures.

4. *Mice become less aggressive if they have had a seizure while young. Along with the other findings, this is believed to suggest a connection between the seizure mechanism and various forms of behavior under stress.*

In some human beings with mental disorders, therapy involving convulsive seizures—induced by shock treatment—is followed by a return to normal behavior. Dr. Ginsburg wondered whether or not seizures would affect the later behavior of mice. As the trait to be studied, he and his co-workers chose aggressiveness, measured by the proportion of times two mice with the same backgrounds attempt to fight when given the opportunity.

The mice came from two strains highly susceptible to seizures. Members of both these strains, as well as those of a third seizure-prone strain, had been shown to be considerably more aggressive than members of three seizure-resistant strains.

Seizures were induced when the animals were 28 days old. Each mouse was then housed alone until its 75th day, when the fighting trials started. Results: In one strain the mice that had had seizures tried to fight on only 37 percent of the occasions as against 72 percent for the control mice. In the other strain the figure was 56 percent as against 80.

5. *The effects of stressful situations during infancy are governed at least in part by heredity.*

In so-called "handling" experiments, a young mouse is lifted from its home cage every day and placed for a few minutes by itself in an unfamiliar place, or it is briefly exposed to cold or pain. When mice that have been subjected to such stress reach adulthood, their behavior is compared with that of mice reared without the stress. A common criterion is aggressiveness.

As noted earlier in this report, Dr. Ginsburg's group has found that in most cases studied, the results—a significant increase in aggressiveness, a significant decrease, or no change—depend both upon the strain of mice and the period of stress. For instance, one strain becomes more aggressive if handled during its second 2 weeks of life but not if handled only during its first 2. Another becomes less aggressive if handled during its first 2 weeks but not if handled only during its second 2.

The grantee compares the implication of these findings with the interpretation given to the results of earlier handling experiments, principally with rats. The older results had been taken to show that early experience profoundly affected various kinds of behavior, including aggressiveness, in a stereotyped way. Thus, the grantee observes, animal experimentation had seemed to bear out Freudian theory.

But the findings of the older work were in most cases the averages of the results obtained from experimenting with mixed—or average— populations. "When you break down a population into a number of components by using pure strains," Dr. Ginsburg continues, "you find that early experience in one genetic situation has a very different effect on later measures of behavior from early experience in another genetic situation. One individual may be so well buffered that early stressful experiences show no effect later on. But they may decidedly change another individual in either one direction or the other.

"One mouse is not the same as another mouse, and certainly one person is not the same as another person. This is true in respect not only to the experiences an individual has had but also to his potentiality for reacting to such experiences."

Consequently, in Dr. Ginsburg's opinion, the way drugs and other forms of therapy affect behavior can be expected to show considerable variation.

Inherited Aggressiveness

A tendency to engage in certain kinds of aggressive behavior, the grantee notes, is definitely inherited. For example, rabbits of one particular strain, first found at the Jackson Memorial Laboratories, Bar Harbor, Maine, will almost invariably fight an intruder. A person who pokes a hand toward them or tries to pick them up will be clawed. This happens no matter how the animals have been raised. Dr. Ginsburg has given young ones away as Easter bunnies to see what would happen if they were brought up with tender, loving care. They turned out mean.

Terriers have been selected for aggressiveness—and so successfully that investigators at Bar Harbor have found it almost impossible to raise a litter of four or more wirehaired fox terrier pups under natural conditions. If the litter is kept together after weaning and one puppy goes down in a fight, the others gang up on him. One puppy can defend itself against two of its littermates, but not three. Eventually it is mutilated or killed. On the other hand, when wirehaireds are raised in isolation from mother and littermates and placed together only after having been weaned from the bottle, no fights develop. The innate genetic aggressiveness is not expressed under these conditions.

Dr. Ginsburg has been associated for years with a breeding program to produce guide dogs for blind persons. The dogs are German shepherds. These have shown a tendency to stick with one person, which is good, often coupled with a tendency toward aggressiveness, which, under the circumstances, is bad. By genetic selection the program now produces a high proportion of German shepherds that have only the desirable trait.

Eventually, the University of Chicago geneticists hope to learn the physiological basis for aggressiveness in rabbits, for the differences in aggressiveness of strains of mice exposed to stress, and for differences in the aggressiveness of a wild animal, the wolf, and a related domestic animal, the dog.

The Socialization of Wolves

Preliminary work with wolves has been underway for several years. It aims at noting marked behavioral differences between wolves and some of their relatives, principally coyotes and dogs, and then eventually at learning the physiological bases for these differences. The wolves come from the Chicago Zoological Park and are wild, in the sense that they have not been handled by human beings. (They were first housed in pens that had been occupied by the university's watchdogs. The watchdogs never learned to work the latches; the wolves learned easily, and the first wolf out would open all the other pens. The researchers had to install locks.)

So far the investigators have learned, among other things, that wolves can be socialized at any age and that tranquilizing drugs have no permanent effect on the process by which this is done. The first part of this finding, Dr. Ginsburg reports, demands a reinterpretation of the widely held hypothesis of a critical period for socialization—a limited time early in life during which, and only during which, an animal can learn to accept human beings. That hypothesis is based mainly on work with dogs and birds.

Socializing an adult wolf is a heroic job. As the grantee outlines it, you begin by entering the pen. The wolf, becoming extremely upset, trembles, moves away, defecates, tries to get out. You have to accustom it to your presence by going to the pen time and again and just sitting there. This phase is known as *the aversive, emotional stage.*

As the animal gets over its extreme fear, Dr. Ginsburg continues, it enters the stage of *the slightly aggressive approach.* It takes cautious steps to investigate you. Now is a critical time because you want to establish contact, yet any move may provoke either fear or aggression. So you watch for the signs that tell how far you may go. Curled lips, raised hair, growls, and, especially, bared canine teeth are all warnings that the wolf is in a fighting humor. In addition to these signs, if the tail droops and the ears are back, you know that the animal is still quite frightened and that you may approach it—very slowly, in full view, and without jerky movements.

If the tail is held high, however, and the ears forward, the wolf means to attack. Stand your ground, and you'll be snapped at and nosed. Retreat, and the wolf will be at you every time you enter the pen. Is there an odor of fear? "We don't think so," answers Dr. Ginsburg, "because we've all been as frightened as we could be. But the animal doesn't know that. How

it reacts to us is not a matter of how we feel but of what we do."
Apparently what the experimenter wears has a bearing, too. Gloves and
other protective clothing are not worn because in the beginning they
appear to frighten the animal and then to make it more aggressive.

Next comes the *investigative stage,* during which the animal rubs
against you, tugs at your clothing and may mark you with urine.

Attempts to domesticate the animal during the second or third phase
will bring back the fear response and retard the socialization process.

Finally you are accepted. The wolf greets you by wagging its tail, and it
comes up to be patted and scratched and to mouth your chin. Then,
having accepted you, it soon comes to accept other human beings. It has
been socialized.

Once socialized, the grantee reports, adult wolves remain friendly with
human beings—for a considerable time, anyway—even after taking up life
again with their brethren. Eighteen months after a socialized adult has
been returned to the zoo, where it ran with wild wolves and was not
handled by the keepers, the Ginsburg group took it back. It was still easy
to handle.

In contrast, when a thoroughly socialized young wolf was left alone
with an unsocialized littermate at the age of 4½ months, it regressed.
Eighteen months later it was as wild as the unhandled wolf and had to be
socialized all over again.

Tranquilizers, over the long run, do not speed the process. Under any
of three quite different compounds—chlorpromazine, reserpine,
chlordiazepoxide—adult wolves can be socialized in a matter of days
rather than months, but when the drugs are withdrawn, the socialized
behavior drops away and the animal is back where it started from. In
other words, tranquilizers can help a wolf overcome fear and aggressive
tendencies but only during the period of tranquilization. The answer to
the important question, *Does learning carry over to the undrugged
state?,* is—in this situation—*no.*

With dogs, the story appears to be different. When tranquilizers are
given to dogs that have been reared in isolation and are, in consequence,
extremely frightened, the animals adjust to the world of man much more
rapidly than untranquilized dogs, and they do not regress when the drug is
dropped.

The grantee views the dog as an incomplete wolf. About the only thing
a dog has that a wolf has not, he says, is a tendency to attach to just one
or a few persons. The coyote is like a dog in that respect; so, too, is the
Australian wild dog, the dingo. But a wolf is gregarious—whether it is with
wolves or, when socialized, people. Most important for an experimenter,
wolf signs are clear. A person can watch any wolf and know what to
expect.

The communications system of wolves and many other wild animals,
Dr. Ginsburg explains, include an elaborate series of warning signs that are
intended to lead not to an attack but to peaceful settlement of the issue at

hand. They comprise a ritual, each element of which elicits an appropriate, built-in response. This symbolic behavior serves to establish dominance and to defend or claim territory—usually without the need of fighting. Other symbolic behavior governs courtship.

The grantee finds an analogy here to the behavior of human beings. He points out that psychoanalysis is largely based on the proposition that a mental event, as in a dream or a fantasy, can be a symbol of whose meaning the individual is not consciously aware. Animals, too, deal in symbols, Dr. Ginsburg observes, and the level at which these may have meaning is analogous to, if not identical with, a level generally considered to exist "only in our own psyche."

Dogs have no dependable series of signals; the grantee says domestication has cost them part of their inheritance. Until the experimenter gets to know the individual animal, he cannot tell whether or not a given posture has the same meaning it would have in a wolf.

To get back to tranquilizers: The investigators reported during the early part of this work that chlordiazepoxide seemed to eliminate a wolf's fear and bring out its aggressiveness. Much the same effect was being observed with human beings, a psychiatrist told the grantee. Certain patients taking that tranquilizer tended to attack people, and the patients, it developed, were usually those with records of assault and other violence. Since wolves, too, have violence in their background, the psychiatrist wondered if the situations might not be analogous.

Dr. Ginsburg doesn't know what conclusions the psychiatrist eventually reached. His own continued observations, however, showed that the tranquilizer was not releasing a wolf's aggressiveness; instead, it was greatly shortening all the stages of socialization, including the first one, in which the animal is afraid, and the second, in which it is aggressive. As noted earlier, the drug's effect does not hold.

Tranquilizers did have one lasting effect. Experimenters who thought they were working with tranquilized wolves—as sometimes they were and sometimes they were not—handled the animals more confidently and got better results.

Work To Be Done

The grantee and his group will continue to search for the underlying biochemical reasons for different behavior. One project aims at exploring other genetic pathways (besides the one that apparently involves the breakdown of ATP or related compounds) involved in audiogenic seizures. Another hopes to learn why seizure-prone mice can differ from one another in such matters as the age of greatest susceptibility and the effect of early, stressful experiences upon later aggressiveness. Studies of the adrenal gland, the catecholamines, the acetylcholine-cholinesterase system in the hipocampal area, and the metabolism of phenylalanine—all of which are known or believed to influence brain function—are underway in one or another of the strains showing behavior differences.

510

In trying to establish a connection between a difference in behavior and a difference in some biochemical characteristic, Dr. Ginsburg observes, research has relied mainly on statistical methods. The grantee prefers to emphasize breeding experiments designed to show whether or not the behavioral difference appears only in animals showing the biochemical difference. He believes that genetically controlled strains must be used if the physiological reasons for variant behaviors are to be demonstrated clearly.

Research Grant: MH 3361

References:

Ginsburg, Benson E. Genetics as a tool in the study of behavior. *Perspectives in Biology and Medicine,* 1(4), 1958.
Ginsburg, Benson E. Causal mechanisms in audiogenic seizures, In: Psychophysi-ologie, *Neuropharmacologie, et Biochemie de la Crise Audiogene,* 112:227–240, 1963. (Colloques Internationaux du Centre National de la Recherche Scientifique, Paris, 1963.)
Ginsburg, Benson E. Genetics and personality. In: Wepman, Joseph M. and Heine, Ralph W., eds. *Concepts of personality.* Chicago, Aldine Press, 1963, p. 63–78.
Ginsburg, Benson E. and Slatis, Herman. The use of pure-bred dogs in problems. *Proceedings of the Animal Care Panel,* 12(4):151–156, 1962.
Ginsburg, Benson E. and Miller, D. Starbuck. Genetic factors in audiogenic seizures. In: *Psychophysiologie, Neuropharmacologie, et Biochemie de la Crise Audiogene.* (Colloques Internationaux du Centre National de la Recherche Scientifique, Paris, 1963.)

Genetics of Human Behavior

Investigator:
Steven G. Vandenberg, Ph. D.
University of Louisville School of Medicine
Louisville, Ky.

prepared by:
Herbert Yahraes

Information about the influence of heredity on the behavior of human beings is being obtained by an Institute grantee through a long-time study of twins, one of the most comprehensive investigations of the kind ever attempted.

Coupled with the findings of other investigators, the results of the study are expected to answer with greater assurance than is now possible such questions as:

• Just where, in the broad fields of intelligence and personality, does heredity have its principal influence?

• Should emphasis on family-child relationships as a major cause of mental illness give way in part to a strengthened emphasis on hereditary factors?

• What hereditary characteristics seem to be involved in the development of mental illness?

• In predicting whether or not a child will later deviate from normal behavior, which tests of his intelligence and personality and which aspects of his early life are most useful?

The grantee is Dr. Steven G. Vandenberg, research associate professor of child development at the University of Louisville and director of psychological research for the university's Louisville twin study. In one part of this project, all pairs of twins of the same sex born in Louisville's eight hospitals are studied during infancy and the preschool years. In another part of the project, like-sexed twins already in the public and parochial school systems are picked up as they become high school freshmen and, once a year until they leave school, given a battery of psychological tests. Under plans for expanding the project, information about the home environment of these older twins will be obtained through visits and questionnaires, and the twins may be followed after they leave school.

Psychologists and geneticists have turned to twin studies many times in the past for light on the roles played by heredity and environment, but the current project promises to be especially valuable because (*a*) it uses more advanced statistical techniques to estimate the strength of hereditary factors and to select tests that most clearly bring out hereditary influences; (*b*) it uses a relatively large sample of twins (about 120 pairs in the baby study and 250 pairs in the high school study—numbers that may be considerably increased if plans for expansion go through), thus strengthening the validity of the findings; and (c) unlike most earlier studies, it uses a reliable technique for distinguishing between fraternal and identical twins, another factor adding to the validity of the results.

Obstetricians and parents often make mistakes in identifying types of twins, but analysis of blood groups—the technique used in this study—is reliable at least 90 percent of the time. This means that in possibly 1 pair of fraternal twins out of 10, both twins will have the same blood factors and will appear on this basis to be identical. Such cases can virtually always be classified correctly, however, by differences in the structure of the heads, hands, and teeth, in the shape of the ears, or in the color and shape of the eyes. (In a doubtful case, absolute proof could be offered only by the skin-graft test.)

The study of baby twins was instituted by Frank Falkner, M.D., now head of the Department of Pediatrics in the University's School of Medicine, to obtain fuller information on how heredity affects physical development. Dr. Falkner brought in Dr. Vandenberg, who added the study of high school twins. In addition to NIMH research grants to Dr. Vandenberg and his appointment as a research career development investigator, the work as a whole has been supported by other NIH and USPHS grants[1] and by a small National Science Foundation grant. Under a new grant from the Institute of Child Health and Human Development, Dr. Vandenberg hopes eventually to establish a Center for Human Behavior Genetics, where additional studies would be undertaken.

Before going to Louisville in 1961, Dr. Vandenberg had already done considerable work on heredity and behavior, principally as director of psychological studies for the hereditary abilities study of the University of Michigan, which NIMH and the McGregor Fund of Detroit supported. That project, too, studied twins—82 pairs, mainly from high schools. The grantee's findings discussed in this report are based in part on preliminary results from the Louisville study of high school twins, but in greater part on recently published reports of the Michigan project and on new analyses by Dr. Vandenberg of data from a review of other twin studies.

The findings may be summed up as follows:

1. Heredity influences human behavior in many of the aspects commonly measured by psychological tests. Its influence shows up strongly even in some types of behavior, such as performance in arithmetic and spelling, in which people have had a good deal of training.

2. Four of the six factors found by the late Dr. L. L. Thurstone to be essential aspects of intelligence and included in the widely used Primary Mental Abilities test are under strong genetic control. These are the factors making for the abilities described as *numerical, verbal* (understanding of words), *spatial* (the ability to perceive patterns and structures and to move them around in the mind, keeping the relationships intact), and *word fluency*. Two other abilities included in the test, *reasoning* and

---

[1] RG 5527, A 4847, H 7233, HD 482.

memory, do not show a strong hereditary influence—quite possibly because the test does not deal with enough of the factors comprising them. Memory for names, as an example, is included in the test, but it has been found unrelated to memory for faces, which is not. Further, a person's willingness to memorize the items during the testing session is highly influenced by his attitude towards the testing, so the test measures his motivation as much as his memory.

3. Motor skills decidedly affected by heredity include dexterity in using tweezers to place small pins into holes, the ability to sort cards fast and accurately, and the ability to walk a beam without losing balance. But tests of hand steadiness and body sway give insignificant results.

4. In the area of personality, one group of tests shows a high degree of heritability for the factors of activity, vigor, impulsiveness, and sociability—but not for dominance, stability, or reflectiveness. Other tests indicate a relatively strong hereditary influence upon neuroticism, the display of nervous tension, and control of the will; and there is some evidence that the degree to which a person is an extrovert or an introvert is partially determined by heredity. However, most measures of personality traits fail to disclose any significant genetic role for them—evidence, Dr. Vandenberg believes, not that personality is little affected by heredity but that present tests are measuring traits primarily affected by environment. He points out that such tests are right and good for most applications but not for studies of hereditary factors.

5. Tests of musical ability and preference have been even less successful than those of personality in pointing to a hereditary factor. Perhaps only the exceptional talent of great composers and musicians has such a factor, the investigator suggests. Perhaps, in the case of the musical and certain other abilities, heredity studies might make greater headway if they looked for innate defects in basic skills rather than for innate proficiencies.

6. Some of the ways in which the body reacts to stressful situations appear to be influenced by heredity. In a laboratory situation, most of the twins in the Michigan study responded to mild stress—induced by a sudden flash of light and the fall of a hammer—by changes in (*a*) the rate of the heartbeat, (*b*) the rate of breathing, and (*c*) the galvanic skin resistance. The changes in the heartbeat and breathing rates, but not in the galvanic skin resistance, were much more alike in the identical twins than in the fraternals, indicating heritability factors at work in the first two responses. The grantee would like to see more research along this line because he believes that the evidence for a genetic factor in some types of responses by the autonomic nervous system may also be partial evidence for a genetic factor in psychosomatic illness. The person who naturally responds to stress by an above-normal increase in his heart beat, Dr. Vandenberg asks—may he not be the one most likely to develop a psychosomatic heart ailment? Other investigators have suggested that persons with different personalities develop different kinds of psychosomatic complaints. Hence, Dr. Vandenberg believes, research might well find a close

514

relationship among illness and two factors controlled in part by heredity—personality and the activity of the autonomic nervous system.

Fraternal and Identical Twins: Analyzing the Differences

Since a pair of identical twins have developed from the same fertilized egg, they have the same heredity, and any difference between them must have been caused by environment alone. But a pair of fraternal twins, having developed from two fertilized eggs, have different heredities; hence the differences between them have been caused by both heredity and environment. Through statistical analysis of these differences, investigators are able to say whether a given aspect of intelligence (for example, facility in using numbers) appears to be strongly or weakly controlled by heredity.

Like earlier researchers, the Louisville group assumes that the differences in the environment of a pair of twins are roughly the same for identical as for like-sexed fraternal. The investigators know that this is not quite true. For one thing, the difference in the prenatal environments of identical twins, taken all together, is probably greater because of the greater possibility of an imbalance in placental circulation. For another, identical twins are more likely than fraternals to be treated alike by their families. The Louisville studies may eventually help to show whether or not these differences are significant. At the most, Dr. Vandenberg believes, they make for either a slight overestimate or a slight underestimate of heredity's role.

In analyzing the differences between the two types of twins, the grantee uses an index based on a statistical concept (the F-ratio) developed by the British statistician, R. A. Fisher. For each test, he subtracts Johnnie's score from Jimmy's, Ronald's from Donald's, Ellen's from Helen's, and so on. Then, for each kind of twins, he adds the squared differences and uses the results to get an index of the strength of the hereditary factor. The index, or F-ratio, is obtained by dividing each sum by the number of pairs and then dividing the figure for the fraternal twins by the figure for the identical twins. The result is almost invariably greater than 1, indicating that the within-pair variance of the fraternal twins is greater than that of the identical twins. If the ratio is statistically significant—meaning that the probability it could have occurred by chance is very slight—the particular ability being tested probably has a strong hereditary element.

By this technique the contribution of environment to the expression of a particular ability is subtracted, loosely speaking, from the contribution of heredity. The method is most reliable when fairly large numbers of twins are studied. The findings for a group, since they give the average picture, do not necessarily apply to any particular pair within the group; they simply point to those aspects of intelligence and personality in which a genetic factor is involved. The grantee believes that the results will prove to have wide validity, inasmuch as a characteristic that can be inherited in Kentucky presumably can be inherited anywhere else. However, the way the characteristic is expressed, if at all, may depend in large part upon the environment. He has found that tests commonly used for measuring basic mental abilities give much the same results whether administered to American college students or to young people who, though going to college in the United States, have been brought up in quite different cultural backgrounds—South American and Chinese. This finding is considered by Dr. Vandenberg to be evidence that the abilities measured by the tests are cross-cultural and perhaps innate.

In spite of their value, Dr. Vandenberg describes twin studies as only "an economical first step in human behavior genetics." They are only a first step because they can be used to deduce *what* traits are inherited but not *how*. Eventually, when enough reliable tests for assessing the influence of heredity are available, researchers will have to look for the *how* by undertaking family studies. They will have to search for the appearance, over generations, of behavioral characteristics related to psychological functioning much as medical geneticists have searched for evidence of hereditary factors in phenylketonuria, hemophilia, diabetes, and other physical disorders.

"If we remember that a rather clear-cut and, one would think, rather noticeable defect such as color blindness has been known to science for little more than a century," Dr. Vandenberg observes, "it does not seem unreasonable to expect that we are overlooking other anomalies." As a possible case in point, he notes the suggestion by a Swedish investigator that severe reading difficulties may stem from a hereditary factor controlled by a single gene.

If an inherited characteristic is harmful, perhaps we can learn how to prevent its full expression, as we have learned how to prevent phenylketonuria from leading still further to permanent mental retardation. Emotional illness, however, is a far more complex problem than phenylketonuria, partly because many genes may be involved instead of only one, and partly because the biochemical mechanism can be fully activated, perhaps, only by certain stressful environmental conditions.

Of the present psychological and biochemical measures, the grantee believes we shall probably find that no single one is clearly related to such complex conditions as schizophrenia and obsessive compulsive neurosis. More likely, statistical analyses of the results of many tests given to large numbers of patients will eventually succeed in isolating a variety of factors involved. Efficient tests of these factors can then be developed.

If the influence on behavior of heredity, environment, and the two of them acting together is to be clearly understood, Dr. Vandenberg suggests that we may need at least a nationwide system of storing information about individuals and families. But we can start on a smaller scale. For example, we can go after proof of the theory that schizophrenia has a rather strong hereditary component. The grantee thinks that a carefully planned 10-year study of several thousand patients and their family backgrounds—a research project in connection with an existing service project—would come up with a definite answer. It might even supply an inkling of the genetic mechanism.

516

Tests of Intelligence

It is widely agreed that heredity plays a large role in intelligence, but intelligence is many things. In fact, one authority attending the recent Conference on Research in Human Behavior Genetics (supported by the Institute through a grant to Dr. Vandenberg) reported that he had preliminary evidence of two entirely different kinds of intelligence, one depending mainly on heredity and the other on culture. Dr. Vandenberg prefers to say that certain of the factors or abilities comprising intelligence can be developed through training to a much greater extent than others.

Psychologists do not agree on the number of different abilities contributing to intelligence—more than 100, by one estimate—or on the exact nature of many of them. However, five of the factors in the frequently used commercial test referred to earlier, the Primary Mental Abilities test (PMA), are generally considered to represent in fact distinct characteristics. This is because, on the average, the scores made in tests of any one of these five abilities—numerical, verbal, spatial, word fluency, and memory—do not correlate highly with the scores made in tests of any of the others. As previously noted, Dr. Vandenberg has found that the first four of these abilities are not only independent but also strongly influenced by heredity.

The grantee began by administering the standard version of the PMA as an important part of his tests, but this year he is using an expanded version drawn from Dr. Thurstone's original material. The new version covers perhaps 14 separate abilities. The complete Louisville battery includes a number of other "intelligence" tests, and several tests of personality—about three dozen tests in all, some widely accepted, others experimental. The tests are made up of about 125 measures, or subtests.

Through a method similar to factor analysis, the investigator can infer whether or not the differences between fraternal twins on a number of the tests can be attributed to the same hereditary factor. He can also estimate what percentage of the variation within all the pairs of fraternal twins on, say, the verbal ability factor, is accounted for by a given test. Thus he can combine and weigh—and discard and add to—tests until he has put together the battery that makes for the best possible separation of fraternal and identical twins. In sum, when he is considering many factors of intelligence and personality, he can say which ones appear to be under strong genetic control, and, when he is considering many tests, which ones most clearly differentiate between the two types of twins, and therefore are of most value to studies of the heritability of psychological characteristics.

A number of provocative findings about psychological tests as indicators of inherited characteristics were turned up by the University of Michigan study with which the grantee was connected.

Close to half of all the psychological measures used in that project, but less than a third of those in the area of personality, Dr. Vandenberg has found, gave statistically significant evidence that the characteristics being measured had a hereditary component. Sometimes the heritability estimate was strongly influenced by the type of measure being used. For

517

instance, one vocabulary test calling upon the subject himself to supply the definitions yielded results showing a decided hereditary influence, while two other vocabulary tests, one giving a choice of answers and one asking the students to match words with pictures, produced opposite results. The Michigan group found half a dozen instances of this sort, and conceivably would have found more if each ability or trait had been measured by two or more tests. It also found some characteristics that showed a strong hereditary component but have little or no practical application—so far as anyone knows now. One of these is the ability to trace a pattern while watching one's work in the mirror. Dr. Vandenberg cites these findings as evidence of the need for wider experimentation in psychological testing if the hereditary elements of behavior are to be pinned down. Tests that work well in predicting success in certain studies or professions, he suggests, are not necessarily the best ones for research in genetics. It may well be that some inherited psychological differences are lying undiscovered because they have no applied usefulness or because we have not been measuring them.

Of particular interest to the grantee right now are the spatial tests because he thinks spatial visualization, an important ability in engineers, may prove to have a stronger hereditary element—and therefore depend less on training—than most other facets of intelligence. (Present tests of this ability include putting a puzzle together in the head, imagining what a given object would look like if cut in half, finding a given pattern among other patterns, and saying where the holes will occur in a piece of paper when it has been folded several times and punched.) A test of vocational preferences also seems to get at things having a hereditary basis—a finding that probably can be traced to the influence on occupational choice of temperament and ability, which are to some extent genetically governed.

Another aspect of intelligence, or perhaps of both personality and intelligence, seems to be *closure,* an ability to round out or complete things. Some types of brain-damaged persons lack it. In the closure tests used by Dr. Vandenberg, developed by the Canadian, C. M. Mooney, the twins are presented with incomplete drawings of faces and asked to identify each face as male or female and say in which direction it is looking. Though closure is at present not known to be related to any other ability, some people do better than others on such a test. Closure items have been included in intelligence measures, Dr. Vandenberg explains, mainly because they do not seem to be influenced by verbal ability, a factor strongly affected by environment and generally difficult to control for. Dr. Vandenberg guesses that high scores on closure tests perhaps indicate some artistic ability, but he may have to wait a long time before he knows.

In experimental use, as well, is a test of the long-held theory that some people react more to color and others more to form, the difference being traceable to a deep-seated personality difference. Preliminary findings by Dr. Vandenberg indicate that scores on the form-color test, developed by Thurstone, show a marked hereditary influence.

518

Tests developed by J. P. Guilford to measure various aspects of creativity are also used. (One asks the student to suggest, among other items, new uses for old newspapers and two improvements each to various social institutions, such as marriage.) Whether or not the tests really do measure creativity in the common sense of the word is in question. Preliminary Louisville findings indicate that whatever they measure is not under strong hereditary control.

Among the measures is one developed by the grantee himself while working with the Schizophrenia and Psychopharmacology Project of the University of Michigan and Ypsilanti State Hospital.[2] In this test a person looks at pictures of faces and chooses a word that best describes their expressions. One of the major characteristics of schizophrenia, Dr. Vandenberg explains, is a loss of social sensitivity of social perception, marked by a withdrawal from other persons and a lessened ability to communicate. As used in the Michigan schizophrenia study, the test apparently provided a measure of this loss: schizophrenic patients performed significantly worse than nonschizophrenic mental patients, while the nonschizophrenic patients did almost as well as normal persons. Perhaps the schizophrenic cannot make the kind of social judgment demanded by the test because he cannot bring himself to look at the pictures long enough; perhaps some other disability is involved. In any event, Dr. Vandenberg thinks that the inability of schizophrenics to make such a judgment is related to their tendency toward withdrawal. Preliminary findings of the Louisville twin study indicate that social sensitivity as measured by this test is more influenced by environment than heredity.

Heredity and Handedness

Dr. Vandenberg is much interested in handedness, a psychophysiological characteristic that may well be controlled by only a few genes. If just two alternative genes are involved, for right-handedness and for left-handedness, a person who received two doses of the one would be right handed; two doses of the other, left handed; one dose of each, either right or left handed, depending mostly on the training received from his parents. A number of right-handed persons, the investigator believes, are perhaps naturally left-handed or ambidextrous—but don't know it.

The biggest difficulty in studying the heredity of this trait is the lack of a good test for natural handedness. A simple test for brain dominance might be the answer, because a person whose left hemisphere was shown to be dominant might be expected to be naturally right-handed. But there is no such test. In fact, we generally do things the other way around and use handedness as an indicator of dominance. Dr. Vandenberg expects to work with the so-called Pulfrich phenomenon in an effort to help develop the needed test. In this phenomenon a luminous pendulum swinging in a darkened room appears to move in the shape of an ellipse when the

---

[2] Supported by Grant MH 1972 to Ralph W. Gerard.

illumination reaches one of the eyes through a filter. The shorter axis of the apparent ellipse is greater when the filter is held in front of the more dominant eye.

The grantee is concerned with handedness, he explains, because information about its genetic mechanism would increase interest in—and provide another model for—research in the heritability of more "psychological" characteristics. Besides, it would be useful in answering that old question about the effects of forcing a naturally left-handed person to become right-handed. In tests involving motor skills, incidentally, performance with the right hand generally shows a stronger hereditary influence than performance with the left.

Genetic Control of Physical Characteristics

The Michigan study, like the Louisville project, to some extent was concerned with the degree of hereditary control over physical as well as psychological development. Recently Dr. Vandenberg compared the Michigan findings in this respect with those of five other twin studies since 1926 and found a high degree of heritability for virtually all the measures that had been included. Among these were height, arm length, middle finger length, leg length, foot length, chest girth, neck girth, head length and breadth and girth, eye spacing, nose height and breadth, face length, and ear breadth. Measures of length generally had higher heritability values than measures of width—perhaps, the grantee notes, because the latter are more affected by "such environmental excesses" as obesity and malnutrition. Perhaps for the same reason, the studies did not agree as to the influence of heredity upon the waist measurement and upon weight.

When twin differences in body measurements were related to twin differences on certain intelligence tests, the Michigan group found that the larger the head, the higher the test score. This relationship was statistically significant among the identical twins but weaker and not significant among the fraternals. Among the general population, Dr. Vandenberg points out, the relationship is obscured by other factors and cannot be observed. It is only when differences in age, sex, background, and education are controlled, as they can be in comparing twins, that the relationship shows up.

Among the fraternal twins studied in the Michigan project, the one who had been born first was found usually to have made the higher score, and there was a tendency among both types of twins for the one who had been born first to have the larger head.

Some Research Needs

Dr. Vandenberg considers research looking toward the following goals, some of them indicated earlier, to be highly important:

- A better understanding of the basic elements making up intelligence and personality.

520

- Better information about the characteristics measured by present psychological tests.
- New tests or combinations of tests that bring out clearly the hereditary elements in our abilities and personalities.
- Better tests of motor skills in children, particularly those under six. (At least during babyhood, the grantee observes, motor development and mental development are related, and he points to work by another NIMH grantee indicating that disturbances of motor development in infancy may be followed by psychological disorders, including schizophrenia.)
- Better evidence than we now have as to the role, if any, played by hereditary factors in schizophrenia and other mental disorders.
- Better information on how learning or training interacts with heredity in the development of a given characteristic. (As an example of how this might be obtained, the grantee suggests that one twin of a 3-year-old pair of identical twins might be given intensive training in reading, the twins then being followed up to learn whether or not any lasting difference resulted.)

Dr. Vandenberg remarks that while he himself is primarily interested in the contribution of heredity, complete understanding of how human behavior is controlled by genes will be reached only through the work of scientists in many fields. Studies of the role of the environment are just as important as studies of hereditary factors.

Research Grants: MH 6203, MH 7033, MH 7708, MH 7880, K3-MH 18,382

References:

Clark, Philip J., Vandenberg, Steven G., and Proctor, Charles H. On the relationship of scores on certain psychological tests with a number of anthropometric characters and birth order in twins. *Human Biology,* 33(2), 1961.
Cohen, William, Vandenberg, Steven G., and Falkner, Frank. *Aims of Louisville Twin Study.* Report No. 2, Child Development Unit, University of Louisville, 1962.
Fish, Barbara. The study of motor development in infancy and its relationship to psychological functioning. *American Journal of Psychiatry,* 117(12), 1961.
Sutton, H. Eldon, Vandenberg, Steven G., and Clark, Philip J. The hereditary abilities study: selection of twins, diagnosis of zygosity and program measurements. *American Journal of Human Genetics,* 14(1), 1962.
Vandenberg, Steven G. Behavioral methods for assessing neuroses and psychoses. In: Uhr and Miller, eds. *Drugs and Behavior.* New York, Wiley, 1960.
Vandenberg, Steven G. The hereditary abilities study: hereditary components in a psychological test battery. *American Journal of Human Genetics,* 14(2), 1962.
Vandenberg, Steven G. How "stable" are heritability estimates? A comparison of heritability estimates from six anthropometric studies. *American Journal of Physical Anthropology,* 20(3), 1962.
Vandenberg, Steven G. *Innate Abilities, One or Many? A New Method and Some Results.* Report No. 3, Child Development Unit, University of Louisville, 1963.
Vandenberg, Steven G. *Contributions of Twin Research to Child Development.* Report No. 5, Child Development Unit, University of Louisville, 1964. Draft of chapter from Lipsitt, L. P., and Spiker, C. C., eds. *Advances in Child Development and Behavior* II, New York, Academic Press.
Vandenberg, Steven G. Multivariate analysis of twin differences. *Methods and Goals in Human Behavior Genetics,* New York, Academic Press, 1964.
Vandenberg, Steven G. *The Primary Mental Abilities of South American Students. A Comparative Study of the Stability of a Factor Structure.* (In press.)

Vandenberg, Steven G., and Mattsson, Eira. The interpretation of facial expressions by schizophrenics, other mental patients, normal adults and children. *Acta Psychologica*, 19, 1961.

Vandenberg, Steven G., Clark, Philip J., and Samuels, Ina. *Psychophysiological Reactions of Twins: Heritability Estimates of Galvanic Skin Resistance, Heartbeat and Breathing Rates.* (In press.)

Patterns of Sleep
Over a Lifetime

Investigator:
Irwin Feinberg, M.D.*
New York Downstate Medical Center
Brooklyn, N.Y.

Co-contributors:
Howard Roffwarg, M.D.,
Montefiore Hospital, New York City
H. W. Agnew, Jr.,
University of Florida
Anthony Kales, M.D.,
University of California at Los Angeles
D. R. Hawkins, M.D.,
University of Virginia
Arthur Parmelee, M.D.,
University of California at Los Angeles

Preprared by:
Gay Luce

Background

From the darkness of the womb the newborn child only slowly emerges: As if incapable of plunging into consciousness for too long at once, he sleeps and awakens in brief alternations. At the other end of life, as if reluctant to let go of consciousness for too long at one time, the aged brain shows a sleep that is punctuated with awakenings. The depth of infant sleep and the alterations brought by youth, adulthood, and age reveal, like indirect mirrors, changes that inevitably take place in the nervous system during the span of a lifetime.

At birth the nervous system is incompletely developed. The brain triples in weight after birth, reaching almost adult proportions by about age 6. During these preadolescent years the brain has its greatest plasticity and presumably the greatest capacity for learning. The plasticity of the brain can be inferred by the ability of very young brains to transfer such functions as speech after significant damage or surgery. During adolescence this plasticity diminishes, and hormonal events make their great impact on the sexually maturing human being. Later, after the plateau of maturity, the middle-aged hormonal system again begins to change. An

---

*Now at Veteran's Hospital, San Francisco, California

individual may then begin to notice in himself a trend that has actually transpired throughout his adulthood: It has become more difficult for him to change his habits, to learn a language, to acquire the skill of a new sport, or adopt a new profession. Nor is he sleeping as soundly as in youth. In old age, finally, this trend accelerates, and the individual begins to find that he can no longer practice his old skills and no longer remembers what once he knew. His sleep, punctuated by wakeful moments, knits night and day together in a prolongation of consciousness.

The relationships between the underlying brain physiology and lifetime behavioral development are now being explored by using the electro-encephalogram (EEG) of sleep to depict the sleep patterns of each age, from birth to senescence.

The overall picture of lifetime sleep, as compiled by Dr. Feinberg and his associates, also includes research conducted by other NIMH grantees, who have concentrated upon particular age groups. In correlating lifetime behavioral changes with sleep patterns, the researchers expect that these sleep-behavioral relationships may offer clues about the biological function of sleep and its various stages. Knowledge of sleep patterns is, moreover, of clinical importance. Dr. Marvin Schultz of UCLA has demonstrated that sleep patterns can now be used to confirm very early diagnoses of illness such as hypothyroidism or of retardation in infants. A knowledge of sleep patterns is only beginning to reveal why elderly people complain of insomnia, and what, indeed, this insomnia looks like and augurs. An understanding of nighttime insomnia and delirious wanderings in the senile may finally lead to the development of rational therapy, rather than the current practice of liberal and unconsidered drug use for insomnia and of institutionalization for the senile. Base line studies of sleep, at different ages, now offer a yardstick against which researchers are looking at the effects of hypnotics and other drugs, and from which they are judging the impressions the various illnesses mark upon nighttime sleep. The base line of sleep patterns—for life—as compiled by these investigators will undoubtedly be refined again in the near future. It is nonetheless the foundation, the bedrock, on which many clinical studies of sleep will increasingly rely.

The formulation presented here he is not solely the substance of one laboratory, but includes the data of other research teams, and offers a reformulation of the age-sleep picture.

The Sleeping Population

For half a dozen years, many infants born in the bright new hospital at UCLA have been subjects for Dr. Arthur Parmelee and his associates, while other infants who were born at Columbia-Presbyterian Hospital in New York were observed by Dr. Howard Roffwarg and his associates. In one of the laboratories at UCLA, infants are being followed into the preschool and early school years, with sleep records and testing at regular intervals. The data contributing to the base line for childhood have been

524

collected for a variety of reasons For instance, Dr. Anthony Kales and his associates compared normal and somnambulistic children, while Dr. David Hawkins, then at the University of North Carolina, and Drs. Chester Pierce and Roy Whitman of Cincinnati were interested in enuresis. Dr. David Foulkes has studied sleep in young school children, moved by particular interest in their dreams. In the course of burgeoning sleep research, adolescents, young adults, and middle-aged people have become the subjects of diverse studies. Dr. Wilse Webb and H. W. Agnew, Jr., at the University of Florida, and Dr. Anthony Kales and his associates at UCLA have studied normal sleep in some elderly subjects for the purpose of obtaining a norm. Dr. Charles Fisher at Mt. Sinai, and Dr. Ismet Karacan now of the University of Florida, were correlating the occurrence of erections with rapid-eye-movement sleep throughout the lifetime, and were thus moved to examine the sleep of quite elderly men.

This laboratory conducted its own studies of young adults, normal older people, and deteriorated elderly people out of an interest in the relation between sleep patterns, intellectual function, and age. As there began to be data of disparate sorts from laboratories all around the country and also in Europe, the investigators were challenged by the need for a summary picture, a lifeline of sleep. They added to their own data a study of sleep in children who were 5 to 10 years old. This filled in the picture of sleep at a time of life when the brain is physically almost mature, yet at its most plastic.

It is difficult to obtain normative data on human sleep, and while a lifetime scale of sleep patterns promises to become an invaluable diagnostic yardstick, it will be hard to acquire. The difficulty in amassing such a yardstick can be seen from the human investment in a single study. Dr. Feinberg and his associates have given the better part of 4 years to their study. Yet they studied only 38 normal people and 15 abnormal elderly persons. The age span was 5−96. It would be hard to make these 38 people evenly represent those 91 years. Ideally, a graph of changing sleep patterns would evolve from records taken from several normal people, one group of subjects for each year in the lifespan. Discounting the time it takes to find and acclimatize subjects, discounting the tediousness of consecutive nights of sleep recording, it would probably take 20 man-years to run the ideal study of 400-odd people—five for each year under study. Some researchers are indeed studying numbers of subjects representing a few years. For obvious reasons there is no wholesale endeavor to encompass the lifetime. The approximate graphs drawn from small and scattered samples are apparently adequate to outline the relation between sleep patterns and age.

The Volunteers of This Study

The young adults and elderly patients were studied at St. Elizabeths—a huge Federal mental hospital located in the southeast portion of Washington, D.C. There, a special ward was established within a modern building, where patients and normal outsiders might live while their nightly sleep was being studied. Nine young men and six young women were recruited from among the hospital nurses and aides at the hospital and persuaded to sleep in the laboratory for five or six nights in succession, and to comply with rules by not drinking alcohol or napping on those days. These people were between 19 and 36 years of age.

Normal Elderly

Nine men and six women who were between 65 and 95 years old—an average age of 77—were studied on a volunteer ward at the large modern hospital on the NIH campus in Bethesda, the Clinical Center. These unusual people were members of a club called the Fossils, a wry version of the Golden Age clubs for retired and elderly persons. In contrast with the young adults, these people were comfortable suburbanites, retired professionals, and generally cultured and highly educated people. Nobody has been able to ascertain that educational level in any way alters sleep patterns, but the good health of these older people may indeed be attributable to their social class. This group was thoroughly screened for even premonitory signs of impairment, and each individual was brought into the research ward for 5 days of acclimatization before the sleep studies began. These people also observed the no-napping and no-alcohol rules.

Chronic Brain Syndrome

Although this group, studied at St. Elizabeths, was matched for age with the Bethesdans, it presented a sad contrast between a healthy old age and old age attended by severe brain impairment. These were intellectually damaged people, some of them professionals retired from exceedingly responsible jobs, others were firemen and small businessmen. At the time of the study they were incompetent to take care of themselves, some wandered around in a disoriented manner, and all needed institutional care. Most of them were not comparable with their healthy Bethesda peers in either education or economic status, although the research team had tried very hard to recruit volunteers of equivalent cultural status.

Children

Eight boys and girls, aged 4½ to 6½ and 9 to 10 years, slept in the laboratory atop the Downstate Medical Center's large new hospital, a laboratory that is often referred to as the Dream Lab. The children were brought by their parents to the laboratory before bedtime, coming on several nights to accustom themselves to the laboratory, and for three nights of recording.

526

All of the subjects, old and young, were carefully and lullingly decorated with electrodes around the scalp and face (in standardized placement) before retiring. They were wired up to the electroencephalograph
amplifier system, through a cable system permitting them to sleep in a
private room, where they were undisturbed by the comings and goings of
researchers in the control room. In each hospital, the undeviating hospital
routine dictated the hour at which the sleep subjects had, perforce, to rise.
At St. Elizabeths the rising hour was 6:30, while at NIH and Downstate
the subjects slept until 7 or 7:30.

The High Water Marks

Throughout the night, changing brain waves and physiological functions
leave a sea of data, marked by only a few distinguishable tides, rhythms
that are recurrent and obvious. Within this sea of data, the investigators
selected certain intervals to act as the high water marks of the night. How
long did the volunteer sleep? How often did he awaken from sleep? How
long did it take him to fall asleep when the lights went out? How long did
it take to reach the first rapid-eye-movement period, and to show not only
the irregular low-voltage brain waves but also an eye movement? How
much of the night did he spend in REM sleep, and how much in slow-wave
sleep?

The investigators subdivided the usual EEG categories of sleep into
more refined intervals which they defined quantitatively. When they
looked for the amounts of deep delta sleep (stages 3 and 4), they would
count the number of slow waves of at least 50 microvolts in a 20-second
interval: They called it stage 3 if there were between 10 and 15 waves, and
stage 4 if the interval contained more than 15 such waves. They also
examined the EEG for bursts of activity that visually resemble wire
spindles, bursts that last about half a second or more, and contain 12–14
cycles a second. This is a configuration that does not occur in the EEG of
sleep until after about age 3 months. It is reduced or absent in old age.

The investigators looked at intervals of rapid-eye-movement sleep in
several ways. Within the REM period are many moments when the eyes
are not moving at all, and the EEG shows a pattern of light, low-voltage
sleep. The researchers looked at density of eye movements. They measured the intervals of stage 1 sleep preceding and succeeding the eye
movements, and the percentage of the night's sleep spent in this variegated
REM period. They measured the night's total REM sleep. They looked at
the amount of time an individual slept, next to the amount of time he
spent in bed. They looked at the periodicity of nightly events—the timing
of recurrent stages of EEG. Their breakdown differed from that of various
colleagues, but the emerging picture from various laboratories has been
amazingly consonant.

527

The Infant

In 1955 Drs. Eugene Aserinsky and Nathaniel Kleitman observed that infants in their first 7 months alternated predictably between active and quiet periods in sleep, roughly every hour. Eight years later Dr. Howard Roffwarg was able to report in considerable detail what happens during an infant's sleep. Using tiny sensors they were able to track the heart rate, the brain waves, the respiration, and muscle tone of the newborn baby as he slept. A year later Dr. Arthur H. Parmelee and his colleagues at UCLA confirmed these findings from their own detailed study of infants beginning on the first day of life. During the quiet phase of sleep the infants showed a regular respiration and scarcely any body movements, but during the active sleep that has resemblance to REM sleep, the infants smiled, kicked, grimaced, made eye movements and sudden gestures with their arms or legs.

For about his first 3 months, an infant naps. Only slowly does he begin to sleep primarily at night. As infants have been recorded and observed around the clock, during their first week of life, it was clear that there were already some important individual differences in the amount of sleep and the length of the baby's cycle. One infant would sleep for 40-minute intervals, 16 times a day, while another would sleep in 14 longer periods. The UCLA laboratory has studied about 25 infants between birth and 3 months, and found that in this period babies generally show a sleep cycle of about 40–45 minutes, which lengthens as the infant matures.

Although many people imagine that infants sleep most of the time and that they are awake more as they mature, this is not really the major change in the first 2 years of life. A newborn infant who sleeps 14 hours a day in his first weeks, may still be sleeping about 12 hours a day at age 2 years. The primary change is in the distribution of his sleep and waking: He begins to sleep continuously through the night and be awake by day, in the almost 24-hour rhythmic pattern of his parents.

The EGG stages of sleep are shifting in their periodicity too. The brain waves of a premature or full-term infant are not so coherent and defined as those of the child or adult. EGG studies by Dr. Parmelee and his associates at UCLA, and independent studies by Drs. Howard Roffwarg, Joseph Muzio, and William Dement suggest that the infant spends about one-third of his existence in a state resembling REM sleep. Premature babies show even greater proportions of this sleep. In the first days of life, this stage occupies about 50 percent of the baby's sleep, declining as the infant's nervous system matures. The infant, like no normal adult, will fall directly from waking into this rapid-eye-movement sleep, so characterized by dreaming in adults, and by subtle facial expressions and extraordinary physical activity on the part of infants. Children over 1½ or 2 years will sleep for almost 3 hours, and adults will sleep for about an hour before falling into a rapid-eye-movement state. Although children and adults may speak out, grimace, or exhibit certain twitches of muscles, they do not wave their arms or legs, nor thrash about wildly during their REM dreams as do infants. Signs of exaggerated activity, like those of the infant during

528

REM sleep, are highly abnormal in adults. Indeed, the only adults who have exhibited as much REM sleep as a newborn infant have been drug addicts, alcoholics during withdrawal, or people who were experimentally deprived of this sleep stage on prior nights. Some of these people have been recorded during a night that was half given over to REM sleep.

Children studied by Dr. Feinberg and his associates, like children studied by Dr. Roffwarg, et al., Dr. Kales et al., H. W. Agnew, Jr. et al., spent around 25 percent of their sleeping time in the REM state; this was about the same proportion as the young adults. The amount of REM sleep declined slightly in the older people, and noticeably in the patients with chronic brain syndrome, but without greatly changing the relative proportions of REM and non-REM sleep. The impaired old people sometimes reacted to REM sleep in the manner of an alcoholic suffering withdrawal symptoms. Three of the patients often awakened from a REM dream with a start. They would try to pull off their electrodes and leave, saying they had to make a train, be at work on time, or meet a business associate. They were in effect delirious and had to be restrained from racing out of the building to do the prosaic errands of their dreams.

It has been conjectured that the intensity of the dream experience may be detected by the density of rapid eye movements. When a person has been deprived of REM sleep, he compensates later by indulging in more than usual REM sleep with more intense eye movements. The paucity of eye movements in the REM sleep of retarded children is one bit of data suggesting that the eye-movement activity of REM sleep may be related to brain metabolism.

Curiously enough, the direction of the dreamer's eye movements changes with age. Newborn babies and infants make many more vertical eye movements than horizontal movements in their active sleep. Elderly people and senile patients were found to make mainly horizontal eye movements during their REM experiences. Children and young adults showed both, although their eye movements have been reported to be primarily horizontal by Dr. J. Antrobus.

Memory of the REM experience also seems to change with age, although pure memory is hardly what the sleep researcher determines when he awakens a sleepy child or an old person and asks what he was thinking. Neither young children nor old people seem to recall—or to be able to recite—dream experiences as well as young adults.

This has been an observation in a recent study by Drs. Edwin Kahn and Charles Fisher at Mount Sinai Hospital in New York City. In contrast to Dr. Feinberg's study, they found no correlation between age and the amount of REM sleep in 11 old men. This discrepancy may be due to differences in sampling or in procedure. The elderly gentlemen studied by Drs. Kahn and Fisher slept with a strain gauge attached to the penis. They still showed some degree of the erections that are seen in all males during REM periods, but when they were awakened from REM sleep they had far less dream recall than a young adult. The investigators conjectured that vitality and psychological vigor may determine the amount of REM sleep obtained at a later age in life.

Rapid-eye-movement sleep has been linked with activity in a primitive portion of the lower brain, the pons. It is not surprising that brain stem activity might be dominant in premature babies, whose brains are in the early stages of development. It has been speculated that this rudimentary brain activity, occurring in the womb, constitutes a state that would not be dreaming in an adult's sense, but which stimulates brain experiences in preparation for life. Dr. Feinberg and other researchers have speculated that the high amount of dreaming found during early childhood is related to the enormous amount that a child must learn—for in early life the brain must absorb more than it ever will later. One emerging theory about REM sleep suggests that this is a time when newly learned material is stored and filed in the brain.

The rhythm of infant sleep and waking has been traced back into the womb in a recording from a mother during her sleep. Until about 7 months' gestation, the activity of the fetus was often changing. After 8 months, there was a regular 44-minute activity period, with a roughly half-hour rest in between. After delivery, the infant showed the same cycle of activity during his first days.

The newborn infant's sleep rhythm only faintly resembles that of children and adults, although the EEG of REM sleep even in very young infants bears a striking resemblance to REM and stage 2 in adults. The sleep records have been compared by three main criteria: The amounts and percentages of REM sleep and slow-wave sleep; the length of intervals such as the transition from waking into active sleep; the periodicity of the complete sleep cycle.

Striking changes occur in the first 3 months, as the proportion of rapid-eye-movement sleep declines in the infant and the baby begins to sleep at night. The child of 6 months or a year spends about a third of his sleep in REM dreaming. By age 2 this has dropped to about a quarter. Somewhere between 3 and 5 years the proportion of REM sleep falls to about 20–25 percent, which is close to the norm throughout much of adulthood. The total amount of sleep obtained by a child decreases very slowly.

Drs. J. Mendels and D. R. Hawkins, at the University of North Carolina, have begun an extensive study of children from 2 to 16 years in which they expect to study five children for each year. They find, in their first recordings, that there is a slow diminution of actual sleep time, proportionately diminishing the time spent in each stage of sleep, but without changing the proportion to the total night of sleep. A very noticeable difference between the sleep of young children and adults is the time spent in a deep stage-4 oblivion.

A child not only obtains more of this slow-wave sleep, but he is much slower to awaken. While the old person will awaken from sleep with alacrity, almost with a nervous promptness, the child tends to be a somnambulist for quite a while, fumbling around sleepily if awakened, and often drifting back to sleep while on his feet or in the lap of a parent. Delta sleep, which occupies much of the first 3 to 4 hours of a 2-year-old's sleep, is the stage from which a child will sleepwalk, and this phenomenon, which is not uncommon among 2- and 3-year-olds, becomes progressively more rare with age—until a new and different kind of somnambulism emerges in senility. The senile person perambulates out of REM sleep: He has no stage-4 sleep.

The youngster between 2 and 10 is particularly hard to awaken early in the night when he is drowned in the depths of delta sleep. His stage 4 sleep differs from that of his parents not only in the subjective experience: The delta waves of a child are of extremely high amplitude. A 5-year-old spends around 2 hours a night in this deepest forgetfulness, whereas the adolescent spends only about 75—80 minutes. The first nightly REM period may not appear for 3 to 4 hours in a 7-year-old, whereas it will arrive within 50—70 minutes after an adult has fallen asleep. The speed with which a person reaches his first REM dream after falling asleep becomes more rapid as he matures. The child begins to show an adult pattern of REM latency around mid-adolescence.

When H. W. Agnew, Jr., and Drs. Wilse B. Webb and R. L. Williams compared 10-year-olds with teenage youths, they found only slight differences in their sleep records. The 10-year-olds slept longer—averaging around 9½ hours. The teenagers slept about 2 hours less. The 10-year-olds showed a higher amplitude activity on their EGG's than the teenagers. If, as some researchers speculate, the power represented by the amplitude of a brain wave is related to the intensity of sleep, then it may be possible to watch the intensity of stage-4 sleep decline steadily over a lifetime.

Young Adults

Sleep has been well documented for the young man between 20 and 28. There are, to be sure, notable differences among individuals, but the general picture of a night's sleep in the twenties is by now familiar. The so-called average person falls asleep, taking about 7—15 minutes. He drifts down through lighter sleep, stages 1, 2, 3, into stage 4. Then he drifts back up toward light sleep and enters a REM dream in 70 minutes from the time he went to sleep. The first REM dream is apt to be short, in the neighborhood of 10 minutes. Once more, the person dives into the depths, rising again so that after about 75 minutes he is ready to dream at greater length. The dive into slow-wave sleep, which happens about five times, goes less deep in the last cycle of night. The four last REM periods of the night run about 20—25 minutes, but the intervals between REM sleeps have diminished.

Delta sleep, and particularly stage 4, provides a visible demarcation between childhood, youth, and that point at which adulthood slips over the edge into old age. Even the young adult receives far less delta sleep than he did before adolescence or during adolescence. His delta sleep, as seen on the EEG, is much lower in amplitude. His complete sleep cycles run between 70 and 90 minutes, yet within the basic pattern lurk many variations.

531

In one preliminary study of good and poor sleepers there appeared to be unmistakable physiological differences between them, differences in body temperature, pulse, vasoconstriction, amount of REM sleep, and the distribution of stage 4, as well as marked personality differences. One young adult in the comparative study of Dr. Feinberg and his associates showed no delta sleep at all, yet seemed normal during his waking hours.

For the most part, however, a number of researchers observe that the EEG amplitude of stage-4 sleep declines with age. Not only is there less stage 4 until it disappears altogether, but it diminishes in what might be called intensity, and which would be defined on the EEG as prolonged trains of high amplitude delta waves. The duration of stage 4 diminishes toward a vanishing point that may occur as early as the late thirties or early forties.

The decline of stage 4 has been observed by Dr. Wilse B. Webb and H. W. Agnew, Jr., at the University of Florida. They have observed that as delta sleep declines, sleep may become less continuous, and its fabric becomes punctured with awakenings. At about age 45 people are likely to awaken three times in a night. People who were allowed to go on sleeping in the morning in the Florida laboratory until they were "slept out" found themselves awakening five and six times toward the end, when their sleep was largely the light stage 2 and REM. The absence of stage-4 sleep in the aged and increased awakenings were also observed at UCLA by Drs. Anthony Kales and Allen Jacobson in their study of elderly people.

As Dr. Feinberg and his associates compared children, young adults, and elderly people, they found that an adult, once beyond adolescence, does not sleep longer at age 20–30 than his counterpart of 70–80. The young adults recorded at St. Elizabeths, who were between 19 and 36, slept about the same amount of time as their counterparts in Bethesda, the aged members of the Fossils Club. However, they took less time falling asleep than either the normal older counterpart or the patient with brain damage. They did not awaken so much at night. The older person obtained an equivalent amount of sleep only by staying in bed a longer time. The person with chronic brain damage, who took a long time falling asleep, did not really obtain as much sleep as his peer in age. The normal older person in this study awakened so often that he spent 17 percent of his time in bed wakeful. The young adult spent his supine hours asleep, but the institutionalized person with symptoms of senility lay awake for a third of his time in bed.

The studies conducted by Dr. Feinberg and his associates enumerated many of the differences between the young and old that make anecdotes in the conversations of large families. For instance, it is common for an older person to rise and go to the bathroom once, or even more often, during the night. Young adults do not, unless they are in exceptional states: for instance, women in late pregnancy find their sleep interrupted and do visit the bathroom. A UCLA study indicates that some enuretic youngsters are never even awakened by their need. On the other hand, some children with enuresis present problems, for even if they awaken with a need, they would rather wet a bed and return to sleep than get up out of bed.

The sleep records obtained from children, young adults, and both the normal and abnormal older people show precisely the expected pattern: Neither the youngsters nor young adults interrupt their sleep to go to the bathroom during the night, but the older persons rose once on the average and the senile patients slightly more often.

Quite apart from rising to visit the toilet during the night, adults do awaken from sleep intermittently. The normal young adult will awaken, albeit briefly, around three times a night. The awakenings may be so brief that he will not remember them. A normal older person will awaken five or more times a night. However, the elderly person with chronic brain syndrome will awaken eight or nine times a night.

Perhaps some of these differences in the number of sleep interruptions stem from the different arousal speeds of the young and old. Youngsters are typically very hard to awaken, especially during the first half of the night when they are so much immersed in intense delta sleep. Older people, by contrast, have less slow-wave sleep, no intense stage 4, and often awaken like a shot. Children are virtually somnambulistic for a long time after awakening, but the oldster is alert at once, his brain having turned off sleep like a faucet.

The insomnia of age is a frequently discussed affliction. Most older people would appear to have no stage-4 sleep and less deep delta sleep. They are more easily awakened than the young. Indeed, they do take longer to fall asleep, awaken more often during the night, and spend considerable time lying in bed sleeplessly. This insomnia has been observed by Dr. Feinberg and his associates, by Dr. Anthony Kales and his associates at UCLA, and by Dr. Wilse B. Webb and his associates at the University of Florida. From childhood on, as the Webb group in Florida has shown, there is a decrease in delta sleep and an increase in awakenings. The proportion of the night spent without sleep increases as a person grows older, but as Dr. Feinberg and his colleagues have shown, the most egregious symptoms of insomnia are found in patients with chronic brain syndrome, far worse than in normal persons of the same advanced age. The children studied by this team were a marked contrast: They fell asleep fast and slept soundly and long. The 5-year-olds averaged about 9½ hours, while the 10-year-olds averaged about 8½ hours. The patients with chronic brain syndrome averaged approximately 5 hours of sleep, while the young adults and normal older people slept around 7 hours a night.

Although a great many older people complain of the insomnia of their waning years, they are not accurate judges of their own sleep. It has become clear in the laboratory, where the EEG record, like the snore of the sleeper, indicates that a person who may think himself awake is not actually awake. Dr. Feinberg has said, "A lot of people who think they're awake are just aware of their mental activity, which to the EEG appears to be sleep. Therefore they think they are awake."

People do not even estimate very accurately the amount of sleep they obtain. Dr. Feinberg asked his elderly volunteers from the Fossils Club how much sleep they usually got at home. "There was zero correlation between what they thought and the amount of sleep they did get. Some of them would just take the time they spent in bed and say that was how much sleep they got. Others would say that they were awake most of the night but that they'd simply lie there. They were both wrong."

In the lifespan picture of sleep, certain invariances are striking. One thing that seemed not to change between ages 5 and 95 was the number of REM periods during a night's sleep. Subjects studied by Dr. Feinberg, et al. consistently showed 4–5 REM periods. The children would sleep between 2 and 3 hours before their first REM period; the young adults took about an average of 70 minutes; the aged people about 58 minutes average; and the chronic brain syndrome patients dropped into REM sleep relatively rapidly—within an average of 46 minutes. The amount of rapid-eye-movement sleep, on the other hand, distributed over the night, showed considerable changes with age.

Similarly there was a pronounced reduction in delta sleep—stages 3 and 4—from childhood to old age. Throughout life, whether the sleeper is child or octogenarian, it appears that most of the delta or slow-wave sleep occurs mainly at the beginning of the night, and there is virtually none during the last period of non-REM sleep. At that time, the intense oblivion seems to have run its course.

When Dr. Wilse B. Webb and H. W. Agnew, Jr., at the University of Florida invited subjects to return to the sleep laboratory for a nap in the morning after a full night's sleep, they found that there was virtually no slow-wave sleep and no stage 4 in the naps of these young adults. REM sleep, on the other hand, occurred more readily in the morning than it did at night. The distribution of stage 4 throughout the night might seem related to some roughly 24-hour rhythm with a peak coming toward the onset of sleep rather than at the end. But, the decrease of stage-4 sleep over a lifetime is striking.

The children and young adults exhibited long stretches of rhythmic delta sleep whereas these slow-wave movements were always interrupted by fast rhythms in the EEGs of the older persons. Dr. Feinberg has suggested that stage 3, which persists in lessened form into old age, may be a less intense form of stage 4. In general, the older people showed a flattened EEG tracing, meaning rhythms of lower amplitude. The stage 3 of the very young, the adult, and the aged remained much the same in quantity although qualitative differences were noted. Even in the senile, stage 3 activity was distributed similarly across the night, as if controlled by some unchanging and inherent periodicity.

Sleep: The Aging Process, Performance, and Pathology

The motivating interest of this work reaches toward the meaning of the changing sleep patterns of age. Data lie like pieces of a jigsaw puzzle, tantalizingly close to revealing some fundamental facts about the development of the mind in youth and the decay of the nervous system in age—and the way this life trend can be read in the EEG patterns of sleep. Although waking EEGs for highly abnormal senile patients often show little deviation from the normal, sleep EEGs display changes so gross they cannot be missed. The senile patient, who seems to represent an extreme of the normal process of aging, shows a sleep pattern that is also an exaggeration of the changes observed in normal elderly people. The investigators began to ask whether certain changes in the sleep record might also correlate with intellectual functioning, memory, and performance on certain tests.

All of the older subjects were given a Wechsler Adult Intelligence Scale, a Wechsler Memory Scale, and another test. How did these test scores correlate with particular changes in the prevailing stages of sleep? Among the senile patients it was possible to see that a person who slept longer, lay awake less than his fellow subjects, but had more REM sleep, also gave a higher showing on the intelligence test. The normal older person, who awakened often from sleep and showed a decline of REM sleep, also did correspondingly less well on the psychometric tests. Since some senile persons did so absurdly on the psychometric tests that it was impossible to rate their performances, an observer was set the task of rating these patients' abilities to carry out the simple chores of life. The more awakenings and less REM sleep they showed, the less intact they seemed during these daily observations. Awakenings and REM sleep appeared to be two indicators that told approximately how much intellectual impairment to expect in an individual. Among patients with chronic brain syndrome, the sleep shows a proportionately greater reduction in REM sleep than in slow-wave sleep.

In earlier work, Dr. Feinberg had noted that lifetime change in the rate of cerebral metabolism was strikingly similar to the lifetime curves for total sleep time, and amount of REM sleep. Not all of the changes in sleep patterns parallel the changing cerebral metabolic rate. However, a decline in cerebral metabolic rate commensurate with the sleep-changes exhibited in senility also spells intellectual impairment. But subtle changes in intellect occur earlier in the normal elderly person. These changes, which cannot be detected by measurement of overall cerebral metabolic rate or in waking EEG, are nevertheless reflected in the EEG of sleep.

One suggestive parallel in the age graph of sleep is that the decline of stage-4 sleep occurs as a person's mental agility also declines and as it becomes difficult for him to learn psychomotor skills. The investigators postulate that in some fashion the intensity of non-REM sleep, particularly as represented by long trains of high-synchronous delta waves, represents the plasticity of the individual's learning capacity. Stage-4 sleep declines as this plasticity also declines in age. The relation between the known sleep stages and an individual's cognitive ability will be the focus of further study.

The relationship between cognitive power and sleep patterns in elderly people may evoke a profoundly different attitude toward some of the deteriorations we now accept as the usual penalties for growing old. As one researcher has conjectured, it may be that the hyperarousability of the aged and their repeated awakenings in sleep cause a reduction in REM sleep and even in stage 4. Loss of cognitive power may in some way be related to an inability to maintain continuous sleep. As other researchers point out, "insomnia," disturbed sleep patterns, and intellectual deterioration are not found in all old people. Perhaps these sleep and mental factors also have a very strong psychological component and relate to the sources of depression in so many old people. Perhaps such deterioration should be considered pathological even in its most usual form, instead of accepted as normal for a given age. During the Elizabethan era, a person had normally lost most of his teeth and might be considered old after age 25. We would hardly accept this as normal today.

A very practical outcome of these studies will be felt in the treatment of the senile. By documenting the changed sleep patterns which occur in old age and chronic brain syndrome, clinicians are acquiring a rational basis for treating the insomnia of the elderly. It is necessary to reverse these age changes in sleep or to alter the sleep schedule so that the effects are minimized. Dramatic vagaries shown by some chronic brain syndrome subjects as they awakened from REM sleep suggest that nocturnal delirium and wandering may result from a confusion of dream and reality in an impaired cerebrum, or perhaps from the lingering of dreams and other REM experiences into the waking state. Drugs that reduce the intensity of REM processes could be valuable in the treating of these symptoms. Since nocturnal disturbances are often the main cause for hospitalization, such treatment might allow elderly people to remain in their homes and communities instead of spending their last days in an institution. As Dr. Feinberg has commented, "The changes in the sleep electroencephalogram which occur in normal old age as well as in chronic brain syndrome, and the correlation of these changes with intellectual function, suggest that the EEG of sleep may provide a far more powerful diagnostic tool for geriatric psychiatry than any which has been hitherto available."

Figure 1.—Total sleep time as a function of age. In this and subsequent figures, the crosses represent data points, the dots represent the best-fitting curve chosen according to standard statistical techniques. The number of subjects contributing to the mean for each data point is as follows: 6 years, 4; 10 years, 4; 21 years, 6; 30 years, 9; 69 years, 7; 84 years, 6. A cubic curve provided the best fit for the changes in total sleep time with age. This measure is high in childhood, declines to a plateau which is maintained during maturity, and then shows a further decline in very old age. The slight dip and subsequent rise shown by the theoretical curve may be artifactual.

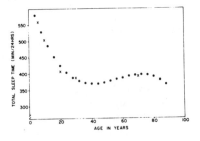

536

Figure 2.—Number of awakenings during sleep as a function of age. Awakening here refers to changes in the EEG and was not necessarily accompanied by gross behavioral arousal. This measure is low in childhood but shows a steady, linear increase with age which is apparent during maturity, where total sleep time is constant.

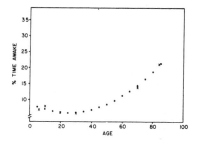

Figure 3.—Percent of time in bed spent awake as a function of age. This measure which is an index of insomnia remains low throughout life and then shows a sharp, positively accelerated increase after age 50 years. The data of Williams et al., on subjects in the sixth decade of life, suggest that the increase starts a few years later than shown by the present parabolic curve.

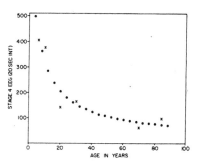

Figure 4.—Stage 4 EEG as a function of age. This measure of the high-voltage, slow-wave EEG of sleep shows a hyperbolic decline with age. However, appreciable change is manifested during maturity, as may be seen by comparing the values at age 20 and age 50 years.

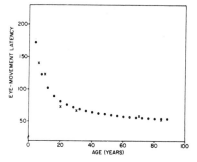

Figure 5.—Stage 1 latency as a function of age. This measure represents the total sleep time recorded prior to the onset of the first period of emergent stage 1 EEG of REM sleep. It shows a hyperbolic decline with age; part of this decline is probably related to the declining need for stage 4 EEG, half of which precedes the first period of emergent stage 1. The curve for the onset of another indicator of REM sleep, the first rapid-eye-movement, is essentially the same as that shown here for emergent stage 1 EEG.

537

Figure 6.–Total time spent nightly in stage 1
EEG (REM sleep) as a function of age.
This measure shows a hyperbolic decline
with little appreciable change during
maturity. The curve for amount of
rapid-eye-movement activity is essentially
the same as that for emergent stage 1
EEG.

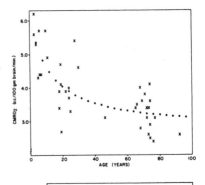

Figure 7.–Cerebral oxygen uptake as a
function of age. These data are taken
from various sources in the literature and
are based on the Kety-Schmidt method
for measuring oxygen uptake ($CMRO^2$).
This variable shows a hyperbolic decline
with age with little change during the
mature years. Since the data did not fall
into well-defined age subgroups, individual values, rather than mean values for
the different ages, are shown here. This
largely accounts for the apparent
increased scatter shown.

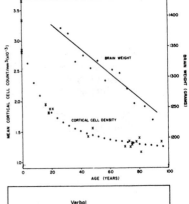

Figure 8.–Cortical cell density and brain
weight as a function of age. The decline
in cell density during maturity is considerable, whereas that for brain weight
is, in percentage terms, less marked.

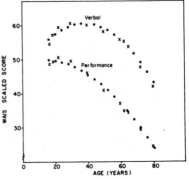

Figure 9.–Wechsler Adult Intelligence Scale
(WAIS) verbal and performance scores as
a function of age. Both measures show a
parabolic decline. However, the verbal
scores show little change during maturity
whereas the performance scores show a
reduction of about 30 percent between
age 20 and age 50 years.

Research Grant: MH 10927
Date of Interview: Apr. 26, 1967

538

The Physiological Imprint of Learning

Investigators:
Mark R. Rosenzweig, Ph.D.*
Edward L. Bennett, Ph.D.
David Krech, Ph.D.
Marian C. Diamond, Ph.D.
University of California
Berkeley, Calif.

Prepared by:
Gay Luce

In the last dozen years a Berkeley team of psychologists, biochemists, and anatomists has demonstrated that learning alters chemical activity and increases cell growth in the cerebral cortex—changes that are correlated with an enhanced problem-solving ability. Thus, experiments with young and with adult animals show that mental activity produces detectable brain growth and that specific kinds of activity may develop particular regions of the brain. Although there may be limits to an animal's responsiveness to its environment, a stimulating environment appears to maximize the rate of learning.

Using rats as experimental subjects, the scientists maximized environmental contrast by segregating littermates into two extreme situations. Some were reared in isolation in small barren cages in a dim, quiet room. Their brothers matured in groups of 10–12 in large complex cages supplied with toys, exercise wheels, and other diversions, as well as daily training on laboratory apparatus. These enriched rats erred less on problem-solving tests, and postmortem analyses showed that their brains differed from the brains of their impoverished siblings. The cerebral cortex had grown larger in relation to the rest of the brain. It contained more glial cells and showed greater activity in a particular biochemical system.

Animals exposed to the differential environments after adulthood exhibited much the same differences in brain growth.

A variety of genetic studies indicated that the proportion of the brain occupied by cerebral cortex and also certain chemical attributes of the brains of enriched rats were characteristic of "bright" strains, while "dull" strains more nearly resembled impoverished animals.

---

*Now at the Department of Psychology, Washington University, St. Louis, Missouri.

The experimenters are now testing for the role of formal training in brain development. Will a rat reared alone in an empty cage show brain growth and an improved problem-solving ability after intensive daily training on an automated teaching apparatus? Can formal training be used to compensate for lack of environmental complexity and stimulation?

The grantees have begun to push this field forward during a time when it was believed impossible to detect physical effects of learning in the brain. Their data may help to explain many baffling statistical observations about human beings, among them the role of environment in intelligence, the accomplishments of people with median childhood IQ, and the curious incidence of eminence among first-born children. The laboratory has seen some evidence that specific kinds of environmental manipulation enhance growth in specific brain areas, suggesting that we may learn to provide rehabilitation training for persons with brain injury or sensory deficiencies—giving exercise to develop brain regions.

Since the brain is measurably modified by use, in a manner that can be correlated with adaptiveness and learning capacity, the laboratory's findings have strong implications for the education of children. However, the extreme impoverishment of the experimental rat should not be translated as if it were synonymous with cultural deprivation. A vacuum of experience is rare among human infants, unless they are deaf-blind. However, there is no escaping the conclusion that we literally modify our brains according to the use we make of them. Through research programs like this one, we may gain the impetus to deliberately improve the education and mental equipment of our young, for there is some potency in the knowledge that we are measurably altering their brains.

Background

Scientists in the past have felt that use of the brain might affect its very size and composition. Charles Darwin, for instance, observed that domestic rabbits had smaller brains than wild rabbits. He surmised that the domestic rabbit had been so confined and protected for many generations that it exercised its intellect and instincts very little. He implied that lack of mental activity and stimulation had caused brain atrophy. In the late 19th century, the autopsy of Laura Bridgman, a deaf-blind mute, showed deficient development in visual, auditory, and speech regions of the brain. Recently, animals reared in darkness have been given careful post mortem examinations. They showed shrinkage in the visual part of the cortex.

The notion that thinking might cause the brain to grow was suggested during the 18th and 19th centuries. A German phrenologist, J. G. Spurzheim, believed that the brain grew by exercise, but he had no means of demonstrating the phenomenon. Even in his day the brain was known to be relatively stable, and there was no equipment for testing subtle changes. Ideally, it was proposed, one should examine the same person after a long period of intense brainwork and after long periods of desuetude; or perhaps compare twins, after keeping one isolated and idle, while the other lived a rich and mentally active life. This experiment was hardly suited for human beings. It had to await the modern animal laboratory, with its refined instruments.

Today, people are aware that the brain is the physical machinery of the mind and that it can be affected by physical means—by drugs, electrical stimulation, etc. The rate of brain activity, memory, and emotions are related to the actions of chemicals in the brain; and when we alter behavior, memory, and emotions by drugs, we thus change many factors in what we consider to be intelligence. In the last century intelligence was presumptively equated with brain size. Many attempts were made to compare the brain size of men with distinguished intellects and with those of inferior intelligence. Gross brain sizes were found to be inconsistent, however, and an idiot can have a larger brain than Einstein. Thus, this unsuccessful approach was abandoned. The notion of anatomical change and actual increase in brain weight as a result of cerebration became so widely debunked that the grantees, themselves, ignored this possibility until they were well along in their research program.

In 1953 they began search for some of the physiochemical correlates of learning, an approach that required considerable courage in the skeptical atmosphere of that time. They had started by observing the behavior of hungry laboratory rats who were placed in a problem-solving test box invented by Dr. Krech. The Krech Hypothesis Apparatus Box is a simple piece of equipment that has been widely used for a number of purposes. This is a long box, divided into four successive chambers. In each chamber the hungry animal chooses between a left and a right alley. He must make four correct choices to reach the food compartment at the end. In each vestibule he may face a darkened alley on one side and a well-lighted alley on the other. Which side has the open door? In one problem the light may be a clue to the correct side. That is, the animal may find he is rewarded when he chooses the lighted alley, whichever side this happens to be. When he almost invariably chooses this avenue and quickly runs to his food reward without digressions, he suddenly finds that light is no longer the rules of the game. He must now learn to choose the dark avenue. At first he has learned a simple discrimination, and then he must learn how to reverse his discrimination. From the animal's point of view it may seem that, as soon as he adopts the profitable habit, the rules are changed. His adaptability—and presumably his survival in the outside world—depend in part upon his ability in this reversal discrimination learning. Thus, in many experiments, reversal discrimination provides a crucial performance test.

In the laboratory's original studies, the hungry rats were bucking an insoluble problem in the Krech apparatus. The choices were prearranged so that there was no correct solution. It was observed, however, that individual rats had interesting choice patterns. They acted as if following some hypothesis about the rules of the game. When, later, the situation was made progressively more solvable—for instance when light became the correct cue 70 percent of the time—an animal might still prefer to go down the left side, much of the time, disregarding the light cue. Some

541

animals acted as if the visual cues of light and dark were irrelevant and would make a spatial choice, running down the right avenue each time. Others seemed to fixate on visual cues, ignoring the possibility that these did not indicate the correct exit. Because the hypothesis box revealed these individual differences in the rats' ability to restrict their attention to the pertinent cues, it seemed to provide an excellent test of problem-solving ability.

When rats were allowed to run through the alley as they wished, no cue being uniformly correct, some animals followed the light and others a spatial pattern. The population seemed to divide into rats with a preference for visual cues and rats with a proclivity for spatial cues. On reversal tests in the alley, the "spatial" rats proved better at adapting to the new rules. Thus, in a sense, they seemed brighter. The experimenters postulated that these rats might have brains that were richer in an important enzyme—related in its quantity to a chemical that helps transmit excitement from one brain cell to the next. At the time it seemed plausible that quick-learning animals might have an abundant supply of this chemical so important in nervous activity. The experimenters expected to find that rat strains which demonstrated superior learning ability would show more of a particular brain enzyme, but the dumber animals actually showed more. In testing more strains of rats, they began to wonder if the neurotransmitter and enzyme were genetically independent, or indeed whether they were seeking the right chemical to correlate with behavior.

Biochemical Indices: The Acetylcholine System

Brain activity is both electrical and chemical. When a person thinks or takes an action, neurons pulse out rhythmic coded messages. Each brain cell influences neighboring cells biochemically. As it fires, it releases a chemical at the infinitesimal gaps or synapses between itself and surrounding cells. This chemical, known as a neurotransmitter, bridges the gap. It can change the excitability of the neighboring cells so that they are readied to fire. The safeguard that prevents cells from continuous excitability and exhaustion is an inactivating chemical. Each time a transmitter is released, it is quickly neutralized by an enzyme.

One of the first neurotransmitters to be studied was acetylcholine. It is released at nerve endings throughout the body, in the regulation of muscular contraction and relaxation, throughout the periphery and in the heart and other organs. Acetylcholine is released at a synapse, then hydrolyzed by the enzymes acetylcholinesterase (AChE) and cholinesterase (ChE)—whereupon the excitability of junction points subsides and they return to their resting state. Acetylcholine and its inactivating enzymes are found throughout the brain.

A high rate of brain activity, as in learning, might require a rapid and constant output of the transmitter and the enzymes that destroy it.

542

In the mid-1950's the grantees began to explore the possibility that bright animals had brains richer in acetylcholine and that an environment enforcing a great deal of learning might change the output of this transmitter in the brain. It was then technically difficult to obtain precise evaluations of acetylcholine in brain tissue, and so they worked by indirection. Presumably the activity of the destroying enzymes was related to acetylcholine concentration.

Because the enzymes AChE and ChE would remain relatively stable in frozen brain tissue, it was possible to measure their speed of activity in a relatively direct way. A sample of homogenized brain tissue was injected into a fluid containing a great deal of acetythiolcholine, which the enzyme breaks down at the same rate as acetylcholine. When light was passed through the fluid, and an indicator was added, its color would change as the enzymes acted, producing a yellow compound; the color change could be measured, and told how fast the enzymes were destroying the transmitter.

Originally, acetylcholinesterase was the better known enzyme. Its activity was first used in an attempt to find a chemical index of brain efficiency. However, as many strains of rat were tested on problem-solving apparatus, the poorest performers often showed the highest AChE activity. Yet some strains, with excellent learning records, showed high ChE activity.

During the late 1950's the experimenters were able to directly evaluate the relation between the transmitter, acetylcholine, and the activity of the enzyme AChE in two rat strains. Although one strain had significantly greater amounts of acetylcholine, the AChE enzyme was not proportionately more active. They found that learning experience or that "brightness" in an animal was indicated in the ratio between ChE and AChE activity in different portions of the brain. AChE activity bore more directly upon the output of the transmitter, and the role of the other less specific enzyme ChE was not clear.

By selective breeding the researchers acquired strains of rats whose brains differed in acetylcholine concentration, or in its enzyme, AChE. On successive tests there has been considerable uncertainty about the relative intelligence of different rat strains and their brain characteristics. Students in the laboratory, and consultants, have begun to amass information about the different rat strains. For example, a strain with high brain acetylcholine would react differently to electric shock than another strain. This fact has some importance to other researchers, especially those who might employ these animals in experiments using shock punishment. The genetic studies have continued to be part of the laboratory program. The team has attempted to control as much as possible for heredity, as it has begun to track the way in which environment might change brain biochemistry.

Experience and Learning Capacity

During the 1950's a number of laboratory experiments suggested that early experience would make an enormous difference in an animal's ability to cope with learning problems. In one laboratory, animals reared in isolation with a minimum of handling turned out to have different adrenal responses and skittery reactions to tests or stresses, in comparison with littermates raised in groups with considerable stimulation. Isolated animals performed poorly in comparison with handled littermates, but were their nervous systems different?

The Enriched and the Impoverished

Over almost a decade the grantees have employed a method that maximized the contrast between their animals, prior to testing and brain assay. Littermates were segregated into extreme environments. In each case rats of a particular age, strain, and sex were used. During subsequent brain assays, the rats were identified only by codes so that the experimenters would not know from which group they came. This procedure, initially used with weanling rats, has since been used with adults and other species.

In general the infant rats were segregated when they were 25 days old. At this point, some pups would land in barren individual cages in a dim, quiet room unable to see or touch other animals, being handled only during biweekly weighing. Their littermates, in groups of 10–12, found themselves surrounded by toys and were handled each day as they were set to play in a square box with wooden barriers or mazes. In many experiments, the rats lived their extraordinarily different lives for 80 days—well into maturity. At this point they were tested and analyzed. In some experiments the environmental exposure lasted only a month or 50 days.

By 1966, the laboratory had amassed data on well over 200 pairs of littermates. The evidence was consistent. Enriched rats were superior to their impoverished brothers on reversal discrimination learning. Along with their greater problem-solving abilities, they had a far different brain. The cerebral cortex, often colloquially termed the thinking brain, had grown larger relative to the rest of the brain, and they showed a different balance in the activities of the enzymes cholinesterase (ChE) and acetylcholinesterase (AChE).

Brain Growth

The research team had already found consistent biochemical changes before they began to look at changes in brain weight. As Dr. Rosenzweig has explained:

Brain anatomy was disregarded since we had inherited from our predecessors the dogma of absolute stability of brain weight. Fortunately we had to record the weights of our brain samples in order to measure chemical activity per unit of tissue weight. After about 2 years of contemplating the chemical effects, it finally dawned on us that the

544

weights of the brain samples were also being altered by the environmental manipulations.

Had the researchers been comparing the weights of whole brains they would have noticed no differences. Indeed, from outside, one might have judged that the impoverished animals showed the advantage. When phrenologists practiced their art of measuring intelligence and personality by comparing proportions of the skull, there had been some expectation that a large skull encompassed a larger brain. The large forehead and cranium which appear to encase a more sizable intelligence turns out to be a poor index of intelligence. The experimenters compared the inner cranial capacity of some of their enriched and impoverished animals and found that the two groups did not differ. By making meticulous rubber casts of the skulls and measuring facial bones, after weighing the brains, they saw that the larger facial bones were those of the impoverished animals and were related to body size rather than to brain development. The impoverished and inactive creatures were both heavier and larger than their littermates.

Comparisons of whole-brain weights would not have defined the anatomical differences between the enriched and impoverished rats. However, in preparing brains for chemical analysis, the experimenters have been dissecting the cerebral cortex into four sections and treating these separately from all the rest of the brain beneath. They had reasoned, plausibly, that the cerebral cortex should be the part of the brain to show the most changes as a result of learning.

Indeed, as they soon saw, the enriched animals had a heavier cortex than did their impoverished brothers. When 141 pairs of littermates of a particular genetic strain were compared, the enriched animal had a cortex that was, on the average, 4 percent heavier than that of his impoverished brother. The impoverished animals showed their growth—a very slight one—in the more primitive subcortex. The delicacy of these procedures is difficult to convey. Altogether, a rat brain is not much larger than a healthy Brazil nut. Still, if the percentage differences do not sound enormous, the brain is generally so stable that these signs of growth, relative to experience, are impressive.

As the experiments were varied, and as the scientists looked closely at the several regions of the cortex, they found that certain portions of the cortex were changing more than others. The occipital region, the visual area located at the back of the brain, showed the most growth. The enriched animal had an occipital cortex that was 6 percent heavier than that of his impoverished littermate. Other regions showed less difference. A number of experiments were conducted in order to see whether specific cortical areas could be caused to grow through the use of specific training and environment.

Animals reared in darkness have been found to show a lack of growth in the visual cortex. When the researchers segregated blinded animals into extreme environments, they found that the complex environment and training of the enriched animals did compensate somewhat for lack of sight. Although the blind animals showed enzymatic differences that distinguished them from the sighted animals, they too responded to impoverishment or stimulating surroundings in very much the same manner. Signs of growth in the visual cortex of enriched blind rats suggested that it must participate in nonvisual functions. Thus, blind animals benefited from the environmental stimulation.

All of the enriched rats have shown a thickening in the gray outer bark of the brain and also in a subcortical region that has been associated with memory functions and refinement of emotion—the hippocampus. Stimulation, enforcing active use of the brain, had caused palpable growth in the cerebral cortex of the enriched animal. Just as specific sensory deprivation such as blindness or deafness would cause a deficiency in the related cortical region, particular experience seemed to produce growth in a relevant cortical area.

Chemical Changes

Originally, the investigators had expected to find that their enriched animals showed increases in the specific activity of the enzyme (AChE), indicating greater concentrations of the neurotransmitter acetylcholine. Indeed, the enriched creatures did have a cortex whose tissue showed more enzyme activity than that of their impoverished brethren. On the other hand, the AChE activity was a smaller percent per unit weight in the cortex of the enriched. The growth of the cortex outdistanced the increase in this particular enzymatic activity. However, it showed a proportional increase in the subcortex. If AChE activity declined in the cortex, it increased in the subcortex.

In order to pinpoint the biochemical change in the cortex, the researchers began looking at the proportions of the specific enzyme AChE to the nonspecific enzyme ChE in the cortex and rest of the brain: in the brains of the enriched animal, there was more cortical ChE relative to AChE. The relative proportions of these two enzymes thus indicated the difference between the enriched and impoverished animals.

When the scientists looked at these enzyme ratios in specific portions of the brain, they found especially striking differences between their enriched and impoverished animals in the visual cortex.

They were more than a little curious to find that the cholinesterase activity was exceeding that of the more specific enzyme in their enriched animals. Cholinesterase is known to be concentrated in the glial—or nonnerve cells—of the brain. As they searched to see precisely what tissue growth accounted for the heavier cortex of the enriched animals, they suspected a proliferation of these important small cells.

A Multiplication of Brain Cells

The experimenters measured the diameter of capillaries in the brains and found them to have grown larger in the enriched animals than in the

546

impoverished animals. But this enlargement in the brain's blood supply network did not explain the amount of cortical growth. They subsequently made a cell count in the cortex—the region that showed most growth in the enriched animal. Frozen tissue, stained and cut paper thin, was made into slides, and sizable photographic enlargements were made of each slide. Now began the count of individual cells.

Two anatomists would make separate counts. A technician using colored pencils would mark the location of each glial and neuronal cell on a sheet of plastic placed on the photographic enlargement of a brain section. The same process would be repeated by a second technician. When the two sheets were superimposed, the discrepancies could be seen and discussed, and finally all the brain cells would be classified and counted.

A comparison was made of the visual cortex of 17 pairs of littermates. The enriched animals had more glial cells than did the impoverished, a higher ratio of glial cells to neurons. Glia are not well understood, but they are believed to nourish the neuron and to modulate the brain activity by altering the excitability of the neurons. Environmental complexity and stimulation had caused a proliferation of these cells, thus perhaps enhancing the efficiency of the neuronal activity.

The proliferation of the glia was confirmed at MIT by Drs. Joseph Altman and Gopal D. Das. Using the same extreme environments, they analyzed their animals' brains by a different method. Each animal was injected with a radioactive substance that is used in formation of new cells. This substance acts as a label. Wherever it was absorbed by a brain cell, there would be slight emissions of nuclear particles which affect a photographic emulsion in the manner that light darkens the silver grains of any ordinary photographic emulsion. When the experiment was concluded and brain sections were dipped in emulsion, photomicrographs showed a significant increase in glial cells in the cortex and neocortex of the enriched animals. The density of these labeled cells—showing up as dark spots on the film—can be measured automatically.

Drs. Altman and Das have shown that in the rat neural cells also multiply after birth. It has long been supposed that an animal possesses its entire lifetime supply of neurons at birth. By injecting a radioactive component of the genetic molecule, DNA, they have observed that the radioactive substance was incorporated in the formation of many new brain cells in adult animals. These cells—so small they are known as microneurons—appear to migrate as they differentiate, moving into new brain areas. It now seems possible that some of these small neural cells have been mistaken for glia. The MIT team has opened a new question in the role of experience in shaping the brain. Will older adults show an increase in these microneurons? Do they multiply in response to the exercise of the brain?

Even if glial cells are the only population to increase in the brain as a result of environmental challenge, they may enhance brain efficiency in a number of ways. Glia are important in the fatty white matter that sheathes nerves. They surround the dendritic tentacles that interconnect each neuron with multitudes of others. Perhaps their multiplication permits the sprouting of new dendrites, new contacts from one neuron to others. Perhaps their proliferation allows greater nourishment of neural cells, or more refined modulation of neuron excitability. All that can be said at present is that environmental manipulation adds to the tissue of the cerebral cortex in part by the multiplication of glia and that animals exhibiting this brain growth excel on problem-solving tests.

How Do the Different Environmental Factors Cause Brain Changes?

Clearly, when an animal's entire environment is manipulated in the laboratory, it is difficult to pinpoint the particular factors responsible for this change. Isolation, for instance, has a potent effect upon man and beast. People who have undergone tests in silent chambers, or in tanks of water at about blood temperature, have noted that the sensory deprivation began to evoke odd psychological experiences. Some people quickly leave such an experiment, while others have suffered little. Some strains of rats, reared in isolation, have become increasingly aggressive and difficult to handle in the laboratory. They suffer enlarged adrenal glands, skin irritations, and other symptoms known as isolation stress. None of the Berkeley animals showed any of these signs. Nonetheless, the team inevitably wanted to ascertain what role isolation contributed to the contrasting brain and behavior effects of the impovereshed and enriched rats.

Social controls.—Some experiments were run with a third group of littermates, reared neither in isolation nor in a complex environment. These rats grew up in the ordinary animal laboratory cages in groups of three. The only sign that the social life was better than isolation was detected in the visual cortex, where growth exceeded that of the impoverished littermates. On other counts, the brains more closely resembled those of the impoverished animals than of the enriched.

Extreme isolation.—In recent studies a condition has been created approaching a sensory vacuum. Some littermates have lived where light is dim and temperature constant. The rat cannot see outside the cage, not even having contact with the experimenter as he changes food and water. The only change is the alternation of light and darkness every 12 hours.

As might have been expected, rats who spent 80 days in this environment proved to be extremely different from their littermates in the enriched condition. The differences in cortical weight and enzyme activity were markedly enhanced. Indeed, these extremely isolated and impoverished animals were different from rats merely raised in the original loneliness of unadorned cages.

Isolated pairs.—Was social isolation, or lack of a stimulating environment, the overriding factor in the lack of brain development in the extreme isolates? Pairs of rats were now placed in the extreme isolation, each one from a different litter. Post mortem analyses of these animals indicated that paired living could not compensate for the rarified surroundings. The cerebral consequences were striking. These pairs did not differ significantly in cortical weight or enzyme activity from those who had lived in a solitary state in these cages, devoid of interest and stimulation.

As they created graded situations, to test for the role of social interaction in learning and brain growth, the researchers saw that the extremely impoverished lone animal was not much worse off than pairs in the same kind of cage. Moreover, triads, raised in barren cages, hardly differed from their isolated littermates, although they did show a ratio of enzyme activity which approached that of the enriched rats. A close comparison of the visual and somesthetic regions of the cortex showed the researchers that the effects of an impoverished environment were somewhat mitigated by placing groups of rats together. Groups of 10–12 rats have been studied after rearing in large cages, devoid of complexity or stimulation. Sheer numbers do not appear to compensate for lack of environmental complexity. These rats fall somewhere between their impoverished and enriched littermates.

The addition of toys, variation, and training appears to add some further element—causing the animal to use his brain more actively—with concomitant biochemical and anatomical changes in the brain.

Formal training.—What is the role of pure learning, of training? In current experiments, the laboratory is rearing animals in isolation in cages devoid of toys or social contact, but for an hour or two each day the animal receives intensive training. Can formal training alone produce cerebral growth commensurate with that observed from life in a rich and varied environment?

Differential Environment: Impact on Adults

Environment during the earliest, most formative years of life appears to leave more of a mark than experience after maturity. Surely this has been a tenet of human clinical psychology. It has been demonstrated in some animal experiments, too.

The Berkeley team demonstrated that adult rats as well as weanlings show cerebral effects of experience. Therefore, the cerebral consequences of environment were not merely effects of normal growth processes accelerated by the impact of environment during infancy.

Between the time of weaning (at about 25 days) and 105 days, a rat's brain grows appreciably. If he is kept in a standard colony cage, there will be a 20-percent increase in cortical weight and a 40-percent increase in the rest of the brain by the time the animal is 105 days old. After that, little growth is observed. In the next 80 days there will be only a 5-percent increment in brain weight. Since brain growth contributes little after 105 days, rats of this age were selected for exposure to impoverished and enriched environments. They had been sexually mature for over a month.

549

Adult rats, left for 80 days in an enriched or impoverished environment, diverge even more than young rats in their ultimate cortical weights. The effects of enriched environment upon adult rats do, however, differ slightly from the effects on young rats. Adults gain more total brain weight than does the immature animal, and they show some weight gain in the subcortical regions.

This difference between young and old is notable in assays of enzyme activity. The older animals show a more pronounced drop in their cortical AChE activity. Nonetheless, the adult rat exhibits an encouraging plasticity, suggesting that the effects of mental activity and a challenging environment can be induced long after maturity. The cerebral growth produced environmentally in this laboratory would not seem to be a result of accelerated maturation, since enriched adult rats, compared with their adult isolates, showed brain growth as did the young.

Nor are these effects of differential environment restricted to rats. Comparable studies with mice have offered very similar results.

Heredity and Environmental Manipulation

Within any family, variations among children vividly display how much an individual's response to his surroundings depends upon his inherited structure. Inbred rats show only slight variation among littermates. However, inbred strains differ exceedingly from each other.

Genetic studies and selective breeding have played an important part in the laboratory's program during the last dozen years. Using performance on certain learning tests as a criterion for brightness or dullness, the laboratory developed two strains: One that was consistently bright, the other consistently dull. In each strain, an impoverished and an enriched littermate will show the behavioral, biochemical, and anatomical impress of environment. However, some rat strains show a greater brain growth and enzymatic change than others when exposed to environmental complexity and training.

When 240 rats—24 from each of 10 different strains—were tested on reversal discrimination, their errors were compared with brain analyses. The individual rats who made the most errors had a smaller cortex relative to the rest of their brains. Their ratio of AChE/ChE activity was also closer to that of the rat from an impoverished cage. Even within any given strain, there was a consistent correlation between an animal's performance and the relative weight of his cortex and his enzyme ratio. The bright animals more nearly resembled animals from an enriched environment.

Both heredity and environment appear to influence an animal's adaptiveness and problem-solving ability through common biochemical and anatomical pathways in the brain. Whether from environmental manipulation or endowment, the good problem solver has a brain with a cortex that is larger in proportion to the rest of his brain and a ratio of enzyme activity that now seems to characterize the efficient learner.

Other experiments have confirmed the correspondence between the laboratory's brain measures and problem-solving capacities.

In 1962 the team left littermates in their extreme environments for only 30 days. Then they regrouped them in colony cages, under the care of an experimenter who had no way of knowing which rats had been enriched and which impoverished. For 10 days they received preparatory training on test apparatus and were acclimated to doing without food so that they could be given a food reward on their performance tests. In order to maintain control for possible weight loss due to food deprivation, a third group of littermates was maintained with food and water always available. These rats received no training or testing and, as it turned out, body weight was not a factor.

The enriched and impoverished animals were then tested in the hypothesis apparatus. On their first trials they appeared similar. But these were easy runs, merely asking that they run down the lighted side at each choice point. When the cues were reversed and the problem became more difficult, the impoverished group performed poorly, the animals many times taking the wrong turn. The enriched group performed significantly better.

Only 30 days of environmental difference had made a pronounced difference. This was especially striking, since the impoverished group had received the benefits of 10 days' pretraining and handling. This short period of relative stimulation probably attenuated the differences between the two groups.

After the discrimination-reversal test had been scored for errors, brain analyses showed that there was a correlation between the number of errors an animal made and the size of his cortex relative to the rest of his brain. Ratios of enzyme activity also distinguished the poor performer from his more efficient littermates. On the brain measures there was no longer any difference between the two groups, indicating that the impoverished group had benefited from their 10 days of pretraining and the 20 days of testing.

Environment and Other Brain Components

In the course of a long and varied research program, these findings have been so consistent as to become predictive. On the basis of problem-solving scores, the experimenters can estimate the activity of the certain enzymes in the animal's brain and the ratio of cortex to the rest of the brain. From these brain indicators, they can estimate how a purebred strain will perform on reversal learning tests. The concentration of acetylcholine and level of activity in its inhibitors has proven to be quite relevant in understanding the impact of environment upon adaptability. This has been borne out in genetic studies and performance studies. Activity in this biochemical system increases in the animal exposed to learning, stimulation, and in whom problem-solving capacity is enhanced.

551

The laboratory has traced other biochemical systems as well. Hexokinase, an enzyme important in cell metabolism, did not seem to be altered by differential experience. Nor did serotonin activity appear to change. In other laboratories, scientists have used differential environments to measure for changes in other brain constituents.

Dr. Edward Geller and a team of scientists at UCLA have found that the transmitter substance, norepinephrine (also known as noradrenalin), exists in greater concentration in the brains of enriched rats. An assay of specific brain regions has revealed, however, that the impoverished animals had about five times as much norepinephrine in a subcortical region sometimes described as the brain's chemical storehouse—the caudate nucleus.

The Berkley team had initially expected to find that protein metabolism increased in the brain as a result of mental activity and thus expected to find higher protein turnover in the brains of enriched rats. Percent protein did not differentiate the enriched from the impoverished groups. Recently, however, Dr. Joseph Altman and his MIT coworkers have found that protein turnover is actually lower in the enriched animals. They injected radioactive leucine into their enriched and impoverished littermates. Leucine is an amino acid used throughout the brain in the construction of protein. Cells that utilized the radioactive leucine created dark spots on a photographic emulsion. On examination, the slides were a surprise, for the brains of the impoverished animals had absorbed the most of the radioactive label and thus indicated a higher rate of protein metabolism. Altman and his coworkers have speculated that this high rate of protein metabolism may be a sign of stress and that the isolated animals may have experienced stress each time they were handled in the laboratory. Perhaps a lower rate of brain metabolism is a sign of greater efficiency.

Memory is, inevitably, a crucial factor in learning, and some experimenters have enhanced retention and speed of learning in animals by chemicals. Under certain conditions oral doses of magnesium pemoline have been reported to cause rats to learn conditioned responses four to five times faster than their untreated controls. Moreover, the treated rats showed no signs of forgetting after 2 weeks. Recently this drug has been tested on senile patients, and preliminary reports suggest that it may improve memory.

Conclusion

From many quarters, diverse scientists of behavior are beginning to illustrate the same proposition. An individual's behavior depends upon the anatomical and chemical attributes of his brain. To a large extent this is dictated by heredity, but many of the brain's characteristics can be altered by experience as well as by drugs.

A rich and complex environment would seem to cause brain growth, in infancy and also in adulthood. Some initial evidence suggests that it is

552

possible to selectively modify the brain by selective environmental demands. Blinded animals, for instance, have shown some development in the visual cortex after an interval in an enriched surrounding. Since adult animals also show brain plasticity, it would seem that people with brain damage might be rehabilitated by special training designed to cause growth in specific portions of the brain. A recent study of elderly patients with aphasia indicates that brain-damaged persons can be reached and possibly rehabilitated by carefully designed training. Aphasics, who are unable to read or understand speech, have been given intensive training in visual discrimination, a fundamental function in reading. Following automated training, they have shown improved performance in discriminating the geometric shapes that make up the English alphabet and have given signs of retention on subsequent followup tests. It appears that programmed training might become an effective tool, helping disabled patients to function once more, perhaps by causing growth in intact portions of the brain. Surely, the Berkeley studies suggest that experience can improve a creature's capacity for learning and adapting, by promoting change in certain anatomical and biochemical pathways of the brain. These appear to be pathways by which cultivation can enlarge the individual's capacities, whatever his hereditary limits initially may seem to be.

These studies have interesting implications for education. Perhaps we can begin to understand factors in the development of the young, which at present yield puzzling statistics. Many studies of birth order and life achievement (for instance) suggest that the first-born child in a family is more likely to be gifted and eminent. Twins, indeed, are found to have lower IQ's than single-born children or pairs of children spaced farther apart. On the other hand, studies conducted in orphanages suggest that institutionally reared babies lag behind their counterparts raised in families. Could these differences reflect the relative enrichment and stimulation the children receive as they are growing? Does the first child in a family receive far more attention and handling on the average than the subsequent children? A scattering of studies suggests that this may be the case. One cannot probe the development of the cortex in human infants; still a difference has been seen in the visual performance of orphan infants who were given visual stimulation and toys in their cribs. Cross-cultural studies have indicated that the early precocity of a very young child in Uganda, for instance, may be related to the constant company and attention of the mother.

A dramatic case in point has been reported recently. Thirty years ago Dr. Harold M. Skeels of NIMH experimented with 13 toddlers who were classed as mentally retarded. They were orphans in an Iowa institution, where the usual procedure was to keep retarded children for a while and then transfer them to a special institution. By chance two youngsters got transferred early. Within a year they were mentally normal. Because they were much younger they attracted a great deal of attention and care from the older inmates, and this apparently accounted for their improved intelligence. Dr. Skeels noted that the orphanage was so efficient that infants received little individual attention. He placed 13 retarded orphans as "houseguests" in a state institution at a very early age. Three of them were categorized as imbeciles. Eleven of the children so profited from the extra play and care that they became "normally" intelligent, were put up for adoption, and later became self-supporting middle-class adults. A control group of the same age had been left in the orphanage. These children had average intelligence. After a number of years both groups were tested. The normal children, within the orphanage, lost IQ points, whereas the supposedly retarded children had gained in IQ. The two groups had, indeed, switched positions, and one child who began with a rating of good average intelligence had become an imbecile by age 19, after a life in the orphanage. The impact of environment on intelligence was heartbreakingly palpable.

In the rearing and education of our young, we can now see that the environment we provide may enhance or retard brain growth—and perhaps intelligence. However, one cannot liken the culturally deprived person to the impoverished laboratory rat. Except for those people who are deaf and blind, or seriously handicapped, a vacuum of experience is rare. Rather, the experience of our young is random. We have done only little to discover how a human education should be programed and placed to maximize the potential of each individual. It is no news to say that the resources of our population could be increased by an education that induced mental growth. Now this same proposition has been put into physiological language. We can deliberately cultivate more effective brains and cause growth in the cerebral cortex.

Research Grants: MH 1292, MH 7903
Dates of Interviews: December 1965, May 1966

References:

Altman, J. Are new neurons formed in the brains of adult mammals? *Science,* 1962, 135, 3509.

Altman. J. Autoradiographic investigation of cell proliferation in the brains of rats and cats. *Anat. Rec.,* 1963, 145, 4.

Altman, J. Differences in the utilization on tritiated leucine by single neurones in normal and exercised rats: on autoradiographic investigation with microdensitometry. *Nature,* 1963, 199, 4895.

Altman, J. The use of fine-resolution autoradiography in neurological and psycho-biological research. In Haley & Snider (Eds.), *Response of the nervous system to ionizing radiation.* Little, Brown, 1964.

Altman, J. Autoradiographic examination of behaviorally induced changes in the protein and nucleic acid metabolism in the brain. In F. A. O. Schmitt (Ed.), *Macromolecules and behavior.*

Altman, J., and Das, G. D. Autoradiographic examination of the effects of enriched environment on the rate of glial multiplication in the adult rat brain. *Nature,* 1964, 204, 4964.

Altman, J., and Das, G. D. Postnatal origin of microneurones in the rat brain. *Nature,* 1965, 207, 5000.

Altman, J., and Das, G. D. Autoradiographic and histological evidence of postnatal hippocampal neurogenesis in rats. *J. Comp. Neurol.,* 1965, 124, 3.

Altman, J., Das., G. D., and Chang, J. Behavioral manipulations and protein metabolism of the brain: effects of visual training on the utilization of Leucine-H^3. *Physiology and Behavior,* 1966, vol. 1, Pergamon Press.

Bennett, E. L., Crossland, J., Krech, D., and Rosenzweig, M. R. Strain differences in acetylcholine concentrations in rat brain. *Nature,* 1960, 187, 787.

Bennett, E. L., Diamond, M. C., Krech, D., and Rosenzweig, M. R. Chemical and anatomical plasticity of brain. *Science,* 1964, 146, 610–619.

Bennett, E. L., Diamond, M. C., Krech, D., and Rosenzweig, M. R. Heredity environment, learning, and the brain. AAAS Symposium, *Behavior, Brain, and Biochemistry.* Berkeley, Calif., Dec. 28, 1965.

Bennett, E. L., Drori, J. B., Krech, D., Rosenzweig, M. R., and Abraham, S. Hexokinase activity in brain. *J. Biol. Chem.,* 1962, 237, 1758–1763.

Bennett, E. L., Drori, J. B., Krech, D., Rosenzweig, M. R., Diamond, M. C., and Abraham, S. Determination of hexokinase activity in brain. *Fed. Proc.,* 1961, 20, 343 (abstract).

Bennett, E. L., Herbert, M., Rosenzweig, M. R., and Krech, D. Genetic selection of rats for cerebral acetylcholine concentration. *Proc. Sixth Int. Congr. Biochem.,* New York, 1964.

Bennett, E. L., Krech, D., and Rosenzweig, M. R. Reliability and regional specificity of cerebral effects of environmental complexity and training. *J. Comp. Physiol. Psychol.,* 1964, 57, 440–441.

Bennett, E. L., Rosenzweig, M. R., Krech, D., Karlsson, H., Dye, N., and Ohlander, A. Individual, strain, and age differences in cholinesterase activity of the rat brain. *J. Neurochem.,* 1958, 3, 144–152.

Das, G. D., and Altman, J. Behavioral manipulations and protein metabolism of the brain: effects of motor exercise on the utilization of Leucine-H³. *Physiology and Behavior,* 1966, vol. 1, Permagon Press.

Das, G. D., and Altman, J. Behavioral manipulations and protein metabolism of the brain: effects of restricted and enriched environments on the utilization of Leucine-H³, *Physiology and Behavior.* 1966, vol. 1, Permagon Press.

Diamond, M. C., Diamond, R. M., Bennett, E. L., Krech, D., and Rosenzweig, M. R. Distribution of acetylcholinesterase in cerebral cortical tissue slices from maze bright and maze dull strains of rats. *Anat. Rec.,* 1961, 139, 221 (abstract).

Diamond, M. C., Rosenzweig, M. R., and Krech, D. Relationships between body weight and skull development in rats raised in enriched and impoverished conditions. *J. Exp. Zool.,* 1965, 160, 29–35.

Krech, D. Heredity, environment, brain and problem solving, *Internatl. Cong. Psych.,* Moscow, August 1966.

Krech, D., Rosenzweig, M. R., Bennett, E. L., and Krueckel, B. Enzyme concentrations in the brain and adjustive behavior patterns. *Science,* 1954, 120, 994–996.

Krech, D., Rosenzweig, M. R., and Bennett, E. L. Dimensions of discrimination and level of cholinesterase activity in the cerebral cortex of the rat. *J. Comp. Physiol. Psychol.,* 1956, 49, 261–268.

Krech, D., Rosenzweig, M. R., and Bennett, E. L. Cholinesterase activity. *Science,* 1958, 128, 1176.

Krech, D., Rosenzweig, M. R., and Bennett, E. L. Correlations between brain cholinesterase and brain weight within two strains of rats. *Amer. J. Physiol.,* 1959, 196, 31–32.

Krech, D., Rosenzweig, M. R., and Bennett, E. L. Effects of environmental complexity and training on brain chemistry. *J. Comp. Physiol. Psychol.,* 1960, 53, 509–519.

Krech, D., Rosenzweig, M. R., and Bennett, E. L. Interhemispheric effects of cortical lesions on brain biochemistry. *Science,* 1960, 132, 352–353.

Krech, D., Rosenzweig, M. R., and Bennett, E. L. Relations between brain chemistry and problem solving, among rats raised in enriched and impoverished environments. *J. Comp. Physiol. Psychol.,* 1962, 55, 801–807.

Krech, D., Rosenzweig, M. R., and Bennett, E. L. Effects of complex environment and blindness on rat brain. *Arch. Neurol.,* 1963, 8, 403–412.

Rosenzweig, M. R. Environmental complexity, cerebral change, and behavior, *APA* Chicago, Sept. 5, 1965.

Rosenzweig, M. R. Evidence for anatomical and chemical changes in the brain during primary learning. *Symposium on Biological Bases of Memory Traces, Internatl. Cong. Psych.,* Moscow, August 1966.

Rosenzweig, M. R., Bennett. E. L., and Krech, D. Cerebral effects of environmental complexity and training among adult rats. *J. Comp. Physiol. Psychol.,* 1964, 57, 438–439.

Rosenzweig, M. R., Krech, D., and Bennett, E. L. Acetylcholine metabolism and behavior of rats. *Science,* 1959, 129, 62–64.

Rosenzweig, M. R., Krech, D., and Bennett, E. L. A search for relations between brain chemistry and behavior. *Psychol. Bull.,* 1960, 57, 476–492.

Rosenzweig, M. R., Krech, D., Bennett, E. L., and Diamond, M. C. Effects of environmental complexity and training on brain chemistry and anatomy: a replication and extension. *J. Comp. Physiol. Psychol.,* 1962, 55, 429–437.

Rosenzweig, M. R., Krech, D., and Bennett, E. L. Effects of environmental complexity and training on brain anatomy and cholinesterase in rat. *Fed. Proc.,* 1962, 21, 358 (abstract).

Rosenzweig, M. R., Krech, D., and Bennett, E. L., Effects of environmental complexity and training on brain chemistry and anatomy among mature rats. *Fed. Proc.,* 1963, 22, 515 (abstract).

Rosenzweig, M. R., Krech, D., and Bennett, E. L. Effects of differential experience on brain. AChE and ChE and brain anatomy in the rat, as a function of strain and age. *Amer. Psychologist,* 1963, 18, 430.

Rosenzweig, M. R., Krech, D., and Bennett, E. L. Strain differences in cerebral responses to environmental complexity and training. *Fed. Proc.,* 1964, 23, 255 (abstract).

Rosenzweig, M. R., Krech, D., and Bennett, E. L. Modifying brain chemistry and anatomy by enrichment or impoverishment of experience. In G. Newton and S. Levine (Eds.), *Readings in early experience,* 1965, in press.

Woolley, D. E., Rosenzweig, M. R., Krech, D., Bennett, E. L., and Timiras, P. S. Strain and sex differences in threshold and pattern of electroshock convulsions in rats. *The Physiologist,* 1960, 3, 182 (abstract).

Woolley, D. E., Timiras, P. S., Rosenzweig, M. R., Krech, D., and Bennett, E. L. Strain and sex differences in electroshock convulsions of the rat. *Nature,* 1961, 190, 515–516.

Woolley, D. E., Timiras, P. S., Rosenzweig, M. R., Krech, D., and Bennett, E. L. Strain differences in seizure responses and brain cholinesterase activity in rats. *Proc. soc. exp. biol. Med.,* 1963, 112, 781–785.

Biological Bases of Memory

Investigator:
James L. McGaugh, Ph. D.
University of California
Irvine, Calif.

Prepared by:
Gay Luce

Introduction

The survival of mankind may now hang upon how well we can educate each coming generation, since the capacity for sophisticated and coopera- tive behavior has become the essential of modern civilization. Ironically, our educational institutions lag behind us. Agriculture and medicine have been transformed by modern scientific research while the schools remain virtually untouched by the 20th century. One aspect of the scientific harvest that might indeed influence the training of the young is the exploration of biological bases for learning and memory. We can no longer afford the luxury of ignoring important problems of memory and their implications for the manner in which we teach.

The social implications of some researches in this area are just beginning to be known. Experiments with rats have divulged a genetic base for learning. As University of California Professors Krech and Rosenzweig and their associates have demonstrated, it is possible to influence the learning ability of rodents by enriching or impoverishing the environment, thereby also altering brain biochemistry. Without stimulation, there can be little learning. Without memory, there can be no learning. There appear to be many processes in memory, some related to short-term memory, some related to long-term storage, and others related to retrieval. There are some patients with brain damage, for example, who appear to be normal, with unaffected IQ's, yet they cannot learn anything new, not even a new home address. Dr. McGaugh and his associates have used electroconvulsive shock to produce a similar amnesia for new experience in animals. By this device he has seen evidence that there may be two separate stages in the implantation of any memory.

The potentiality for improving education by using such research has been demonstrated by Prof. Millard Madsen of UCLA. He has shown how knowledgeable timing of information will permit children with low IQ scores to learn quite as well and almost as fast as children with high IQ's.

In studying biochemical influences upon memory, Doctor McGaugh has recently found that biological time of day may also influence learning behavior.

History

In 1917, the psychologist William Lashley observed that rats would learn to run a maze with more celerity than usual if they were first given low doses of strychnine sulfate. The implication that drugs might influence learning or be useful in exploring memory processes was ignored for several decades. Then, stimulant drugs, known as analeptics, were again observed to facilitate learning.

In recent experiments strychnine, picrotoxin, pentylenetetrazole, and diazadamantanol have been used on animals performing prescribed and measurable tasks. Some have been discrimination problems, in which the animals learned to choose among alternative paths in a maze in order to reach a goal and to discriminate between black and white gates, while in others they had to escape from a situation in which they would be punished or learn restraint in order to avoid electric shock. The situations, while limited, were precisely controlled and therefore quantifiable. In most of the early studies, animals were first given stimulants a few minutes before their first encounter with the training, and were trained under drug influence. Did the drug influence the process we call memory? Perhaps not. Perhaps it improved performance by making the animal more attentive, by sharpening his perceptions, by enhancing his motivation, or by improving muscular coordination. Research on learning resembles the divergent reports from six blind men describing an elephant, each touching a different part of the beast. The impact of a drug upon "learning" is partly dependent upon the measure of learning. One easily quantified part of performance is the response latency—how long it takes the animal to get around to making a response. When this measure is the criterion of learning, a drug that increases response speed or alertness will also seem to improve learning. Since no experimenter can afford to use many criteria of performance, studies of learning and memory typically contain some knotty problems of method and measurement. Doctor McGaugh and his associates began to train undrugged animals, but gave them "memory" tests while they were drugged. Perhaps drugs altered dimensions of performance, although they did not act upon memory processes during learning. It soon appeared that the memory process, itself, was exceedingly subtle.

Retrograde Amnesia

One means of exploring memory is by training a creature on a narrowly prescribed performance and administering drugs or convulsive shock at intervals directly after the training. Will they interfere with the consolidation of memory? Does it matter how soon after training the shock or drug is given? In the course of many such experiments, the grantee and his associates found that animals shocked immediately, or at short intervals after training, seemed later not to recall. By strategically varying their treatment of the animals, they saw that training or experience seemed to initiate a kind of potential residue for memory. Yet this potentially permanent memory would remain labile for long periods, perhaps hours, before being permanently etched into the neural code of memory. These studies in which memory was impaired by drug or shock interference led Dr. McGaugh to wonder about enhancing memory in a similar manner. If there is a long period after training in which memory processes are active, a memory-enhancing drug could be given in this interval after training and should improve performance or make the animal resistant to calculated amnesia-electroshock.

Drugs After Training

The training procedures were straightforward. Animals were conditioned to push a lever or avoid a grid, etc. Then, after training, they were injected with drugs. After a suitable interval allowing the drugs to be metabolized, the animals were tested on the original procedure. A number of drugs appeared to enhance performance when injected after training—and by implication seemed to be acting upon the mysterious processes of memory. Strychnine, picrotoxin (at low doses), and amphetamine all seemed to enhance the learning of animals who received doses directly after training: on tests they outperformed the animals who had received only a placebo.

During the last few years, several drugs have been given to animals on a wide range of learning tasks, measured by various criteria. Clearly, the outcome is some blend of the kind of learning (it is vastly different to learn to discriminate between two colors than to learn to avoid a shock at the toll of a bell), the experimental conditions, the drug, and the amount of the drug used. Results from laboratories around the country are not all in accordance, but most of the evidence suggests that certain drugs enhance learning. If so, presumably, they are acting upon memory storage in its labile period. Presumably, these same drugs would do nothing for memory if they were injected at some maximum time after training. By carefully graded experiments, therefore, one might expect to delineate how long the labile period of memory lasts.

The procedure in this laboratory was straightforward. One group of animals would be injected with a drug 5 seconds after they responded to a learning procedure. Another group would be injected after 1 minute, still another after 5 minutes, and so on. During 1962, Doctor McGaugh was injecting strychnine at various intervals after training: he found that one strain of mice "learned" better if injected immediately after training, yet injections given a half hour after training were ineffective. On a discrimination task, one group of mice showed the greatest facilitation—by comparison with undrugged controls—if they were injected between 5 and 15 minutes *before* training.

The results of these studies of effects of time of administration of drugs indicate that the effects are time-dependent. The magnitude of the facilitating effect decreases with the interval between training and drug administration. These findings are consistent with the studies of experimentally induced retrograde amnesia. Together, these two lines of evidence provide very strong support for the view that memory storage processes are susceptible to both facilitating and impairing influences for a relatively long period of time following training.

Environment

The elusiveness and delicacy of the process of memory—and the sensitivity of rodents—has forced the investigators to take all kinds of precautions against slamming doors and disturbance in the laboratory. The need for constant temperature, quiet, etc., was underscored by an experiment in which mice, given strychnine, were given a discrimination problem and were disrupted by environmental stimulation. Like students trying to memorize a lesson in an "acid-rock" discotheque under strobe lights, half these mice were rocked back and forth in their cage, exposed to flashing lights and bursts of sound for 20 minutes. On tests, it was the other half of the animals—who remained in dark quiet cages—who showed enhanced learning from strychnine while the stimulated animals did worse than controls. It was an encouragement for control in the learning laboratory and perhaps also a hint for humans.

Drug Attenuation of Retrograde Amnesia

Inevitably, the investigator wondered whether strychnine and other drugs enhanced learning by accelerating the rate at which memory traces were consolidated into permanent memory. If so, the drugs should prevent or attenuate the kind of retrograde amnesia that is caused by convulsive shock. Animals were given saline solution or strychnine just before or just after training: then, within a few minutes each animal was shocked. A day later each mouse was tested on the training task. The drug-injected animals did a little better on tests than did the controls who received only saline solution. It appeared that drugs attenuated the amnesia, but the reason was not clear.

Recently, the experimenters have used a different kind of task, one on which a single exposure is sufficient for a test of learning. It is known as a "one trial inhibitory test."

Each mouse is placed on a small cantilevered platform on the outside wall of a box. There is an entry hole leading to the dark interior. The mouse is a nocturnal animal. In his search for comfort and security he will soon step inside the hole. Most mice hesitate for no more than 10 seconds. Their predicament resembles that of a human being, stuck in the dead of night on a small porch without rails, hundreds of feet above ground on a skyscraper, with an open window leading to a well-lit room. What person would not try to enter that room?

The mouse, seeking the comfort and security of a dark box, would step in the hole and immediately get a shock on the foot. Twenty-four hours later he would be placed on the platform again. Would he remember that the hole leads to a "forbidden" place? Would he restrain his natural urge for security? The length of time that he would hesitate on the platform before attempting to enter the box would represent a degree of learning. This time, resisting temptation, as it were, was measured as the criterion of learning.

Each mouse was placed on the platform, received a footshock when it transgressed the boundary and then received electroconvulsive shock. For some, the shock came within 18 seconds; for some, it came after 18 seconds; and other animals received it an hour or 3 hours later. Some of these mice were on saline solution, whereas half the mice received strychnine either 10 minutes before or a minute after the platform training.

Twenty-four hours later, each mouse was put to the test, placed on the platform, and clocked. The amount of time an animal stayed on the platform without moving through the hole was directly proportional to the amount of time he had been allowed between his first experience and electroconvulsive shock. The animals given shock 3 hours after training showed to amnesia at all. Control animals given shock 18 seconds or a minute after their training experience seemed to have forgotten that entry was forbidden. Those pretested with strychnine were not rendered so completely amnesic by shock at the same short intervals. Oddly enough, some memory also persisted in the animals who had injections of strychnine *after the electroshock.*

If strychnine affects learning by acclerating consolidation processes, these injections should have no effect. However, as can be seen, retention of these animals was superior to that of controls.

Why should strychnine counteract the amnesia effects when injected *after* electroshock?

In the next series of experiments, strychnine was administered at varying intervals after the electroshock. Evidently the critical interval was the timing of the shock. Strychnine did not improve the retention of an animal given shock 8 seconds after training; yet if shock was delayed a minute or 3 hours, strychnine made a difference. In subsequent experiments, it became evident that the timing of the strychnine was also pertinent. The longer the interval between the drug and the shock, the less effect the drug had in improving memory. If injected 9 hours after shock, it was totally ineffective. Further studies showed the same effects with other stimulants such as picrotoxin.

It appeared that these drugs did not act—as previously believed—by accelerating memory consolidation. Otherwise, why should they cancel the amnesic effects of electroshock?

Doctor McGaugh and his associates conjectured that there might be two distinct phases in memory consolidation. Perhaps the first step is a formation of a pattern in the brain which is then used to "empattern" storage material in the permanent "files" of the mind. Electroshock might prevent

561

the first step if given instantly, within 8 seconds of an experience, perhaps eradicating that initial pattern. However, if that first pattern were permitted time to form—taking more than 8 seconds—then shock blocks the second stage of permanent storage. This means that if one were to wait a sufficiently long time after a training trial, the first phase of memory would be impervious to erasure by shock. What shock does, at longer intervals, is to obliterate the second stage—and it was the second stage that was influenced by drugs.

Drugs might affect learning in many ways, and as we come to understand them it may be possible to evolve chemotherapies for defective memory, such as those of the elderly or the retarded child, or disorders like those of brain-damaged patients. In recent years many experimenters have postulated that the synthesis of nucleic acids must be involved in memory. Antibiotics can inhibit the synthesis of RNA, yet injections do not impair learning in animals. Puromysin inhibits protein synthesis, and when injected into the brain of a goldfish has produced effects resembling those of electroshock. Some researchers have postulated that memory depends upon changing levels of neurotransmitters such as acetylcholine. Using chemicals that effectually raise the levels of acetylcholine in the brain, one laboratory found that there were extraordinary effects upon memory—an injection might eradicate memory of a task learned 11 days earlier but enhance a performance learned 30 days before. Clearly, memory processes are time-dependent, and changes occur in some mysterious but presumably regular order.

A new dimension has been added to the study of time-and-memory by the finding that biological time of day influences memory.

Daily Rhythms of Memory

In recent studies with Dr. Gwen Stephens, the grantee has found that mice retain inhibitory training best if trained at night, when they are at the peak of their body temperature and motor activity for the 24 hours. Indeed, just as training seems more vividly impressed at this time, the obliterating effects of shock are also more pronounced when they follow 3 minutes after training at this peak time.

Mice were placed on the platform, and within 10 seconds most of them would set foot through the hole into the box, only to be shocked. Now, if replaced on the platform within 5 seconds, some seemed not to remember and would step again into the forbidden place. However, if they were given their second experience on the platform after a delay, they would hover there for a long time before venturing in. A day later they would again hover, resisting the urge to enter the dark and comfortable hole. The criterion for remembering was set at 30 seconds—for if the animal hovered that long without entering he clearly recalled the shock. If he restrained himself for less than 30 seconds, there was some loss in the strength of his memory. The gradient between 30 seconds and zero seconds was taken to

562

measure the loss of memory, since animals placed on the platform the first time would often hesitate for a few seconds before exploring.

A recent series of experiments was run in several ways. Some animals never received more than one experience on the platform. Others were placed there several times in succession. Groups of animals destined for the same schedule of treatment were trained and tested at trough and crest of the 24-hour temperature-activity rhythm.

Ironically, much of the study of memory and the impact of drugs has been conducted with rodents. They are nocturnal animals, whose peak activity occurs in darkness. Yet these animals are treated in most laboratories as if they were diurnal. Usually they are tested at times when they would normally be resting and sleeping.

The influence of experimental order within a training and treatment session was noticed in 60 mice who were put on the platform, given shock, and later tested. It seemed to matter whether the mice had been in the early part, the middle, or the late portion of an experiment, since the training and treatment of 60 animals stretched out across 2 or 3 hours. Were the animals responding to noise in the laboratory, to lighting, to the experimenters?

Under the suggestion that time of day might matter, experimental data for one study were submitted to a double analysis. The usual analysis scored groups of animals for their retention, grouping them according to the elapsed time between training and shock. Those animals shocked within 5 seconds of training showed almost no retention; those shocked after 15 seconds or many minutes later showed signs of memory in proportion to the interval between training and shock. However, the neat correlation between retention and elapsed time before shock was thrown into complication, if the data were grouped differently. If averages were taken by cage of four animals in the order trained—regardless of the interval between training and shock—the retest scores show a striking fluctuation. No longer is there a clean straight line, suggesting the direct correlation between elapsed time before shock and retention. Instead, it would seem that physiologic status of the individual animal at the time of training and treatment is a big factor in the retention of the animal—regardless of the length of time between training and shock.

The experimenters discovered, for instance, that the animals trained in the first 20 minutes of a 2-hour experiment were very different from those trained in the last third of the experiment. They showed no correlation between retention and the interval between training and shock. Yet those animals processed later did show a correlation. Was this due to the experimenters, to noise in the laboratory, to time of day?

In these "time of day" experiments, the animals have been housed in quiet cages, protected from disturbance, and maintained at a constant temperature on a rigid lighting schedule. The mice live in darkness from 4 p.m. to 4 a.m. and in light between 4 a.m. and 4 p.m. This entrains the animals' temperature rhythm so that at the 1 p.m. experimental hour they are at trough values; at the 9 p.m. session they are at crest.

Time of Day and Amnesia

Recently, an experimental population of 72 mice was divided into six groups. Half were processed at 1 p.m., the middle of the animals' rest period; the other half were processed at 9 p.m. at about the peak of activity. In each time period, for each of three conditions there was a control group of animals who received only a sham electroshock, while the others were put into convulsion. Each animal went through three trials on the platform, one group receiving shock at 3 minutes and another an hour after the training. The amnesia following shock was most pronounced in the animals treated at 9 p.m. This surprised the experimenters who commented:

> "This could mean either that memory consolidation varies inversely with metabolic activities or susceptibility to electroconvulsive shock varies directly with metabolic activity. Whatever the basis, such variations must be considered in experimental investigations of memory storage processes."

The greatest response to shock occurred at the time when the animal's temperature reached its daily peak, at a time when there would be a high concentration of adrenal steroids in the blood. A correspondence between biological time of day and the strength of conditoned fear and also extinction has been observed by Dr. Charles Stroebel of the Institute of Living in Hartford. He postulated that certain emotional conditioning might show a time-lock—linking strength of memory and the biological time of day at which the conditioning took place.

In a series of experiments conducted in Doctor McGaugh's laboratory, it was found that animals treated by day differed from the animals treated at night. Indeed, animals who were put into shock right after multiple experiences on the platform were unusually resistant to the amnesic effects of shock if they had been trained between 9 and 11 o'clock in the evening—their period of high temperature and peak activity. This suggested again that retention of avoidance reactions must be strongly influenced by physiological cycles.

An animal's temperature curve over 24 hours is not a sine wave. Temperatures were obtained from 72 animals on a schedule of 12 hours of light and 12 hours of darkness. These animals were protected from disturbance and maintained on a steady, even room temperature. In the course of 3 days, it was clear that the rectal temperature would show a 2° to 3° change each 24 hours. The peak would occur around 9 p.m., and the nadir at about 1 p.m. These were now the hours selected for experimental trials.

In repeated trials on the platform, with shock or sham shock delivered at varying intervals, it was possible to examine the animals' rates of learning. How quickly did they learn and how resistant were they to forgetting that they must hover on that platform and not enter the forbidden hole? In several replications of the experiment at different hours of day and night, the animals' rates of learning and persistence of memory were scored. Both seemed to fluctuate, rising and falling rhythmically around

564

the clock. It suggested that the animals were fluctuating in some basic level of arousal.

Clearly, retrograde amnesia did not simply depend upon the time allowed between the acquisition of some new learning and an electroconvulsive shock. Indeed, it depended upon the phase of the animal's temperature rhythms and other factors. The most sizable fluctuation seemed to correspond with the daily rise and fall in adrenal steroids and temperature. Almost every system in the body is known to show a roughly 24-hour fluctuation in function.

Recently, the investigators have been shifting the lighting schedule 3 hours in order to see how animals learn and remember during periods of biological transition. If the lighting is shifted by 3 hours, there are some days in which the animals are readjusting to the new day-night cycle, and they no longer show their former crest of activity and temperature. Now, when the experiments are run at 1 p.m. and 9 p.m., the memory gradients are no longer the same. Perhaps the disruption of sleep schedules, as this experiment suggests, also disrupts some memory functions.

Implications

All of these facets in the exploration of the biology of memory are bound to have their impact upon education. Clearly, the more we understand about a student and his properties as a learner, the more effectively he can be taught. Unfortunately, today's classrooms are not run according to knowledge about the nature of memory and learning. Educators generally assume that such information is irrelevant despite the fact that memory is one of the most important aspects of a child's learning. One of the few contributions accepted by educators from psychology has been the IQ test. This is not used as it should be, for diagnostic purposes. This test attempts to say something about the child as a learner and to predict something about the child's capacity to learn. But the current use of IQ tests reminds one of a physician who examines his patient and says. "You have a very bad liver and you are likely to die an early death. Very interesting, you have 3 days to live."

In a very crude sense, the IQ test appears to measure some adaptability that is biologically based. Many deficiencies as well as talents are biologically based. Some are metabolic, like phenylketonuria, which can be counteracted by a diet starting at birth. If it is not corrected, the defect leads to mental retardation. Biological variations of normal intelligence and learning are not presently analyzed and used for the purposes of education. Where there is strong evidence that family resemblances and intelligence have a genetic basis, general notions of intelligence are useless. There are diverse reasons why a person may be a good or a poor learner. For example, a child's learning efficiency depends on many different processes. He might be a poor learner because he has a deficiency in several systems of storage and retrieval. He might have no short-term memory or he may not be able to retrieve information. Some people have good immediate memory but have lost the ability to memorize; that is, to learn any new material and store it for any length of time.

Dr. Brenda Milner of the Montreal Neurological Institute has studied memory in patients with brain damage in both temporal lobes. Often these people seem to be quite normal and their IQ scores are unaffected. Some of them have completely lost the ability to acquire and retain new information. For instance, one man had suffered brain damage 10 years ago. While in many respects he seems normal, his family moved and he never was able to learn the address of his new house. He does the same jigsaw puzzles day after day without ever showing any effect from practice. He reads the same magazine over and over again, but doesn't find the contents familiar. This type of amnesia has proved to be very helpful in understanding various aspects of memory. Some of the problems of school children may stem from kinds of memory-retrieval defects that normal school techniques never overcome.

As Dr. Millard Madsen of UCLA has shown, high IQ and low IQ children can be induced to learn at about the same rate under the appropriate conditions. Under the usual schoolroom conditions, the children with high IQ's seem to learn much faster. However, if the low IQ children are permitted a longer interval between the introduction of new information, they learn at about the same rate as the high IQ children. Thus, rearranging the school environment to meet the individual's needs can eliminate the differences predicted by IQ scores. The role of our present diagnostic tests, such as the IQ test, should allow us to find out what information-storing process is deficient and how to compensate for it.

The day of the memory pill is not quite here, but it is coming soon. In the future it may be just as common to give Johnny his pill when he leaves the house as it is to remind him to brush his teeth and to put on his glasses.

The relation between long-term memory and the intervals between training, the influence of shock, of drugs, may indeed revolutionize the intellectual capacity of humankind. We may also learn how biological rhythms enhance or detract from learning and may schedule learning for the optimum time of day. We may learn how to encounteract memory deficiencies with drugs—thus opening the doors for almost half of mankind more fully to realize their potential. Children may receive a more compact and rich education when we begin to respond to the way they learn. For the elderly, too, the advent of memory drugs may prolong the philosophical years of intellectual activity now curtailed by poor memory.

Research Grant: MH 12526
Date of Interview: September 1968

Hormones in the
Development of Behavior

Investigator:
Seymour Levine, Ph. D.
Stanford University Medical School
Stanford, Calif.

Prepared by:
Gay Luce

How Experience Shapes the Infant

A dominant child-rearing philosophy—often accredited to Freud—warns that trauma and distress in infancy and childhood may be the source of neurosis and adult instability. As Americans have become more affluent, increasing numbers of financially secure and devoted parents have absorbed the popular distillations of child-rearing theories, and have been striving to protect their offspring from some of the nastier realities and contretemps that they themselves encountered in early life. A variety of protections have been built into the environment of the middle-class child. The amount of stimulation in infancy has been reduced by bottles and pacifiers. In extreme designs for infant care with minimal handling there are thermostatically controlled glass cribs with cloth rollers that obviate even the necessity of changing diapers.

What are the consequences of increasingly automated infant care followed by a highly protected childhood? There is no way of telling from case histories in retrospect. Instability and neurosis do not appear to have decreased notably. Some observers have cited the Korean war as evidence that Americans were growing soft, for jarring and exaggerated analyses of American soldiers had implied that they capitulated to the enemy under only moderate stress. Some reporters thought these POW's had been rendered unduly vulnerable to stress by comfortable and protected backgrounds. For a time, the middle-class home was blamed for defections and surrenders in Korea although they were not statistically different from defections and surrenders in other wars and among other groups—but this attempt to understand and explain behavior was not enlightening, for in retrospect there could be no measure of the precise child-rearing tactics that affected the POW's and might have been relevant to their behavior in war. It was an object lesson in the difficulty of determining cause and effect, and might have thrown into question the case study basis for prevailing theories of rearing the young.

Until the last decade there was remarkably little scientific study of the developmental process. There was a small literature containing a few controlled studies of human infants, observations by ethologists, and a few neurophysiological studies. But extensive developmental research had to await an instrumentation that was not yet developed, and also a change of attitudes. A good many explorations could not be conducted upon human infants; the physiological effects of infant experience had to be learned in laboratory experiments on animals. Initially, these studies of infant experience made the presumption that the most important, most scarring effects might be blamed on trauma—which was roughly assumed to be equivalent to any intense and unpleasant experience. Scientists searched for the effects of trauma.

Many early attempts to find the effects of trauma in infancy were often conducted with mice or rats, but the methodology left the question of effects unanswered. During the 1950's Dr. Levine and his various colleagues began to compare groups of infant animals: one group would be subjected to handling, shock, and other treatments while the control group was strictly exempt from all treatment and handling. Comparisons of these groups clearly suggested that even a seemingly mild experience would leave perceptible traces in the animal's behavior and physiology.

In some studies the infant mice or rats were shaken in bottles, shocked, or vibrated in their cages. The investigators expected their tests to show that these manhandled infants were neurotic and emotional while the controls behaved properly and matured faster. The effect seemed to occur in reverse. Rats handled in infancy might be placed in a large open container as adults and would show little timidity. They would rummage about—while the controls cowered in corners. It seemed, indeed, that the handled animal was less emotional.

One measure of distress and emotionality in rodents has been the open field test. When taken from a cage and placed in a larger barren container, the emotional and distressed rat will tend to crouch and cower in one spot rather than wander around. He will also defecate and urinate a great deal. The calmer animal will eliminate much less and will explore his new setting. Involuntary elimination under fear and stress has provided a good many battle jokes, for it has been a relatively common experience among fighting men. It is one of the responses of the sympathetic nervous system when activated by the neurochemical network that functions during stress. The indices of nervous elimination and activity in open field tests have been useful measures of behavioral-physiological differences among rodents.

Another criterion used to judge a rat's adaptive behavior is avoidance conditioning, a procedure in which the animal must press a bar or perform some action in order to escape being shocked. A traumatized animal might be expected to learn avoidance very slowly. With this expectation, an early experiment divided the infant rats into three groups. One group was shocked, one group was put through all the motions preparatory to shock but not the shock itself, and the third group was left to rest quietly in isolated cages—never handled at all. The shock was evidently painful

568

enough that the infant rats squeaked and tried to escape, and the experimenters expected that these creatures might later show signs of trauma. When they became mature they were placed in an avoidance cage. The previously shocked animals learned to avoid shock most rapidly, with the other handled animals performing nearly as well. However, when the totally untreated animals were put to the test they did not react normally at all. Instead of running and jumping when shocked they would tend to freeze and defecate. Their lack of infantile experience had apparently left them incapable of confronting a new situation, and they were so flustered that they showed what might be called, in human terms, the signs of a paralyzing fear.

Infant experience, even if quite noxious, seemed to gear the animal to meet new situations and stress in adulthood, enhancing his capacity to survive in a changing environment. As subsequent experiments indicated, lack of infant experience was indeed a severe handicap in the survival behavior of the rat. Even when quite thirsty the unhandled rats would drink little in a new situation. When shocked they became so flustered they drank less and less. Here again, the rats had been divided into three groups. All were deprived of water for nearly a day. Then they were given water and the amount they drank was measured. The untreated rats drank least.

Later, when the thirsty rats were shocked before receiving water, all of the groups drank less, but as this procedure continued the untreated group drank least of all. Throughout the study this naive group persisted in drinking very little, whereas the shocked and handled groups apparently got used to the situation and began drinking more. The creature with an infancy empty of varying experience appeared so overcome when confronted with stress that it would not even drink when very thirsty.

Further experiments began to suggest that the inexperienced animal might react poorly to an aversive test, but if it were merely novel, the animals would perform more adequately as they grew accustomed to it. They simply took much longer to adjust than did the handled creatures.

A deeper exploration of the animals's reaction to shock indicated that the handled animals would learn avoidance faster at low levels of shock. Although these creatures were supposed to be less emotional, they gave signs of being *more* responsive than the untreated creatures to acute shock. Infantile stimulation did not merely make an animal less emotional: apparently it enabled him to make discriminations about relevant attributes of the environment and adjust his responses accordingly.

By what physiological process was this experience altering the emotional reactivity and learning ability to the animals? The effects of infantile stimulation were explored by Dr. Levine and others in a multitude of experiments. They soon found themselves examining the endocrine system which suffuses the animal with emergency chemicals during stress. One measure of stress in an animal is the level of certain adrenal steroids in the blood.

When crisis occurs and an animal is threatened, the central nervous system transmits the alarm to two important and interconnected glandular systems. Messages from the brain will set into action the pituitary, an inconspicuous egg-shaped gland which in man resides just above the nasal passages, at the base of the brain. The pituitary controls quite a few specialized sex hormones, exerts influence upon the thyroid gland, controls growth hormones. On occasions of stress it releases ACTH, adrenocorticotropic hormone, which mobilizes the adrenal glands far distant. The adrenals, two small yellowish capsules above the kidneys, respond to ACTH by releasing several hormones into the system. One of these is the familiar stimulant adrenalin, whose action increases the available blood sugar. When a stress outpouring continues for some time, the adrenal glands will enlarge. Thus a good deal can be learned about an animal's intensity of stress reaction by measuring adrenal steroids in the blood or by weighing the adrenal glands themselves, and analyzing their content. These measures indeed may be used to predict how an animal will behave, although not invariably, for many genetic factors must be taken into account.

As Dr. Levine and his associates probed the consequences of infant handling, they found that a detectable and sometimes exceedingly large physiological change occurs and persists into adulthood. In recent studies they have been examining the differences between handled and untreated rats after shock—now by a combination of behavioral and physical tests.

Manipulated infant rats and untouched controls were subjected to shock: during the first 15 minutes after shock it was clear that the handled animals produced more adrenal steroids. At first it looked as if handling had made the animal overreactive, but in fact it simply caused him to respond fast. When shocked, he would summon his adrenal forces rapidly, receiving a rich suffusion of emergency steroids for the period of stress, but the steroid level would subside quickly back to normal. The unhandled rats, by contrast, were reacting slowly to stress. They continued pouring emergency fuel into their systems long after the crisis had passed. They might be like the person who awakens slowly to disaster and remains perturbed and anxious long after it has passed. They are not geared to act promptly but endure a prolonged aftermath of stress physiology which might indeed incur damages, perhaps causing ulcers or susceptibility to infection.

Handling in infancy, as a long program of studies began to show, improved the stress physiology in the maturing animal and adult. The investigators began to find that the handled animals matured far more rapidly than the unhandled controls. There were many indices for the maturation rate. Ordinarily the pituitary gland of the laboratory rat does not release ACTH until the animal is about 16 days old. Handled rats, however, were producing and releasing ACTH by about 12 days.

The brains differed. As the infant brain matures, all the nerve fibers in the brain and body that link neural cells become ensheathed in a fatty substance, myelin. This white matter, as it is often called, is largely composed of cholesterol. When the brains of handled infant rats were compared with those of the unmanipulated controls, the handled rats showed considerably more cholesterol, perhaps indicating that myelinization was occurring faster.

Experiments with deliberately induced brain damage again pointed up the difference between the handled and unhandled animals. Lesions within the septal region of the hippocampus cause hyperexcitability and even viciousness. After lesions were made, however, the handled animals did not become as excitable and certainly not as vicious as did the unhandled controls. These brain-damaged innocents, the experimenters noted, were the most vicious little rodents they had ever seen and would pursue people around the laboratory, attacking their ankles and legs.

The overt maturation rate of the handled infants was well in advance of the unhandled controls. They simply grew faster, opened their eyes sooner, moved in a coordinated fashion earlier, developing a good coat of fur and gaining weight rapidly. Since these handled rats did not appear to be eating more than their naive controls, it was speculated that they might have developed a more efficient protein metabolism. The handled group survived the longest. The infant who had been moved around, joggled, shocked, and subjected to various stresses was clearly better equipped to survive than the creature who had been raised in a completely sterile fashion.

There is, of course, a huge difference between the laboratory environment of the protected animal and the environment he would enjoy living in a cage with his mother and littermates or, surely, in the natural environment. His is a world composed of a temperature-controlled cage, aseptic and barren, with light and sound artificially regulated. Thus, the laboratory study of infant experience compares animals subjected to extreme and purified conditions. The experimenters have consequently been very cautious about generalizing their findings to human beings. What they have indicated, in their purification of environments, is that some range of stimulation even if noxious must be necessary to the normal maturation of a mammal and will leave its imprint upon the physiology and behavior of the adult animal. Ordinarily neither animals nor infant humans pass their earliest months in an environmental vacuum. Perhaps the closest approximation to a vacuum in the life of the human baby is that of the orphanage. Orphanage babies are rarely picked upon, spoken to, played with, and moved around.

Clinical studies of orphans have indicated that they were often retarded in development, timid, unable to adapt to changing situations, and indeed more susceptible to disease than the home child of the same age. Some investigators attributed the debilities of the orphan to the lack of a mother. Today, however, animal studies make it possible to offer another conjecture. It is the mother who lifts and handles a child, speaking to it, feeding, playing, and expending upon it a prodigious amount of "attention." Perhaps the missing element in the orphan's development is the motion, the stimulation ordinarily provided by a devoted parent. Very recently, in the first controlled study of its kind, White and Held have shown that aspects of visual acuity and adaptation in very young infants in orphanages can be "speeded up" by enriching the visual environments of the crib. Only longitudinal studies will tell whether the infant in his usual orphanage environment will later catch up with the experimental infants and whether, indeed, effects of early visual experience can be detected in future behavior.

In the animal studies of Dr. Levine and his associates, employing a purified situation, it has become increasingly clear that manipulation during infancy has produced more responsive adult animals. Rats that were left strictly alone in infancy were shocked as adults: they took considerable amounts of shock before they would learn to avoid it. Their counterparts, handled during infancy, required little shock to teach them avoidance. These handled rats appeared to be making more sensitive discriminations about events impinging on them.

The experimenters predicted that early handling would help the creature respond to new situations, and one measure of response would be the amount of stress registered physically—the output of steroids. Rats at the weaning stage were set down in a new cage for a few minutes and then their steroids were measured. The handled rats showed a much lower output of stress steroids than did the nonhandled controls. Laboratory tests of this kind may seem remote from their human analogy—in part because we have precious little empathy for rats. It may be possible to imagine the experience of the infant rat by recalling the reactions of a small infant. He is accustomed to sleeping in his own crib and he is suddenly transported to a new house where he is left upon a large open bed. Some infants will cry and fuss showing signs of fear and distress. The first time an infant is lifted up and held by strangers he may produce a fearful wail. Surely, the infant human shows signs of intense distress when first exposed to a night in a hospital, and many parents comment that their babies are generally resistant to change. One may imagine that the laboratory rat endures drastic experiences when he is first picked up by a giant, removed from his familiar cage, and set down in a new place with unfamiliar smells. The first time he confronts the open-field test he must experience some of the emotional upheavals that might occur in an infant who is lifted from his crib and set into a gigantic baby-pen the size of a huge room.

Both handled and unhandled rats reacted similarly to their first open-field test, if judged by their movements around the container and amount of elimination. But when the experience was repeated, the effects of handling were apparent. The handled rats now acted more "at home" and explored more and eliminated less. The "protected" rats, on the contrary, acted more emotional than before. They reduced their activity and defecated more. They did not seem to have benefited from their first experience but acted as if this were a new and even more threatening situation.

The effects of infant handling have been studied in other species than the rat. The monkey is, of course, much closer to man phylogentically, and quite a number of investigators have been looking with interest at the effects of early experience on monkeys. Recently, in collaboration with Dr. William Mason of the Delta Primate Center, Dr. Levine and his colleagues have been able to follow the behavioral and physiological effects of handling in infant monkeys. They have recently compared the stress and learning responses of three pairs of monkeys. One pair was raised with only a stationary dummy for a mother. Another pair had a robot mother that was motorized and capable of certain motions. The third pair had been raised naturally by their mothers in the wild. When the six animals arrived at the Stanford laboratory they bore no identification tags saying which was which. Their behavioral differences were so great, however, that it was quickly apparent. One of the first examinations required placing each monkey in a restraining chair while blood samples were drawn and steroid levels analyzed. The experimenters wanted to determine something about the baseline responses of the animals to ordinary laboratory handling and to get some reactions to very minor and standard stimulation.

When seated in the restraining chair, a small blood sample was taken from the leg. A half hour later, electrodes were applied so that galvanic skin responses could be obtained as tones were played. Another blood sample was drawn at this time. The motherless monkeys gave a low-galvanic skin response and at first their steroid levels were also very low. As the procedure continued, the steroid response rose high above the others. When this procedure was repeated, the reactions of the feral and motherless monkeys were more nearly the same. The experimenters began to look at behavior.

Now the animals were placed in a choice situation. They were presented with two different visual patterns on two panels. When the monkey pushed the right panel he automatically received a peanut. The feral monkeys, once they mastered the notion of pressing panels, learned the correct discrimination in few trials. The monkeys raised with robot mothers took more practice but learned the problem in far less time than did the monkeys raised with stationary dummies.

When the monkeys were transferred to a new discrimination apparatus, the differences again became evident. The wild monkeys learned with their former speed. The monkeys mothered by robots learned, also. But the monkeys raised on stationary dummies never learned. Now the problem was reversed so that the formerly wrong choice was correct and rewarded. This taxed the adaptiveness and resilience of the monkeys. On the first day of reversal there was no reinforcement. The feral and robot-raised monkeys continued responding rapidly as before. On the next day, when reward was offered for the formerly wrong choice, the feral monkeys adapted with no show of difficulty. The robot-raised monkeys took twice as long, behaving as if this were a totally new situation. The monkeys raised on stationary dummies never did learn. The experimenters observed that the maternally deprived monkeys reacted to each change, each variation in a situation as if it were now totally novel and inimical. Characteristically, steroid samples indicated that these deprived monkeys were both sluggish in responding and then overreactive.

An initial look at these three pairs of monkeys suggested that infant experience might have far-reaching and subtle effects upon the animal's later ability to learn, to generalize from one situation to its variant. From the very first it was clear that novelty of any kind presented the mother-less monkeys with a painful problem of adjustment. They would crouch and cower and scream when placed in the learning cage—as if learning to push a panel were a wretched torture. When they finally mastered a discrimination between two panels and were asked to make the reverse choice among the alternatives, they acted as if they had been dropped into an entirely new situation.

These maternally deprived animals have, of course, lacked more than just the handling, training, and affection that their mothers would have bestowed during critical periods. They lacked, as well, whatever biochemical modulation they might have received through their mother's milk. A program of controlled studies with monkeys, beginning in 1967, may begin to illuminate the weight of these many factors in mature adjustment. These studies may also begin to explain why the inexperienced infant fails to become adept at making discriminations later. Is he handicapped by a physiological system that is slow to react to a stimulus and then overreactive? Is he thus placed in a state of anxiety, feeling so continually overwrought that he cannot take note of the subtle distinctions in his surroundings and must react to everything?

In a decade of animal studies, the investigator has consistently observed that infant handling influences later behavior by adjusting the animal's level of physiological response to stress. What is the physiological mechanism through which experience regulates the stress sensitivity of the mature animal? Why does early handling instill responses to "crisis" that are prompt and brief? Why does lack of infant experience create an adrenal response that is sluggish and disproportionate?

Adrenal Hormones and Experience

Early studies of internal responses were often, of necessity, acute, and the animal had to be killed to find the physical effects. Determinations of adrenal responses were made by examining the glands themselves and by measuring steroid levels in sizable quantities of blood. More recently the experimenters have devised a method of determining steroid levels in very small amounts of tissue, in a drop of blood. Very precise determinations can be made on one drop of blood by fluorescence measurement, following this new method—a distinct advantage when several measures are required and the experimental animal is a small rat or mouse. Using this technique, it has been possible to follow the steroid responses in handled and nonhandled animals over repeated tests without harming the animal. Now it is possible to obtain frequent steroid determinations during stimulation and behavior.

Since adrenal steroids seem to correspond to a level "emotionality" or reactivity, the experimenters have inevitably asked what role these steroids play in behavior. Early studies suggested that steroids appeared to alert the animal for emergency action. When the steroid levels were excessively high, however, the animal appeared to be too keyed up to make

574

sensitive discriminations. One of the best vehicles for observing the effects of steroid levels on behavior was the avoidance situation. Rats placed in a small cage or maze with an electrified floor grid would learn quite a variety of behaviors to avoid getting shocked. In a recent variant on this avoidance conditioning, rats have had to learn a temporal rhythm. This has allowed the experimenters to measure changes in behavior with great precision.

When shocks were paced to arrive every 20 seconds, the animal had to press a bar before the shock in order to prevent it. He would quickly learn that he did not need to press the bar continuously. He would develop a rhythm, pressing about every 18 or 19 seconds. Each day, when he was first placed in the avoidance chamber, the animal would receive a few shocks as he readjusted to the apparatus, but his performance would soon become steady, his rhythm accurate. Given an injection of ACTH, then when his performance was already stable, he would become even more efficient. When placed in the chamber, he would receive fewer shocks during the warmup period. He also made fewer responses, more accurately timed. The priming steroid appeared to enhance his precision. When the rat was injected with an even more potent steroid, he would become perceptibly more efficient. The steroid seemed to be enhancing the alertness of the animal.

In the normal course of events, the adrenal steroids suffuse the body by a chain of reactions. A stimulus causes the brain to send signals to the pituitary, which releases ACTH, thus causing the adrenals to release their stimulating chemicals into the bloodstream and gear the body for action. The immediate supply of blood sugar is increased by a breakdown of stored glycogen, giving the body extra energy to use. But the alerting effects, the potent influence upon behavior, must come from the effects of steroids upon the central nervous system itself. One step in ascertaining how these steroid hormones might shape neural responses, has been to watch behavior when steroids are administered directly to the brain. Does the brain respond to these steroids?

Dr. Levine and his associates have begun a series of experiments in which they are implanting steroids directly into the brain through tiny hollow cannulae. In effect, this causes the brain to "believe" that the steroid level of the body is a great deal higher than it is an actuality. If so, the experimenters have postulated that the animal should be exceedingly alert and learn to avoid punishment very swiftly. When hydrocortisone, one of the adrenal steroids, has been injected into the hypothalamus of a rat, ether no longer causes a stress response. Moreover, when this animal is placed in a shuttlebox, it will learn to avoid shock very quickly and will maneuver to escape being shocked 48 times out of 60. A control rat, whose brain has received instead of steroid an implant of cholesterol, will avoid this same shock much less efficiently and therefore receive more shocks in the shuttlebox. It would appear that the adrenal steroids exert their influence upon the brain, thus enhancing the ability to discriminate in avoidance situations—situations in which the stakes must be high from the animal's point of view, for the failure to respond means a very unpleasant consequence.

These studies of adrenal steroids, as they directly influence the central nervous system, are filling in the puzzle of infant handling and its consequences in adulthood. Handling, a wide variety of stimulations, and indeed stresses, appears to alter a basic hormonal system during infancy. Without handling and stress, the infant and the adult animal learns avoidance slowly, does not discriminate readily, and exhibits disproportionate emotionality when placed in a novel situation for the first time. He exhibits a slow but inordinate level of adrenal steroids whenever confronted with a challenge or shock. His excessive output after repeated stress is reflected in adrenal glands that are unusually large and heavy, by stunted growth, by susceptibility to disease. How does experience create the different and healthier pattern of the handled infant?

The experimenters have postulated that handling during critical periods of infancy must allow the system to adjust its "stress" system by a series of approximations. Perhaps the system operates in a manner analogous to a thermostat. The animal reacts to an event and pours out adrenal steroids by which the brain responds according to their level, thus regulating further behavior. The shaping that occurs is in the organization of emotional responses via the pattern of released corticosteroids, a pattern that is thought to be controlled by the hypothalamus. Release of these fear-inspired steroids may have a permanent effect upon the hypothalamus during critical periods of infancy, thus calibrating the animal's level of response to stimuli. Without experience, there can be no comparison, none of the raw material by which the central nervous system could establish a ratio of response and event—setting up an internal sense of proportion. If the nervous system of the experienced infant is calibrated so that responses are rapid, brief, and create little aftermath—cues to this development must lie within the steroid levels of the newborn and infant animal.

A number of factors—among them size and cost—have made rodents the most convenient animals for many of these studies. Different strains of inbred rats and mice show distinctive characteristics in their stress responses, their normal excitability, and their responses to handling. When laboratory animals are purchased, moreover, it is hard to determine exactly how the infants have been handled by the breeder and, therefore, how much of their response pattern is genetic, how much due to experience. Genetic differences exert a profound influence upon the development of the individual animal as he interacts with his environment. For this reason, the laboratory has engaged in a number of genetic studies and has compared quite a few strains of rodents on a number of criteria. There have been studies of differences in adult emotionality, studies of the effects of infant handling, and of the adrenal output of various strains of mice under stress. These genetic studies add some important dimensions to the study of infant development.

No creature is completely plastic at birth. The shape of the body, the color of its fur, the arrangement of vital organs, and many other internal patterns are clearly laid out by the genes. Many behaviors are determined by the structure of the nervous system, and neural circuitry is preset. The nervous system contains a network of communication fibers determining which cells shall receive and transmit impulses to other particular cells. These nerve circuits determine how cells in the eye shall transmit to the visual brain thus structuring the animal's vision. Even relatively specific predilections such as preferred kinds of food may be determined before birth. Early studies have indicated that experience in infancy may perform the next modification, adjusting factors that control the readiness of an emergency response, the extent of a reaction, and the length of time that an animal is alerted, his intensity. Here, too, the animal has some genetic predilections. Steroid measurements are being used to distinguish some of the basic differences which appear in the magnitude of the animal's reactions to handling. Some strains of mouse, for example, exhibit a hyper-reactiveness and a strong steroid response to stress. These animals show great differenes in the production and release of steroids following shocks. The reactive mice, placed in an open-field test, exhibit a notable tendency to cower in corners, to defecate. The others show less emotionality.

The genetic foundations of a response pattern are important if the effects of experimental manipulation are to be measured precisely. In working with mice it has been advisable to explore this baseline of responsiveness and a number of studies have been undertaken recently. Wild mice, as compared with domestic mice, show differences that may tell a good deal about the way in which the creature becomes tailored to the particular demands of his environment. Wild mice, for instance, show a much larger steroid response to laboratory tests, and have, indeed, larger adrenals than domestic mice.

In a current study, genetic differences showed up when the creatures were presented with a conflict situation. The mice were given no water to drink in their cages. They were placed in a special cage where they had to drink from a water bottle. After 5 days they received a shock while drinking from the bottle. The strain with a high-steroid response quit drinking after 5 shocks, but the low-steroid strain took 15 shocks before it would give up. After an injection of a substance that blocks steroid output, the high-steroid strain would behave like the low reactors and would also require 15 shocks to prevent them from drinking on.

A very interesting adrenal adaptation was discovered in a variety of desert mouse that showed none of the usual elevation in stress steroids after shock and other tests. Here, as it turned out, the assays that were suitable for most of the laboratory mice were totally inappropriate. It was not that this mouse lacked a stress response, but that his glandular functions were differently organized. Steroids usually indicative of stress were, in this mouse, functioning to maintain water in tissue.

577

Some recent experiments have indicated that the startle response of a mouse may be a good indicator of his steroid level. Two strains, one high steroid and another low, have been tested in a delicate little box that registers the height and impact of a jump. At 1-minute intervals a cap pistol is fired. The reactive mice leap high at first and take some time before they get used to the noise so that they no longer jump. The other strain consistently shows a much smaller startle jump and takes little time to habituate.

A recent study of four strains has indicated that the reactive mice (showing the most marked steroid response to shock and novelty) are the ones in whom infant handling makes the greatest change. Handled mice from these two strains have indicated the greatest reduction in stress upon testing. The two strains initially showing least response to shock and novelty in steroid output have also least change after handling.

Current studies of genetic factors in the developing responses of animals do suggest a variety of differences in initial responsiveness to environment. Experience makes little dent upon the adrenal response of low-steroid strains. However, the high-steroid strains appear to become "less emotional" with experience and show less reaction to stress. It seems likely that analogous genetic differences operate within human beings. Parents, certainly, speak as if the "high strung" infant makes his presence known in early infancy. The intimations of a temperament seem to be conveyed by the baby in the first weeks of life. Tests, such as the startle test used with laboratory animals, might indeed give a very early estimate of the infant's adrenal responsiveness. Even so, one would not know whether the infant's intensity of reaction were truly genetic or whether it were influenced by its mother's own steroid levels prior to delivery and throughout the nursing period. In addition, maternal behavior presumably plays its role in shaping of the infant.

Concurrent with a number of genetic studies, the laboratory has also been investigating the mother's own prenatal and postpartum adrenal reactivity and the effects on the young.

The Development of Endocrine Responses in Critical Periods

Whatever the genes that formed him, a child does spend almost a year in the chemical bath of his mother's womb. In the first months after birth he will be nourished by her milk and suffused with her chemicals. Most of his experience will derive from her ministrations. Will he feel the consequences if his mother endures an ordeal while she is bearing him? Will he suffer from the debilities of a high-steroid start in life if she is high strung while nursing him? Does her stress chemistry give the infant's own physiology a push, helping him to set the level of his endocrine responses to life?

There is a period in the life of an infant rat which seems to be strongly influenced by the mother's chemistry—perhaps through her milk, perhaps through her behavior. It was discovered when rat pups were being tested for their steroid responses to shock and other stresses. The experimenters noticed that the neonate, on the day of birth and for 3 days of life, gave a marked response to stress. But after the third day, there was no sign of adrenal stress hormones. The usual response had vanished. Ether, electric shock, exposure to cold—all of the standard laboratory stresses failed to elicit a steroid response in the infant. They injected ACTH—the hormone that instructs the adrenals to release stress steroids—but nothing seemed to happen. There was no detectable release of steroids from the adrenals. The animal was in a dormant period, and it lasted somewhere between 6 and 12 days.

Handling the infant seemed to shorten this dormant period. Creatures handled in the laboratory would again show a steroid response to shock after about 6 days. Protected creatures would not resume their response for about 12 days.

Why did the animal give a shock response right after birth and then exhibit none for almost 2 weeks? The probable answer was that the first responses depended upon an endowment of steroids from the mother, but thereafter the creature was in a state of transition. His endocrine system might be setting up its steroid response levels dictated, in part, by genetic endowment mediated by the mother and by his experiences during the critical period. The experimenters postulated that the infant animal must adjust his adrenal hormone release to the stresses of the outside world, after a fashion—setting a glandular thermostat that would dictate the intensity of his responses to events.

The research team began to take a close look at the mother's influence upon this critical adjustment—a glandular calibration that would seriously affect the animal's rate of growth, his learning ability, his resistance to disease, and his long-term ability to adapt and survive.

They saw, with mice, that the mother's steroid levels appeared to exert far more influence than the father's. Genetically identical mothers bred to antipodal fathers bore infants whose steroid response patterns inevitably followed those of the mothers—not the fathers.

If the mother's own steroid levels were mediating the endocrine responses of her newborn, the experimenters expected that a shift in her own steroid levels might show up in the young. After delivery, in one study, they injected the mother with ACTH. The newborn showed a higher steroid response than did the neonates whose mothers received only saline injections. The next test was to drastically reduce the mother's steroid level with a chemical that blocks the release of ACTH. Her young, as might be expected, exhibited decidedly lower steroid levels. She was undoubtedly still capable of transmitting steroids, for an ACTH blocker would prevent further release of the hormones but would not reduce the high level already circulating in her system. The steroid level of the mother distinctly influenced that of her young.

Ordinarily a mother's stress responses are at their lowest just after delivery. The steroid levels rise before labor and diminish after delivery and during nursing. After the offspring are weaned, there is a radical increase in steroid levels. A similar pattern of steroid decrease after birth is found in human beings. Perhaps this is a built-in safety device. It works to insure low-stress responses in the mother directly after birth. Since high levels in the infant will stunt growth, it is essential that the newborn not experience high-steroid concentrations too early. After birth and throughout the nursing period nature has provided a mechanism for generating a particular calm in the mother. This appears to be the period in which she mediates the initial steroid levels of the young, perhaps through her behavior and her milk.

Within the laboratory, in a study of mice, the calmest, low-steroid mothers had offspring who showed a sluggish response to shock. It has not yet been determined whether these low-steroid infants will learn discriminations faster than the more excitable creatures. One thing was clear—the infants reflected, in their steroid respones, the steroid levels of their mothers. A good many factors might be responsible for the base steroid level of the mother.

In a study of rats, the experimenters started at the beginning—in the infancy of the mothers. They handled one group of females in infancy, and protected another group. Now the effects of handling might be traced through to the next generation, for all the mothers were of the same genetic strain. Would the infant experience of the mother show up in her own offspring? The study seemed to answer in the affirmative. The handled mothers had lower resting levels of steroids, and their young showed low-stress responses. The protected, or nonhandled mothers had higher resting levels of steroids, and their young showed higher stress responses. The handling of the infant female appeared to help set an endocrine level that was then transmitted to the next generation.

Although a round of different studies has not yet indicated whether the mother's steroid influence comes mainly through her milk or from her behavior—it seems clear that her steroid levels dictate the early levels of the infant. A cross-fostering study of rats indicated very dramatically the importance of the mother's role in mediating the early steroid levels of the young. The offspring of high-steroid mothers were given to low-steroid mothers, and vice versa. Initially, it seems that the offspring of high-steroid mothers show a very low-steroid response to stress when they are raised by low-steroid mothers.

The importance of the mother's steroid level has been evident throughout these studies and raises many questions about infant care and the postnatal experience of the mother. Is the nursing period a time in which shock to mothers will raise their steroid levels and transmit to the young a tendency for emotionality that would reverberate throughout infancy, retard growth, and even appear in the adult responses to alarm? Although many questions must be answered about the mother's own experience and her steroid state—the other half of the question must be answered by determining what the infant body is doing during this critical time after birth.

His mother's steroid levels give him an initial presetting, yet during these first weeks experience will shorten the transition period and may alter his glandular calibration of intensity and stimulus. The process might be likened to the setting of an automatic thermostat, so that it will turn on only when the temperature drops below a certain point.

If a kind of hormonostat is developed during the time when the infant begins producing his own steroids, its effect upon his behavior may come about through a feedback to the central nervous system. When his steroid levels rise, his brain will move him in the direction of alertness, of excitability. This early development of the hormonal system, according to the data now amassed, would seem to exert a profound and endless effect on the growth, the adaptability, and health of the animal. Basic metabolic processes may be altered through this system and so the steroid response to shock or other stress may be the key to many of the adult animal's adaptive capacities.

The hormones issued by the adrenals, in response to pituitary command during situations of potential danger, are evidently affected by the sex hormones. Normal male rodents when shocked show a lower stress response than do the normal females. The typical pattern of reaction differs according to sex. The male reacts by pouring steroids into his system much more rapidly and more rapidly declines when the stimulus is over. The female takes longer to respond and characteristically shows high-steroid levels for some time after the shock. This description of stress reaction may sound familiar for it describes a male-female difference in reaction that is encountered in the human species. The typical emotional female remains emotional long after her baby has returned home safely or the near accident has been averted. One might almost expect that the difference between the male and female stress pattern is a pivot of conflict between the sexes. Surely it is clear that the hormones of stress are in some way related to the apportionment of sex hormones.

Just as the stress responses of an organism appear to be shaped during critical periods of infancy and remain irreversible thereafter, the shaping of sexual traits by hormonal settings is irreversible after a critical period in infancy.

Sex Hormones and Behavior

The sex of a child can be determined very early—while still in the womb. The overt sexual features are pronounced by birth, and a doctor can after one glance say, "It's a boy." Nevertheless, the maleness of the child may be deceptive. His internal hormonal states will determine whether he acts like a boy or a girl. Quite a number of experiments have demonstrated that sex can be altered after birth.

Sexual differentiation determines the behavior and reproductive ability of the adult, also the nature of physical responses to stress, and this differentiation appears to depend upon neonatal hormones. Perhaps as current studies indicate, the crucial hormone may be testosterone. Observations that sexual capacity and behavior were not differentiated by physical morphology was made by ethologists long ago. In the mid-1930's, testes from newborn males were transplanted to females. These ostensibly

581

female animals grew up without any sign of the usual estrus cycle, but rather seemed to be in a continuous estrus. They did not, however, show cyclical release of important hormones and never became pregnant although given ample opportunity, and so it was thought that these animals refused to mate. As later studies were to demonstrate, the transplanting of testes was unnecessary. A single injection of testosterone in a female during her first 5 days of life sufficed to create a lack of estrus cycle and an inability to be impregnated. Hormone treatments to the mother in other studies indicated that prenatal estrogen could produce feminization in the male offspring, and testosterone resulted in male behaviors in females. By the mid-1950's, it seemed clear that in the life of the guinea pig there was a critical period during its first week when sex hormones could enter the brain and influence the sexual differentiation of the animal.

Dr. Levine's laboratory has been using several techniques to find out how, indeed, the hormones cause sexual differentiation and thereby influence behavior. The investigator had found that when male rats were given the ovarian hormone, estrogen, their gonads atrophied, and they were forever feminized. Indeed, if the male rat was castrated during his first 24 hours, it was possible to implant an ovary in him in adulthood and the ovary would ovulate in the cyclical fashion typical of female estrus.

Further transplantation studies suggested that hormones must influence the brain. The cyclic pattern of ovulation is stimulated by the pituitary gland in the base of the brain. This gland produces the follicle-stimulating hormone that prepares the ovary to produce egg cells. When this process is finished, the pituitary issues a luteinizing hormone which ripens the follicles so that they rupture and release the eggs. When a female ovary is transplanted into a male who has been castrated neonatally, that ovary will ovulate. This suggests that neither the ovary nor the pituitary alone is responsible for the cycle. It would appear that other brain areas must react to hormonal stimulation and that during critical periods these brain regions cause the unformed nervous system to generate either maleness or femaleness.

Once again it would seem that the infant's final hormonal adjustments must not be genetic but are made during some critical periods of development. The balance determining ultimate sexual behavior and sexual function appears to develop by a hormonostat—subject to influence in early infancy and presumably affected by the mother's hormones. When female rats were injected with small doses of the male gonadal hormone, testosterone, in infancy, they never ovulated on maturity and exhibited abnormal sex behaviors. If they were given very high doses of testosterone, they would grow into adulthood with no trace of usual female behaviors. Any observer watching one of these hormonally treated females as she interacted with another female in the cage would have to conclude that she was a male. The mounting behavior would even conclude in the appearance of ejaculation. Shots of female hormone—estrogen—in adulthood would not reverse the effect. This female, given testosterone in infancy, ever after would behave as a male.

582

These studies suggested that hormonal balance in infancy was crucial, and that its effects upon the central nervous system would subsequently influence behavior and reproduction. The castrated neonate—effectively losing his testosterone—appeared to be suffering from an alteration in the brain tissues which would later become receptive to male hormones. This male, it should be said, was being feminized in many ways. He would subsequently show feminine responses in nonsexual behaviors. His hormonal balance, causing differentiation within brain tissue would also affect his adrenal system.

Male and female rats differ in their open-field behavior, but the difference can be reversed with a single hormone shot. A castrated neonate will act like a female in the open field. A female injected with testosterone will act like a male. The activity cycles of the male and female rat ordinarily show characteristic differences, for the female becomes quite active before estrus and inactive afterwards. A castrated neonate with transplanted ovary will show female activity cycles.

A variety of studies has indicated that these changes in sexual orientation occur during a very short time after birth in the rat. Moreover, the critical period is especially brief for the male. Male differentiation seems to occur during the first 48 hours, while female differentiation takes as long as 120 hours in the same species. The investigators have postulated that the female state is in some sense more primitive and that without the addition of a particular male hormone every rat remains a female.

The evidence comes from a number of studies. In essence, it seems to be lack of testosterone that creates female differentiation. A newborn male rat, if castrated, will not produce testosterone. If he is given no supplementing injections of testosterone he will behave as a female, exhibit female sex behavior with the lordosis position of receptivity; he will accept implanted ovaries, show ovulation, and behave like a female on open-field tests, in response to shock, and with other females. Injections of the female hormone, estrogen, do not have the overwhelming impact on a male that is caused by lack of testosterone. Estrogen causes the testes to wither, however, and creates some female behavior.

Hormonal influences can be profound after birth, for it appears that sexual functions and behaviors are exceedingly malleable during critical periods. Rats in prenatal development, are structurally developed in part by the influence of androgen. Written into the very chromosomes are the directions that determine whether the animal will have testes or ovaries. Once the testes and ovaries develop, however, their hormones exert the final influence upon the sexual nature of the animal. During infancy, the hormones perform an organizational function, perhaps by creating a regulatory system within the brain that finally governs sex behavior and biological function. Gonadal hormones appear to act upon the brain, thus dictating whether the creature shall be male or female.

By this differentiation, the sex hormones dictate many behaviors that are not strictly sexual. Recent studies within this laboratory have indicated how estrogen and testosterone injections will influence the emotional behavior of the animal. Inbred strains of highly reactive rats and unreactive rats, as defined by open-field behavior, were injected with hormones and observed in their subsequent open-field behavior. Before injection, the reactive males defecated more than the females. In all the strains tested, the females were more active. Neonatal hormone injection had a profound effect on the nonsexual behavior of the animals. Estrogen caused considerably more defecation and activity, producing what might be called a more emotional rat, and affected both sexes by heightening this reactivity. Testosterone, on the other hand, produced a more male response by one criteria; it increased defecation in the reactive females to roughly the level of the males. In another study, male neonates had been injected with estrogen, and when stressed, their output of corticosterone was like that of the female.

In current studies, the investigators have been exploring for reliable behavior differences among male and female rats. It will then be possible to perform more sensitive tests of the effects of hormone changes. In mice, aggressive behavior is exhibited mainly by males. Males fight when placed together but females do not. Females given testosterone, however, will engage in some fighting. Further studies may indicate whether neonatal castration will remove fighting from the behavior repertoire of the male and whether neonatal injection of testosterone produces an adult female who does battle like a male. Female rodents show more rapid avoidance conditioning than males and this, too, may turn out to be amenable to hormonal change.

Stress responses have been altered by hormonal treatment. In measuring the adrenal steroids in the blood, samples are drawn from the jugular vein under ether. This procedure, in itself, constitutes a stress for the animal. Ordinarily, the normal male will respond to the ether and surgical cut by a rise in corticosterone lasting about 20-45 minutes. The male treated with neonatal estrogen shows almost double the normal concentration of adrenal stress hormone, but his response is still considerably less than that generated by the normal female. If, however, the female has been given testosterone during the initial days of life, her output of adrenal stress steroid will fall between that of the normal male and the estrogen-treated male. It might seem that testosterone, acting upon the central nervous system, mediates the response of the emergency system, the emotional, or stress output of the animal. There are many questions and one very striking conclusion to be drawn from this program of research. The environment of the newborn animal and its changes have a very significant and life-long effect upon his adult biology and behavior. Sex hormones, the interplay of environment factors, and adrenal steroids, all appear to have an organizing influence upon the central nervous system of the newborn. Hormones cause the infant to become a male or female in function. And infantile stimulation appears to organize the emotional responses of the creature.

Both neonatal manipulation and hormonal treatment may have an effect upon the neuroendocrine system as a whole, for they are interlinked. An event occurs, and a brain activity signals the pituitary to release ACTH, which in turn stimulates the adrenal cortex to produce steroids.

The pituitary produces growth hormone, and hormones enabling the ovary to produce eggs, and a male hormone that stimulates the production of testosterone in the cells of the testes. The hormones of the pituitary stimulate the thyroid gland. Thus the systems of endocrine regulation and hormonal regulation of mating behavior and specific sexual functions are to some extent joined. The neonate, at critical periods, can be shifted in his responses to stress by manipulation, treatment with adrenal steroids, or by gonadal hormones. These neurophysiological systems, with their enormous impact upon adult behavior, lie at the hub of the formative periods.

The mysterious and vast influence of the hormones has been probed at the cellular level by many biologists. Today there is a growing body of data that suggests how the hormones exert their influence. Hormones within the tissues appear to direct the activity of the genes, the controllers of individual cells. It is by their influence upon the gene that the hormones appear to steer cell differentiation. Thus the hormone, while external to the cell, can alter the pattern of gene activity and thereby influence protein synthesis. This influence is nowhere more clearly seen than in some of the recent transplantation experiments in which a castrated male wears a healthy, cyclically nourished ovary in an eye-socket, while a testosterone-treated female remains anovulatory and shows no cycles.

These studies demonstrate the power of neonatal hormones in shaping the sexual differentiation of the animal. Insofar as the mother's own balance may influence the infant, there are some very strong implications for medicine. It would seem that an indiscriminate use of prenatal hormones holds some possible dangers for the differentiation of male infants, since the male appears particularly vulnerable to lack of testosterone or to an overbalance of female hormones. Because neonatal hormones appear to play such a decisive role in sexual differentiation, hormone studies of infancy should instigate new approaches and research into sexual deviation and its possible treatments. If it is possible to develop sensitive hormone assays for the infant and child, it seems possible that preventive treatment might be attempted. Surely, these studies raise important questions about the extent to which deviant behaviors are the result of hormonal imbalances that have gone undetected in the clinic but have led to a life of social castigation and punishment. To what extent might these hormonal imbalances be caused by the steroids ingested by pregnant mothers? To what extent might they be altered after the critical and formative periods have passed. Sexual differentiation is crucial to human adjustment. It may seem amazing that the story of neonatal hormones and their bearing on differentiation and behavior have just begun to be explored in the animal laboratory, but the human being for whom these mechanisms have long social and personal reverberations is far less understood and studied.

The psychophysiology of the human formative period will undoubtedly take its guidelines from the animal laboratory. Already studies performed by this laboratory suggest techniques that should enable safe and illuminating studies of human infants. It should be possible to devise an equivalent of the startle apparatus permitting measurements of the amplitude of an infant's response and the detection of early signs of overreactivity. By techniques allowing a determination of steroid concentrations within a drop of blood, it should be possible to measure the steroid elevations an infant shows in response to mild stimulation. Thus we may hope to discover something about the critical periods in which the neuroendocrine system sets up its hierarchy. Controlled studies of infants and mothers should give us information about the prenatal and postnatal influences and how they are molded by outside events. It should be possible to detect the early warning signals of hyperreactivity in a child pretending susceptibility to sickness and perhaps to psychosomatic illness. We can finally hope to establish child-watching and child-rearing practices that will enhance the adaptability and health of the individual.

Some of the more mysterious questions of large populations may finally be answered as more data become available from studies of the ways in which hormone mechanisms influence differentiation. Indeed, it may be possible to answer some of the recurrent questions of the demographer. During war and its aftermath, for instance, it has been noticed that there is an increase in male births. Is this a response of the parents' hormonal systems to stress?

These studies of the neuroendocrine system in its developmental stages have far-reaching implications, but perhaps the ones that fall closest to home are really hopeful questions—what do high doses of steroids do to the pregnant mother and her young? How could our clinics begin to obtain predictive information about the endocrine adjustments of the newborn? Can we begin to look for hormone balance and stress-steroid concentrations as usefully as we look for blood types?

Research Grants: MH 1051, MH 1630, K3—MH 19,936, MH 7435
Dates of Interviews: Fall, 1965; spring, 1966

References:

Davidson, E. H. Hormones and genes. *Scient. American,* 1965, 212, 36-45.
Harris, G. W., & Levine, S. Sexual differentiation of the brain and its experimental control. *J. Physiol.,* 1962, 163, 42-43.
Glick, D., Von Redlich, Dorothy, & Levine, S. Fluorometric determination of corticosterone and cortisol in 0.02-0.05 milliliters of plasma or submilligram samples of adrenal tissue. *Endocrinology,* 1964, 74, 653-655.
Gray, J. A., & Levine, S. Effect of induced oestrus on emotional behavior in selected strains of rats. *Nature,* 1964, 201, 1198-1200.
Gray, J. A., Levine, S., & Broadhurst, P. L. Gonadal hormone injections in infancy and adult emotional behavior. *Anim. Behav.,* 1965, 13, 1, 33-45.
Levine, S. Stimulation in infancy. *Scient. American,* 1960, 202, 80-86.
Levine, S. The effects of infantile experience on adult behavior. In A. J. Bachrach (Ed.), *Experimental foundations of clinical psychology.* New York: Basic Books, 1962.
Levine, S. The psychophysiological effects of infantile stimulation. In E. Bliss (Ed.), *Roots of behavior.* New York: Hoeber, 1962.
Levine, S. Some effects of stimulation in infancy. In S. H. Bartlett (Ed.), *Lessons from Animal Behavior for the Clinician.* London: Nat'l Spastics Soc. (Little Club Clinics in Developmental Medicine, No. 7), 1962, 18-24.

Levine, S., & Broadhurst, P. L. Genetic and ontogenetic determinants of adult behavior in the rat. *J. Comp. Physiol. Psychol.*, 1963, 56, 423-428.

Levine, S., & Mullins, R. Estrogen administered neonatally affects adult sexual behavior in male and female rats. *Science*, 1964, 144, 185-187.

Levine, S., & Treiman, D. M. Differential plasma corticosterone response to stress in four inbred strains of mice. *Endocrinology*, 1964, 75, 142-144.

Levine, S. & Wetzel, A. Infantile experiences, strain differences, and avoidance learning. *J. Comp. Physiol. Psychol.*, 1963, 56, 879-881.

ACKNOWLEDGEMENTS

Major contributions in the editing and preparation of this volume were made by Sherry Prestwich and Muriel Reich. They were assisted by Emily Barron, Lillian Becker, Mary Carmody, Helen Fussell, and Sandy Snider.

☆ U.S. GOVERNMENT PRINTING OFFICE : 1971 O—424-320